Routing Protocols and Concepts
CCNA Exploration Companion Guide

Rick Graziani
Allan Johnson

Cisco Press

800 East 96th Street

Indianapolis, Indiana 46240 USA

Routing Protocols and Concepts, CCNA Exploration Companion Guide

Rick Graziani, Allan Johnson

Copyright© 2008 Cisco Systems, Inc.

Published by:
Cisco Press
800 East 96th Street
Indianapolis, IN 46240 USA

Printed in the United States of America

First Printing December 2007

Library of Congress Cataloging-in-Publication Data

Graziani, Rick.
  Routing protocols and concepts : CCNA exploration companion guide/Rick Graziani,
Allan Johnson.
     p. cm.
  ISBN 978-1-58713-206-3 (hbk. : CD-ROM) 1. Routers (Computer networks) 2.
Routing protocols (Computer network protocols) I. Johnson, Allan, 1962- II. Title.
  TK5105.543.G73 2007
  004.6—dc22
                          2007042619

ISBN-13: 978-1-58713-206-3
ISBN-10: 1-58713-206-0

Publisher
Paul Boger

Associate Publisher
Dave Dusthimer

Cisco Representative
Anthony Wolfenden

Cisco Press Program Manager
Jeff Brady

Executive Editor
Mary Beth Ray

Managing Editor
Patrick Kanouse

Senior Development Editor
Christopher Cleveland

Senior Project Editor
Tonya Simpson

Copy Editor
Written Elegance, Inc.

Technical Editors
Nolan Fretz
Charles Hannon
Matt Swinford

Editorial Assistant
Vanessa Evans

Book and Cover Designer
Louisa Adair

Composition
Bronkella Publishing, LLC

Indexer
Tim Wright

Proofreader
Gill Editorial Services

This book is part of the Cisco Networking Academy® series from Cisco Press. The products in this series support and complement the Cisco Networking Academy curriculum. If you are using this book outside the Networking Academy, then you are not preparing with a Cisco trained and authorized Networking Academy provider.

For more information on the Cisco Networking Academy or to locate a Networking Academy, please visit www.cisco.com/edu.

CISCO.

Warning and Disclaimer

This book is designed to provide information about routing protocols and concepts of the Cisco Network Academy CCNA Exploration curriculum. Every effort has been made to make this book as complete and as accurate as possible, but no warranty or fitness is implied.

The information is provided on an "as is" basis. The authors, Cisco Press, and Cisco Systems, Inc. shall have neither liability nor responsibility to any person or entity with respect to any loss or damages arising from the information contained in this book or from the use of the discs or programs that may accompany it.

The opinions expressed in this book belong to the author and are not necessarily those of Cisco Systems, Inc.

Trademark Acknowledgments

All terms mentioned in this book that are known to be trademarks or service marks have been appropriately capitalized. Cisco Press or Cisco Systems, Inc. cannot attest to the accuracy of this information. Use of a term in this book should not be regarded as affecting the validity of any trademark or service mark.

Corporate and Government Sales

The publisher offers excellent discounts on this book when ordered in quantity for bulk purchases or special sales, which may include electronic versions and/or custom covers and content particular to your business, training goals, marketing focus, and branding interests. For more information, please contact: **U.S. Corporate and Government Sales**   1-800-382-3419   corpsales@pearsontechgroup.com

For sales outside the United States please contact: **International Sales**   international@pearsoned.com

Feedback Information

At Cisco Press, our goal is to create in-depth technical books of the highest quality and value. Each book is crafted with care and precision, undergoing rigorous development that involves the unique expertise of members from the professional technical community.

Readers' feedback is a natural continuation of this process. If you have any comments regarding how we could improve the quality of this book, or otherwise alter it to better suit your needs, you can contact us through e-mail at feedback@ciscopress.com. Please make sure to include the book title and ISBN in your message.

We greatly appreciate your assistance.

Americas Headquarters	Asia Pacific Headquarters	Europe Headquarters
Cisco Systems, Inc.	Cisco Systems, Inc.	Cisco Systems International BV
170 West Tasman Drive	168 Robinson Road	Haarlerbergpark
San Jose, CA 95134-1706	#28-01 Capital Tower	Haarlerbergweg 13-19
USA	Singapore 068912	1101 CH Amsterdam
www.cisco.com	www.cisco.com	The Netherlands
Tel: 408 526-4000	Tel: +65 6317 7777	www-europe.cisco.com
800 553-NETS (6387)	Fax: +65 6317 7799	Tel: +31 0 800 020 0791
Fax: 408 527-0883		Fax: +31 0 20 357 1100

Cisco has more than 200 offices worldwide. Addresses, phone numbers, and fax numbers are listed on the Cisco Website at **www.cisco.com/go/offices.**

©2007 Cisco Systems, Inc. All rights reserved. CCVP, the Cisco logo, and the Cisco Square Bridge logo are trademarks of Cisco Systems, Inc.; Changing the Way We Work, Live, Play, and Learn is a service mark of Cisco Systems, Inc.; and Access Registrar, Aironet, BPX, Catalyst, CCDA, CCDP, CCIE, CCIP, CCNA, CCNP, CCSP, Cisco, the Cisco Certified Internetwork Expert logo, Cisco IOS, Cisco Press, Cisco Systems, Cisco Systems Capital, the Cisco Systems logo, Cisco Unity, Enterprise/Solver, EtherChannel, EtherFast, EtherSwitch, Fast Step, Follow Me Browsing, FormShare, GigaDrive, GigaStack, HomeLink, Internet Quotient, IOS, IP/TV, iQ Expertise, the iQ logo, iQ Net Readiness Scorecard, iQuick Study, LightStream, Linksys, MeetingPlace, MGX, Networking Academy, Network Registrar, Packet, PIX, ProConnect, RateMUX, ScriptShare, SlideCast, SMARTnet, StackWise, The Fastest Way to Increase Your Internet Quotient, and TransPath are registered trademarks of Cisco Systems, Inc. and/or its affiliates in the United States and certain other countries.

All other trademarks mentioned in this document or Website are the property of their respective owners. The use of the word partner does not imply a partnership relationship between Cisco and any other company. (0609R)

About the Authors

Rick Graziani teaches computer science and computer networking courses at Cabrillo College in Aptos, California. Rick has worked and taught in the computer networking and information technology field for almost 30 years. Prior to teaching, Rick worked in IT for various companies including Santa Cruz Operation, Tandem Computers, and Lockheed Missiles and Space Corporation. He holds an M.A. in computer science and systems theory from California State University Monterey Bay. Rick also does consulting work for Cisco and other companies. When Rick is not working, he is most likely surfing. Rick is an avid surfer who enjoys longboarding at his favorite Santa Cruz surf breaks.

Allan Johnson entered the academic world in 1999 after 10 years as a business owner/operator to dedicate his efforts to his passion for teaching. He holds both an M.B.A. and an M.Ed. in occupational training and development. He is an information technology instructor at Del Mar College in Corpus Christi, Texas. In 2003, Allan began to commit much of his time and energy to the CCNA Instructional Support Team, providing services to Networking Academy instructors worldwide and creating training materials. He now works full time for the Academy in Learning Systems Development.

About the Technical Reviewers

Nolan Fretz is a college professor in network and telecommunications engineering technology at Okanagan College in Kelowna, British Columbia. He has almost 20 years of experience in implementing and maintaining IP networks and has been sharing his experiences by educating students in computer networking for the past nine years. He holds a master's degree in information technology.

Charles Hannon is an assistant professor of network design and administration at Southwestern Illinois College. He has been a Cisco Certified Academy instructor since 1998. Charles has a master of arts in education from Maryville University, St. Louis, Missouri, currently holds a valid CCNA certification, and has eight years' experience in management of information systems. Charles' priority is to empower students to become successful and compassionate lifelong learners.

Matt Swinford, associate professor of network design and administration at Southwestern Illinois College, has been an active Cisco Certified Academy instructor since 1999. Matt is dedicated to fostering a learning environment that produces certified students and quality IT professionals. Matt has a master of business administration from Southern Illinois University at Edwardsville in Edwardsville, Illinois, and currently holds CCNP, A+, and Microsoft certifications.

Acknowledgments

From Rick Graziani:

First of all, I want to thank my good friend Allan Johnson for the pleasure of writing this book with him. I can't imagine a better team of two writers contributing to a book that worked so well together to the benefit of its readers. Allan's unique combination of technical knowledge, writing skills, and graphic skills, along with his commitment to quality, is evident throughout the curriculum and this book.

Cindy Ciriello was a critical member of the development team as an instructional designer, and her assistance and perspective were invaluable to the project. Thank you, Cindy, for all of your help.

The more you know about computer networking, the more you realize what you don't know. Over the years, friends and network engineers Mark Boolootian and Jim Warner, at the University of California Santa Cruz, and Dave Barnett, Santa Cruz County Office of Education, have been vital resources for me. Our late-night discussions at various restaurants, writing topologies and protocols out on napkins, and discussing a variety of scenarios and issues have been invaluable to me over our many years of friendship. It is always a classic case of four geeks talking nerd-stuff.

Thank you to Fred Baker, Cisco Fellow and former IETF chair, for his support and encouragement over the years. I greatly appreciate his time and the insight he has always graciously provided.

A special thank you to Alex Zinin, author of the book *Cisco IP Routing*. His book and generous correspondence has detailed routing protocol processes and algorithms for me that I could find nowhere else. His impact and influence can be found throughout this book. Thanks again, Alex!

Special thanks to Mary Beth Ray for her patience and understanding throughout this long process. Mary Beth always provided that voice of calm assurance and guidance whenever needed.

Thank you Dayna Isley and Chris Cleveland for your help in the editing and production stages. I am amazed at the level of cooperation and teamwork required to produce a technical book, and I am grateful for all of your help.

Thanks to all of the technical editors for providing feedback and suggestions. I will take full responsibility for any remaining technical errors in the book.

Special thanks to Pat Farley, who made sure that I continued to get my surf time in every week during this project and therefore maintained my sanity. For those of you who surf, you know how important this is. Thank you, Pat, for your friendship and support.

Finally, I want to thank all of my students over the years. For some reason, I always get the best students. You make my job fun and the reason why I love teaching.

From Allan Johnson:

Thank you, Rick Graziani, for graciously sharing the work of this project with me. It has truly been an honor to serve our students together. Rick has been my teacher for many years. Now I am proud to call him my friend. Fellow students and readers, you might not realize just how dedicated Rick is to "getting it right." During development, when I would ask him a really tough technical question, his answer many times was, "Let me go look at the algorithm, and I'll get back to you."

Cindy Ciriello rounded out the talents of our development effort, insisting on improving the way we present very technical material. As "Agent 99," you were able to "geek out" with the best of us and helped maintain my sanity during some very crazy days.

Mary Beth Ray, executive editor, you amaze me with your ability to juggle multiple projects at once, steering each from beginning to end. I can always count on you to make the tough decisions.

Thank you to all my students—past and present—who have helped me over the years to become a better teacher. There is no better way to test the effectiveness of a teaching strategy than to present it to a team of dedicated students. They excel at finding the obscurest of errors! I could have never done this without all of your support.

Dedications

For my wife, Teri. Without her patience and understanding, I would not have been able to participate in this project. Thank you for your love and support throughout the countless hours it took me to complete this book and for your understanding that I still needed time to surf.

—Rick Graziani

For my wife, Becky. Without the sacrifices you made during the project, this work would not have come to fruition. Thank you for providing me the comfort and resting place only you can give.

—Allan Johnson

Contents at a Glance

Contents

Icons Used in This Book

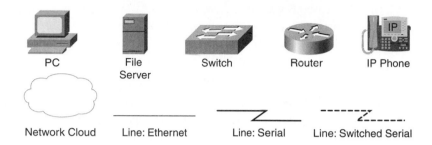

Command Syntax Conventions

The conventions used to present command syntax in this book are the same conventions used in the IOS Command Reference. The Command Reference describes these conventions as follows:

- **Boldface** indicates commands and keywords that are entered literally as shown. In actual configuration examples and output (not general command syntax), boldface indicates commands that are manually input by the user (such as a **show** command).

- *Italics* indicate arguments for which you supply actual values.

- Vertical bars (|) separate alternative, mutually exclusive elements.

- Square brackets [ ] indicate optional elements.

- Braces { } indicate a required choice.

- Braces within brackets [{ }] indicate a required choice within an optional element.

Introduction

The Cisco Networking Academy is a comprehensive e-learning program that provides students with Internet technology skills. A Networking Academy delivers web-based content, online assessment, student performance tracking, and hands-on labs to prepare students for industry-standard certifications. The CCNA curriculum includes four courses oriented around the topics of the Cisco Certified Network Associate (CCNA) certification.

Routing Protocols and Concepts, CCNA Exploration Companion Guide is the official supplement textbook to be used with v4 of the CCNA Exploration Routing Protocols and Concepts online curriculum of the Networking Academy.

This book goes beyond earlier editions of the Cisco Press *Companion Guides* by providing many alternate explanations and examples as compared to the course. You can use the online curriculum as normal and use this companion guide to help solidify your understanding of all the topics through the alternate examples.

The basis for this book as well as the online curriculum is to provide you with a thorough understanding of routing protocols and concepts beyond that necessary for the CCNA certification exam. The commands used for configuring routing protocols are not very difficult. The challenge is to understand the operation of those protocols and their effect upon the network.

The objective of this book is to explain routing protocols and concepts. Every concept is methodically explained with no assumptions made of the reader's knowledge of routing protocols. The only exceptions are, if a concept is beyond the scope of this course or is covered in CCNP, it is noted within the text.

Readers are welcome to use the resources on Rick Graziani's website: http://www.cabrillo.edu/~rgraziani. You can e-mail Rick Graziani at graziani@cabrillo.edu to obtain the username and password to access his resources for this course and all other CCNA and CCNP courses, including PowerPoint presentations.

Goal of This Book

First and foremost, by providing a fresh, complementary perspective on the content, this book is intended to help you learn all the required materials of the Routing Protocols and Concepts course in the Networking Academy CCNA Exploration curriculum. As a secondary goal, the text is intended as a mobile replacement for the online curriculum for individuals who do not always have Internet access. In those cases, you can instead read the appropriate sections of the book, as directed by your instructor, and learn the same material that is covered in the online curriculum. Another secondary goal is to serve as your offline study material to prepare for the CCNA exam.

Audience for This Book

This book's main audience is anyone taking the CCNA Exploration Routing Protocols and Concepts course of the Cisco Networking Academy curriculum. Many Academies use this textbook as a required tool in the course, while other Academies recommend the *Companion Guides* as an additional source of study and practice materials.

Book Features

The educational features of this book focus on supporting topic coverage, readability, and practice of the course material to facilitate your full understanding of the course material.

Topic Coverage

The following features give you a thorough overview of the topics covered in each chapter so that you can make constructive use of your study time:

- **Objectives**—Listed at the beginning of each chapter, the objectives reference the core concepts covered in the chapter. The objectives match the objectives stated in the corresponding chapters of the online curriculum; however, the question format in the *Companion Guide* encourages you to think about finding the answers as you read the chapter.

- **"How-to" feature:** When this book covers a set of steps that you need to perform for certain tasks, it lists the steps as a how-to list. When you are studying, the icon helps you easily refer to this feature as you skim through the book.

- **Notes, tips, cautions, and warnings:** These are short sidebars that point out interesting facts, timesaving methods, and important safety issues.

- **Chapter summaries:** At the end of each chapter is a summary of the chapter's key concepts. It provides a synopsis of the chapter and serves as a study aid.

Readability

The authors have compiled, edited, and in some cases, rewritten the material so that it has a more conversational tone that follows a consistent and accessible reading level. In addition, the following features have been updated to assist your understanding of the networking vocabulary:

- **Key terms:** Each chapter begins with a list of key terms, along with a page-number reference from inside the chapter. The terms are listed in the order in which they are explained in the chapter. This handy reference allows you to find a term, flip to the page where the term appears, and see the term used in context. The Glossary defines all the key terms.

- **Glossary:** This book contains an all-new Glossary, with more than 150 terms.

Practice

Practice makes perfect. This new *Companion Guide* offers you ample opportunities to put what you learn to practice. You will find the following features valuable and effective in reinforcing the instruction that you receive:

- **Check Your Understanding questions and answer key:** Updated review questions are presented at the end of each chapter as a self-assessment tool. These questions match the style of questions that you see in the online course. The appendix, "Check Your Understanding and Challenge Questions Answer Key," provides an answer key to all the questions and includes an explanation of each answer.

- **(NEW) Challenge questions and activities:** Additional—and more challenging— review questions and activities are presented at the end of chapters. These questions are purposefully designed to be similar to the more complex styles of questions you might see on the CCNA exam. This section might also include activities to help prepare you for the exams. The appendix provides the answers.

- **Packet Tracer Activities:** Interspersed throughout the chapters, you'll find many activities that allow you to work with the Cisco Packet Tracer tool. Packet Tracer allows you to create networks, visualize how packets flow in the network, and use basic testing tools to determine whether the network would work. When you see this icon, you can use Packet Tracer with the listed file to perform a task suggested in this book. The activity files are available on this book's CD-ROM; Packet Tracer software, however, is available through the Academy Connection website. Ask your instructor for access to Packet Tracer.

Labs and Study Guide

The supplementary book *Routing Protocols and Concepts, CCNA Exploration Labs and Study Guide*, by Cisco Press (ISBN 1-58713-204-4), contains all the labs from the curriculum plus additional challenge labs and study guide material. The end of each chapter of this *Companion Guide* indicates with icons what labs, activities, and Packet Tracer Activities are available in the Labs and Study Guide.

- **Lab and Activity references:** This icon notes the hands-on labs and other activities created for this chapter in the online curriculum. Within *Routing Protocols and Concepts, CCNA Exploration Labs and Study Guide,* you will also find additional labs and study guide material created by the author of that book.

- **(NEW) Packet Tracer Companion activities:** Many of the hands-on labs include Packet Tracer Companion activities, where you can use Packet Tracer to complete a simulation of the lab. Look for this icon in *Routing Protocols and Concepts, CCNA Exploration Labs and Study Guide*, by Cisco Press (ISBN 1-58713-204-4), for hands-on labs that have a Packet Tracer Companion.

■ **(NEW) Packet Tracer Skills Integration Challenge activities:** These activities require you to pull together several skills learned from the chapter to successfully complete one comprehensive exercise. Look for this icon in *Routing Protocols and Concepts, CCNA Exploration Labs and Study Guide*, by Cisco Press (ISBN 1-58713-204-4) for instructions on how to perform the Packet Tracer Skills Integration Challenge for this chapter.

A Word About Packet Tracer Software and Activities

Packet Tracer is a self-paced, visual interactive teaching and learning tool developed by Cisco. Lab activities are an important part of networking education. However, lab equipment can be a scarce resource. Packet Tracer provides a visual simulation of equipment and network processes to offset the challenge of limited equipment. Students can spend as much time as they like completing standard lab exercises through Packet Tracer, and have the option to work from home. Although Packet Tracer is not a substitute for real equipment, it allows students to practice using a command-line interface. This "e-doing" capability is a fundamental component of learning how to configure routers and switches from the command line.

Packet Tracer v4.x is available only to Cisco Networking Academies through the Academy Connection website. Ask your instructor for access to Packet Tracer.

The course includes essentially three different types of Packet Tracer activities. This book uses an icon system to indicate which type of Packet Tracer activity is available. The icons are intended to give you a sense of the purpose of the activity and the amount of time you need to allot to complete it. The three types of Packet Tracer activities follow:

■ **Packet Tracer Activity:** This icon identifies straightforward exercises interspersed throughout the chapters where you can practice or visualize a specific topic. The activity files for these exercises are available on this book's CD-ROM. These activities take less time to complete than the Packet Tracer Companion and Challenge activities.

■ **Packet Tracer Companion:** This icon identifies exercises that correspond to the hands-on labs of the course. You can use Packet Tracer to complete a simulation of the hands-on lab or complete a similar "lab." The Companion Guide points these out at the end of each chapter, but look for this icon and the associated exercise file in *Routing Protocols and Concepts CCNA Exploration Labs and Study Guide* for hands-on labs that have a Packet Tracer Companion.

■ **Packet Tracer Skills Integration Challenge:** This icon identifies activities that require you to pull together several skills learned from the chapter to successfully complete one comprehensive exercise. The *Companion Guide* points these out at the end of each chapter, but look for this icon in *Routing Protocols and Concepts CCNA Exploration Labs and Study Guide* for instructions on how to perform the Packet Tracer Skills Integration Challenge for this chapter.

How This Book Is Organized

The book covers the major topic headings in the same sequence as the online curriculum for the CCNA Exploration Routing Protocols and Concepts course. This book has 11 chapters, with the same numbers and similar names as the online course chapters.

Each routing protocol chapter and the static routing chapter begin with a single topology that is used throughout the chapter. The single topology per chapter allows better continuity and easier understanding of routing commands, operations, and outputs.

- **Chapter 1, "Introduction to Routing and Packet Forwarding,"** provides an overview of the router hardware and software, along with an introduction to directly connected networks, static routing, and dynamic routing protocols. The process of packet forwarding is also reviewed, including the path determination and switching functions.

- **Chapter 2, "Static Routing,"** examines static routing in detail. The use of static routes and the role they play in modern networks are discussed. This chapter describes the advantages, uses, and configuration of static routes using next-hop IP addresses and/or exit interfaces. Basic Cisco IOS commands are reviewed, along with an introduction to the Cisco IP routing table.

- **Chapter 3, "Introduction to Dynamic Routing Protocols,"** provides an overview of dynamic routing protocols and the various methods used to classify them. The terms *metrics* and *administrative distance* are introduced. This chapter serves as an introduction to terms and concepts that are examined more fully in later chapters.

- **Chapter 4, "Distance Vector Routing Protocols,"** covers the theory behind distance vector routing protocols. The algorithm used by distance vector routing protocols, along with the process of network discovery and routing table maintenance, is discussed.

- **Chapter 5, "RIP Version 1,"** examines the distance vector routing protocol RIPv1. Although it is the oldest IP routing protocol, RIPv1 is the ideal candidate for discussing distance vector technology and classful routing protocols. This chapter includes the configuration, verification, and troubleshooting of RIPv1.

- **Chapter 6, "VLSM and CIDR,"** discusses VLSM (variable-length subnet masks) and CIDR (classless interdomain routing), including how to allocate IP addresses according to need rather than by class, and how IP addresses can be summarized as a single address, which is known as *supernetting*.

- **Chapter 7, "RIPv2,"** discusses RIPv2, a distance vector routing protocol. RIPv2 is a classless routing protocol as compared to RIPv1, which is a classful routing protocol. This chapter examines the benefits of using a classless routing protocol and describes how it supports both VLSM and CIDR. This chapter includes the configuration, verification, and troubleshooting of RIPv2.

- **Chapter 8, "The Routing Table: A Closer Look,"** examines the Cisco IPv4 routing table in detail. Understanding the structure and lookup process of the routing table provides a valuable tool in verifying and troubleshooting networks.

- **Chapter 9, "EIGRP,"** discusses the classless routing protocol EIGRP. EIGRP is a Cisco-proprietary, advanced distance vector routing protocol. This chapter examines DUAL (Diffusing Update Algorithm) and describes how DUAL determines best paths and loop-free backup paths. This chapter includes the configuration, verification, and troubleshooting of EIGRP.

- **Chapter 10, "Link-State Routing Protocols,"** provides an introduction to link-state terms and concepts. This chapter compares link-state and distance vector routing protocols, discussing the benefits and requirements of using a link-state routing protocol.

- **Chapter 11, "OSPF,"** examines the classless, link-state routing protocol OSPF. OSPF operations are discussed, including link-state updates, adjacency, and the DR/BDR election process. This chapter includes the configuration, verification, and troubleshooting of OSPF.

- **Appendix, "Check Your Understanding and Challenge Questions Answer Key,"** provides the answers to the Check Your Understanding questions that you find at the end of each chapter. It also includes answers for the Challenge Questions and Activities that conclude most chapters.

- The **Glossary** provides a compiled list of all the key terms that appear throughout this book.

About the CD-ROM

The CD-ROM included with this book provides many useful tools and information to support your education:

- **Packet Tracer Activity files:** These are files to work through the Packet Tracer Activities referenced throughout the book, as indicated by the Packet Tracer Activity icon.

- **Taking Notes:** This section includes a .txt file of the chapter objectives to serve as a general outline of the key topics of which you need to take note. The practice of taking clear, consistent notes is an important skill not only for learning and studying the material but for on-the-job success as well. Also included in this section is "A Guide to Using a Networker's Journal" PDF booklet providing important insight into the value of the practice of using a journal, how to organize a professional journal, and some best practices on what, and what not, to take note of in your journal.

- **IT Career Information:** This section includes a student guide to applying the toolkit approach to your career development. Learn more about entering the world of Information Technology as a career by reading two informational chapters excerpted from *The IT Career Builder's Toolkit:* "Defining Yourself: Aptitudes and Desires" and "Making Yourself Indispensable."

- **Lifelong Learning in Networking:** As you embark on a technology career, you will notice that it is ever-changing and evolving. This career path provides new and exciting opportunities to learn new technologies and their applications. Cisco Press is one of the key resources to plug into on your quest for knowledge. This section of the CD-ROM provides an orientation to the information available to you and tips on how to tap into these resources for lifelong learning.

CHAPTER 1

Introduction to Routing and Packet Forwarding

Objectives

Upon completion of this chapter, you should be able to answer the following questions:

- What features do routers and computers have in common?

- How do you configure Cisco devices and apply addresses?

- Can you describe the basic structure of a routing table?

- Can you describe, in detail, how a router determines the best path and then switches a packet?

Key Terms

This chapter uses the following key terms. You can find the definitions in the Glossary at the end of the book.

power-on self test (POST)   page 12

console port   page 18

DSL   page 18

ISDN   page 18

cable   page 19

LED   page 19

NIC   page 20

hosts   page 20

gateway   page 22

privileged EXEC mode   page 25

Telnet   page 26

next-hop   page 34

neighbor   page 35

metric   page 36

administrative distance   page 36

hub-and-spoke   page 39

IGRP   page 41

BGP   page 42

asymmetric routing   page 43

TTL   page 44

datagrams   page 45

NAT   page 45

equal-cost metric   page 48

equal-cost load balancing   page 48

unequal-cost load balancing   page 49

Today's networks have a significant impact on our lives, changing the way we live, work, and play. Today's networks and, in a larger context, the Internet allow people to communicate, collaborate, and interact in ways they never did before. We use the network in a variety of ways, including web applications, *IP* telephony, videoconferencing, interactive gaming, electronic commerce, education, and more.

At the center of the network is the *router*. Routers are used to connect multiple networks. The router is responsible for the delivery of *packets* across different networks. The destination of the IP packet can be a web server in another country or an e-mail server on the local-area network. It is the router's responsibility to deliver those packets in a timely manner. The effectiveness of internetwork communications for a large part depends on the ability of the routers to forward packets in the most efficient way possible. Whether it is a packet sent between two LANs within a company's intranetwork or a packet sent thousands of miles away to a remote network in another country, it is the router that forwards the packet from network to network, from sending host to destination host.

Routers are even being added to satellites in space. These routers will have the ability to route IP traffic between satellites in space in much the same way that packets are moved on earth, therefore reducing delays and offering greater networking flexibility.

The services that a router provides go well beyond those of just packet forwarding. Because of the demands on today's network, the router also is used for

- Ensuring 24/7 (24 hours a day, 7 days a week) availability to help guarantee network reachability using alternate paths in case the primary path fails

- Providing integrated services of data, video, and voice over wired and wireless networks using quality of service (QoS) prioritization of IP packets to ensure that real-time traffic, such as voice and video or critical data, is not dropped or delayed

- Mitigating the impact of worms, viruses, and other attacks on the network by permitting or denying the forwarding of packets

All this is built around the router and its capability to forward packets from one network to the next, from the original source to the final destination. It is only because of the router's capability to route packets between networks that devices on different networks can communicate. This chapter introduces you to the router, its role in the networks, its main hardware and software components, and the routing process itself.

Inside the Router

A router is a computer and has many of the common hardware components found on other types of computers. A router also includes an operating system. Examining some of the basic hardware and software components will give you a better understanding of the routing and packet-forwarding process.

Routers Are Computers

A router is a computer, just like any other computer, including a PC. The first router, which was used for the Advanced Research Projects Agency Network (ARPANET), was the IMP (Interface Message Processor). The IMP was a Honeywell 516 minicomputer that brought the ARPANET to life on August 30, 1969.

The ARPANET was developed by the Advanced Research Projects Agency (ARPA) of the United States Department of Defense. The ARPANET was the world's first operational packet-switching network and the predecessor of today's Internet.

Figure 1-1 shows the front side of a Cisco 1800 series Integrated Services Router, which is the recommended router for use with this course. Routers have many of the same hardware and software components that are found in other computers, including

- CPU
- *RAM*
- *ROM*
- *Operating system*

Figure 1-1   Cisco 1841 Integrated Services Router

Routers Are at the Network Center

A typical user might be unaware of the presence of numerous routers in his or her own network or in the Internet. Users expect to be able to access web pages, send e-mails, and download music, whether the server they are accessing is on their own network or on another network halfway around the world. However, networking professionals know that it is the router that is responsible for forwarding packets from network to network, from the original source to the final destination.

A router connects multiple networks. This means that it has interfaces that belong to different IP networks. When a router receives an IP packet on one interface, it determines which interface to forward the packet on its way to its destination. The interface that the router uses to forward the packet can be the network of the final destination of the packet (the network with the destination IP address of this packet), or it can be a network connected to another router that is used to reach the destination network.

Each network that a router connects to typically requires a separate interface. These interfaces are used to connect a combination of both *local-area networks (LAN)* and *wide-area networks (WAN)*. LANs are commonly *Ethernet* networks that contain devices such as PCs, printers, and servers. WANs are used to connect networks over a large geographical area. For example, a WAN connection is commonly used to connect a LAN to the *Internet service provider (ISP)* network.

Figure 1-2 shows that Routers R1 and R2 are responsible for receiving the packet on one network and forwarding the packet out another network toward the packet's destination network.

Figure 1-2   What Is a Router?

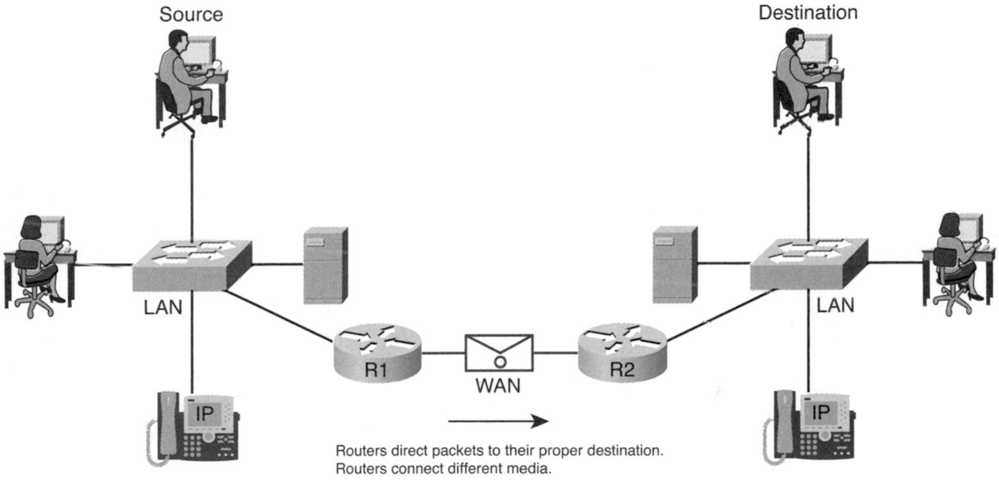

Routers direct packets to their proper destination.
Routers connect different media.

Routers Determine the Best Path

The router's primary responsibility is to forward packets destined for local and remote networks by

- Determining the *best path* to send packets
- Forwarding packets toward their destination

The router uses its *routing table* to determine the best path to forward the packet. When the router receives a packet, it examines the destination IP address and searches for the best match with a network address in the router's routing table. The routing table will include the interface to be used to forward the packet. When a match is found, the router encapsulates the IP packet into the data-link frame of the outgoing or exit interface, and the packet is then forwarded toward its destination.

A router will likely receive a packet encapsulated in one type of data-link frame, such as an Ethernet frame, and when forwarding the packet, encapsulate it in a different type of data-link frame, such as *Point-to-Point Protocol (PPP)*. The data-link encapsulation depends on the type of interface on the router and the type of medium to which it connects. The different data-link technologies that a router connects to can include LAN technologies, such as Ethernet, and WAN *serial* connections, such as a T1 connection using PPP, *Frame Relay*, and *ATM*.

In Figure 1-3, notice that it is the router's responsibility to find the destination network in its routing table and forward the packet toward the destination. In the figure, R1 receives the packet encapsulated in an Ethernet frame. After decapsulating the packet, the router uses the destination IP address of the packet to search the routing table for a matching network address. R2 found the static route 192.168.3.0/24, which can be reached out its Serial 0/0/0 interface. R2 will encapsulate the packet in a frame format appropriate for the outbound interface and then forward the packet.

Figure 1-3   Routers Determine the Best Path

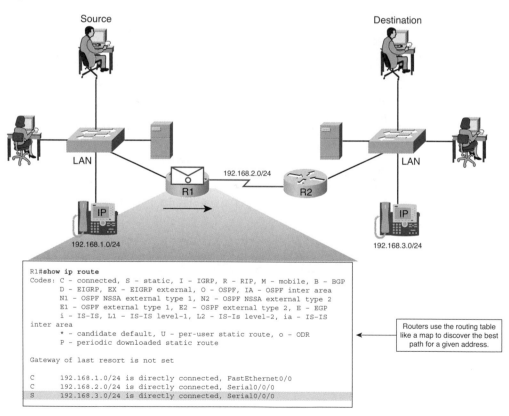

```
R1#show ip route
Codes: C - connected, S - static, I - IGRP, R - RIP, M - mobile, B - BGP
       D - EIGRP, EX - EIGRP external, O - OSPF, IA - OSPF inter area
       N1 - OSPF NSSA external type 1, N2 - OSPF NSSA external type 2
       E1 - OSPF external type 1, E2 - OSPF external type 2, E - EGP
       i - IS-IS, L1 - IS-IS level-1, L2 - IS-Is level-2, ia - IS-IS
inter area
       * - candidate default, U - per-user static route, o - ODR
       P - periodic downloaded static route

Gateway of last resort is not set

C       192.168.1.0/24 is directly connected, FastEthernet0/0
C       192.168.2.0/24 is directly connected, Serial0/0/0
S       192.168.3.0/24 is directly connected, Serial0/0/0
```

Routers use the routing table like a map to discover the best path for a given address.

Static routes and *dynamic routing protocols* are used by routers to learn about remote networks and build their routing tables. This is the primary focus of the course. It will be discussed in detail in later chapters, along with the process routers use in searching their routing tables and forwarding the packets.

More Info

Visit websites such as http://www.howstuffworks.com, http://www.techweb.com/encyclopedia, and http://whatis.techtarget.com to see the definitions of a router and related terms.

Today's router is much more than just a packet-forwarding and network-interconnecting device. Modern routers incorporate many other features, such as security, QoS, and voice functionalities. Routers play an important role in the current trend toward *unified communications*. To learn more about Cisco unified communications, see http://www.cisco.com/go/unifiedcommunications _solutions_unified_communications_ home.html.

Corporate Network Simulation (1.1.1)

This Packet Tracer Activity shows a complex network of routers with many different technologies. Be sure to view the activity in simulation mode so that you can see the traffic traveling from multiple sources to multiple destinations over various types of *media*. Detailed instructions are provided within the activity. Use file e2-111.pka on the CD-ROM that accompanies this book to perform this activity using Packet Tracer.

Router CPU and Memory

Although there are several different types and models of routers, every router has the same general hardware components. Depending on the model, those components are located in different places inside the router. Figure 1-4 shows the inside of an 1841 router. To see the internal router components, you must unscrew the metal cover and take it off the router. Usually you do not need to open the router unless you are upgrading memory.

Similar to a PC, a router also includes

- CPU
- RAM
- ROM
- Flash memory
- NVRAM

Figure 1-5 is a schematic of the hardware components of an 1841 router.

Figure 1-4   Inside a Router

Figure 1-5   Hardware Components of a Router

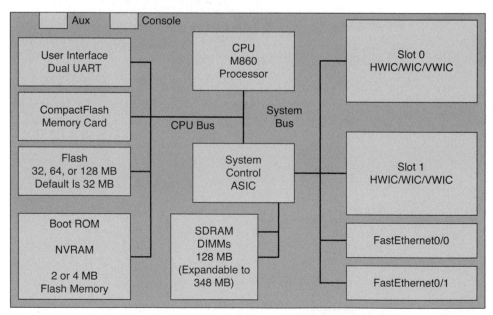

Logical diagram of the Internal Components of a Cisco 1841 router.

CPU

The CPU executes operating system instructions, such as system initialization, routing functions, and network interface control.

RAM

Similar to other computers, RAM stores the instructions and data needed to be executed by the CPU. RAM is used to store

- **Operating system:** Cisco IOS (Internetwork Operating System) is copied into RAM during bootup.

- **Running configuration file:** This is the configuration file that stores the configuration commands that the router's IOS is currently using. With few exceptions, all commands configured on the router are stored in the running configuration file known as the running-config.

- **IP routing table:** This is the file that stores information about directly connected and remote networks.

- *ARP* **cache:** This cache stores IP address–to–*MAC address* mappings, similar to the ARP cache on a PC. ARP cache would be used on routers that have Ethernet interfaces.

- **Packet buffering:** Packets are temporarily stored in a buffer when received on an interface or before they exit an interface.

RAM is volatile memory and loses its contents when the router is powered down or restarted. For this reason, the router also contains permanent storage areas such as ROM, flash, and NVRAM.

ROM

ROM is a form of permanent storage. Cisco devices use ROM to store

- Bootstrap instructions

- Basic diagnostic software

- Scaled-down version of IOS

ROM uses firmware, which is software embedded inside the integrated circuit. Firmware, such as the bootup instructions, does not normally need to be modified or upgraded. Many of these features, including ROM monitor software, will be discussed in a later course. ROM does not lose its contents when the router loses power or is restarted.

Flash Memory

Flash memory is nonvolatile computer memory that can be electrically erased and reprogrammed. Flash is used as permanent storage for the operating system, Cisco IOS. In most models of Cisco routers, the IOS is permanently stored in flash memory and copied into RAM during the bootup process. Flash consists of SIMM or PC cards (PCMCIA cards), which can be upgraded to increase the amount of flash memory.

Flash memory does not lose its contents when the router loses power or is restarted.

NVRAM

NVRAM is nonvolatile random-access memory, which does not lose its information when the power is turned off. This is in contrast to the most common forms of RAM such as DRAM, which requires continual power to maintain its information. NVRAM is used by Cisco IOS Software as permanent storage for the startup configuration file (startup-config). All configuration changes are stored in the running-config file in RAM and, with few exceptions, are implemented immediately by the IOS. To save those changes in case the router is restarted or loses power, the running-config file must be copied to NVRAM, where it is stored as the startup-config file. NVRAM retains its contents even when the router is powered off.

ROM, RAM, NVRAM, and flash are discussed in the following sections, which introduce IOS and the bootup process. They are also discussed in more detail in a later course with regard to managing IOS.

For a networking professional, it is more important to understand the *function* of the main internal components of a router than the exact location of those components inside a particular model of router. Physical architecture differs among the models.

More Info

View the "Cisco 1800 Series Portfolio Multimedia Demo" at http://www.cisco.com/en/ US/products/ps5875/index.html.

Internetwork Operating System (IOS)

The operating system software used in Cisco routers is known as Cisco Internetwork Operating System (IOS). Like any operating system on any other computer, Cisco IOS Software is responsible for managing the hardware and software resources of the router, including allocating memory, managing processes and security, and managing file systems. Cisco IOS is a multitasking operating system that is integrated with routing, switching, internetworking, and telecommunications functions.

Although the Cisco IOS might appear to be the same on many routers, there are many different IOS images. An IOS image is a file that contains the entire IOS for that router. Cisco creates many different IOS images, depending on the model and the features within the IOS. Typically, additional features require more flash and RAM to store and load the IOS. For example, some features can include the ability to run Internet Protocol version 6 (*IPv6*) or a routing protocol such as Intermediate System–to–Intermediate System (*IS-IS*).

As with other operating systems, Cisco IOS has its own user interface. Although some routers provide a GUI (graphical user interface), the CLI (command-line interface) is a much more common method of configuring Cisco routers and is used throughout this curriculum.

Upon bootup, the startup-config file in NVRAM is copied into RAM and stored as the running-config file. IOS executes the configuration commands in the running-config file. Any changes entered by the network administrator are stored in the running-config file and immediately implemented by the IOS. In this chapter, we will review some of the basic IOS commands used to configure a Cisco router. In later chapters, you will learn the commands used to configure, verify, and troubleshoot *static routing* and various routing protocols, such as Routing Information Protocol (*RIP*), Enhanced Interior Gateway Routing Protocol (*EIGRP*), and Open Shortest Path First (*OSPF*).

Note

Cisco IOS is discussed in more detail in a later course.

Router Bootup Process

Like all computers, a router uses a systematic process to boot. This involves testing the hardware, loading the operating system software, and performing any saved configuration commands in the startup configuration file. Some of the details of this process have been excluded and are examined more completely in a later course.

Bootup Process

Figure 1-6 shows the six major phases in the bootup process:

1. POST: Testing the router hardware

2. Loading the bootstrap program

3. Locating Cisco IOS

4. Loading Cisco IOS

5. Locating the configuration file

6. Loading the startup configuration file or entering *setup mode*

Figure 1-6   How a Router Boots Up

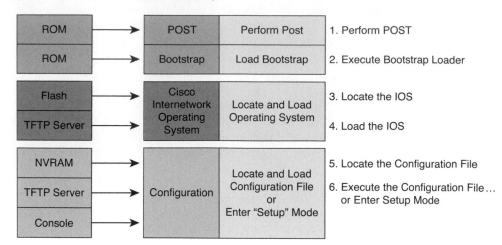

Step 1: Performing the POST

A *power-on self test (POST)* is a common process that occurs on most every computer during bootup. The POST process is used to test the router hardware. When the router is powered on, software on the ROM chip conducts the POST. During this self test, the router executes diagnostics from ROM on several hardware components, including the CPU, RAM, and NVRAM. After the POST has been completed, the router executes the bootstrap program.

Step 2: Loading the Bootstrap Program

After the POST, the bootstrap program is copied from ROM into RAM. When the bootstrap program is in RAM, the CPU executes the instructions in the bootstrap program. The main task of the bootstrap program is to locate the Cisco IOS and load it into RAM.

At this point, if you have a console connection to the router, you will begin to see output on the screen.

Step 3: Locating Cisco IOS

The bootstrap program is responsible for locating the Cisco IOS and copying it into RAM. The IOS is typically stored in flash memory, but it can be stored in other places such as a TFTP server.

If a full IOS image cannot be located, a scaled-down version of the IOS is copied from ROM into RAM. This version of IOS is used to help diagnose any problems and can be used to load a complete version of the IOS into RAM.

Note

A TFTP server is typically used as a backup server for IOS, but it can also be used as a central point for storing and loading the IOS. IOS management and using the TFTP server are discussed in a later course.

Step 4: Loading Cisco IOS

Some of the older Cisco routers ran the IOS directly from flash, but current models copy the IOS into RAM for execution by the CPU. When the IOS begins to load, you might see a string of pound signs (#) while the image decompresses.

Step 5: Locating the Configuration File

After the IOS is loaded, the bootstrap program searches for the startup configuration file, known as the startup-config file, in NVRAM. This file has the previously saved configuration commands and parameters, including the following:

- Interface addresses
- Routing information
- Passwords
- Any other configurations saved by the network administrator

If the startup configuration file, startup-config, is located in NVRAM, it is then copied into RAM as the running configuration file, running-config.

Note

If the startup configuration file does not exist in NVRAM, the router can search for a TFTP server. If the router detects that it has an active link to another configured router, it will send a broadcast searching for a configuration file across the active link. This condition will cause the router to pause, but you will eventually see a console message like the following:

```
<router pauses here while it broadcasts for a configuration file across an
active link>
%Error opening tftp://255.255.255.255/network-confg (Timed out)
%Error opening tftp://255.255.255.255/cisconet.cfg (Timed out)
```

Step 6: Loading the Startup Configuration File or Entering Setup Mode

If a startup configuration file is found in NVRAM, the IOS loads it into RAM as the running-config file and executes the commands in the file one line at a time. The running-config commands contain interface addresses, start routing processes, configure router passwords, and define other characteristics of the router.

If the startup configuration file cannot be located, the router will prompt the user to enter setup mode. Setup mode is a series of questions prompting the user for basic configuration information. Setup mode is not intended to enter complex router configurations, nor is it commonly used by network administrators. Setup mode will not be used in this course.

When booting a router that does not contain a startup configuration file, you will see the following question after the IOS has been loaded:

```
Would you like to enter the initial configuration dialog? [yes/no]: no
```

Setup mode will not be used in this course to configure the router. When prompted to enter setup mode, always answer **no**. If you answer **yes** and enter setup mode, you can press **Ctrl-C** at any time to terminate the setup process.

When setup mode is not used, IOS will create a default running-config file. The default running-config file is a basic configuration file that includes the router interfaces, management interfaces, and certain default information. The default running-config file does not contain interface addresses, routing information, passwords, or other specific configuration information.

Command-Line Interface

Depending on the platform and IOS, the router might ask the following question before displaying the prompt:

```
Would you like to terminate autoinstall? [yes]: <Enter>

Press the Enter key to accept the default answer.

Router>
```

If a startup configuration file was found, the running configuration can include a host name, which means that the prompt will display the host name of the router.

After the prompt is displayed, the router is now running IOS with the current running configuration file. The network administrator can now begin using IOS commands on this router.

Note

The bootup process is discussed in more detail in a later course.

Verifying Router Bootup Process

The **show version** command can be used to help verify and troubleshoot some of the basic hardware and software components of the router. The **show version** command in Example 1-1 displays information about the version of Cisco IOS Software currently running on the router, the version of the bootstrap program, and information about the hardware configuration, including the amount of system memory.

Example 1-1 show version Command Output

```
Router# show version

Cisco Internetwork Operating System Software
IOS (tm) C2600 Software (C2600-I-M), Version 12.2(28), RELEASE SOFTWARE (fc5)
Technical Support: http://www.cisco.com/techsupport
Copyright (c) 1986-2005 by cisco Systems, Inc.
Compiled Wed 27-Apr-04 19:01 by miwang
Image text-base: 0x8000808C, data-base: 0x80A1FECC

ROM: System Bootstrap, Version 12.1(3r)T2, RELEASE SOFTWARE (fc1)
Copyright (c) 2000 by cisco Systems, Inc.
ROM: C2600 Software (C2600-I-M), Version 12.2(28), RELEASE SOFTWARE (fc5)

System returned to ROM by reload
System image file is "flash:c2600-i-mz.122-28.bin"

cisco 2621 (MPC860) processor (revision 0x200) with 60416K/5120K bytes of memory.
Processor board ID JAD05190MTZ (4292891495)
M860 processor: part number 0, mask 49
Bridging software.
X.25 software, Version 3.0.0.
2 FastEthernet/IEEE 802.3 interface(s)
2 Low-speed serial(sync/async) network interface(s)
32K bytes of non-volatile configuration memory.
16384K bytes of processor board System flash (Read/Write)

Configuration register is 0x2102
```

The output from the **show version** command includes information about the following:

- IOS version

- ROM bootstrap program

- Location of IOS

- CPU and amount of RAM

- Interfaces

- Amount of NVRAM

- Amount of flash

- Configuration register information

The sections that follow dissect these pieces of information in further detail.

IOS Version

```
Cisco Internetwork Operating System Software
IOS (tm) C2600 Software (C2600-I-M), Version 12.2(28), RELEASE SOFTWARE (fc5)
```

This is the version of Cisco IOS Software in RAM and being used by the router.

ROM Bootstrap Program

```
ROM: System Bootstrap, Version 12.1(3r)T2, RELEASE SOFTWARE (fc1)
```

This is the version of the system bootstrap software, stored in ROM, that was initially used to boot up the router.

Location of IOS

```
System image file is "flash:c2600-i-mz.122-28.bin"
```

This is the location from which the boostrap program located and loaded the Cisco IOS, along with the complete filename of the IOS image.

CPU and Amount of RAM

```
cisco 2621 (MPC860) processor (revision 0x200) with 60416K/5120K bytes of memory
```

The first part of this line displays the type of CPU on this router. The last part of this line displays the amount of DRAM. Some series of routers like the 2600 use a fraction of DRAM as packet memory. Packet memory is used for buffering packets.

You must add both numbers to find out the total amount of DRAM on the router. In this example, the Cisco 2621 router has 60,416 KB (kilobytes) of free DRAM used for temporarily storing the Cisco IOS and other system processes. The other 5120 KB is dedicated to packet memory. Adding the two numbers gives you 60,416 KB + 5120 KB = 65,536 KB, or 64 megabytes (MB), of total DRAM.

It might be necessary to upgrade the amount of RAM when upgrading the IOS.

Interfaces

```
2 FastEthernet/IEEE 802.3 interface(s)
2 Low-speed serial(sync/async) network interface(s)
```

This section of the output displays the physical interfaces on the router. In this example, the Cisco 2621 router has two Fast Ethernet interfaces and two low-speed serial interfaces.

Amount of NVRAM

```
32K bytes of non-volatile configuration memory.
```

This is the amount of NVRAM on the router. NVRAM is used to store the startup-config file.

Amount of Flash

```
16384K bytes of processor board System flash (Read/Write)
```

This is the amount of flash memory on the router. Flash is used to permanently store the Cisco IOS. It might be necessary to upgrade the amount of flash when upgrading the IOS.

Configuration Register

```
Configuration register is 0x2102
```

The last line of the **show version** command displays the current configured value of the software configuration register in hexadecimal. If a second value is displayed in parentheses, this is the configuration register value that will be used during the next reload.

The configuration register has several uses, including password recovery. The factory default setting for the configuration register is 0x2102. This value indicates that the router will attempt to load a Cisco IOS Software image from flash memory and load the startup configuration file from NVRAM.

Note

The configuration register is discussed in more detail in a later course.

Packet Tracer
☐ Activity

Using Setup Mode (1.1.4)

Setup mode is available when a router is started for the first time to provide a basic configuration for the router. Packet Tracer supports only basic management setup. This limits you to configuring only a single interface that can connect to a management system to supply the remainder of the configuration. In this activity, R2 is an existing router already added to the network. You will clear any existing configuration and use setup mode to connect R2 to another router. Detailed instructions are provided within the activity. Use file e2-114.pka on the CD-ROM that accompanies this book to perform this activity using Packet Tracer.

Router Ports and Interfaces

Although there are no "hard and fast" rules, the term *port*, when referring to a router, normally means one of the management ports used for administrative access. The term *interface* normally refers to interfaces that are capable of sending and receiving user traffic. However, these terms are often used interchangeably in the industry and even with IOS output.

Management Ports

Figure 1-7 shows the back side of a 2621 router. Routers have management ports, which are physical connectors used to manage the router. Management ports are not used for packet forwarding like Ethernet and serial interfaces. The most common of the management ports is the *console port*. The console port is used to connect a terminal, or most likely a PC running terminal emulator software, to configure the router without the need for network access to that router. The console port must be used during initial configuration of the router.

Figure 1-7   Router Interfaces: Physical Representation

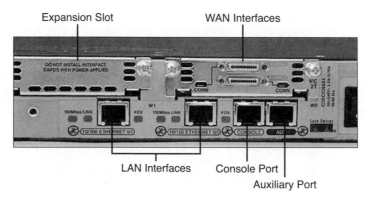

Each interface connects to a different network;
thus, each interface has an IP address/mask from that network.

Another management port is the auxiliary (AUX) port. Not all routers have auxiliary ports. At times, the auxiliary port can be used similarly to a console port but can also be used to attach a modem. Auxiliary ports will not be used in this curriculum.

Router Interfaces

The term *interface* on Cisco routers refers to a physical connector on the router whose main purpose is to receive and forward packets. Routers have multiple interfaces used to connect to multiple networks. It is common that the interfaces will connect to various types of networks, which means different types of media and connectors. Often a router will need to have different types of interfaces. For example, a router will most likely have Fast Ethernet interfaces for connections to different LANs and also have different types of WAN interfaces used to connect a variety of serial links, including T1, *DSL*, and *ISDN*. Figure 1-8 shows the Fast Ethernet and serial interfaces on the router.

Figure 1-8   Router Interfaces: Logical Representation

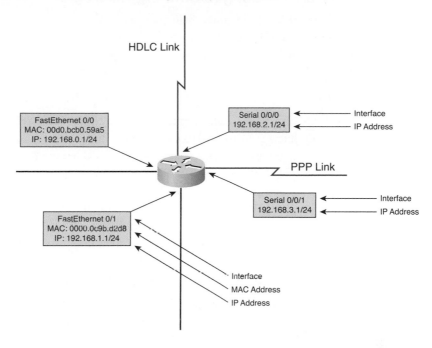

Like the interfaces on a PC, the ports and interfaces on a router are located on the outside of the router. This makes sense, because the appropriate network *cable* and connector will need to be connected to this interface.

> **Note**
>
> A single interface on a router can be used to connect to multiple networks; however, this is beyond the scope of this course and is discussed in a later course.

Like most networking devices, Cisco routers use *LED* indicators to provide status information. An interface LED indicates the activity of the corresponding interface. If an LED is off when the interface is active and the interface is correctly connected, this might be an indication of a problem with that interface. If an interface is extremely busy, its LED will always be on. Depending on the router, there might be other LEDs as well.

More Info

For more information on reading LEDs on the 1841 series routers, see "Troubleshooting Cisco 1800 Series Routers (Modular)" at http://www.cisco.com/en/US/products/ps5853/ products_installation_guide_chapter09186a00802c36b8.html.

Interfaces Belong to Different Networks

Every interface on the router belongs to a different network. In other words, each interface is a host on a different IP network, as shown previously in Figure 1-8. Each interface must be configured with an IP address and subnet mask of a different network. Cisco IOS will not allow two active interfaces on the same router to belong to the same network.

Router interfaces can be divided into two major groups:

- **LAN interfaces**, such as Ethernet and Fast Ethernet interfaces. As the name indicates, LAN interfaces are used to connect the router to the LAN, similar to how a PC's Ethernet network interface card (*NIC*) is used to connect the PC to the Ethernet LAN. Like a PC's Ethernet NIC, a router's Ethernet interface also has a Layer 2 MAC address and participates in the Ethernet LAN the same way as any other *hosts* on that LAN. For example, a router's Ethernet interface participates in the Address Resolution Protocol (ARP) process for that LAN. The router will maintain an ARP cache for that interface, send ARP requests when needed, and respond with ARP replies when required.

  A router's Ethernet interface typically uses an RJ-45 jack that supports unshielded twisted-pair (UTP) cabling. When a router is connected to a switch, a straight-through cable is used. When two routers are connected directly through the Ethernet interfaces, or when a PC's NIC is connected directly to a router's Ethernet interface, a crossover cable is used.

- **WAN interfaces**, such as serial, ISDN, and Frame Relay interfaces. WAN interfaces are used to connect routers to external networks, usually over a larger geographical distance. The Layer 2 encapsulation can be different types including PPP, Frame Relay, and HDLC (High-Level Data Link Control). Similar to LAN interfaces, each WAN interface has its own IP address and subnet mask, making it a member of a specific network. Remember, MAC addresses are used only on Ethernet interfaces and are not on WAN interfaces. However, WAN interfaces use their own Layer 2 addresses depending on the technology. Layer 2 WAN encapsulation types and addresses are covered in a later course.

Example of Router Interfaces

The router in Figure 1-8 has four interfaces. Each interface has a Layer 3 IP address and subnet mask that configures it for a different network. The Ethernet interfaces also have Layer 2 Ethernet MAC addresses.

The WAN interfaces are using different Layer 2 encapsulations. Serial 0/0/0 is using HDLC and Serial 0/0/1 is using PPP. Both of these serial point-to-point protocols use a broadcast address for the Layer 2 destination address when encapsulating the IP packet into a data-link frame.

In the lab environment, you are restricted to how many LAN and WAN interfaces you can use to configure "hands-on" labs. With Packet Tracer, however, you have the flexibility to create more complex network designs.

Cabling Devices (1.1.5.3)

To successfully complete this activity, you must select the proper cables to connect the various devices. Detailed instructions are provided within the activity. Use file e2-1153.pka on the CD-ROM that accompanies this book to perform this activity using Packet Tracer.

Using Packet Tracer Device Tabs (1.1.5.4)

The configuration window in Packet Tracer for Cisco devices, such as routers and switches, consists of three tabs. The Physical tab is used to add and remove modules. The Config tab is used to configure Packet Tracer–specific settings and a limited number of other settings. The CLI tab is used to configure all the settings supported by Packet Tracer. The CLI tab simulates the command-line interface of a Cisco IOS device. In this activity, you will add a router to the lab topology, install a module, configure the router using the Config tab, and complete the configuration using the CLI tab. Detailed instructions are provided within the activity. Use file e2-1154.pka on the CD-ROM that accompanies this book to perform this activity using Packet Tracer.

Routers and the Network Layer

The key to understanding the role of a router in the network is to understand that a router is a Layer 3 device responsible for forwarding packets. However, a router also operates at Layers 1 and 2.

Routing Is Forwarding Packets

The main purpose of a router is to connect multiple networks and forward packets destined for its own networks or other networks. A router is considered a Layer 3 device because its primary forwarding decision is based on the information in the Layer 3 IP packet, specifically the destination IP address. This is known as *routing*.

When a router receives a packet, it examines the destination IP address. If the destination IP address does not belong to any of the router's directly connected networks, the router must forward this packet to another router. In Figure 1-9, R1 examines the packet's destination IP address and, after searching the routing table, forwards the packet onto R2. When R2 receives the packet, it also examines the packet's destination IP address and, after searching its routing table, forwards the packet out its directly connected Ethernet network to PC2.

Figure 1-9   Packet Forwarding

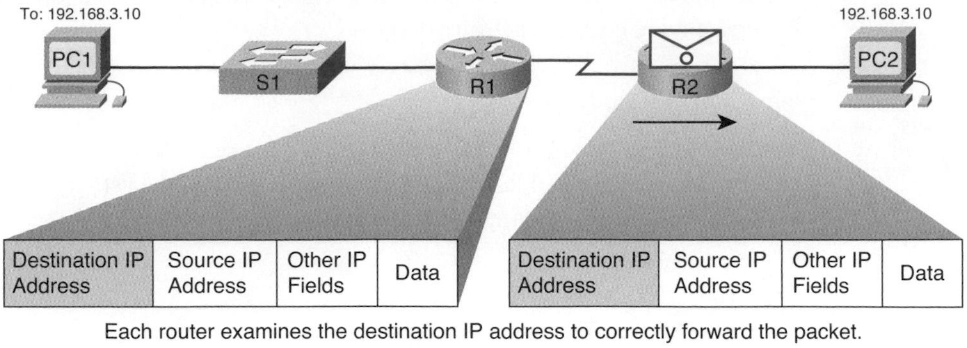

Each router examines the destination IP address to correctly forward the packet.

When each router receives a packet, it searches the routing table to find the best match between the destination IP address of the packet and one of the network addresses in the routing table. When a match is found, the packet is encapsulated in the Layer 2 data-link frame for that outgoing interface. The type of data-link encapsulation depends on the type of interface, such as Ethernet or HDLC.

Eventually the packet reaches a router, where the destination IP address of the packet belongs to the same network as one of the router's directly connected interfaces. In this example, Router R2 receives the packet from Router R1. Router R2 forwards the packet out its Ethernet interface, which belongs to the same network as the destination device, PC2.

This sequence of events is explained in more detail later in this chapter.

Routers Operate at Layers 1, 2, and 3

A router makes its primary forwarding decision at Layer 3, but as you saw earlier, it also participates in Layer 1 and Layer 2 processes. After a router has examined the destination IP address of a packet and consulted its routing table to make its forwarding decision, it can then forward that packet out the appropriate interface toward its destination. The router will encapsulate the Layer 3 IP packet into the data portion of a Layer 2 data-link frame appropriate for the exit interface. This can be an Ethernet frame, an HDLC frame, or some other Layer 2 encapsulation, depending on the encapsulation used on that particular interface. The Layer 2 frame will then be encoded into the Layer 1 physical signals used to represent these bits over the physical link.

To understand this better, refer to Figure 1-10. Notice that PC1 operates at all seven layers, encapsulating the data and sending the frame out as a stream of encoded bits to R1, its default *gateway*.

Figure 1-10   Routers Operate at Layers 1, 2, and 3

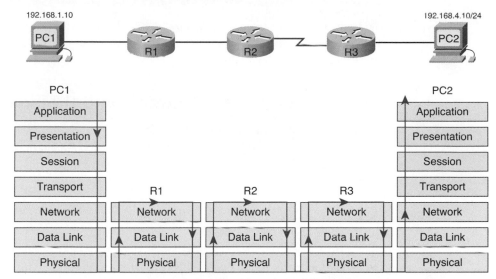

Arrows indicate flow through the OSI layers.

R1 receives the stream of encoded bits on its interface. The bits are decoded and passed up to Layer 2, where R1 decapsulates the frame. The router examines the destination address of the data-link frame to determine whether it matches the receiving interface, including a broadcast or multicast address. If there is a match, the data portion of the frame, the IP packet, is then passed up to Layer 3, where R1 makes its routing decision. R1 then reencapsulates the packet into a new Layer 2 data-link frame and forwards it out the outbound interface as a stream of encoded bits. The new Layer 2 data-link address is associated with that of the interface of the next-hop router.

R2 then receives the stream of bits, and the process repeats itself. R2 decapsulates the frame and passes the data portion of the frame, the IP packet, to Layer 3, where R2 makes its routing decision. R2 then reencapsulates the packet into a new Layer 2 data-link frame and forwards it out the outbound interface as a stream of encoded bits.

This process is repeated once again by Router R3, where R3 forwards the IP packet, encapsulated inside a data-link frame and encoded as bits to PC2.

Each router in the path from source to destination performs this same process of decapsulation, searching the routing table, and then reencapsulation. This process is important to your understanding of how routers participate in networks. Therefore, we will revisit this discussion in more depth in a later section.

CLI Configuration and Addressing

The basic addressing and configuration of Cisco devices was covered in a previous course. However, we will spend some time reviewing these topics as well as preparing you for the hands-on lab experience in this course.

Implementing Basic Addressing Schemes

When designing a new network or mapping an existing network, it is important to document the network. As a starting point, the documentation should include a topology map of the network and an addressing table that lists the following information:

- Device names

- Interface

- IP address and subnet mask

- Default gateway address for end devices such as PCs

Populating an Address Table

Figure 1-11 shows the topology used for the rest of the chapter, with devices interconnected and configured with IP addresses. Below the network topology in the figure is a table used to document the network. The table is populated with the data documenting the network (devices, IP addresses, subnet masks, and interfaces).

Figure 1-11   Documenting an Addressing Scheme

Device	Interface	IP Address	Subnet Mask	Default Gateway
R1	Fa0/0	192.168.1.1	255.255.255.0	N/A
	S0/0/0	192.168.2.1	255.255.255.0	N/A
R2	Fa0/0	192.168.3.1	255.255.255.0	N/A
	S0/0/0	192.168.2.2	255.255.255.0	N/A
PC1	N/A	192.168.1.10	255.255.255.0	192.168.1.1
PC2	N/A	192.168.3.10	255.255.255.0	192.168.3.1

Packet Tracer
☐ **Activity**

Connecting and Identifying Devices (1.2.1)

Use the Packet Tracer Activity to connect the devices and configure the device names, and use the "Place Note" feature to add network address labels. Detailed instructions are provided within the activity. Use file e2-121.pka on the CD-ROM that accompanies this book to perform this activity using Packet Tracer. Detailed instructions are provided within the activity.

Basic Router Configuration

When configuring a router, certain basic tasks are performed, including the following:

- Naming the router
- Setting passwords
- Configuring interfaces
- Configuring a banner
- Saving changes on a router
- Verifying basic configuration and router operations

You should already be familiar with these commands. However, this section will provide a brief review with the assumption that the router does not have a current startup-config file.

The first prompt is at user mode:

```
Router>
```

User mode will allow you to view the state of the router but will not allow you to modify its configuration. Don't confuse "user mode" with "users of the network." "User mode" is intended for the network technicians, operators, and engineers who have the responsibility to configure network devices.

The **enable** command is used to enter *privileged EXEC mode*. This mode allows the user to make configuration changes on the router. The router prompt will change from a > to a # in this mode:

```
Router> enable
Router#
```

Host Name and Passwords

Table 1-1 shows the basic router configuration command syntax used to configure R1 in the following example. You can open Packet Tracer Activity 1.2.2 and follow along or wait until the end of this section to open it.

Table 1-1   Basic Router Configuration Command Syntax

Naming the router	Router(config)# **hostname** *name*
Setting passwords	Router(config)# **enable secret** *password*
	Router(config)# **line console 0**
	Router(config-line)# **password** *password*
	Router(config-line)# **login**
	Router(config)# **line vty 0 4**
	Router(config-line)# **password** *password*
	Router(config-line)# **login**
Configuring a message-of-the-day banner	Router(config)# **banner motd** # *message* #
Configuring an interface	Router(config)# **interface** *type number*
	Router(config-if)# **ip address** *address mask*
	Router(config-if)# **description** *description*
	Router(config-if)# **no shutdown**
Saving changes on a router	Router# **copy running-config startup-config**
Examining the output of **show** commands	Router# **show running-config**
	Router# **show ip route**
	Router# **show ip interface brief**
	Router# **show interfaces**

First, enter global configuration mode:

```
Router# config t
```

Next, apply a unique host name to the router:

```
Router(config)# hostname R1
```

Now, configure a password that is to be used to enter privileged EXEC mode. In our lab environment, we will use the password **class**. However, in production environments, routers should have strong passwords. See the links at the end of this section for more information on creating and using strong passwords.

```
R1(config)# enable secret class
```

Next, configure the console and *Telnet* lines with the password **cisco**. Once again, the password **cisco** is used only in our lab environment. The **login** command enables password checking on the line. If you do not enter the **login** command on the console line, the user will be granted access to the line without entering a password. The console commands follow:

```
R1(config)# line console 0
R1(config-line)# password cisco
R1(config-line)# login
```

The Telnet lines use similar commands:

```
R1(config)# line vty 0 4
R1(config-line)# password cisco
R1(config-line)# login
```

Configuring a Banner

From global configuration mode, configure the message-of-the-day (MOTD) banner. A delimiting character such as a # is used at the beginning and at the end of the message. The delimiter allows you to configure a multiline banner as shown here:

```
R1(config)# banner motd #

Enter TEXT message.  End with the character '#'.
*****************************************
WARNING!! Unauthorized Access Prohibited!!
*****************************************
#
```

Configuring an appropriate banner is part of a good security plan. At a minimum, a banner should warn against unauthorized access. A good security policy would prohibit configuring a banner that "welcomes" an unauthorized user.

Router Interface Configuration

You will now configure the individual router interfaces with IP addresses and other information. First, enter interface configuration mode by specifying the interface type and number. Next, configure the IP address and subnet mask:

```
R1(config)# interface Serial0/0/0
R1(config-if)# ip address 192.168.2.1 255.255.255.0
```

It is good practice to configure a description on each interface to help document the network information. The description text is limited to 240 characters. On production networks, a description can be helpful in troubleshooting by providing information about the type of network the interface is connected to and whether any other routers are on that network. If the interface connects to an ISP or service carrier, it is helpful to enter the third party's connection and contact information. For example:

```
Router(config-if)# description Circuit#VBN32696-123 (help desk:1-800-555-1234)
```

In lab environments, enter a simple description that will help in troubleshooting situations. For example:

```
R1(config-if)# description Link to R2
```

After configuring the IP address and description, the interface must be activated with the **no shutdown** command. This is similar to powering on the interface. The interface must also be connected to another device (a hub, a switch, another router, and so on) for the physical layer to be active.

```
R1(config-if)# no shutdown
```

Note

When cabling a point-to-point serial link in our lab environment, one end of the cable is marked DTE and the other end is marked DCE. The router that has the DCE end of the cable connected to its serial interface will need the additional **clock rate** command configured on that serial interface, as follows:

```
R1(config-if)# clock rate 64000
```

This step is only necessary in a lab environment and will be explained in more detail in Chapter 2, "Static Routing."

Repeat the interface configuration commands on all other interfaces that need to be configured. In our example topology, the Fast Ethernet interface needs to be configured:

```
R1(config)# interface FastEthernet0/0
R1(config-if)# ip address 192.168.1.1 255.255.255.0
R1(config-if)# description R1 LAN
R1(config-if)# no shutdown
```

Each Interface Belongs to a Different Network

At this point, note that each interface must belong to a different network. Although IOS allows you to configure an IP address from the same network on two different interfaces, the router will not activate the second interface.

For example, what if you attempt to configure the FastEthernet 0/1 interface on R1 with an IP address on the 192.168.1.0/24 network? FastEthernet 0/0 has already been assigned an address on that same network. If you attempt to configure another interface, FastEthernet 0/1, with an IP address that belongs to the same network, you will get the following message:

```
R1(config)# interface FastEthernet0/1
R1(config-if)# ip address 192.168.1.2 255.255.255.0
192.168.1.0 overlaps with FastEthernet0/0
```

If there is an attempt to enable the interface with the **no shutdown** command, the following message will appear:

```
R1(config-if)# no shutdown

192.168.1.0 overlaps with FastEthernet0/0
FastEthernet0/1: incorrect IP address assignment
```

In Example 1-2, notice that the **show ip interface brief** command output displays that the FastEthernet 0/1 interface is still down, even though the **no shutdown** command was used on that interface. Again, this is because FastEthernet 0/1 belongs to the same 192.168.1.0/24 network as the previously configured IP address on FastEthernet 0/0. Therefore, it will remain in the down state until one of these two interfaces is reconfigured with a non-overlapping IP address.

Example 1-2 show ip interface brief Command Output

```
R1# show ip interface brief

Interface        IP-Address      OK? Method Status                Protocol
FastEthernet0/0  192.168.1.1     YES manual up                    up
Serial0/0        192.168.2.1     YES manual up                    up
FastEthernet0/1  192.168.1.2     YES manual administratively down down
Serial0/1        unassigned      YES unset  administratively down down
```

More Info

For discussions about using strong passwords, see the following articles:

- "Strong passwords: How to create and use them" at http://www.microsoft.com/athome/security/privacy/password.mspx

- "Simple formula for strong passwords" at http://www.sans.org/reading_room/whitepapers/authentication/1636.php

---

Verifying Basic Router Configuration

All the previous basic router configuration commands entered were immediately stored in the running configuration file of R1. The running-config file is stored in RAM and is the configuration file used by IOS. Verify the commands entered by displaying the running configuration with the **show running-config** command, as shown in Example 1-3.

Example 1-3 show running-config Command Output

```
R1# show running-config

!
```

```
version 12.3
!
hostname R1
!
interface FastEthernet0/0
 description R1 LAN
 ip address 192.168.1.1 255.255.255.0
!
interface Serial0/0
 description Link to R2
 ip address 192.168.2.1 255.255.255.0
 clock rate 64000
!
banner motd ^C
*********************************************
WARNING!! Unauthorized Access Prohibited!!
*********************************************
^C
!
line con 0
 password cisco
 login
line vty 0 4
 password cisco
 login
!
end
```

Now that the basic configuration commands have been entered, it is important to save the running-config file to nonvolatile memory, the router's NVRAM. In case of a power outage or an accidental reload, the router will be able to boot with the current configuration. After the router's configuration has been completed and tested, it is important to save the running-config file to the startup-config file as the permanent configuration file:

```
R1# copy running-config startup-config
```

After you apply and save the basic configuration, several commands will help you verify that you have correctly configured the router. All of these commands are discussed in detail in later chapters. For now, begin to become familiar with the output.

The **show running-config** command displays the current running configuration that is stored in RAM. With a few exceptions, any configuration commands that were used will be entered into the running-config file and implemented immediately by IOS.

The **show startup-config** command, demonstrated in Example 1-4, displays the startup configuration file stored in NVRAM. This is the configuration that the router will use on the next reboot. This configuration does not change unless the current running configuration is saved to NVRAM with the **copy running-config startup-config** command.

Example 1-4 show startup-config Command Output

```
R1# show startup-config

Using 728 bytes
!
version 12.3
!
hostname R1
!
interface FastEthernet0/0
 description R1 LAN
 ip address 192.168.1.1 255.255.255.0
!
interface Serial0/0
 description Link to R2
 ip address 192.168.2.1 255.255.255.0
 clock rate 64000
!
banner motd ^C
*******************************************
WARNING!! Unauthorized Access Prohibited!!
*******************************************
^C
line con 0
 password cisco
 login
line vty 0 4
 password cisco
 login
!
end
```

When comparing the output from the **show running-config** command and the **show startup-config** command, notice that the startup configuration and the running configuration are identical. They are identical because the running configuration has not changed since the last time it was saved. Also notice that the **show startup-config** command displays how many bytes of NVRAM the saved configuration is using: 728 bytes in Example 1-4.

The **show ip route** command, demonstrated in Example 1-5, displays the routing table that IOS is currently using to choose the best path to its destination networks. At this point, R1 only has routes for its directly connected networks, its own interfaces.

Example 1-5 show ip route Command Output

```
R1# show ip route

Codes: C - connected, S - static, I - IGRP, R - RIP, M - mobile, B - BGP
       D - EIGRP, EX - EIGRP external, O - OSPF, IA - OSPF inter area
       N1 - OSPF NSSA external type 1, N2 - OSPF NSSA external type 2
       E1 - OSPF external type 1, E2 - OSPF external type 2, E - EGP
       i - IS-IS, L1 - IS-IS level-1, L2 - IS-IS level-2, ia - IS-IS inter area
       * - candidate default, U - per-user static route, o - ODR
       P - periodic downloaded static route

Gateway of last resort is not set

C    192.168.1.0/24 is directly connected, FastEthernet0/0
C    192.168.2.0/24 is directly connected, Serial0/0
```

The **show interfaces** command, demonstrated in Example 1-6, displays all the interface configuration parameters and statistics. Some of this information will be discussed in later chapters and in later courses.

Example 1-6 show interfaces Command Output

```
R1# show interfaces

<some interfaces not shown>
FastEthernet0/0 is up, line protocol is up (connected)
  Hardware is Lance, address is 0007.eca7.1511 (bia 00e0.f7e4.e47e)
  Description: R1 LAN
  Internet address is 192.168.1.1/24
  MTU 1500 bytes, BW 100000 Kbit, DLY 100 usec, rely 255/255, load 1/255
  Encapsulation ARPA, loopback not set
  ARP type: ARPA, ARP Timeout 04:00:00,
  Last input 00:00:08, output 00:00:05, output hang never
  Last clearing of "show interface" counters never
  Queueing strategy: fifo
  Output queue :0/40 (size/max)
  5 minute input rate 0 bits/sec, 0 packets/sec
  5 minute output rate 0 bits/sec, 0 packets/sec
```

```
        0 packets input, 0 bytes, 0 no buffer
        Received 0 broadcasts, 0 runts, 0 giants, 0 throttles
        0 input errors, 0 CRC, 0 frame, 0 overrun, 0 ignored, 0 abort
        0 input packets with dribble condition detected
        0 packets output, 0 bytes, 0 underruns
        0 output errors, 0 collisions, 1 interface resets
        0 babbles, 0 late collision, 0 deferred
        0 lost carrier, 0 no carrier
        0 output buffer failures, 0 output buffers swapped out
Serial0/0 is up, line protocol is up (connected)
   Hardware is HD64570
   Description: Link to R2
   Internet address is 192.168.2.1/24
   MTU 1500 bytes, BW 1544 Kbit, DLY 20000 usec, rely 255/255, load 1/255
   Encapsulation HDLC, loopback not set, keepalive set (10 sec)
   Last input never, output never, output hang never
   Last clearing of "show interface" counters never
   Input queue: 0/75/0 (size/max/drops); Total output drops: 0
   Queueing strategy: weighted fair
   Output queue: 0/1000/64/0 (size/max total/threshold/drops)
      Conversations  0/0/256 (active/max active/max total)
      Reserved Conversations 0/0 (allocated/max allocated)
   5 minute input rate 0 bits/sec, 0 packets/sec
   5 minute output rate 0 bits/sec, 0 packets/sec
      0 packets input, 0 bytes, 0 no buffer
      Received 0 broadcasts, 0 runts, 0 giants, 0 throttles
      0 input errors, 0 CRC, 0 frame, 0 overrun, 0 ignored, 0 abort
      0 packets output, 0 bytes, 0 underruns
      0 output errors, 0 collisions, 0 interface resets
      0 output buffer failures, 0 output buffers swapped out
      0 carrier transitions
      DCD=up  DSR=up  DTR=up  RTS=up  CTS=up
```

The **show ip interface brief** command, demonstrated in Example 1-7, displays abbreviated interface configuration information, including IP address and interface status. This command is a useful tool for troubleshooting and is a quick way to determine the status of all router interfaces.

Example 1-7 show ip interface brief Command Output

```
R1# show ip interface brief

Interface          IP-Address      OK? Method Status                 Protocol
FastEthernet0/0    192.168.1.1     YES manual up                     up
FastEthernet0/1    unassigned      YES manual administratively down  down
Serial0/0          192.168.2.1     YES manual up                     up
Serial0/1          unassigned      YES manual administratively down  down
Vlan1              unassigned      YES manual administratively down  down
```

Configure and Verify R1 (1.2.2)

In this activity, all devices on the network are configured with the exception of R1. You will configure R1 and then verify the configuration. Detailed instructions are provided within the activity. Use file e2-122.pka on the CD-ROM that accompanies this book to perform this activity using Packet Tracer.

Building the Routing Table

The primary function of a router is to forward packets toward their destination network, the destination IP address of the packet. To do this, a router needs to search the routing information stored in its routing table. In the following sections, you will learn how a router builds the routing table. Then, you will learn the three basic routing principles.

Introducing the Routing Table

A *routing table* is a data file in RAM that is used to store route information about directly connected and remote networks. The routing table contains network/next-hop associations that tell a router that a particular destination can be optimally reached by sending the packet to a particular router representing the "next hop" on the way to the final destination. The **next-hop** association can also be the outgoing or exit interface to the final destination.

The network/exit interface association can represent the destination network address of the IP packet. This would be one of the router's directly connected networks.

A *directly connected network* is a network that is directly attached to one of the router interfaces. When a router's interface is configured with an IP address and subnet mask, the interface becomes a host on that attached network. The network address and subnet mask of the interface, along with the interface type and number, are entered into the routing table as a directly connected network. When a router forwards a packet to a host such as a web server, that host is on the same network as a router's directly connected network.

A *remote network* is a network that is not directly connected to the router. In other words, a remote network is a network that can only be reached by sending the packet to another router. Remote networks are added to the routing table using a dynamic routing protocol or by configuring static routes. *Dynamic routes* are routes to remote networks that were learned automatically by the router, using a dynamic routing protocol. *Static routes* are routes to networks that a network administrator manually configured.

Note

The routing table—with its directly connected networks, static routes, and dynamic routes—will be introduced in the following sections and discussed in even greater detail throughout this course.

The following analogies can help clarify the concept of connected, static, and dynamic routes:

- **Directly connected routes:** To visit a *neighbor*, you only have to go down the street on which you already live. This path is similar to a directly connected route because the "destination" is available directly through your "connected interface"—the street.

- **Static routes:** A train uses the same railroad tracks every time for a specified route. This path is similar to a static route because the path to the destination is always the same.

- **Dynamic routes:** When driving a car, you can "dynamically" choose a different path based on traffic, weather, or other conditions. This path is similar to a dynamic route because you can choose a new path at many different points on your way to the destination.

show ip route Command

You can use the **show ip route** command to display the routing table for a router, as demonstrated in Example 1-8.

Example 1-8 Connected Routes in the Routing Table

```
R1# show ip route

Codes: C - connected, S - static, I - IGRP, R - RIP, M - mobile, B - BGP
       D - EIGRP, EX - EIGRP external, O - OSPF, IA - OSPF inter area
       N1 - OSPF NSSA external type 1, N2 - OSPF NSSA external type 2
       E1 - OSPF external type 1, E2 - OSPF external type 2, E - EGP
       i - IS-IS, L1 - IS-IS level-1, L2 - IS-IS level-2, ia - IS-IS inter area
       * - candidate default, U - per-user static route, o - ODR
```

```
        P - periodic downloaded static route

Gateway of last resort is not set

C    192.168.1.0/24 is directly connected, FastEthernet0/0
C    192.168.2.0/24 is directly connected, Serial0/0/0
```

At this point, no static routes have been configured nor any dynamic routing protocols enabled. Therefore, the routing table for R1 only shows the router's directly connected networks. For each network listed in the routing table, the following information is included:

- **C:** The information in this column denotes the source of the route information, directly connected network, static route, or a dynamic routing protocol. The C represents a directly connected route.

- **192.168.1.0/24:** This is the network address and subnet mask of the directly connected or remote network. In this example, both entries in the routing table, 192.168.1./24 and 192.168.2.0/24, are directly connected networks.

- **FastEthernet 0/0:** The information at the end of the route entry represents the exit interface and/or the IP address of the next-hop router. In this example, both FastEthernet 0/0 and Serial 0/0/0 are the exit interfaces used to reach these networks.

When the routing table includes a route entry for a remote network, additional information is included, such as the routing *metric* and the *administrative distance*. Routing metrics, administrative distance, and the **show ip route** command are explained in more detail in later chapters.

PCs also have a routing table. In Example 1-9, you can see the **route print** command output. The command reveals the configured or acquired default gateway and connected, loopback, multicast, and broadcast networks.

Example 1-9 route print Command Output in Windows

```
C:\> route print


===========================================================================
Interface List
0x1 ........................ MS TCP Loopback interface
0x2 ...00 11 25 af 40 9b ...... Intel(R) PRO/1000 MT Mobile Connection
===========================================================================
===========================================================================
Active Routes:
```

```
Network Destination          Netmask          Gateway          Interface   Metric
             0.0.0.0          0.0.0.0      192.168.1.1      192.168.1.1       10
           127.0.0.0        255.0.0.0        127.0.0.1        127.0.0.1        1
         192.168.1.0    255.255.255.0      192.168.1.1      192.168.1.1       10
        192.168.1.10    255.255.255.0        127.0.0.1      192.168.1.1       10
           224.0.0.0        240.0.0.0     192.168.1.10     192.168.1.10       10
     255.255.255.255  255.255.255.255     192.168.1.10     192.168.1.10        1
Default Gateway:       192.168.1.1
========================================================================
Persistent Routes:
  None
```

The output from the **route print** command will not be analyzed during this course. It is shown here to emphasize the point that all IP-configured devices should have a routing table. The **route –n** command is a similar command used with Linux operating systems.

Directly Connected Networks

When a router's interface is configured with an IP address and subnet mask, that interface becomes a host on that network. When the FastEthernet 0/0 interface on R1 is configured with the IP address 192.168.1.1 and the subnet mask 255.255.255.0, the FastEthernet 0/0 interface is now a member of the 192.168.1.0/24 network. Hosts that are attached to the same LAN, like PC1, are also configured with an IP address that belongs to the 192.168.1.0/24 network.

When a PC is configured with a host IP address and subnet mask, the PC uses the subnet mask to determine what network it now belongs to. This is done by the operating system performing an AND operation using the host IP address and subnet mask. A router uses the same logic when an interface is configured.

A PC is normally configured with a single host IP address because it only has a single network interface, usually an Ethernet NIC. Routers have multiple interfaces; therefore, each interface must be a member of a different network. In Example 1-10, R1 is a member of two different networks: 192.168.1.0/24 and 192.168.2.0/24. Although not shown in the example, R2 is also a member of two networks: 192.168.2.0/24 and 192.168.3.0/24.

Example 1-10   Connected Routes in the Routing Table for R1

```
R1# show ip route

Codes: C - connected, S - static, I - IGRP, R - RIP, M - mobile, B - BGP
       D - EIGRP, EX - EIGRP external, O - OSPF, IA - OSPF inter area
```

```
          N1 - OSPF NSSA external type 1, N2 - OSPF NSSA external type 2
          E1 - OSPF external type 1, E2 - OSPF external type 2, E - EGP
          i - IS-IS, L1 - IS-IS level-1, L2 - IS-IS level-2, ia - IS-IS inter area
          * - candidate default, U - per-user static route, o - ODR
          P - periodic downloaded static route

Gateway of last resort is not set

C    192.168.1.0/24 is directly connected, FastEthernet0/0
C    192.168.2.0/24 is directly connected, Serial0/0/0
```

After the router's interface is configured and the interface is activated with the **no shutdown** command, the interface must receive a carrier signal from another device (another router, switch, hub, and so on) before the interface state is considered as "up." After the interface is up, the network of that interface is added to the routing table as a directly connected network.

Before any static or dynamic routing is configured on a router, the router only knows about its own directly connected networks. These are the only networks that are displayed in the routing table until static or dynamic routing is configured. Directly connected networks are of prime importance for routing decisions. Static and dynamic routes cannot exist in the routing table without a router's own directly connected networks. The router cannot send packets out an interface if that interface is not enabled with an IP address and subnet mask, just as a PC cannot send IP packets out its Ethernet interface if that interface is not configured with an IP address and subnet mask.

Note

The process of configuring router interfaces and adding the network address to the routing table is discussed in the following chapter.

Directly Connected Routes (1.3.2)

This activity focuses on the routing table and how it is built. A router builds routing tables by first adding the networks for the IP addresses configured on its own interfaces. These networks are the directly connected networks for the router. The focus of this activity is two routers, R1 and R2, and the networks supported through the configuration of the router interfaces. Initially, all interfaces have been configured with correct addressing, but the interfaces are shut down. Detailed instructions are provided within the activity. Use file e2-132.pka on the CD-ROM that accompanies this book to perform this activity using Packet Tracer.

Static Routing

Remote networks are added to the routing table by configuring static routes or enabling a dynamic routing protocol. When the IOS routing process learns about a remote network and the interface it will use to reach that network, it adds that route to the routing table as long as the exit interface is enabled.

A static route includes the network address and subnet mask of the remote network, along with the IP address of the next-hop router or exit interface. Static routes are denoted with the code S in the routing table, as shown in Example 1-11. Static routes are examined in detail in the next chapter.

Example 1-11   Static Route in the Routing Table for R1

```
R1# show ip route

Codes: C - connected, S - static, I - IGRP, R - RIP, M - mobile, B - BGP
       D - EIGRP, EX - EIGRP external, O - OSPF, IA - OSPF inter area
       N1 - OSPF NSSA external type 1, N2 - OSPF NSSA external type 2
       E1 - OSPF external type 1, E2 - OSPF external type 2, E - EGP
       i - IS-IS, L1 - IS-IS level-1, L2 - IS-IS level-2, ia - IS-IS inter area
       * - candidate default, U - per-user static route, o - ODR
       P - periodic downloaded static route

Gateway of last resort is not set

C    192.168.1.0/24 is directly connected, FastEthernet0/0
C    192.168.2.0/24 is directly connected, Serial0/0/0
S    192.168.3.0/24 [1/0] via 192.168.2.2
```

When to Use Static Routes

Static routes should be used in the following cases:

- **A network consists of only a few routers:** Using a dynamic routing protocol in such a case does not present a substantial benefit. On the contrary, dynamic routing can add more administrative overhead.

- **A network is connected to the Internet only through a single ISP:** There is no need to use a dynamic routing protocol across this link because the ISP represents the only exit point to the Internet.

- **A large network is configured in a hub-and-spoke topology:** A *hub-and-spoke* topology consists of a central location (the hub) and multiple branch locations (spokes), with each spoke having only one connection to the hub. Using a dynamic routing protocol would be unnecessary because each branch only has one path to a given destination: through the central location.

Typically, most routers' routing tables contain a combination of static routes and dynamic routes. But, as stated earlier, the routing table must first contain the directly connected networks used to access these remote networks before any static or dynamic routing can be used.

Packet Tracer ☐ Activity

Static Routing (1.3.3)

Routers can learn of remote networks through static or dynamic routing. This activity focuses on how remote networks are added to the routing table using static routes. Detailed instructions are provided within the activity. Use file e2-133.pka on the CD-ROM that accompanies this book to perform this activity using Packet Tracer.

Dynamic Routing

Remote networks can also be added to the routing table by using a dynamic routing protocol. In Example 1-12, R1 has automatically learned about the 192.168.4.0/24 network from R2 through the dynamic routing protocol RIP (Routing Information Protocol). RIP was one of the first IP routing protocols and will be fully discussed in later chapters.

Example 1-12   Dynamic Route in the Routing Table for R1

```
R1# show ip route

Codes: C - connected, S - static, I - IGRP, R - RIP, M - mobile, B - BGP
       D - EIGRP, EX - EIGRP external, O - OSPF, IA - OSPF inter area
       N1 - OSPF NSSA external type 1, N2 - OSPF NSSA external type 2
       E1 - OSPF external type 1, E2 - OSPF external type 2, E - EGP
       i - IS-IS, L1 - IS-IS level-1, L2 - IS-IS level-2, ia - IS-IS inter area
       * - candidate default, U - per-user static route, o - ODR
       P - periodic downloaded static route


Gateway of last resort is not set

C    192.168.1.0/24 is directly connected, FastEthernet0/0
C    192.168.2.0/24 is directly connected, Serial0/0/0
S    192.168.3.0/24 [1/0] via 192.168.2.2
R    192.168.4.0/24 [120/1] via 192.168.2.2, 00:00:20, Serial0/0/0
```

Note

In Example 1-12, R1's routing table shows that R1 has learned about two remote networks: one route dynamically using RIP and a static route that was manually configured. This is an example of how routing tables can contain routes learned dynamically and configured statically and is not necessarily representative of the best configuration for this network.

Dynamic routing protocols are used by routers to share information about the reachability and status of remote networks. Dynamic routing protocols perform several activities, including the following:

- Network discovery

- Updating and maintaining routing tables

Automatic Network Discovery

Network discovery is a routing protocol's capability to share information about the networks it knows about with other routers that are also using the same routing protocol. Instead of configuring static routes to remote networks on every router, a dynamic routing protocol allows the routers to automatically learn about these networks from other routers. These networks and the best path to each network are added to the router's routing table and denoted as a network learned by a specific dynamic routing protocol.

Maintaining Routing Tables

After the initial network discovery, dynamic routing protocols will also update and maintain the networks in their routing tables. Dynamic routing protocols not only make a best-path determination to various networks but also determine a new best path if the initial path becomes unusable (or if the topology changes). For these reasons, dynamic routing protocols have an advantage over static routes. Routers that use dynamic routing protocols automatically share routing information with other routers and compensate for any topology changes without involving the network administrator.

IP Routing Protocols

There are several dynamic routing protocols for IP. Here are some of the more common dynamic routing protocols for routing IP packets:

- RIP (Routing Information Protocol)

- *IGRP* (Interior Gateway Routing Protocol)

- EIGRP (Enhanced Interior Gateway Routing Protocol)

- OSPF (Open Shortest Path First)

- IS-IS (Intermediate System–to–Intermediate System)

- *BGP* (Border Gateway Protocol)

Note

RIP (versions 1 and 2), EIGRP, and OSPF are covered in this course. EIGRP and OSPF are also covered in more detail in CCNP, along with IS-IS and BGP. IGRP is a legacy routing protocol and has been replaced by EIGRP. Both IGRP and EIGRP are Cisco-proprietary routing protocols, whereas all other routing protocols listed are nonproprietary protocols based on open standards.

Remember, in most cases, routers contain a combination of static routes and dynamic routes in the routing tables. Dynamic routing protocols will be discussed in more detail in Chapter 3, "Introduction to Dynamic Routing Protocols."

Dynamic Routing (1.3.4)

Use the Packet Tracer Activity to learn how IOS installs and removes dynamic routes. Detailed instructions are provided within the activity. Use file e2-134.pka on the CD-ROM that accompanies this book to perform this activity using Packet Tracer.

Routing Table Principles

At times, this course refers to three principles regarding routing tables that will help you understand, configure, and troubleshoot routing issues. These principles, listed as follows, are from Alex Zinin's book, *Cisco IP Routing*[1]:

- Every router makes its decision alone, based on the information it has in its own routing table.

- The fact that one router has certain information in its routing table does not mean that other routers have the same information.

- Routing information about a path from one network to another does not provide routing information about the reverse, or return, path.

What is the effect of these principles? Consider the example in Figure 1-12.

After making its routing decision, R1 forwards the packet destined for PC2 to R2. R1 only knows about the information in its own routing table, which indicates that Router R2 is the next-hop router. R1 does not know whether R2 actually has a route to the destination network.

It is the network administrator's responsibility to make sure that all routers within their control have complete and accurate routing information so that packets can be forwarded between any two networks. This can be done using static routes, a dynamic routing protocol, or a combination of both.

Figure 1-12   Routing Principle Example

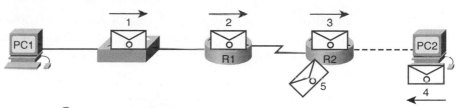

① PC1 sends ping to PC2.

② R1 has a route to PC2's network.

③ R2 is directly connected to PC2's network.

④ PC2 sends reply ping to PC1.

⑤ R2 does NOT have a route to PC1's network, so it drops the packet.

Because R2 is directly connected to the destination network, it was able to forward the packet to PC2. However, the packet from PC2 to PC1 was dropped by R2. Although R2 had information in its routing table about the destination network of PC1's original ping request, that does not mean it has the information for the return path to PC1's network.

Asymmetric Routing

Because routers do not necessarily have the same information in their routing tables, packets can traverse the network in one direction, using one path, and return through another path. This is called *asymmetric routing*. Asymmetric routing is more common in the Internet, which uses the BGP routing protocol, than it is in most internal networks.

This example implies that when designing and troubleshooting a network, the network administrator should check the following:

- Is there a path from source to destination available in both directions?

- Is the path taken in both directions the same path? (Asymmetrical routing is not uncommon but sometimes can pose additional issues.)

Comprehensive Routing Simulation (1.3.5)

Packets are forwarded through the network from one router to another router on a hop-by-hop basis.

Each router makes an independent forwarding decision based on that router's knowledge of destination paths. Although packets might reach the destination network, the return path might be unknown to the destination router. When this occurs, the router will be unable to route traffic back to the source. This is known as *black hole* routing. Use File e2-135.pka on the CD-ROM that accompanies this book to perform this activity using Packet Tracer.

Path Determination and Switching Functions

The following sections focus on exactly what happens to data as it moves from source to destination. First, these sections review the packet and frame field specifications, and then they discuss in detail how the frame fields change from hop to hop, whereas the packet fields remain unchanged.

Packet Fields and Frame Fields

As previously discussed, routers make their primary forwarding decision by examining the destination IP address of a packet. Before sending that packet out the proper exit interface, the IP packet needs to be encapsulated into a Layer 2 data-link frame. In later sections, you will follow an IP packet from source to destination, examining the encapsulation and decapsulation process at each router. But first, you need to review the format of a Layer 3 IP packet and a Layer 2 Ethernet frame.

Internet Protocol (IP) Packet Format

The Internet Protocol specified in RFC 791 defines the IP packet format. As shown in Figure 1-13, the IP packet header has specific fields that contain information about the packet and about the sending and receiving hosts.

Figure 1-13   Field Specifications for the IP Header

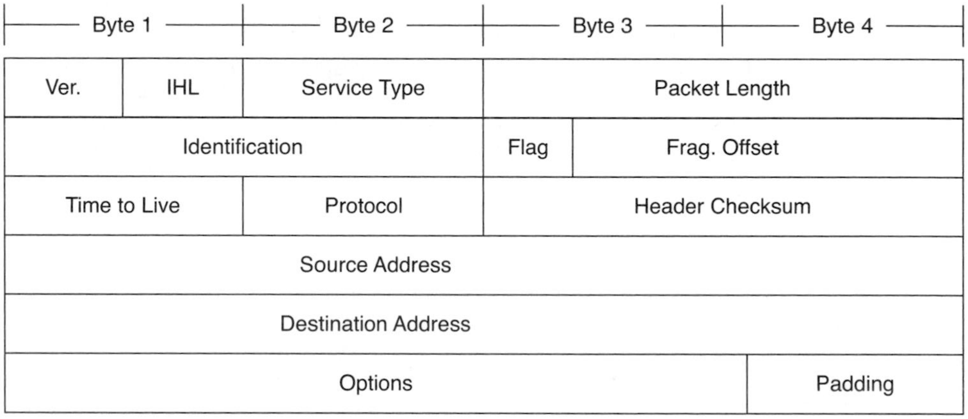

Byte 1		Byte 2	Byte 3	Byte 4
Ver.	IHL	Service Type	Packet Length	
Identification			Flag	Frag. Offset
Time to Live		Protocol	Header Checksum	
Source Address				
Destination Address				
Options				Padding

The following list describes the fields in the IP header. You should already be familiar with destination IP address, source IP address, version, and Time to Live *(TTL)* fields. The other fields are important but are outside the scope of this course.

- **Version:** Version number (4 bits); predominant version is IP version 4 (IPv4).

- **IHL:** IP header length in 32-bit words (4 bits).

- **Service Type:** How the datagram should be handled (8 bits); the first 3 bits are precedence bits. (This use has been superseded by Differentiated Services Code Point [DSCP], which uses the first 6 bits [last 2 reserved].)

- **Packet Length:** Packet length (header + data) (16 bits).

- **Identification:** Unique IP datagram value (16 bits).

- **Flag:** Controls fragmenting (3 bits).

- **Frag. Offset:** Supports fragmentation of *datagrams* to allow differing maximum transmission units (MTU) in the Internet (13 bits).

- **Time to Live: (TTL)** Identifies how many routers can be traversed by the datagram before being dropped (8 bits).

- **Protocol:** Upper-layer protocol sending the datagram (8 bits).

- **Header Checksum:** Integrity check on the header (16 bits).

- **Source Address:** 32-bit source IP address (32 bits).

- **Destination Address:** 32-bit destination IP address (32 bits).

- **Options:** IP options for network testing, debugging, security, and others (multiple of 32 bits).

MAC Layer Frame Format

The Layer 2 data-link frame usually contains header information with a data-link source and destination address, trailer information, and the actual transmitted data. The data-link source address is the Layer 2 address of the interface that sent the data-link frame. The data-link destination address is the Layer 2 address of the interface of the destination device. Both the source and destination data-link interfaces are on the same network. As a packet is forwarded from router to router, the Layer 3 source and destination IP addresses will not change; however, the Layer 2 source and destination data-link addresses will change. This process will be examined more closely in later sections.

Note

When *NAT* (Network Address Translation) is used, the destination IP address does change, but this process is of no concern to IP and is a process performed within a company's network. Routing with NAT is discussed in a later course.

The Layer 3 IP packet is encapsulated in the Layer 2 data-link frame associated with that interface. In this example, we will show the Layer 2 Ethernet frame. Figure 1-14 shows the two compatible versions of Ethernet.

Figure 1-14   Field Specification for Ethernet Frames

Ethernet

Field Length in Bytes

8	6	6	2	46-1500	4
Preamble	Destination Address	Source Address	Type	Data	FCS

IEEE 802.3

Field Length in Bytes

7	1	6	6	2	46-1500	4
Preamble	S O F	Destination Address	Source Address	Length	802.2 Header and Data	FCS

The following list describes the fields in an Ethernet frame:

- **Preamble:** Seven bytes of alternating 1s and 0s, used to synchronize signals

- **Start of Frame (SOF) delimiter:** 1 byte signaling the beginning of the frame

- **Destination Address:** 6-byte MAC address of the sending device on the local segment

- **Source Address:** 6-byte MAC address of the receiving device on the local segment

- **Type/Length:** 2 bytes specifying either the type of upper-layer protocol (Ethernet II frame format) or the length of the data field (IEEE 802.3 frame format)

- **Data and Pad:** 46 to 1500 bytes of data; 0s used to pad any data packet less than 46 bytes

- **Frame Check Sequence (FCS):** 4 bytes used for a cyclic redundancy check to make sure that the frame is not corrupted

Best Path and Metrics

A router determines the best path by evaluating metrics.

Best Path

A router's best-path determination involves evaluating multiple paths to the same destination network and selecting the optimum or "shortest" path to reach that network. Whenever there are multiple paths to reach the same network, this means that each path uses a different exit interface on that router to reach that network. The best path is selected by a routing protocol based on the value or metric it uses to determine the distance to reach a network. Some routing protocols, such as RIP, use simple hop count, which is the number of routers between a router and the destination network. Other routing protocols, such as OSPF, determine the shortest path examining the bandwidth of the links, therefore using links with the fastest bandwidth from a router to the destination network.

Dynamic routing protocols typically use their own rules and metrics to build and update routing tables. A metric is the quantitative value used to measure the distance to a given route. The best path to a network is the path with the lowest metric. For example, a router will prefer a path that is five hops away over a path that is ten hops away.

The primary objective of the routing protocol is to determine the best paths for each route to include in the routing table. The routing algorithm generates a value, a metric for each path through the network. Metrics can be based on either a single characteristic or several characteristics of a path. Some routing protocols can base route selection on multiple metrics, combining them into a single metric. The smaller the value of the metric, the better the path.

Comparing Hop Count and Bandwidth Metrics

Two metrics that are used by some dynamic routing protocols are

- **Hop count:** This is the number of routers that a packet must travel through before reaching its destination. Each router is equal to one hop. A hop count of 4 indicates that a packet must pass through four routers to reach its destination. If multiple paths are available to a destination, the routing protocol, such as RIP, picks the path with the least number of hops.

- **Bandwidth:** Bandwidth is the data capacity of a link, sometimes referred to as the "speed" of the link. For example, the Cisco implementation of the OSPF routing protocol uses bandwidth as its metric. The best path to a network is determined by the path that has an accumulation of links with the highest bandwidth values, that is, the fastest links. Chapter 11, "OSPF," explains the use of bandwidth in OSPF.

Note
"Speed" is technically not an accurate description because all bits travel at the same speed over the same physical medium. Bandwidth is more accurately defined as the number of bits that can be transmitted over that link per second.

When hop count is used as the metric, the resulting path can sometimes be suboptimal. For example, consider the network shown in Figure 1-15.

Figure 1-15   Hop Count Versus Bandwidth as a Metric

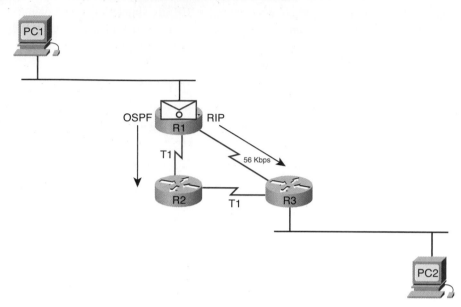

If RIP is the routing protocol used by the three routers, R1 will choose the suboptimal route through R3 to reach PC2 because this path has fewer hops. Bandwidth is not considered. However, if OSPF is used as the routing protocol, R1 will choose the route based on bandwidth. Packets will be able to reach their destination sooner using the two, faster T1 links as compared to the single, slower 56-kbps link.

Discovering Packet and Frame Fields (1.4.2)

Use the Packet Tracer Activity to investigate the contents of the IP and frame headers. Detailed instructions are provided within the activity. Use file e2-142.pka on the CD-ROM that accompanies this book to perform this activity using Packet Tracer.

Equal-Cost Load Balancing

You might be wondering what happens if a routing table has two or more paths with the same metric to the same destination network. When a router has multiple paths to a destination network and the value of that metric (hop count, bandwidth, and so on) is the same, this is known as an *equal-cost metric*, and the router will perform *equal-cost load balancing*, as shown in Figure 1-16. Because both paths to the destination have the same metric, R1 will send the first packet to R2 and the second packet to R4. The routing table will contain the single destination network but will have multiple exit interfaces, one for each equal-cost path. The router will forward packets using the multiple exit interfaces as listed in the routing table.

Figure 1-16   Equal-Cost Load Balancing

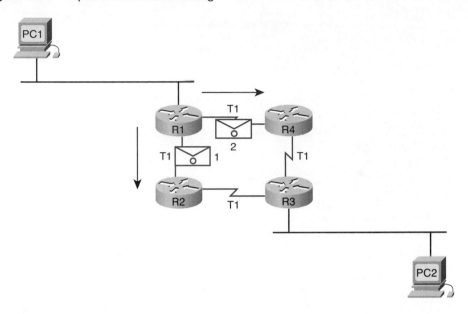

If configured correctly, load balancing can increase the effectiveness and performance of the network. Equal-cost load balancing can be configured to use both dynamic routing protocols and static routes. Equal-cost load balancing is discussed in more detail in Chapter 8, "The Routing Table: A Closer Look."

Equal-Cost Paths Versus Unequal-Cost Paths

Just in case you are wondering, a router can send packets over multiple networks even when the metric is not the same if it is using a routing protocol that has this capability. This is known as *unequal-cost load balancing*. EIGRP and IGRP are the only routing protocols that can be configured for unequal-cost load balancing. Unequal-cost load balancing in EIGRP is not discussed in any of the CCNA-related courses, but is covered in the CCNP-related courses.

Determine Best Path Using Routing Tables (1.4.3)

Use the Packet Tracer Activity to explore a routing table that is using equal-cost load balancing. Detailed instructions are provided within the activity. Use file e2-143.pka on the CD-ROM that accompanies this book to perform this activity using Packet Tracer.

Path Determination

Packet forwarding involves two functions:

- Path determination function

- Switching function

The path determination function is the process of how the router determines which path to use when forwarding a packet, as illustrated in Figure 1-17. To determine the best path, the router searches its routing table for a network address that matches the packet's destination IP address.

Figure 1-17   Routers Determine the Best Path to the Destination

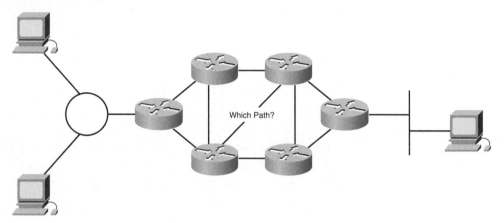

One of three path determinations results from this search:

- **Directly connected network:** If the destination IP address of the packet belongs to a device on a network that is directly connected to one of the router's interfaces, that packet is forwarded directly to that device. This means that the destination IP address of the packet is a host address on the same network as this router's interface.

- **Remote network:** If the destination IP address of the packet belongs to a remote network, the packet is forwarded to another router. Remote networks can only be reached by forwarding packets to another router.

- **No route determined:** If the destination IP address of the packet does not belong to either a connected or remote network, and the router does not have a default route, the packet is discarded. The router sends an Internet Control Message Protocol (ICMP) Unreachable message to the source IP address of the packet.

In the first two results, the router reencapsulates the IP packet into the Layer 2 data-link frame format of the exit interface. The type of Layer 2 encapsulation is determined by the type of interface. For example, if the exit interface is Fast Ethernet, the packet is encapsulated in an Ethernet frame. If the exit interface is a serial interface configured for PPP, the IP packet is encapsulated in a PPP frame.

The following section demonstrates this process.

More Info

For more information on how a router using Cisco IOS performs route lookup, see the Cisco Press book *Inside Cisco IOS Software Architecture*, by Vijay Bolapragada, Curtis Murphy, and Russ White.

Switching Function

After the router has determined the exit interface using the path determination function, the router needs to encapsulate the packet into the data-link frame of the outgoing interface.

The switching function is the process used by a router to accept a packet on one interface and forward it out another interface. A key responsibility of the switching function is to encapsulate packets in the appropriate data-link frame type for the outgoing data link.

What does a router do with a packet received from one network and destined for another network? The router performs the following three major steps:

1. Decapsulates the Layer 3 packet by removing the Layer 2 frame header and trailer

2. Examines the destination IP address of the IP packet to find the best path in the routing table

3. Encapsulates the Layer 3 packet into a new Layer 2 frame and forwards the frame out the exit interface

As the Layer 3 IP packet is forwarded from one router to the next, the IP packet remains unchanged, with the exception of the TTL (Time to Live) field. When a router receives an IP packet, it decrements the TTL by 1. If the resulting TTL value is 0, the router discards the packet. The TTL is used to prevent IP packets from traveling endlessly over networks because of a routing loop or other misfunction in the network. Routing loops are discussed in a later chapter.

As the IP packet is decapsulated from one Layer 2 frame and encapsulated into a new Layer 2 frame, the data-link destination address and source address will change as the packet is forwarded from one router to the next. The Layer 2 data-link source address represents the Layer 2 address of the outbound interface. The Layer 2 destination address represents the Layer 2 address of the next-hop router. If the next hop is the final destination device, it will be the Layer 2 address of that device.

The packet might be encapsulated in a different type of Layer 2 frame than the one in which it was received. For example, the packet might be received by the router on a Fast Ethernet interface, encapsulated in an Ethernet frame, and forwarded out a serial interface, encapsulated in a PPP frame.

Remember, as a packet travels from the source device to the final destination device, the Layer 3 IP addresses do not change. However, the Layer 2 data-link addresses change at every hop as the packet is decapsulated and reencapsulated in a new frame by each router.

Path Determination and Switching Function Details

Can you describe the exact details of what happens to a packet at Layer 2 and Layer 3 as it travels from source to destination? If not, study Figures 1-18 through 1-23 along with the following discussion until you can describe the process on your own.

Step 1: PC1 Has a Packet to Be Sent to PC2

Refer to Figure 1-18. PC1 encapsulates the IP packet into an Ethernet frame with the destination MAC address of R1's FastEthernet 0/0 interface.

Figure 1-18 Day in the Life of a Packet: Step 1

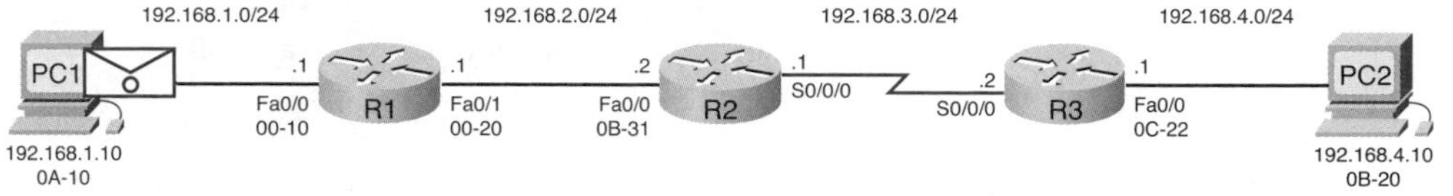

Layer 2 Data Link Frame | Packet's Layer 3 Data

Destination MAC 00-10	Source MAC 0A-10	Type 800	Destination IP 192.168.4.10	Source IP 192.168.1.10	IP Fields	Data	Trailer

PC1's ARP Cache for R1	
IP Address	MAC Address
192.168.1.1	00-10

How does PC1 know to forward the packet to R1 and not directly to PC2? PC1 has determined that the IP source and IP destination addresses are on different networks.

PC1 knows what network it belongs to by doing an AND operation on its own IP address and subnet mask, which results in its network address. PC1 does this same AND operation using the packet's destination IP address and PC1's subnet mask. If the result is the same as its own network, PC1 knows that the destination IP address is on its own network, and it does not need to forward the packet to the default gateway, the router. If the AND operation results in a different network address, PC1 knows that the destination IP address is not on its own network, and it must forward this packet to the default gateway, the router.

Note

If an AND operation with the packet's destination IP address and PC1's subnet mask results in a different network address than what PC1 has determined to be its own network address, this address does not necessarily reflect the actual remote network address. PC1 only knows that if the destination IP address is on its own network, the masks would be the same and the network addresses would be the same. The mask of the remote network can very well be a different mask. If the destination IP address results in a different network address, PC1 doesn't know the actual remote network address, only that it is not on its own network.

How does PC1 determine the MAC address of the default gateway, router R1? PC1 checks its ARP table for the IP address of the default gateway and its associated MAC address.

What if this entry does not exist in the ARP table? PC1 sends an ARP request, and Router R1 sends back an ARP reply.

Step 2: Router R1 Receives the Ethernet Frame

Router R1 examines the destination MAC address, which matches the MAC address of the receiving interface, FastEthernet 0/0. R1 will therefore copy the frame into its buffer.

R1 sees that the Ethernet Type field is 0x800, which means that the Ethernet frame contains an IP packet in the data portion of the frame.

R1 decapsulates the Ethernet frame.

Because the destination IP address of the packet does not match any of R1's directly connected networks, the router consults its routing table to route this packet. As shown in Figure 1-19, R1 searches the routing table for a network address and subnet mask that would include this packet's destination IP address as a host address on that network.

Figure 1-19 Day in the Life of a Packet: Step 2a

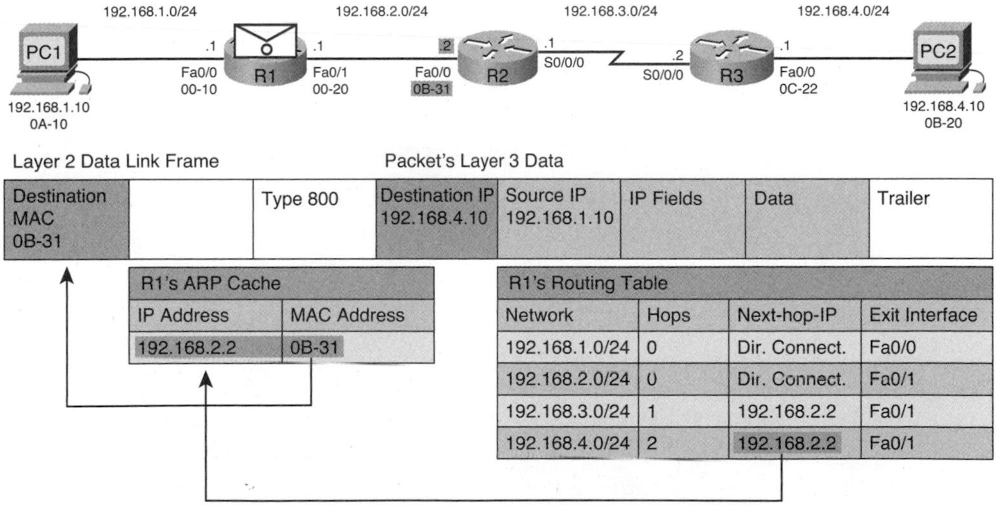

In this example, the routing table has a route for the 192.168.4.0/24 network. The destination IP address of the packet is 192.168.4.10, which is a host IP address on that network. R1's route to the 192.168.4.0/24 network has a next-hop IP address of 192.168.2.2 and an exit interface of FastEthernet 0/1. This means that the IP packet will be encapsulated in a new Ethernet frame, with the destination MAC address being that of the next-hop router's IP address. Because the exit interface is on an Ethernet network, R1 must resolve the next-hop IP address with a destination MAC address.

Refer to Figure 1-20. R1 looks up the next-hop IP address of 192.168.2.2 in its ARP cache for its FastEthernet 0/1 interface. If the entry is not in the ARP cache, R1 sends an ARP request out its FastEthernet 0/1 interface. R2 would then send back an ARP reply. R1 then updates its ARP cache with an entry for 192.168.2.2 and the associated MAC address.

Figure 1-20   Day in the Life of a Packet: Step 2b

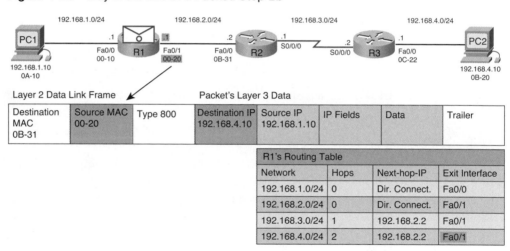

The IP packet is now encapsulated into a new Ethernet frame and forwarded out R1's FastEthernet 0/1 interface.

Step 3: Packet Arrives at Router R2

Router R2 examines the destination MAC address, which matches the MAC address of the receiving interface, FastEthernet 0/0. R1 will therefore copy the frame into its buffer.

R2 sees that the Ethernet Type field is 0x800, which means that the Ethernet frame contains an IP packet in the data portion of the frame.

R2 decapsulates the Ethernet frame.

Because the destination IP address of the packet does not match any of R2's interface addresses, the router consults its routing table to route this packet. As shown in Figure 1-21,

R2 searches the routing table for the packet's destination IP address using the same process as discussed in R1.

Figure 1-21   Day in the Life of a Packet: Step 3a

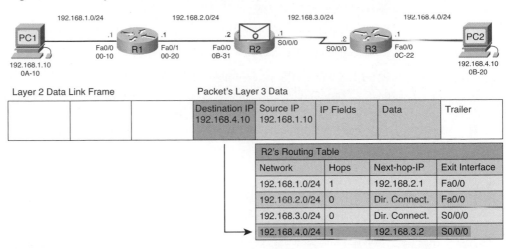

R2's routing table has a route to the 192.168.4.0/24 route, with a next-hop IP address of 192.168.3.2 and an exit interface of Serial 0/0/0. Because the exit interface is not an Ethernet network, R2 does not have to resolve the next-hop IP address with a destination MAC address. When the interface is a point-to-point serial connection, R2 encapsulates the IP packet into the proper data-link frame format used by the exit interface (HDLC, PPP, and so on). The Layer 2 encapsulation shown in Figure 1-22 is HDLC. Therefore, the data-link destination address is set to 0x8F. Remember, there are no MAC addresses on serial interfaces.

Figure 1-22   Day in the Life of a Packet: Step 3b

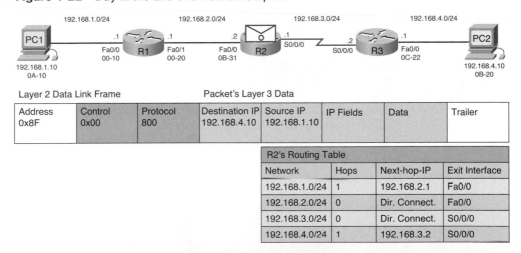

The IP packet is now encapsulated into a new data-link frame, PPP, and sent out the Serial 0/0/0 exit interface.

Step 4: Packet Arrives at R3

R3 receives and copies the data-link HDLC frame into its buffer.

R3 decapsulates the data-link HDLC frame.

Refer to Figure 1-23. R3 searches the routing table for the destination IP address of the packet. The search of the routing table results in a network that is one of R3's directly connected networks. This means that the packet can be sent directly to the destination device and does not need to be sent to another router. Because the exit interface is a directly connected Ethernet network, R3 needs to resolve the destination IP address of the packet with a destination MAC address.

Figure 1-23   Day in the Life of a Packet: Step 4

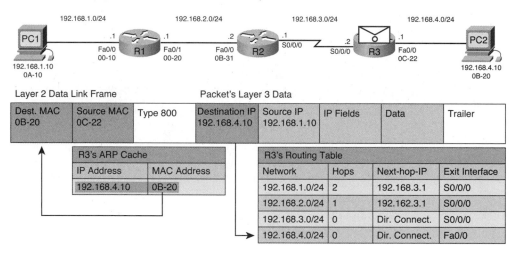

R3 searches for the packet's destination IP address of 192.168.4.10 in its ARP cache. If the entry is not in the ARP cache, R3 sends an ARP request out its FastEthernet 0/0 interface. PC2 sends back an ARP reply with its MAC address. R3 updates its ARP cache with an entry for 192.168.4.10 and the MAC address returned in the ARP reply.

The IP packet is encapsulated into a new data-link Ethernet frame and sent out R3's FastEthernet 0/0 interface.

Step 5: Ethernet Frame with Encapsulated IP Packet Arrives at PC2

Refer to Figure 1-24. PC2 examines the destination MAC address, which matches the MAC address of the receiving interface, that is, its own Ethernet NIC. PC2 will therefore copy the rest of the frame.

Figure 1-24   Day in the Life of a Packet: Step 5

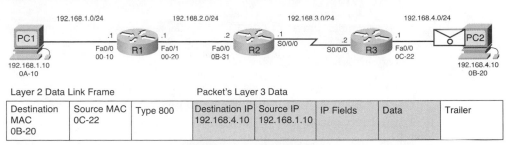

Destination MAC 0B-20	Source MAC 0C-22	Type 800	Destination IP 192.168.4.10	Source IP 192.168.1.10	IP Fields	Data	Trailer

PC2 sees that the Ethernet Type field is 0x800, which means that the Ethernet frame contains an IP packet in the data portion of the frame.

PC2 decapsulates the Ethernet frame and passes the IP packet to its operating system's IP process.

Path Determination and Switching Function Summary

We have just examined the encapsulation and decapsulation process of a packet as it is forwarded from router to router, from the originating source device to the final destination device. We have also introduced the routing table lookup process, which will be discussed more thoroughly in a later chapter. You have seen that routers are not just involved in Layer 3 routing decisions, but also participate in Layer 2 processes, including encapsulation, and on Ethernet networks, ARP. Router interfaces also participate in Layer 1 used to transmit and receive the bits over the physical medium. Layer 1 is used to convert the bit stream into a physical signal, which then is transmitted over the cable or wireless medium.

Routing tables contain both directly connected networks and remote networks. It is because routers contain addresses for remote networks in their routing tables that routers know how and where to send packets destined for other networks, including the Internet. In the following chapters, you will learn how the routers build and maintain these routing tables, either by the use of manually entered static routes or through the use of a dynamic routing protocol.

More Info

For more information about how routers using Cisco IOS forward packets and the packet-switching mechanisms that exist, refer to the Cisco Press book *Inside Cisco IOS Software Architecture*, by Vijay Bolapragada, Curtis Murphy, and Russ White.

Summary

This chapter introduced the router. Routers are computers and include many of the same hardware and software components found in a typical PC, such as CPU, RAM, ROM, and an operating system.

The main purpose of a router is to connect multiple networks and forward packets from one network to the next. This means that a router typically has multiple interfaces. Each interface is a member or host on a different IP network.

The router has a routing table, which is a list of networks known by the router. The routing table includes network addresses for its own interfaces, which are the directly connected networks, as well as network addresses for remote networks. A remote network is a network that can only be reached by forwarding the packet to another router.

Remote networks are added to the routing table in two ways: either by the network administrator manually configuring static routes or by implementing a dynamic routing protocol. Static routes do not have as much overhead as dynamic routing protocols; however, static routes can require more maintenance if the topology is constantly changing or is unstable.

Dynamic routing protocols automatically adjust to changes with no intervention from the network administrator. Dynamic routing protocols require more CPU processing and also use a certain amount of link capacity for routing updates and messages. In many cases, a routing table will contain both static and dynamic routes.

Routers make their primary forwarding decision at Layer 3, the network layer. However, router interfaces participate in Layers 1, 2, and 3. Layer 3 IP packets are encapsulated into a Layer 2 data-link frame and encoded into bits at Layer 1. Router interfaces participate in Layer 2 processes associated with their encapsulation. For example, an Ethernet interface on a router participates in the ARP process like other hosts on that LAN.

The next chapter examines the configuration of static routes and introduces the IP routing table.

Labs

The labs available in the companion *Routing Protocols and Concepts, CCNA Exploration Labs and Study Guide* (ISBN 1-58713-204-4) provide hands-on practice with the following topics introduced in this chapter:

Lab 1-1: Cabling a Network and Basic Router Configuration (1.5.1)

Complete this lab if you need a solid review of device cabling, establishing a console connection, and command-line interface (CLI) basics. If you are comfortable with these skills, you can substitute Lab 1-2: Basic Router Configuration (1.5.2) for this lab.

Lab 1-2: Basic Router Configuration (1.5.2)

Complete this lab if you have solid skills in device cabling, establishing a console connection, and CLI basics. If you need a review of these skills, you can substitute Lab 1-1: Cabling a Network and Basic Router Configuration (1.5.1) for this lab.

Lab 1-3: Challenge Router Configuration (1.5.3)

This lab challenges your subnetting and configuration skills. Given an address space and network requirements, you are expected to design and implement an addressing scheme in a two-router topology.

Many of the hands-on labs include Packet Tracer Companion Activities, where you can use Packet Tracer to complete a simulation of the lab. Look for this icon in *Routing Protocols and Concepts, CCNA Exploration Labs and Study Guide* (ISBN 1-58713-204-4) for hands-on labs that have a Packet Tracer Companion.

Check Your Understanding

Complete all the review questions listed here to test your understanding of the topics and concepts in this chapter. The appendix, "Check Your Understanding and Challenge Questions Answer Key," lists the answers.

1. Which of the following matches a router component with its function?

   A. Flash: Permanently stores the bootstrap program

   B. ROM: Permanently stores the startup configuration file

   C. NVRAM: Permanently stores the operating system image

   D. RAM: Stores the routing tables and ARP cache

2. Which two commands can a technician use to determine whether router serial ports have IP addresses that are assigned to them?

   A. **show interfaces**

   B. **show interfaces ip brief**

   C. **show controllers all**

   D. **show ip config**

   E. **show ip interface brief**

3. Which of the following commands will set the privileged mode password to "quiz"?

    A. R1(config)# **enable secret quiz**

    B. R1(config)# **password secret quiz**

    C. R1(config)# **enable password secret quiz**

    D. R1(config)# **enable secret password quiz**

4. Which routing principle is correct?

    A. If one router has certain information in its routing table, all adjacent routers have the same information.

    B. Routing information about a path from one network to another implies routing information about the reverse, or return, path.

    C. Every router makes its routing decisions alone, based on the information it has in its own routing table.

    D. Every router makes its routing decisions based on the information it has in its own routing table and its neighbor routing tables.

5. What two tasks do dynamic routing protocols perform?

    A. Discover hosts

    B. Update and maintain routing tables

    C. Propagate host default gateways

    D. Network discovery

    E. Assign IP addressing

6. A network engineer is configuring a new router. The interfaces have been configured with IP addresses and activated, but no routing protocols or static routes have been configured yet. What routes are present in the routing table?

    A. Default routes.

    B. Broadcast routes.

    C. Direct connections.

    D. No routes; the routing table is empty.

7. What two statements are correct regarding how a router forwards packets?

    A. If the packet is destined for a remote network, the router forwards the packet out all interfaces that might be a next hop to that network.

    B. If the packet is destined for a directly connected network, the router forwards the packet out the exit interface indicated by the routing table.

    C. If the packet is destined for a remote network, the router forwards the packet based on the information in the router host table.

    D. If the packet is destined for a remote network, the router sends the packet to the next-hop IP in the routing table.

    E. If the packet is destined for a directly connected network, the router forwards the packet based on the destination MAC address.

    F. If the packet is destined for a directly connected network, the router forwards the packet to the switch on the next-hop VLAN.

8. Which statement is true regarding metrics used by routing protocols?

    A. A metric is the quantitative value that a routing protocol uses to measure a given route.

    B. A metric is a Cisco-proprietary means to convert distances to a standard unit.

    C. Metrics represent a composite value of the amount of packet loss occurring for all routing protocols.

    D. Metrics are used by the router to determine whether a packet has an error and should be dropped.

9. The network administrator configured the **ip route 0.0.0.0 0.0.0.0 serial 0/0/0** command on the router. How will this command appear in the routing table, assuming that the Serial 0/0/0 interface is up?

    A. D 0.0.0.0/0 is directly connected, Serial0/0/0

    B. S* 0.0.0.0/0 is directly connected, Serial0/0/0

    C. S* 0.0.0.0/0 [1/0] via 192.168.2.2

    D. C 0.0.0.0/0 [1/0] via 192.168.2.2

10. Describe the internal and external router hardware components, and outline the purpose of each.

11. Describe the router bootup process from power on to final configuration.

12. What important features does a router add to the network?

13. Describe the steps necessary to apply a basic configuration to a router.

14. Describe the importance of the routing table. What purposes does it serve?

15. What are the three basic ways a router learns about networks?

16. What fields in the IP header were the most relevant to the information presented in this chapter?

17. Describe the encapsulation/decapsulation process as a packet travels from source to destination.

Challenge Questions and Activities

These questions require a deeper application of the concepts covered in this chapter and are similar to the style of questions you might see on a CCNA certification exam. You can find the answers to these questions in the appendix, "Answers to Check Your Understanding and Challenge Questions and Activities."

1. When you think about the difference between the hardware and software of a PC and a router, what do you see as the strengths and weaknesses of each device? Which device do you think is the more powerful and why?

2. As you study, learn, and use the command-line interface on a Cisco router, do you see a time when you cannot need to use the CLI to configure routers and switches? What does your vision of network configuration tasks look like without the CLI?

3. If you could design your own routing protocol algorithm to route packets, what would its main features be? How would your protocol decide on the best route? Remember, a computer is going to implement your idea; therefore, be specific.

4. Although the Internet Protocol is now considered the only protocol to use for Layer 3 addressing, this was not always the case. Investigate and report on some other Layer 3 protocols that serve the same purpose. What features do they share in common with IP? How are they different?

To Learn More

Create a topology similar to that presented in Figure 1-18 earlier in the chapter, with several routers and a LAN at each end. On one LAN, add a client host, and on the other end, add a web server. On each LAN, include a switch between the computer and the router. Assume that each router has a route to each of the LANs, similar to that shown in Figure 1-18.

What happens when the host requests a web page from the web server? Look at all the processes and protocols involved, starting with the user entering a URL such as http://www.cisco.com. This includes protocols learned in *Network Fundamentals, CCNA Exploration* as well as information learned in this chapter.

See whether you can determine each of the processes that happen, starting with the client needing to resolve http://www.cisco.com to an IP address, which results in the client having to do an ARP request for the DNS server. What are all the protocols and processes involved, starting with the DNS request, in getting the first packet with http information from the web server?

- How is DNS involved?

- How is ARP involved?

- What effect does TCP have on the client and the server? Is the first packet the web server receives from the client the request for the web page?

- What do the switches do when they receive an Ethernet frame? How do they update their MAC address tables, and how do they determine how to forward the frame?

- What do the routers do when they receive an IP packet?

- What is the decapsulation and encapsulation process of each frame received and forwarded by the router?

- Are any ARP processes required by the web server and its default gateway (its router)?

End Notes

1. Zinin, A. *Cisco IP Routing: Packet Forwarding and Intra-domain Routing Protocols*. Indianapolis, IN: Addison-Wesley; 2002.

CHAPTER 2

Static Routing

Objectives

Upon completion of this chapter, you should be able to answer the following questions:

- What is the role of a router in the network?

- Can you describe the relationship between router interfaces, directly connected networks, and the routing table?

- How can CDP be used with directly connected networks?

- How can static routes be used with exit interfaces?

- Can you describe the use and configuration of summary and default routes?

- How do packets get forwarded using static routes?

- What commands would you use to manage and troubleshoot static routes?

Key Terms

This chapter uses the following key terms. You can find the definitions in the Glossary at the end of the book.

Routing is at the core of every data network, moving information across an internetwork from source to destination. Routers are the devices responsible for the transfer of packets from one network to the next.

As you learned in the previous chapter, routers learn about remote networks either dynamically using routing protocols or manually using static routes. A remote network is a network that is not one of the router's directly connected networks. In many cases, routers use a combination of both dynamic routing protocols and static routes. This chapter focuses on static routing.

Static routes are very common and do not require the same amount of processing and overhead as do dynamic routing protocols.

This chapter follows a sample topology as you learn to configure static routes and learn troubleshooting techniques. In the process, you will examine several key IOS commands and the results they display. You will also learn about the routing table using both directly connected networks and static routes.

As you work through the Packet Tracer Activities associated with these commands, take the time to experiment with the commands and examine the results. Reading the routing tables will soon become second nature.

Routers and the Network

Routers have always played a key role in larger networks and the Internet. Over the past several years, routers have become more common in smaller and home networks. This is because of several reasons, including the need to connect multiple devices to the Internet, security, and quality of service.

Role of the Router

The router is a special-purpose computer that plays a key role in the operation of any data network. Routers are primarily responsible for interconnecting networks by

- Determining the best path to send packets
- Forwarding packets toward their destination

Routers make routing decisions by learning about remote networks and maintaining routing information. The router is the junction or intersection that connects multiple IP networks. The router's primary forwarding decision is based on Layer 3 information, the destination IP address.

The router's routing table is used to find the best match between the destination IP of a packet and a network address in the routing table. The routing table will ultimately determine the exit interface to forward the packet from, and the router will encapsulate that packet in the appropriate data-link frame for that outgoing interface.

Introducing the Topology

Figure 2-1 shows the topology used in this chapter. The topology consists of three routers, labeled R1, R2, and R3. Routers R1 and R2 are connected through one WAN link, and routers R2 and R3 are connected through another WAN link. Each router is connected to a different Ethernet LAN, represented by a switch and a PC. Table 2-1 outlines the addressing scheme of these devices.

Figure 2-1   Chapter Topology

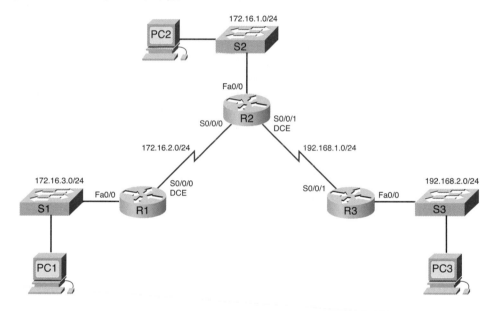

Table 2-1   Chapter Topology Addressing Scheme

Device	Interface	IP Address	Subnet Mask	Default Gateway
R1	Fa0/0	172.16.3.1	255.255.255.0	—
	S0/0/0	172.16.2.1	255.255.255.0	—
R2	Fa0/0	172.16.1.1	255.255.255.0	—
	S0/0/0	172.16.2.2	255.255.255.0	—
	S0/0/1	192.168.1.2	255.255.255.0	—

continues

Table 2-1   Chapter Topology Addressing Scheme   *continued*

Device	Interface	IP Address	Subnet Mask	Default Gateway
R3	Fa0/0	192.168.2.1	255.255.255.0	—
	S0/0/0	192.168.1.1	255.255.255.0	—
PC1	NIC	172.16.3.10	255.255.255.0	172.16.3.1
PC2	NIC	172.16.1.10	255.255.255.0	172.16.1.1
PC3	NIC	192.168.2.10	255.255.255.0	192.168.2.1

Each router in this example is a Cisco 1841. A Cisco 1841 router has the following interfaces:

- Two Fast Ethernet interfaces: FastEthernet 0/0 and FastEthernet 0/1

- Two serial interfaces: Serial 0/0/0 and Serial0/0/1

The interfaces on your routers can vary from those on the 1841, but you should be able to follow the commands in this chapter—with some slight modifications—and complete the hands-on labs. In addition, Packet Tracer Activities are referenced throughout the discussion of static routing so that you can practice skills as they are presented. Lab 2-1: Basic Static Route Configuration (2.8.1) mirrors the topology, configurations, and commands discussed in this chapter.

Examining the Connections of the Router

Unlike most user PCs, a router will have multiple network interfaces. These interfaces can include a variety of connectors.

Router Connections

Connecting a router to a network requires a router interface connector to be coupled with a cable connector. As you can see in Figure 2-2, Cisco routers support many different connector types.

Serial Connectors

Figure 2-2 shows various LAN and WAN connectors. For WAN connections, Cisco routers support the EIA/TIA-232, EIA/TIA-449, V.35, X.21, and EIA/TIA-530 standards for serial connections, as shown. Memorizing these connection types is not important. Just know that a router has a DB-60 port that can support five different cabling standards. Because five different cable types are supported with this port, the port is sometimes called a five-in-one serial port. The other end of the serial cable is fitted with a connector that is appropriate to one of the five possible standards.

Figure 2-2   Connections and Connectors

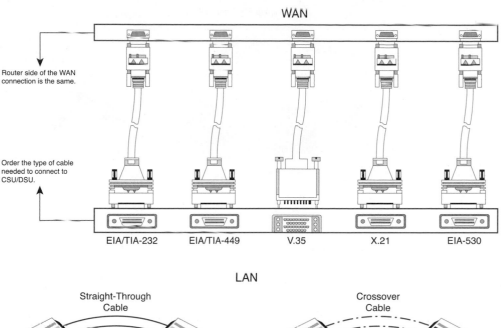

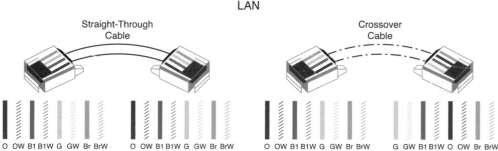

Note

The documentation for the device to which you want to connect should indicate the standard for that device.

Figure 2-3 shows the two types of DB-60 serial connectors commonly used with Cisco router serial interfaces.

If your lab has 2500 series routers, you will use the cable on the right with the larger router connector. Newer routers support the *smart serial* interface, which allows more data to be forwarded across fewer cable pins. Your lab might have this type of cable to support 1700, 2600, and 1800 platforms. The serial end of the smart serial cable is a 26-pin connector. It is much smaller than the DB-60 connector used to connect to a five-in-one serial port. These transition cables support the same five serial standards and are available in either data terminal equipment (DTE) or data communications equipment (DCE) configurations.

Figure 2-3   DTE Serial DB-60 Cables

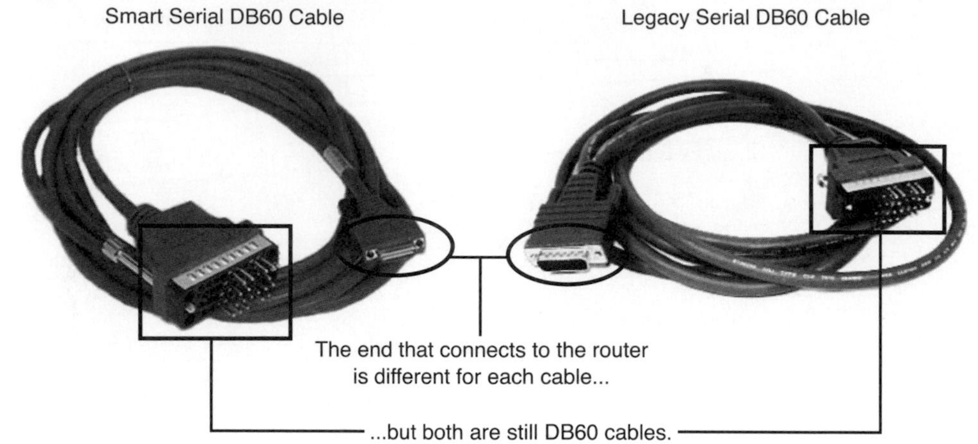

Smart Serial DB60 Cable   Legacy Serial DB60 Cable

The end that connects to the router
is different for each cable...

...but both are still DB60 cables.

Note

For a thorough explanation of DTE and DCE, see Lab 1-1: Cabling a Network and Basic Router
Configuration (1.5.1).

These cable designations are only important to you when configuring your lab equipment to
simulate a "real-world" environment. In a production setting, the cable type is determined
for you by the WAN service you are using.

Ethernet Connectors

A different connector is used in an Ethernet-based LAN environment (see Figure 2-4). An
RJ-45 connector for the unshielded twisted-pair (UTP) cable is the most common connector
used to connect LAN interfaces. At each end of an RJ-45 cable, you should be able to see
eight colored wires, or conductors, ending in eight metal pins or contacts. An Ethernet
cable uses pins 1, 2, 3, and 6 for transmitting and receiving data.

Figure 2-4   TIA/EIA 568B UTP Ethernet Cable

Two types of cables can be used with Ethernet LAN interfaces:

- A straight-through, or patch, cable, with the order of the colored pins the same on each end of the cable

- A crossover cable, with pin 1 connected to pin 3 and pin 2 connected to pin 6

Straight-through cables are used for the following connections:

- Switch-to-router

- Hub-to-router

- Switch-to-PC/server

- Hub-to-PC/server

Crossover cables are used for the following connections:

- Switch-to-switch

- PC/server-to-PC/server

- Switch-to-hub

- Hub-to-hub

- Router-to-router

- Router-to-PC/server

Note

Wireless connectivity is discussed in another course.

Build the Chapter Topology (2.1.3)

Use the Packet Tracer Activity to build the topology that you will use for the rest of this chapter. You will add all the necessary devices and connect them with the correct cabling. Use file e2-213.pka on the CD-ROM that accompanies this book to perform this activity using Packet Tracer.

Router Configuration Review

To configure static routing and dynamic routing protocols, you only need to know the basic IOS commands. You should already be familiar with these commands. The following sections are only meant as a review. For more detailed explanations, see Chapter 1, "Introduction to Routing and Packet Forwarding," and the Network Fundamentals, CCNA Exploration course.

Examining Router Interfaces

As you learned in Chapter 1, the **show ip route** command is used to display the routing table. Initially, the routing table is empty if no interfaces have been configured.

As you can see in Example 2-1, the routing table for Router R1, no interfaces have been configured with an IP address and subnet mask.

Example 2-1 Routing Table Has No Routes

```
R1# show ip route

Codes: C - connected, S - static, I - IGRP, R - RIP, M - mobile, B - BGP
       D - EIGRP, EX - EIGRP external, O - OSPF, IA - OSPF inter area
       N1 - OSPF NSSA external type 1, N2 - OSPF NSSA external type 2
       E1 - OSPF external type 1, E2 - OSPF external type 2, E - EGP
       i - IS-IS, L1 - IS-IS level-1, L2 - IS-IS level-2, ia - IS-IS inter area
       * - candidate default, U - per-user static route, o - ODR
       P - periodic downloaded static route

Gateway of last resort is not set

R1#
```

Note

Static routes and dynamic routes cannot be added to the routing table until the appropriate local interfaces, also known as the *exit interfaces*, have been configured on the router. This procedure will be examined more closely in later chapters.

Interfaces and Their Statuses

The status of each interface can be examined by using several commands.

Example 2-2 displays the **show interfaces** command for R1. The **show interfaces** command shows the status and gives a detailed description for all interfaces on the router.

Example 2-2 show interfaces Command Output Provides Detailed Interface
                Information

```
R1# show interfaces

FastEthernet0/0 is administratively down, line protocol is down
  Hardware is AmdFE, address is 000c.3010.9260 (bia 000c.3010.9260)
```

```
   MTU 1500 bytes, BW 100000 Kbit, DLY 100 usec,
       reliability 255/255, txload 1/255, rxload 1/255
   Encapsulation ARPA, loopback not set
   Keepalive set (10 sec)
   Auto-duplex, Auto Speed, 100BaseTX/FX
   ARP type: ARPA, ARP Timeout 04:00:00
   Last input never, output never, output hang never
   Last clearing of "show interface" counters never
   Input queue: 0/75/0/0 (size/max/drops/flushes); Total output drops: 0
   Queueing strategy: fifo
   Output queue :0/40 (size/max)
   5 minute input rate 0 bits/sec, 0 packets/sec
   5 minute output rate 0 bits/sec, 0 packets/sec
      0 packets input, 0 bytes
      Received 0 broadcasts, 0 runts, 0 giants, 0 throttles
      0 input errors, 0 CRC, 0 frame, 0 overrun, 0 ignored
      0 watchdog
      0 input packets with dribble condition detected
      0 packets output, 0 bytes, 0 underruns
      0 output errors, 0 collisions, 0 interface resets
      0 babbles, 0 late collision, 0 deferred
      0 lost carrier, 0 no carrier
      0 output buffer failures, 0 output buffers swapped out
Serial0/0/0 is administratively down, line protocol is down
   Hardware is PowerQUICC Serial
   MTU 1500 bytes, BW 1544 Kbit, DLY 20000 usec,
       reliability 255/255, txload 1/255, rxload 1/255
   Encapsulation HDLC, loopback not set
   Keepalive set (10 sec)
   Last input never, output never, output hang never
   Last clearing of "show interface" counters never
   Input queue: 0/75/0/0 (size/max/drops/flushes); Total output drops: 0
   Queueing strategy: weighted fair
   Output queue: 0/1000/64/0 (size/max total/threshold/drops)
       Conversations  0/0/256 (active/max active/max total)
       Reserved Conversations 0/0 (allocated/max allocated)
       Available Bandwidth 1158 kilobits/sec
   5 minute input rate 0 bits/sec, 0 packets/sec
   5 minute output rate 0 bits/sec, 0 packets/sec
      0 packets input, 0 bytes, 0 no buffer
      Received 0 broadcasts, 0 runts, 0 giants, 0 throttles
      0 input errors, 0 CRC, 0 frame, 0 overrun, 0 ignored, 0 abort
      0 packets output, 0 bytes, 0 underruns
      0 output errors, 0 collisions, 0 interface resets
      0 output buffer failures, 0 output buffers swapped out
```

```
      1 carrier transitions
      DCD=down  DSR=down  DTR=down  RTS=down  CTS=down
<remaining output omitted for brevity>
R1#
```

Only the first two interfaces are shown. But as you can see, the output from the command can be rather lengthy. To view the same information, but for a specific interface, such as FastEthernet 0/0, use the **show interfaces** command with a parameter that specifies the interface. For example:

```
R1# show interfaces fastethernet 0/0

FastEthernet0/0 is administratively down, line protocol is down
<remaining output omitted for brevity>
```

Notice that the interface is administratively down and the line protocol is down. Administratively down means that the interface is currently in the shutdown mode, or turned off. Line protocol down means, in this case, that the interface is not receiving a carrier signal from a switch or the hub. This condition might also be because of the fact that the interface is in shutdown mode.

You will notice that the **show interfaces** command does not show any IP addresses on R1's interfaces. This is because you have not yet configured IP addresses on any of the interfaces.

Additional Commands for Examining Interface Status

Example 2-3 displays the **show ip interface brief** command output for R1. This command can be used to see a portion of the interface information in a condensed format.

Example 2-3 Summary of Interface Status with the **show ip interface brief** Command

```
R1# show ip interface brief

Interface          IP-Address      OK? Method Status                Protocol
FastEthernet0/0    unassigned      YES manual administratively down  down
Serial0/0          unassigned      YES unset  administratively down  down
FastEthernet0/1    unassigned      YES unset  administratively down  down
Serial0/1          unassigned      YES unset  administratively down  down
```

Example 2-4 displays the **show running-config** command output for R1.

Example 2-4 Interface Information with the **show running-config** Command

```
R1# show running-config
!
version 12.3
!
hostname R1
!
!
enable secret 5 $1$.3RO$VLUOdBF2OqNBn0EjQBvR./
!
!
interface FastEthernet0/0
 mac-address 000c.3010.9260
 no ip address
 duplex auto
 speed auto
 shutdown
!
interface FastEthernet0/1
 mac-address 000c.3010.9261
 no ip address
 duplex auto
 speed auto
 shutdown
!
interface Serial0/0/0
 no ip address
 shutdown
!
interface Serial0/0/1
 no ip address
 shutdown
!
interface Vlan1
 no ip address
 shutdown
!
ip classless
!
!
line con 0
 password cisco
 login
line vty 0 4
```

```
 password cisco
 login
!
end
```

The **show running-config** command is used to display the current configuration file that the router is using. Configuration commands are temporarily stored in the running configuration file and implemented immediately by the router. Using this command is another way to verify the configuration of an interface such as FastEthernet 0/0:

```
R1# show running-config

<some output omitted>
interface FastEthernet0/0
  no ip address
  shutdown
<some output omitted>
```

However, using **show running-config** is not necessarily the best way to verify interface configurations. Use the **show ip interface brief** command to quickly verify that interfaces are up and up (administratively up and line protocol is up).

Configuring an Ethernet Interface

One common type of interface on many routers is an Ethernet interface. Ethernet interfaces are commonly used to connect to the corporate LAN.

Configuring an Ethernet Interface

As shown earlier in Example 2-1, R1 does not yet have any routes. Add a route by configuring an interface with an IP address/subnet mask, and explore exactly what happens when that interface is activated. By default, all router interfaces are shut down or turned off. To enable this interface, use the **no shutdown** command, which changes the interface from administratively down to up:

```
R1(config)# interface fastethernet 0/0
R1(config-if)# ip address 172.16.3.1 255.255.255.0
R1(config-if)# no shutdown
```

The following message is returned from the IOS:

```
*Mar 1 01:16:08.212: %LINK-3-UPDOWN: Interface FastEthernet0/0, changed state to up
*Mar 1 01:16:09.214: %LINEPROTO-5-UPDOWN: Line protocol on Interface
   FastEthernet0/0, changed state to up
```

Both of these messages are important. The first **changed state to up** message indicates that, physically, the connection is good. If you do not get this first message, be sure that the interface is properly connected to a switch or a hub.

Note

Although enabled with the **no shutdown** command, an Ethernet interface will not be active, or up, unless it is receiving a carrier signal from another device (switch, hub, PC, or another router).

The second **changed state to up** message indicates that the data link layer is operational. On LAN interfaces, you do not normally change the data link layer parameters. However, WAN interfaces in a lab environment require clocking on one side of the link, as discussed in Lab 1-1: Cabling a Network and Basic Router Configuration (1.5.1), as well as the section "Configuring a Serial Interface," later in this chapter. If you do not correctly set the clock rate, the line protocol (the data link layer) will not change to up.

Unsolicited Messages from IOS

Example 2-5 shows the output from an unsolicited message from the IOS.

Example 2-5 Command Input Interrupted by IOS

```
R1(config)# int fa0/0
R1(config-if)# ip address 172.16.3.1 255.255.255.0
R1(config-if)# no shutdown
R1(config-if)# descri

*Mar  1 01:16:08.212: %LINK-3-UPDOWN: Interface FastEthernet0/0, changed state to
  up
*Mar  1 01:16:09.214: %LINEPROTO-5-UPDOWN: Line protocol on Interface
  FastEthernet0/0, changed state to upption
R1(config-if)#
```

The IOS often sends unsolicited messages similar to the **changed state to up** messages just discussed. As you can see in the previous example, sometimes these messages will occur when you are in the middle of typing a command. In Example 2-5, this occurred while the user was entering the **description** command. The IOS message does not affect the command, but it can cause you to lose your place when typing.

To keep the unsolicited output separate from your input, enter line configuration mode for the console port and add the **logging synchronous** command, as shown in Example 2-6. Notice that the messages returned by IOS no longer interfere with the user's entry of the **description** command. Instead, the IOS copies the command, midstream, to the next router prompt. The user then is able to easily finish the command as well as read the unsolicited message.

Example 2-6 Synchronizing IOS Messages and Command Output

```
R1(config)# line console 0
R1(config-line)# logging synchronous
R1(config-if)# descri


*Mar  1 01:28:04.242: %LINK-3-UPDOWN: Interface FastEthernet0/0, changed state to
  up
*Mar  1 01:28:05.243: %LINEPROTO-5-UPDOWN: Line protocol on Interface
  FastEthernet0/0, changed state to up
R1(config-if)# description
```

Reading the Routing Table

Now look at routing table shown in Example 2-7. Notice that R1 now has a "directly connected" FastEthernet 0/0 interface along with a new network.

Example 2-7 Directly Connected Route

```
R1# show ip route

Codes: C - connected, S - static, I - IGRP, R - RIP, M - mobile, B - BGP
       D - EIGRP, EX - EIGRP external, O - OSPF, IA - OSPF inter area
       N1 - OSPF NSSA external type 1, N2 - OSPF NSSA external type 2
       E1 - OSPF external type 1, E2 - OSPF external type 2, E - EGP
       i - IS-IS, L1 - IS-IS level-1, L2 - IS-IS level-2, ia - IS-IS inter area
       * - candidate default, U - per-user static route, o - ODR
       P - periodic downloaded static route


Gateway of last resort is not set


     172.16.0.0/24 is subnetted, 1 subnets
C       172.16.3.0 is directly connected, FastEthernet0/0
```

The interface was configured with the 172.16.3.1/24 IP address, which makes it a member of the 172.16.3.0/24 network.

Examine the following line of output from the table:

```
C       172.16.3.0 is directly connected, FastEthernet0/0
```

The **C** at the beginning of the route indicates that this is a directly connected network. In other words, R1 has an interface that belongs to this network. The meaning of **C** is defined in the list of codes at the top of the routing table.

The /24 subnet mask for this route is displayed in the line above the actual route:

```
     172.16.0.0/24 is subnetted, 1 subnets
C       172.16.3.0 is directly connected, FastEthernet0/0
```

Routers Usually Store Network Addresses

With very few exceptions, routing tables have routes for network addresses rather than individual host addresses. The 172.16.3.0/24 route in the routing table means that this route matches all packets with a destination address belonging to this network. Having a single route represent an entire network of host IP addresses makes the routing table smaller, with fewer routes, which results in faster routing table lookups. The routing table could contain all 254 individual host IP addresses for the 172.16.3.0/24 network, but that is an inefficient way of storing addresses.

A phone book is a good analogy for a routing table structure. A phone book is a list of names and phone numbers, sorted in alphabetical order by last name. When looking for a number, you can assume that the fewer names there are in the book, the faster it will be to find a particular name. A phone book of 20 pages and perhaps 2000 entries will be much easier to search than a book of 200 pages and 20,000 entries.

The phone book only contains one listing for each phone number. For example, the Stanford family might be listed as

Stanford, Harold, 742 Evergreen Terrace, 555-1234

This is the single entry for everyone who lives at this address and has the same phone number. The phone book could contain a listing for every individual, but this would increase the size of the phone book. For example, there could be a separate listing for Harold Stanford, Margaret Stanford, Brad Stanford, Leslie Stanford, and Maggie Stanford—all with the same address and phone number. If this were done for every family, the phone book would be larger and take longer to search.

Routing tables work the same way: One entry in the table represents a "family" of devices that all share the same network or address space. (The difference between a network and an address space will become clearer as you move through the course.) The fewer the entries in the routing table, the faster the lookup process. To keep routing tables smaller, network addresses with subnet masks are listed instead of individual host IP addresses.

Note

Occasionally, a "host route" is entered in the routing table; the host route represents an individual host IP address. The host route is listed with the device's host IP address and a /32 (255.255.255.255) subnet mask. The topic of host routes is discussed in another course.

Verifying Ethernet Addresses

After an interface is configured, it can be verified using various commands.

Commands to Verify Interface Configuration

The **show interfaces fastethernet 0/0** command in Example 2-8 now shows that the interface is up and the line protocol is up. The **no shutdown** command changed the interface from administratively down to up. Notice that the IP address is now displayed.

Example 2-8 Verifying Interface Status with the **show interfaces** Command

```
R1# show interfaces fastethernet 0/0

FastEthernet0/0 is up, line protocol is up
  Hardware is AmdFE, address is 000c.3010.9260 (bia 000c.3010.9260)
  Internet address is 172.16.3.1/24
  <output omitted>
```

The **show ip interface brief** command output in Example 2-9 also verifies this same information. Under the status and protocol, you should see "up."

Example 2-9 Verifying Interface Status with the **show ip interface brief** Command

```
R1# show ip interface brief

Interface          IP-Address      OK? Method Status                Protocol
FastEthernet0/0    172.16.3.1      YES manual up                    up
Serial0/0/0        unassigned      YES unset  administratively down down
FastEthernet0/1    unassigned      YES unset  administratively down down
Serial0/0/1        unassigned      YES unset  administratively down down
```

The following partial **show running-config** command output also shows the current configuration of this interface. When the interface is disabled, the **show running-config** command displays **shutdown**; however, when the interface is enabled, **no shutdown** is not displayed.

```
R1# show running-config

<output omitted>
interface FastEthernet0/0
ip address 172.16.3.1 255.255.255.0
<output omitted>
```

As explained in Chapter 1, a router cannot have multiple interfaces that belong to the same IP subnet. Each interface must belong to a separate subnet. For example, a router cannot have both its FastEthernet 0/0 interface configured as 172.16.3.1/24 address and mask and its FastEthernet 0/1 interface configured as 172.16.3.2/24.

IOS will return the following error message if you attempt to configure the second interface with the same IP subnet as the first interface:

```
R1(config-if)# int fa0/1
R1(config-if)# ip address 172.16.3.2 255.255.255.0

172.16.3.0 overlaps with FastEthernet0/0
R1(config-if)#
```

Typically, the router's Ethernet or Fast Ethernet interface will be the default gateway IP address for any devices on that LAN. For example, PC1 would be configured with a host IP address belonging to the 172.16.3.0/24 network, with the default gateway IP address 172.16.3.1. 172.16.3.1 is Router R1's Fast Ethernet IP address. Remember, a router's Ethernet or Fast Ethernet interface will also participate in the Address Resolution Protocol (ARP) process as a member of that Ethernet network.

Ethernet Interfaces Participate in ARP

A router's Ethernet interface participates in a LAN network just like any other device on that network. This means that these interfaces have a Layer 2 MAC address. As shown in Example 2-8, the **show interfaces** command displays the MAC address for the Ethernet interfaces.

As demonstrated in Chapter 1, an Ethernet interface participates in ARP requests and replies and maintains an ARP table. If a router has a packet destined for a device on a directly connected Ethernet network, it checks the ARP table for an entry with that destination IP address to map it to the MAC address. If the ARP table does not contain this IP address, the Ethernet interface sends out an ARP request. The device with the destination IP address sends back an ARP reply that lists its MAC address. The IP address and MAC address information is then added to the ARP table for that Ethernet interface. The router is now able to encapsulate the IP packet into an Ethernet frame with the destination MAC address from its ARP table. The Ethernet frame, with the encapsulated packet, is then sent through that Ethernet interface.

Configure Ethernet Interfaces for IP on Hosts and Routers (2.2.3)

Use the Packet Tracer Activity to practice configuring Ethernet interfaces. Follow the additional instructions provided in the activity to examine the ARP process in simulation mode. Use file e2-223.pka on the CD-ROM that accompanies this book to perform this activity using Packet Tracer.

Configuring a Serial Interface

Next, configure the Serial 0/0/0 interface on Router R1. This interface is on the 172.16.2.0/24 network and is assigned the IP address and subnet mask of 172.16.2.1/24. The process to use for the configuration of the serial interface 0/0/0 is similar to the process you used to configure the FastEthernet 0/0 interface:

```
R1(config)# interface serial 0/0/0
R1(config-if)# ip address 172.16.2.1 255.255.255.0
R1(config-if)# no shutdown
```

Example 2-10 shows the output from the **show interfaces serial 0/0/0** command.

Example 2-10   Serial Interface with down and down

```
R1# show interfaces serial 0/0/0

Serial0/0/0 is down, line protocol is down
  Hardware is PowerQUICC Serial
  Internet address is 172.16.2.1/24
  MTU 1500 bytes, BW 1544 Kbit, DLY 20000 usec,
<output omitted>
```

After entering the commands in Example 2-10, the state of the serial interface might vary depending on the type of WAN connection. For purposes here, we will be using dedicated, serial point-to-point connections between two routers. The serial interface will be in the up state only after the other end of the serial link has also been properly configured. You can display the current state of Serial 0/0/0 using the **show interfaces serial 0/0/0** command:

```
R2# show interfaces serial 0/0/0

Serial0/0/0 is administratively down, line protocol is down
```

As you can see, the link is still down. The link is down because you have not yet configured and enabled the other end of the serial link on R2.

You will now configure the other end of this link, Serial 0/0/0, for Router R2.

Note

There is no requirement that both ends of the serial link use the same interface, in this case, Serial 0/0/0. However, because both interfaces are members of the same network, they both must have IP addresses that belong to the 172.16.2.0/24 network. (The terms *network* and *subnet* can be used interchangeably in this case.)

R2's interface Serial 0/0/0 is configured with the IP address and subnet mask 172.16.2.2/24:

```
R2(config)# interface serial 0/0/0
R2(config-if)# ip address 172.16.2.2 255.255.255.0
R2(config-if)# no shutdown
```

If you now issue the **show interfaces serial 0/0/0** command on either router, you still see that the link is up/down:

```
R2# show interfaces serial 0/0/0

Serial0/0/0 is up, line protocol is down
<output omitted>
```

The physical link between R1 and R2 is up because both ends of the serial link have been configured correctly with an IP address/mask and enabled with the **no shutdown** command. However, the line protocol is still down. This is because the interface is not receiving a clock signal. There is still one more command that you need to enter, the **clock rate** command, on the router with the DCE cable. The **clock rate** command will set the clock signal for the link. Configuring the clock signal will be discussed in the next sections.

Examining Serial Interfaces

Serial interfaces can take various forms and use additional equipment such as a channel service unit/data service unit (CSU/DSU). This might also require additional commands on the router.

Physically Connecting a WAN Interface

The WAN physical layer describes the interface between the DTE and the DCE. Generally, the DCE is the service provider and the DTE is the attached device. In this model, the services offered to the DTE are made available either through a modem or a CSU/DSU.

Figure 2-5 shows a router connected to a CSU/DSU. Typically, the router is the DTE device and is connected to a CSU/DSU, which is the DCE device. The CSU/DSU (DCE device) is used to convert the data from the router (DTE device) into a form acceptable to the WAN service provider. The CSU/DSU (DCE device) is also responsible for converting the data from the WAN service provider into a form acceptable by the router (DTE device). The router is usually connected to the CSU/DSU using a serial DTE cable.

Serial interfaces require a clock signal to control the timing of the communications. In most environments, the service provider (a DCE device such as a CSU/DSU) will provide the clock. By default, Cisco routers are DTE devices. However, in a lab environment, we are not using CSU/DSUs and, of course, we do not have a WAN service provider.

Figure 2-5   CSU/DSU Connection Using a DTE Cable

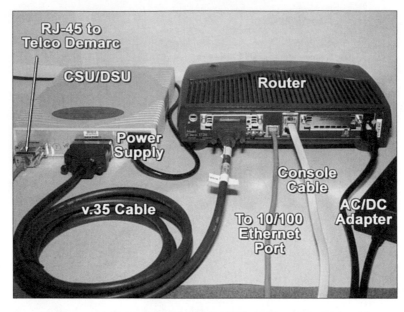

Source: http://www.more.net/technical/netserv/routers/cisco1720/images/dsu-router-connection-w.jpg

Configuring Serial Links in a Lab Environment

For serial links that are directly interconnected, as in a lab environment, one side of a connection must be considered a DCE and provide a clocking signal. Although Cisco serial interfaces are DTE devices by default, they can be configured as DCE devices.

To configure a router to be the DCE device, follow these steps:

Step 1.   Connect the DCE end of the cable to the serial interface.

Step 2.   Configure the clock signal on the serial interface using the **clock rate** command.

The serial cables used in the lab are typically one of two types:

- A DTE/DCE crossover cable on which one end is DTE and the other end is DCE

- A DTE cable connected to a DCE cable

In our chapter topology, the Serial 0/0/0 interface on R1 is connected to the DCE end of the cable, and the Serial 0/0/0 interface on R2 is connected to the DTE end of the cable. The cable should be labeled either DTE or DCE.

You can also distinguish DTE from DCE by looking at the connector between the two cables. The DTE cable has a male connector, whereas the DCE cable has a female connector.

If a cable is connected between the two routers and neither end of the cable is labeled, you can use the **show controllers** command to determine which end of the cable is attached to that interface. In the following command output, notice that R1 has the DCE cable attached to its Serial 0/0/0 interface and that no clock rate is set.

```
R1# show controllers serial 0/0/0


Interface Serial0/0/0
Hardware is PowerQUICC MPC860
DCE V.35, no clock
<output omitted>
```

When the cable is attached, the clock can now be set with the **clock rate** command. The available clock rates, in bits per second, are 1200, 2400, 9600, 19200, 38400, 56000, 64000, 72000, 125000, 148000, 500000, 800000, 1000000, 1300000, 2000000, and 4000000. Some bit rates might not be available on certain serial interfaces. Because the Serial 0/0/0 interface on R1 has the DCE cable attached, we will configure that interface with a clock rate:

```
R1(config)# interface serial 0/0/0
R1(config-if)# clock rate 64000


01:10:28: %LINEPROTO-5-UPDOWN: Line protocol on Interface Serial0/0/0, changed state
    to up
```

Note

If a router's interface with a DTE cable is configured with the **clock rate** command, the IOS will disregard the command and there will be no ill effects.

Verifying the Serial Interface Configuration

As you can see from Example 2-11, you can determine that the line protocol is now up and verify this on both ends of the serial link by using the **show interfaces** and **show ip interface brief** commands. Remember, the serial interface will be up only if both ends of the link are configured correctly. In our lab environment, we have configured the clock rate on the end with the DCE cable.

Example 2-11   Verifying the Serial Interface Configuration

```
R1# show interfaces serial 0/0/0


Serial0/0/0 is up, line protocol is up
  Hardware is PowerQUICC Serial
```

```
   Internet address is 172.16.2.1/24
<output omitted>


R1# show ip interface brief

Interface              IP-Address      OK? Method Status          Protocol
FastEthernet0/0        172.16.3.1      YES manual up                   up
Serial0/0/0            172.16.2.1      YES manual up                   up
<output omitted>
```

You can further verify that the link is up/up by pinging the remote interface, as shown in Example 2-12.

Example 2-12   Using the **ping** Command to Verify Connectivity

```
R1# ping 172.16.2.2

Type escape sequence to abort.
Sending 5, 100-byte ICMP Echos to 172.16.2.2, timeout is 2 seconds:
!!!!!
Success rate is 100 percent (5/5), round-trip min/avg/max = 28/28/28 ms
R1#
```

Finally, you can see in Example 2-13 that the 172.16.2.0/24 serial network is now in the routing table for R1. If you issued the **show ip route** command on R2, you would also see the directly connected route for the 172.16.2.0/24 network.

Example 2-13   Using the **show ip route** Command to Verify Connectivity

```
R1# show ip route

Codes: C - connected, S - static, I - IGRP, R - RIP, M - mobile, B - BGP
       D - EIGRP, EX - EIGRP external, O - OSPF, IA - OSPF inter area
       N1 - OSPF NSSA external type 1, N2 - OSPF NSSA external type 2
       E1 - OSPF external type 1, E2 - OSPF external type 2, E - EGP
       i - IS-IS, L1 - IS-IS level-1, L2 - IS-IS level-2, ia - IS-IS inter area
       * - candidate default, U - per-user static route, o - ODR
       P - periodic downloaded static route

Gateway of last resort is not set

     172.16.0.0/24 is subnetted, 2 subnets
C       172.16.2.0 is directly connected, Serial0/0/0
C       172.16.3.0 is directly connected, FastEthernet0/0
```

Now verify the interface's configurations by using the **show running-config** command on R1, as shown in Example 2-14.

Example 2-14   Verifying the Configuration with the **show running-config** Command

```
R1# show running-config

Building configuration...

Current configuration : 1130 bytes
!
hostname R1
!
<output omitted>
!
interface FastEthernet0/0
 description R1 LAN
 ip address 172.16.3.1 255.255.255.0
!
interface Serial0/0/0
 description Link to R2
 ip address 172.16.2.1 255.255.255.0
 clockrate 64000
!
<output omitted>
R1#
```

Note

Although the **clock rate** command is two words, IOS spells clockrate as a single word in the running configuration and startup configuration files.

Exploring Directly Connected Networks

Before a router can forward packets to a remote network, it must have active directly connected networks. Each directly connected network on the router is a member of a different network or subnet.

Verifying Changes to the Routing Table

The routing table is a key component in routing operations. Several commands can be used to help verify and troubleshoot the routing table.

Routing Table Concepts

As you can see in Examples 2-15 and 2-16, the **show ip route** command reveals the content of the routing tables for R1 and R2.

Example 2-15   Current Routing Table for R1

```
R1# show ip route

Codes: C - connected, S - static, I - IGRP, R - RIP, M - mobile, B - BGP
       D - EIGRP, EX - EIGRP external, O - OSPF, IA - OSPF inter area
       N1 - OSPF NSSA external type 1, N2 - OSPF NSSA external type 2
       E1 - OSPF external type 1, E2 - OSPF external type 2, E - EGP
       i - IS-IS, L1 - IS-IS level-1, L2 - IS-IS level-2, ia - IS-IS inter area
       * - candidate default, U - per-user static route, o - ODR
       P - periodic downloaded static route

Gateway of last resort is not set

     172.16.0.0/24 is subnetted, 2 subnets
C       172.16.2.0 is directly connected, Serial0/0/0
C       172.16.3.0 is directly connected, FastEthernet0/0
R1#
```

Example 2-16   Current Routing Table for R2

```
R2# show ip route

Codes: C - connected, S - static, I - IGRP, R - RIP, M - mobile, B - BGP
       D - EIGRP, EX - EIGRP external, O - OSPF, IA - OSPF inter area
       N1 - OSPF NSSA external type 1, N2 - OSPF NSSA external type 2
       E1 - OSPF external type 1, E2 - OSPF external type 2, E - EGP
       i - IS-IS, L1 - IS-IS level-1, L2 - IS-IS level-2, ia - IS-IS inter area
       * - candidate default, U - per-user static route, o - ODR
       P - periodic downloaded static route

Gateway of last resort is not set

     172.16.0.0/24 is subnetted, 2 subnets
C       172.16.2.0 is directly connected, Serial0/0/0
R2#
```

A routing table is a data structure used to store routing information acquired from different sources. The main purpose of a routing table is to provide the router with paths to different destination networks.

The routing table consists of a list of "known" network addresses—that is, those addresses that are directly connected, configured statically, and learned dynamically. R1 and R2 only have routes for directly connected networks.

Observing Routes as They Are Added to the Routing Table

This section takes a closer look at how directly connected routes are added to, and deleted from, the routing table. In contrast to **show** commands, **debug** commands can be used to monitor router operations in real time. The **debug ip routing** command will display any changes that the router performs when adding or removing routes. You will configure the interfaces on Router R2 and examine this process. The following discussion will refer to Example 2-17.

Example 2-17   Using the **debug ip routing** Command to Observe a Route Installed

```
R2# debug ip routing

IP routing debugging is on

R2(config)#int fa0/0
R2(config-if)#ip address 172.16.1.1 255.255.255.0
R2(config-if)#no shutdown

%LINK-3-UPDOWN: Interface FastEthernet0/0, changed state to up
%LINEPROTO-5-UPDOWN: Line protocol on Interface FastEthernet0/0, changed state to
  up

RT: add 172.16.1.0/24 via 0.0.0.0, connected metric [0/0]
RT: interface FastEthernet0/0 added to routing table
```

First, you enable debugging with the **debug ip routing** command so that you can see the directly connected networks as they are added to the routing table.

Next, you configure the IP address and subnet mask for the FastEthernet 0/0 interface on R2 and use the **no shutdown** command. Because the Fast Ethernet interface connects to the 172.16.1.0/24 network, it must be configured with a host IP address for that network.

In Example 2-17, notice that the following message is returned from the IOS:

```
02:35:30: %LINK-3-UPDOWN: Interface FastEthernet0/0, changed state to up
02:35:31: %LINEPROTO-5-UPDOWN: Line protocol on Interface FastEthernet0/0, changed
  state to up
```

After the **no shutdown** command is entered and the router determines that the interface and line protocol are in the up and up state, the **debug** output shows R2 adding this directly connected network to the routing table.

```
02:35:30: RT: add 172.16.1.0/24 via 0.0.0.0, connected metric [0/0]
02:35:30: RT: interface FastEthernet0/0 added to routing table
```

The routing table for R2 now shows the route for the directly connected network 172.16.1.0/24, as shown in Example 2-18.

```
Example 2-18    Routing Table for R2 with New Route Installed
R2# show ip route

Codes: C - connected, S - static, I - IGRP, R - RIP, M - mobile, B - BGP
       D - EIGRP, EX - EIGRP external, O - OSPF, IA - OSPF inter area
       N1 - OSPF NSSA external type 1, N2 - OSPF NSSA external type 2
       E1 - OSPF external type 1, E2 - OSPF external type 2, E - EGP
       i - IS-IS, L1 - IS-IS level-1, L2 - IS-IS level-2, ia - IS-IS inter area
       * - candidate default, U - per-user static route, o - ODR
       P - periodic downloaded static route

Gateway of last resort is not set

     172.16.0.0/24 is subnetted, 2 subnets
C       172.16.1.0 is directly connected, FastEthernet0/0
C       172.16.2.0 is directly connected, Serial0/0
```

The **debug ip routing** command displays routing table processes for any route, whether that route is a directly connected network, a static route, or a dynamic route.

You can disable **debug ip routing** by using either the **undebug ip routing** command or the **undebug all** command, as shown in Example 2-19.

```
Example 2-19    Disabling Debug
R2# undebug all

All possible debugging has been turned off
!
or
!
R2# undebug ip routing

IP routing debugging is off
R2#
```

Changing an IP Address

To change an IP address or subnet mask for an interface, reconfigure the IP address and subnet mask for that interface. This change will overwrite the previous entry. There are ways to configure a single interface with multiple IP addresses, as long as each address is on a different subnet. This topic will be discussed in a later course.

To remove a directly connected network from a router, use these two commands: **shutdown** and **no ip address**, as demonstrated in Example 2-20. The **shutdown** command is used to disable interfaces. This command can be used by itself if you want to retain the IP address/mask configuration on the interface but want to shut it down temporarily. In our example, this command will disable R2's Fast Ethernet interface. The IP address, however, will still be in the configuration file, running-config.

After the **shutdown** command is used, you can remove the IP address and subnet mask from the interface. The order in which you perform these two commands does not matter.

Again, using **debug ip routing**, you can see the routing table process. We will delete the configuration for R2's FastEthernet 0/0 interface. In Example 2-20, you can see the routing table process removing the directly connected route.

Example 2-20   Removing Interface Configurations

```
R2# debug ip routing

IP routing debugging is on
R2# config t

Enter configuration commands, one per line.  End with CNTL/Z.
R2(config)# int fa0/0
R2(config-if)# shutdown

%LINK-5-CHANGED: Interface FastEthernet0/0, changed state to administratively down
%LINEPROTO-5-UPDOWN: Line protocol on Interface FastEthernet0/0, changed state to
  down

is_up: 0 state: 6 sub state: 1 line: 1
RT: interface FastEthernet0/0 removed from routing table
RT: del 172.16.1.0/24 via 0.0.0.0, connected metric [0/0]
RT: delete subnet route to 172.16.1.0/24

<some ouput omitted>

R2(config-if)# no ip address
R2(config-if)# end
```

```
%SYS-5-CONFIG_I: Configured from console by console
R2# undebug all

All possible debugging has been turned off
```

First, you shut down the interface. The IOS output also indicates that the interface and line protocol are now down. Then, the output from debugging shows the route being deleted from the routing table. Finally, to completely remove the configuration, enter **no ip address** and turn off debugging.

To verify that the route was removed from the routing table, use the **show ip route** command. In Example 2-21, notice that the route to 172.16.1.0/24 has been removed.

Example 2-21   Routing Table for R2 with Route Deleted

```
R2# show ip route

Codes: C - connected, S - static, I - IGRP, R - RIP, M - mobile, B - BGP
       D - EIGRP, EX - EIGRP external, O - OSPF, IA - OSPF inter area
       N1 - OSPF NSSA external type 1, N2 - OSPF NSSA external type 2
       E1 - OSPF external type 1, E2 - OSPF external type 2, E - EGP
       i - IS-IS, L1 - IS-IS level-1, L2 - IS-IS level-2, ia - IS-IS inter area
       * - candidate default, U - per-user static route, o - ODR
       P - periodic downloaded static route

Gateway of last resort is not set

     172.16.0.0/24 is subnetted, 1 subnets
C       172.16.2.0 is directly connected, Serial0/0/0
```

For the purposes of the rest of this chapter, we will assume that the addressing for FastEthernet 0/0 was not removed. To reconfigure the interface, simply enter the commands again:

```
R2(config)# interface fastethernet 0/0
R2(config-if)# ip address 172.16.1.1 255.255.255.0
R2(config-if)# no shutdown
```

> **Caution**
>
> The **debug** commands, especially the **debug all** command, should be used sparingly. These commands can disrupt router operations. The **debug** commands are useful when configuring or troubleshooting a network; however, they can make intensive use of CPU and memory resources. It is recommended that you run as few debug processes as necessary and disable them immediately when they are no longer needed. The **debug** commands should be used with caution on production networks because they can affect the performance of the device.

Configure Serial Interfaces and Verify the Routing Table (2.3.1)

Use the Packet Tracer Activity to practice configuring serial interfaces. You will also use the **debug ip routing** command to observe the routing table processes. Use file e2-231.pka on the CD-ROM that accompanies this book to perform this activity using Packet Tracer.

Devices on Directly Connected Networks

Before configuring static routes or a dynamic routing protocol, it is recommended that you verify connectivity with devices on the directly connected networks. Hosts on different networks will not be able to communicate with each other if they cannot communicate with their own default gateway, the local router.

Accessing Devices on Directly Connected Networks

To return to the configuration in the sample topology, assume that all directly connected networks are configured for all three routers. Example 2-22 shows the rest of the configurations for Routers R2 and R3.

Example 2-22   Remaining Interface Configurations for R2 and R3

```
R2(config)# interface serial 0/0/1
R2(config-if)# ip address 192.168.1.2 255.255.255.0
R2(config-if)# clock rate 64000
R2(config-if)# no shutdown
R3(config)# interface fastethernet 0/0
R3(config-if)# ip address 192.168.2.1 255.255.255.0
R3(config-if)# no shutdown
R3(config-if)# interface serial 0/0/1
R3(config-if)# ip address 192.168.1.1 255.255.255.0
R3(config-if)# no shutdown
```

The output from the **show ip interface brief** command shown in Example 2-23 verifies that all configured interfaces are up and up.

Example 2-23   Verifying That All Interfaces Are up and up

```
R1# show ip interface brief

Interface            IP-Address      OK? Method Status                Protocol
FastEthernet0/0      172.16.3.1      YES manual up                         up
Serial0/0/0          172.16.2.1      YES manual up                         up
FastEthernet0/1      unassigned      YES manual administratively down down
Serial0/0/1          unassigned      YES manual administratively down down
```
```
R2# show ip interface brief

Interface            IP-Address      OK? Method Status                Protocol
FastEthernet0/0      172.16.1.1      YES manual up                         up
Serial0/0/0          172.16.2.2      YES manual up                         up
FastEthernet0/1      unassigned      YES manual administratively down down
Serial0/0/1          192.168.1.2     YES manual up                         up
```
```
R3# show ip interface brief

Interface            IP-Address      OK? Method Status                Protocol
FastEthernet0/0      192.168.2.1     YES manual up                         up
Serial0/0/0          unassigned      YES manual administratively down down
FastEthernet0/1      unassigned      YES manual administratively down down
Serial0/0/1          192.168.1.1     YES manual up                         up
```

By reviewing the routing tables in Example 2-24, you can verify that all directly connected networks are installed for routing.

Example 2-24   Verifying That Directly Connected Routes Are Installed

```
R1# show ip route

<output omitted>
     172.16.0.0/24 is subnetted, 2 subnets
C       172.16.2.0 is directly connected, Serial0/0/0
C       172.16.3.0 is directly connected, FastEthernet0/0
```
```
R2# show ip route

172.16.0.0/24 is subnetted, 2 subnets
```

```
C        172.16.1.0 is directly connected, FastEthernet0/0
C        172.16.2.0 is directly connected, Serial0/0/0
C     192.168.1.0/24 is directly connected, Serial0/0/1
R3# show ip route


C     192.168.1.0/24 is directly connected, Serial0/0/1
C     192.168.2.0/24 is directly connected, FastEthernet0/0
```

The crucial step in configuring your network is to verify that all the interfaces are up and up and that the routing tables are complete. Regardless of what routing scheme you ultimately configure—static, dynamic, or a combination of both—verify your initial network configurations with the **show ip interface brief** command and the **show ip route** command before proceeding with more complex configurations.

When a router only has its interfaces configured, and the routing table contains the directly connected networks but no other routes, only devices on those directly connected networks are reachable:

- R1 can communicate with any device on the 172.16.3.0/24 and 172.16.2.0/24 networks.

- R2 can communicate with any device on the 172.16.1.0/24, 172.16.2.0/24, and 192.168.1.0/24 networks.

- R3 can communicate with any device on the 192.168.1.0/24 and 192.168.2.0/24 networks.

Because these routers know only about their directly connected networks, the routers can communicate only with those devices on their own directly connected LANs and serial networks.

For example, PC1 in the chapter topology (see Figure 2-1) has been configured with the IP address 172.16.3.10 and the subnet mask 255.255.255.0. PC1 has also been configured with the default gateway IP address 172.16.3.1, which is the router's FastEthernet 0/0 interface IP address. Because R1 only knows about directly connected networks, it can forward packets from PC1 to devices on the 172.16.2.0/24 network, such as 172.16.2.1 and 172.16.2.2. Packets from PC1 with any other destination IP address, such as PC2 at 172.16.1.10, would be dropped by R1.

Take a look at the routing table for R2 in Example 2-24. R2 only knows about its three directly connected networks. Try to predict what will happen if you ping the Fast Ethernet interfaces on the other routers.

In Example 2-25, notice that the pings failed, as indicated by the series of five periods.

Example 2-25   Remote Networks Are Unreachable

```
R2# ping 172.16.3.1

Type escape sequence to abort.
Sending 5, 100-byte ICMP Echos to 172.16.3.1, timeout is 2 seconds:
.....
Success rate is 0 percent (0/5)
R2#ping 192.168.2.1

Type escape sequence to abort.
Sending 5, 100-byte ICMP Echos to 192.168.2.1, timeout is 2 seconds:
.....
Success rate is 0 percent (0/5)
```

The pings failed because R2 does not have a route in its routing table that matches either 172.16.3.1 or 192.168.2.1, which is the ping packet's destination IP address. To have a match between the packet's destination IP address of 172.16.3.1 and a route in the routing table, the address must match the number of leftmost bits of the network address as indicated by the prefix of the route. For R2, all the routes have a /24 prefix; therefore, the leftmost 24 bits are checked for each route.

The sections that follow further investigate what is happening.

Pings from R2 to 172.16.3.1

Figure 2-6 shows the unsuccessful ping output along with the unmatched routes in the routing table.

The first route in the table for R1 is 172.16.1.0/24:

```
     172.16.0.0/24 is subnetted, 2 subnets
C       172.16.1.0 is directly connected, FastEthernet0/0
```

The IOS routing table process checks to see whether the 24 leftmost bits of the packet's destination IP address, 172.16.3.1, match the 172.16.1.0/24 network.

If you convert these addresses to binary and compare them, as shown in Figure 2-6, you will see that the first 24 bits of this route do not match because the twenty-third bit does not match. Therefore, this route is rejected:

```
     172.16.0.0/24 is subnetted, 2 subnets
C       172.16.2.0 is directly connected, Serial0/0/0
```

Figure 2-6   No Route: Pings Are Discarded

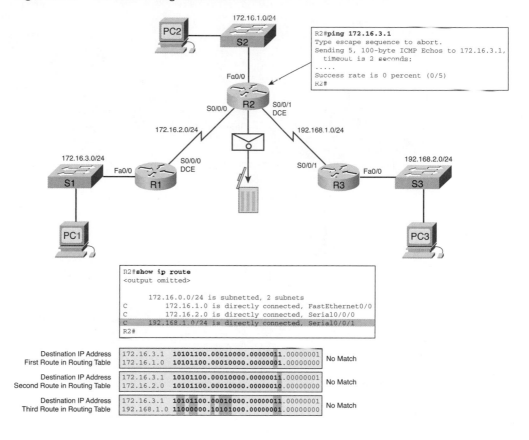

In Figure 2-6, you see that the first 24 bits of the second route do not match because the twenty-fourth bit does not match. Therefore, this route is also rejected, and the process moves on to the next route in the routing table:

```
C 192.168.1.0/24 is directly connected, Serial0/0/1
```

The third route is also not a match. As shown, 10 of the first 24 bits do not match. Therefore, this route is rejected. Because there are no more routes in the routing table, the pings are discarded. The router makes its forwarding decision at Layer 3, a "best effort" to forward the packet, but it makes no guarantees.

Pings from R2 to 192.168.1.1

Look at Figure 2-7 to see what happens if Router R2 pings the 192.168.1.1 interface on Router R3.

Figure 2-7   Route Exists: Pings Are Sent

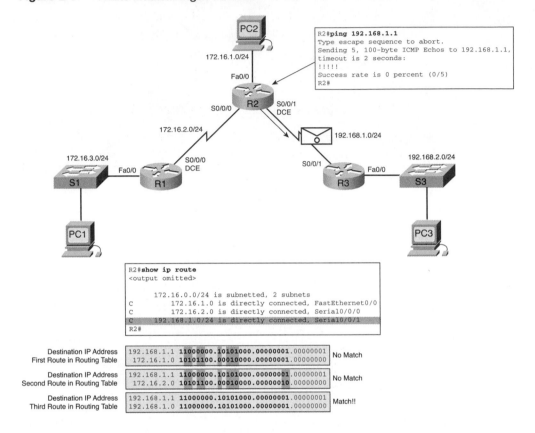

This time the ping succeeds! It is successful because R2 has a route in its routing table that matches 192.168.1.1, which is the ping packet's destination IP address. The first two routes, 172.16.1.0/24 and 172.16.2.0/24, are rejected. But the last route, 192.168.1.0/24, matches the first 24 bits of the destination IP address. The ping packet is encapsulated in the Layer 2 High-Level Data Link Control (HDLC) protocol of Serial 0/0/1, the exit interface, and forwarded through the Serial 0/0/1 interface. R2 is now done making the forwarding decisions for this packet; the decisions made by other routers regarding this packet are not its concern.

Note

The routing table lookup process will be discussed in further detail in Chapter 8, "The Routing Table: A Closer Look."

Verify Connectivity of Directly Connected Devices (2.3.2)

Use the Packet Tracer Activity to test connectivity between directly connected devices. Use file e2-232.pka on the CD-ROM that accompanies this book to perform this activity using Packet Tracer.

Cisco Discovery Protocol (CDP)

Cisco Discovery Protocol (CDP) is a powerful network-monitoring and -troubleshooting tool. CDP is an information-gathering tool used by network administrators to get information about directly connected Cisco devices. CDP is a proprietary tool that enables you to access a summary of protocol and address information about Cisco devices that are directly connected.

Network Discovery with CDP

By default, each Cisco device sends periodic messages to directly connected Cisco devices, as shown in Figure 2-8. These messages are known as CDP advertisements. These advertisements contain information such as the types of devices that are connected, the router interfaces they are connected to, the interfaces used to make the connections, and the model numbers of the devices.

Most network devices, by definition, do not work in isolation. A Cisco device frequently has other Cisco devices as *neighbors* on the network. Information gathered from other devices can assist you in making network design decisions, in troubleshooting, and in making changes to equipment. CDP can be used as a network discovery tool, helping you to build a logical topology of a network when such documentation is missing or lacking in detail.

Familiarity with the general concept of neighbors is important for understanding CDP as well as for future discussions about dynamic routing protocols.

Layer 3 Neighbors

At this point in the chapter topology configuration, you only have directly connected neighbors. At Layer 3, routing protocols consider neighbors to be devices that share the same network address space.

For example, in the chapter topology (Figure 2-1), R1 and R2 are neighbors. Both are members of the 172.16.1.0/24 network. R2 and R3 are also neighbors because they both share the 192.168.1.0/24 network. But R1 and R3 are not neighbors because they do not share network address space. If you connected R1 and R3 with a cable and configured each with an IP address from the same network, they would be neighbors.

Figure 2-8   CDP Advertisements

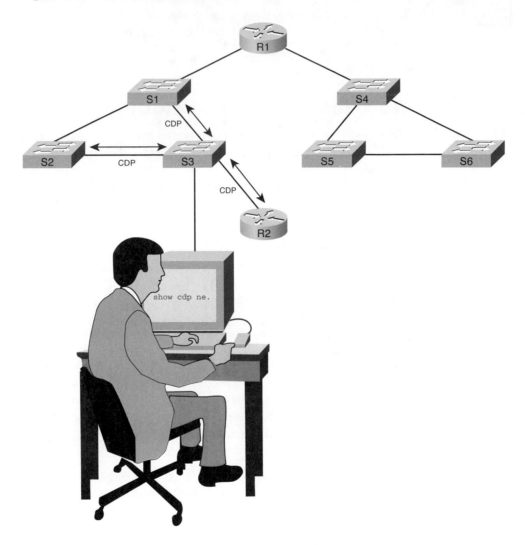

Layer 2 Neighbors

CDP operates at Layer 2 only. Therefore, CDP neighbors are Cisco devices that are directly connected physically and share the same data link. In Figure 2-8, the network administrator is logged in to S3. S3 will receive CDP advertisements from S1, S2, and R2 only.

Assuming that all routers and switches are Cisco devices running CDP, what neighbors would R1 have? Can you determine the CDP neighbors for each device?

In the chapter topology (Figure 2-1), you can see the following CDP neighbor relationships:

- R1 and S1 are CDP neighbors

- R1 and R2 are CDP neighbors

- R2 and S2 are CDP neighbors

- R2 and R3 are CDP neighbors

- R3 and S3 are CDP neighbors

Notice the difference between Layer 2 and Layer 3 neighbors. The switches are not neighbors to the routers at Layer 3, because the switches are operating at Layer 2 only. However, the switches are Layer 2 neighbors to their directly connected routers.

The section that follows shows how CDP can be helpful to a network administrator.

CDP Operation

Examine the output from the **show cdp neighbors** and **show cdp neighbors detail** commands in Example 2-26. Notice that R3 has gathered some detailed information about R2 and the switch connected to the Fast Ethernet interface on R3.

Example 2-26   Examining CDP Neighbors

```
R3# show cdp neighbors

Capability Codes: R - Router, T - Trans Bridge, B - Source Route Bridge
                  S - Switch, H - Host, I - IGMP, r - Repeater, P - Phone

Device ID       Local Intrfce    Holdtme    Capability  Platform  Port ID
S3              Fas 0/0          151          S I       WS-C2950  Fas 0/6
R2              Ser 0/0/1        125          R         1841      Ser 0/0/1

R3# show cdp neighbors detail

-------------------------
Device ID: R2
Entry address(es):
  IP address: 192.168.1.2
Platform: Cisco 1841,  Capabilities: Router Switch IGMP
Interface: Serial0/0/1,  Port ID (outgoing port): Serial0/0/1
Holdtime : 161 sec

Version :
Cisco IOS Software, 1841 Software (C1841-ADVIPSERVICESK9-M), Version 12.4(10b),
```

```
  RELEASE SO
FTWARE (fc3)
Technical Support: http://www.cisco.com/techsupport
Copyright (c) 1986-2007 by Cisco Systems, Inc.
Compiled Fri 19-Jan-07 15:15 by prod_rel_team

advertisement version: 2
VTP Management Domain: ''

-----------------------
Device ID: S3
Entry address(es):
Platform: cisco WS-C2950-24,   Capabilities: Switch IGMP
Interface: FastEthernet0/0,  Port ID (outgoing port): FastEthernet0/11
Holdtime : 148 sec

Version :
Cisco Internetwork Operating System Software
IOS (tm) C2950 Software (C2950-I6Q4L2-M), Version 12.1(9)EA1, RELEASE SOFTWARE
  (fc1)
Copyright (c) 1986-2002 by cisco Systems, Inc.
Compiled Wed 24-Apr-02 06:57 by antonino

advertisement version: 2
Protocol Hello:  OUI=0x00000C, Protocol ID=0x0112; payload len=27,
  value=00000000FFFFFFFF0
10231FF000000000000000AB769F6C0FF0000
VTP Management Domain: 'CCNA3'
Duplex: full

R3#
```

CDP runs at the data link layer connecting the physical media to the upper-layer protocols. Because CDP operates at the data link layer, two or more Cisco network devices, such as routers that support different network layer protocols (for example, IP and Novell IPX) can learn about each other.

When a Cisco device boots up, CDP starts up by default. CDP automatically discovers neighboring Cisco devices running CDP, regardless of which protocol or suites are running. CDP exchanges hardware and software device information with its directly connected CDP neighbors.

CDP provides the following information about each CDP neighbor device:

- **Device identifiers:** For example, the configured host name of a switch

- **Address list:** Up to one network layer address for each protocol supported

- **Port identifier:** The name of the local and remote port, in the form of an ASCII character string such as ethernet0

- **Capabilities list:** For example, whether this device is a router or a switch

- **Platform:** The hardware platform of the device; for example, a Cisco 7200 series router

Cisco Discovery Protocol (CDP) (2.3.3)

Use the Packet Tracer Activity to explore the features of the Cisco Discovery Protocol (CDP). Practice enabling and disabling CDP both globally and on a per-interface basis. Investigate the power of using CDP to discover the topology of a network. Use file e2-233.pka on the CD-ROM that accompanies this book to perform this activity using Packet Tracer.

Using CDP for Network Discovery

CDP can be used to discover a variety of information about directly connected networks. CDP can be a useful tool in helping analyze and document existing networks.

CDP show Commands

The information gathered by the CDP protocol can be examined with the **show cdp neighbors** command, as shown previously in Example 2-26. For each CDP neighbor, the following information is displayed:

- Neighbor device ID

- Local interface

- Holdtime value, in seconds

- Neighbor device capability code

- Neighbor hardware platform

- Neighbor remote port ID

The **show cdp neighbors detail** command also reveals the IP address of a neighboring device. In Example 2-26, R3 learned through CDP that R2 is using IP address 192.168.1.2. CDP will reveal the neighbor's IP address regardless of whether you can ping the neighbor.

This command is very helpful when two Cisco routers cannot route across their shared data link. The **show cdp neighbors detail** command will help determine whether one of the CDP neighbors has an IP configuration error.

For network discovery situations, knowing the IP address of the CDP neighbor is often all the information needed to telnet into that device. With an established Telnet session, information can be gathered about a neighbor's directly connected Cisco devices. In this fashion, you can telnet around a network and build a logical topology. In the next Packet Tracer Activity, "Mapping a Network with CDP and Telnet (2.3.4)," you will do just that.

Disabling CDP

Could CDP be a security risk? Yes, it could be. You might already have seen CDP packets in your packet capturing labs from a previous course. Because some IOS versions send out CDP advertisements by default, it is important to know how to disable CDP.

To disable CDP globally, for the entire device, use this command:

```
Router(config)# no cdp run
```

If you want to use CDP but need to stop CDP advertisements on a particular interface, use this command:

```
Router(config-if)# no cdp enable
```

Mapping a Network with CDP and Telnet (2.3.4)

CDP **show** commands can be used to discover information about unknown devices in a network. CDP **show** commands display information about directly connected Cisco devices, including an IP address that can be used to reach the device. You can then telnet to the device and repeat the process until the entire network is mapped.

Use the Packet Tracer Activity to discover and map an unknown network using CDP and Telnet. Use file e2-234.pka on the CD-ROM that accompanies this book to perform this activity using Packet Tracer.

Static Routes with "Next-Hop" Addresses

As discussed previously, a router can learn about remote networks in one of two ways:

- Manually, from configured static routes

- Automatically, from a dynamic routing protocol

The rest of this chapter focuses on configuring static routes. Dynamic routing protocols are introduced in the next chapter.

Purpose and Command Syntax of the ip route Command

Static routes are commonly used when routing from a network to a stub network. A ***stub network*** is a network accessed by a single route. For an example, see Figure 2-9. Here you see that any network attached to R1 would only have one way to reach other destinations, whether to networks attached to R2 or to destinations beyond R2. Therefore, network 172.16.3.0 is a stub network and R1 is a ***stub router***.

Figure 2-9   Stub Network Example

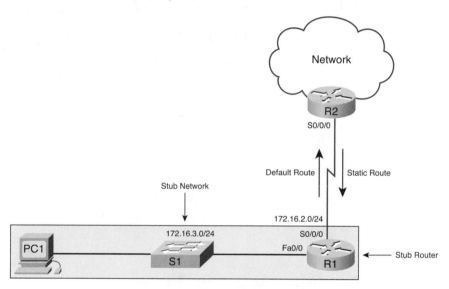

Running a routing protocol between R1 and R2 is a waste of resources because R1 has only one way out for sending nonlocal traffic. Therefore, static routes are configured for connectivity to remote networks that are not directly connected to a router. Again, referring to the figure, you would configure a static route on R2 to the LAN attached to R1. You will also see how to configure a default static route from R1 to R2 later in the chapter so that R1 can send traffic to any destination beyond R2.

ip route Command

The command for configuring a static route is **ip route**. The complete syntax for configuring a static route is

```
ip route prefix mask {ip-address | interface-type interface-number [ip-address]}
    [dhcp] [distance] [name next-hop-name] [permanent | track number] [tag tag]
```

Most of these parameters are not relevant for this chapter or for your CCNA studies. We will use a simpler version of the syntax:

```
Router(config)# ip route network-address subnet-mask {ip-address | exit-interface}
```

The following parameters are used:

- *network-address*: Destination network address of the remote network to be added to the routing table. (Equivalent to the *prefix* parameter in the complete syntax.)

- *subnet-mask*: Subnet mask of the remote network to be added to the routing table. The subnet mask can be modified to summarize a group of networks. (Equivalent to the *mask* parameter in the complete syntax.)

One or both of the following parameters must also be used:

- *ip-address*: Commonly referred to as the next-hop router's IP address. (Equivalent to the *ip-address* parameter in the complete syntax.)

- *exit-interface*: Outgoing interface that would be used in forwarding packets to the destination network. (Equivalent to the **interface-type** *interface-number* parameter in the complete syntax.)

Note

The *ip-address* parameter is commonly referred to as the "next-hop" router's IP address. The actual next-hop router's IP address is commonly used for this parameter. However, the *ip-address* parameter could be any IP address, as long as it is resolvable in the routing table. This is beyond the scope of this course, but we've added this point to maintain technical accuracy.

Configuring Static Routes

Remember that R1 in our chapter topology knows about its directly connected networks. Example 2-24 showed the routes currently in R1's routing table. The remote networks that R1 does not know about are as follows:

- **172.16.1.0/124:** The LAN on R2

- **192.168.1.0/24:** The serial network between R2 and R3

- **192.168.2.0/24:** The LAN on R3

Use the **ip route** command syntax to configure static routes to these remote networks. Example 2-27 shows the command syntax.

Example 2-27   R1 Static Route Configuration to R2's LAN

```
R1# debug ip routing

<some debug output omitted>
R1# conf t
```

```
R1(config)# ip route 172.16.1.0 255.255.255.0 172.16.2.2


00:20:15: RT: add 172.16.1.0/24 via 172.16.2.2, static metric [1/0]


R1# show ip route


Codes: C - connected, S - static, I - IGRP, R - RIP, M - mobile, B - BGP
       D - EIGRP, EX - EIGRP external, O - OSPF, IA - OSPF inter area
       N1 - OSPF NSSA external type 1, N2 - OSPF NSSA external type 2
       E1 - OSPF external type 1, E2 - OSPF external type 2, E - EGP
       i - IS-IS, L1 - IS-IS level-1, L2 - IS-IS level-2, ia - IS-IS inter area
       * - candidate default, U - per-user static route, o - ODR
       P - periodic downloaded static route


Gateway of last resort is not set


     172.16.0.0/24 is subnetted, 3 subnets
S       172.16.1.0 [1/0] via 172.16.2.2
C       172.16.2.0 is directly connected, Serial0/0/0
C       172.16.3.0 is directly connected, FastEthernet0/0
R1#
```

To have IOS messages display when the new route is added to the routing table, you can use the **debug ip routing** command.

Then, use the **ip route** command to configure static routes on R1 for each of these networks. Example 2-27 shows the first route configured.

Examining each element in this output reveals the following:

- **ip route:** Static route command

- **172.16.1.0:** Network address of remote network

- **255.255.255.0:** Subnet mask of remote network

- **172.16.2.2:** Serial 0/0/0 interface IP address on R2, which is the next hop to this network

When the IP address is the actual next-hop router's IP address, this IP address is reachable from one of this router's directly connected networks. In other words, the next-hop IP address 172.16.2.2 belongs to Router R1's directly connected Serial 0/0/0 network 172.16.2.0/24.

Verifying the Static Route

The output from the **debug ip routing** command shows that this route has been added to the routing table:

```
00:20:15: RT: add 172.16.1.0/24 via 172.16.2.2, static metric [1/0]
```

Entering **show ip route** on R1 displays the new routing table. The static route entry is highlighted.

Examine this output:

- **S:** Routing table code for static route.

- **172.16.1.0:** Network address for the route.

- **/24:** Subnet mask for this route; this is displayed in the line above, known as the parent route, and discussed in Chapter 8.

- **[1/0]:** Administrative distance and metric for the static route (explained in a later chapter).

- **via 172.16.2.2:** IP address of the next-hop router, the IP address of R2's Serial 0/0/0 interface.

Any packets with a destination IP address that have the 24 leftmost bits matching 172.16.1.0 will use this route.

Configuring Routes to Two More Remote Networks

Example 2-28 shows the commands to configure the routes for the other two remote networks. Debugging has been disabled.

Example 2-28   Configuring Routes for Remote Networks

```
R1(config)# ip route 192.168.1.0 255.255.255.0 172.16.2.2
R1(config)# ip route 192.168.2.0 255.255.255.0 172.16.2.2
R1(config)# end
R1# show ip route

Codes: C - connected, S - static, I - IGRP, R - RIP, M - mobile, B - BGP
       D - EIGRP, EX - EIGRP external, O - OSPF, IA - OSPF inter area
       N1 - OSPF NSSA external type 1, N2 - OSPF NSSA external type 2
       E1 - OSPF external type 1, E2 - OSPF external type 2, E - EGP
       i - IS-IS, L1 - IS-IS level-1, L2 - IS-IS level-2, ia - IS-IS inter area
       * - candidate default, U - per-user static route, o - ODR
       P - periodic downloaded static route

Gateway of last resort is not set
```

```
      172.16.0.0/24 is subnetted, 3 subnets
S        172.16.1.0 [1/0] via 172.16.2.2
C        172.16.2.0 is directly connected, Serial0/0/0
C        172.16.3.0 is directly connected, FastEthernet0/0
S     192.168.1.0/24 [1/0] via 172.16.2.2
S     192.168.2.0/24 [1/0] via 172.16.2.2
```

Notice that all three static routes configured on R1 have the same next-hop IP address: 172.16.2.2. Using the chapter topology as a reference (Figure 2-1), you can see that this is true because packets for all the remote networks must be forwarded to Router R2, the next-hop router.

In Example 2-28, the **show ip route** command is used again to examine the new static routes in the routing table:

```
S 192.168.1.0/24 [1/0] via 172.16.2.2
S 192.168.2.0/24 [1/0] via 172.16.2.2
```

The /24 subnet masks are located on the same line as the network address. For now, this difference is not important. It will be explained in detail in Chapter 8.

The static routes that have been configured can also be verified by examining the running configuration with the **show running-config** command, as shown in Example 2-29. Now is a good time to save the configuration to NVRAM with the **copy running-config startup-config** command.

Example 2-29   Verifying Static Route Commands

```
R1# show running-config

Building configuration...

Current configuration : 849 bytes
!
hostname R1
!
<output omitted>
!
ip classless
ip route 172.16.1.0 255.255.255.0 172.16.2.2
ip route 192.168.1.0 255.255.255.0 172.16.2.2
ip route 192.168.2.0 255.255.255.0 172.16.2.2
!
<output omitted>
```

```
!
end

R1#copy running-config startup-config
Destination filename [startup-config]?
Building configuration...
[OK]
R1#
```

Routing Table Principles and Static Routes

Refer to the chapter topology (see Figure 2-1). Now that three static routes are configured on R1, can you predict whether packets destined for these networks will reach their destination? If so, will return packets from all these networks be successfully routed back to R1?

Review the three routing table principles, as described by Alex Zinin in his book *Cisco IP Routing*[1]:

Principle 1: Every router makes its decision alone, based on the information it has in its own routing table.

R1 has three static routes in its routing table and makes forwarding decisions based solely on the information in the routing table. R1 does not consult the routing tables in any other routers, nor does it know whether those routers have routes to other networks. Making each router aware of remote networks is the responsibility of the network administrator.

Principle 2: The fact that one router has certain information in its routing table does not mean that other routers have the same information.

R1 does not know what information other routers have in their routing table. For example, R1 has a route to the 192.168.2.0/24 network through Router R2. Any packets that match this route belong to the 192.168.2.0/24 network and will be forwarded to Router R2. R1 does not know whether R2 has a route to the 192.168.2.0/24 network. Again, the network administrator would be responsible for ensuring that the next-hop router also has a route to this network.

Using Principle 2, you still need to configure the proper routing on the other routers (R2 and R3) to make sure that they have routes to these three networks.

Principle 3: Routing information about a path from one network to another does not provide routing information about the reverse, or return, path.

Most of the communication over networks is bidirectional. This means that packets must travel in both directions between the end devices involved. A packet from PC1 can reach PC3 because all the routers involved have routes to the destination network 192.168.2.0/24.

However, the success of any returning packets going from PC3 to PC1 depends on whether the routers involved have a route to the return path, PC1's 172.16.3.0/24 network.

Using Principle 3 as guidance, you will configure proper static routes on the other routers to make sure that they have routes back to the 172.16.3.0/24 network.

Applying the Principles

With these principles in mind, how would you answer the questions posed regarding packets that originate from PC1?

Would packets from PC1 reach their destination?

In this case, packets destined for 172.16.1.0/24 and 192.168.1.0/24 networks would reach their destination. This is because Router R1 has a route to these networks through R2. When packets reach Router R2, these networks are directly connected on R2 and are routed using its routing table.

However, packets destined for the 192.168.2.0/24 network would not reach their destination. R1 has a static route to this network through R2. However, when R2 receives a packet, it will drop it because R2 does not yet contain a route for this network in its routing table.

Does this mean that any return packets from remote networks destined for the 172.16.3.0/24 network will reach their destination?

If R2 or R3 receives a packet destined for 172.16.3.0/24, the packet will not reach its destination, because neither router has a route to the 172.16.3.0/24 network.

We finish the static routing configuration for the chapter topology by configuring static routes on R2 and R3. With the commands shown in Example 2-30, all routers now have routes to all remote networks.

Example 2-30   Configure R2 and R3 Static Routes

```
R2(config)# ip route 172.16.3.0 255.255.255.0 172.16.2.1
R2(config)# ip route 192.168.2.0 255.255.255.0 192.168.1.1
R3(config)# ip route 172.16.1.0 255.255.255.0 192.168.1.2
R3(config)# ip route 172.16.2.0 255.255.255.0 192.168.1.2
R3(config)# ip route 172.16.3.0 255.255.255.0 192.168.1.2
```

Examine the routing tables in Example 2-31 to verify that all routers now have routes to all remote networks.

Example 2-31   Verify Static Routes Are in Routing Tables

```
R1# show ip route

<output omitted>
     172.16.0.0/24 is subnetted, 3 subnets
S       172.16.1.0 [1/0] via 172.16.2.2
C       172.16.2.0 is directly connected, Serial0/0/0
C       172.16.3.0 is directly connected, FastEthernet0/0
S     192.168.1.0/24 [1/0] via 172.16.2.2
S     192.168.2.0/24 [1/0] via 172.16.2.2
R2# show ip route

<output omitted>
     172.16.0.0/24 is subnetted, 3 subnets
C       172.16.1.0 is directly connected, FastEthernet0/0
C       172.16.2.0 is directly connected, Serial0/0/0
S       172.16.3.0 [1/0] via 172.16.2.1
C     192.168.1.0/24 is directly connected, Serial0/0/1
S     192.168.2.0/24 [1/0] via 192.168.1.1
R3# show ip route

<output omitted>
     172.16.0.0/24 is subnetted, 3 subnets
S       172.16.1.0 [1/0] via 192.168.1.2
S       172.16.2.0 [1/0] via 192.168.1.2
S       172.16.3.0 [1/0] via 192.168.1.2
C     192.168.1.0/24 is directly connected, Serial0/0/1
C     192.168.2.0/24 is directly connected, FastEthernet0/0
```

Connectivity can be further verified by pinging remote router interfaces from Router R1, as shown in Example 2-32.

Example 2-32   Verify End-to-End Connectivity

```
R1# ping 172.16.1.1

Type escape sequence to abort.
Sending 5, 100-byte ICMP Echos to 172.16.1.1, timeout is 2 seconds:
!!!!!
Success rate is 100 percent (5/5), round-trip min/avg/max = 28/28/32 ms
R1# ping 192.168.1.1

Type escape sequence to abort.
```

```
Sending 6, 100-byte ICMP Echos to 192.168.1.1, timeout is 2 seconds:
!!!!!
Success rate is 100 percent (5/5), round-trip min/avg/max = 56/56/56 ms
R1# ping 192.168.1.2

Type escape sequence to abort.
Sending 5, 100-byte ICMP Echos to 192.168.1.2, timeout is 2 seconds:
!!!!!
Success rate is 100 percent (5/5), round-trip min/avg/max = 28/29/32 ms
R1# ping 192.168.2.1

Type escape sequence to abort.
Sending 5, 100-byte ICMP Echos to 192.168.2.1, timeout is 2 seconds:
!!!!!
Success rate is 100 percent (5/5), round-trip min/avg/max = 56/56/56 ms
R1#
```

Full connectivity is now achieved for the devices in our topology. Any PC, on any LAN, can now access PCs on all other LANs.

Resolving to an Exit Interface with a Recursive Route Lookup

Before any packet is forwarded by a router, the routing table process must determine the exit interface to use to forward the packet. This is known as *route resolvability*. Examine this process by looking at the routing table for R1 in Example 2-31. R1 has a static route for the remote network 192.168.2.0/24, which forwards all packets to the next-hop IP address 172.16.2.2:

```
S      192.168.2.0/24 [1/0] via 172.16.2.2
```

Finding a route is only the first step in the lookup process. R1 must determine how to reach the next-hop IP address 172.16.2.2. It will do a second search looking for a match for 172.16.2.2. In this case, the IP address 172.16.2.2 matches the route for the directly connected network 172.16.2.0/24:

```
C      172.16.2.0 is directly connected, Serial0/0/0
```

The 172.16.2.0 route is a directly connected network with the exit interface Serial 0/0/0. This lookup tells the routing table process that this packet will be forwarded out that interface. Therefore, it takes two routing table lookup processes to forward any packet to the

192.168.2.0/24 network. When the router has to perform multiple lookups in the routing table before forwarding a packet, it is performing a process known as a *recursive route lookup*. In this example:

1. The packet's destination IP address is matched to the static route 192.168.2.0/24 with the next-hop IP address 172.16.2.2.

2. The next-hop IP address of the static route, 172.16.2.2, is matched to the directly connected network 172.16.2.0/24, with the exit interface of Serial 0/0/0.

Every route that references only a next-hop IP address and does not reference an exit interface must have the next-hop IP address resolved using another route in the routing table that has an exit interface.

Typically, these routes are resolved to routes in the routing table that are directly connected networks, because these entries will always contain an exit interface. In the next section, you will see that static routes can be configured with an exit interface. This means that they do not need to be resolved using another route entry.

Exit Interface Is Down

Consider what would happen if an exit interface went down. For example, what would happen to R1's static route to 192.16.2.0/24 if its Serial 0/0/0 interface went down? If the static route cannot be resolved to an exit interface, in this case Serial 0/0/0, the static route is removed from the routing table.

Examine this process with the **debug ip routing** command on R1, and then configure the Serial 0/0/0 to **shutdown**, as shown in Example 2-33.

Example 2-33   R1 Static Routes Depend on Exit Interface

```
R1# debug ip routing

IP routing debugging is on
R1# config t

Enter configuration commands, one per line.  End with CNTL/Z.
R1(config)# int s0/0/0
R1(config-if)# shutdown
R1(config-if)# end

is_up: 0 state: 6 sub state: 1 line: 0
RT: interface Serial0/0/0 removed from routing table
RT: del 172.16.2.0/24 via 0.0.0.0, connected metric [0/0]
RT: delete subnet route to 172.16.2.0/24
RT: del 192.168.1.0 via 172.16.2.2, static metric [1/0]
```

```
RT: delete network route to 192.168.1.0
RT: del 172.16.1.0/24 via 172.16.2.2, static metric [1/0]
RT: delete subnet route to 172.16.1.0/24
R1# show ip route

<output omitted>
Gateway of last resort is not set
     172.16.0.0/24 is subnetted, 1 subnets
C       172.16.3.0 is directly connected, FastEthernet0/0
```

From Chapter 1, you know that the network attached to the Serial 0/0/0 interface is removed from the routing table. But also notice from the debug output that all three static routes were deleted, because all three static routes were resolved to Serial 0/0/0. Now R1 only has one route in its routing table.

However, the static routes are still in R1's running configuration. If the interface comes back up (is enabled again with **no shutdown**), the IOS routing table process will reinstall these static routes into the routing table.

Static Routes with Exit Interfaces

In the previous section, you saw how a static route can be configured with a next-hop address. Using a next-hop address is a correct method in configuring static routes. However, in some situations, using an exit interface can result in a more efficient route lookup process.

The simpler **ip route** command syntax is repeated here for easy reference:

```
Router(config)# ip route network-address subnet-mask {ip-address | exit-interface}
```

Configuring a Static Route with an Exit Interface

Consider another way to configure the same static routes. Currently, R1's static route for the 192.168.2.0/24 network is configured with the next-hop IP address of 172.16.2.2. In the running configuration, note the following line:

```
ip route 192.168.2.0 255.255.255.0 172.16.2.2
```

This static route requires a second routing table lookup to resolve the 172.16.2.2 next-hop IP address to an exit interface. However, most static routes can be configured with an exit interface, which allows the routing table to resolve the exit interface in a single search instead of two searches.

Static Route and an Exit Interface

Reconfigure this static route to use an exit interface instead of a next-hop IP address. The first thing to do is to delete the current static route. This is done using the **no ip route** command, as shown in Example 2-34.

Example 2-34   Static Route with an Exit Interface

```
R1(config)# no ip route 192.168.2.0 255.255.255.0 172.16.2.2
R1(config)# ip route 192.168.2.0 255.255.255.0 serial 0/0/0
R1(config)# end
R1# show ip route

Codes: C - connected, S - static, I - IGRP, R - RIP, M - mobile, B - BGP
       D - EIGRP, EX - EIGRP external, O - OSPF, IA - OSPF inter area
       N1 - OSPF NSSA external type 1, N2 - OSPF NSSA external type 2
       E1 - OSPF external type 1, E2 - OSPF external type 2, E - EGP
       i - IS-IS, L1 - IS-IS level-1, L2 - IS-IS level-2, ia - IS-IS inter area
       * - candidate default, U - per-user static route, o - ODR
       P - periodic downloaded static route

Gateway of last resort is not set

     172.16.0.0/24 is subnetted, 3 subnets
S       172.16.1.0 [1/0] via 172.16.2.2
C       172.16.2.0 is directly connected, Serial0/0/0
C       172.16.3.0 is directly connected, FastEthernet0/0
S    192.168.1.0/24 [1/0] via 172.16.2.2
S    192.168.2.0/24 is directly connected, Serial0/0/0
R1#
```

Next, configure R1's static route to 192.168.2.0/24 using the exit interface Serial 0/0/0.

Then use the **show ip route** command to examine the change in the routing table. Notice that the entry in the routing table no longer refers to the next-hop IP address but refers directly to the exit interface. This exit interface is the same one that the static route was resolved to when it used the next-hop IP address:

```
S    192.168.2.0/24 is directly connected, Serial0/0/0
```

Now, when the routing table process matches a packet to this static route, it will be able to resolve the route to an exit interface in a single lookup. As you can see from the routing table, the other two static routes still must be processed in two steps, resolving to the same Serial 0/0/0 interface.

Note

The static route displays the route as directly connected. It is important to understand that this does not mean that this route is a directly connected network or a directly connected route. This route is still a static route. The next chapter examines the importance of this fact when it discusses administrative distances in the next chapter. You will learn that this type of static route still has an administrative distance of 1. For now, just note that this route is still a static route with an administrative distance of 1 and is not a directly connected network.

Static Routes and Point-to-Point Networks

Static routes that are configured with exit interfaces instead of next-hop IP addresses are ideal for most serial point-to-point networks. Point-to-point networks that use protocols such as HDLC and PPP do not use the next-hop IP address in the packet-forwarding process. The routed IP packet is encapsulated in an HDLC Layer 2 frame with a broadcast Layer 2 destination address.

These types of point-to-point serial links are like pipes. A pipe has only two ends. What enters one end can only have a single destination: the other end of the pipe. Any packets that are sent through R1's Serial 0/0/0 interface can only have one destination: R2's Serial 0/0/0 interface. R2's serial interface happens to be the IP address 172.16.2.2.

Note

Under certain conditions, the network administrator will not want to configure the static route with an exit interface but with the next-hop IP address. This type of situation is beyond the scope of this course but is important to note.

Modifying Static Routes

There are times when a previously configured static route needs to be modified:

- The destination network no longer exists, and therefore the static route should be deleted.

- There is a change in the topology, and either the intermediate address or the exit interface has to be changed.

There is no way to modify an existing static route. The static route must be deleted and a new one configured.

To delete a static route, add **no** in front of the **ip route** command, followed by the rest of the static route to be removed.

For example, in the previous section, you removed the static route:

```
ip route 192.168.2.0 255.255.255.0 172.16.2.2
```

with the following **no ip route** command:

```
no ip route 192.168.2.0 255.255.255.0 172.16.2.2
```

As you will recall, the static route was deleted because you wanted to modify it to use an exit interface instead of a next-hop IP address. You configured a new static route using the exit interface:

```
R1(config)# ip route 192.168.2.0 255.255.255.0 serial 0/0/0
```

It is more efficient for the routing table lookup process to have static routes with exit interfaces, at least for serial point-to-point outbound networks. Reconfigure the rest of the static routes on R1, R2, and R3 to use exit interfaces as shown in Example 2-35.

Example 2-35   Convert All Static Routes to Exit Interfaces

```
R1(config)# no ip route 172.16.1.0 255.255.255.0 172.16.2.2
R1(config)# ip route 172.16.1.0 255.255.255.0 serial 0/0/0
R1(config)# no ip route 192.168.1.0 255.255.255.0 172.16.2.2
R1(config)# ip route 192.168.1.0 255.255.255.0 serial 0/0/0
R2(config)# no ip route 172.16.3.0 255.255.255.0 172.16.2.1
R2(config)# ip route 172.16.3.0 255.255.255.0 serial 0/0/0
R2(config)# no ip route 192.168.2.0 255.255.255.0 192.168.1.1
R2(config)# ip route 192.168.2.0 255.255.255.0 serial 0/0/1
R3(config)# no ip route 172.16.1.0 255.255.255.0 192.168.1.2
R3(config)# ip route 172.16.1.0 255.255.255.0 serial 0/0/1
R3(config)# no ip route 172.16.2.0 255.255.255.0 192.168.1.2
R3(config)# ip route 172.16.2.0 255.255.255.0 serial 0/0/1
R3(config)# no ip route 172.16.3.0 255.255.255.0 192.168.1.2
R3(config)# ip route 172.16.3.0 255.255.255.0 serial 0/0/1
```

As you can see, as you delete each route, you will configure a new route to the same network using an exit interface.

Verifying the Static Route Configuration

Whenever changes are made to static routes (or to other aspects of the network), verify that the changes took effect and that they produce the desired results.

Verifying Static Route Changes

In the previous section, you deleted and reconfigured the static routes for all three routers, which can be verified with the **show running-config** command, as demonstrated in Example 2-36.

Example 2-36   Verify Static Route Configuration with the **show running-config** Command

```
R1# show running-config

<output omitted>
ip route 172.16.1.0 255.255.255.0 Serial0/0/0
ip route 192.168.1.0 255.255.255.0 Serial0/0/0
ip route 192.168.2.0 255.255.255.0 Serial0/0/0
<output omitted>
```
```
R2# show running-config

<output omitted>
ip route 172.16.3.0 255.255.255.0 Serial0/0/0
ip route 192.168.2.0 255.255.255.0 Serial0/0/1
<output omitted>
```
```
R3# show running-config

<output omitted>
ip route 172.16.1.0 255.255.255.0 Serial0/0/1
ip route 172.16.2.0 255.255.255.0 Serial0/0/1
ip route 172.16.3.0 255.255.255.0 Serial0/0/1
<output omitted>
```

Remember, the running configuration contains the current router configuration—the commands and parameters that the router is currently using. Verify your changes by examining the running configuration. Example 2-36 shows only the static route portion of each router's running configuration.

Example 2-37 shows the routing table for all three routers. Notice that static routes with exit interfaces have been added to the routing table and that the previous static routes with next-hop addresses have been deleted.

Example 2-37   Verify That New Routes Are Installed in the Routing Table

```
R1# show ip route

<output omitted>
     172.16.0.0/24 is subnetted, 3 subnets
S       172.16.1.0 is directly connected, Serial0/0/0
C       172.16.2.0 is directly connected, Serial0/0/0
C       172.16.3.0 is directly connected, FastEthernet0/0
S    192.168.1.0/24 is directly connected, Serial0/0/0
```

```
S     192.168.2.0/24 is directly connected, Serial0/0/0
R2# show ip route

<output omitted>
     172.16.0.0/24 is subnetted, 3 subnets
C        172.16.1.0 is directly connected, FastEthernet0/0
C        172.16.2.0 is directly connected, Serial0/0/0
S        172.16.3.0 is directly connected, Serial0/0/0
C     192.168.1.0/24 is directly connected, Serial0/0/1
S     192.168.2.0/24 is directly connected, Serial0/0/1
R3# show ip route

<output omitted>
     172.16.0.0/24 is subnetted, 3 subnets
S        172.16.1.0 is directly connected, Serial0/0/1
S        172.16.2.0 is directly connected, Serial0/0/1
S        172.16.3.0 is directly connected, Serial0/0/1
C     192.168.1.0/24 is directly connected, Serial0/0/1
C     192.168.2.0/24 is directly connected, FastEthernet0/0
```

The ultimate test is to route packets from source to destination, as shown in Example 2-38.

Example 2-38   Test End-to-End Connectivity with the **ping** Command

```
R1# ping 192.168.2.1

Type escape sequence to abort.
Sending 5, 100-byte ICMP Echos to 172.16.3.1, timeout is 2 seconds:
!!!!!
Success rate is 100 percent (5/5), round-trip min/avg/max = 28/28/32 ms
R2# ping 172.16.3.1

Type escape sequence to abort.
Sending 5, 100-byte ICMP Echos to 172.16.1.1, timeout is 2 seconds:
!!!!!
Success rate is 100 percent (5/5), round-trip min/avg/max = 28/29/32 ms
R2#ping 192.168.2.1

Type escape sequence to abort.
Sending 5, 100-byte ICMP Echos to 192.168.2.1, timeout is 2 seconds:
!!!!!
Success rate is 100 percent (5/5), round-trip min/avg/max = 56/56/60 ms
R3# ping 172.16.3.1
```

```
Type escape sequence to abort.
Sending 5, 100-byte ICMP Echos to 172.16.1.1, timeout is 2 seconds:
!!!!!
Success rate is 100 percent (5/5), round-trip min/avg/max = 28/29/32 ms
```

Using the **ping** command, you can verify that packets from each router are reaching their destination and that the return path is working properly. Example 2-38 shows successful ping outputs.

Now it's time for you to practice configuring and verifying static routes.

Removing and Configuring Static Routes (2.5.3)

Use the Packet Tracer Activity to practice removing static routes and reconfiguring static routes using the exit interface argument. Then verify the new configuration and test connectivity. Use file e2-253.pka on the CD-ROM that accompanies this book to perform this activity using Packet Tracer.

Static Routes with Ethernet Interfaces

Sometimes the exit interface is an Ethernet network. An Ethernet interface on a router participates in the same processes as any other host on that Ethernet network, including ARP.

Ethernet Interfaces and ARP

For this discussion, you need to modify the chapter topology as shown in Figure 2-10.

Suppose the network link between R1 and R2 is an Ethernet link and that each router's FastEthernet 0/1 interface is connected to that network. A static route, using a next-hop IP address for the 192.168.2.0/24 network, can be set using this command:

```
R1(config)# ip route 192.168.2.0 255.255.255.0 172.16.2.2
```

As discussed in the section "Configuring an Ethernet Interface," earlier in this chapter, the IP packet must be encapsulated into an Ethernet frame with an Ethernet destination MAC address. If the packet should be sent to a next-hop router, the destination MAC address will be the address of the next-hop router's Ethernet interface. In this case, the Ethernet destination MAC address will be matched to the next-hop IP address 172.16.2.2. R1 checks its FastEthernet 0/1 ARP table for an entry with 172.16.2.2 and a corresponding MAC address.

Figure 2-10   Modified Chapter Topology

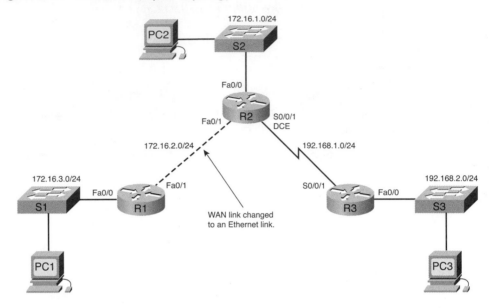

Sending an ARP Request

If this entry is not in the ARP table, R1 sends an ARP request through its FastEthernet 0/1 interface. The Layer 2 broadcast is requesting that if any device has the IP address 172.16.2.2, it should respond with its MAC address. Because R2's FastEthernet 0/1 interface has the IP address 172.16.2.2, it sends back an ARP reply with the MAC address for that interface.

R1 receives the ARP reply and adds the 172.16.2.2 IP address and the associated MAC address to its ARP table. The IP packet is now encapsulated into an Ethernet frame with the destination MAC address found in the ARP table. The Ethernet frame with the encapsulated packet is then sent out the FastEthernet 0/1 interface to Router R2.

Static Routes and Ethernet Exit Interfaces

Configure a static route with an Ethernet exit interface instead of a next-hop IP address. Change the static route for 192.168.2.0/24 to use an exit interface with this command:

```
R1(config)# ip route 192.168.2.0 255.255.255.0 fastethernet 0/1
```

The difference between an Ethernet network and a point-to-point serial network is that a point-to-point network has only one other device on that network: the router at the other end of the link. With Ethernet networks, many different devices can be sharing the same multiaccess network, including hosts and even multiple routers. By only designating the Ethernet exit interface in the static route, the router will not have sufficient information to determine which device is the next-hop device.

R1 knows that the packet needs to be encapsulated in an Ethernet frame and sent out the FastEthernet 0/1 interface. However, R1 does not know the next-hop IP address, and therefore it cannot determine the destination MAC address for the Ethernet frame.

Depending on the topology and the configurations on other routers, this static route might or might not work. Recommended practice dictates that when the exit interface is an Ethernet network, you do not use only the exit interface in the static route.

You might ask: Is there any way to configure a static route over an Ethernet network so that it does not have to use the recursive lookup of the next-hop IP address? Yes, this can be done by configuring the static route to include both the exit interface and the next-hop IP address.

As you can see in Figure 2-10, the exit interface would be FastEthernet 0/1, and the next-hop IP address would be 172.16.2.2:

```
R1(config)# ip route 192.168.2.0 255.255.255.0 fastethernet 0/1 172.16.2.2
```

The routing table entry for this route would be

```
S     192.168.2.0/24 [1/0] via 172.16.2.2 FastEthernet0/1
```

The routing table process will only need to perform a single lookup to get both the exit interface and the next-hop IP address.

Advantages of Using an Exit Interface with Static Routes

There is an advantage to using exit interfaces in static routes for both serial point-to-point and Ethernet outbound networks. The routing table process only has to perform a single lookup to find the exit interface instead of a second lookup to resolve a next-hop address.

For static routes with outbound point-to-point serial networks, it is best to configure static routes with only the exit interface. For point-to-point serial interfaces, the next-hop address in the routing table is never used by the packet delivery procedure, so it is not needed.

For static routes with outbound Ethernet networks, it is best to configure the static routes with both the next-hop address and the exit interface.

Note

For more information about the issues that can occur with static routes that only use an Ethernet or Fast Ethernet exit interface, see *Cisco IP Routing*, by Alex Zinin.

Summary and Default Static Routes

A router might have a specific route entry in its routing table for a destination network, or that same network can be part of a less specific route entry. The less specific route entry might be a summary route or a default route.

Summary Static Routes

A *summary route* is a single route that can be used to represent multiple routes. Summary routes are generally a set of contiguous networks that have the same exit interface or next-hop IP address.

Note

The networks represented in a summary route do not have to be contiguous. This is explained later in Chapter 8.

Summarizing Routes to Reduce the Size of the Routing Table

Creating smaller routing tables makes the routing table lookup process more efficient, because there are fewer routes to search. If one static route can be used instead of multiple static routes, the size of the routing table will be reduced. In many cases, a single static route can be used to represent dozens, hundreds, or even thousands of routes.

You can use a single network address to represent multiple subnets. For example, the networks 10.0.0.0/16, 10.1.0.0/16, 10.2.0.0/16, 10.3.0.0/16, 10.4.0.0/16, 10.5.0.0/16, all the way through 10.255.0.0/16 can be represented by a single network address: 10.0.0.0/8.

Route Summarization

Multiple static routes can be summarized into a single static route if they meet both of the following criteria:

- The destination networks can be summarized into a single network address.

- All the multiple static routes use the same exit interface or next-hop IP address.

This is called *route summarization*.

In our static route configuration of the chapter topology (Figure 2-1), R3 has three static routes. All three routes are forwarding traffic out the same Serial 0/0/1 interface. The three static routes on R3 are

```
ip route 172.16.1.0 255.255.255.0 Serial0/0/1
ip route 172.16.2.0 255.255.255.0 Serial0/0/1
ip route 172.16.3.0 255.255.255.0 Serial0/0/1
```

If possible, you'll want to summarize all of these routes into a single static route. The networks 172.16.1.0/24, 172.16.2.0/24, and 172.16.3.0/24 can be summarized to the 172.16.0.0/22 network. Because all three routes use the same exit interface, they can be summarized to the single 172.16.0.0 255.255.252.0 network, and you can create a single summary route.

Calculating a Summary Route

Here's the process of creating the summary route 172.16.1.0/22, as shown in Figure 2-11:

Figure 2-11   Summarizing Routes

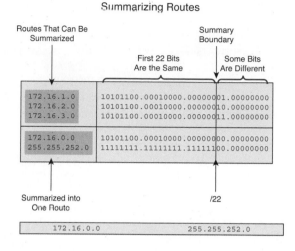

Summarizing Routes

Routes That Can Be Summarized

Summary Boundary

First 22 Bits Are the Same

Some Bits Are Different

```
172.16.1.0      10101100.00010000.00000001.00000000
172.16.2.0      10101100.00010000.00000010.00000000
172.16.3.0      10101100.00010000.00000011.00000000

172.16.0.0      10101100.00010000.00000000.00000000
255.255.252.0   11111111.11111111.11111100.00000000
```

Summarized into One Route

/22

```
172.16.0.0              255.255.252.0
```

Step 1.   Write out the networks that you want to summarize in binary.

Step 2.   To find the subnet mask for summarization, start with the leftmost bit.

Step 3.   Work your way to the right, finding all the bits that match consecutively.

Step 4.   When you find a column of bits that do not match, stop. You are at the summary boundary.

Step 5.   Count the number of leftmost matching bits, which in our example is 22. This number becomes your subnet mask for the summarized route, /22 or 255.255.252.0.

Step 6.   To find the network address for summarization, copy the matching 22 bits and add all 0 bits to the end to make 32 bits.

By following these steps, you can discover that the three static routes on R3 can be summarized into a single static route, using the summary network address of 172.16.0.0 255.255.252.0:

```
ip route 172.16.0.0 255.255.252.0 Serial0/0/1
```

Configuring a Summary Route

To implement the summary route, you must first delete the three current static routes:

```
R3(config)# no ip route 172.16.1.0 255.255.255.0 serial0/0/1
R3(config)# no ip route 172.16.2.0 255.255.255.0 serial0/0/1
R3(config)# no ip route 172.16.3.0 255.255.255.0 serial0/0/1
```

Next, you will configure the summary static route:

```
R3(config)# ip route 172.16.0.0 255.255.252.0 serial0/0/1
```

Example 2-39 shows the change in the routing table with three static routes now represented by a single summary static route. To verify the new static route, examine R3's routing table with the **show ip route** command, as shown in the example.

Example 2-39   Three Static Routes Summarized into One Summary Route

```
R3# show ip route

<output omitted>

Gateway of last resort is not set

 172.16.0.0/24 is subnetted, 3 subnets
S        172.16.1.0 is directly connected, Serial0/0/1
S        172.16.2.0 is directly connected, Serial0/0/1
S        172.16.3.0 is directly connected, Serial0/0/1
C    192.168.1.0/24 is directly connected, Serial0/0/1
C    192.168.2.0/24 is directly connected, FastEthernet0/0

R3# show ip route

<output omitted>

Gateway of last resort is not set

     172.16.0.0/22 is subnetted, 1 subnets
S        172.16.0.0 is directly connected, Serial0/0/1
C    192.168.1.0/24 is directly connected, Serial0/1
C    192.168.2.0/24 is directly connected, FastEthernet0/0
```

With this summary route, the destination IP address of a packet only needs to match the leftmost 22 bits of the 172.16.0.0 network address. Any packet with a destination IP address belonging to the 172.16.1.0/24, 172.16.2.0/24, or 172.16.3.0/24 network matches this summarized route.

As shown in Example 2-40, you can test the reconfiguration using the **ping** command to verify that proper connectivity exists throughout the network.

Example 2-40   Verify the Summary Route with the **ping** Command

```
R3# ping 172.16.1.1

Type escape sequence to abort.
Sending 5, 100-byte ICMP Echos to 172.16.1.1, timeout is 2 seconds:
!!!!!
Success rate is 100 percent (5/5), round-trip min/avg/max = 28/29/32 ms
R3#ping 172.16.2.1

Type escape sequence to abort.
Sending 5, 100-byte ICMP Echos to 172.16.2.1, timeout is 2 seconds:
!!!!!
Success rate is 100 percent (5/5), round-trip min/avg/max = 56/56/60 ms
R3#ping 172.16.3.1

Type escape sequence to abort.
Sending 5, 100-byte ICMP Echos to 172.16.3.1, timeout is 2 seconds:
!!!!!
Success rate is 100 percent (5/5), round-trip min/avg/max = 56/56/60 ms
R3#
```

Note

As of March 2007, there are more than 200,000 routes in the Internet core routers. Most of these are summarized routes.

Default Static Route

A default route is used to represent all routes with zero or no bits matching. In other words, when there are no routes that have a more specific match, the default route will be a match. The following section will discuss a default static route. Default routes will be discussed and used throughout this book.

Most Specific Match

The destination IP address of a packet can match multiple routes in the routing table. For example, consider having the following two static routes in the routing table:

```
      172.16.0.0/24 is subnetted, 3 subnets
S        172.16.1.0 is directly connected, Serial0/0/0
S        172.16.0.0/16 is directly connected, Serial0/0/1
```

Consider a packet with the destination IP address 172.16.1.10. This IP address matches both routes. The routing table lookup process will use the most specific match. Because 24 bits match the 172.16.1.0/24 route, and only 16 bits of the 172.16.0.0/16 route match, the static route with the 24-bit match will be used. This is the most specific or longest match. The packet will then be encapsulated in a Layer 2 frame and sent through the Serial 0/0/0 interface. Remember, the subnet mask in the route entry is what determines how many bits must match the packet's destination IP address for this route to be a match.

Note

This process is the same for all routes in the routing table, including static routes, routes learned from a routing protocol, and directly connected networks. The routing table lookup process will be explained in more detail in Chapter 8.

A default static route is a route that will match all packets. Default static routes are used

- To represent destination networks outside the router's own routing domain. A common use is when connecting a company's edge router to the ISP network.

- When no other routes in the routing table match the packet's destination IP address—in other words, when a more specific match does not exist.

- When a router has only one other router to which it is connected. This condition is known as a *stub router*.

This will become more evident in later chapters when discussing dynamic routing protocols.

Configuring a Default Static Route

The syntax for a default static route is similar to any other static route, except that the network address is 0.0.0.0 and the subnet mask is 0.0.0.0:

```
Router(config)# ip route 0.0.0.0 0.0.0.0 [exit-interface | ip-address ]
```

The 0.0.0.0 0.0.0.0 network address and mask is called a *quad-zero route*.

Look back at Figure 2-9. Remember that in this topology, R1 is a stub router and is connected only to R2. Although the chapter topology (Figure 2-1) shows an R3 router, R1 doesn't need specific routing information to reach R3 networks. Currently R1 has three static routes, which are used to reach all the remote networks in our chapter topology. All three static routes have the exit interface Serial 0/0/0, forwarding packets to the next-hop Router R2.

As a review, the three static routes on R1 are

```
ip route 172.16.1.0 255.255.255.0 serial 0/0/0
ip route 192.168.1.0 255.255.255.0 serial 0/0/0
ip route 192.168.2.0 255.255.255.0 serial 0/0/0
```

As shown in Figure 2-9, R1 is an ideal candidate to have all of its static routes replaced by a single default route. First, delete the three static routes:

```
R1(config)# no ip route 172.16.1.0 255.255.255.0 serial 0/0/0
R1(config)# no ip route 192.168.1.0 255.255.255.0 serial 0/0/0
R1(config)# no ip route 192.168.2.0 255.255.255.0 serial 0/0/0
```

Next, configure the single default static route using the same Serial 0/0/0 exit interface as the three previous static routes:

```
R1(config)# ip route 0.0.0.0 0.0.0.0 serial 0/0/0
```

Verifying a Default Static Route

Verify the change to the routing table with the **show ip route** command. Example 2-41 shows the routing table before the default route configuration.

Example 2-41   R1 Routing Table Before Default Route Is Configured

```
R1# show ip route

<output omitted>

Gateway of last resort is not set

 172.16.0.0/24 is subnetted, 3 subnets
S        172.16.1.0 is directly connected, Serial0/0/0
C        172.16.2.0 is directly connected, Serial0/0/0
C        172.16.3.0 is directly connected, FastEthernet0/0
S     192.168.1.0/24 is directly connected, Serial0/0/0
S     192.168.2.0/24 is directly connected, Serial0/0/0
```

Example 2-42 shows the routing table after the default route configuration.

Example 2-42   R1 Routing Table After Default Route Is Configured

```
R1# show ip route

<some codes omitted>
        * - candidate default, U - per-user static route, o - ODR
        P - periodic downloaded static route

Gateway of last resort is 0.0.0.0 to network 0.0.0.0
      172.16.0.0/24 is subnetted, 2 subnets
C        172.16.2.0 is directly connected, Serial0/0/0
C        172.16.3.0 is directly connected, FastEthernet0/0
S*    0.0.0.0/0 is directly connected, Serial0/0/0
```

Note that the asterisk (*) next to the S code marks the default route. That is why it is called a "default static" route. You will see in later chapters that a default route does not always have to be a static route.

The key to this configuration is the /0 mask. Previously, you learned that it is the subnet mask in the routing table that determines how many bits must match between the destination IP address of the packet and the route in the routing table. A /0 mask indicates that zero or no bits are needed to match. As long as a more specific match doesn't exist, the default static route will match all packets.

Default routes are very common on routers. Instead of routers having to store routes for all the networks in the Internet, they can store a single default route to represent any network that is not in the routing table. This topic will be discussed in more detail in Chapter 3, "Introduction to Dynamic Routing Protocols."

Now it's time for you to practice configuring and verifying default static routes.

Packet Tracer
☐ Activity

Configuring a Default Route (2.6.2)

Use the Packet Tracer Activity to practice configuring summary routes and default routes. Then verify the new configuration by testing for connectivity. Use file e2-262.pka on the CD-ROM that accompanies this book to perform this activity using Packet Tracer.

Managing and Troubleshooting Static Routes

It is important to be able to properly manage and troubleshoot static routes. When a static route is no longer needed, that static route should be deleted from the running and startup configuration files.

Static Routes and Packet Forwarding

Now that you have configured static routes on all three routers in the topology, you need to learn about the process that a packet goes through as it is forwarded by these routers.

Static Routes and Packet Forwarding

Figure 2-12 and the following steps illustrate the packet-forwarding process with static routes. In this example, R1, R2, and R3 are routing traffic between PC1 and PC3. Only the processing of traffic from PC1 to PC3 is shown. However, the same process is used for traffic from PC3 back to PC1.

Figure 2-12   Static Routes and Packet Forwarding

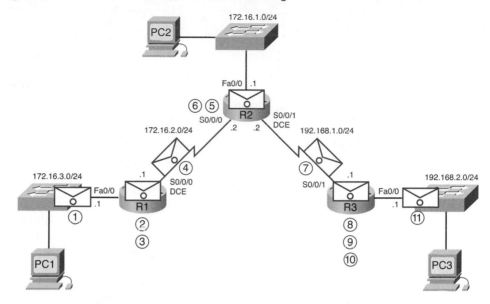

The packet forwarding process of a packet from R1 to R3 is as follows:

1. The packet arrives on the FastEthernet 0/0 interface of R1.

2. R1 does not have a specific route to the destination network, 192.168.2.0/24; therefore, R1 uses the default static route.

3. R1 encapsulates the packet in a new frame. Because the link to R2 is a point-to-point link, R1 adds an "all 1s" address for the Layer 2 destination address.

4. The frame is forwarded out the Serial 0/0/0 interface. The packet arrives on the Serial 0/0/0 interface on R2.

5. R2 decapsulates the frame, examines the packet's destination IP address, and looks for a route to the destination. R2 has a static route to 192.168.2.0/24 out Serial 0/0/1.

6. R2 encapsulates the packet in a new frame. Because the link to R3 is a point-to-point link, R2 adds an "all 1s" address for the Layer 2 destination address.

7. The frame is forwarded out the Serial 0/0/1 interface. The packet arrives on the Serial 0/0/1 interface on R3.

8. R3 decapsulates the frame, examines the packet's destination IP address, and looks for a route to the destination. R3 has a connected route to 192.168.2.0/24 out FastEthernet 0/1.

9. R3 looks up the ARP table entry for 192.168.2.10 to find the Layer 2 MAC address for PC3:

   a. If no entry exists, R3 broadcasts an ARP request out FastEthernet 0/0.

   b. PC3 responds with an ARP reply that includes the PC3 MAC address.

10. R3 encapsulates the packet in a new frame with the MAC address of interface FastEthernet 0/0 as the source Layer 2 address and the MAC address of PC3 as the destination MAC address.

11. The frame is forwarded out the FastEthernet 0/0 interface. The packet arrives on the NIC interface of PC3.

This process is no different from the process demonstrated in Chapter 1. You must be able to describe this process in detail. Knowing how a router performs its two basic functions—path determination and packet forwarding—is fundamental to all routing discussions. In Lab 2-1: Basic Static Route Configuration (2.8.1), you have an opportunity to demonstrate your knowledge of the path determination and packet-forwarding process.

Troubleshooting a Missing Route

Troubleshooting is a skill that develops as you gain more experience. It is always best to look for the most obvious and simplest issues first, such as an interface still in shutdown mode or an interface with the wrong IP address. After these items have been verified, begin looking for more complicated possibilities like an error in the static route configuration.

Troubleshooting a Missing Route

When end-to-end connectivity is a problem, begin by making sure that you can ping your own interface and other devices on your own directly connected networks. When this has been verified, begin testing connectivity to remote networks and from other devices.

Networks are subject to many different forces that can cause their status to change quite often:

- Interface failure

- Dropped connection by a service provider

- Oversaturation of links

- Incorrect configuration entered by an administrator

When there is a change in the network, connectivity might be lost. As a network administrator, you are the one responsible for pinpointing and solving the problem. What steps can you take?

By now, you should be familiar with some tools that can help you isolate routing problems:

- **ping**
- **traceroute**
- **show ip route**

Although this and the preceding chapter have not discussed **traceroute**, you should be familiar with its capabilities from previous studies. Recall that the **traceroute** command will find a break in the path from source to destination.

As you go further into this course, you will discover more tools. For example, the **show ip interface brief** command gives you a quick summary of interface status. CDP can help you gather information about the IP configuration of a directly connected Cisco device using the **show cdp neighbors detail** command.

Solving the Missing Route

The following is an example of solving a missing static route using the network topology from Figure 2-1.

Finding a missing (or misconfigured) route is relatively straightforward if you methodically use the correct tools.

Consider this problem: PC1 cannot ping PC3. A traceroute reveals that R2 is responding but that there is no response from R3. Displaying the routing table shown in Example 2-43, R2 reveals that the 172.16.3.0/24 network is configured incorrectly.

```
Example 2-43    Misconfigured Static Route
R2# show ip route

<output omitted>

Gateway of last resort is not set

     172.16.0.0/24 is subnetted, 3 subnets
C       172.16.1.0 is directly connected, FastEthernet0/0
C       172.16.2.0 is directly connected, Serial0/0/0
S       172.16.3.0 is directly connected, Serial0/0/1
C    192.168.1.0/24 is directly connected, Serial0/1
S*   0.0.0.0/0 is directly connected, Serial0/0/1
```

The exit interface is configured to send packets to R3. Obviously, from the topology, you can see that R1 has the 172.16.3.0/24 network. Therefore, R2 must use Serial 0/0/0 as the exit interface, not Serial 0/0/1.

To remedy the situation, remove the incorrect route and add the route for network 172.16.3.0/24 with Serial 0/0/0 specified as the exit interface:

```
R2(config)# no ip route 172.16.3.0 255.255.255.0 serial0/0/1
R2(config)# ip route 172.16.3.0 255.255.255.0 serial 0/0/0
```

Tip

Always remove the incorrect static route. The command that properly configures the static route will not remove the incorrect command.

The final Packet Tracer Activity associated with this chapter explores another issue with static routes. As you will see, it is possible to inadvertently configure a loop in your network using static routes.

Packet Tracer
☐ Activity

Solving the Missing Route (2.7.3)

Use the Packet Tracer Activity to see how the loop explained in this section can occur. In simulation mode, watch as R2 and R3 loop a packet for 172.16.3.10 until the Time to Live (TTL) field reaches 0. Then fix the problem and test for connectivity between PC1 and PC3. Use file e2-273.pka on the CD-ROM that accompanies this book to perform this activity using Packet Tracer.

Summary

In this chapter, you learned how static routes can be used to reach remote networks. Remote networks are networks that can only be reached by forwarding the packet to another router. Static routes are easily configured. However, in large networks, this manual operation can become quite cumbersome. As you will see in later chapters, static routes are still used, even when a dynamic routing protocol is implemented.

Static routes can be configured with a next-hop IP address, which is commonly the IP address of the next-hop router. When a next-hop IP address is used, the routing table process must resolve this address to an exit interface. On point-to-point serial links, it is usually more efficient to configure the static route with an exit interface. On multiaccess networks such as Ethernet, both a next-hop IP address and an exit interface should be configured on the static route.

Static routes have a default administrative distance of 1. This administrative distance also applies to static routes configured with a next-hop address as well as an exit interface.

A static route will only be entered in the routing table if the next-hop IP address can be resolved through an exit interface. Regardless of whether the static route is configured with a next-hop IP address or exit interface, if the exit interface—the directly connected network that is used to forward that packet—is not in the routing table, the static route will not be included in the routing table.

In many cases, several static routes can be configured as a single summary route. This means fewer entries in the routing table and results in a faster routing table lookup process. The ultimate summary route is a default route, configured with a 0.0.0.0 network address and a 0.0.0.0 subnet mask. If there is not a more specific match in the routing table, the routing table will use the default route to forward the packet to another router.

Note
The routing table lookup process is examined more closely in Chapter 8.

Labs

The labs available in the companion *Routing Protocols and Concepts, CCNA Exploration Labs and Study Guide* (ISBN 1-58713-204-4) provide hands-on practice with the following topics introduced in this chapter:

Lab 2-1: Basic Static Route Configuration (2.8.1)

In this lab activity, you will create a network like the one used in this chapter. You will cable the network and perform the initial router configurations required for connectivity. After completing the basic configuration, you will test connectivity among the devices on the network. You will then configure the static routes that are needed to allow communication between the hosts.

Lab 2-2: Challenge Static Route Configuration (2.8.2)

In this lab activity, you will be given a network address that must be subnetted to complete the addressing of the network. The addressing for the LAN connected to the ISP router and the link between the HQ and ISP routers have already been completed. Static routes will also need to be configured so that hosts on networks that are not directly connected will be able to communicate with each other.

Lab 2-3: Troubleshooting Static Routes (2.8.3)

In this lab, you will begin by loading corrupted configuration scripts on each of the routers. These scripts contain errors that will prevent end-to-end communication across the network. You will need to troubleshoot each router to determine the configuration errors, and then use the appropriate commands to correct the configurations. When you have corrected all the configuration errors, all the hosts on the network should be able to communicate with each other.

Many of the hands-on labs include Packet Tracer Companion Activities, where you can use Packet Tracer to complete a simulation of the lab. Look for this icon in *Routing Protocols and Concepts, CCNA Exploration Labs and Study Guide* (ISBN 1-58713-204-4) for hands-on labs that have a Packet Tracer Companion.

Check Your Understanding

Complete all the review questions listed here to test your understanding of the topics and concepts in this chapter. The appendix, "Check Your Understanding and Challenge Questions Answer Key," lists the answers.

1. Refer to Figure 2-13. Which two commands must be configured to allow communication between the 192.168.1.0/24 and 10.0.0.0/8 networks?

Figure 2-13   Topology for Quiz Question #1

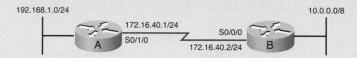

192.168.1.0/24   172.16.40.1/24   10.0.0.0/8
                                                              S0/0/0
                                              S0/1/0
                                     A   172.16.40.2/24   B

   A. A(config)# **ip route 10.0.0.0 255.0.0.0 172.16.40.2**

   B. A(config)# **ip route 10.0.0.0 255.0.0.0 s0/0/0**

   C. A(config)# **ip route 10.0.0.0 255.0.0.0 10.0.0.1**

   D. B(config)# **ip route 192.168.1.0 255.255.255.0 172.16.40.1**

   E. B(config)# **ip route 192.168.1.0 255.255.255.0 172.16.40.2**

   F. B# **ip route 192.168.1.0 255.255.255.0 192.168.1.1**

2. Which statement is true concerning configuring static routes using next-hop addresses?

   A. Routers cannot use more than one static route with a next-hop address.

   B. When the router identifies that a packet is destined for a route associated with a next-hop address in the routing table, the router requires no further information and can immediately forward the packet.

   C. Routers configured with the static route using a next-hop address must either have the exit interface listed in the route or have another route with the network of the next hop and an associated exit interface.

   D. Routes associated with a next-hop address are more efficient than routes going to exit interfaces.

3. Refer to the following command output. The network administrator must remove the route to the 10.0.0.0 network. What command will accomplish this task?

```
R1# show ip route

<output omitted>

Gateway of last resort is not set

S    10.0.0.0/8 [1/0] via 172.16.40.2
     64.0.0.0/16 is subnetted, 1 subnets
C      64.100.0.0 is directly connected, Serial0/1
C    128.107.0.0/16 is directly connected, Loopback2
     172.16.0.0/24 is subnetted, 1 subnets
S      172.16.40.0 is directly connected, Serial0/0
C    192.168.1.0/24 is directly connected, FastEhternet0/0
C    192.168.2.0/24 [1/0] via 172.16.40.2
C    198.133.219.0/24 is directly connected, Loopback0
```

A. **no ip address 10.0.0.1 255.255.255.0 172.16.40.2**

B. **no static-route 10.0.0.0 255.0.0.0**

C. **no ip route 10.0.0.0 255.0.0.0 172.16.40.2**

D. **no ip route 10.0.0.1 255.255.255.0**

4. Refer to Figure 2-14. What command was used on Router R1 to produce the output shown in the graphic?

Figure 2-14 Topology for Quiz Question #4

A. **traceroute**

B. **extended ping**

C. **show ip route**

D. **show cdp neighbor detail**

5. Refer to Figure 2-15. Which command correctly configures a static default route on R1?

Figure 2-15   Topology for Quiz Question #5

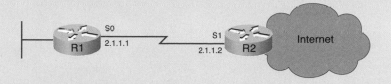

A. R1(config-if)# **ip route 0.0.0.0 0.0.0.0 s0**

B. R1(config)# **ip route 0.0.0.0 0.0.0.0 s1**

C. R1(config-if)# **ip route 0.0.0.0 0.0.0.0 2.1.1.2**

D. R1(config)# **ip route 0.0.0.0 0.0.0.0 2.1.1.2**

E. R1(config-router)# **default-information originate**

6. Which of the following are three characteristics of a static route?

A. Reduces the memory and processing burdens on a router

B. Ensures that there is always a path available

C. Used to dynamically find the best path to a destination network

D. Used for routers that connect to stub networks

E. Used for networks with a single route to a destination network

F. Reduces configuration time

7. Which of the following is a function of the IOS command **show cdp neighbors**?

A. It displays the port type and platform of neighboring Cisco routers.

B. It displays the device capability code of all non-Cisco routers.

C. It displays platform information for all devices in the network.

D. It displays the protocol encapsulation used by neighboring routers.

8. Refer to Figure 2-16. What type of connector is shown in the exhibit?

Figure 2-16   Graphic for Quiz Question #8

A. The DB-60 DTE end of the serial cable for 1600 and 2500 series routers

B. The DTE end of a smart serial cable used with newer routers

C. The EIA/TIA-530 DCE end of a serial cable that plugs into the CSU/DSU

D. The V.35 DCE end of a serial cable that plugs into the CSU/DSU

E. The EIA/TIA-232 DCE end of a serial cable that plugs into the CSU/DSU

F. The EIA/TIA-449 DCE end of a serial cable that plugs into the CSU/DSU

9. Which statement is true concerning directly connected routes?

A. They appear in the routing table as soon as cables are connected to the router.

B. They appear in the routing table when an IP address is configured on an interface.

C. They appear in the routing table when the **no shutdown** command is entered in router interface configuration mode.

D. They appear in the routing table when the **show interface** command shows that the interface is up, line protocol is up.

10. Choose the proper command that is associated with each of the following configuration tasks.

Configuration tasks:

Enter global configuration mode

Enter interface configuration mode

Configure an IP address

Activate the interface

Commands:

A. **interface fastethernet 0/0**

B. **ip address 192.168.35.11 255.255.255.0**

C. **ip address 192.168.35.11/24**

D. **config terminal**

E. **ip 192.168.35.11 255.255.255.0**

F. **ip 192.168.35.11/24**

G. **no shutdown**

H. **show interfaces fastethernet 0/0**

11. Match the following **show/debug** commands with the proper outputs.

show ip route:

show ip interface brief:

show interfaces:

show controllers:

debug ip routing:

show cdp neighbors:

Output:

A. Display all known networks

B. Display detailed port information

C. Display routing troubleshooting information

D. Display basic port information

E. Display directly connected routers

F. Display DTE/DCE information

12. Describe the cabling used to connect devices to an Ethernet LAN.

13. List three commands used to display interface configuration information.

14. Explain the difference between attaching a serial interface to a service provider in a production environment and attaching a serial interface to another router in a lab environment.

15. What is CDP, and why would you want to disable it?

16. What is the simpler form used for the **ip route** syntax?

17. What is a recursive route lookup, and when does it occur?

18. Why must you remove a static route from the configuration before modifying it?

19. Explain the value of summary and default routes.

20. List the commands used to test and troubleshoot a network implementation.

Challenge Questions and Activities

These questions require a deeper application of the concepts covered in this chapter and are similar to the style of questions you might see on a CCNA certification exam. You can find the answers to these questions in the appendix, "Answers to Check Your Understanding and Challenge Questions and Activities."

1. On some newer computers, it does not matter whether you attach a straight-through or crossover cable to the device. The computer successfully connects to the other device. Why do you think this happens?

2. All network interfaces are up and up. PC1, PC2, and PC3 have full connectivity. Pings from R1 to R2 and R3 are successful. However, although pings from R3 to R2 are successful, R3 cannot ping either address on R1. Using Figure 2-17 and the following command output, identify the problem, explain why the ping fails, and suggest a solution.

Figure 2-17   Topology for Challenge Question #2

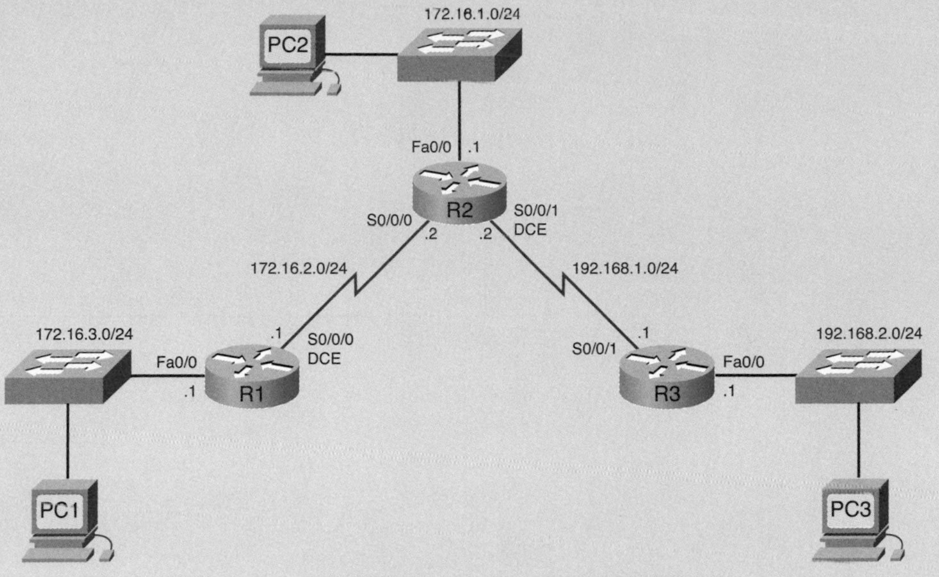

```
R1# show ip interface brief

Interface          IP-Address      OK? Method Status                 Protocol
FastEthernet0/0    172.16.3.1      YES manual up                         up
Serial0/0/0        172.16.2.1      YES manual up                         up
FastEthernet0/1    unassigned      YES manual administratively down down
Serial0/0/1        unassigned      YES manual administratively down down
```
```
R2# show ip interface brief

Interface          IP-Address      OK? Method Status                 Protocol
FastEthernet0/0    172.16.1.1      YES manual up                         up
Serial0/0/0        172.16.2.2      YES manual up                         up
FastEthernet0/1    unassigned      YES manual administratively down down
Serial0/0/1        192.168.1.1     YES manual up                         up
```
```
R3# show ip interface brief

Interface          IP-Address      OK? Method Status                 Protocol
FastEthernet0/0    192.168.2.1     YES manual up                         up
Serial0/0/0        unassigned      YES manual administratively down down
FastFthernet0/1    unassigned      YES manual administratively down down
Serial0/0/1        192.168.1.1     YES manual up                         up
```

3. Use the output from the **show cdp neighbors** commands that follow to draw the topology on a piece of paper. Show connections between devices and label the interfaces. All devices are unique. For example, there is only one EAST router and one S1 switch.

HQ# **show cdp neighbors**

```
Capability Codes: R - Router, T - Trans Bridge, B - Source Route Bridge
                  S - Switch, H - Host, I - IGMP, r - Repeater, P - Phone
Device ID    Local Intrfce     Holdtme    Capability    Platform    Port ID
S4           FastEthernet0/0   151            S          WS-C2960    Fas 0/16
EAST         Serial0/0         163            R          C1841       Ser 0/1
WEST         Serial0/1         169            R          C1841       Ser 0/0
```

EAST# **show cdp neighbors**

```
Capability Codes: R - Router, T - Trans Bridge, B - Source Route Bridge
                  S - Switch, H - Host, I - IGMP, r - Repeater, P - Phone
Device ID    Local Intrfce     Holdtme    Capability    Platform    Port ID
S1           FastEthernet0/1   177            S          WS-C2960    Fas 0/3
HQ           Serial0/1         128            R          C1841       Ser 0/0
S2           FastEthernet0/0   133            S          WS-C2960    Fas 0/3
```

WEST# **show cdp neighbors**

```
Capability Codes: R - Router, T - Trans Bridge, B - Source Route Bridge
                  S - Switch, H - Host, I - IGMP, r - Repeater, P - Phone
Device ID    Local Intrfce     Holdtme    Capability    Platform    Port ID
S1           FastEthernet0/0   176            S          WS-C2960    Fas 0/4
HQ           Serial0/0         126            R          C1841       Ser 0/1
S3           FastEthernet0/1   156            S          WS-C2960    Fas 0/12
```

4. In Figure 2-18, all the Branch routers need to be configured with a default route to RegionA. RegionA needs a default route to HQ, and HQ needs a default route to ISP. RegionA can summarize each of the LANs attached to each Branch router with one static route pointing to each of the Branch routers. HQ and ISP can summarize all the LANs with just one static route. Using the exit interface argument, what are the static default routes for each Branch router, for RegionA, and for HQ? What are the summary static routes configured on RegionA, HQ, and ISP? Build the topology in Packet Tracer, and test your static and default routing commands. The Web Server should be able to ping every interface on every router.

Figure 2-18   Topology for Challenge Question #4

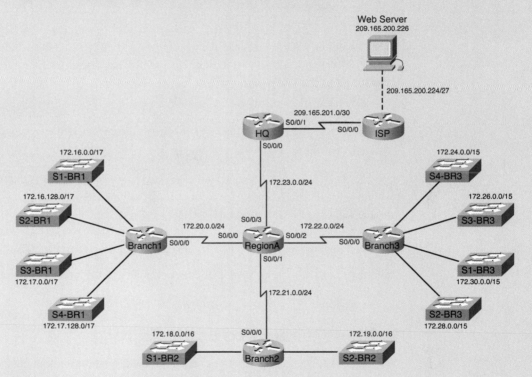

To Learn More

Static routes can have other uses besides what you have seen in this chapter. Other common static routes include floating static routes and discard routes.

Floating Static Routes

A floating static route is a backup route to a route that is either a dynamic route or another static route. The default administrative distance of a static route is 1. See whether you can create a static route using a different exit interface or next-hop IP address, which would only be added to the routing table if the primary static route fails.

Hint: Remember, if the router has two routes to the same destination network with two different administrative distance values, it will add the route with the lower administrative distance. A static route will be removed from the routing table if the exit interface or next-hop IP address is no longer available.

Discard Route

A common configuration in many networks is to have a static default route on the edge router forwarding packets to the ISP. The ISP router then has a static route pointing to the customer's network.

For example, customer A has the network address of 172.16.0.0/16, which is subnetted into several /24 subnets. The edge router of customer A has a static default route forwarding all other traffic to the ISP router:

```
ip route 0.0.0.0 0.0.0.0 serial 0/0/0
```

The ISP router has a static default route for forwarding traffic to customer A's network:

```
ip route 172.16.0.0 255.255.0.0 serial 0/0/1
```

A problem can occur when packets are originated from the customer A's network for a subnet that does not exist. Customer A's edge router will use its default route to forward those packets onto the ISP. The ISP router will receive those packets and send them back to customer A's edge router because they are part of the 172.16.0.0/16 network. The edge router will once again send them back to the ISP. The packets are caught in a loop until the TTL of the packet expires.

Configure a static route on customer A's edge router to discard those packets instead of forwarding them onto the ISP router.

Further Reading on Static Routing

Although static routes can be easily understood and configured, there are some situations when the IOS processing of static routes can be quite complex. This is especially true when there are various static routes configured that cover the same range of networks.

Alex Zinin's book, *Cisco IP Routing*, covers static routing and IOS's static route processing in detail. This book goes beyond just the configuration and looks at the inner workings of the Cisco IOS and its routing processes.

End Notes

1. Zinin, A. *Cisco IP Routing: Packet Forwarding and Intra-domain Routing Protocols*. Indianapolis, IN: Addison-Wesley; 2002.

CHAPTER 3

Introduction to Dynamic Routing Protocols

Objectives

Upon completion of this chapter, you should be able to answer the following questions:

- Can you describe the role of dynamic routing protocols and place these protocols in the context of modern network design?

- What are several ways to classify routing protocols?

- How are metrics used by routing protocols, and what are the metric types used by dynamic routing protocols?

- How do you determine the administrative distance of a route, and what is its importance in the routing process?

- What are the different elements in the routing table?

- Given realistic constraints, can you devise and apply subnetting schemes?

Key Terms

This chapter uses the following key terms. You can find the definitions in the Glossary at the end of the book.

scale   page 149

algorithm   page 151

autonomous system   page 154

routing domain   page 154

interior gateway protocols   page 154

exterior gateway protocols   page 154

path vector protocol   page 156

distance vector   page 156

vectors   page 156

link-state   page 157

link-state router   page 157

converged   page 157

classful routing protocols   page 158

VLSM   page 158

discontiguous   page 158

classless routing protocols   page 159

convergence   page 159

administrative distance   page 165

The data networks that we use in our everyday lives to learn, play, and work range from small, local networks to large, global internetworks. At home, you might have a router and two or more computers. At work, your organization might have multiple routers and switches servicing the data communication needs of hundreds or even thousands of PCs.

In Chapters 1 and 2, you discovered how routers are used in packet forwarding and that routers learn about remote networks using both static routes and dynamic routing protocols. You also know how routes to remote networks can be configured manually using static routes.

This chapter introduces dynamic routing protocols, including how different routing protocols are classified, what metrics they use to determine best path, and the benefits of using a dynamic routing protocol.

Dynamic routing protocols are typically used in larger networks to ease the administrative and operational overhead of using only static routes. Typically, a network uses a combination of both a dynamic routing protocol and static routes. In most networks, a single dynamic routing protocol is used; however, there are cases where different parts of the network can use different routing protocols.

Since the early 1980s, several different dynamic routing protocols have emerged. This chapter begins to discuss some of the characteristics and differences in these routing protocols; however, this will become more evident in later chapters, with a discussion of several of these routing protocols in detail.

Although many networks will use only a single routing protocol or use only static routes, it is important for a network professional to understand the concepts and operations of all the different routing protocols. A network professional must be able to make an informed decision regarding when to use a dynamic routing protocol and which routing protocol is the best choice for a particular environment.

Introduction to Dynamic Routing Protocols

Dynamic routing protocols play an important role in today's networks. The following sections describe several important benefits that dynamic routing protocols provide. In many networks, dynamic routing protocols are typically used with static routes.

Perspective and Background

Dynamic routing protocols have evolved over several years to meet the demands of changing network requirements. Although many organizations have migrated to more recent routing protocols such as Enhanced Interior Gateway Routing Protocol (EIGRP) and Open Shortest Path First (OSPF), many of the earlier routing protocols, such as Routing Information Protocol (RIP), are still in use today.

Evolution of Dynamic Routing Protocols

Dynamic routing protocols have been used in networks since the early 1980s. The first version of RIP was released in 1982, but some of the basic algorithms within the protocol were used on the ARPANET as early as 1969.

As networks have evolved and become more complex, new routing protocols have emerged. Figure 3-1 shows the classification of routing protocols.

Figure 3-1   Routing Protocols' Evolution and Classification

	Distance Vector Routing Protocols		Link State Routing Protocols		Path Vector
Classful	RIP	IGRP			EGP
Classless	RIPv2	EIGRP	OSPFv2	IS-IS	BGPv4
IPv6	RIPng	EIGRP for IPv6	OSPFv3	IS-IS for IPv6	BGPv4 for IPv6

Highlighted routing protocols are the focus of this course.

Figure 3-1 shows a timeline of IP routing protocols, with a chart that helps classify the various protocols. This chart will be referred to several times throughout this book.

One of the earliest routing protocols was RIP. RIP has evolved into a newer version: RIPv2. However, the newer version of RIP still does not *scale* to larger network implementations. To address the needs of larger networks, two advanced routing protocols were developed: OSPF and Intermediate System–to–Intermediate System (IS-IS). Cisco developed Interior Gateway Routing Protocol (IGRP) and Enhanced IGRP (EIGRP). EIGRP also scales well in larger network implementations.

Additionally, there was the need to interconnect different internetworks and provide routing among them. Border Gateway Protocol (BGP) is now used between Internet service providers (ISP) as well as between ISPs and their larger private clients to exchange routing information.

With the advent of numerous consumer devices using IP, the IPv4 addressing space is nearly exhausted. Thus IPv6 has emerged. To support the communication based on IPv6, newer versions of the IP routing protocols have been developed (see the IPv6 row in Figure 3-1).

Note

This chapter presents an overview of the different dynamic routing protocols. More details about RIP, EIGRP, and OSPF routing protocols will be discussed in later chapters. The IS-IS and BGP routing protocols are explained in the CCNP curriculum. IGRP is the predecessor to EIGRP and is now considered obsolete.

Role of Dynamic Routing Protocol

What exactly are dynamic routing protocols? Routing protocols are used to facilitate the exchange of routing information between routers. Routing protocols allow routers to dynamically learn information about remote networks and automatically add this information to their own routing tables, as shown in Figure 3-2.

Figure 3-2   Routers Dynamically Pass Updates

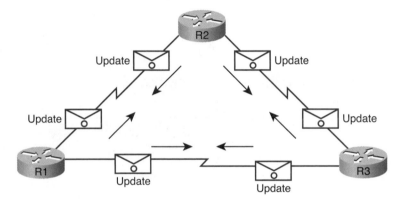

Routing protocols determine the best path to each network, which is then added to the routing table. One of the primary benefits of using a dynamic routing protocol is that routers exchange routing information whenever there is a topology change. This exchange allows routers to automatically learn about new networks and also to find alternate paths if there is a link failure to a current network.

Compared to static routing, dynamic routing protocols require less administrative overhead. However, the expense of using dynamic routing protocols is dedicating part of a router's resources for protocol operation, including CPU time and network link bandwidth. Despite the benefits of dynamic routing, static routing still has its place. There are times when static routing is more appropriate and other times when dynamic routing is the better choice. More often than not, you will find a combination of both types of routing in any network that has a moderate level of complexity. You will learn about the advantages and disadvantages of static and dynamic routing later in this chapter.

Network Discovery and Routing Table Maintenance

Two important processes concerning dynamic routing protocols are initially discovering remote networks and maintaining a list of those networks in the routing table.

Purpose of Dynamic Routing Protocols

A routing protocol is a set of processes, algorithms, and messages that are used to exchange routing information and populate the routing table with the routing protocol's choice of best paths. The purpose of a routing protocol includes

- Discovering remote networks

- Maintaining up-to-date routing information

- Choosing the best path to destination networks

- Having the ability to find a new best path if the current path is no longer available

The components of a routing protocol are as follows:

- **Data structures:** Some routing protocols use tables or databases for their operations. This information is kept in RAM.

- **Algorithm:** An *algorithm* is a finite list of steps used in accomplishing a task. Routing protocols use algorithms for processing routing information and for best-path determination.

- **Routing protocol messages:** Routing protocols use various types of messages to discover neighboring routers, exchange routing information, and do other tasks to learn and maintain accurate information about the network.

Dynamic Routing Protocol Operation

All routing protocols have the same purpose: to learn about remote networks and to quickly adapt whenever there is a change in the topology. The method that a routing protocol uses to accomplish this depends on the algorithm it uses and the operational characteristics of that protocol. The operations of a dynamic routing protocol vary depending on the type of routing protocol and the specific operations of that routing protocol. The specific operations of RIP, EIGRP, and OSPF are examined in later chapters. In general, the operations of a dynamic routing protocol can be described as follows:

1. The router sends and receives routing messages on its interfaces.

2. The router shares routing messages and routing information with other routers that are using the same routing protocol.

3. Routers exchange routing information to learn about remote networks.

4. When a router detects a topology change, the routing protocol can advertise this change to other routers.

Note

Understanding dynamic routing protocol operation and concepts and using these protocols in real networks require a solid knowledge of IP addressing and subnetting. Three subnetting scenarios are available in *Routing Protocols and Concepts, CCNA Exploration Labs and Study Guide* (ISBN 1-58713-204-4) for your practice.

Dynamic Routing Protocol Advantages

Dynamic routing protocols provide several advantages, which will be discussed in this section. In many cases, the complexity of the network topology, the number of networks, and the need for the network to automatically adjust to changes require the use of a dynamic routing protocol.

Before examining the benefits of dynamic routing protocols in more detail, you need to consider the reasons why you would use static routing. Dynamic routing certainly has several advantages over static routing; however, static routing is still used in networks today. In fact, networks typically use a combination of both static and dynamic routing.

Table 3-1 compares dynamic and static routing features. From this comparison, you can list the advantages of each routing method. The advantages of one method are the disadvantages of the other.

Table 3-1   Dynamic Versus Static Routing

Feature	Dynamic Routing	Static Routing
Configuration complexity	Generally independent of the network size	Increases with network size
Required administrator knowledge	Advanced knowledge required	No extra knowledge required
Topology changes	Automatically adapts to topology changes	Administrator intervention required
Scaling	Suitable for simple and complex topologies	Suitable for simple topologies
Security	Less secure	More secure
Resource usage	Uses CPU, memory, and link bandwidth	No extra resources needed
Predictability	Route depends on the current topology	Route to destination is always the same

Static Routing Usage, Advantages, and Disadvantages

Static routing has several primary uses, including the following:

- Providing ease of routing table maintenance in smaller networks that are not expected to grow significantly.

- Routing to and from stub networks (see Chapter 2).

- Using a single default route, used to represent a path to any network that does not have a more specific match with another route in the routing table.

Static routing advantages are as follows:

- Minimal CPU processing

- Easier for administrator to understand

- Easy to configure

Static routing disadvantages are as follows:

- Configuration and maintenance are time-consuming.

- Configuration is error-prone, especially in large networks.

- Administrator intervention is required to maintain changing route information.

- Does not scale well with growing networks; maintenance becomes cumbersome.

- Requires complete knowledge of the entire network for proper implementation.

Dynamic Routing Advantages and Disadvantages

Dynamic routing advantages are as follows:

- Administrator has less work in maintaining the configuration when adding or deleting networks.

- Protocols automatically react to the topology changes.

- Configuration is less error-prone.

- More scalable; growing the network usually does not present a problem.

Dynamic routing disadvantages are as follows:

- Router resources are used (CPU cycles, memory, and link bandwidth).

- More administrator knowledge is required for configuration, verification, and troubleshooting.

Classifying Dynamic Routing Protocols

Figure 3-1 showed how routing protocols can be classified according to various characteristics. This chapter will introduce you to these terms, which will be discussed in more detail in later chapters.

This section gives an overview of the most common IP routing protocols. Most of these routing protocols will be examined in detail later in this book. For now, we will give a very brief overview of each protocol.

Routing protocols can be classified into different groups according to their characteristics:

- IGP or EGP

- Distance vector or link-state

- Classful or classless

The sections that follow discuss these classification schemes in more detail.

The most commonly used routing protocols are as follows:

- **RIP:** A distance vector interior routing protocol

- **IGRP:** The distance vector interior routing protocol developed by Cisco (deprecated from Cisco IOS Release 12.2 and later)

- **OSPF:** A link-state interior routing protocol

- **IS-IS:** A link-state interior routing protocol

- **EIGRP:** The advanced distance vector interior routing protocol developed by Cisco

- **BGP:** A path vector exterior routing protocol

Note

IS-IS and BGP are beyond the scope of this book.

IGP and EGP

An *autonomous system* (AS)—otherwise known as a *routing domain*—is a collection of routers under a common administration. Typical examples are a company's internal network and an ISP's network. Because the Internet is based on the autonomous system concept, two types of routing protocols are required: interior and exterior routing protocols. These protocols are

- *Interior gateway protocols (IGP):* Used for intra-autonomous system routing, that is, routing inside an autonomous system

- *Exterior gateway protocols (EGP):* Used for inter-autonomous system routing, that is, routing between autonomous systems

Figure 3-3 is a simplified view of the difference between IGPs and EGPs. The autonomous system concept will be explained in more detail later in the chapter. Even though this is an oversimplification, for now, think of an autonomous system as an ISP.

Figure 3-3   IGP Versus EGP Routing Protocols

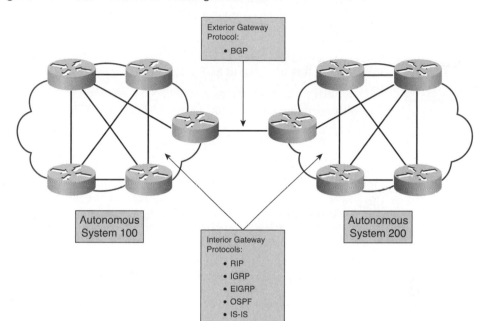

IGPs are used for routing within a routing domain, those networks within the control of a single organization. An autonomous system is commonly composed of many individual networks belonging to companies, schools, and other institutions. An IGP is used to route within the autonomous system and also used to route within the individual networks themselves. For example, The Corporation for Education Network Initiatives in California (CENIC) operates an autonomous system composed of California schools, colleges, and universities. CENIC uses an IGP to route within its autonomous system to interconnect all of these institutions. Each of the educational institutions also uses an IGP of its own choosing to route within its own individual network. The IGP used by each entity provides best-path determination within its own routing domains, just as the IGP used by CENIC provides best-path routes within the autonomous system itself. IGPs for IP include RIP, IGRP, EIGRP, OSPF, and IS-IS.

Routing protocols (and more specifically, the algorithm used by that routing protocol) use a metric to determine the best path to a network. The metric used by the routing protocol RIP is *hop count*, which is the number of routers that a packet must traverse in reaching another network. OSPF uses *bandwidth* to determine the shortest path.

EGPs, on the other hand, are designed for use between different autonomous systems that are under the control of different administrations. BGP is the only currently viable EGP and is the routing protocol used by the Internet. BGP is a *path vector protocol* that can use many different attributes to measure routes. At the ISP level, there are often more important issues than just choosing the fastest path. BGP is typically used between ISPs and sometimes between a company and an ISP. BGP is not part of this course or CCNA; it is covered in CCNP.

Packet Tracer □ Activity	**Characteristics of IGP and EGP Routing Protocols (3.2.2)**

In this activity, the network has already been configured within the autonomous systems. You will configure a default route from AS2 and AS3 (two different companies) to the ISP (AS1) to simulate the exterior gateway routing that would take place from both companies to their ISP. Then you will configure a static route from the ISP (AS1) to AS2 and AS3 to simulate the exterior gateway routing that would take place from the ISP to its two customers, AS2 and AS3. View the routing table before and after both static routes and default routes are added to observe how the routing table has changed. Use file e2-322.pka on the CD-ROM that accompanies this book to perform this activity using Packet Tracer.

Distance Vector and Link-State Routing Protocols

Interior gateway protocols (IGP) can be classified as two types:

- Distance vector routing protocols
- Link-state routing protocols

Distance Vector Routing Protocol Operation

Distance vector means that routes are advertised as *vectors* of distance and direction. Distance is defined in terms of a metric such as hop count, and direction is simply the next-hop router or exit interface. Distance vector protocols typically use the Bellman-Ford algorithm for the best-path route determination.

Some distance vector protocols periodically send complete routing tables to all connected neighbors. In large networks, these routing updates can become enormous, causing significant traffic on the links.

Although the Bellman-Ford algorithm eventually accumulates enough knowledge to maintain a database of reachable networks, the algorithm does not allow a router to know the exact topology of an internetwork. The router only knows the routing information received from its neighbors.

Distance vector protocols use routers as signposts along the path to the final destination. The only information a router knows about a remote network is the distance or metric to reach that network and which path or interface to use to get there. Distance vector routing protocols do not have an actual map of the network topology.

Distance vector protocols work best in situations where

- The network is simple and flat and does not require a hierarchical design.

- The administrators do not have enough knowledge to configure and troubleshoot link-state protocols.

- Specific types of networks, such as hub-and-spoke networks, are being implemented.

- Worst-case convergence times in a network are not a concern.

Chapter 4, "Distance Vector Routing Protocols," covers distance vector routing protocol functions and operations in greater detail. You will also learn about the operations and configuration of the distance vector routing protocols RIP and EIGRP.

Link-State Protocol Operation

In contrast to distance vector routing protocol operation, a router configured with a *link-state* routing protocol can create a "complete view," or topology, of the network by gathering information from all the other routers. Think of using a link-state routing protocol as having a complete map of the network topology. The signposts along the way from source to destination are not necessary, because all link-state routers are using an identical "map" of the network. A *link-state router* uses the link-state information to create a topology map and to select the best path to all destination networks in the topology.

With some distance vector routing protocols, routers send periodic updates of their routing information to their neighbors. Link-state routing protocols do not use periodic updates. After the network has *converged*, a link-state update is only sent when there is a change in the topology.

Link-state protocols work best in situations where

- The network design is hierarchical, usually occurring in large networks.

- The administrators have a good knowledge of the implemented link-state routing protocol.

- Fast convergence of the network is crucial.

Link-state routing protocol functions and operations will be explained in later chapters. You will also learn about the operations and configuration of the link-state routing protocol OSPF in Chapter 11, "OSPF."

Classful and Classless Routing Protocols

All routing protocols can also be classified as either

- Classful routing protocols
- Classless routing protocols

Classful Routing Protocols

Classful routing protocols do not send subnet mask information in routing updates. The first routing protocols, such as RIP, were classful. This was at a time when network addresses were allocated based on classes: Class A, B, or C. A routing protocol did not need to include the subnet mask in the routing update because the network mask could be determined based on the first octet of the network address.

Classful routing protocols can still be used in some of today's networks, but because they do not include the subnet mask, they cannot be used in all situations. Classful routing protocols cannot be used when a network is subnetted using more than one subnet mask. In other words, classful routing protocols do not support variable-length subnet masks (***VLSM***). Figure 3-4 shows an example of a network using the same subnet mask on all its subnets for the same major network address. In this situation, either a classful or classless routing protocol could be used.

Figure 3-4   Classful Routing

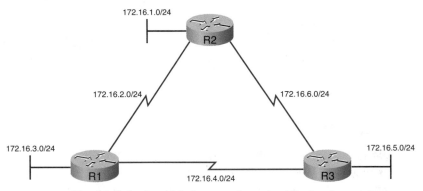

Classful: Subnet mask is the same throughout the topology.

There are other limitations to classful routing protocols, including their inability to support ***discontiguous*** networks. Later chapters discuss classful routing protocols, discontiguous networks, and VLSM in greater detail.

Classful routing protocols include RIPv1 and IGRP.

Classless Routing Protocols

Classless routing protocols include the subnet mask with the network address in routing updates. Today's networks are no longer allocated based on classes, and the subnet mask cannot be determined by the value of the first octet. Classless routing protocols are required in most networks today because of their support for VLSM, discontiguous networks, and other features that will be discussed in later chapters.

In Figure 3-5, notice that the classless version of the network is using both /30 and /27 subnet masks in the same topology. Also notice that this topology is using a discontiguous design.

Figure 3-5   Classless Routing

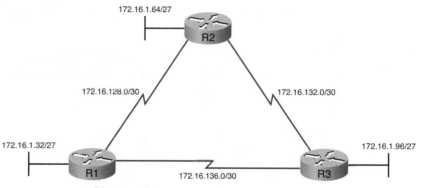

Classless: Subnet mask can vary in the topology.

Classless routing protocols are RIPv2, EIGRP, OSPF, IS-IS, and BGP.

Dynamic Routing Protocols and Convergence

An important characteristic of a routing protocol is how quickly it converges when there is a change in the topology.

Convergence is when the routing tables of all routers are at a state of consistency. The network has converged when all routers have complete and accurate information about the network. Convergence time is the time it takes routers to share information, calculate best paths, and update their routing tables. A network is not completely operable until the network has converged; therefore, most networks require short convergence times.

Convergence is both collaborative and independent. The routers share information with each other but must independently calculate the impacts of the topology change on their own routes. Because they develop an agreement with the new topology independently, they are said to *converge* on this consensus.

Convergence properties include the speed of propagation of routing information and the calculation of optimal paths. Routing protocols can be rated based on the speed to convergence; the faster the convergence, the better the routing protocol. Generally, RIP and IGRP are slow to converge, whereas EIGRP, OSPF, and IS-IS are faster to converge.

<table>
<tr><td>Packet Tracer
☐ Activity</td></tr>
</table>

Convergence (3.2.5)

In this activity, the network has already been configured with two routers, two switches, and two hosts. A new LAN will be added, and you will watch the network converge. Use file e2-325.pka on the CD-ROM that accompanies this book to perform this activity using Packet Tracer.

Metrics

Metrics are a way to measure or compare. Routing protocols use metrics to determine which route is the best path.

Purpose of a Metric

There are cases when a routing protocol learns of more than one route to the same destination. To select the best path, the routing protocol must be able to evaluate and differentiate among the available paths. For this purpose, a metric is used. A metric is a value used by routing protocols to assign costs to reach remote networks. The metric is used to determine which path is most preferable when there are multiple paths to the same remote network.

Each routing protocol calculates its metric in a different way. For example, RIP uses hop count, EIGRP uses a combination of bandwidth and delay, and the Cisco implementation of OSPF uses bandwidth. Hop count is the easiest metric to envision. The *hop count* refers to the number of routers a packet must cross to reach the destination network.

For Router R3 in Figure 3-6, network 172.16.3.0 is two hops, or two routers, away. For Router R2, network 172.16.3.0 is one hop away, and for Router R1, it is 0 hops (because the network is directly connected).

Note

The metrics for a particular routing protocol and a discussion of how they are calculated will be presented in the chapter for that routing protocol.

Figure 3-6   Metrics

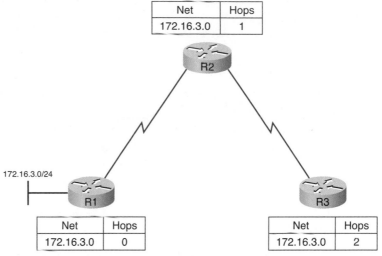

Net	Hops
172.16.3.0	1

Net	Hops
172.16.3.0	0

Net	Hops
172.16.3.0	2

172.16.3.0/24

Metrics and Routing Protocols

Different routing protocols use different metrics. The metric used by one routing protocol is not comparable to the metric used by another routing protocol.

Metric Parameters

Two different routing protocols might choose different paths to the same destination because of using different metrics.

Figure 3-7 shows how R1 would reach the 172.16.1.0/24 network. RIP would choose the path with the least amount of hops through R2, whereas OSPF would choose the path with the highest bandwidth through R3.

Metrics used in IP routing protocols include the following:

- **Hop count:** A simple metric that counts the number of routers a packet must traverse.

- **Bandwidth:** Influences path selection by preferring the path with the highest bandwidth.

- **Load:** Considers the traffic utilization of a certain link.

- **Delay:** Considers the time a packet takes to traverse a path.

- **Reliability:** Assesses the probability of a link failure, calculated from the interface error count or previous link failures.

- **Cost:** A value determined either by the IOS or by the network administrator to indicate preference for a route. Cost can represent a metric, a combination of metrics, or a policy.

Figure 3-7   Hop Count Versus Bandwidth

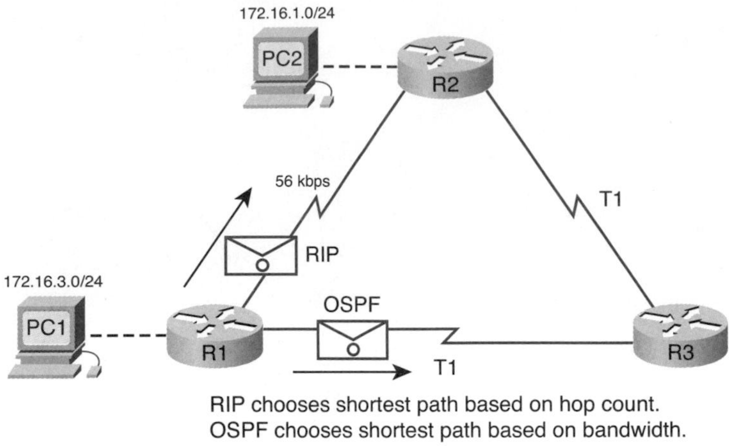

RIP chooses shortest path based on hop count.
OSPF chooses shortest path based on bandwidth.

Note

At this point, it is not important to completely understand these metrics; they will be explained in later chapters.

Metric Field in the Routing Table

The routing table displays the metric for each dynamic and static route. Remember from Chapter 2 that static routes always have a metric of 0.

The list that follows defines the metric for each routing protocol:

- **RIP: Hop count:** Best path is chosen by the route with the lowest hop count.

- **IGRP and EIGRP: Bandwidth, delay, reliability, and load:** Best path is chosen by the route with the smallest composite metric value calculated from these multiple parameters. By default, only bandwidth and delay are used.

- **IS-IS and OSPF: Cost:** Best path is chosen by the route with the lowest cost. The Cisco implementation of OSPF uses bandwidth to determine the cost. IS-IS is discussed in CCNP.

Routing protocols determine best path based on the route with the lowest metric.

In Figure 3-8, all the routers are using the RIP routing protocol.

The metric associated with a certain route can be best viewed using the **show ip route** command. The metric value is the second value in the brackets for a routing table entry. In Example 3-1, R2 has a route to the 192.168.8.0/24 network that is two hops away. The highlighted **2** in the command output is where the routing metric is displayed.

Figure 3-8   Best Path Determined in a Network Using RIP

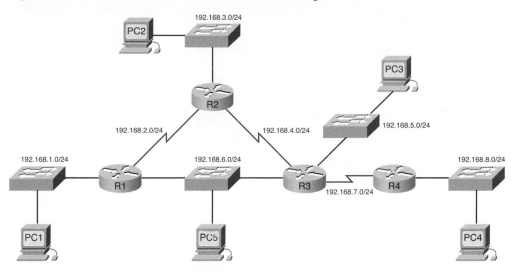

Example 3-1 Routing Table for R2

```
R2# show ip route

<output omitted>

Gateway of last resort is not set

R    192.168.1.0/24 [120/1] via 192.168.2.1, 00:00:24, Serial0/0/0
C    192.168.2.0/24 is directly connected, Serial0/0/0
C    192.168.3.0/24 is directly connected, FastEthernet0/0
C    192.168.4.0/24 is directly connected, Serial0/0/1
R    192.168.5.0/24 [120/1] via 192.168.4.1, 00:00:26, Serial0/0/1
R    192.168.6.0/24 [120/1] via 192.168.2.1, 00:00:24, Serial0/0/0
                     [120/1] via 192.168.4.1, 00:00:26, Serial0/0/1
R    192.168.7.0/24 [120/1] via 192.168.4.1, 00:00:26, Serial0/0/1
R    192.168.8.0/24 [120/2] via 192.168.4.1, 00:00:26, Serial0/0/1
```

Load Balancing

You now know that individual routing protocols use metrics to determine the best route to reach remote networks. But what happens when two or more routes to the same destination have identical metric values? How will the router decide which path to use for packet forwarding? In this case, the router does not choose only one route. Instead, the router *load-balances* between these equal-cost paths. The packets are forwarded using all equal-cost paths.

To see whether load balancing is in effect, check the routing table. Load balancing is in effect if two or more routes are associated with the same destination.

Note

Load balancing can be done either per packet or per destination. How a router actually load-balances packets between the equal-cost paths is governed by the switching process. The switching process will be discussed in greater detail in a later chapter.

Figure 3-9 shows an example of load balancing, assuming that R2 load-balances traffic to PC5 over two equal-cost paths.

Figure 3-9   Load Balancing Across Equal-Cost Paths

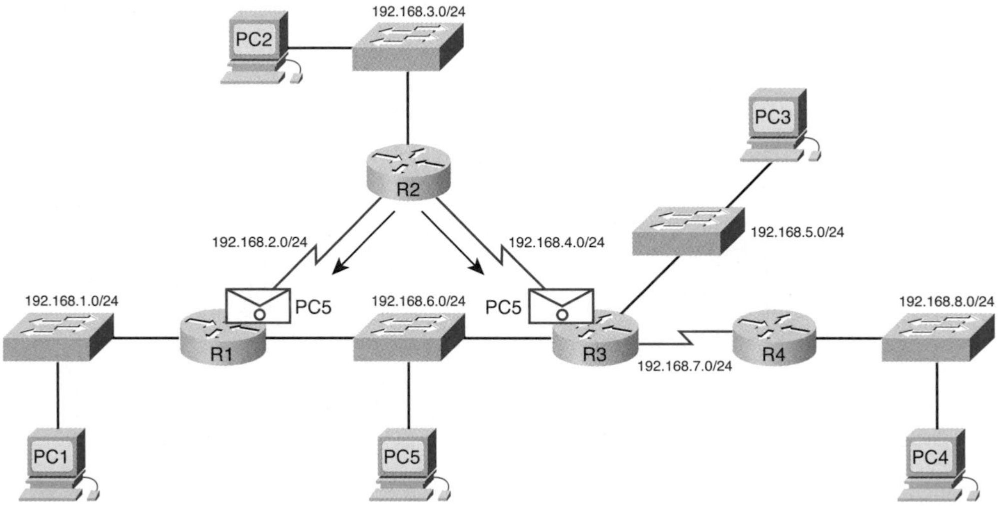

R2 load balances traffic destined for the 192.168.6.0/24 network.

The **show ip route** command in Example 3-1 reveals that the destination network 192.168.6.0 is available through 192.168.2.1 (Serial 0/0/0) and 192.168.4.1 (Serial 0/0/1). The equal-cost routes are shown again here:

```
R2# show ip route

<output omitted>
R    192.168.6.0/24 [120/1] via 192.168.2.1, 00:00:24, Serial0/0/0
                    [120/1] via 192.168.4.1, 00:00:26, Serial0/0/1
```

All the routing protocols discussed in this course are capable of automatically load-balancing traffic for up to four equal-cost routes by default. EIGRP is also capable of load-balancing across unequal-cost paths. This feature of EIGRP is discussed in the CCNP courses.

Administrative Distance

The following sections introduce the concept of administrative distance. Administrative distance will also be discussed within each chapter that focuses on a particular routing protocol.

Purpose of Administrative Distance

Before the routing process can determine which route to use when forwarding a packet, it must first determine which routes to include in the routing table. There can be times when a router learns a route to a remote network from more than one routing source. The routing process will need to determine which routing source to use. *Administrative distance* is used for this purpose.

Multiple Routing Sources

You know that routers learn about adjacent networks that are directly connected and about remote networks by using static routes and dynamic routing protocols. In fact, a router might learn of a route to the same network from more than one source. For example, a static route might have been configured for the same network/subnet mask that was learned dynamically by a dynamic routing protocol, such as RIP. The router must choose which route to install.

> **Note**
>
> You might be wondering about equal-cost paths. Multiple routes to the same network can only be installed when they come from the same routing source. For example, for equal-cost routes to be installed, they both must be static routes or they both must be RIP routes.

Although less common, more than one dynamic routing protocol can be deployed in the same network. In some situations, it might be necessary to route the same network address using multiple routing protocols such as RIP and OSPF. Because different routing protocols use different metrics—RIP uses hop count and OSPF uses bandwidth—it is not possible to compare metrics to determine the best path.

So, how does a router determine which route to install in the routing table when it has learned about the same network from more than one routing source? Cisco IOS makes the determination based on the administrative distance of the routing source.

Purpose of Administrative Distance

Administrative distance (AD) defines the preference of a routing source. Each routing source—including specific routing protocols, static routes, and even directly connected networks—is prioritized in order of most to least preferable using an administrative distance value. Cisco routers use the AD feature to select the best path when they learn about the same destination network from two or more different routing sources.

Administrative distance is an integer value from 0 to 255. The lower the value, the more preferred the route source. An administrative distance of 0 is the most preferred. Only a directly connected network has an administrative distance of 0, which cannot be changed.

Note

It is possible to modify the administrative distance for static routes and dynamic routing protocols. This is discussed in CCNP courses.

An administrative distance of 255 means the router will not believe the source of that route, and it will not be installed in the routing table.

Note

The term *trustworthiness* is commonly used when defining administrative distance. The lower the administrative distance value, the more trustworthy the route.

Figure 3-10 shows a topology with R2 running both EIGRP and RIP. R2 is running EIGRP with R1 and RIP with R3.

Figure 3-10 Comparing Administrative Distances

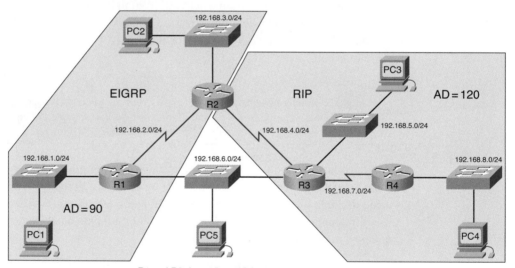

R1 and R3 do not "speak" the same routing protocol.

Example 3-2 displays the **show ip route** command output for R2.

```
Example 3-2  Routing Table for R2
R2# show ip route

<output omitted>

Gateway of last resort is not set

D    192.168.1.0/24 [90/2172416] via 192.168.2.1, 00:00:24, Serial0/0
C    192.168.2.0/24 is directly connected, Serial0/0/0
C    192.168.3.0/24 is directly connected, FastEthernet0/0
C    192.168.4.0/24 is directly connected, Serial0/0/1
R    192.168.5.0/24 [120/1] via 192.168.4.1, 00:00:08, Serial0/0/1
D    192.168.6.0/24 [90/2172416] via 192.168.2.1, 00:00:24, Serial0/0/0
R    192.168.7.0/24 [120/1] via 192.168.4.1, 00:00:08, Serial0/0/1
R    192.168.8.0/24 [120/2] via 192.168.4.1, 00:00:08, Serial0/0/1
```

The AD value is the first value in the brackets for a routing table entry. Notice that R2 has a route to the 192.168.6.0/24 network with an AD value of 90.

```
D    192.168.6.0/24 [90/2172416] via 192.168.2.1, 00:00:24, Serial0/0/0
```

R2 is running both RIP and EIGRP routing protocols. Remember, it is not common for routers to run multiple dynamic routing protocols, but is used here to demonstrate how administrative distance works. R2 has learned of the 192.168.6.0/24 route from R1 through EIGRP updates and from R3 through RIP updates. RIP has an administrative distance of 120, but EIGRP has a lower administrative distance of 90. So, R2 adds the route learned using EIGRP to the routing table and forwards all packets for the 192.168.6.0/24 network to Router R1.

What happens if the link to R1 becomes unavailable? Would R2 not have a route to 192.168.6.0? Actually, R2 still has RIP route information for 192.168.6.0 stored in the RIP database. This can be verified with the **show ip rip database** command, as shown in Example 3-3.

```
Example 3-3  Verifying RIP Route Availability
R2# show ip rip database

192.168.3.0/24    directly connected, FastEthernet0/0
192.168.4.0/24    directly connected, Serial0/0/1
```

```
192.168.5.0/24
    [1] via 192.168.4.1, Serial0/0/1
192.168.6.0/24
    [1] via 192.168.4.1, Serial0/0/1
192.168.7.0/24
    [1] via 192.168.4.1, Serial0/0/1
192.168.8.0/24
    [2] via 192.168.4.1, Serial0/0/1
```

The **show ip rip database** command shows all RIP routes learned by R2, whether or not the RIP route is installed in the routing table. Now you can answer the question as to what would happen if the EIGRP route to 192.168.6.0 became unavailable. RIP has a route, and it would be installed in the routing table. If the EIGRP route is later restored, the RIP route would be removed and the EIGRP route would be reinstalled because it has a better AD value.

Dynamic Routing Protocols and Administrative Distance

You already know that you can verify AD values with the **show ip route** command, as shown previously in Example 3-2.

Example 3-4 shows that the AD value can also be verified with the **show ip protocols** command. This command displays all pertinent information about routing protocols operating on the router.

Example 3-4 Verify Administrative Distance with the **show ip protocols** Command

```
R2# show ip protocols

Routing Protocol is "eigrp  100 "
  Outgoing update filter list for all interfaces is not set
  Incoming update filter list for all interfaces is not set
  Default networks flagged in outgoing updates
  Default networks accepted from incoming updates
  EIGRP metric weight K1=1, K2=0, K3=1, K4=0, K5=0
  EIGRP maximum hopcount 100
  EIGRP maximum metric variance 1
  Redistributing: eigrp 100
  Automatic network summarization is in effect
```

```
    Automatic address summarization:
    Maximum path: 4
    Routing for Networks:
        192.168.2.0
        192.168.3.0
        192.168.4.0
    Routing Information Sources:
      Gateway          Distance       Last Update
      192.168.2.1       90             2366569
    Distance: internal 90 external 170

Routing Protocol is "rip"
  Sending updates every 30 seconds, next due in 12 seconds
  Invalid after 180 seconds, hold down 180, flushed after 240
  Outgoing update filter list for all interfaces is not set
  Incoming update filter list for all interfaces is not set
  Redistributing: rip
  Default version control: send version 1, receive any version
    Interface              Send  Recv  Triggered RIP  Key-chain
    Serial0/0/1             1     2 1
    FastEthernet0/0         1     2 1
  Automatic network summarization is in effect
  Maximum path: 4
  Routing for Networks:
      192.168.3.0
      192.168.4.0
Passive Interface(s):
Routing Information Sources:
    Gateway          Distance       Last Update
    192.168.4.1         120           
Distance: (default is 120)
```

You will see additional coverage of the **show ip protocols** command many times during the rest of the course. However, for now, notice the highlighted output: R2 has two routing protocols listed, and the AD value is called Distance.

Table 3-2 shows the different administrative distance values for various routing protocols.

Table 3-2   Default Administrative Distances

Route Source	AD
Connected	0
Static	1
EIGRP summary route	5
External BGP	20
Internal EIGRP	90
IGRP	100
OSPF	110
IS-IS	115
RIP	120
External EIGRP	170
Internal BGP	200

Static Routes and Administrative Distance

As you know from Chapter 2, static routes are entered by an administrator who wants to manually configure the best path to the destination. For that reason, static routes have a default AD value of 1. This means that after directly connected networks, which have a default AD value of 0, static routes are the most preferred route source.

There are situations when an administrator will configure a static route to the same destination that is learned using a dynamic routing protocol, but using a different path. The static route will be configured with an AD greater than that of the routing protocol. If there is a link failure in the path used by the dynamic routing protocol, the route entered by the routing protocol is removed from the routing table. The static route will then become the only source and will automatically be added to the routing table. This is known as a *floating static route* and is discussed in CCNP courses.

A static route using either a next-hop IP address or an exit interface has a default AD value of 1. However, the AD value is not listed in the **show ip route** output when you configure a static route with the exit interface specified. When a static route is configured with an exit interface, the output shows the network as directly connected through that interface.

Using the topology shown in Figure 3-11 and the **show ip route** command for R2 shown in Example 3-5, you can examine the two types of static routes.

Figure 3-11   Administrative Distances and Static Routes

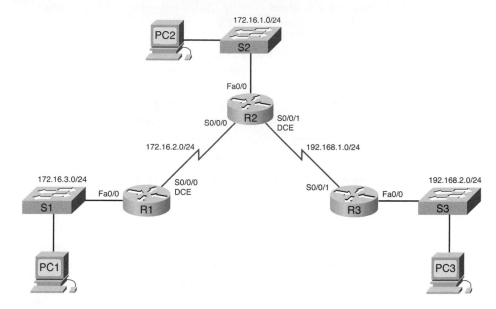

```
Example 3-5  Routing Table for R2
R2# show ip route

<output omitted>

Gateway of last resort is not set

     172.16.0.0/24 is subnetted, 3 subnets
C       172.16.1.0 is directly connected, FastEthernet0/0
C       172.16.2.0 is directly connected, Serial0/0/0
S       172.16.3.0 is directly connected, Serial0/0/0
C    192.168.1.0/24 is directly connected, Serial0/0/1
S    192.168.2.0/24 [1/0] via 192.168.1.1
```

The static route to 172.16.3.0 is listed as directly connected. However, there is no information on what the AD value is. It is a common misconception to assume that the AD value of this route must be 0 because it states "directly connected." However, that is a false assumption. The default AD of any static route, including those configured with an exit interface, is 1. Remember, only a directly connected network can have an AD of 0. This can be verified by extending the **show ip route** command with the [*route*] option. Specifying the [*route*] reveals detailed information about the route, including its distance, or AD value.

The **show ip route 172.16.3.0** command in Example 3-6 reveals that, in fact, the administrative distance for static routes—even with the exit interface specified—is 1.

Example 3-6 show ip route Command with the [*route*] Option

```
R2# show ip route 172.16.3.0

Routing entry for 172.16.3.0/24
Known via "static", distance 1, metric 0 (connected)
  Routing Descriptor Blocks:
  * directly connected, via Serial0/0/0
      Route metric is 0, traffic share count is 1
```

Directly Connected Networks and Administrative Distance

Directly connected networks appear in the routing table as soon as the IP address on the interface is configured and the interface is enabled and operational. The AD value of directly connected networks is 0, meaning that this is the most preferred routing source. There is no better route for a router than having one of its interfaces directly connected to that network. For that reason, the administrative distance of a directly connected network cannot be changed, and no other route source can have an administrative distance of 0.

The output of the **show ip route** command in Example 3-7 highlights the directly connected networks with no information about the AD value.

Example 3-7 Directly Connected Networks in Routing Table Do Not Show AD Value

```
R2# show ip route

Codes: C - connected, S - static, I - IGRP, R - RIP, M - mobile, B - BGP
       D - EIGRP, EX - EIGRP external, O - OSPF, IA - OSPF inter area
       N1 - OSPF NSSA external type 1, N2 - OSPF NSSA external type 2
       E1 - OSPF external type 1, E2 - OSPF external type 2, E - EGP
       i - IS-IS, L1 - IS-IS level-1, L2 - IS-IS level-2, ia - IS-IS inter area
       * - candidate default, U - per-user static route, o - ODR
       P - periodic downloaded static route

Gateway of last resort is not set

     172.16.0.0/24 is subnetted, 3 subnets
C       172.16.1.0 is directly connected, FastEthernet0/0
C       172.16.2.0 is directly connected, Serial0/0/0
S       172.16.3.0 is directly connected, Serial0/0/0
C    192.168.1.0/24 is directly connected, Serial0/0/1
S    192.168.2.0/24 [1/0] via 192.168.1.1
```

The output is similar to the output for static routes that point to an exit interface. The only difference is the letter C at the beginning of the entry, which indicates that this is a directly connected network.

To see the AD value of a directly connected network, use the [*route*] option, as shown in Example 3-8.

Example 3-8 Directly Connected Route with AD Value Shown

```
R2# show ip route 172.16.3.0

Routing entry for 172.16.1.0/24
Known via "connected", distance 0, metric 0 (connected, via interface)
  Routing Descriptor Blocks:
  * directly connected, via FastEthernet0/0
      Route metric is 0, traffic share count is 1
```

The **show ip route 172.16.1.0** command reveals that the distance is 0 for that directly connected route.

Viewing Routing Table Information—show ip route (3.4.4)

In this activity, you will use a version of the **show ip route** command to see details of routing table entries. Use file e2-344.pka on the CD-ROM that accompanies this book to perform this activity using Packet Tracer.

Packet Tracer
☐ Activity

Summary

Dynamic routing protocols are used by routers to automatically learn about remote networks from other routers. In this chapter, you were introduced to several different dynamic routing protocols.

You learned the following about routing protocols:

- They can be classified as classful or classless.

- They can be a distance vector, link-state, or path vector type.

- They can be an interior gateway protocol or an exterior gateway protocol.

The differences in these classifications will become better understood as you learn more about these routing concepts and protocols in later chapters.

Routing protocols not only discover remote networks but also have a procedure for maintaining accurate network information. When there is a change in the topology, it is the function of the routing protocol to inform other routers about this change. When there is a change in the network topology, some routing protocols can propagate that information throughout the routing domain faster than other routing protocols.

The process of bringing all routing tables to a state of consistency is called convergence. Convergence is when all the routers in the same routing domain or area have complete and accurate information about the network.

Metrics are used by routing protocols to determine the best path or shortest path to reach a destination network. Different routing protocols can use different metrics. Typically, a lower metric means a better path. Five hops to reach a network is better than ten hops.

Routers sometimes learn about multiple routes to the same network from both static routes and dynamic routing protocols. When a Cisco router learns about a destination network from more than one routing source, it uses the administrative distance value to determine which source to use. Each dynamic routing protocol has a unique administrative value, along with static routes and directly connected networks. The lower the administrative value, the more preferred the route source. A directly connected network is always the preferred source, followed by static routes and then various dynamic routing protocols.

All the classifications and concepts in this chapter will be discussed more thoroughly in the rest of the chapters of this course. At the end of this course, you might want to review this chapter to get a review and overview of this information.

Activities and Labs

The activities and labs available in the companion *Routing Protocols and Concepts, CCNA Exploration Labs and Study Guide* (ISBN 1-58713-204-4) provide hands-on practice with the following topics introduced in this chapter:

Activity 3-1: Subnetting Scenario 1 (3.5.2)

In this activity, you have been given the network address 192.168.9.0/24 to subnet and provide the IP addressing for the network shown in the topology diagram.

Activity 3-2: Subnetting Scenario 2 (3.5.3)

In this activity, you have been given the network address 172.16.0.0/16 to subnet and provide the IP addressing for the network shown in the topology diagram.

Activity 3-3: Subnetting Scenario 3 (3.5.4)

In this activity, you have been given the network address 192.168.1.0/24 to subnet and provide the IP addressing for the network shown in the topology diagram.

Many of the hands-on labs include Packet Tracer Companion Activities, where you can use Packet Tracer to complete a simulation of the lab. Look for this icon in *Routing Protocols and Concepts, CCNA Exploration Labs and Study Guide* (ISBN 1-58713-204-4) for hands-on labs that have a Packet Tracer Companion.

Check Your Understanding

Complete all the review questions listed here to test your understanding of the topics and concepts in this chapter. Answers are listed in the appendix, "Check Your Understanding and Challenge Questions Answer Key."

1. What are two advantages of static routing over dynamic routing?

   A. The configuration is less error prone.

   B. Static routing is more secure because routers do not advertise routes.

   C. Growing the network usually does not present a problem.

   D. No computing overhead is involved.

   E. The administrator has less work maintaining the configuration.

2. Match the description to the proper routing protocol.

Routing protocols:

RIP

IGRP

OSPF

EIGRP

BGP

Description:

A. Path vector exterior routing protocol:

B. Cisco advanced interior routing protocol:

C. Link-state interior routing protocol:

D. Distance vector interior routing protocol:

E. Cisco distance vector interior routing protocol:

3. Which statement best describes convergence on a network?

A. The amount of time required for routers to share administrative configuration changes, such a password changes, from one end of a network to the other end

B. The time required for the routers in the network to update their routing tables after a topology change has occurred

C. The time required for the routers in one autonomous system to learn routes to destinations in another autonomous system

D. The time required for routers running disparate routing protocols to update their routing tables

4. Which of the following parameters are used to calculate metrics? (Choose two.)

A. Hop count

B. Uptime

C. Bandwidth

D. Convergence time

E. Administrative distance

5. Which routing protocol has the most trustworthy administrative distance by default?

A. EIGRP internal routes

B. IS-IS

C. OSPF

D. RIPv1

E. RIPv2

6. How many equal-cost paths can a dynamic routing protocol use for load balancing by default?

   A. 2

   B. 3

   C. 4

   D. 6

7. Which command will show the administrative distance of routes?

   A. R1# **show interfaces**

   B. R1# **show ip route**

   C. R1# **show ip interfaces**

   D. R1# **debug ip routing**

8. When do directly connected networks appear in the routing table?

   A. When they are included in a static route

   B. When they are used as an exit interface

   C. As soon as they are addressed and operational at Layer 2

   D. As soon as they are addressed and operational at Layer 3

   E. Always when a **no shutdown** command is issued

9. Router R1 is using the RIPv2 routing protocol and has discovered multiple unequal paths to reach a destination network. How will Router R1 determine which path is the best path to the destination network?

   A. Lowest metric.

   B. Highest metric.

   C. Lowest administrative distance.

   D. Highest administrative distance.

   E. It will load-balance between up to four paths.

10. Enter the proper administrative distance for each routing protocol.

   A. eBGP:

   B. EIGRP (Internal):

   C. EIGRP (External):

   D. IS-IS:

   E. OSPF:

   F. RIP:

11. Designate the following characteristics as belonging to either a classful routing protocol or a classless routing protocol.

A. Does not support discontiguous networks:

B. EIGRP, OSPF, and BGP:

C. Sends subnet mask in its routing updates:

D. Supports discontiguous networks:

E. RIP version 1 and IGRP:

F. Does not send subnet mask in its routing updates:

12. Explain why static routing might be preferred over dynamic routing.

13. What are four ways of classifying dynamic routing protocols?

14. What are the most common metrics used in IP dynamic routing protocols?

15. What is administrative distance, and why is it important?

Challenge Questions and Activities

These questions require a deeper application of the concepts covered in this chapter and are
similar to the style of questions you might see on a CCNA certification exam. You can find
the answers to these questions in the appendix, "Answers to Check Your Understanding and
Challenge Questions and Activities."

1. It can be said that every router must have at least one static route. Explain why this
statement might be true.

2. Students new to routing sometimes assume that bandwidth is a better metric than hop
count. Why might this be a false assumption?

To Learn More

Border Gateway Protocol (BGP) is an inter-autonomous routing protocol—the routing protocol of the Internet. Although BGP is only briefly discussed in this course (it is discussed
more fully in CCNP), you might find it interesting to view routing tables of some of the
Internet core routers.

Route servers are used to view BGP routes on the Internet. Various websites provide access
to these route servers, for example, http://www.traceroute.org. When choosing a route server in a specific autonomous system, you will start a Telnet session on that route server. This
server is mirroring an Internet core router, which is most often a Cisco router.

You can then use the **show ip route** command to view the actual routing table of an Internet router. Use the **show ip route** command followed by the public or global network address of your school, for example, **show ip route 207.62.187.0**.

You will not be able to understand much of the information in this output, but these commands should give you a sense of the size of a routing table on a core Internet router.

Distance Vector Routing Protocols

Objectives

Upon completion of this chapter, you should be able to answer the following questions:

- Can you identify the characteristics of distance vector routing protocols?

- What is the network discovery process of distance vector routing protocols using Routing Information Protocol (RIP)?

- What are the processes for maintaining accurate routing tables that are used by distance vector routing protocols?

- What are the conditions leading to a routing loop, and can you explain the implications for router performance?

- Which types of distance vector routing protocols are in use today?

Key Terms

This chapter uses the following key terms. You can find the definitions in the Glossary at the end of the book.

The dynamic routing protocol chapters of this book focus on interior gateway protocols (IGP). As discussed in Chapter 3, "Introduction to Dynamic Routing Protocols," IGPs are classified as either distance vector or link-state routing protocols.

Figure 4-1 shows a chart of the most common IP routing protocols used today. Those that are highlighted will be discussed in this book.

Figure 4-1   Dynamic Routing Protocols

| | Interior Gateway Protocols | | | | Exterior Gateway Protocols |
	Distance Vector Routing Protocols		Link State Routing Protocols		Path Vector
Classful	RIP	IGRP			EGP
Classless	RIPv2	EIGRP	OSPFv2	IS-IS	BGPv4
IPv6	RIPng	EIGRP for IPv6	OSPFv3	IS-IS for IPv6	BGPv4 for IPv6

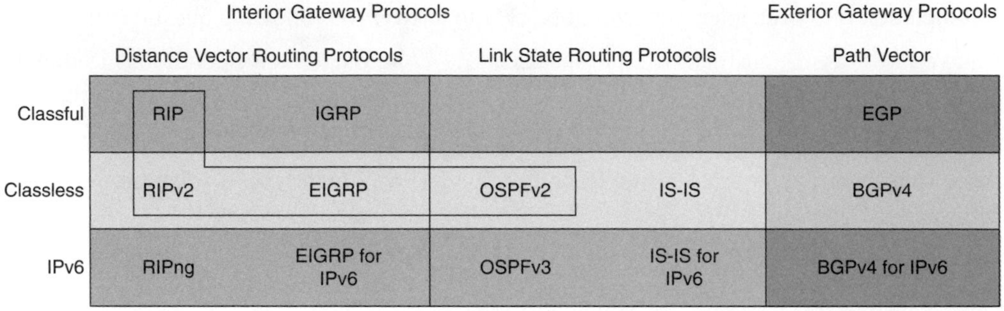

This chapter describes the characteristics, operations, and functionality of distance vector routing protocols. There are advantages and disadvantages to using any type of routing protocol. This chapter covers the operations of distance vector protocols, some of their inherent pitfalls, and the remedies to these pitfalls. Understanding the operation of distance vector routing is critical to enabling, verifying, and troubleshooting these protocols.

Introduction to Distance Vector Routing Protocols

One way to characterize routing protocols is by the type of routing algorithm they use to build and maintain their routing table. By doing this, routing protocols can be differentiated as a distance vector, link-state, or path vector routing protocol. This chapter will introduce you to the characteristics of a distance vector routing protocol. Chapter 10, "Link-State Routing Protocols," will introduce you to link-state routing protocols. Path vector routing protocols are beyond the scope of this book and are discussed in CCNP.

Figure 4-2 shows a network with a moderate number of routers and links.

Figure 4-2   Network That Would Use Dynamic Routing

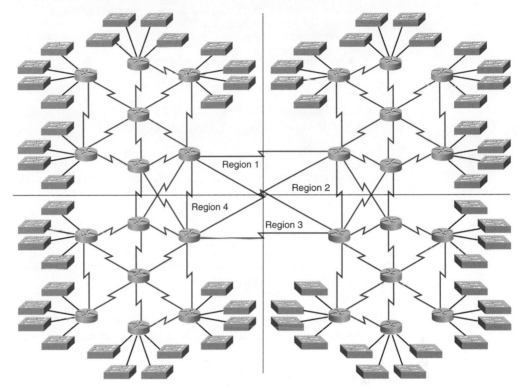

Dynamic routing protocols help the network administrator overcome the time-consuming and exacting process of configuring and maintaining static routes. For example, can you imagine maintaining the static routing configurations of the 28 routers shown in Figure 4-2? What happens when a link goes down? What happens when that link goes down at 3:00 a.m.? How do you ensure that redundant paths are available 24 hours a day, 7 days a week? Dynamic routing is the most common choice for large networks like the one shown.

Distance vector routing protocols include the following:

- **RIP:** Routing Information Protocol (RIP) was originally specified in RFC 1058. It has the following key characteristics:
  - Hop count is used as the metric for path selection.
  - If the hop count for a network is greater than 15, RIP cannot supply a route to that network.
  - Routing updates are broadcast or multicast every 30 seconds, by default.

- **IGRP:** Interior Gateway Routing Protocol (IGRP) is a proprietary protocol developed by Cisco. IGRP has the following key design characteristics:

  - Bandwidth, delay, load, and reliability are used to create a composite metric.

  - Routing updates are broadcast every 90 seconds, by default.

  - IGRP is the predecessor of EIGRP and is now obsolete.

- **EIGRP:** Enhanced IGRP (EIGRP) is a Cisco-proprietary distance vector routing protocol. EIGRP has these key characteristics:

  - It can perform unequal-cost load balancing.

  - It uses *Diffusing Update Algorithm (DUAL)* to calculate the shortest path.

  - There are no periodic updates as with RIP and IGRP. Routing updates are sent only when there is a change in the topology.

Note

There are no RFCs for IGRP or EIGRP, because Cisco never submitted these routing protocols to the Internet Engineering Task Force (IETF) for comments.

RIP and EIGRP will be discussed in more detail in later chapters. IGRP is not discussed and is considered obsolete. IGRP will be referred to for comparison purposes only.

Distance Vector Technology

Distance vector technology is one way to characterize routing protocols based on the type of routing algorithm they use to build and maintain their routing table. The other two methods are link-state and path vector.

Meaning of Distance Vector

As the name implies, distance vector means that routes are advertised as vectors of distance and direction. Distance is defined in terms of a metric, such as hop count, and direction is simply the next-hop router or exit interface.

A router using a distance vector routing protocol does not have the knowledge of the entire path to a destination network. Instead the router knows only

- The direction in which or interface to which packets should be forwarded

- The distance to the destination network

For example, in Figure 4-3, R1 knows that the distance to reach network 172.16.3.0/24 is one hop and that the direction is out interface S0/0/0 toward R2.

Figure 4-3   Meaning of Distance Vector

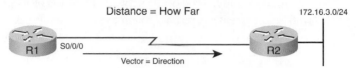

For R1, 172.16.3.0/24 is one hop away (distance).
It can be reached through S0/0/0 (vector).

Operation of Distance Vector Routing Protocols

Some distance vector routing protocols call for the router to periodically broadcast the entire routing table to each of its neighbors. This method is inefficient because the updates not only consume bandwidth but also consume router CPU resources to process the updates.

Distance vector routing protocols share certain characteristics. Periodic updates are sent at regular intervals (30 seconds for RIP and 90 seconds for IGRP). Even if the topology has not changed in several days, periodic updates continue to be sent to all neighbors.

Figure 4-4 shows an example of a periodic update. The routing protocol for each router maintains a local timer. When that timer expires, a routing update is sent. In the figure, the timer for R1 has expired. When the local timer on each of the other routers reaches 0, it will also send its respective periodic updates. These periodic updates are entries from all or part of the routing table. This will be examined more thoroughly in Chapter 5, "RIP Version 1."

Figure 4-4   Distance Vector Periodic Updates

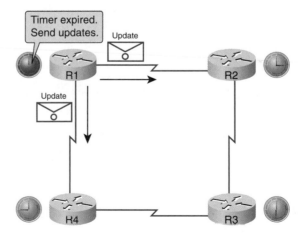

Neighbors are routers that share a link and are configured to use the same routing protocol. The router is only aware of the network addresses of its own interfaces and the remote network addresses it can reach through its neighbors. It has no broader knowledge of the network topology. Routers using distance vector routing are not aware of the network topology.

Broadcast updates are sent to 255.255.255.255. Neighboring routers that are configured with the same routing protocol will process the updates. Other devices such as host computers will also process the update up to Layer 3 before discarding it. Some distance vector routing protocols use multicast addresses instead of broadcast addresses.

Entire routing table updates are sent, with some exceptions to be discussed later, periodically to all neighbors. Neighbors receiving these updates must process the entire update to find pertinent information and discard the rest. Some distance vector routing protocols like EIGRP do not send periodic routing table updates.

Routing Protocol Algorithms

Remember that an algorithm is a rule or process for arriving at a solution to a problem. In networking, algorithms are commonly used to determine the best route to forward traffic to a particular destination. The algorithm used by a particular routing protocol is responsible for building and maintaining the router's routing table.

At the core of the distance vector protocol is the algorithm, which is used to calculate the best paths. Routers then send this information to neighboring routers.

An algorithm is a procedure for accomplishing a certain task, starting at a given initial state and terminating in a defined end state. Different routing protocols use different algorithms and processes to install routes in the routing table, send updates to neighbors, and make path determination decisions.

The algorithm used for the routing protocols defines the following processes:

- Mechanism for sending and receiving routing information

- Mechanism for calculating the best paths and installing routes in the routing table

- Mechanism for detecting and reacting to topology changes

In Figure 4-5, R1 and R2 are configured with RIP. The algorithm sends and receives updates.

Both R1 and R2 then glean new information from the update. In this case, each router learns about a new network, as shown in Figure 4-6. The new networks are highlighted.

The algorithm on each router makes its calculations independently and updates the routing table with the new information.

Figure 4-7 illustrates what happens when there is a topology change. When the LAN on R2 goes down, the algorithm constructs a "triggered" update and sends it to R1. R1 then removes the network from the routing table. Triggered updates will be discussed later in this chapter.

Figure 4-5   Sending and Receiving Updates

172.16.1.0/24   172.16.2.0/24   172.16.3.0/24

Network	Interface	Hop
172.16.1.0/24	Fa0/0	0
172.16.2.0/24	S0/0/0	0

Network	Interface	Hop
172.16.2.0/24	S0/0/0	0
172.16.3.0/24	Fa0/0	0

Figure 4-6   Calculating the Best Path and Installing Routes

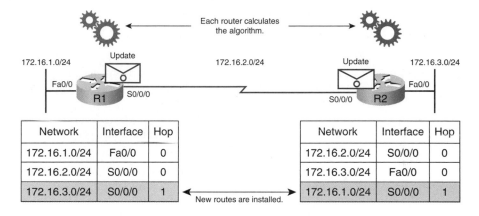

Network	Interface	Hop
172.16.1.0/24	Fa0/0	0
172.16.2.0/24	S0/0/0	0
172.16.3.0/24	S0/0/0	1

Network	Interface	Hop
172.16.2.0/24	S0/0/0	0
172.16.3.0/24	Fa0/0	0
172.16.1.0/24	S0/0/0	1

Figure 4-7   Detecting and Reacting to Topology Changes

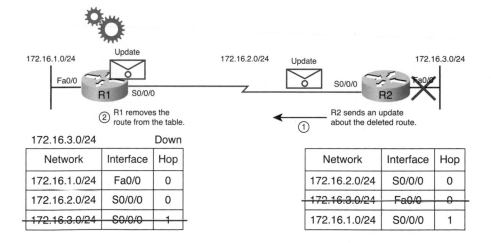

172.16.3.0/24   Down

Network	Interface	Hop
172.16.1.0/24	Fa0/0	0
172.16.2.0/24	S0/0/0	0
~~172.16.3.0/24~~	~~S0/0/0~~	~~1~~

Network	Interface	Hop
172.16.2.0/24	S0/0/0	0
~~172.16.3.0/24~~	~~Fa0/0~~	~~0~~
172.16.1.0/24	S0/0/0	1

Routing Protocol Characteristics

There are several ways to differentiate routing protocols. The chart in Figure 4-1 shows some of the ways to characterize these routing protocols. Another way to compare routing protocols is by using other characteristics such as time to convergence and scalability.

Routing protocols can be compared based on the following characteristics:

- **Time to convergence:** Time to convergence defines how quickly the routers in the network topology share routing information and reach a state of consistent knowledge. The faster the convergence, the more preferable the protocol. Routing loops can occur when inconsistent routing tables are not updated because of slow convergence in a changing network.

- **Scalability:** Scalability defines how large a network can become based on the routing protocol that is deployed. The larger the network is, the more scalable the routing protocol needs to be.

- **Classless (use of VLSM) or classful:** Classless routing protocols include the subnet mask in the updates. This feature supports the use of variable-length subnet masking (VLSM) and better route summarization. Classful routing protocols do not include the subnet mask and cannot support VLSM.

- **Resource usage:** Resource usage includes the requirements of a routing protocol such as memory space, CPU utilization, and link bandwidth utilization. Higher resource requirements necessitate more powerful hardware to support the routing protocol operation in addition to the packet-forwarding processes.

- **Implementation and maintenance:** Implementation and maintenance describe the level of knowledge that is required for a network administrator to implement and maintain the network based on the routing protocol deployed.

Table 4-1 outlines the advantages and disadvantages of distance vector routing protocols.

Table 4-1   Advantages and Disadvantages of Distance Vector Routing Protocols

Advantages	Disadvantages
Simple implementation and maintenance. The level of knowledge required to deploy and later maintain a network with distance vector protocols is not high.	Slow convergence. The use of periodic updates can cause slower convergence. Even if some advanced techniques are used, like triggered updates which are discussed later, the overall convergence is still slower compared to link-state routing protocols.

Advantages	Disadvantages
Low resource requirements. Distance vector protocols typically do not need large amounts of memory to store the information, nor do they require a powerful CPU.	Limited scalability. Slow convergence can limit the size of the network because larger networks require more time to propagate routing information.
Depending on the network size and the IP addressing implemented, distance vector protocols typically do not require a high level of link bandwidth to send routing updates. However, this can become an issue if you deploy a distance vector protocol in a large network.	Routing loops. Routing loops can occur when inconsistent routing tables are not updated because of slow convergence in a changing network.

Comparing Routing Protocol Features

In Table 4-2, all the routing protocols discussed in the course are compared based on these characteristics. Although IGRP is no longer supported by Cisco IOS Software, it is shown here to compare it with EIGRP. Also, although the Intermediate System–to–Intermediate System (IS-IS) routing protocol is covered in the CCNP courses, it is shown here because it is a commonly used interior gateway protocol.

Table 4-2   Comparing Routing Protocol Features

	Distance Vector				Link-State	
	RIPv1	**RIPv2**	**IGRP**	**EIGRP**	**OSPF**	**IS-IS**
Speed of Convergence	Slow	Slow	Slow	Fast	Fast	Fast
Scalability— Size of Network	Small	Small	Small	Large	Large	Large
Use of VLSM	No	Yes	No	Yes	Yes	Yes
Resource Usage	Low	Low	Low	Medium	High	High
Implementation and Maintenance	Simple	Simple	Simple	Complex	Complex	Complex

Network Discovery

Network discovery is part of the process of the routing protocol algorithm that enables routers to first learn about remote networks.

Cold Start

When a router cold-starts or powers up, it knows nothing about the network topology. It does not even know that there are devices on the other end of its links. The only information that a router has is from its own saved configuration file stored in NVRAM. After a router boots successfully, it applies the saved configuration. As described in Chapter 1, "Introduction to Routing and Packet Forwarding," and Chapter 2, "Static Routing," if the IP addressing is configured correctly and active, the router will initially discover its own directly connected networks.

After a cold start and before the exchange of routing information, the routers initially discover their own directly connected networks and subnet masks. As shown in Figure 4-8, this information is added to their routing tables:

- **R1:**

    - 10.1.0.0 available through interface FastEthernet 0/0

    - 10.2.0.0 available through interface Serial 0/0/0

- **R2:**

    - 10.2.0.0 available through interface Serial 0/0/0

    - 10.3.0.0 available through interface Serial 0/0/1

- **R3:**

    - 10.3.0.0 available through interface Serial 0/0/0

    - 10.4.0.0 available through interface FastEthernet 0/0

Figure 4-8   Network Discovery: Cold Start

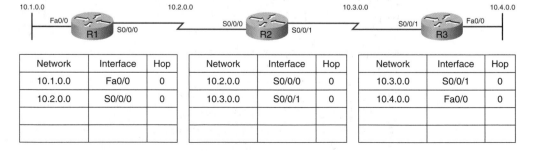

Network	Interface	Hop
10.1.0.0	Fa0/0	0
10.2.0.0	S0/0/0	0

Network	Interface	Hop
10.2.0.0	S0/0/0	0
10.3.0.0	S0/0/1	0

Network	Interface	Hop
10.3.0.0	S0/0/1	0
10.4.0.0	Fa0/0	0

With this initial information, the routers start to exchange routing information.

Initial Exchange of Routing Information

If a routing protocol is configured, the routers begin exchanging routing updates, as shown in Figure 4-9. Initially, these updates include information only about their directly connected networks. Upon receiving an update, the router checks it for new information. Any routes that are not currently in its routing table are added.

Figure 4-9   Network Discovery: Initial Exchange of Routing Updates

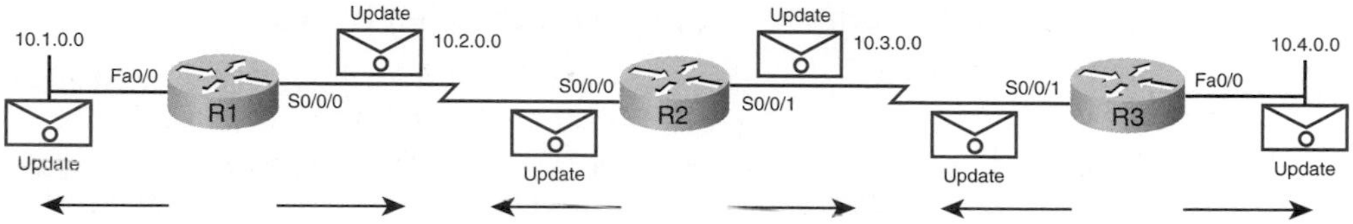

Network	Interface	Hop
10.1.0.0	Fa0/0	0
10.2.0.0	S0/0/0	0

Network	Interface	Hop
10.2.0.0	S0/0/0	0
10.3.0.0	S0/0/1	0

Network	Interface	Hop
10.3.0.0	S0/0/1	0
10.4.0.0	Fa0/0	0

In Figure 4-9, Routers R1, R2, and R3 start their initial exchange. All three routers send their routing tables to their neighbors, which at this point only contain the directly connected networks.

Each router processes updates in the following manner:

- **R1:**

    - Sends an update about network 10.1.0.0 out the Serial 0/0/0 interface with a metric of 1

    - Sends an update about network 10.2.0.0 out the FastEthernet 0/0 interface with a metric of 1

    - Receives an update from R2 about network 10.3.0.0 on Serial 0/0/0 with a metric of 1

    - Stores network 10.3.0.0 in the routing table with a metric of 1

- **R2:**

    - Sends an update about network 10.3.0.0 out the Serial 0/0/0 interface with a metric of 1

    - Sends an update about network 10.2.0.0 out the Serial 0/0/1 interface with a metric of 1

■ Receives an update from R1 about network 10.1.0.0 on Serial 0/0/0 with a metric of 1

■ Stores network 10.1.0.0 in the routing table with a metric of 1

■ Receives an update from R3 about network 10.4.0.0 on Serial 0/0/1 with a metric of 1

■ Stores network 10.4.0.0 in the routing table with a metric of 1

■ **R3:**

■ Sends an update about network 10.4.0.0 out the Serial 0/0/1 interface with a metric of 1

■ Sends an update about network 10.4.0.0 out the FastEthernet 0/0 interface with a metric of 1

■ Receives an update from R2 about network 10.2.0.0 on Serial 0/0/1 with a metric of 1

■ Stores network 10.2.0.0 in the routing table with a metric of 1

As shown in Figure 4-10, after this first round of update exchanges, each router knows about the connected networks of its directly connected neighbors.

Figure 4-10   Network Discovery: Updated Tables After Initial Exchange

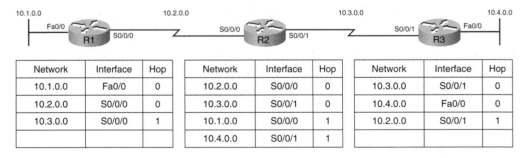

Network	Interface	Hop
10.1.0.0	Fa0/0	0
10.2.0.0	S0/0/0	0
10.3.0.0	S0/0/0	1

Network	Interface	Hop
10.2.0.0	S0/0/0	0
10.3.0.0	S0/0/1	0
10.1.0.0	S0/0/0	1
10.4.0.0	S0/0/1	1

Network	Interface	Hop
10.3.0.0	S0/0/1	0
10.4.0.0	Fa0/0	0
10.2.0.0	S0/0/1	1

However, did you notice that R1 does not yet know about 10.4.0.0 and that R3 does not yet know about 10.1.0.0? Full knowledge and a converged network will not take place until there is another exchange of routing information.

Exchange of Routing Information

At this point, the routers have knowledge about their own directly connected networks and about the connected networks of their immediate neighbors. Continuing the journey toward convergence, the routers exchange the next round of periodic updates. Each router again checks the updates for new information.

In Figure 4-11, R1, R2, and R3 send their latest routing tables to their neighbors.

Figure 4-11 Network Discovery—Next Update

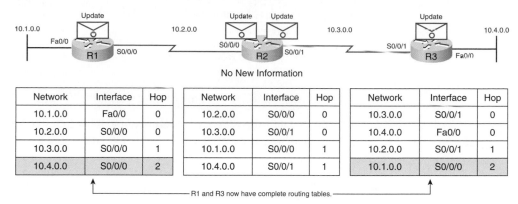

Network	Interface	Hop
10.1.0.0	Fa0/0	0
10.2.0.0	S0/0/0	0
10.3.0.0	S0/0/0	1
10.4.0.0	S0/0/0	2

Network	Interface	Hop
10.2.0.0	S0/0/0	0
10.3.0.0	S0/0/1	0
10.1.0.0	S0/0/0	1
10.4.0.0	S0/0/1	1

Network	Interface	Hop
10.3.0.0	S0/0/1	0
10.4.0.0	Fa0/0	0
10.2.0.0	S0/0/1	1
10.1.0.0	S0/0/0	2

R1 and R3 now have complete routing tables.

Each router processes updates in the following manner:

- **R1:**

    - Sends an update about network 10.1.0.0 out the Serial 0/0/0 interface with a metric of 1.

    - Sends an update about networks 10.2.0.0 with a metric of 1 and 10.3.0.0 with a metric of 2 out the FastEthernet 0/0 interface.

    - Receives an update from R2 about network 10.4.0.0 on Serial 0/0/0 with a metric of 2.

    - Stores network 10.4.0.0 in the routing table with a metric of 2.

    - Same update from R2 contains information about network 10.3.0.0 on Serial 0/0/0 with a metric of 1. There is no change; therefore, the routing information remains the same.

- **R2:**

    - Sends an update about networks 10.3.0.0 with a metric of 1 and 10.4.0.0 with a metric of 2 out the Serial 0/0/0 interface.

    - Sends an update about networks 10.1.0.0 with a metric of 2 and 10.2.0.0 with a metric of 1 out the Serial 0/0/1 interface.

    - Receives an update from R1 about network 10.1.0.0 on Serial 0/0/0. There is no change; therefore, the routing information remains the same.

    - Receives an update from R3 about network 10.4.0.0 on Serial 0/0/1. There is no change; therefore, the routing information remains the same.

- **R3:**

  - Sends an update about network 10.4.0.0 out the Serial0/0/1 interface.

  - Sends an update about networks 10.2.0.0 with a metric of 2 and 10.3.0.0 with a metric of 1 out the FastEthernet 0/0 interface.

  - Receives an update from R2 about network 10.1.0.0 on Serial 0/0/1 with a metric of 2.

  - Stores network 10.1.0.0 in the routing table with a metric of 2.

  - Same update from R2 contains information about network 10.2.0.0 on Serial 0/0/1 with a metric of 1. There is no change; therefore, the routing information remains the same.

Note

Distance vector routing protocols typically implement a technique known as *split horizon*. Split horizon prevents information from being sent out the same interface from which it was received. For example, R2 would not send an update out Serial 0/0/0 containing the network 10.1.0.0 because R2 learned about that network through Serial 0/0/0. This mechanism will be explained in more detail later in this chapter.

Convergence

The amount of time it takes for a network to converge is directly proportional to the size of that network. In Figure 4-12, a branch router in Region 4 (B2-R4) cold-starts and sends out an update with information about its four directly connected LANs.

The shaded areas in the figure show the propagation of new routing information as updates are sent between neighboring routers. It takes five rounds of periodic update intervals before most of the branch routers in regions 1, 2, and 3 learn about the new routes advertised by B2-R4. Routing protocols are compared based on how fast they can propagate this information—their speed to convergence.

The speed of achieving convergence consists of

- How quickly the routers propagate a change in the topology in a routing update to their neighbors

- The speed of calculating best-path routes using the new routing information collected

A network is not completely operable until it has converged. Therefore, network administrators prefer routing protocols with shorter convergence times.

Figure 4-12   Convergence Time

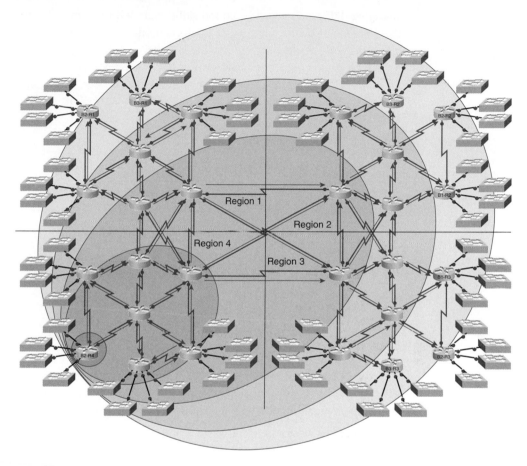

Routing Table Maintenance

After the routers have initially learned about remote networks, routing protocols must maintain the routing tables so that they have the most current routing information. How the routing protocol maintains the routing table depends on the type of routing protocol (distance vector, link-state, or path vector) as well as the routing protocol itself (RIP, EIGRP, and so on).

Periodic Updates

Many distance vector protocols employ periodic updates to exchange routing information with their neighbors and to maintain up-to-date routing information in the routing table. RIP and IGRP are examples of two such protocols.

Maintaining the Routing Table

In Figure 4-13, the routers are periodically sending the routing table to neighbors. Even though none of the routers have new information to share, periodic updates are sent anyway. The term *periodic updates* refers to the fact that a router sends the complete routing table to its neighbors at a predefined interval. For RIP, these updates are sent every 30 seconds as a broadcast (255.255.255.255), whether or not there has been a topology change. This 30-second interval is a route update timer that also aids in tracking the age of routing information in the routing table.

Figure 4-13   Periodic Updates

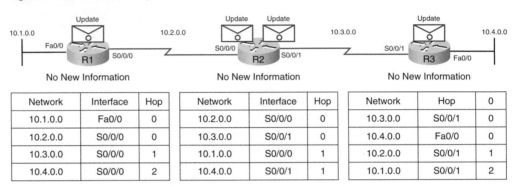

Network	Interface	Hop
10.1.0.0	Fa0/0	0
10.2.0.0	S0/0/0	0
10.3.0.0	S0/0/0	1
10.4.0.0	S0/0/0	2

Network	Interface	Hop
10.2.0.0	S0/0/0	0
10.3.0.0	S0/0/1	0
10.1.0.0	S0/0/0	1
10.4.0.0	S0/0/1	1

Network	Hop	0
10.3.0.0	S0/0/1	0
10.4.0.0	Fa0/0	0
10.2.0.0	S0/0/1	1
10.1.0.0	S0/0/1	2

The age of routing information in a routing table is refreshed each time an update is received. This way, information in the routing table can be maintained when there is a topology change. Changes might occur for several reasons, including

- Failure of a link
- Introduction of a new link
- Failure of a router
- Change of link parameters

RIP Timers

In addition to the update timer, IOS implements three additional timers for RIP:

- **Invalid:** If an update has not been received to refresh an existing route after 180 seconds (the default), the route is marked as invalid by setting the metric to 16. The route is retained in the routing table until the flush timer expires.

- **Flush:** By default, the flush timer is set for 240 seconds, which is 60 seconds longer than the invalid timer. When the flush timer expires, the route is removed from the routing table.

- **Hold-down:** This timer stabilizes routing information and helps prevent routing loops during periods when the topology is converging on new information. When a route is marked as unreachable, it must stay in holddown long enough for all routers in the topology to learn about the unreachable network. By default, the hold-down timer is set for 180 seconds. The hold-down timer is discussed in more detail later in this chapter.

Figure 4-14 shows the three-router topology we have been using to demonstrate routing protocol updates.

Figure 4-14 Three-Router Topology

Examples 4-1 and 4-2 show that the timer values can be verified with two commands: **show ip route** and **show ip protocols**.

Example 4-1 RIP Timers in the **show ip route** Command Output

```
R1# show ip route

<output omitted>

Gateway of last resort is not set

     10.0.0.0/16 is subnetted, 4 subnets
C       10.2.0.0 is directly connected, Serial0/0/0
R       10.3.0.0 [120/1] via 10.2.0.2, 00:00:04, Serial0/0/0
C       10.1.0.0 is directly connected, FastEthernet0/0
R       10.4.0.0 [120/2] via 10.2.0.2, 00:00:04, Serial0/0/0
```

Notice in the output from **show ip route** that each route learned through RIP shows the elapsed time since the last update, expressed in seconds.

Example 4-2 RIP Timers in the **show ip protocols** Command Output

```
R1# show ip protocols

Routing Protocol is "rip"
  Sending updates every 30 seconds, next due in 13 seconds
  Invalid after 180 seconds, hold down 180, flushed after 240
  <output omitted>
```

```
Routing for Networks:
  10.0.0.0
Routing Information Sources:
  Gateway          Distance      Last Update
  10.3.0.1              120       00:00:27
Distance: (default is 120)
```

This information is also repeated in the **show ip protocols** command output under the heading Last Update. The **show ip protocols** command details when this router, R1, is due to send out its next round of updates. It also lists the invalid, hold-down, and flush timer default values.

Bounded Updates

Unlike other distance vector routing protocols, EIGRP does not send periodic updates. Instead, EIGRP sends *bounded updates* about a route when a path changes or the metric for that route changes. When a new route becomes available or when a route needs to be removed, EIGRP sends an update only about that network instead of the entire table. This information is sent only to those routers that need it.

EIGRP uses updates that are

- Nonperiodic, because they are not sent out on a regular basis

- Partial, because they are sent only when there is a change in topology that influences routing information

- Bounded, meaning that the propagation of partial updates is automatically bounded so that only those routers that need the information are updated

Note

Chapter 9, "EIGRP," provides more detailed information on how EIGRP operates.

Triggered Updates

To speed the convergence when there is a topology change, RIP uses triggered updates. A *triggered update* is a routing table update that is sent immediately in response to a routing change. Triggered updates do not wait for update timers to expire. The detecting router immediately sends an update message to adjacent routers. The receiving routers, in turn, generate triggered updates that notify their neighbors of the change.

Triggered updates are sent when one of the following events occurs:

- An interface changes state (up or down).

- A route has entered (or exited) the unreachable state.

- A route is installed in the routing table.

Using only triggered updates would be sufficient if there were a guarantee that the wave of updates would reach every appropriate router immediately. However, there are two problems with triggered updates:

- Packets containing the update message can be dropped.

- Packets containing the update message can be corrupted by some link in the network.

The triggered updates do not happen instantaneously. A router that has not yet received the triggered update could issue a regular update at just the wrong time, causing the bad route to be reinserted in a neighbor that had already received the triggered update.

Figure 4-15 shows how a network topology change is propagated through the network by sending a triggered update.

Figure 4-15   Triggered Updates

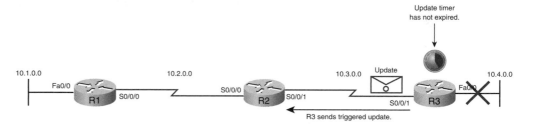

When network 10.4.0.0 becomes unavailable and R3 becomes aware of that, R3 sends out the information to its neighbors before the update timer expires. The information is then propagated through the network.

Random Jitter

When multiple routers transmit routing updates at the same time on multiaccess LAN segments, the update packets can collide and cause delays or consume too much bandwidth.

Note

Collisions are an issue only with hubs and not with switches.

Sending updates at the same time is known as the *synchronization* of updates. Synchronization can become a problem with distance vector routing protocols because of their usage of periodic updates. As more routers' timers become synchronized, more collisions of updates and more delays occur in the network. Initially, the updates of routers will not be synchronized. But over time, the timers across a network will become globally synchronized.

To prevent the synchronization of updates between routers, Cisco IOS uses a random variable, called RIP_JITTER, which subtracts a variable amount of time to the update interval for each router in the network. This random jitter, or variable amount of time, ranges from 0 to 15 percent of the specified update interval. In this way, the update interval varies randomly in a range from 25.5 to 30 seconds for the default 30-second interval.

Routing Loops

Routing loops can cause a severe impact on network performance. The following sections discuss the causes and solutions of routing loops with distance vector routing protocols.

Defining a Routing Loop

A routing loop is a condition in which a packet is continuously transmitted within a series of routers without ever reaching its intended destination network. A routing loop can occur when two or more routers have inaccurate routing information to a destination network.

The loop can be a result of

- Incorrectly configured static routes

- Incorrectly configured route redistribution (*redistribution* is a process of handing the routing information from one routing protocol to another routing protocol and is discussed in CCNP-level courses)

- Inconsistent routing tables not being updated because of slow convergence in a changing network

Distance vector routing protocols are simple in their operations. Their simplicity results in protocol drawbacks like routing loops. Routing loops are less of a problem with link-state routing protocols but can occur under certain circumstances.

Note

IP has its own mechanism to prevent the possibility of a packet traversing the network endlessly. IP has a Time to Live (TTL) field, and its value is decremented by 1 at each router. If the TTL is 0, the router drops the packet. The TTL is set by the operating system of the host that originated the packet. TTL values are typically much higher than the hop count limit of 15, with a maximum value of 255.

Implications of Routing Loops

A routing loop can have a devastating effect on a network, resulting in degraded network performance or even network downtime.

A routing loop can create the following conditions:

- Link bandwidth will be used for traffic looping back and forth between the routers in a loop.

- A router's CPU will be burdened with useless packet forwarding that will negatively impact the convergence of the network.

- Routing updates might get lost or not be processed in a timely manner. These conditions would introduce additional routing loops, making the situation even worse.

- Packets might get lost in "black holes," never reaching their intended destinations.

Figure 4-16 shows a possible routing loop scenario in which mechanisms to prevent such loops do not exist.

Figure 4-16   Routing Loop

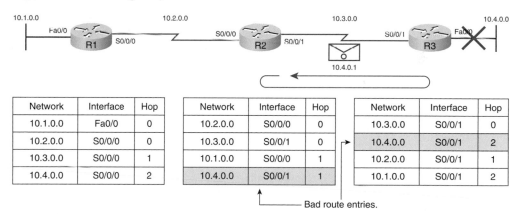

In this scenario, R2 sent R3 a route to 10.4.0.0 *before* R3 could inform R2 that the network is down. R3—not knowing the R2 does not have a route to 10.4.0.0—installs the new route for 10.4.0.0, pointing to R2 as the vector with a distance of 2. R2 and R3 now believe that the other router is the next hop for traffic to 10.4.0.0. The result of these bad routes is that traffic to destinations of the 10.4.0.0 network will loop between R2 and R3 until one of the routers drops the packet (the TTL expires).

As you can see, routing loops consume bandwidth and router resources, resulting in a slow or even unresponsive network.

There are a number of mechanisms available to eliminate routing loops, primarily with distance vector routing protocols. These mechanisms include

- Defining a maximum metric to prevent count to infinity

- Hold-down timers

- Split horizon

- Route poisoning or poison reverse

- Triggered updates

Triggered updates were discussed in the previous section. The other loop-avoidance mechanisms are discussed later in this chapter.

Routing Loops (4.4.1)

Use the Packet Tracer Activity to experience how a routing loop might occur with misconfigured static routes. Use file e2-441.pka on the CD-ROM that accompanies this book to perform this activity using Packet Tracer.

Count-to-Infinity Condition

Count to infinity is a condition that exists when inaccurate routing updates increase the metric value to "infinity" for a network that is no longer reachable. Figure 4-17 shows what happens to the routing tables when all three routers continue to send inaccurate updates about the downed 10.4.0.0 network to each other. The routers will continue to increment the metric until infinity for that protocol is reached. Each protocol defines infinity at a different value.

Figure 4-17   Count to Infinity

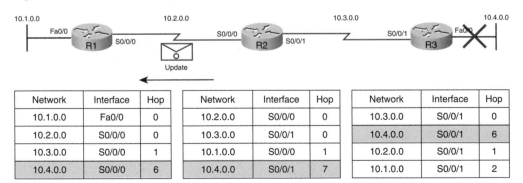

Network	Interface	Hop
10.1.0.0	Fa0/0	0
10.2.0.0	S0/0/0	0
10.3.0.0	S0/0/0	1
10.4.0.0	S0/0/0	6

Network	Interface	Hop
10.2.0.0	S0/0/0	0
10.3.0.0	S0/0/1	0
10.1.0.0	S0/0/0	1
10.4.0.0	S0/0/1	7

Network	Interface	Hop
10.3.0.0	S0/0/1	0
10.4.0.0	S0/0/1	6
10.2.0.0	S0/0/1	1
10.1.0.0	S0/0/1	2

Preventing Routing Loops by Setting a Maximum Metric Value

To eventually stop the incrementing of the metric, "infinity" is defined by setting a maximum metric value. For example, in Figure 4-18, RIP defines infinity as 16 hops—an "unreachable" metric. When the routers "count to infinity," they mark the route as unreachable.

Figure 4-18   10.4.0.0 Is Unreachable—Hop Count Is 16

Network	Interface	Hop
10.1.0.0	Fa0/0	0
10.2.0.0	S0/0/0	0
10.3.0.0	S0/0/0	1
10.4.0.0	S0/0/0	16

Network	Interface	Hop
10.2.0.0	S0/0/0	0
10.3.0.0	S0/0/1	0
10.1.0.0	S0/0/0	1
10.4.0.0	S0/0/1	16

Network	Interface	Hop
10.3.0.0	S0/0/1	0
10.4.0.0	S0/0/1	16
10.2.0.0	S0/0/1	1
10.1.0.0	S0/0/1	2

Preventing Routing Loops with Hold-Down Timers

Earlier you learned that distance vector protocols employ triggered updates to speed the convergence process. Remember that in addition to triggered updates, routers using distance vector routing protocols also send periodic updates. Imagine that a particular network is unstable. The interface resets as up, then down, and then up again in rapid succession. The route is flapping. Using triggered updates, the routers might react too quickly and unknowingly create a routing loop. A routing loop could also be created by a periodic update that is sent by the routers during the instability. Hold-down timers prevent routing loops from being created by these conditions. Hold-down timers also help prevent the count-to-infinity condition.

Hold-down timers are used to prevent regular update messages from inappropriately reinstating a route that might have gone bad. Hold-down timers instruct routers to hold any changes that might affect routes for a specified period of time. If a route is identified as down or possibly down, any other information for that route containing the same status, or worse, is ignored for a predetermined amount of time (the hold-down period). This means that routers will leave a route marked as unreachable in that state for a period of time that is long enough for updates to propagate the routing tables with the most current information.

Figures 4-19 through 4-23, along with the following discussion of steps, illustrate how hold-down timers work:

1. Network 10.4.0.0 attached to R3 goes down. R3 sends a triggered update (see Figure 4-19).

Figure 4-19 Triggered Update Sent to R2

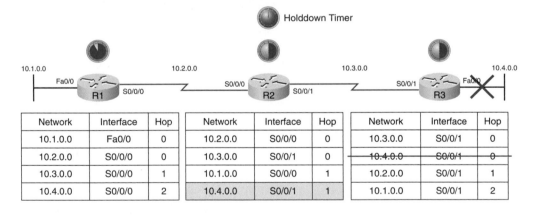

Network	Interface	Hop
10.1.0.0	Fa0/0	0
10.2.0.0	S0/0/0	0
10.3.0.0	S0/0/0	1
10.4.0.0	S0/0/0	2

Network	Interface	Hop
10.2.0.0	S0/0/0	0
10.3.0.0	S0/0/1	0
10.1.0.0	S0/0/0	1
10.4.0.0	S0/0/1	1

Network	Interface	Hop
10.3.0.0	S0/0/1	0
~~10.4.0.0~~	~~S0/0/1~~	~~0~~
10.2.0.0	S0/0/1	1
10.1.0.0	S0/0/1	2

2. R2 receives the update from R3 indicating that network 10.4.0.0 is now no longer accessible. R3 marks the network as possibly down and starts the hold-down timer (see Figure 4-20).

Figure 4-20 R2 Places 10.4.0.0 in Holddown

Holddown Timer

Network	Interface	Hop
10.1.0.0	Fa0/0	0
10.2.0.0	S0/0/0	0
10.3.0.0	S0/0/0	1
10.4.0.0	S0/0/0	2

Network	Interface	Hop
10.2.0.0	S0/0/0	0
10.3.0.0	S0/0/1	0
10.1.0.0	S0/0/0	1
10.4.0.0	S0/0/1	1

Network	Interface	Hop
10.3.0.0	S0/0/1	0
~~10.4.0.0~~	~~S0/0/1~~	~~0~~
10.2.0.0	S0/0/1	1
10.1.0.0	S0/0/1	2

3. If an update with a better metric for that network is received from any neighboring router during the hold-down period, R2 will reinstate the network and the hold-down timer will be removed.

4. If an update from any other neighbor is received during the hold-down period with the same or worse metric for that network, that update is ignored (see Figure 4-21). Thus, more time is allowed for the information about the change to be propagated.

Figure 4-21   R2 Ignores Update from R1

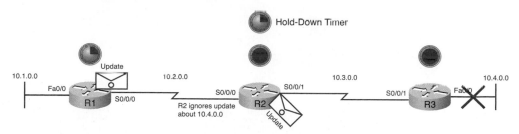

Network	Interface	Hop
10.1.0.0	Fa0/0	0
10.2.0.0	S0/0/0	0
10.3.0.0	S0/0/0	1
10.4.0.0	S0/0/0	2

Network	Interface	Hop
10.2.0.0	S0/0/0	0
10.3.0.0	S0/0/1	0
10.1.0.0	S0/0/0	1
10.4.0.0	S0/0/1	1

Network	Interface	Hop
10.3.0.0	S0/0/1	0
~~10.4.0.0~~	~~S0/0/1~~	~~0~~
10.2.0.0	S0/0/1	1
10.1.0.0	S0/0/1	2

5. R1 and R2 still forward packets to 10.4.0.0, even though it is marked as possibly down (see Figure 4-22). This allows the router to overcome any issues associated with inter-mittent connectivity. If the destination network is truly unavailable and the packets are forwarded, black-hole routing is created and lasts until the hold-down timer expires.

Figure 4-22   Traffic to 10.4.0.0 Is Still Routed

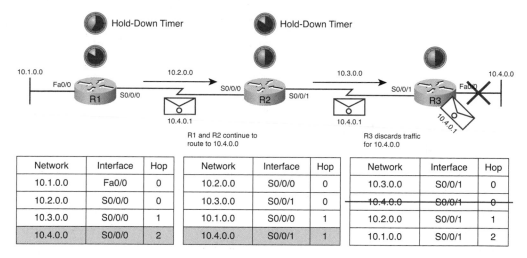

Network	Interface	Hop
10.1.0.0	Fa0/0	0
10.2.0.0	S0/0/0	0
10.3.0.0	S0/0/0	1
10.4.0.0	S0/0/0	2

Network	Interface	Hop
10.2.0.0	S0/0/0	0
10.3.0.0	S0/0/1	0
10.1.0.0	S0/0/0	1
10.4.0.0	S0/0/1	1

Network	Interface	Hop
10.3.0.0	S0/0/1	0
~~10.4.0.0~~	~~S0/0/1~~	~~0~~
10.2.0.0	S0/0/1	1
10.1.0.0	S0/0/1	2

6. When the hold-down timers expire on R1 and R2, 10.4.0.0 is removed from the routing table. No traffic to 10.4.0.0 will be routed (see Figure 4-23).

Figure 4-23 Network Is Now Converged

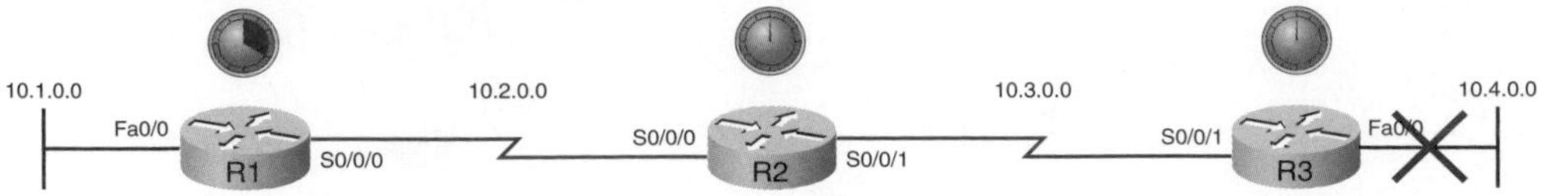

Network	Interface	Hop
10.1.0.0	Fa0/0	0
10.2.0.0	S0/0/0	0
10.3.0.0	S0/0/0	1
~~10.4.0.0~~	~~S0/0/0~~	~~2~~

Network	Interface	Hop
10.2.0.0	S0/0/0	0
10.3.0.0	S0/0/1	0
10.1.0.0	S0/0/0	1
~~10.4.0.0~~	~~S0/0/1~~	~~1~~

Network	Interface	Hop
10.3.0.0	S0/0/1	0
~~10.4.0.0~~	~~S0/0/1~~	~~0~~
10.2.0.0	S0/0/1	1
10.1.0.0	S0/0/1	2

Preventing Routing Loops with the Split Horizon Rule

Another method used to prevent routing loops caused by slow convergence of a distance vector routing protocol is split horizon. The split horizon rule says that a router should not advertise a network through the interface from which the update came.

Applying split horizon to the previous example of route 10.4.0.0 produces the following actions:

1. R3 advertises the 10.4.0.0 network to R2.

2. R2 receives the information and updates its routing table.

3. R2 then advertises the 10.4.0.0 network to R1 out S0/0/0. R2 does not advertise 10.4.0.0 to R3 out S0/0/1, because the route originated from that interface.

4. R1 receives the information and updates its routing table.

5. Because of split horizon, R1 also does not advertise the information about network 10.4.0.0 back to R2.

Complete routing updates are exchanged, with the exception of routes that violate the split horizon rule. The results look like this:

- R2 advertises networks 10.3.0.0 and 10.4.0.0 to R1.

- R2 advertises networks 10.1.0.0 and 10.2.0.0 to R3.

- R1 advertises network 10.1.0.0 to R2.

- R3 advertises network 10.4.0.0 to R2.

Figure 4-24 illustrates this example of the split horizon rule. Notice that R2 sends different routing updates to R1 and R3. Also notice that each router increments the hop count *before* sending the update.

Figure 4-24   Split Horizon Rule

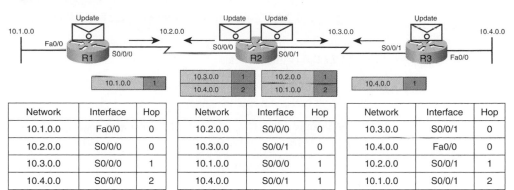

Network	Interface	Hop
10.1.0.0	Fa0/0	0
10.2.0.0	S0/0/0	0
10.3.0.0	S0/0/0	1
10.4.0.0	S0/0/0	2

Network	Interface	Hop
10.2.0.0	S0/0/0	0
10.3.0.0	S0/0/1	0
10.1.0.0	S0/0/0	1
10.4.0.0	S0/0/1	1

Network	Interface	Hop
10.3.0.0	S0/0/1	0
10.4.0.0	Fa0/0	0
10.2.0.0	S0/0/1	1
10.1.0.0	S0/0/1	2

Note

Split horizon can be disabled by an administrator. Under certain conditions, this has to be done to achieve the proper routing. These conditions are discussed in later courses.

Split horizon can be combined with route poisoning or poison reverse to specifically mark a route as unreachable, as described in the sections that follow.

Route Poisoning

Route poisoning is used to mark the route as unreachable in a routing update that is sent to other routers. Unreachable is interpreted as a metric that is set to the maximum. For RIP, a poisoned route has a metric of 16.

Figure 4-25 shows route poisoning in effect.

Figure 4-25   Route Poisoning

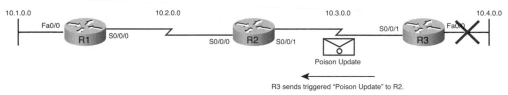

Network	Interface	Hop
10.1.0.0	Fa0/0	0
10.2.0.0	S0/0/0	0
10.3.0.0	S0/0/0	1
10.4.0.0	S0/0/0	2

Network	Interface	Hop
10.2.0.0	S0/0/0	0
10.3.0.0	S0/0/1	0
10.1.0.0	S0/0/0	1
10.4.0.0	S0/0/1	1

Network	Interface	Hop
10.3.0.0	S0/0/1	0
10.4.0.0	Fa0/0	16
10.2.0.0	S0/0/1	1
10.1.0.0	S0/0/1	2

The following process occurs:

1. Network 10.4.0.0 becomes unavailable because of a link failure.

2. R3 poisons the metric with a value of 16 and then sends out a triggered update stating that 10.4.0.0 is unavailable.

3. R2 processes that update. Because the metric is 16, R2 invalidates the routing entry in its routing table.

4. R2 then sends the poison update to R1, indicating that route is unavailable, again by setting the metric value to 16.

5. R1 processes the update and invalidates the routing entry for 10.4.0.0 in its routing table.

Route poisoning speeds the convergence process because the information about 10.4.0.0 spreads through the network more quickly than waiting for the hop count to reach "infinity."

Split Horizon with Poison Reverse

Poison reverse can be combined with the split horizon technique. The method is called split horizon with poison reverse. The rule for split horizon with poison reverse states that when sending updates out a specific interface, you should designate any networks that were learned on that interface as unreachable.

The concept of split horizon with poison reverse is that explicitly telling a router to ignore a route is better than not telling it about the route in the first place.

Figure 4-26 shows an example of split horizon with poison reverse in effect.

Figure 4-26   Poison Reverse

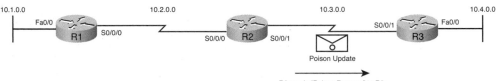

Network	Interface	Hop
10.1.0.0	Fa0/0	0
10.2.0.0	S0/0/0	0
10.3.0.0	S0/0/0	1
10.4.0.0	S0/0/0	2

Network	Interface	Hop
10.2.0.0	S0/0/0	0
10.3.0.0	S0/0/1	0
10.1.0.0	S0/0/0	1
10.4.0.0	S0/0/1	1

Network	Interface	Hop
10.3.0.0	S0/0/1	0
10.4.0.0	Fa0/0	0
10.2.0.0	S0/0/1	1
10.1.0.0	S0/0/1	2

The following process occurs:

1. R3 sends out a periodic update to R2 with the network 10.4.0.0 and a metric of 1 (RIP hop count).

2. When R2 sends out its periodic update, the 10.4.0.0 update to R3 will be marked unreachable with a metric of 16 (RIP hop count). This poison reverse update explicitly tells R3 that it will not be able to reach the 10.4.0.0 network through R2.

3. R3 processes the poison reverse update from R2, keeping its better route entry for 10.4.0.0 with a metric of 0.

Poison reverse is a specific circumstance that overrides split horizon. It occurs to ensure that R3 is not susceptible to incorrect updates about network 10.4.0.0.

Note

Split horizon is enabled by default. However, split horizon with poison reverse might not be the default on all IOS implementations.

Preventing Routing Loops with IP and TTL

The Time to Live (TTL) is an 8-bit field in the IP header that limits the number of hops a packet can traverse through the network before it is discarded. The purpose of the TTL field is to avoid a situation in which an undeliverable packet keeps circulating on the network endlessly. With TTL, the 8-bit field is set with a value by the source device of the packet. The TTL is decreased by 1 by every router on the route to its destination. If the TTL field reaches 0 before the packet arrives at its destination, the packet is discarded and the router sends an Internet Control Message Protocol (ICMP) error message back to the source of the IP packet.

Figure 4-27 shows a situation where the routing tables do not have accurate information about the downed 10.4.0.0 network. Even in the case of this routing loop, packets will not loop endlessly in the network. Eventually the TTL value will be decreased to 0 and the packet will be discarded by the router.

Figure 4-27   TTL in Effect

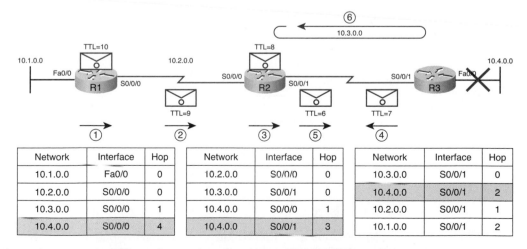

Network	Interface	Hop
10.1.0.0	Fa0/0	0
10.2.0.0	S0/0/0	0
10.3.0.0	S0/0/0	1
10.4.0.0	S0/0/0	4

Network	Interface	Hop
10.2.0.0	S0/0/0	0
10.3.0.0	S0/0/1	0
10.4.0.0	S0/0/0	1
10.4.0.0	S0/0/1	3

Network	Interface	Hop
10.3.0.0	S0/0/1	0
10.4.0.0	S0/0/1	2
10.2.0.0	S0/0/1	1
10.1.0.0	S0/0/1	2

The sequence of events, as depicted in Figure 4-27, is as follows:

1. R1 receives a packet with a TTL value of 10.

2. R1 decrements the TTL value to 9 and sends the packet to R2.

3. R2 decrements the TTL value to 8 and sends the packet to R3.

4. R3 decrements the TTL value to 7 and sends the packet back to R2.

5. R2 decrements the TTL value to 6 and sends the packet back to R3.

6. The packet loops between R2 and R3 until the TTL value reaches 0. Then the packet is discarded.

Distance Vector Routing Protocols Today

Later in this book, you will learn about link-state routing protocols. Although link-state routing protocols have several advantages over distance vector routing protocols, distance vector routing protocols are still in use today. In Chapter 9, you will learn that EIGRP is an "enhanced" distance vector routing protocol. These enhancements make EIGRP a viable choice for a routing protocol in many environments.

RIP and EIGRP

For distance vector routing protocols, there really are only two choices: RIP or EIGRP. The decision about which routing protocol to use in a given situation is influenced by a number of factors, including

- Size of the network

- Compatibility between models of routers

- Administrative knowledge required

Table 4-3 compares distance vector routing protocol features.

Table 4-3   Comparing Distance Vector Routing Protocol Features

	RIPv1	RIPv2	IGRP	EIGRP
Speed of Convergence	Slow	Slow	Slow	Fast
Scalability—Size of Network	Small	Small	Small	Large
Use of VLSM	No	Yes	No	Yes
Resource Usage	Low	Low	Low	Medium
Implementation and Maintenance	Simple	Simple	Simple	Complex

RIP

Over the years, RIP has evolved from a classful routing protocol (RIPv1) to a classless routing protocol (RIPv2). RIPv2 is a standardized routing protocol that works in a mixed-vendor router environment. Routers made by different companies can communicate using RIP. It is one of the easiest routing protocols to configure, making it a good choice for small networks. However, RIPv2 still has limitations. Both RIPv1 and RIPv2 have a route metric that is based only on hop count and that is limited to 15 hops.

Features of RIP include

- Supports split horizon and split horizon with poison reverse to prevents loops.

- Is capable of load-balancing up to six equal-cost paths. The default is four equal-cost paths.

RIPv2 introduced the following improvements to RIPv1:

- Includes the subnet mask in the routing updates, making it a classless routing protocol

- Has an authentication mechanism to secure routing table updates

- Supports variable-length subnet mask (VLSM)

- Uses multicast addresses instead of broadcast

- Supports manual route summarization

EIGRP

EIGRP was developed from IGRP, another distance vector protocol. EIGRP is a classless, distance vector routing protocol with features found in link-state routing protocols. However, unlike RIP or OSPF, EIGRP is a proprietary protocol developed by Cisco and runs only on Cisco routers.

EIGRP features include

- Triggered updates (EIGRP has no periodic updates).

- Use of a *topology table* to maintain all the routes received from neighbors (not only the best paths).

- Establishment of adjacencies with neighboring routers using the EIGRP Hello protocol.

- Support for VLSM and manual route summarization. These allow EIGRP to create hierarchically structured large networks.

Advantages of EIGRP are as follows:

- Although routes are propagated in a distance vector manner, the metric is based on minimum bandwidth and cumulative delay of the path, rather than hop count.

- Fast convergence because of Diffusing Update Algorithm (DUAL) route calculation. DUAL allows the insertion of backup routes into the EIGRP topology table, which are used in case the primary route fails. Because it is a local procedure, the switchover to the backup route is immediate and does not involve the action in any other routers.

- Bounded updates mean that EIGRP uses less bandwidth, especially in large networks with many routes.

- EIGRP supports multiple network layer protocols through Protocol Dependent Modules, which include support for IP, *IPX*, and AppleTalk.

Summary

One way of classifying routing protocols is by the type of algorithm they use to determine the best path to a destination network. Routing protocols can be classified as distance vector, link-state, or path vector. Distance vector means that routes are advertised as vectors of distance and direction. Distance is defined in terms of a metric, such as hop count, and direction is simply the next-hop router or exit interface.

Distance vector routing protocols include

- RIPv1

- RIPv2

- IGRP

- EIGRP

Routers that use distance vector routing protocols determine the best path to remote networks based on the information they learn from their neighbors. If Router X learns of two paths to the same network, one through Router Y at seven hops and another through Router Z at ten hops, the router will choose the shorter path using Router Y as the next-hop router. Router X has no knowledge of what the network looks like beyond Routers Y and Z, and it can only make its best-path decision based on the information sent to it by these two routers. Distance vector routing protocols do not have a map of the topology as do link-state routing protocols.

Network discovery is an important process of any routing protocol. Some distance vector routing protocols such as RIP go through a step-by-step process of learning and sharing routing information with their neighbors. As routes are learned from one neighbor, that information is passed on to other neighbors with an increase in the routing metric.

Routing protocols also need to maintain their routing tables to keep them current and accurate. RIP exchanges routing table information with its neighbors every 30 seconds. EIGRP, another distance vector routing protocol, does not send these periodic updates and only sends a "bounded" update when there is a change in the topology and only to those routers that need that information. EIGRP is discussed in a later chapter.

RIP also uses timers to determine when a neighboring router is no longer available, or when some of the routers might not have current routing information. This is typically because the network has not yet converged because of a recent change in the topology. Distance vector routing protocols also use triggered updates to help speed convergence time.

One disadvantage of distance vector routing protocols is the potential for routing loops. Routing loops can occur when the network is in an unconverged state. Distance vector routing protocols use hold-down timers to prevent the router from using another route to a recently down network until all the routers have had enough time to learn about this change in the topology.

Split horizon and split horizon with poison reverse are also used by routers to help prevent routing loops. The split horizon rule states that a router should never advertise a route through the interface from which it learned that route. Split horizon with poison reverse means that it is better to explicitly state that this router does not have a route to this network by poisoning the route with a metric stating that the route is unreachable.

Distance vector routing protocols are sometimes referred to as "routing by rumor," although this can be somewhat of a misnomer. Distance vector routing protocols are popular with many network administrators because they are typically easily understood and simple to implement. This does not necessarily mean that link-state routing protocols are any more complicated or difficult to configure.

Unfortunately, link-state routing protocols have received this somewhat unwarranted reputation. You will learn in later chapters that link-state routing protocols are as easy to understand and configure as distance vector routing protocols.

Activities and Labs

The activities and labs available in the companion *Routing Protocols and Concepts, CCNA Exploration Labs and Study Guide* (ISBN 1-58713-204-4) provide hands-on practice with the following topics introduced in this chapter:

Lab 4-1: Routing Table Interpretation Lab (4.6.1)

In this lab activity, you re-create a network based only on the output from the **show ip route** command. Then, to verify your answer, you configure the routers and compare the actual routing table to the routing table shown in the lab documentation.

Many of the hands-on labs include Packet Tracer Companion Activities, where you can use Packet Tracer to complete a simulation of the lab. Look for this icon in *Routing Protocols and Concepts, CCNA Exploration Labs and Study Guide* (ISBN 1-58713-204-4) for hands-on labs that have a Packet Tracer Companion.

Check Your Understanding

Complete all the review questions listed here to test your understanding of the topics and concepts in this chapter. Answers are listed in the appendix, "Check Your Understanding and Challenge Questions Answer Key."

1. Which four statements are true regarding some distance vector routing protocols?

   A. Hop counts can be used for path selection.

   B. They scale well.

   C. Routing updates are broadcast at intervals.

   D. EIGRP can do unequal-cost load balancing.

   E. RIPv1 multicasts its routing updates.

   F. RIP sends its entire routing table to directly connected neighbors (except for any routes affected by split horizon).

2. Which conditions cause some distance vector routing protocols to send routing table updates? (Choose three.)

   A. When the hold-down timer expires

   B. When a change occurs in the network topology

   C. When the update timer value expires

   D. When a triggered update is received from another router

   E. When a packet is received that is destined for an unknown network

   F. When there have been no routing table changes for 30 minutes

3. What are two characteristics of EIGRP updates?

   A. Include all EIGRP routes

   B. Include the full routing table

   C. Independent of architecture

   D. Only triggered for route topology changes

   E. Broadcast to affected neighbors

   F. Bounded only to those routers that need the update

4. What feature was added to RIP to help with synchronization errors?

   A. Hold-down timer

   B. RIP_JITTER

   C. RIP_DELAY

   D. Jitter control

5. Which two of the following are timers used for RIP?

   A. Invalid

   B. Refresh

   C. Flush

   D. Deadlink

   E. Hello

6. Which statement is true concerning the advantages of a distance vector protocol?

   A. Periodic updates speed convergence.

   B. Convergence times make routing loops impossible.

   C. Ease of implementation makes configuration simple.

   D. They work well in complex networks.

   E. Their convergence times are faster than link-state routing protocols.

7. Which mechanism can be used to avoid a count-to-infinity loop?

   A. Split horizon

   B. Route poisoning

   C. Hold-down timers

   D. Triggered updates

   E. Split horizon with poison reverse

8. Refer to Figure 4-28. The network shown is running the RIP routing protocol. What mechanism will keep Router R4 from sending updates about the 10.0.0.0 network back to Router R5?

Figure 4-28   Check Your Understanding, Question #8

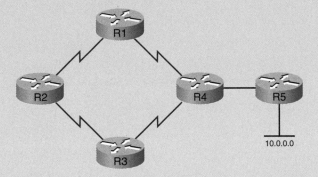

   A. Split horizon

   B. Poison reverse

   C. Route poisoning

   D. Hold-down timers

   E. Maximum hop count

9. What allows RIP to avoid routing loops by advertising a metric of infinity?

   A. Split horizon

   B. Route poisoning

   C. Hold-down timers

   D. Maximum hop count

   E. Time to Live (TTL) field of the IP header

10. Which field in the IP header ensures that packets will not loop endlessly on a network?

    A. CRC

    B. TOS

    C. TTL

    D. Checksum

11. Match the loop-preventing mechanism with its corresponding function.

    Loop-prevention mechanism:

    Split horizon:

    Route poisoning:

    Hold-down timers:

    Triggered updates:

    Function:

    A. Routes learned through an interface are not advertised out that same interface.

    B. Routes learned through an interface are advertised back out the same interface as unreachable.

    C. Topology changes are immediately sent to adjacent routers.

    D. This allows time for topology changes to travel through an entire network.

Challenge Questions and Activities

These questions require a deeper application of the concepts covered in this chapter and are similar to the style of questions you might see on a CCNA certification exam. You can find the answers to these questions in the appendix, "Answers to Check Your Understanding and Challenge Questions and Activities."

1. Briefly explain the basic operation of RIP and IGRP.

2. Explain convergence and why it is important.

3. What are the four main timers used by RIP? How many seconds are in each timer? What is the purpose of each timer?

4. What five techniques do distance vector routing protocols use to prevent routing loops?

To Learn More

Understanding the distance vector algorithm is not difficult. There are many books and online sources that show how algorithms such as the Bellman-Ford algorithm are used in networking. There are several websites devoted to explaining how these algorithms work. Seek out some of the resources and familiarize yourself with how this algorithm works.

Here are some suggested resources:

- *Interconnections, Bridges, Routers, Switches, and Internetworking Protocols*, by Radia Perlman

- *Cisco IP Routing*, by Alex Zinin

- *Routing the Internet*, by Christian Huitema

CHAPTER 5

RIP Version 1

Objectives

Upon completion of this chapter, you should be able to answer the following questions:

- What are the functions, characteristics, and operation of the RIPv1 protocol?

- Can you configure a device for RIPv1?

- Can you verify proper RIPv1 operations?

- How does RIPv1 perform automatic summarization?

- Can you configure, verify, and troubleshoot default routes propagated in a routed network implanting RIPv1?

- What are the recommended techniques to solve problems related to RIPv1?

Key Terms

This chapter uses the following key terms. You can find the definitions in the Glossary at the end of the book.

XNS   page 221

automatic summarization   page 238

boundary router   page 242

discontiguous network   page 248

Over the years, routing protocols have evolved to meet the increasing demands of complex networks. The first protocol used was Routing Information Protocol (RIP). RIP still enjoys popularity because of its simplicity and widespread support.

Figure 5-1 shows a chart of the most common IP routing protocols, with the routing protocols that will be discussed in this book highlighted. Notice in the chart that RIP (RIP version 1) is a classful, distance vector routing protocol.

Figure 5-1   Chart of Routing Protocols

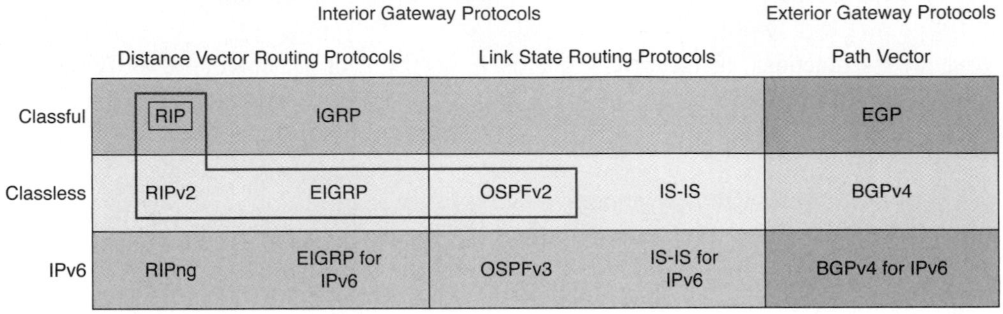

| | Interior Gateway Protocols | | Exterior Gateway Protocols |
	Distance Vector Routing Protocols	Link State Routing Protocols	Path Vector
Classful	RIP IGRP		EGP
Classless	RIPv2 EIGRP	OSPFv2 IS-IS	BGPv4
IPv6	RIPng EIGRP for IPv6	OSPFv3 IS-IS for IPv6	BGPv4 for IPv6

Understanding RIP is important to your networking studies for two reasons:

- RIP is still in use today. You might encounter a network implementation that is large enough to need a routing protocol, yet simple enough to use RIP effectively.

- Familiarity with many of the fundamental concepts of RIP will help you to compare RIP with other protocols. Understanding how RIP operates and knowing its implementation will make learning other routing protocols easier.

This chapter covers the details of RIP version 1, including a bit of history, RIPv1 characteristics, operation, configuration, verification, and troubleshooting. Throughout the chapter, you can use Packet Tracer Activities to practice what you learn. *Routing Protocols and Concepts, CCNA Exploration Labs and Study Guide* and the online curriculum provide three hands-on labs and a Packet Tracer Skills Integration Challenge Activity to help you integrate RIPv1 into your growing set of networking knowledge and skills.

RIPv1: Distance Vector, Classful Routing Protocol

RIPv1 is a distance vector routing protocol for IPv4. RIPv1 is also a classful routing protocol. This chapter begins to examine the limitations of a classful routing protocol. Chapter 6, "VLSM and CIDR," and Chapter 7, "RIPv2," will discuss classless routing protocols and compare them to classful routing protocols.

Background and Perspective

RIP is the oldest of the distance vector routing protocols. Although RIP lacks the sophistication of more advanced routing protocols, its simplicity and continued widespread use is a testament to its longevity. RIP is not a protocol "on the way out." In fact, an IPv6 form of RIP called RIPng (next generation) is now available.

Figure 5-2 compares RIP and other network protocol developments over time.

Figure 5-2   Overview of RIP Historical Impact

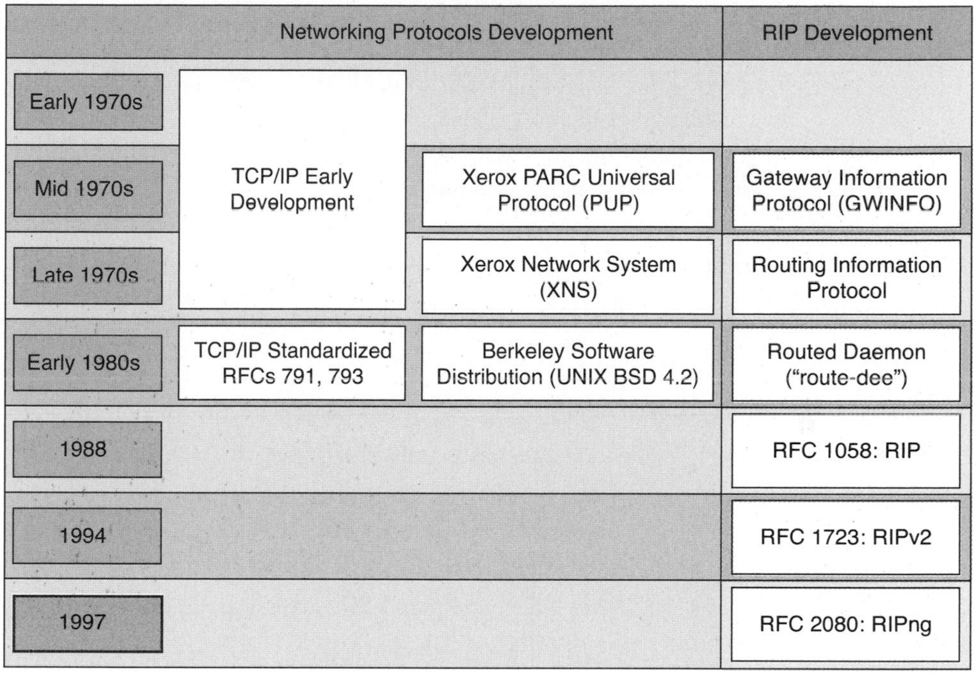

	Networking Protocols Development			RIP Development
Early 1970s	TCP/IP Early Development			
Mid 1970s		Xerox PARC Universal Protocol (PUP)		Gateway Information Protocol (GWINFO)
Late 1970s		Xerox Network System (XNS)		Routing Information Protocol
Early 1980s	TCP/IP Standardized RFCs 791, 793	Berkeley Software Distribution (UNIX BSD 4.2)		Routed Daemon ("route-dee")
1988				RFC 1058: RIP
1994				RFC 1723: RIPv2
1997				RFC 2080: RIPng

RIP evolved from an earlier protocol developed at Xerox, called Gateway Information Protocol (GWINFO). With the development of Xerox Network System (*XNS*), GWINFO evolved into RIP. It later gained popularity because it was implemented in the Berkeley Software Distribution (BSD) as a daemon named routed (pronounced *route-dee*, not *routed*). Various other vendors made their own, slightly different implementations of RIP. Recognizing the need for standardization of the protocol, Charles Hedrick wrote RFC 1058 in 1988, in which he documented the existing protocol and specified some improvements. RFC 1058 can be found at http://www.ietf.org/rfc/rfc1058.txt. Since then, RIP has been improved with RIPv2 in 1994 and with RIPng in 1997.

> **Note**
>
> The first version of RIP is often called RIPv1 to distinguish it from RIP Version 2 (RIPv2). However, both versions share many of the same features. When discussing features common to both versions, we will refer to RIP. When discussing features unique to each version, we will use RIPv1 and RIPv2. RIPv2 is discussed in Chapter 7.

RIPv1 Characteristics and Message Format

RIPv1 is a routing protocol and, like other protocols, has a format with fields containing specific information. For example, the IP protocol has fields containing information such as source IP address and destination IP address. Routing protocols also have fields containing information. One of the fields in the RIPv1 routing protocol is the IP Address field, which contains an IP network address. Using the information in these fields is how routers share routing information. Examining some of these fields can help take some of the mystery out of the protocol and its operations.

RIP Characteristics

As discussed in Chapter 4, "Distance Vector Routing Protocols," RIP has the following key characteristics:

- RIP is a distance vector routing protocol.

- RIP uses hop count as its only metric for path selection.

- Advertised routes with hop counts greater than 15 are considered unreachable.

- Response messages (routing table updates) are broadcast every 30 seconds.

Figure 5-3 shows an encapsulated RIPv1 message.

The data portion of a RIP message is encapsulated into a User Datagram Protocol (UDP) segment, with both source and destination port numbers set to 520. The IP header and data-link headers add broadcast destination addresses before the message is sent out all RIP-configured interfaces.

RIP Message Format: RIP Header

Figure 5-4 shows the detail of a RIPv1 message. Table 5-1 lists and describes the main fields of the message.

Figure 5-3   Encapsulated RIPv1 Message

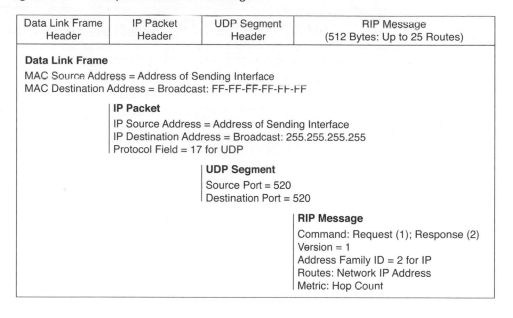

Figure 5-4   RIPv1 Message Format

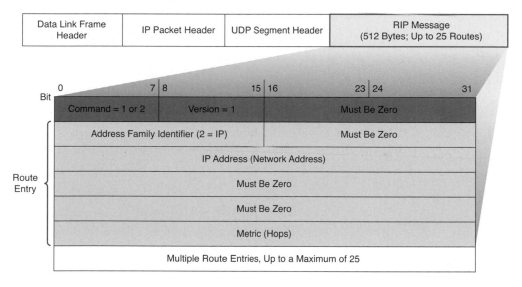

Table 5-1   RIPv1 Message Field Descriptions

Field	Description
Command	1 for a Request or 2 for a Response.
Version	1 for RIPv1 or 2 for RIPv2.
Address Family Identifier	2 for IP unless a Request is for the full routing table, in which case the field is set to 0.
IP Address	The address of the destination route, which can be a network, subnet, or host address.
Metric	Hop count between 1 and 16. The sending router increases the metric before sending out the message.

Three fields are specified in the 4-byte header portion shown in blue in the figure. The Command field specifies the message type, discussed in more detail in the next section. The Version field is set to 1 for RIP Version 1. The third field is labeled "Must be zero." "Must be zero" fields provide room for future expansion of the protocol.

RIP Message Format: Route Entry

The route entry portion of the message includes three fields with content:

- Address Family Identifier (set to 2 for IP unless a router is requesting a full routing table, in which case the field is set to 0)

- IP Address

- Metric

This route entry portion represents one destination route with its associated metric. One RIP update can contain up to 25 route entries. The maximum datagram size is 512 bytes, not including the IP or UDP headers.

Why Are So Many Fields Set to Zero?

RIP was developed before IP and was used for other network protocols (like XNS). BSD also had its influence. Initially, the extra space was added with the intention of supporting larger address spaces in the future. As you will see in Chapter 7, RIPv2 has now used most of these empty fields.

RIP Operation

The following sections introduce the basic operations of RIPv1. Later sections will discuss these operations in more detail.

RIP Request/Response Process

RIP uses two message types specified in the Command field: Request message and Response message.

Figure 5-5 shows the RIPv1 request/response process.

Figure 5-5   RIP Request/Response Example

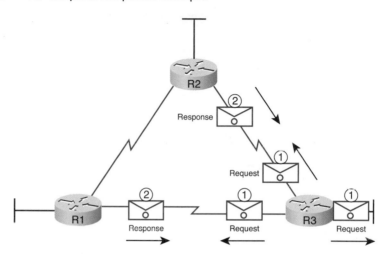

Each RIP-configured interface sends out a Request message on startup, requesting that all RIP neighbors send their complete routing tables. A Response message is sent back by RIP-enabled neighbors. When the requesting router receives the responses, it evaluates each route entry. If a route entry is new, the receiving router installs the route in the routing table. If the route is already in the table, the existing entry is replaced if the new entry has a better hop count. The startup router then sends a triggered update out all RIP-enabled interfaces containing its own routing table so that RIP neighbors can be informed of any new routes.

IP Address Classes and Classful Routing

You might recall from previous studies that IP addresses assigned to hosts were initially divided into three classes: Class A, Class B, and Class C. Each class was assigned a default subnet mask, as shown in Figure 5-6. Knowing the default subnet mask for each class is important to understanding how RIP operates.

RIP is a classful routing protocol. As you might have realized from the previous message format discussion, RIPv1 does not send subnet mask information in the update. Therefore, a router either uses the subnet mask configured on a local interface or applies the default subnet mask based on the address class. Because of this limitation, RIPv1 networks cannot be discontiguous, nor can they implement VLSM.

IP addressing is discussed further in Chapter 6.

Figure 5-6   Default Subnet Masks for Address Classes

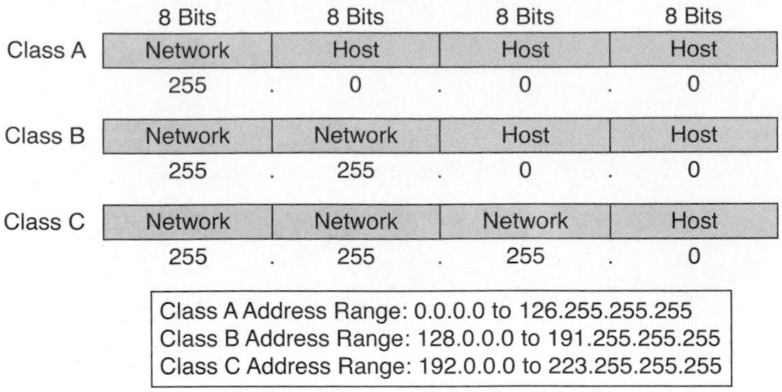

Class A Address Range: 0.0.0.0 to 126.255.255.255
Class B Address Range: 128.0.0.0 to 191.255.255.255
Class C Address Range: 192.0.0.0 to 223.255.255.255

Administrative Distance

As discussed in Chapter 3, "Introduction to Dynamic Routing Protocols," *administrative distance* (AD) is the trustworthiness (or preference) of the route source. RIP has a default administrative distance of 120. When compared to other interior gateway protocols, RIP is the least-preferred routing protocol. Intermediate System–to–Intermediate System (IS-IS), Open Shortest Path First (OSPF), Interior Gateway Routing Protocol (IGRP), and Enhanced IGRP (EIGRP) all have lower default AD values.

Remember, you can check the administrative distance using the **show ip route** command (see Example 5-1) or **show ip protocols** command (see Example 5-2).

Example 5-1 AD Values in the **show ip route** Command

```
R3# show ip route

Codes: C - connected, S - static, I - IGRP, R - RIP, M - mobile, B - BGP
       D - EIGRP, EX - EIGRP external, O - OSPF, IA - OSPF inter area
       N1 - OSPF NSSA external type 1, N2 - OSPF NSSA external type 2
       E1 - OSPF external type 1, E2 - OSPF external type 2, E - EGP
       i - IS-IS, L1 - IS-IS level-1, L2 - IS-IS level-2, ia - IS-IS inter area
       * - candidate default, U - per-user static route, o - ODR
       P - periodic downloaded static route

Gateway of last resort is not set

R    192.168.1.0/24 [120/1] via 192.168.6.2, 00:00:05, Serial0/0/0
R    192.168.2.0/24 [120/1] via 192.168.6.2, 00:00:05, Serial0/0/0
                    [120/1] via 192.168.4.2, 00:00:05, Serial0/0/1
R    192.168.3.0/24 [120/1] via 192.168.4.2, 00:00:05, Serial0/0/1
```

```
C    192.168.4.0/24 is directly connected, Serial0/0/1
C    192.168.5.0/24 is directly connected, FastEthernet0/0
C    192.168.6.0/24 is directly connected, Serial0/0/0
```

Example 5-2 AD Values in the **show ip protocols** Command

```
R3# show ip protocols

Routing Protocol is "rip"
  Sending updates every 30 seconds, next due in 22 seconds
  Invalid after 180 seconds, hold down 180, flushed after 240
  Outgoing update filter list for all interfaces is
  Incoming update filter list for all interfaces is
  Redistributing: rip
  Default version control: send version 1, receive any version
    Interface            Send  Recv  Triggered RIP  Key-chain
    FastEthernet0/0       1     1 2
    Serial0/0/0           1     1 2
    Serial0/0/1           1     1 2
  Automatic network summarization is in effect
  Routing for Networks:
    192.168.4.0
    192.168.5.0
    192.168.6.0
  Routing Information Sources:
    Gateway         Distance      Last Update
    192.168.6.2       120         00:00:10
    192.168.4.2       120         00:00:18
  Distance: (default is 120)
```

Basic RIPv1 Configuration

The following sections introduce the first of three topologies that will be used in this chapter.

RIPv1 Scenario A

Figure 5-7 shows the three router topologies used in Chapter 2, "Static Routing." Physically, the topology is the same, except that you will not need PCs attached to the LANs. Logically, however, the addressing scheme is different; this topology uses five Class C network addresses.

Figure 5-7   RIP Topology: Scenario A

192.168.3.0/24

Fa0/0   .1

S0/0/0   **R2**   S0/0/1
DCE
.2   .2

192.168.2.0/24   192.168.4.0/24

192.168.1.0/24   .1   .1   192.168.5.0/24
                              S0/0/0   S0/0/1
        Fa0/0   DCE   Fa0/0
        .1   **R1**   **R3**   .1

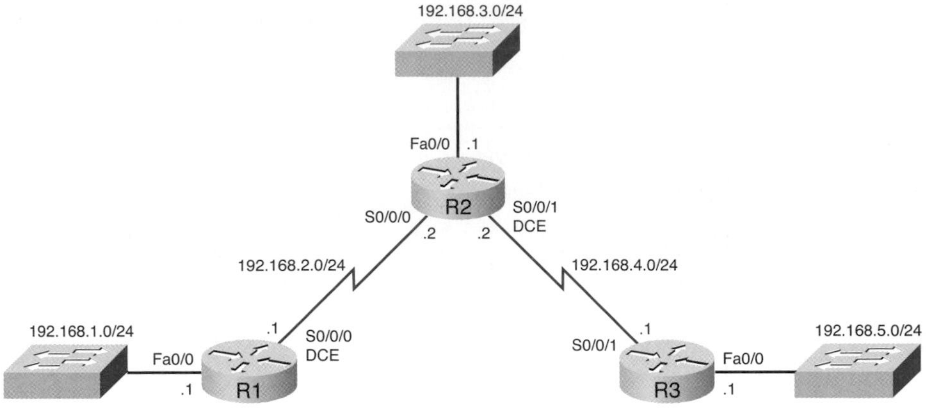

Table 5-2 displays the interface addressing for each router.

Table 5-2   Addressing Table: Scenario A

Device	Interface	IP Address	Subnet Mask
R1	Fa0/0	192.168.1.1	255.255.255.0
	S0/0/0	192.168.2.1	255.255.255.0
R2	Fa0/0	192.168.3.1	255.255.255.0
	S0/0/0	192.168.2.2	255.255.255.0
	S0/0/1	192.168.4.2	255.255.255.0
R3	Fa0/0	192.168.5.1	255.255.255.0
	S0/0/1	192.168.4.1	255.255.255.0

Packet Tracer
☐ Activity

Configure IP Addresses on Router Interfaces (5.2.1)

Use the Packet Tracer Activity to configure and activate all the interfaces for the RIP Topology: Scenario A. Detailed instructions are provided within the activity. Use file e2-521.pka on the CD-ROM that accompanies this book to perform this activity using Packet Tracer.

Enabling RIP: router rip Command

To enable a dynamic routing protocol, enter global configuration mode and use the **router** command. As shown in Example 5-3, if you type a space followed by a question mark, a list of all the available routing protocols supported by IOS displays.

Example 5-3 RIP Router Configuration Mode

```
R1# conf t

Enter configuration commands, one per line.  End with CNTL/Z.
R1(config)# router ?

  bgp       Border Gateway Protocol (BGP)
  egp       Exterior Gateway Protocol (EGP)
  eigrp     Enhanced Interior Gateway Routing Protocol (EIGRP)
  igrp      Interior Gateway Routing Protocol (IGRP)
  isis      ISO IS-IS
  iso-igrp  IGRP for OSI networks
  mobile    Mobile routes
  odr       On Demand stub Routes
  ospf      Open Shortest Path First (OSPF)
  rip       Routing Information Protocol (RIP)

R1(config)# router rip

R1(config-router)#
```

To enter router configuration mode for RIP, enter **router rip** at the global configuration prompt. Notice that the prompt changes from a global configuration prompt to the following:

```
R1(config-router)#
```

This command does not directly start the RIP process. Instead, it provides access to configure routing protocol settings. No routing updates are sent until additional commands are configured.

If you need to remove the RIP routing process from a device, negate the command with **no router rip**. This command stops the RIP process and erases all existing RIP configuration commands.

Specifying Networks

By entering RIP router configuration mode, the router is enabled for RIP. But the router still needs to know which local interfaces it should use for communication with other routers, as well as which locally connected networks it should advertise to those routers. To enable RIP routing for a network, use the **network** command in router configuration mode and enter the classful network address for each directly connected network.

```
Router(config-router)# network directly-connected-classful-network-address
```

The **network** command performs the following functions:

- Enables RIP on all interfaces that belong to a specific network. Associated interfaces will now both send and receive RIP updates.

- Advertises the specified network in RIP routing updates sent to other routers every 30 seconds.

Note

If you enter a subnet address, IOS automatically converts it to a classful network address. For example, if you enter the command **network 192.168.1.32**, the router will convert it to **network 192.168.1.0**.

Example 5-4 shows the **network** command configured on all three routers for the directly connected networks. Notice that only classful networks were entered.

Example 5-4 Enabling RIP with the **network** Command

```
R1(config)# router rip
R1(config-router)# network 192.168.1.0
R1(config-router)# network 192.168.2.0
R2(config)# router rip
R2(config-router)# network 192.168.2.0
R2(config-router)# network 192.168.3.0
R2(config-router)# network 192.168.4.0
R3(config)# router rip
R3(config-router)# network 192.168.4.0
R3(config-router)# network 192.168.5.0
```

What happens if you enter a subnet address or interface IP address instead of the classful network address when using the **network** command for RIP configurations?

```
R3(config)# router rip
R3(config-router)# network 192.168.4.0
R3(config-router)# network 192.168.5.1
```

This example uses an interface IP address instead of the classful network address. Notice that IOS does not give an error message. Instead, IOS corrects the input and enters the classful network address, as you can see in the following output for verification.

```
R3# show running-config
!
router rip
 network 192.168.4.0
 network 192.168.5.0
!
```

Packet Tracer
☐ Activity

Configure RIP Routing on a Network (5.2.3)

Use the Packet Tracer Activity to practice configuring RIP routing on all three routers in the topology. Detailed instructions are provided within the activity. Use file e2-523.pka on the CD-ROM that accompanies this book to perform this activity using Packet Tracer.

Verification and Troubleshooting

It is important to be able to verify and troubleshoot your routing configuration. Verifying routing operations immediately after configuration will help solve any potential troubleshooting issues that might arise later.

To verify and troubleshoot routing, first use the **show ip route** and **show ip protocols** commands. If you cannot isolate the problem using these two commands, use the **debug ip rip** command to see exactly what is happening. These three commands are discussed in a suggested order that you might use to verify and troubleshoot a routing protocol configuration. Remember, before you configure any routing—whether static or dynamic—make sure that all necessary interfaces are up and up with the **show ip interface brief** command.

Verifying RIP: show ip route Command

Examining the routing table is an easy way to see whether the routing protocol and commands have been properly configured. Be sure to look for any routes that you expect to see in the routing table, along with any routes that should not be there.

Example 5-5 shows the routing tables for R1, R2, and R3 by using the **show ip route** command.

Example 5-5 Verifying RIP Convergence with the **show ip route** Command

```
R1# show ip route

Codes: C - connected, S - static, I - IGRP, R - RIP, M - mobile, B - BGP
<output omitted>

Gateway of last resort is not set

R    192.168.4.0/24 [120/1] via 192.168.2.2, 00:00:02, Serial0/0/0
R    192.168.5.0/24 [120/2] via 192.168.2.2, 00:00:02, Serial0/0/0
C    192.168.1.0/24 is directly connected, FastEthernet0/0
C    192.168.2.0/24 is directly connected, Serial0/0/0
R    192.168.3.0/24 [120/1] via 192.168.2.2, 00:00:02, Serial0/0/0
```

```
R2# show ip route

Codes: C - connected, S - static, I - IGRP, R - RIP, M - mobile, B - BGP
<output omitted>

Gateway of last resort is not set

C    192.168.4.0/24 is directly connected, Serial0/0/1
R    192.168.5.0/24 [120/1] via 192.168.4.1, 00:00:12, Serial0/0/1
R    192.168.1.0/24 [120/1] via 192.168.2.1, 00:00:24, Serial0/0/0
C    192.168.2.0/24 is directly connected, Serial0/0/0
C    192.168.3.0/24 is directly connected, FastEthernet0/0
R3# show ip route

Codes: C - connected, S - static, I - IGRP, R - RIP, M - mobile, B - BGP
<output omitted>

Gateway of last resort is not set

C    192.168.4.0/24 is directly connected, Serial0/0/1
C    192.168.5.0/24 is directly connected, FastEthernet0/0
R    192.168.1.0/24 [120/2] via 192.168.4.2, 00:00:08, Serial0/0/1
R    192.168.2.0/24 [120/1] via 192.168.4.2, 00:00:08, Serial0/0/1
R    192.168.3.0/24 [120/1] via 192.168.4.2, 00:00:08, Serial0/0/1
```

The **show ip route** command verifies that routes received by RIP neighbors are installed in a routing table. An **R** in the output indicates RIP routes. Because this command displays the entire routing table, including directly connected and static routes, it is normally the first command used to check for convergence. Routes might not immediately appear when you execute the command because networks take some time to converge. However, when routing is correctly configured on all routers, the **show ip route** command will reflect that each router has a full routing table, with a route to each network in the topology.

In the topology shown earlier in Figure 5-7, you can see there are five networks. Each router lists five networks in the routing table; therefore, you can say that all three routers are converged because each router has a route to every network shown in the topology.

To better understand the output from the **show ip route** command, focus on one RIP route learned by R1 and interpret the output shown in the routing table:

```
R    192.168.5.0/24 [120/2] via 192.168.2.2, 00:00:23, Serial0/0/0
```

The listing of routes with an R code is a quick way to verify that RIP is running on this router. If RIP is not at least partially configured, you will not see RIP routes.

Next, the remote network address and subnet mask are listed (**192.168.5.0/24**).

The AD value (**120** for RIP) and the distance to the network (**2** hops) are shown in brackets.

The next-hop IP address of the advertising router is listed (R2 at **192.168.2.2**) as well as the number of seconds elasped since the last update (**00:00:23**, in this case).

Finally, the exit interface that this router will use for traffic destined for the remote network is listed (**Serial 0/0/0**).

Table 5-3 lists the output and description of each part.

Table 5-3   Interpreting a Route

Output	Description
R	Identifies the source of the route as RIP.
192.168.5.0	Indicates the address of the remote network.
/24	Indicates the subnet mask used for this network.
[120/2]	Shows the administrative distance (120) and the metric (2 hops).
via 192.168.2.2,	Specifies the address of the next-hop router (R2) to send traffic to for the remote network.
00:00:23,	Specifies the amount of time since the route was updated (here, 23 seconds). Another update is due in 7 seconds.
Serial0/0/0	Specifies the local interface through which the remote network can be reached.

Verifying RIP: show ip protocols Command

Another useful command in verifying RIP or other routing protocols is the **show ip protocols** command. If a network is missing from the routing table, check the routing configuration using **show ip protocols**.

The **show ip protocols** command displays the routing protocol that is currently configured on the router. This output can be used to verify most RIP parameters to confirm that

- RIP routing is configured.
- The correct interfaces send and receive RIP updates.
- The router advertises the correct networks.
- RIP neighbors are sending updates.

This command is also useful when verifying the operations of other routing protocols, as you will see later with EIGRP and OSPF.

Figure 5-8 shows the output from the **show ip protocols** command, with numbers by each portion of the output. The descriptions that follow the figure correspond to the numbers in the figure.

Figure 5-8   Interpreting **show ip protocols** Output

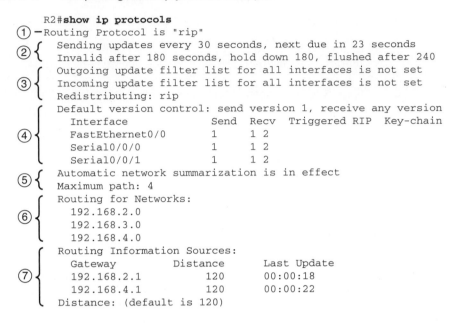

```
                R2#show ip protocols
  ①─Routing Protocol is "rip"
       Sending updates every 30 seconds, next due in 23 seconds
  ②    Invalid after 180 seconds, hold down 180, flushed after 240
       Outgoing update filter list for all interfaces is not set
  ③    Incoming update filter list for all interfaces is not set
       Redistributing: rip
       Default version control: send version 1, receive any version
         Interface            Send  Recv  Triggered RIP  Key-chain
  ④     FastEthernet0/0        1     1 2
         Serial0/0/0           1     1 2
         Serial0/0/1           1     1 2
  ⑤    Automatic network summarization is in effect
       Maximum path: 4
       Routing for Networks:
  ⑥     192.168.2.0
         192.168.3.0
         192.168.4.0
       Routing Information Sources:
         Gateway          Distance      Last Update
  ⑦     192.168.2.1          120        00:00:18
         192.168.4.1          120        00:00:22
       Distance: (default is 120)
```

1. The first line of output verifies that RIP routing is configured and running on Router R2. As you saw in the section "Basic RIPv1 Configuration," earlier in this chapter, at least one active interface with an associated **network** command is needed before RIP routing will start.

2. These are the timers that show when the next round of updates will be sent out from this router—23 seconds from now, in the example.

3. This information relates to filtering updates and redistributing routes, if configured on this router. Filtering and redistribution are both CCNP-level topics.

4. This block of output contains information about which RIP version is currently configured and which interfaces are participating in RIP updates.

5. This part of the output shows that Router R2 is currently summarizing at the classful network boundary and, by default, will use up to four equal-cost routes to load-balance traffic. Automatic summarization is discussed later in this chapter.

6. The classful networks configured with the **network** command are listed next. These are the networks that R2 will include in its RIP updates.

7. Here, the RIP neighbors are listed as Routing Information Sources. Gateway is the next-hop IP address of the neighbor that is sending R2 updates. Distance is the AD that R2 uses for updates sent by this neighbor. Last Update is the seconds since the last update was received from this neighbor.

Verifying RIP: debug ip rip Command

The **debug** command is a useful tool to help diagnose and resolve networking problems, providing real-time, continuous information. Because debugging output is assigned high priority in the CPU process, it can render the system unusable. For this reason, use **debug** commands only to troubleshoot specific problems. Moreover, it is best to use **debug** commands during periods of lower network traffic and fewer users.

Most RIP configuration errors involve an incorrect **network** statement configuration, a missing **network** statement configuration, or the configuration of discontiguous subnets in a classful environment. As shown in Figure 5-9, an effective command used to find issues with RIP updates is **debug ip rip**.

Figure 5-9   Interpreting **debug ip rip** Output

```
      R2#debug ip rip
      RIP protocol debugging is on
①  {  RIP: received v1 update from 192.168.2.1 on Serial0/0/0
            192.168.1.0 in 1 hops
②  {  RIP: received v1 update from 192.168.4.1 on Serial0/0/1
            192.168.5.0 in 1 hops
      RIP: sending  v1 update to 255.255.255.255 via FastEthernet0/0
            (192.168.3.1)
      RIP: build update entries
③  {     network 192.168.1.0 metric 2
            network 192.168.2.0 metric 1
            network 192.168.4.0 metric 1
            network 192.168.5.0 metric 2
      RIP: sending  v1 update to 255.255.255.255 via Serial0/0/1
            (192.168.4.2)
④  {  RIP: build update entries
            network 192.168.1.0 metric 2
            network 192.168.2.0 metric 1
            network 192.168.3.0 metric 1
      RIP: sending  v1 update to 255.255.255.255 via Serial0/0/0
            (192.168.2.2)
⑤  {  RIP: build update entries
            network 192.168.3.0 metric 1
            network 192.168.4.0 metric 1
            network 192.168.5.0 metric 2
⑥  {  R2#undebug all
      All possible debugging has been turned off
```

This command displays RIP routing updates as they are sent and received. Because updates are periodic, you need to wait for the next round of updates before seeing any output.

The list that follows corresponds to the numbers in Figure 5-9.

1. First you see an update coming in from R1 on interface Serial 0/0/0. Notice that R1 only sends one route to the 192.168.1.0 network. No other routes are sent because doing so would violate the split horizon rule. R1 is not allowed to advertise networks back to R2 that R2 previously sent to R1.

2. The next update that is received is from R3. Again, because of the split horizon rule, R3 only sends one route: the 192.168.5.0 network.

3. R2 sends out its own updates. First, R2 builds an update to send out the FastEthernet 0/0 interface. The update includes the entire routing table except for network 192.168.3.0, which is attached to FastEthernet 0/0.

4. Next, R2 builds an update to send to R3. Three routes are included. R2 does not advertise the network R2 and R3 share, nor does it advertise the 192.168.5.0 network because of split horizon.

5. Finally, R2 builds an update to send to R1. Three routes are included. R2 does not advertise the network that R2 and R1 share, nor does it advertise the 192.168.1.0 network because of split horizon.

Note

If you waited another 30 seconds, you would see all the debug output shown in the figure repeat because RIP sends out periodic updates every 30 seconds.

6. To stop monitoring RIP updates on R2, enter the **no debug ip rip** command or simply **undebug all**, as shown in figure.

Reviewing this debug output, you can verify that RIP routing is fully operational on R2. But do you see a way to optimize RIP routing on R2? Does R2 need to send updates out FastEthernet 0/0? You will see in the next topic how to prevent unnecessary updates.

Passive Interfaces

Some routers can have interfaces that do not connect to another router; therefore, there is no reason to send routing updates out that interface. You can use the **passive-interface** command with RIP to configure an interface not to send those updates.

Unnecessary RIP Updates Impact Network

As you saw in the previous example, R2 is sending updates out FastEthernet 0/0 even though no RIP router exists on that LAN. R2 has no way of knowing this and, as a result, sends an update every 30 seconds. Sending out unneeded updates on a LAN impacts the network in three ways:

- Bandwidth is wasted transporting unnecessary updates. Because RIPv1 updates are broadcast, switches will forward the updates out all ports.

- All devices on the LAN must process the RIPv1 update up to the transport layers, where the receiving device will discard the update.

- Advertising updates on a broadcast network is a security risk. RIP updates can be intercepted with packet-sniffing software. Routing updates can be modified and sent back to the router, corrupting the routing table with false metrics that misdirect traffic.

Stopping Unnecessary RIP Updates

You might think you could stop the updates by removing the 192.168.3.0 network from the configuration using the **no network 192.168.3.0** command, but then R2 would not advertise this LAN as a route in updates sent to R1 and R3. The correct solution is to use the **passive-interface** command, which prevents the transmission of routing updates through a router interface but still allows that network to be advertised to other routers. Enter the **passive-interface** command in router configuration mode:

```
Router(config-router)# passive-interface interface-type interface-number
```

This command stops routing updates out the specified interface. However, the network that the specified interface belongs to will still be advertised in routing updates that are sent out other interfaces.

In Example 5-6, R2 is first configured with the **passive-interface** command to prevent routing updates on FastEthernet 0/0 because no RIP neighbors exist on the LAN. The **show ip protocols** command is then used to verify the passive interface.

Example 5-6 Disabling Updates with the **passive-interface** Command

```
R2(config)# router rip
R2(config-router)# passive-interface FastEthernet 0/0
R2(config-router)# end
R2# show ip protocols

Routing Protocol is "rip"
  Sending updates every 30 seconds, next due in 14 seconds
  Invalid after 180 seconds, hold down 180, flushed after 240
  Outgoing update filter list for all interfaces is
  Incoming update filter list for all interfaces is
  Redistributing: rip
  Default version control: send version 1, receive any version
    Interface            Send  Recv  Triggered RIP  Key-chain
    Serial0/0/0            1    1 2
    Serial0/0/1            1    1 2
```

```
Automatic network summarization is in effect
Routing for Networks:
   192.168.2.0
   192.168.3.0
   192.168.4.0
Passive Interface(s):
   FastEthernet0/0
Routing Information Sources:
   Gateway          Distance       Last Update
   192.168.2.1           120       00:00:27
   192.168.4.1           120       00:00:23
Distance: (default is 120)
```

Notice that the interface is no longer listed under **Interface** but under a new section called **Passive Interface(s)**. Also notice that the network 192.168.3.0 is still listed under **Routing for Networks:**, which means that this network is still included as a route entry in RIP updates that are sent to R1 and R3.

All routing protocols support the **passive-interface** command. You will be expected to use the **passive-interface** command when appropriate as part of your normal routing configuration.

Configure Passive Interfaces in RIP (5.3.4)

Use the Packet Tracer Activity to verify RIP routing and stop RIP updates using the **passive-interface** command. Detailed instructions are provided within the activity. Use file e2-534.pka on the CD-ROM that accompanies this book to perform this activity using Packet Tracer.

Automatic Summarization

Fewer routes in a routing table means that the routing table process can more quickly locate the route needed to forward the packet. Summarizing several routes into a single route is known as *route summarization* or *route aggregation*. Some routing protocols, such as RIP, automatically summarize routes on certain routers. The following sections discuss how RIP performs this *automatic summarization*.

Modified Topology: Scenario B

To aid the discussion of automatic summarization, refer to the RIP topology shown in Figure 5-10, Scenario B.

Figure 5-10   RIP Topology: Scenario B

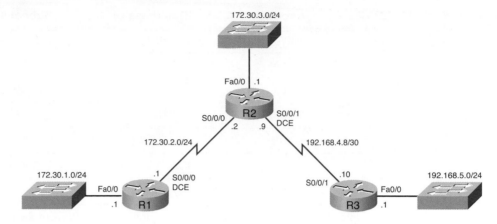

Scenario B is a modification of Scenario A with the following changes:

Three classful networks are used:

- 172.30.0.0/16
- 192.168.4.0/24
- 192.168.5.0/24

The 172.30.0.0/16 network is subnetted into three subnets:

- 172.30.1.0/24
- 172.30.2.0/24
- 172.30.3.0/24

The following devices are part of the 172.30.0.0/16 classful network address:

- All interfaces on R1
- S0/0/0 and Fa0/0 on R2

The 192.168.4.0/24 network is subnetted as a single subnet 192.168.4.8/30.

Table 5-4 shows the addressing scheme for this modified topology.

Table 5-4   Addressing Table: Scenario B

Device	Interface	IP Address	Subnet Mask
R1	Fa0/0	172.30.1.1	255.255.255.0
	S0/0/0	172.30.2.1	255.255.255.0
R2	Fa0/0	172.30.3.1	255.255.255.0
	S0/0/0	172.30.2.2	255.255.255.0
	S0/0/1	192.168.4.9	255.255.255.252
R3	Fa0/0	192.168.5.1	255.255.255.0
	S0/0/1	192.168.4.10	255.255.255.252

Examples 5-7, 5-8, and 5-9 show the configuration changes from Scenario A for Routers R1, R2, and R3, respectively.

Example 5-7 Configuration Changes for R1

```
R1(config)# interface fa0/0
R1(config-if)# ip address 172.30.1.1 255.255.255.0
R1(config-if)# interface S0/0/0
R1(config-if)# ip address 172.30.2.1 255.255.255.0
R1(config-if)# no router rip
R1(config)# router rip
R1(config-router)# network 172.30.1.0
R1(config-router)# network 172.30.2.0
R1(config-router)# passive-interface FastEthernet 0/0
R1(config-router)# end
R1# show run

<output omitted>
!
router rip
 passive-interface FastEthernet0/0
 network 172.30.0.0
!
<output omitted>
```

Example 5-8 Configuration Changes for R2

```
R2(config)# interface S0/0/0
R2(config-if)# ip address 172.30.2.2 255.255.255.0
R2(config-if)# interface fa0/0
R2(config-if)# ip address 172.30.3.1 255.255.255.0
```

```
R2(config-if)# interface S0/0/1
R2(config-if)# ip address 192.168.4.9 255.255.255.252
R2(config-if)# no router rip
R2(config)# router rip
R2(config-router)# network 172.30.0.0
R2(config-router)# network 192.168.4.8
R2(config-router)# passive-interface FastEthernet 0/0
R2(config-router)# end
R2# show run

<output omitted>
!
router rip
 passive-interface FastEthernet0/0
 network 172.30.0.0
 network 192.168.4.0
!
<output omitted>
```

Example 5-9 Configuration Changes for R3

```
R3(config)# interface fa0/0
R3(config-if)# ip address 192.168.5.1 255.255.255.0
R3(config-if)# interface S0/0/1
R3(config-if)# ip address 192.168.4.10 255.255.255.252
R3(config-if)# no router rip
R3(config)# router rip
R3(config-router)# network 192.168.4.0
R3(config-router)# network 192.168.5.0
R3(config-router)# passive-interface FastEthernet 0/0
R3(config-router)# end
R3# show run

<output omitted>
!
router rip
 passive-interface FastEthernet0/0
 network 192.168.4.0
 network 192.168.5.0
!
<output omitted>
```

Notice that the **no shutdown** and **clock rate** commands are not needed because these commands are still configured from Scenario A. However, because new networks were added, the RIP routing process was removed with the **no router rip** command before enabling it again.

In the configuration for R1 (Example 5-7), notice that both subnets were configured with the **network** command. This configuration is technically incorrect because RIPv1 sends the classful network address in its updates and not the subnet. Therefore, IOS changed the configuration to reflect the correct, classful configuration, as you can see from the **show run** output.

In the configuration for R2 (Example 5-8), notice that the subnet 192.168.4.8 was configured with the **network** command. Again, this configuration is technically incorrect, and IOS changed it to 192.168.4.0 in the running configuration.

The routing configuration for R3 is correct (Example 5-9). The running configuration matches what was entered in router configuration mode.

Note

On assessment and certification exams, entering a subnet address instead of the classful network address in a **network** command is considered an incorrect answer, even though Cisco IOS will make the correction.

Boundary Routers and Automatic Summarization

As you know, RIP is a classful routing protocol that automatically summarizes classful networks across major network boundaries. In Figure 5-11, you can see that R2 has interfaces in more than one major classful network. This makes R2 a *boundary router* in RIP. Both Serial 0/0/0 and FastEthernet 0/0 interfaces on R2 are inside the 172.30.0.0 boundary. The Serial 0/0/1 interface is inside the 192.168.4.0 boundary.

Figure 5-11   RIP Boundary Router

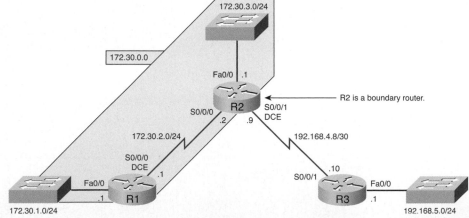

Because boundary routers summarize RIP subnets from one major network to the other, updates for the 172.30.1.0, 172.30.2.0, and 172.30.3.0 networks will automatically be summarized into 172.30.0.0 when sent out R2's Serial 0/0/1 interface.

The next two sections examine how boundary routers perform this summarization.

Processing RIP Updates

Classful routing protocols such as RIPv1 do not include the subnet mask in the routing update. However, the routing table includes RIPv1 routes with both the network address and the subnet mask. So how does a router running RIPv1 determine what subnet mask it should apply to a route when adding it to the routing table? The following section explains this process.

Rules for Processing RIPv1 Updates

The following two rules govern RIPv1 updates:

- If a routing update and the interface on which it is received belong to the same major network, the subnet mask of the interface is applied to the network in the routing update.

- If a routing update and the interface on which it is received belong to different major networks, the classful subnet mask of the network is applied to the network in the routing update.

Example of RIPv1 Processing Updates

In Example 5-10, R2 receives an update from R1 and enters the network in the routing table.

Example 5-10   Boundary Router Receiving RIP Updates

```
R2# debug ip rip

RIP protocol debugging is on
RIP: received v1 update from 172.30.2.1 on Serial0/0/0
      172.30.1.0 in 1 hops
<output omitted>
R2# undebug all

All possible debugging has been turned off
R2# show ip route

<output omitted>
```

```
Gateway of last resort is not set

     172.30.0.0/24 is subnetted, 3 subnets
R       172.30.1.0 [120/1] via 172.30.2.1, 00:00:18, Serial0/0/0
C       172.30.2.0 is directly connected, Serial0/0/0
C       172.30.3.0 is directly connected, FastEthernet0/0
     192.168.4.0/30 is subnetted, 1 subnets
C       192.168.4.8 is directly connected, Serial0/0/1
R    192.168.5.0/24 [120/1] via 192.168.4.10, 00:00:16, Serial0/0/1
```

How does R2 know that this subnet has a /24 (255.255.255.0) subnet mask? It knows because

- R2 received this information on an interface that belongs to the same classful network (172.30.0.0) as that of the incoming 172.30.1.0 update.

- The IP address for which R2 received the **172.30.1.0 in 1 hops** message was on Serial 0/0/0 with an IP address of 172.30.2.2 and a subnet mask of 255.255.255.0 (/24).

- R2 uses its own subnet mask on this interface and applies it to this and all other 172.30.0.0 subnets that it receives on this interface—in this case, 172.30.1.0.

- The 172.30.1.0 /24 subnet was added to the routing table.

Routers running RIPv1 are limited to using the same subnet mask for all subnets with the same classful network.

As you will learn in later chapters, classless routing protocols such as RIPv2 allow the same major (classful) network to use different subnet masks on different subnets, better known as *variable-length subnet masking* (VLSM).

Sending RIP Updates: Using debug to View Automatic Summarization

To verify the network addresses sent and received by a router, you can use the **debug ip rip** command. Then by examining the routing tables, you can see the subnet mask that the receiving router applied to the RIPv1 routes.

Example 5-11 again shows the **debug ip rip** output for R2.

Example 5-11   Additional R2 Debug Output

```
R2# debug ip rip

RIP protocol debugging is on
RIP: sending  v1 update to 255.255.255.255 via Serial0/0/0 (172.30.2.2)
```

```
RIP: build update entries
        network 172.30.3.0 metric 1
        network 192.168.4.0 metric 1
        network 192.168.5.0 metric 2
RIP: sending  v1 update to 255.255.255.255 via Serial0/0/1 (192.168.4.9)
RIP: build update entries
        network 172.30.0.0 metric 1
R2# undebug all


All possible debugging has been turned off
```

When sending an update, boundary Router R2 will include the network address and associated metric. If the route entry is for an update sent out a different major network, the network address in the route entry is summarized to the classful or major network address. This is exactly what R2 does for 192.168.4.0 and 192.168.5.0. It sends these classful networks to R1.

R2 also has routes for the 172.30.1.0/24, 172.30.2.0/24, and 172.30.3.0/24 subnets. In R2's routing update to R3 on Serial 0/0/1, R2 sends only a summary of the classful network address of 172.30.0.0.

If the route entry is for an update sent within a major network, the subnet mask of the outbound interface is used to determine the network address to advertise. R2 sends the 172.30.3.0 subnet to R1 using the subnet mask on Serial 0/0/0 to determine the subnet address to advertise.

R1 receives the 172.30.3.0 update on the Serial 0/0/0 interface, which has an interface address of 172.30.2.1/24. Because both the routing update and interface belong to the same major network, R1 applies its /24 mask to the 172.30.3.0 route.

Compare the routing tables for R1 and R3 in Examples 5-12 and 5-13.

Example 5-12   Routing Table for R1

```
R1# show ip route

<output omitted>

Gateway of last resort is not set

     172.30.0.0/24 is subnetted, 3 subnets
C       172.30.1.0 is directly connected, FastEthernet0/0
C       172.30.2.0 is directly connected, Serial0/0/0
R       172.30.3.0 [120/1] via 172.30.2.2, 00:00:17, Serial0/0/0
R     192.168.4.0/24 [120/1] via 172.30.2.2, 00:00:17, Serial0/0/0
R     192.168.5.0/24 [120/2] via 172.30.2.2, 00:00:17, Serial0/0/0
```

```
Example 5-13    Routing Table for R3
R3# show ip route

<output omitted>

Gateway of last resort is not set

R     172.30.0.0/16 [120/1] via 192.168.4.9, 00:00:15, Serial0/0/1
      192.168.4.0/30 is subnetted, 1 subnets
C        192.168.4.8 is directly connected, Serial0/0/1
C     192.168.5.0/24 is directly connected, FastEthernet0/0
```

Notice that R1 has three routes for the 172.30.0.0 major network, which has been subnetted to /24 or 255.255.255.0. R3 has only one route to the 172.30.0.0 network, and the network has not been subnetted. R3 has the major network in its routing table. However, it would be a mistake to assume that R3 does not have full connectivity. R3 will send any packets destined for the 172.30.1.0/24, 172.30.2.0/24, and 172.30.3.0/24 networks to R2 because all three of those networks belong to 172.30.0.0/16 and are reachable through R2.

Advantages and Disadvantages of Automatic Summarization

Automatic summarization has both advantages and disadvantages. Classful routing protocols such as RIPv1 do not allow you to modify this behavior. However, classless routing protocols such as RIPv2 do permit automatic summarization to be disabled. For now, we examine the advantages and disadvantages of automatic summarization.

Advantages of Automatic Summarization

As you saw with R2 in Example 5-11, RIP automatically summarizes updates between classful networks. Because the 172.30.0.0 update is sent out an interface (Serial 0/0/1) on a different classful network (192.168.4.0), RIP sends out only a single update for the entire classful network instead of one for each of the different subnets. This process is similar to what you did when you summarized several static routes into a single static route. Why is automatic summarization an advantage? It is for the following reasons:

- Smaller routing updates are sent and received, which uses less bandwidth for routing updates between R2 and R3.

- R3 has a single route for the 172.30.0.0/16 network, regardless of how many subnets there are or how it is subnetted. Using a single route results in a faster lookup process in the routing table for R3.

Is there a disadvantage to automatic summarization? Yes, when discontiguous networks are configured in the topology.

Disadvantage of Automatic Summarization

Figure 5-12 shows a topology with discontiguous networks. Discontiguous networks will be explained shortly.

Figure 5-12   Discontiguous Topology

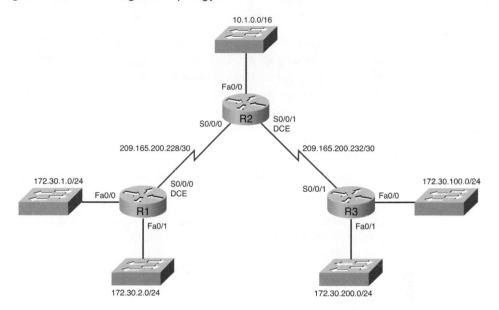

As you can see in Table 5-5, the addressing scheme has been changed.

Table 5-5   Addressing Scheme for Discontiguous Topology

Device	Interface	IP Address	Subnet Mask
R1	Fa0/0	172.30.1.1	255.255.255.0
	Fa0/1	172.30.2.1	255.255.255.0
	S0/0/0	209.165.200.229	255.255.255.252
R2	Fa0/0	10.1.0.1	255.255.0.0
	S0/0/0	209.165.200.230	255.255.255.252
	S0/0/1	209.165.200.233	255.255.255.252
R3	Fa0/0	172.30.100.1	255.255.255.0
	Fa0/0	172.30.200.1	255.255.255.0
	S0/0/1	209.165.200.234	255.255.255.252

This topology will be used to show a main disadvantage with classful routing protocols such as RIPv1: their lack of support for discontiguous networks.

Classful routing protocols do not include the subnet mask in routing updates. Networks are automatically summarized across major network boundaries because the receiving router is unable to determine the mask of the route. This is because the receiving interface might have a different mask than the subnetted routes.

Notice in Figure 5-12 that both R1 and R3 have subnets from the 172.30.0.0/16 major network, whereas R2 does not. Essentially, R1 and R3 are boundary routers for 172.30.0.0/16 because they are separated by another major network, 209.165.200.0/24. This separation creates a *discontiguous network*, because two groups of 172.30.0.0/24 subnets are separated by at least one other major network. 172.30.0.0/16 is a discontiguous network.

Discontiguous Topologies Do Not Converge with RIPv1

Example 5-14 shows the RIP configuration for each router based on the topology shown in Figure 5-12.

Example 5-14   RIP Configuration for the Discontiguous Topology

```
R1(config)# router rip
R1(config-router)# network 172.30.0.0
R1(config-router)# network 209.165.200.0
R2(config)# router rip
R2(config-router)# network 10.0.0.0
R2(config-router)# network 209.165.200.0
R3(config)# router rip
R3(config-router)# network 172.30.0.0
R3(config-router)# network 209.165.200.0
```

The RIPv1 configuration is correct, but it is unable to determine all the networks in this discontiguous topology. To understand why, remember that a router will only advertise major network addresses out interfaces that do not belong to the advertised route. As a result, R1 will not advertise 172.30.1.0 or 172.30.2.0 to R2 across the 209.165.200.0 network. R3 will not advertise 172.30.100.0 or 172.30.200.0 to R2 across the 209.165.200.0 network. Both routers, however, will advertise the 172.30.0.0 major network address, a summary route to R3.

What is the result? Without the inclusion of the subnet mask in the routing update, RIPv1 cannot advertise specific routing information that will allow routers to correctly route for the 172.30.0.0/24 subnets.

Examine the routing tables for R1, R2, and R3 in Examples 5-15, 5-16, and 5-17, respectively.

Example 5-15   Routing Table for R1

```
R1# show ip route

<output omitted>

Gateway of last resort is not set

R    10.0.0.0/8 [120/1] via 209.165.200.230, 00:00:26, Serial0/0/0
     172.30.0.0/24 is subnetted, 3 subnets
R       172.30.0.0 [120/2] via 209.165.200.230, 00:00:26, Serial0/0/0
C       172.30.1.0 is directly connected, FastEthernet0/0
C       172.30.2.0 is directly connected, FastEthernet0/1
     209.165.200.0/30 is subnetted, 2 subnets
C       209.165.200.228 is directly connected, Serial0/0/0
R       209.165.200.232 [120/1] via 209.165.200.230, 00:00:26, Serial0/0/0
```

Example 5-16   Routing Table for R2

```
R2# show ip route

<output omitted>

Gateway of last resort is not set

     10.0.0.0/16 is subnetted, 1 subnets
C       10.1.0.0 is directly connected, FastEthernet0/0
R    172.30.0.0/16 [120/1] via 209.165.200.234, 00:00:14, Serial0/0/1
                   [120/1] via 209.165.200.229, 00:00:19, Serial0/0/0
     209.165.200.0/30 is subnetted, 2 subnets
C       209.165.200.228 is directly connected, Serial0/0/0
C       209.165.200.232 is directly connected, Serial0/0/1
```

Example 5-17   Routing Table for R3

```
R3# show ip route

<output omitted>

Gateway of last resort is not set

R    10.0.0.0/8 [120/1] via 209.165.200.233, 00:00:24, Serial0/0/1
```

```
          172.30.0.0/24 is subnetted, 3 subnets
R         172.30.0.0 [120/2] via 209.165.200.233, 00:00:22, Serial0/0/1
C         172.30.100.0 is directly connected, FastEthernet0/0
C         172.30.200.0 is directly connected, FastEthernet0/1
       209.165.200.0/30 is subnetted, 2 subnets
R         209.165.200.228 [120/1] via 209.165.200.233, 00:00:24, Serial0/0/1
C         209.165.200.232 is directly connected, Serial0/0/1
```

- R1 does not have routes to the LANs attached to R3.

- R3 does not have routes to the LANs attached to R1.

- R2 has two equal-cost paths to the 172.30.0.0 network.

- R2 will load-balance traffic destined for any subnet of 172.30.0.0. This means that R1 will get half of the traffic and R3 will get the other half of the traffic, whether or not the destination of the traffic is for one of their LANs.

In Chapter 7, you will see a version of this topology. It will be used to show the difference between classful and classless routing.

Automatic Route Summarization in RIP (5.4.5)

Use the Packet Tracer Activity to implement the Scenario B addressing scheme and explore the advantages and disadvantages of automatic summarization. Detailed instructions are provided within the activity. Use file e2-545.pka on the CD-ROM that accompanies this book to perform this activity using Packet Tracer.

Default Route and RIPv1

Default routes are used by routers to represent all routes that are not specifically in the routing table. A default route is commonly used to represent routes that are not in the locally administered network, such as the Internet.

Modified Topology: Scenario C

Figure 5-13 shows a modified topology, Scenario C, to demonstrate the use of a default route and show how it is propagated by RIPv1 to other routers.

Figure 5-13   RIP Topology: Scenario C

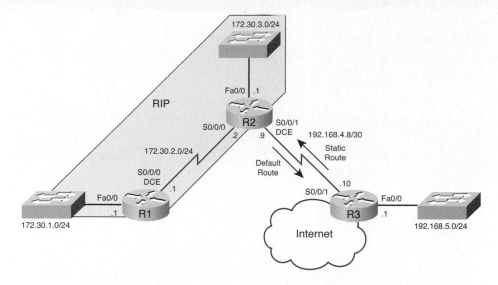

RIP was the first dynamic routing protocol and was used extensively in early implementations between customers and Internet service providers (ISP), as well as between different ISPs. But in today's networks, customers do not necessarily have to exchange routing updates with their ISP. Customer routers that connect to an ISP do not need a listing for every route on the Internet. Instead, these routers have a default route that sends all traffic to the ISP router when the customer router does not have a route to a destination. The ISP configures a static route pointing to the customer router for addresses inside the customer's network.

In Scenario C, R3 is the service provider with access to the Internet, as signified by the cloud. R3 and R2 do not exchange RIP updates. Instead, R2 uses a default route to reach the R3 LAN and all other destinations that are not listed in its routing table. R3 uses a summary static route to reach the subnets 172.30.1.0, 172.30.2.0, and 172.30.3.0.

To prepare the topology, you can leave the addressing in place; it is the same as was used in Scenario B. However, you also need to complete the following steps.

Example 5-18 shows the configuration commands used in the following steps:

Step 1.   Disable RIP routing for network 192.168.4.0 on R2.

Step 2.   Configure R2 with a static default route to send default traffic to R3.

Step 3.   Disable RIP routing on R3.

Step 4.   Configure R3 with a static route to the 172.30.0.0 subnets.

Example 5-18   Configuration Changes for R2 and R3

```
R2(config)# router rip
R2(config-router)# no network 192.168.4.0
R2(config-router)# exit
R2(config)# ip route 0.0.0.0 0.0.0.0 serial 0/0/1
```
```
R3(config)# no router rip
R3(config)# ip route 172.30.0.0 255.255.252.0 serial 0/0/1
```

Examples 5-19, 5-20, and 5-21 show the new routing tables for R1, R2, and R3, respectively.

Example 5-19   Routing Table for R1

```
R1# show ip route

<output omitted>

Gateway of last resort is not set

     172.30.0.0/24 is subnetted, 3 subnets
C       172.30.1.0 is directly connected, FastEthernet0/0
C       172.30.2.0 is directly connected, Serial0/0/0
R       172.30.3.0 [120/1] via 172.30.2.2, 00:00:05, Serial0/0/0
```

Example 5-20   Routing Table for R2

```
R2# show ip route

<output omitted>

Gateway of last resort is 0.0.0.0 to network 0.0.0.0

     172.30.0.0/24 is subnetted, 3 subnets
R       172.30.1.0 [120/1] via 172.30.2.1, 00:00:03, Serial0/0/0
C       172.30.2.0 is directly connected, Serial0/0/0
C       172.30.3.0 is directly connected, FastEthernet0/0
     192.168.4.0/30 is subnetted, 1 subnets
C       192.168.4.8 is directly connected, Serial0/0/1
S*   0.0.0.0/0 is directly connected, Serial0/0/1
```

```
Example 5-21    Routing Table for R3
R3# show ip route

<output omitted>

Gateway of last resort is not set

     172.30.0.0/22 is subnetted, 1 subnets
S       172.30.0.0 is directly connected, Serial0/0/1
     192.168.4.0/30 is subnetted, 1 subnets
C       192.168.4.8 is directly connected, Serial0/0/1
C     192.168.5.0/24 is directly connected, FastEthernet0/0
```

Propagating the Default Route in RIPv1

To provide Internet connectivity to all other networks in the RIP routing domain, the default static route needs to be advertised to all other routers that use the dynamic routing protocol. You could configure a static default route on R1 pointing to R2, but this technique is not scalable. With every router added to the RIP routing domain, you would have to configure another static default route. Why not let the routing protocol do the work for you?

In many routing protocols, including RIP, you can use the **default-information originate** command in router configuration mode to specify that this router is to originate default information, by propagating the static default route in RIP updates. In Example 5-22, R2 has been configured with the **default-information originate** command. Notice from the **debug ip rip** output that it is now sending a "quad-zero" static default route to R1.

```
Example 5-22    Configuring Default Route Propagation
R2(config)# router rip
R2(config-router)# default-information originate
R2(config-router)# end
R2# debug ip rip

RIP protocol debugging is on
RIP: sending v1 update to 255.255.255.255 via Serial0/0/0 (172.30.2.2)
RIP: build update entries
       subnet 0.0.0.0 metric 1
       subnet 172.30.3.0 metric 1
R2# undebug all

All possible debugging has been turned off
```

In the routing table for R1 (Example 5-23), you can see that there is a candidate default route, as denoted by the R* code. Cisco IOS uses the concept of *candidate default routes*, which are one or more routes marked manually or automatically as a candidate to be the default route. The actual default route installed in the routing table depends on factors such as administrative distance of the candidate. For example, a static default route will have precedence over a default route learned through a dynamic routing protocol.

Example 5-23   Verifying Default Route Propagation

```
R1# show ip route

<output omitted>
       * - candidate default, U - per-user static route, o - ODR

Gateway of last resort is 172.30.2.2 to network 0.0.0.0

     172.30.0.0/24 is subnetted, 3 subnets
C       172.30.2.0 is directly connected, Serial0/0/0
R       172.30.3.0 [120/1] via 172.30.2.2, 00:00:16, Serial0/0/0
C       172.30.1.0 is directly connected, FastEthernet0/0
R*   0.0.0.0/0 [120/1] via 172.30.2.2, 00:00:16, Serial0/0/0
```

The static default route on R2 has been propagated to R1 in a RIP update. R1 has connectivity to the LAN on R3 and any destination on the Internet.

Propagating the Default Route in RIP (5.5.2)

Use the Packet Tracer Activity to implement Scenario C with static and default routing, and configure R2 to propagate a default route. Detailed instructions are provided within the activity. Use file e2-552.pka on the CD-ROM that accompanies this book to perform this activity using Packet Tracer.

Summary

RIP (Version 1) is a classful distance vector routing protocol. RIPv1 was one of the first routing protocols developed for routing IP packets. RIP uses hop count for its metric, with a metric of 16 hops, meaning that a route is unreachable. As a result, RIP can only be used in networks where there are no more than 15 routers between any two networks.

RIP messages are encapsulated in a UDP segment, with source and destination ports of 520. RIP routers send their complete routing tables to their neighbors every 30 seconds except for those routes that are covered by the split horizon rule.

RIP is enabled by using the **router rip** command at the global configuration prompt. The **network** command is used to specify which interfaces on the router will be enabled for RIP along with the classful network address for each directly connected network. The **network** command enables the interface to send and receive RIP updates and advertises that network in RIP updates to other routers.

The **debug ip rip** command can be used to view the RIP updates that are sent and received by the router. To prevent RIP updates from being sent out an interface, such as on a LAN where there are no other routers, the **passive-interface** command is used.

RIP entries are displayed in the routing table with the source code of R and have an administrative distance of 120. Default routes are propagated in RIP by configuring a static default route and using the **default-information originate command** in RIP.

RIPv1 automatically summarizes subnets to their classful address when sending an update out an interface that is on a different major network than the subnetted address of the route. Because RIPv1 is a classful routing protocol, the subnet mask is not included in the routing update. When a router receives a RIPv1 routing update, RIP must determine the subnet mask of that route. If the route belongs to the same major classful network as the update, RIPv1 applies the subnet mask of the receiving interface. If the route belongs to a different major classful network from the receiving interface, RIPv1 applies the default classful mask.

The **show ip protocols** command can be used to display information for any routing protocol enabled on the router. Regarding RIP, this command displays timer information, status of automatic summarization, the networks that are enabled on this router for RIP, and other information.

Because RIPv1 is a classful routing protocol, it does not support discontiguous networks or VLSM. Both of these topics are discussed in Chapter 7.

Activities and Labs

The activities and labs available in the companion *Routing Protocols and Concepts, CCNA Exploration Labs and Study Guide* (ISBN 1-58713-204-4) provide hands-on practice with the following topics introduced in this chapter.

Lab 5-1: Basic RIP Configuration (5.6.1)

In this lab, you will work through the configuration and verification commands discussed in this chapter using the same three scenarios. You will configure RIP routing, verify your configurations, investigate the problem with discontiguous networks, observe automatic summarization, and configure and propagate a default route.

Lab 5-2: Challenge RIP Configuration (5.6.2)

In this lab activity, you will be given a network address that must be subnetted to complete the addressing of the network shown in the topology diagram. A combination of RIPv1 and static routing will be required so that hosts on networks that are not directly connected will be able to communicate with each other.

Lab 5-3: RIP Troubleshooting (5.6.3)

In this lab, you will begin by loading configuration scripts on each of the routers. These scripts contain errors that will prevent end-to-end communication across the network. You will need to troubleshoot each router to determine the configuration errors, and then use the appropriate commands to correct the configurations. When you have corrected all the configuration errors, all the hosts on the network should be able to communicate with each other.

Many of the hands-on labs include Packet Tracer Companion Activities, where you can use Packet Tracer to complete a simulation of the lab. Look for this icon in *Routing Protocols and Concepts, CCNA Exploration Labs and Study Guide* (ISBN 1-58713-204-4) for hands-on labs that have a Packet Tracer Companion.

Check Your Understanding

Complete all the review questions listed here to test your understanding of the topics and concepts in this chapter. Answers are listed in the appendix, "Check Your Understanding and Challenge Questions Answer Key."

1. Which statement is true about the **debug ip rip** command?

    A. It searches through the running configuration and shows possible errors in the RIP configuration.

    B. It displays RIP routing updates as they are sent and received.

    C. It automatically identifies routing loops.

    D. It shows the history of RIP updates over the previous 90 seconds.

2. What problem does the **passive-interface** command help resolve?

    A. Prevents confusion if both RIPv1 and RIPv2 are being advertised on a network

    B. Prevents wasted bandwidth and processing from unnecessary updates

    C. Prevents routing loops

    D. Prevents updates from being sent out without a password

3. What makes a router a boundary router in RIP?

    A. If it is on the edge of an autonomous system

    B. If a router has multiple interfaces in more than one major classful network

    C. If it runs both RIP and EIGRP at the same time

    D. If it is configured to be a boundary router by an administrator

4. What command is used with RIP to propagate default routes to neighbors?

    A. **network 0.0.0.0**

    B. **ip summary-address rip address mask**

    C. **ip default-network address**

    D. **default-information originate**

5. What command will create a candidate default route on a RIP router?

    A. **default-information originate**

    B. **ip default-network 0.0.0.0**

    C. **ip default-gateway 192.168.0.1**

    D. **ip route 0.0.0.0 0.0.0.0 serial0/0/0**

6. Refer to Figure 5-14. All routers are running RIPv1. The interfaces on all routers are up and stable. Users on the 10.16.1.0 network cannot access services on the 10.16.1.64 network. What is the cause of this problem?

Figure 5-14 Check Your Understanding: Question #6

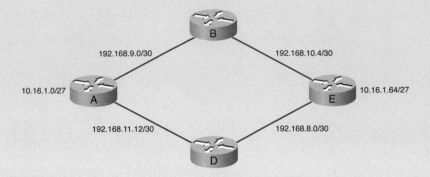

A. The RIP hold-down timer in Router A is not allowing the 10.16.1.64 network into routing updates.

B. The network uses variable-length subnet masking, and RIPv1 does not allow this.

C. The 10.16.1.x subnets are discontiguous.

D. Routers A and B need to have their interfaces configured as passive interfaces.

7. How does a router running RIPv1 determine the subnet mask of the routes that are received in routing updates?

A. The subnet mask is included in the routing update.

B. The router sends a request for the subnet mask to the sending router.

C. The router uses the subnet mask of the local interface or the default subnet mask for the address class in the routing update.

D. The router calculates the subnet mask based on the variable-length subnetting in its own configuration.

E. The router defaults to 255.255.255.0 for all updates.

8. Refer to the following output. What is the administrative distance of the route to the 172.30.3.0 network?

```
<output omitted>
C       172.30.1.0 is directly connected, FastEthernet0/0
C       172.30.2.0 is directly connected, Serial0/0/0
R       172.30.3.0 [120/1] via 172.30.2.2, 00:00:05, Serial0/0/0
<output omitted>
```

    A. 0

    B. 1

    C. 12

    D. 24

    E. 120

9. What is the purpose of the **network** command when RIP is being configured as the routing protocol?

    A. It identifies the networks connected to the neighboring router.

    B. It restricts networks from being used for static routes.

    C. It identifies all the destination networks that the router is allowed to install in its routing table.

    D. It identifies the directly connected networks that will be included in the RIP routing updates.

10. To ensure proper routing in a network, the network administrator should always check the router configuration to verify that appropriate routes are available. Match the commands with their appropriate function.

Command:

debug ip rip

show ip protocols

show running-config

show ip route

show interfaces

Function:

    A. Displays current configuration information for configured routing protocols and interfaces

    B. Checks to see that the interfaces are up and operational

    C. Displays the networks advertised in the updates as the updates are sent and received

    D. Verifies that the routing protocol is running and advertising the correct networks

    E. Verifies that the routes received are installed in the routing table

11. What are the key characteristics of RIPv1?

12. Refer to Figure 5-15. HQ has connections to three branch routers (BR1, BR2, and BR3) and to the Internet through ISP. RIPv1 is configured between HQ and the branch routers. List the commands used to configure RIPv1 routing on the BR1 router.

Figure 5-15   Summary Topology

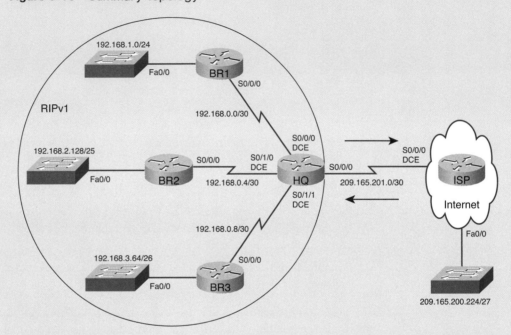

13. List the three commands used to verify and troubleshoot a RIP configuration.

14. What is the purpose of the **passive-interface** command? What is the configuration for BR1 shown in Figure 5-15, including router prompt, for this command?

15. Why would you not want to configure a dynamic routing protocol to exchange updates with your ISP?

Challenge Questions and Activities

These questions require a deeper application of the concepts covered in this chapter and are similar to the style of questions you might see on a CCNA certification exam. You can find the answers to these questions in the appendix, "Answers to Check Your Understanding and Challenge Questions and Activities."

1. What is the full routing configuration for HQ in Figure 5-15, including RIPv1, default routing, and propagating the default route to the branch routers?

2. The network in Figure 5-15 is not fully converged. Using only the following output from **show ip route**, determine the problem and either suggest a solution or suggest the next step in determining the source of the problem.

```
HQ# show ip route

<output omitted>

Gateway of last resort is 0.0.0.0 to network 0.0.0.0

     192.168.0.0/30 is subnetted, 3 subnets
C       192.168.0.0 is directly connected, Serial0/0/1
C       192.168.0.4 is directly connected, Serial0/1/0
C       192.168.0.8 is directly connected, Serial0/1/1
R    192.168.1.0/24 [120/1] via 192.168.0.2, 00:00:04, Serial0/0/1
R    192.168.2.0/24 [120/1] via 192.168.0.6, 00:00:22, Serial0/1/0
     209.165.201.0/30 is subnetted, 1 subnets
C       209.165.201.0 is directly connected, Serial0/0/0
S*   0.0.0.0/0 is directly connected, Serial0/0/0
```

```
BR1# show ip route

<output omitted>

Gateway of last resort is 192.168.0.1 to network 0.0.0.0

     192.168.0.0/30 is subnetted, 3 subnets
C       192.168.0.0 is directly connected, Serial0/0/0
R       192.168.0.4 [120/1] via 192.168.0.1, 00:00:05, Serial0/0/0
R       192.168.0.8 [120/1] via 192.168.0.1, 00:00:05, Serial0/0/0
C    192.168.1.0/24 is directly connected, FastEthernet0/0
R    192.168.2.0/24 [120/2] via 192.168.0.1, 00:00:05, Serial0/0/0
R*   0.0.0.0/0 [120/1] via 192.168.0.1, 00:00:05, Serial0/0/0
```

```
BR2# show ip route

<output omitted>

Gateway of last resort is 192.168.0.5 to network 0.0.0.0

     192.168.0.0/30 is subnetted, 3 subnets
R       192.168.0.0 [120/1] via 192.168.0.5, 00:00:06, Serial0/0/0
C       192.168.0.4 is directly connected, Serial0/0/0
R       192.168.0.8 [120/1] via 192.168.0.5, 00:00:06, Serial0/0/0
R    192.168.1.0/24 [120/2] via 192.168.0.5, 00:00:01, Serial0/0/0
     192.168.2.0/25 is subnetted, 1 subnets
```

```
C        192.168.2.128 is directly connected, FastEthernet0/0
R*    0.0.0.0/0 [120/1] via 192.168.0.5, 00:00:06, Serial0/0/0
```

```
BR3# show ip route

<output omitted>

Gateway of last resort is 192.168.0.9 to network 0.0.0.0

     192.168.0.0/30 is subnetted, 3 subnets
R        192.168.0.0 [120/1] via 192.168.0.9, 00:00:08, Serial0/0/0
R        192.168.0.4 [120/1] via 192.168.0.9, 00:00:08, Serial0/0/0
C        192.168.0.8 is directly connected, Serial0/0/0
R     192.168.1.0/24 [120/2] via 192.168.0.9, 00:00:02, Serial0/0/0
R     192.168.2.0/24 [120/2] via 192.168.0.9, 00:00:08, Serial0/0/0
R*    0.0.0.0/0 [120/1] via 192.168.0.9, 00:00:08, Serial0/0/0
```

3. What static route command on ISP will summarize all the networks (and only those networks) accessible through HQ?

4. Using Packet Tracer, build and configure the topology shown in Figure 5-15.

To Learn More

Requests For Comments (RFC) are a series of documents submitted to the IETF (Internet Engineering Task Force) to propose an Internet standard or convey new concepts, information, or occasionally even humor. RFC 1058 is the original RFC for RIP written by Charles Hedrick.

RFCs can be accessed from several websites, including http://www.ietf.org/rfc/rfc1058.txt. Read all or parts of RFC 1058. Much of this information will now be familiar to you, along with some additional information.

CHAPTER 6

VLSM and CIDR

Objectives

Upon completion of this chapter, you should be able to answer the following questions:

- What are the differences between classful and classless IP addressing?

- What is VLSM, and what are the benefits of classless IP addressing?

- What is the role of the classless interdomain routing (CIDR) standard in making efficient use of scarce IPv4 addresses?

Key Terms

This chapter uses the following key terms. You can find the definitions in the Glossary at the end of the book.

Prior to 1981, IP addresses used only the first 8 bits to specify the network portion of the address, limiting the Internet—then known as ARPANET—to 256 networks. Early on, it became obvious that this was not going to be enough address space.

In 1981, RFC 791 modified the IPv4 32-bit address to allow three different classes or sizes of the networks:

- Class A addresses, which used 8 bits for the network portion of the address

- Class B addresses, which used 16 bits for the network portion of the address

- Class C addresses, which used 24 bits for the network portion of the address

This format became known as *classful IP addressing*.

The initial development of classful addressing solved the 256-network limit problem, for a time. A decade later, it became clear that the IP address space was depleting rapidly. In response, the Internet Engineering Task Force (IETF) introduced classless interdomain routing (CIDR), which used variable-length subnet masking (VLSM) to help conserve address space.

With the introduction of CIDR and VLSM, Internet service providers (ISP) could now assign one part of a classful network to one customer and a different part to another customer. This *discontiguous address assignment* by ISPs was paralleled by the development of classless routing protocols. To compare: Classful routing protocols always summarize on the classful boundary and do not include the subnet mask in routing updates. Classless routing protocols do include the subnet mask in routing updates and are not required to perform summarization. The classless routing protocols discussed in this course are Routing Information Protocol version 2 (RIPv2), Enhanced Interior Gateway Routing Protocol (EIGRP), and Open Shortest Path First (OSPF).

With the introduction of VLSM and CIDR, network administrators had to use additional subnetting skills. VLSM is simply subnetting a subnet. Subnets can be further subnetted in multiple levels, as you will learn in this chapter. In addition to subnetting, it became possible to summarize a large collection of classful networks into an aggregate route, or *supernet*. In this chapter, you will also review route summarization skills.

Classful and Classless Addressing

One of the ways to characterize routing protocols is either as classful or classless. This is a result of the evolution from classful to classless IPv4 addressing. As networks began to use classless addressing, classless routing protocols had to be modified or developed to include the subnet mask in the routing update. The following sections review classful and classless addressing, and introduce classless routing protocols.

Classful IP Addressing

Figure 6-1 shows the exponential growth of hosts in the Internet from 1992 to 2006.

Figure 6-1   Growth of the Internet from 1992 to 2006 (Source: http://en.wikipedia.org/
wiki/Image:Number_of_internet_hosts.svg)

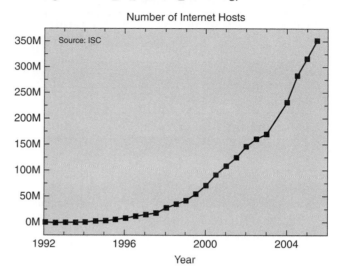

Note

The Internet Software Consortium (ISC) tracks the number of hosts on the Internet. To see more information about ISC's host count, visit "ISC Domain Survey: Number of Internet Hosts," http://www.isc.org/index.pl?/ops/ds/host-count-history.php.

When the ARPANET was commissioned in 1969, no one anticipated that the Internet would explode out of the humble beginnings of this research project. By 1989, ARPANET had been transformed into what we now call the Internet. Over the next decade, the number of hosts on the Internet grew exponentially, from 159,000 in October 1989 to over 72 million by the end of the millennium. As of January 2007, there were over 433 million hosts on the Internet.

Without the introduction of VLSM and CIDR notation in 1993 (RFC 1519), Network Address Translation (NAT) in 1994 (RFC 1631), and *private addressing* in 1996 (RFC 1918), the IPv4 32-bit address space would now be exhausted.

High-Order Bits

IPv4 addresses were initially allocated based on class, as shown in Table 6-1.

Table 6-1   High-Order Bits

Class	High-Order Bits	Start	End
Class A	0	0.0.0.0	127.255.255.255
Class B	10	128.0.0.0	191.255.255.255
Class C	110	192.0.0.0	223.255.255.255
Multicast	1110	224.0.0.0	239.255.255.255
Experimental	1111	240.0.0.0	255.255.255.255

In the original specification of IPv4 (RFC 791, http://www.ietf.org/rfc/rfc791.txt) released in 1981, the authors established the classes to provide three different sizes of networks for large, medium, and small organizations. As a result, Class A, B, and C addresses were defined with a specific format for the *high-order bits*. High-order bits are the leftmost bits in a 32-bit address.

Table 6-1 shows the following details:

- Class A addresses begin with a 0 bit. Therefore, all addresses from 0.0.0.0 to 127.255.255.255 belong to Class A. The 0.0.0.0 address is reserved for default routing, and the 127.0.0.0 address is reserved for loopback testing.

- Class B addresses begin with a 1 bit and a 0 bit. Therefore, all addresses from 128.0.0.0 to 191.255.255.255 belong to Class B.

- Class C addresses begin with two 1 bits and a 0 bit. Class C addresses range from 192.0.0.0 to 223.255.255.255.

The remaining addresses were reserved for multicasting and future uses. Multicast addresses begin with three 1s and a 0 bit. Multicast addresses are used to identify a group of hosts that are part of a multicast group. This helps reduce the amount of packet processing that is done by hosts, particularly on broadcast media. In this course, you will see that the routing protocols RIPv2, EIGRP, and OSPF use designated multicast addresses.

IP addresses that begin with four 1 bits are reserved for future use.

Note

To see the assignment of individual multicast addresses, visit "Internet Multicast Addresses," http://www.iana.org/assignments/multicast-addresses.

IPv4 Classful Addressing Structure

The designations of network bits and host bits were established in RFC 790 (released with RFC 791). Figure 6-2 shows how the subnet mask for a network is determined based on its class.

Figure 6-2   Subnet Mask Based on Class

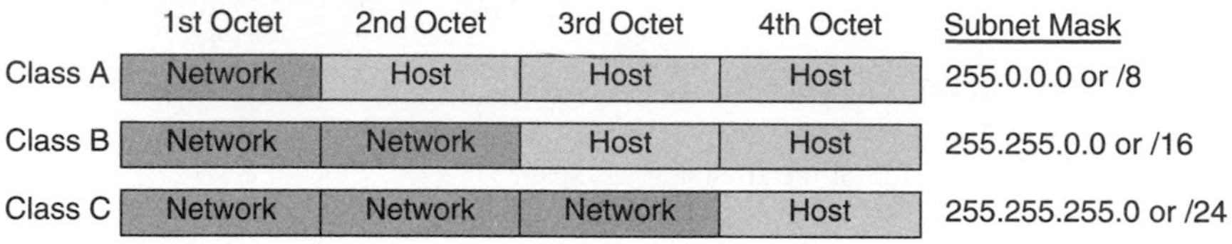

Table 6-2 shows the number of networks available per class as well as the number of hosts per network.

Table 6-2   Number of Networks and Hosts per Network for Each Class

Address Class	First Octet Range	Number of Possible Networks	Number of Hosts per Network
Class A	0 to 127	128 (2 are reserved)	16,777,214
Class B	128 to 191	16,344	65,534
Class C	192 to 223	2,097,152	254

Class A networks used the first octet for network assignment, which translated to a 255.0.0.0 classful subnet mask. Because only 7 bits were left in the first octet (remember, the first bit is always 0), this made 2^7, or 128, networks.

With 24 bits in the host portion, each Class A address had the potential for over 16 million individual host addresses. Before CIDR and VLSM, organizations were assigned an entire classful network address. What was one organization going to do with 16 million addresses? Now you can understand the tremendous waste of address space that occurred in the beginning days of the Internet, when companies received Class A addresses. Some companies and governmental organizations still have Class A addresses. For example, General Electric owns 3.0.0.0/8, Apple Computer owns 17.0.0.0/8, and the U.S. Postal Service owns 56.0.0.0/8. (The note at the end of this section provides a link to a listing of all the IANA assignments.)

Class B was not much better. RFC 790 specified the first two octets as the network portion of the address. With the first 2 bits already established as 1 and 0, 14 bits remained in the first two octets for assigning networks, which resulted in 16,384 Class B network addresses. Because each Class B network address contained 16 bits in the host portion, it controlled 65,534 addresses. (Remember, two addresses were reserved for the network and broadcast addresses.) Only the largest organizations and governments could ever hope to use all 65,000 addresses. Like Class A, Class B address space was wasted.

To make things worse, Class C addresses were often too small! RFC 790 specified the first three octets as the network portion of the address. With the first 3 bits established as 1, 1, and 0, 21 bits remained for assigning networks for over 2 million Class C networks. But, each Class C network only had 8 bits in the host portion, or 254 possible host addresses.

Note

The following links provide some background to the discussion of the IPv4 classful structure and the depletion of the IPv4 address space:

■ "A Brief History of the Internet," http://www.isoc.org/internet/history/brief.shtml

■ "Internet Protocol v4 Address Space," http://www.iana.org/assignments/ipv4-address-space

Classful Routing Protocol

Now that we have reviewed classful addressing, we take another look at classful routing protocol updates. Remember, a classful routing protocol does not include the subnet mask in the routing update.

Using classful IP addresses meant that the subnet mask of a network address could be determined by the value of the first octet, or more accurately, the first 3 bits of the address. Routing protocols, such as RIPv1, only needed to propagate the network address of known routes and did not need to include the subnet mask in the routing update. This is because the router receiving the routing update could determine the subnet mask simply by examining the value of the first octet in the network address, or by applying its ingress interface mask for subnetted routes. The subnet mask was directly related to the network address.

Figure 6-3 illustrates how classful routing determines the subnet mask for a given network.

In the figure, R1 knows that subnet 172.16.1.0 belongs to the same major classful network as the outgoing interface. Therefore, it sends a RIP update to R2 containing subnet 172.16.1.0. When R2 receives the update, it applies the receiving interface subnet mask (/24) to the update because the update belongs to the same major network as the interface. R2 adds 172.16.1.0 to the routing table with the /24 mask.

However, when sending updates to R3, R2 summarizes subnets 172.16.1.0/24, 172.16.2.0/24, and 172.16.3.0/24 into the major classful network 172.16.0.0. Because R3 receives this update on a major network address other than 172.16.0.0, it will apply the classful mask for a Class B network, /16.

Figure 6-3   Classful Routing Updates

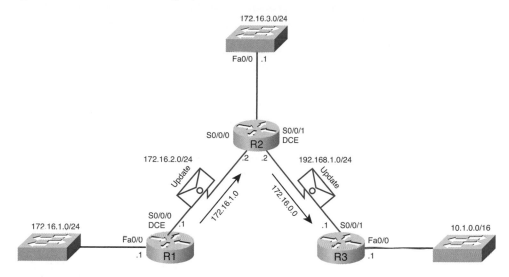

Classless IP Addressing

The previous sections discussed classful addressing and classful routing protocols. The following sections now take a look at the evolution of classless addressing and classless routing protocols.

Moving Toward Classless Addressing

By 1992, members of the IETF had serious concerns about the exponential growth of the Internet and the limited scalability of Internet routing tables. They were also concerned with the eventual exhaustion of 32-bit IPv4 address space. The depletion of the Class B address space was occurring so fast that within two years there would be no more Class B addresses available (RFC 1519). This depletion was occurring because every organization that requested and obtained approval for IP address space received an entire classful network address—either a Class B with 65,534 host addresses or a Class C with 254 host addresses. One fundamental cause of this problem was the lack of flexibility. No class existed to serve a midsized organization that needed thousands of IP addresses but not 65,000.

In 1993, IETF introduced classless interdomain routing (CIDR) (RFC 1517). CIDR allowed the following:

- More efficient use of IPv4 address space

- *Prefix aggregation*, which reduced the size of routing tables

To CIDR-compliant routers, address class is meaningless. The network portion of the address is determined by the network subnet mask, also known as the **network prefix**, or prefix length (/8, /19, and so on). The network address is no longer determined by the class of the address.

ISPs could now more efficiently allocate address space using any prefix length, starting with /8 and larger (/8, /9, /10, and so on). ISPs were no longer limited to a /8, /16, or /24 subnet mask. Blocks of IP addresses could be assigned to a network based on the requirements of the customer, ranging from a few hosts to hundreds or thousands of hosts.

CIDR and Route Summarization

CIDR uses variable-length subnet masking (VLSM) to allocate IP addresses to subnets according to individual need rather than by class. This type of allocation allows the network/host boundary to occur at any bit in the address. Networks can be further divided or subnetted into smaller and smaller subnets.

Just as the Internet was growing at an exponential rate in the early 1990s, so were the size of routing tables that were maintained by Internet routers under classful IP addressing. CIDR allowed prefix aggregation, which you already know as route summarization. Recall from Chapter 2, "Static Routing," that you can create one static route for multiple networks. Internet routing tables were now able to benefit from the same type of aggregation of routes. The capability for routes to be summarized as a single route helped reduce the size of Internet routing tables. Figure 6-4 illustrates a simple example of this capability.

Figure 6-4   Example of CIDR Used to Summarize Routes

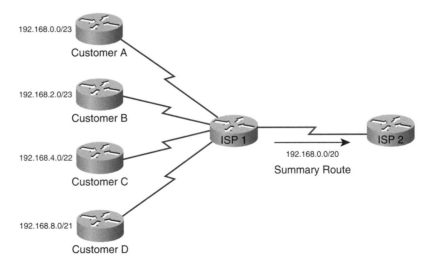

In the figure, notice that ISP 1 has four customers, each with a variable amount of IP address space. However, all the customer address space can be summarized into one advertisement to

ISP 2. The 192.168.0.0/20 summarized or aggregated route includes all the networks belonging to customers A, B, C, and D. This type of route is known as a *supernet route*. A supernet summarizes multiple network addresses with a mask less than the classful mask.

Propagating VLSM and supernet routes requires a classless routing protocol, because the subnet mask can no longer be determined by the value of the first octet. The subnet mask now needs to be included with the network address. Classless routing protocols include the subnet mask with the network address in the routing update.

Classless Routing Protocol

Classless routing protocols include RIPv2, EIGRP, OSPF, Intermediate System–to–Intermediate System (IS-IS), and Border Gateway Protocol (BGP). These routing protocols include the subnet mask with the network address in their routing updates. Classless routing protocols are necessary when the mask cannot be assumed or determined by the value of the first octet.

For example, in Figure 6-5, the networks 172.16.0.0/16, 172.17.0.0/16, 172.18.0.0/16, and 172.19.0.0/16 can be summarized as 172.16.0.0/14, known as a *supernet*.

Figure 6-5   Classless Routing

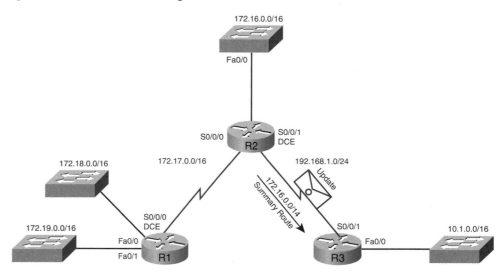

If R2 sends the 172.16.0.0 summary route without the /14 mask, R3 only knows to apply the default classful mask of /16. In a classful routing protocol scenario, R3 is unaware of the 172.17.0.0/16, 172.18.0.0/16, and 172.19.0.0/16 networks.

Note

Using a classful routing protocol, R2 can send these individual networks without summarization, but the benefits of summarization are lost.

Classful routing protocols cannot send supernet routes because the receiving router will apply the default classful mask to the network address in the routing update. If our topology contained a classful routing protocol, R3 would install only 172.16.0.0/16 in the routing table.

> **Note**
>
> When a supernet route is in a routing table, for example, as a static route, a classful routing protocol will not include that route in its updates.

With a classless routing protocol, R2 will advertise the 172.16.0.0 network along with the /14 mask to R3. R3 will then be able to install the supernet route 172.16.0.0/14 in its routing table, giving it reachability to the 172.16.0.0/16, 172.17.0.0/16, 172.18.0.0/16, and 172.19.0.0/16 networks.

VLSM

The Network Fundamentals course described how VLSM allows the use of different masks for each subnet. After a network address is subnetted, those subnets can be further subnetted. As you most likely recall, VLSM is simply subnetting a subnet. VLSM can be thought of as sub-subnetting.

VLSM in Action

Figure 6-6 shows that the network 10.0.0.0/8 has been subnetted using the subnet mask of /16, which gives the potential of 256 subnets:

10.0.0.0/16

10.1.0.0/16

10.2.0.0/16

.

.

.

10.255.0.0/16

In this example, 10.0.0.0/8 has been subnetted into four subnets, 10.0.0.0/16, 10.1.0.0/16, 10.2.0.0/16, and 10.3.0.0/16.

Any of these /16 subnets can be subnetted further. For example, in Figure 6-7, the 10.1.0.0/16 subnet is subnetted again using the /24 mask.

Figure 6-6   VLSM: First Round of Subnets

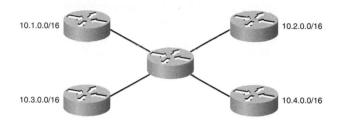

Figure 6-7   VLSM: Subnetting a Subnet

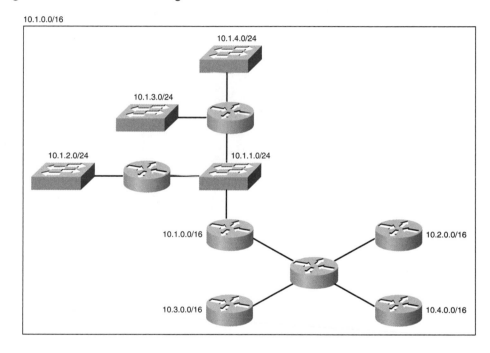

Subnetting 10.1.0.0/16 with a /24 mask results in the following potential subnets:

10.1.1.0/24

10.1.2.0/24

10.1.3.0/24

.

.

.

10.1.255.0/24

Figure 6-8 shows that the 10.2.0.0/16 subnet is also subnetted again with a /24 mask. The 10.3.0.0/16 subnet is subnetted again with the /28 mask, and the 10.4.0.0/16 subnet is subnetted again with the /20 mask.

Figure 6-8   VLSM: Additional Levels of Subnetting

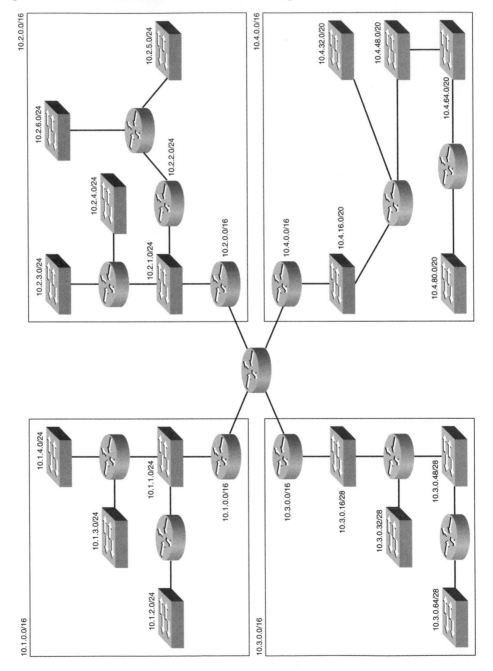

Individual host addresses are assigned from the addresses of "sub-subnets." For example, the figure shows the 10.1.0.0/16 subnet divided into /24 subnets. The 10.1.4.10 address would now be a member of the more specific subnet 10.1.4.0/24.

VLSM and IP Addresses

Another way to view the VLSM subnets is to list each subnet and its sub-subnets. In Figure 6-9, the 10.0.0.0/8 network is the starting address space.

Figure 6-9   Subnets of the Subnet: First Round

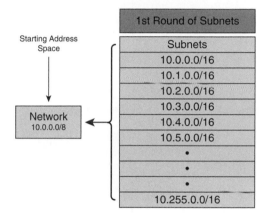

The 10.0.0.0/8 network is subnetted with a /16 mask on the first round of subnetting. You already know that borrowing 8 bits (going from /8 to /16) creates 256 subnets. With classful routing, that is as far as you can go. You can choose only one mask for all your networks. With VLSM and classless routing, you have more flexibility to create additional network addresses and use a mask that fits your needs.

For subnet 10.1.0.0/16 (see Figure 6-10), 8 more bits are borrowed again, to create 256 subnets with a /24 mask.

This mask will allow 254 host addresses per subnet. The subnets ranging from 10.1.0.0/24 to 10.1.255.0/24 are subnets of the subnet 10.1.0.0/16.

Subnet 10.2.0.0/16 is also further subnetted with a /24 mask (see Figure 6-11).

Figure 6-10   Subnets of the Subnet: 10.1.0.0/16

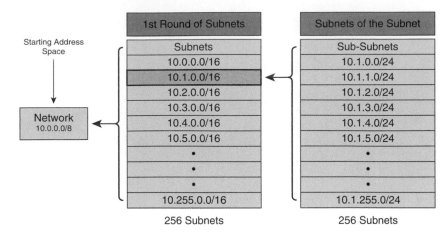

Figure 6-11   Subnets of the Subnet: 10.2.0.0/16

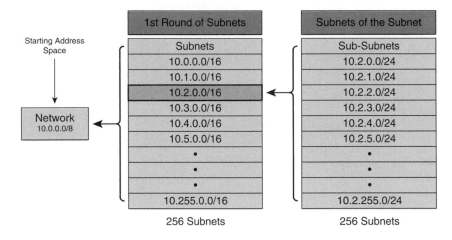

The subnets ranging from 10.2.0.0/24 to 10.2.255.0/24 are subnets of the subnet 10.2.0.0/16.

Subnet 10.3.0.0/16 is further subnetted with a /28 mask (see Figure 6-12).

This mask will allow 14 host addresses per subnet. Twelve bits are borrowed, creating 4096 subnets ranging from 10.3.0.0/28 to 10.3.255.240/28.

Subnet 10.4.0.0/16 is further subnetted with a /20 mask (see Figure 6-13).

Figure 6-12   Subnets of the Subnet: 10.3.0.0/16

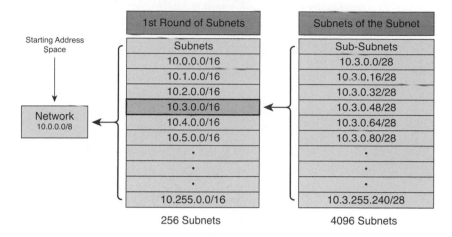

Figure 6-13   Subnets of the Subnet: 10.4.0.0/16

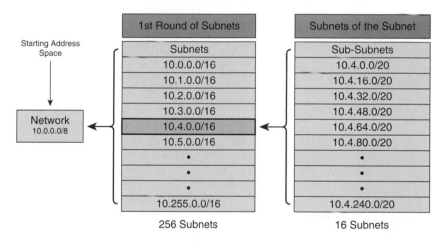

This mask will allow 4094 host addresses per subnet. Four bits are borrowed, creating 16 subnets ranging from 10.4.0.0/20 to 10.4.240.0/20. These /20 subnets are big enough to subnet even further, allowing more networks.

CIDR

Classless interdomain routing (CIDR) is a prefix-based standard for the interpretation of IP addresses. CIDR allows routing protocols to summarize multiple networks, a block of addresses, as a single route. With CIDR, IP addresses and their subnet masks are written as four octets, separated by periods, and followed by a forward slash and a number that represents the subnet mask (slash notation). An example is 172.16.1.0/24.

Route Summarization

As you previously learned, route summarization, also known as route aggregation, is the process of advertising a *contiguous* set of addresses as a single address with a less-specific, shorter subnet mask. Remember that CIDR is a form of route summarization and is synonymous with the term *supernetting*.

You should already be familiar with route summarization that is done by classful routing protocols such as RIPv1. RIPv1 summarizes subnets to a single major network classful address when sending the RIPv1 update out an interface that belongs to another major network. For example, RIPv1 will summarize 10.0.0.0/24 subnets (10.0.0.0/24 through 10.255.255.0/24) as 10.0.0.0/8.

CIDR ignores the limitation of classful boundaries and allows summarization with masks that are less than that of the default classful mask. This type of summarization helps reduce the number of entries in routing updates and reduces the number of entries in local routing tables. It also helps reduce bandwidth utilization for routing updates and results in faster routing table lookups.

Only classless routing protocols can propagate supernets. Classless routing protocols include both the network address and the mask in the routing update. Classful routing protocols cannot include supernets in their routing updates because they cannot apply a mask less than the default classful mask. A static route can be used to configure a supernet route because the network address and mask are configured directly on that router.

Figure 6-14 shows a single static route with the address 172.16.0.0 and the mask 255.248.0.0 summarizing all the 172.16.0.0/16 to 172.23.0.0/16 classful networks.

Figure 6-14   Route Summarization

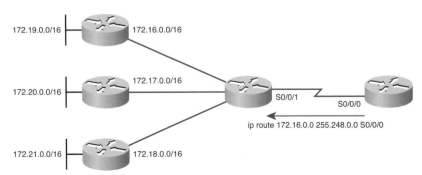

Although 172.22.0.0/16 and 172.23.0.0/16 are not shown in the graphic, these are also included in the summary route. Notice that the /13 mask (255.248.0.0) is less than the default classful mask /16 (255.255.0.0).

Note

You might recall that a supernet is always a route summary, but a route summary is not always a supernet.

A router could have both a specific route entry and a summary route entry covering the same network. Assume that Router X has a specific route for 172.22.0.0/16 using Serial 0/0/1 and a summary route of 172.16.0.0/14 using Serial 0/0/0. Packets with the IP address of 172.22.n.n match both route entries. These packets destined for 172.22.0.0 would be sent out the Serial 0/0/1 interface because there is a more specific match of 16 bits than with the 14 bits of the 172.16.0.0/14 summary route.

Calculating Route Summarization

Calculating route summaries and supernets is identical to the process that you already learned in Chapter 2. Therefore, the following example is presented as a quick review.

Summarizing networks into a single address and mask can be done in three steps, as shown in Figure 6-15.

Figure 6-15 Calculating a Route Summary

Step 1: List networks in binary format.

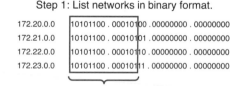

Step 2: Count the number of leftmost matching bits to determine the mask. 14 matching bits, /14 or 255.252.0.0.

Step 3: Copy the matching bits and add zero bits to determine the network address.

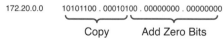

Consider the following four networks:

- 172.20.0.0/16
- 172.21.0.0/16
- 172.22.0.0/16
- 172.23.0.0/16

The steps to summarizing these networks are as follows:

Step 1.   List the networks in binary format. The figure shows all four networks in binary.

Step 2.   Count the number of leftmost matching bits to determine the mask for the summary route. You can see in the figure that the first 14 leftmost bits match. This is the prefix, or subnet mask, for the summarized route: /14 or 255.252.0.0.

Step 3.   Copy the matching bits and then add 0 bits to determine the summarized network address. The figure shows that the matching bits with 0s at the end result in the network address 172.20.0.0. The four networks—172.20.0.0/16, 172.21.0.0/16, 172.22.0.0/16, and 172.23.0.0/16—can be summarized into the single network address and prefix 172.20.0.0/14.

Summary

Classless interdomain routing (CIDR) was introduced in 1993, replacing the previous generation of IP address syntax, classful networks. CIDR allowed more efficient use of IPv4 address space and prefix aggregation, known as route summarization or supernetting.

With CIDR, address classes (Class A, Class B, and Class C) became meaningless. The network address was no longer determined by the value of the first octet, but assigned a prefix length (subnet mask). Address space, the number of hosts on a network, could now be assigned a specific prefix depending on the number of hosts needed for that network.

CIDR allows supernetting. A supernet is a group of major network addresses summarized as a single network address with a mask less than that of the default classful mask.

CIDR uses VLSM (variable-length subnet masks) to allocate IP addresses to subnetworks according to need rather than by class. VLSM allows subnets to be further divided or subnetted into even smaller subnets. Simply put, VLSM is just subnetting a subnet.

Propagating CIDR supernets or VLSM subnets require a classless routing protocol. A classless routing protocol includes the subnet mask along with the network address in the routing update. Classless routing protocols include RIPv2, EIGRP, OSPF, IS-IS, and BGP.

Determining the summary route and subnet mask for a group of networks can be done in three easy steps. The first step is to list the networks in binary format. The second step is to count the number of leftmost matching bits. This will give you the prefix length or subnet mask for the summarized route. The third step is to copy the matching bits and then add 0 bits to the rest of the address to determine the summarized network address. The summarized network address and subnet mask can now be used as the summary route for this group of networks. Summary routes can be used by both static routes and classless routing protocols. Classful routing protocols can only summarize routes to the default classful mask.

Classless routing protocols and their ability to support CIDR supernet, VLSM, and discontiguous networks are described in the following chapters.

Activities and Labs

The activities and labs available in the companion *Routing Protocols and Concepts, CCNA Exploration Labs and Study Guide* [ISBN 1-58713-204-4] provide hands-on practice with the following topics introduced in this chapter:

Activity 6-1: Basic VLSM Calculation and Addressing Design Activity (6.4.1)

In this activity, you will use the network address 192.168.1.0/24 to subnet and provide the IP addressing for a given topology. VLSM will be used so that the addressing requirements can be met using the 192.168.1.0/24 network.

Activity 6-2: Challenge VLSM Calculation and Addressing Design Activity (6.4.2)

In this activity, you will use the network address 172.16.0.0/16 to subnet and provide the IP addressing for a given topology. VLSM will be used so that the addressing requirements can be met using the 172.16.0.0/16 network.

Activity 6-3: Troubleshooting a VLSM Addressing Design Activity (6.4.3)

In this activity, the network address 172.16.128.0/17 was used to provide the IP addressing for a network. VLSM has been used to subnet the address space incorrectly. You will need to troubleshoot the addressing that was assigned to each subnet to determine where errors are present and determine the correct addressing assignments where needed.

Activity 6-4: Basic Route Summarization Activity (6.4.4)

In this activity, you are given a network with subnetting and address assignments already completed. Your task is to determine summarized routes that can be used to reduce the number of entries in routing tables.

Activity 6-5: Challenge Route Summarization Activity (6.4.5)

In this activity, you are given a network with subnetting and address assignments already completed. Your task is to determine summarized routes that can be used to reduce the number of entries in routing tables.

Activity 6-6: Troubleshooting Route Summarization Activity (6.4.6)

In this activity, the LAN IP addressing is already completed for the network. VLSM was used to subnet the address space. The summary routes are incorrect. You will need to troubleshoot the summary routes that have been assigned to determine where errors are present and determine the correct summary routes.

Packet Tracer
☐Companion

Many of the hands-on labs include Packet Tracer Companion Activities, where you can use Packet Tracer to complete a simulation of the lab. Look for this icon in *Routing Protocols and Concepts, CCNA Exploration Labs and Study Guide* (ISBN 1-58713-204-4) for hands-on labs that have a Packet Tracer Companion.

Check Your Understanding

Complete all the review questions listed here to test your understanding of the topics and concepts in this chapter. The section, "Check Your Understanding and Challenge Questions Answer Key" at the end of this chapter lists the answers.

1. For each of the following routing protocols, indicate whether it supports VLSM (VLSM or non-VLSM).

   RIPv1:

   EIGRP:

   IGRP:

   IS-IS:

   OSPF:

   RIPv2:

2. For each of the following definitions, indicate whether it is describing VLSM or route summarization.

   Combining several IP network addresses in one IP address:

   Ability to specify a different subnet mask for the same network number and different subnets:

   Used in supernetting:

   Conserves address space:

   Used to reduce the number of entries in a routing table:

3. What two methods allowed the continued use of IPv4 addressing and helped delay the need to implement IPv6?

   A. Subnetting was variable-length.

   B. The IPv4 address range was expanded.

   C. Private addresses were used with address translation.

   D. Classful routing was implemented.

   E. IPv4 was abandoned in favor of IPv6 for all hosts.

   F. Supernetting was implemented.

4. The following subnet masks have been chosen for use with the 192.168.16.0 network:

255.255.255.252

255.255.255.240

255.255.255.192

Which of the following identify the most efficient use for each of these masks?
(Choose three.)

A. Use the /30 mask for point-to-point links, such as WAN connections.

B. Use the /30 mask for subnetworks of four or more hosts.

C. Use the /28 mask for small subnetworks with up to 14 hosts.

D. Use the /26 mask for larger subnetworks with up to 62 hosts.

E. Use the /25 mask for subnetworks with up to 30 hosts.

F. Use the /24 mask for point-to-point links, such as WAN connections.

5. When using a classful Class A IP address scheme, how many octets are used to designate the network portion of the address?

A. 1

B. 2

C. 3

D. 4

6. Match the VLSM subnet with the network size it is most appropriate for. Each answer can be used only once.

VLSM subnets:

172.16.64.0/18

172.16.16.64/30

172.16.128.0/19

172.16.18.0/24

172.16.5.128/26

Number of hosts:

A. 2

B. 60

C. 250

D. 8000

E. 16,000

7. A network engineer is summarizing the two groups of routes, group A and group B, on Router R1. Which summarization will work for all subnets?

   Group A:

   192.168.0.0/30

   192.168.0.4/30

   192.168.0.8/30

   192.168.0.16/29

   Group B:

   192.168.4.0/30

   192.168.5.0/30

   192.168.6.0/30

   192.168.7.0/29

   A. 192.168.0.0/23
   B. 192.168.0.0/22
   C. 192.168.0.0/21
   D. 192.168.0.0/28

8. How many bits are used in the IPv4 address space?

   A. 8
   B. 12
   C. 16
   D. 30
   E. 32
   F. 64

9. For the following classful network addresses, indicate whether the address is a Class A address or a Class B address.

   191.254.45.0: Class

   123.90.78.45: Class

   128.44.0.23: Class

   129.68.11.45: Class

   126.0.0.0: Class

   125.33.23.56: Class

10. Refer to Figure 6-16. The network administrator wants to minimize the number of entries in Router R1's routing table. What should the administrator implement on the network?

Figure 6-16   Check Your Understanding: Question #10

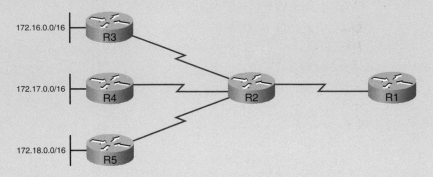

A. VLSM

B. CIDR

C. Private IP addresses

D. Classful routing

11. What distinguishes a classless routing protocol from a classful routing protocol?

12. What are the advantages of using a classless routing protocol?

13. How does a classful routing protocol determine the subnet mask of a routing update?

14. Why did the IETF introduce classless IP addressing, CIDR?

15. What term is used to define the process of subnetting a subnet?

Challenge Questions and Activities

These questions require a deeper application of the concepts covered in this chapter and are similar to the style of questions you might see on a CCNA certification exam. You can find the answers to these questions in the appendix, "Answers to Check Your Understanding and Challenge Questions and Activities."

1. The 172.16.0.0/16 network is subnetted using a /24 subnet mask. What could you do if you needed to divide the 172.16.10.0/24 subnet into three equal subnets with the maximum number of hosts in each subnet?

2. 172.16.10.0/24 is using the following /28 subnets for LANs:

172.16.10.16/28

172.16.10.32/28

172.16.10.48/28

172.16.10.64/28

172.16.10.80/28

172.16.10.96/28

172.16.10.112/28

172.16.10.128/28

172.16.10.144/28

172.16.10.160/28

172.16.10.176/28

172.16.10.192/28

172.16.10.240/28

The network administrator wants to allocate a /28 subnet and subnet it further with a /30 mask for all point-to-point serial links in the network. What /28 subnets are available to be used?

3. What is supernetting? What is required to propagate a supernet route?

4. Summarize the following networks:

192.168.68.0/24

192.168.96.0/24

192.168.80.0/24

Packet Tracer
☐ Challenge

Look for this icon in *Routing Protocols and Concepts, CCNA Exploration Labs and Study Guide* (ISBN 1-58713-204-4) for instructions on how to perform the Packet Tracer Skills Integration Challenge for this chapter.

To Learn More

RFC 1519, Classless Inter-Domain Routing (CIDR)

Requests For Comments (RFC) are a series of documents submitted to the IETF (Internet Engineering Task Force) to propose an Internet standard or convey new concepts, information, or occasionally even humor.

RFCs can be accessed from several websites, including http://www.ietf.org. Read all or parts of RFC 1519 to learn more about the introduction of CIDR to the Internet community.

Internet Core Routers

In the "To Learn More" section of Chapter 3, "Introduction to Dynamic Routing Protocols," you accessed route servers to display BGP routes on the Internet. One such site is http://www.traceroute.org.

Access one of the route servers, and using the **show ip route** command, view the actual routing table of an Internet router. Notice how many routes there are on an Internet core router. As of March 2007, there were over 200,000 routes. Many of these are summarized routes and supernets. Use the **show ip route 207.62.187.0** command to view one such supernet.

CAIDA

An interesting website is CAIDA, the Cooperative Association for Internet Data Analysis, http://www.caida.org. CAIDA "provides tools and analyses promoting the engineering and maintenance of a robust, scalable global Internet infrastructure." There are several sponsors for CAIDA including Cisco Systems. Although much of this information might seem beyond your understanding, you will begin to recognize many of these terms and concepts.

CHAPTER 7

RIPv2

Objectives

Upon completion of this chapter, you will be able to answer the following questions:

- As a classful routing protocol, what are the limitations of RIPv1?

- What are the basic configuration commands used to apply Routing Information Protocol version 2 (RIPv2), and how do you evaluate RIPv2 classless routing updates?

- How do you analyze router output to see RIPv2 support for variable-length subnet masking (VLSM) and classless interdomain routing (CIDR)?

- Which commands are used to verify RIPv2 and identify common issues?

- What are the commands used to configure, verify, and troubleshoot RIPv2?

Key Terms

This chapter uses the following key terms. You can find the definitions in the Glossary at the end of the book.

discontiguous network   *page 291*

redistribution   *page 295*

loopback interface   *page 297*

null interface   *page 298*

ICMP   *page 299*

Figure 7-1 shows a chart of the most common IP routing protocols, with the routing protocols that will be discussed in this book highlighted. Notice in the chart that RIP Version 2 (RIPv2) is a classless distance vector routing protocol.

Figure 7-1   Classification of Routing Protocols

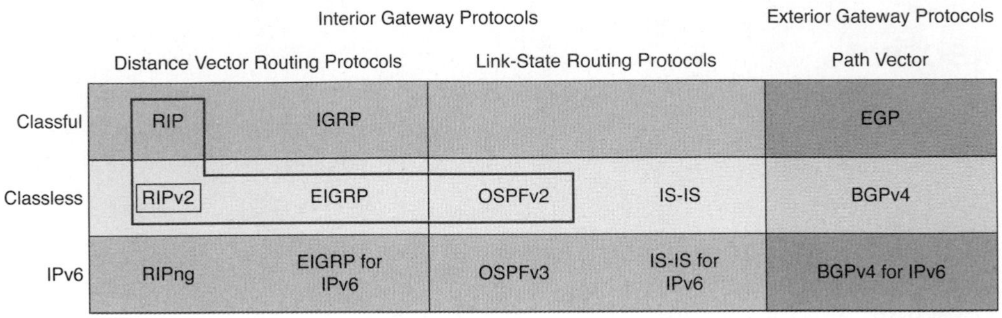

	Distance Vector Routing Protocols		Link-State Routing Protocols		Path Vector
	Interior Gateway Protocols				Exterior Gateway Protocols
Classful	RIP	IGRP			EGP
Classless	RIPv2	EIGRP	OSPFv2	IS-IS	BGPv4
IPv6	RIPng	EIGRP for IPv6	OSPFv3	IS-IS for IPv6	BGPv4 for IPv6

RIP Version 2 (RIPv2) is defined in RFC 1723. RIPv2 is the first classless routing protocol discussed in this book. Although RIPv2 is a suitable routing protocol for some environments, it has lost popularity when compared to other routing protocols such as Enhanced Interior Gateway Routing Protocol (EIGRP), Open Shortest Path First (OSPF), and Intermediate System–to–Intermediate System (IS-IS), which offer more features and are more scalable.

However, both versions of RIP are still used in some situations. Although RIP lacks the capabilities of many of the later protocols, its sheer simplicity and widespread use in multiple operating systems make it an ideal candidate for smaller, homogeneous networks where multivendor support is necessary, especially within UNIX environments.

Even if you do not plan on using RIPv2, it is ideal for explaining the differences between a classful routing protocol (RIPv1) and a classless routing protocol (RIPv2). This chapter will focus on these differences rather than the details of implementing RIPv2. The main limitation of RIPv1 is that it is a classful routing protocol. As you know, classful routing protocols do not include the subnet mask with the network address in routing updates. This can cause problems with discontiguous subnets or networks that use VLSM. Because RIPv2 is a classless routing protocol, subnet masks are included in the routing updates, making RIPv2 more compatible with modern routing environments.

RIPv2 is actually an enhancement of RIPv1's features and extensions rather than an entirely new protocol. Some of these features include

- Next-hop addresses included in the routing updates

- Use of multicast addresses in sending updates

- Authentication option available

Like RIPv1, RIPv2 is a distance vector routing protocol. Both versions of RIP share the following features and limitations:

- Use of hold-down and other timers to help prevent routing loops

- Use of split horizon and split horizon with poison reverse to also help prevent routing loops

- Use of triggered updates when there is a change in the topology for faster convergence

- Maximum hop count of 15 hops, with the hop count of 16 signifying an unreachable network

RIPv1 Limitations

Figure 7-2 shows the topology used in this chapter. Examples 7-1, 7-2, and 7-3 show the startup configuration for each router. This scenario is similar to the routing domain with three routers that was used at the end of Chapter 5, "RIP Version 1." Remember that both the R1 and R3 routers have subnets that are part of the 172.30.0.0/16 major classful network (Class B). Also remember that R1 and R3 are connected to R2 using subnets of the 209.165.200.0/24 major classful network (Class C).

The topology in Figure 7-2 is an example of a *discontiguous network*. In a discontiguous network, a classful major network address, such as 172.30.0.0/16, is separated by one or more other major networks. In this case, 172.30.0.0/16 is divided by the 209.165.200.228/30 and 209.165.200.232/30 networks. As you saw with RIPv1, classful routing protocols do not include enough routing information to route properly for discontiguous networks. Later in this chapter, we will further examine the issue of classful routing protocols and discontiguous networks as well as describe how a classless routing protocol can solve this problem.

Figure 7-2   RIPv2 Topology

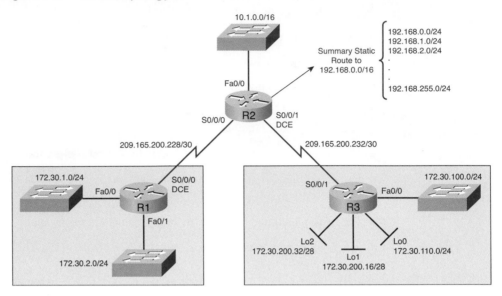

Table 7-1   Addressing Table for RIPv2

Device	Interface	IP Address	Subnet Mask
R1	Fa0/0	172.30.1.1	255.255.255.0
	Fa0/1	172.30.2.1	255.255.255.0
	S0/0/0	209.165.200.230	255.255.255.252
R2	Fa0/0	10.1.0.1	255.255.0.0
	S0/0/0	209.165.200.229	255.255.255.252
	S0/0/1	209.165.200.233	255.255.255.252
R3	Fa0/0	172.30.100.1	255.255.255.0
	Lo0	172.30.110.1	255.255.255.0
	Lo1	172.30.200.17	255.255.255.240
	Lo2	172.30.200.33	255.255.255.240
	S0/0/1	209.165.200.234	255.255.255.252

Example 7-1   R1 Startup Configuration

```
R1# show startup-config

Building configuration...

Current configuration : 434 bytes
!
<some output omitted>
!
hostname R1
!
!
!
interface FastEthernet0/0
 ip address 172.30.1.1 255.255.255.0
!
interface FastEthernet0/1
 ip address 172.30.2.1 255.255.255.0
!
interface Serial0/0/0
 description Link to R2
 ip address 209.165.200.230 255.255.255.252
 clock rate 64000
!
end
```

Example 7-2   R2 Startup Configuration

```
R2# show startup-config

Building configuration...

Current configuration : 502 bytes
!
<some output omitted>
!
hostname R2
```

```
!
!
!
interface FastEthernet0/0
 ip address 10.1.0.1 255.255.0.0
!
interface Serial0/0/0
 description Link to R1
 ip address 209.165.200.229 255.255.255.252
!
interface Serial0/0/1
 description Link to R3
 ip address 209.165.200.233 255.255.255.252
 clock rate 64000
!
end
```

Example 7-3   R3 Startup Configuration

```
R3# show startup-config

Building configuration...

Current configuration : 646 bytes
!
<some output omitted>
!
hostname R3
!
!
!
interface FastEthernet0/0
 ip address 172.30.100.1 255.255.255.0
!
interface Serial0/0/1
 description Link to R2
 ip address 209.165.200.234 255.255.255.252
!
interface Loopback0
```

```
 ip address 172.30.110.1 255.255.255.0
!
interface Loopback1
 ip address 172.30.200.17 255.255.255.240
!
interface Loopback2
 ip address 172.30.200.33 255.255.255.240
!
end
```

Summary Route

Notice in Figure 7-2 that R2 has a static summary route to the 192.168.0.0/16 network. The concept and configuration of static summary routes were discussed in Chapter 2, "Static Routing." You can inject static route information into routing protocol updates. This is called *redistribution* and will be discussed later in this chapter. For now, understand that this summary route will cause problems with RIPv1 because 192.168.0.0/16 is not a major classful address and includes all the /24 versions of 192.168.0.0/16, as shown in the topology.

VLSM

Looking at the chapter topology and Figure 7-3, notice that the R1 and R3 contain VLSM networks. Both R1 and R3 are configured with /24 subnets of the 172.30.0.0/16 network. Four of these /24 subnets are assigned: two to R1 (172.30.1.0/24 and 172.30.2.0/24) and two to R3 (172.30.100.0/24 and 172.30.110.0/24).

On R3, the 172.30.200.0/24 address was subnetted again, using the first 4 bits for subnets and the last 4 for hosts. This gives you a 255.255.255.240 mask, or /28. The configuration on R3 includes two of these subnets: 172.30.200.16/28 and 172.30.200.32/28.

RFC 1918 Private Addresses

You should already be familiar with RFC 1918 and the reasoning behind private addressing. All the examples in the curriculum use private IP addresses for the inside addressing example.

Figure 7-3   VLSM Addressing Scheme for Topology

	Subnet	Network	Host Range	Broadcast
	0	172.30.0.0	172.30.0.1 to 172.30.0.254	172.30.0.255
Assigned to R1 Fa0/0	1	172.30.1.0	172.30.1.1 to 172.30.1.254	172.30.1.255
Assigned to R1 Fa0/1	2	172.30.2.0	172.30.2.1 to 172.30.2.254	172.30.2.255
	3	172.30.3.0	172.30.3.1 to 172.30.3.254	172.30.3.255
	4	172.30.4.0	172.30.4.1 to 172.30.4.254	172.30.4.255
	.			
Assigned to R3 Fa0/0	100	172.30.100.0	172.30.100.1 to 172.30.100.254	172.30.100.255
	.			
Assigned to R3 Lo0	110	172.30.110.0	172.30.110.1 to 172.30.110.254	172.30.110.255
	.			
Subnetted Again	200	172.30.200.0	172.30.200.1 to 172.30.200.254	172.30.200.255
	.			
	255	172.30.255.0	172.30.255.1 to 172.30.255.254	172.30.255.255

256 /24 Subnets

	Subnet	Network	Host Range	Broadcast
	0	172.30.200.0	172.30.200.1 to 172.30.200.14	172.30.200.15
Assigned to R3 Lo1	1	172.30.200.16	172.30.200.17 to 172.30.200.30	172.30.200.31
Assigned to R3 Lo2	2	172.30.200.32	172.30.200.33 to 172.30.200.46	172.30.200.47
	3	172.30.200.48	172.30.200.49 to 172.30.200.62	172.30.200.63
	.			
	15	172.30.200.240	172.30.200.241 to 172.30.200.254	172.30.200.255

16 /28 Subnets

Table 7-2 shows the RFC 1918–compliant addresses. When IP traffic is routed across WAN links through an Internet service provider (ISP), or when inside users need to access outside sites, a public IP address must be used.

Table 7-2   RFC 1918–Compliant Addresses

Class	Prefix/Mask	Address Range
A	10.0.0.0/8	10.0.0.0 to 10.255.255.255
B	172.16.0.0/12	172.16.0.0 to 172.31.255.255
C	192.168.0.0/16	192.168.0.0 to 192.168.255.255

Cisco Example IP Addresses

Notice that the WAN links between R1, R2, and R3 are using public IP addresses. Although these IP addresses are not private addresses according to RFC 1918, Cisco has acquired some public address space to use for example purposes. Table 7-3 lists the Cisco example IP addresses.

Table 7-3   Cisco Example IP Addresses

Prefix/Mask	Address Range
209.165.200.224/27	209.165.200.224 to 209.165.200.255
209.165.201.0/27	209.165.201.0 to 209.165.201.31
209.165.202.128/27	209.165.202.128 to 209.165.202.159

Loopback Interfaces

Notice that R3 is using loopback interfaces (Lo0, Lo1, and Lo2). A *loopback interface* is a software-only interface used to emulate an interface. It can be assigned an IP address. Loopback interfaces also have specific purposes with some routing protocols such as OSPF and will be discussed later in that chapter. A loopback interface can be pinged, and the subnet can be advertised in routing updates. Therefore, loopback interfaces are ideal for simulating multiple networks attached to the same router. In our example, R3 does not need four LAN interfaces to demonstrate multiple subnets and VLSM. Instead, we use loopback interfaces.

RIPv1 Topology Limitations

Example 7-4 shows the RIPv1 configuration for all three routers. Notice that the network statements use the classful major network addresses. R2 contains two commands that require explanation.

Example 7-4   RIPv1 Configuration for All Three Routers

```
R1(config)# router rip
R1(config-router)# network 172.30.0.0
R1(config-router)# network 209.165.200.0
R2(config)# ip route 192.168.0.0 255.255.0.0 null0
R2(config)# router rip
R2(config-router)# redistribute static
R2(config-router)# network 10.0.0.0
R2(config-router)# network 209.165.200.0
R3(config)# router rip
R3(config-router)# network 172.30.0.0
R3(config-router)# network 209.165.200.0
```

Static Routes and Null Interfaces

The first command that needs explanation is R2's static route to the 192.168.0.0/16 network:

```
R2(config)# ip route 192.168.0.0 255.255.0.0 Null0
```

Remember that CIDR allows route aggregation. This means that a single high-level route entry with a subnet mask less than the classful mask can be used to represent many lower-level routes. This results in fewer entries in the routing table. The static route on R2 is using a /16 mask to summarize all 256 networks ranging from 192.168.0.0/24 to 192.168.255.0/24.

The address space represented by the static summary route 192.168.0.0/16 does not actually exist. To simulate this static route, we will use a *null interface* as the exit interface. You do not need to enter commands to create or configure the null interface. It is always up but does not forward or receive traffic. Traffic sent to the null interface is discarded. For our purposes, the null interface will serve as the exit interface for our static route. Remember from Chapter 2 that a static route must have an active exit interface before it will be installed in the routing table. Using the null interface will allow R2 to advertise the static route in RIP, even though networks belonging to the summary 192.168.0.0/16 do not actually exist.

Route Redistribution

The second command that needs explanation is the **redistribute static** command:

```
R2(config-router)# redistribute static
```

Redistribution involves taking the routes from one routing source and sending those routes to another routing source. Routes can only be redistributed into a dynamic routing protocol. In our chapter topology, we want the RIPv1 process on R2 to redistribute our static route (192.168.0.0/16) by importing the route into RIPv1 and then sending it to R1 and R3 using the RIPv1 process. We will see whether this is indeed happening, and if not, why not.

Verifying and Testing Connectivity

To test whether the topology has full connectivity, first verify that both serial links on R2 are up using the **show ip interface brief** command. Example 7-5 shows the output for this command on R2.

Example 7-5 Interface Status for R2
```
R2# show ip interface brief

Interface        IP-Address      OK? Method Status              Protocol
FastEthernet0/0  10.1.0.1        YES manual up                  up
```

```
Serial0/0/0          209.165.200.229 YES manual up                          up
FastEthernet0/1      unassigned      YES unset  administratively down down
Serial0/0/1          209.165.200.233 YES manual up                          up
```

If a link is down, the Status field or the Protocol field (or both fields) will display **down** in the command output. If a link is up, both fields will display **up**, as shown here. R2 has direct connectivity to R1 and R3 across the serial links.

But can R2 ping LANs on R1 and R3? Are there any connectivity problems with a classful routing protocol and the discontiguous subnets of 172.30.0.0? We test the communications between the routers using the **ping** command.

The output in Example 7-6 shows R2 attempting to ping the 172.30.1.1 interface on R1 and the 172.30.100.1 interface on R3. Whenever R2 pings any of the 172.30.0.0 subnets on R1 or R3, only about 50 percent of the Internet Control Message Protocol (*ICMP*) messages are successful.

Example 7-6   R2 Intermittent Pings to Subnets of 172.30.0.0/16

```
R2# ping 172.30.1.1

Type escape sequence to abort.
Sending 5, 100-byte ICMP Echos to 172.30.1.1, timeout is 2 seconds:
!U!.!
Success rate is 60 percent (3/5), round-trip min/avg/max = 28/29/32 ms

R2#ping 172.30.100.1
Type escape sequence to abort.
Sending 5, 100-byte ICMP Echos to 172.30.100.1, timeout is 2 seconds:
!U!.!
Success rate is 60 percent (3/5), round-trip min/avg/max = 28/28/28 ms
R2#
```

The output in Example 7-7 shows that R1 is able to ping 10.1.0.1 but is unsuccessful when attempting to ping the 172.30.100.1 interface on R3.

Example 7-7   R1 Pings Fail to Reach R3 LAN

```
R1# ping 10.1.0.1

Type escape sequence to abort.
Sending 5, 100-byte ICMP Echos to 10.1.0.1, timeout is 2 seconds:
```

```
!!!!!
Success rate is 100 percent (5/5), round-trip min/avg/max = 28/28/28 ms


R1# ping 172.30.100.1


Type escape sequence to abort.
Sending 5, 100-byte ICMP Echos to 172.30.100.1, timeout is 2 seconds:
.....
Success rate is 0 percent (0/5)
R1#
```

The output in Example 7-8 shows that R3 is able to ping 10.1.0.1 but is unsuccessful when attempting to ping the 172.30.1.1 interface on R1.

Example 7-8   R3 Pings to Reach R1 LAN
```
R3# ping 10.1.0.1


Type escape sequence to abort.
Sending 5, 100-byte ICMP Echos to 10.1.0.1, timeout is 2 seconds:
!!!!!
Success rate is 100 percent (5/5), round-trip min/avg/max = 28/28/28 ms


R3#ping 172.30.1.1
Type escape sequence to abort.
Sending 5, 100-byte ICMP Echos to 172.30.1.1, timeout is 2 seconds:
.....
Success rate is 0 percent (0/5)
R3#
```

As you can see, there is an obvious problem when trying to communicate with the 172.30.0.0 discontiguous subnets. The following sections examine routing tables and routing updates to further investigate this problem and attempt to resolve it.

Configuring Discontiguous Routes (7.1.2)

In this activity, you will review how to configure RIP on the network containing discontiguous subnets, introduced in this section. Because Packet Tracer does not support redistribution of static routes or null interfaces, these configurations will not be included. Detailed instructions are provided within the activity. Use file e2-712.pka on the CD-ROM that accompanies this book to perform this activity using Packet Tracer.

RIPv1: Discontiguous Networks

As you learned previously, RIPv1 is a classful routing protocol. It does not include the subnet masks in its routing updates, as you can see in the RIPv1 message format in Figure 7-4. Therefore, RIPv1 cannot support discontiguous networks, VLSM, or CIDR supernets. However, might there be room to expand the RIPv1 message format to include the subnet mask so that you could have a discontiguous network configuration? How would you change the format of this message in the figure to include the subnet mask?

Figure 7-4   RIPv1 Message Format

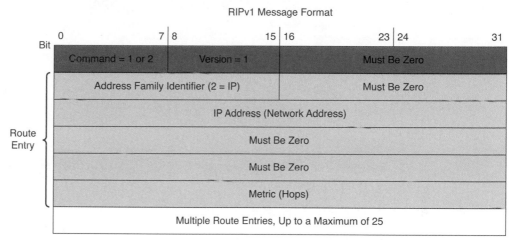

Because the subnet mask is not included in the update, RIPv1 and other classful routing protocols must summarize networks at major network boundaries. As you can see in Figure 7-5, RIPv1 on both Routers R1 and R3 will summarize their 172.30.0.0 subnets to the classful major network address of 172.30.0.0 when sending routing updates to R2.

Examining the Routing Tables

As you saw earlier, R2 gets inconsistent results when attempting to ping an address on one of the 172.30.0.0 subnets.

Example 7-9 shows that R2 has two equal-cost routes to the 172.30.0.0/16 network. This is because both R1 and R3 are sending R2 a RIPv1 update for the 172.30.0.0 network with a metric of 1 hop. Because R1 and R3 automatically summarized the individual subnets, R2's routing table only contains the major classful network address of 172.30.0.0 and adds the Class B subnet mask of /16.

Figure 7-5   Automatic Summarization

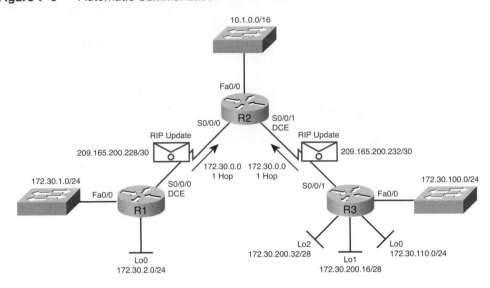

Example 7-9   R2 Assumes Equal Cost to 172.30.0.0/16 Through R1 and R3

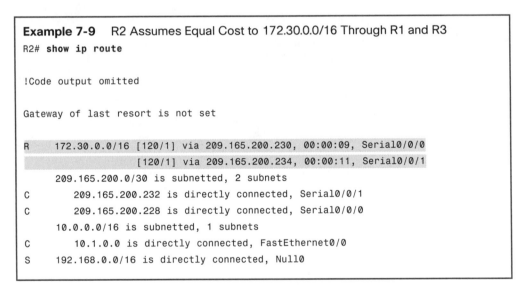

You can examine the contents of the routing updates as the updates are sent and received with **debug ip rip** command, as demonstrated in Example 7-10.

Example 7-10 R2 Output from the **debug ip rip** Command

```
R2# debug ip rip

RIP protocol debugging is on

RIP: received v1 update from 209.165.200.230 on Serial0/0/0
     172.30.0.0 in 1 hops
RIP: received v1 update from 209.165.200.234 on Serial0/0/1
     172.30.0.0 in 1 hops
R2#
RIP: sending v1 update to 255.255.255.255 via Serial0/0/0 (209.165.200.229)
RIP: build update entries
       network 10.0.0.0 metric 1
       subnet 209.165.200.232 metric 1
RIP: sending v1 update to 255.255.255.255 via Serial0/0/1 (209.165.200.233)
RIP: build update entries
       network 10.0.0.0 metric 1
       subnet 209.165.200.228 metric 1
R2#
```

Notice that R2 is receiving two 172.30.0.0 equal-cost routes with a metric of 1 hop: one route on Serial 0/0/0 from R1 and the other route on Serial 0/0/1 from R3. Also notice that the subnet mask is not included with the network address in the update.

What about R1 and R3? Are they receiving each other's 172.30.0.0 subnets?

Example 7-11 shows that R1 has its own 172.30.0.0 routes: 172.30.2.0/24 and 172.30.1.0/24. But R1 does not send R2 those subnets. R3 has a similar routing table. Both R1 and R3 are boundary routers and are only sending the summarized 172.30.0.0 network to R2 in their RIPv1 routing updates. As a result, R2 only knows about the 172.30.0.0/16 classful network and is unaware of any 172.30.0.0 subnets.

Example 7-11 R1 Output from the **show ip route** Command

```
R1# show ip route

!Code output omitted

Gateway of last resort is not set


     172.30.0.0/24 is subnetted, 2 subnets
C       172.30.2.0 is directly connected, Loopback0
```

```
C          172.30.1.0 is directly connected, FastEthernet0/0
       209.165.200.0/30 is subnetted, 2 subnets
R          209.165.200.232 [120/1] via 209.165.200.229, 00:00:16, Serial0/0/0
C          209.165.200.228 is directly connected, Serial0/0/0
R      10.0.0.0/8 [120/1] via 209.165.200.229, 00:00:16, Serial0/0/0
R1#
```

Referring again to the **debug ip rip** output in Example 7-10, notice that R2 is not including the 172.30.0.0 network in its updates to either R1 or R3. Why not? Because the split horizon rule is in effect. R2 learned about 172.30.0.0/16 on both the Serial 0/0/0 and Serial 0/0/1 interfaces. Because R2 learned about the 172.30.0.0 network on these interfaces, it will not include that network in its updates sent out those same interfaces.

How Classful Routing Protocols Determine Subnet Masks

Figure 7-6 shows the classful boundaries in the chapter topology. Do you remember why R1 is sending a summary route and not the subnets? Remember, RIPv1 is a classful routing protocol. The 172.30.1.0/24 and 172.30.2.0/24 routes are in R1's routing table. However, because the update is going out an interface on a different major classful network (209.165.200.0), RIPv1 will summarize these subnets to the Class B address of 172.30.0.0.

Figure 7-6 Classful Boundaries in the Chapter Topology

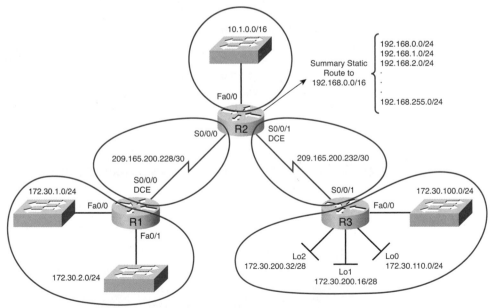

Do you remember how RIPv1 on R2 determines the subnet mask for the 172.30.0.0 update from R1 and R3? Using R1 as an example, R2 receives the 172.30.0.0 update on its Serial 0/0/0 interface, which has an IP address on the 209.165.200.228 network. Because this is a different major network address from the 172.30.0.0 update, RIPv1 applies the classful mask, the Class B /16 mask to the route.

R2 has two routes for the 172.30.0.0/16 network but cannot differentiate between the various subnets. When forwarding packets with a destination IP address belonging to this 172.30.0.0/16 network, R2 does not have specific enough information to determine which exit interface it should use for which subnet. In this case, the routing table has two equal-cost paths for the 172.30.0.0/16 network and will perform load balancing. Load balancing will be discussed in more detail in Chapter 8, "The Routing Table: A Closer Look." For now, realize that unexpected results will occur. Depending on other configurations on this router, it is possible that the packets destined for the 172.30.0.0 network will alternate between the two exit interfaces. For example, some packets for the 172.30.1.0/24 subnet will be sent to R1 and some packets to R2. This means that some packets will reach their destination and others will not. This intermittent performance is precisely what you observed in Example 7-6; some pings succeeded and some pings failed.

RIPv1: No VLSM Support

Because RIPv1 does not send the subnet mask in routing updates, it cannot support VLSM. The R3 router is configured with the following VLSM subnets, all of which are members of the Class B network 172.30.0.0/16:

- 172.30.100.0**/24** (FastEthernet 0/0)
- 172.30.110.0**/24** (Loopback 0)
- 172.30.200.16**/28** (Loopback 1)
- 172.30.200.32**/28** (Loopback 2)

As you saw with the 172.30.0.0/16 updates to R2 by R1 and R3, RIPv1 either summarizes the subnets to the classful boundary or uses the subnet mask of the outgoing interface to determine which subnets to advertise.

To demonstrate how RIPv1 uses the subnet mask of the outgoing interface, R4 is temporarily added to the chapter topology and is connected to R3 through the FastEthernet 0/0 interface on the 172.30.100.0/24 network (see Figure 7-7).

In the **debug ip rip** output for R3 in Example 7-12, notice that the only 172.30.0.0 subnet that is included in the RIPv1 updates leaving the FastEthernet 0/0 interface to the R4 router is 172.30.110.0.

Figure 7-7   Comparing RIPv1 Updates Inside and Across Classful Boundaries

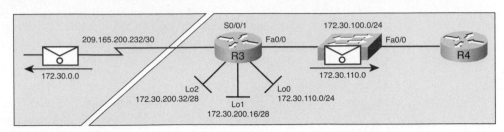

```
Example 7-12  R3 Output from the debug ip rip Command
R3# debug ip rip

RIP protocol debugging is on
R3#
RIP: sending v1 update to 255.255.255.255 via FastEthernet0/0 (172.30.100.1)
RIP: build update entries
        network 10.0.0.0 metric 2
        subnet 172.30.110.0 metric 1
        network 209.165.200.0 metric 1
RIP: sending v1 update to 255.255.255.255 via Serial0/0/1 (209.165.200.234)
RIP: build update entries
        network 172.30.0.0 metric 1
```

Why is RIPv1 on R3 not including the other subnets, 172.30.200.16/28 and
172.30.200.32/28, in updates to R4? When RIPv1 on R3 sends its 172.30.0.0 subnets out its
exit interface FastEthernet 0/0, it will only include those 172.30.0.0 subnets with the same
subnet mask as the exit interface. The 172.30.200.16/28 and 172.30.200.32/28 subnets in
R3's routing table do not have the same /24 subnet mask as FastEthernet 0/0, so they are
not included. Only the 172.30.110.0 subnet in R3's routing table has a /24 mask. This is
why all subnets must use the same subnet mask when a classful routing protocol is implemented in the network.

Also notice that R3 is sending the full 172.30.0.0 major classful network out Serial 0/0/1.

RIPv1: No CIDR Support

So far, most of this information should be somewhat familiar to you from Chapter 5.
However, there is one issue that has not yet been addressed.

192.168.0.0/16 Static Route

Example 7-13 shows the configuration of a static route to the 192.168.0.0/16 network on R2 and instructs RIP to include that route in its updates using the **redistribute static** command. This static route is a summary of the 192.168.0.0/24 subnets ranging from 192.168.0.0/24 to 192.168.255.0/24.

Example 7-13 R2 Static Summary Route Configuration and Redistribution

```
R2(config)# ip route 192.168.0.0 255.255.0.0 null0
R2(config)# router rip
R2(config-router)# redistribute static
R2(config-router)# network 10.0.0.0
R2(config-router)# network 209.165.200.0
R2(config-router)# exit
```

In Example 7-14, you can see that the static route is included in R2's own routing table.

Example 7-14 R2 Routing Table

```
R2# show ip route

!Code output omitted

Gateway of last resort is not set

R    172.30.0.0/16 [120/1] via 209.165.200.230, 00:00:09, Serial0/0/0
                   [120/1] via 209.165.200.234, 00:00:11, Serial0/0/1
     209.165.200.0/30 is subnetted, 2 subnets
C       209.165.200.232 is directly connected, Serial0/0/1
C       209.165.200.228 is directly connected, Serial0/0/0
     10.0.0.0/16 is subnetted, 1 subnets
C       10.1.0.0 is directly connected, FastEthernet0/0
S    192.168.0.0/16 is directly connected, Null0
```

Looking at the routing table for R1 in Example 7-15, notice that R1 is not receiving this 192.168.0.0/16 route in its RIP updates from R2, although you might expect that it should.

Example 7-15 R1 Routing Table

```
R1# show ip route

!Code output omitted

Gateway of last resort is not set

     172.30.0.0/24 is subnetted, 2 subnets
C        172.30.2.0 is directly connected, FastEthernet0/1
C        172.30.1.0 is directly connected, FastEthernet0/0
     209.165.200.0/30 is subnetted, 2 subnets
R        209.165.200.232 [120/1] via 209.165.200.229, 00:00:16, Serial0/0/0
C        209.165.200.228 is directly connected, Serial0/0/0
R    10.0.0.0/8 [120/1] via 209.165.200.229, 00:00:16, Serial0/0/0
```

Using **debug ip rip** on R2, as shown in Example 7-16, notice that RIPv1 is not including the 192.168.0.0/16 route in its RIP updates to either R1 or R3. Do you know why this route is not being included? Look at the route 192.168.0.0/16. What is the class of the route: A, B, or C? What is the mask used in the static route? Does it match the class? Is the mask in the static route less than the classful mask?

Example 7-16 R2 **debug ip rip** Output Verifies 192.168.0.0/16 Is Not Sent to R1 and R3

```
R2# debug ip rip

RIP protocol debugging is on
<some output omitted>
RIP: received v1 update from 209.165.200.230 on Serial0/0/0
     172.30.0.0 in 1 hops
RIP: received v1 update from 209.165.200.234 on Serial0/0/1
     172.30.0.0 in 1 hops
R2#
RIP: sending v1 update to 255.255.255.255 via Serial0/0/0 (209.165.200.229)
RIP: build update entries
        network 10.0.0.0 metric 1
        subnet 209.165.200.232 metric 1
RIP: sending v1 update to 255.255.255.255 via Serial0/0/1 (209.165.200.233)
RIP: build update entries
        network 10.0.0.0 metric 1
        subnet 209.165.200.228 metric 1
R2#
```

We configured the static route 192.168.0.0 with a /16 mask. This is fewer bits than the classful Class C mask of /24. Because the mask does not match the class or a subnet of the class, RIPv1 will not include this route in its updates to other routers.

RIPv1 and other classful routing protocols cannot support CIDR routes that are summarized routes with a smaller subnet mask than the classful mask of the route. RIPv1 ignores these supernets in the routing table and does not include them in updates to other routers. This is because the receiving router would only be able to apply the larger classful mask to the update and not the shorter /16 mask.

Note

If the 192.168.0.0 static route were configured with a /24 mask or greater, this route would be included in the RIP updates. The receiving routers would apply the classful /24 mask to this update.

As discussed in Chapter 6, "VLSM and CIDR," CIDR allows networks to have masks without regard to the class, hence the name *classless*. The network 192.168.0.0 could have a mask of /8, /10, /20, /24, /30, or something else. CIDR also allows routes to be aggregated with a subnet mask that includes all the routes being summarized, even if that mask is less than the classful mask. This point was discussed previously in Chapter 6.

Verify Nonconvergence Using Commands (7.1.5)

Use the Packet Tracer Activity in simulation mode to see that updates are not sent across classful network boundaries with RIPv1. In real-time mode, verify nonconvergence with the **show ip route**, **ping**, and **debug ip rip** commands. Detailed instructions are provided within the activity. Use file e2-715.pka on the CD-ROM that accompanies this book to perform this activity using Packet Tracer.

Configuring RIPv2

Configuring RIPv2 is similar to configuring RIPv1, with the addition of a single RIP command, **version 2**. This command will be explained in the next section. Although RIPv2 uses the same basic configuration commands as RIPv1, the results of using RIPv2 are different, allowing both CIDR and VLSM to be used in the network.

Enabling and Verifying RIPv2

RIPv2 is defined in RFC 1723. Like Version 1, RIPv2 is encapsulated in a User Datagram Protocol (UDP) segment using port 520 and can carry up to 25 routes. Figure 7-8 shows the RIPv1 and RIPv2 message formats. Although RIPv2 has the same basic message format as RIPv1, two significant extensions are added.

Figure 7-8   Comparing RIPv1 and RIPv2 Message Formats

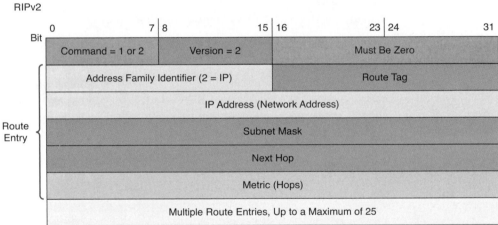

The first significant extension in the RIPv2 message format is the subnet mask field that allows a 32-bit mask to be included in the RIP route entry. As a result, the receiving router no longer depends on the subnet mask of the inbound interface or the classful mask when determining the subnet mask for a route.

The second significant extension to the RIPv2 message format is the addition of the next-hop address. The next-hop address is used to identify a better next-hop address—if one exists—than the address of the sending router. If the field is set to all 0s (0.0.0.0), the address of the sending router is the best next-hop address. Detailed information about how the next-hop address is used is beyond the scope of this course. However, an example can be found in RFC 1722, "RIP Version 2 Protocol Applicability Statement" or *Routing TCP/IP, Volume 1*, by Jeff Doyle.

By default, when a RIP process is configured on a Cisco router, it is running RIPv1. However, even though the router only sends RIPv1 messages, it can process both RIPv1 and RIPv2 messages. A RIPv1 router will just ignore the RIPv2 fields in the route entry.

In Example 7-17, the **show ip protocols** command verifies that R2 is configured for RIPv1 but receives RIP messages for both versions.

Example 7-17 R2 **show ip protocols** Command Verifies the Sending of RIPv1
Updates, but Can Receive Both RIPv1 and RIPv2 Updates

```
R2# show ip protocols

Routing Protocol is "rip"
  Sending updates every 30 seconds, next due in 1 seconds
  Invalid after 180 seconds, hold down 180, flushed after 240
  Outgoing update filter list for all interfaces is
  Incoming update filter list for all interfaces is
  Redistributing: static, rip
  Default version control: send version 1, receive any version
    Interface           Send  Recv  Triggered RIP   Key-chain
    Serial0/0/0         1       1 2
    Serial0/0/1         1       1 2
  Automatic network summarization is in effect
  <output omitted for brevity>
```

Interestingly, a router configured with RIPv2 will ignore RIPv1 updates. The interface commands **ip rip send** and **ip rip receive** can be used to force compatibility between different versions.

In Example 7-18, notice that the **version 2** command is used to modify RIP to use Version 2. This command should be configured on all routers in the routing domain. The RIP process will now include the subnet mask in all updates, making RIPv2 a classless routing protocol.

Example 7-18 Configuring RIP as a Classless Routing Protocol with the **version 2**
Command

```
R1(config)# router rip
R1(config-router)# version 2

R2(config)# router rip
R2(config-router)# version 2

R3(config)# router rip
R3(config-router)# version 2
```

As you can see from the output in Example 7-19, when a router is configured for Version 2, only RIPv2 messages are sent and received.

Example 7-19 R2 **show ip protocols** Command Verifies the Sending and Receiving of RIPv2 Updates Only

```
R2# show ip protocols

Routing Protocol is "rip"
  Sending updates every 30 seconds, next due in 1 seconds
  Invalid after 180 seconds, hold down 180, flushed after 240
  Outgoing update filter list for all interfaces is
  Incoming update filter list for all interfaces is
  Redistributing: static, rip
  Default version control: send version 2, receive version 2
    Interface           Send  Recv  Triggered RIP  Key-chain
    Serial0/0/0          2     2
    Serial0/0/1          2     2
  Automatic network summarization is in effect
  <output omitted for brevity>
```

The default behavior of RIPv1 can be restored by using either the **version 1** command or the **no version** command in router configuration mode, as shown in Example 7-20.

Example 7-20 Restoring RIP to Version 1

```
R1(config)# router rip
R1(config-router)# version 1

!or

R1(config)# router rip
R1(config-router)# no version
```
```
R2(config)# router rip
R2(config-router)# version 1

!or

R2(config)# router rip
R2(config-router)# no version
```
```
R3(config)# router rip
R3(config-router)# version 1
```

```
!or

R3(config)# router rip
R3(config-router)# no version
```

Auto-Summary and RIPv2

Because RIPv2 is a classless routing protocol, you might expect to see the individual 172.30.0.0 subnets in the routing tables. However, when you examine the routing table for R2 in Example 7-21, you still see the summarized 172.30.0.0/16 route with the same two equal-cost paths. Routers R1 and R3 still do not include the 172.30.0.0 subnets of the other router.

Example 7-21 RIPv2 Still Summarizes to the Classful Boundary

```
R2# show ip route

!Code output omitted

Gateway of last resort is not set

R    172.30.0.0/16 [120/1] via 209.165.200.230, 00:00:28, Serial0/0/0
                    [120/1] via 209.165.200.234, 00:00:18, Serial0/0/1
     209.165.200.0/30 is subnetted, 2 subnets
C       209.165.200.232 is directly connected, Serial0/0/1
C       209.165.200.228 is directly connected, Serial0/0/0
     10.0.0.0/16 is subnetted, 1 subnets
C       10.1.0.0 is directly connected, FastEthernet0/0
S    192.168.0.0/16 is directly connected, Null0
```

The only difference so far between RIPv1 and RIPV2 is that R1 and R3 each have a route to 192.168.0.0/16, as shown in Example 7-22. This route was the static route configured on R2 and redistributed by RIP.

Example 7-22 R1 Now Has a Summary Route to 192.168.0.0/16

```
R1# show ip route

!Code output omitted

Gateway of last resort is not set
```

```
        172.30.0.0/24 is subnetted, 2 subnets
C          172.30.2.0 is directly connected, Loopback0
C          172.30.1.0 is directly connected, FastEthernet0/0
        209.165.200.0/30 is subnetted, 2 subnets
R          209.165.200.232 [120/1] via 209.165.200.229, 00:00:04, Serial0/0/0
C          209.165.200.228 is directly connected, Serial0/0/0
R       10.0.0.0/8 [120/1] via 209.165.200.229, 00:00:04, Serial0/0/0
R       192.168.0.0/16 [120/1] via 209.165.200.229, 00:00:04, Serial0/0/0
```

So, what is happening? To examine which RIPv2 routes are being sent and received, we will use the **debug ip rip** command. Example 7-23 shows the **debug ip rip** output for R1. Notice that RIPv2 is sending both the network address and subnet mask.

Example 7-23 R1 **debug ip rip** Output Verifies That Subnet Mask Is Now Sent but Classful Summarization Is Still in Effect

```
R1# debug ip rip

RIP protocol debugging is on
R1#
RIP: sending v2 update to 224.0.0.9 via Serial0/0/0 (209.165.200.230)
RIP: build update entries
        172.30.0.0/16 via 0.0.0.0, metric 1, tag 0
R1#
<output omitted for brevity>
RIP: received v2 update from 209.165.200.229 on Serial0/0/0
      10.0.0.0/8 via 0.0.0.0 in 1 hops
      192.168.0.0/16 via 0.0.0.0 in 1 hops
      209.165.200.232/30 via 0.0.0.0 in 1 hops
<output omitted for brevity>
R1#
```

However, in Example 7-23, notice that the route sent is the summarized classful network address, 172.30.0.0/16, and not the individual 172.30.1.0/24 and 172.30.2.0/24 subnets.

By default, RIPv2 automatically summarizes networks at major network boundaries, just like RIPv1. Both R1 and R3 routers are still summarizing their 172.30.0.0 subnets to the Class B address of 172.30.0.0 when sending updates out their interfaces on the 209.165.200.228 and 209.165.200.232 networks, respectively. The **show ip protocols** command in Example 7-24 verifies that "automatic network summarization is in effect."

Example 7-24 R1 **show ip protocols** Output Verifies That Automatic Summarization
                        Is in Effect

```
R1# show ip protocols

Routing Protocol is "rip"
  Sending updates every 30 seconds, next due in 20 seconds
  Invalid after 180 seconds, hold down 180, flushed after 240
  Outgoing update filter list for all interfaces is not set
  Incoming update filter list for all interfaces is not set
  Redistributing: rip
  Default version control: send version 2, receive version 2
    Interface              Send  Recv  Triggered RIP  Key-chain
    FastEthernet0/0         2     2
    FastEthernet0/1         2     2
    Serial0/1/0             2     2
  Automatic network summarization is in effect
  <output omitted for brevity>
```

The only change resulting from the **version 2** command is that R2 is now including the
192.168.0.0/16 network in its updates. This is because RIPv2 includes the 255.255.0.0
mask with the 192.168.0.0 network address in the update. Both R1 and R3 will now receive
this redistributed static route through RIPv2 and enter it into their routing tables.

Note

Remember, the 192.168.0.0/16 route could not be distributed with RIPv1 because the subnet mask
was less than the classful mask. Because the mask is not included in RIPv1 updates, there was no
way for RIPv1 to determine what that mask should be.

Disabling Auto-Summary in RIPv2

As you can see in Example 7-25, to modify the default RIPv2 behavior of automatic
summarization, use the **no auto-summary** command in router configuration mode.
This command is not valid with RIPv1. Even though Cisco IOS will let you configure
no auto-summary for RIPv1, the command has no effect. You must also configure
version 2 before IOS will change the way it sends RIP updates.

Example 7-25 Disable Automatic Summarization with the **no auto-summary**
               Command

```
R2(config)# router rip
R2(config-router)# no auto-summary

R3(config)# router rip
R3(config-router)# no auto-summary

R1(config)# router rip
R1(config-router)# no auto-summary
```

After automatic summarization is disabled, RIPv2 will no longer summarize networks to their classful address at boundary routers. RIPv2 will now include all subnets and their appropriate masks in its routing updates. Example 7-26 demonstrates how the **show ip protocols** command is used to verify that "automatic network summarization is not in effect."

Example 7-26 R1 **show ip protocols** Output Verifies That Automatic Summarization
               Is Not in Effect

```
R1# show ip protocols

Routing Protocol is "rip"
  Sending updates every 30 seconds, next due in 11 seconds
  Invalid after 180 seconds, hold down 180, flushed after 240
  Outgoing update filter list for all interfaces is not set
  Incoming update filter list for all interfaces is not set
  Redistributing: rip
  Default version control: send version 2, receive version 2
    Interface          Send  Recv  Triggered RIP  Key-chain
    FastEthernet0/0     2     2
    FastEthernet0/1     2     2
    Serial0/1/0         2     2
  Automatic network summarization is not in effect
  <output omitted for brevity>
```

Verifying RIPv2 Updates

Now that you are using the classless routing protocol RIPv2 and you have disabled automatic summarization, what should you expect to see in the routing tables?

In Example 7-27, the routing table for R2 now contains the individual subnets for 172.30.0.0/16. Notice that a single summary route with two equal-cost paths no longer exists. Each subnet and mask has its own specific entry, along with the exit interface and next-hop address to reach that subnet.

Example 7-27 R2 Routing Table Fully Converged on 172.30.0.0/16 Subnets

```
R2# show ip route

!Code output omitted

Gateway of last resort is not set

     172.30.0.0/16 is variably subnetted, 6 subnets, 2 masks
R        172.30.200.32/28 [120/1] via 209.165.200.234, 00:00:09, Serial0/0/1
R        172.30.200.16/28 [120/1] via 209.165.200.234, 00:00:09, Serial0/0/1
R        172.30.2.0/24 [120/1] via 209.165.200.230, 00:00:03, Serial0/0/0
R        172.30.1.0/24 [120/1] via 209.165.200.230, 00:00:03, Serial0/0/0
R        172.30.100.0/24 [120/1] via 209.165.200.234, 00:00:09, Serial0/0/1
R        172.30.110.0/24 [120/1] via 209.165.200.234, 00:00:09, Serial0/0/1
     209.165.200.0/30 is subnetted, 2 subnets
C        209.165.200.232 is directly connected, Serial0/0/1
C        209.165.200.228 is directly connected, Serial0/0/0
     10.0.0.0/16 is subnetted, 1 subnets
C        10.1.0.0 is directly connected, FastEthernet0/0
S    192.168.0.0/16 is directly connected, Null0
```

The routing table for R1, shown in Example 7-28, contains all the subnets for
172.30.0.0/16, including those subnets from R3.

Example 7-28 R1 Routing Table Fully Converged on 172.30.0.0/16 Subnets

```
R1# show ip route

!Code output omitted

Gateway of last resort is not set

     172.30.0.0/16 is variably subnetted, 6 subnets, 2 masks
R        172.30.200.32/28 [120/2] via 209.165.200.229, 00:00:01, Serial0/0/0
R        172.30.200.16/28 [120/2] via 209.165.200.229, 00:00:01, Serial0/0/0
C        172.30.2.0/24 is directly connected, Loopback0
C        172.30.1.0/24 is directly connected, FastEthernet0/0
R        172.30.100.0/24 [120/2] via 209.165.200.229, 00:00:01, Serial0/0/0
R        172.30.110.0/24 [120/2] via 209.165.200.229, 00:00:01, Serial0/0/0
     209.165.200.0/30 is subnetted, 2 subnets
R        209.165.200.232 [120/1] via 209.165.200.229, 00:00:02, Serial0/0/0
```

```
C         209.165.200.228 is directly connected, Serial0/0/0
      10.0.0.0/16 is subnetted, 1 subnets
R          10.1.0.0 [120/1] via 209.165.200.229, 00:00:02, Serial0/0/0
R     192.168.0.0/16 [120/1] via 209.165.200.229, 00:00:02, Serial0/0/0
```

The routing table for R3, shown in Example 7-29, contains all the subnets for 172.30.0.0/16, including those subnets from R1. This network is converged.

Example 7-29 R3 Routing Table Fully Converged on 172.30.0.0/16 Subnets

```
R3# show ip route

!Code output omitted

Gateway of last resort is not set

     172.30.0.0/16 is variably subnetted, 6 subnets, 2 masks
C         172.30.200.32/28 is directly connected, Loopback2
C         172.30.200.16/28 is directly connected, Loopback1
R         172.30.2.0/24 [120/2] via 209.165.200.233, 00:00:01, Serial0/0/1
R         172.30.1.0/24 [120/2] via 209.165.200.233, 00:00:01, Serial0/0/1
C         172.30.100.0/24 is directly connected, FastEthernet0/0
C         172.30.110.0/24 is directly connected, Loopback0
     209.165.200.0/30 is subnetted, 2 subnets
C         209.165.200.232 is directly connected, Serial0/0/1
R         209.165.200.228 [120/1] via 209.165.200.233, 00:00:02, Serial0/0/1
     10.0.0.0/16 is subnetted, 1 subnets
R          10.1.0.0 [120/1] via 209.165.200.233, 00:00:02, Serial0/0/1
R     192.168.0.0/16 [120/1] via 209.165.200.233, 00:00:02, Serial0/0/1
```

In Example 7-30, using the **debug ip rip** command, we can verify that the classless routing protocol RIPv2 is indeed sending and receiving routing updates, which are individual routes with their subnet mask instead of a single summary route with the classful mask. Notice that each route entry now includes the slash notation for the subnet mask.

Example 7-30 R2 Is Sending and Receiving Subnet Mask Information

```
R2# debug ip rip

 RIP protocol debugging is on
<some output omitted for brevity>
R2#
RIP: received v2 update from 209.165.200.234 on Serial0/0/1
```

```
      172.30.100.0/24 via 0.0.0.0 in 1 hops
      172.30.110.0/24 via 0.0.0.0 in 1 hops
      172.30.200.16/28 via 0.0.0.0 in 1 hops
      172.30.200.32/28 via 0.0.0.0 in 1 hops
R2#
RIP: sending v2 update to 224.0.0.9 via Serial0/0/0 (209.165.200.229)
RIP: build update entries
      10.1.0.0/16 via 0.0.0.0, metric 1, tag 0
      172.30.100.0/24 via 0.0.0.0, metric 2, tag 0
      172.30.110.0/24 via 0.0.0.0, metric 2, tag 0
      172.30.200.16/28 via 0.0.0.0, metric 2, tag 0
      172.30.200.32/28 via 0.0.0.0, metric 2, tag 0
      192.168.0.0/16 via 0.0.0.0, metric 1, tag 0
      209.165.200.232/30 via 0.0.0.0, metric 1, tag 0
R2#
```

You can also see that an update on one interface has its metric incremented before it is sent out another interface. For example, the update received on Serial 0/0/1 for the 172.30.100.0/24 network with 1 hop is sent out other interfaces, such as Serial 0/0/0 with a metric of 2, or 2 hops:

```
RIP: received v2 update from 209.165.200.234 on Serial0/0/1
       172.30.100.0/24 via 0.0.0.0 in 1 hops
RIP: sending v2 update to 224.0.0.9 via Serial0/0/0 (209.165.200.229)
       172.30.100.0/24 via 0.0.0.0, metric 2, tag 0
```

Notice also that the updates are sent using the multicast address 224.0.0.9. RIPv1 sends updates as a broadcast 255.255.255.255. There are several advantages to using a multicast address. These details are beyond the scope of this course; in general, however, multicasts can take up less bandwidth on the network. In addition, multicasting updates require less processing by devices that are not RIP enabled. Under RIPv2, any device that is not configured for RIP will discard the frame at the data link layer. With broadcast updates under RIPv1 configurations, all devices on a broadcast network like Ethernet must process a RIP update all the way up to the transport layer, where the device finally discovers that the packet is destined for a process that does not exist.

Configure RIPv2 (7.2.4)

RIPv2 is an updated version that supports VLSM and CIDR by carrying subnet mask information in its routing update packets. However, the default behavior of RIPv2 is to automatically summarize routes on classful boundaries. In this activity, you will use Packet Tracer to configure RIPv2 and disable automatic summarization in the network introduced in this section containing discontiguous subnets. Then you will examine the changes in the operation of the network. Use file e2-724.pka on the CD-ROM that accompanies this book to perform this activity using Packet Tracer.

VLSM and CIDR

Classless routing protocols such as RIPv2 include the subnet mask in their routing updates. This allows classless routing protocols to support both VLSM and CIDR.

RIPv2 and VLSM

Because classless routing protocols like RIPv2 can carry both the network address and the subnet mask, they do not need to summarize these networks to their classful addresses at major network boundaries. Therefore, classless routing protocols support VLSM. Routers using RIPv2 no longer need to use the inbound interface's mask to determine the subnet mask in the route advertisement. The network and the mask are explicitly included in every routing update.

In networks that use a VLSM addressing scheme, a classless routing protocol is essential to propagate all the networks along with their correct subnet masks. In Figure 7-9, we temporarily added back the R4 router to illustrate how RIPv2 operates within a classful boundary. Although the boundary is shown as a reminder, with automatic summarization disabled, RIPv2 ignores classful boundaries. Remember, with RIPv1, R3 would only send R4 the 172.30.0.0 routes that had the same mask as the FastEthernet 0/0 exit interface. Because the interface is 172.30.100.1 with a /24 mask, RIPv1 only included 172.30.0.0 subnets with a /24 mask. The only route that met this condition was 172.30.110.0.

Figure 7-9   RIPv2 Updates Inside Classful Boundaries

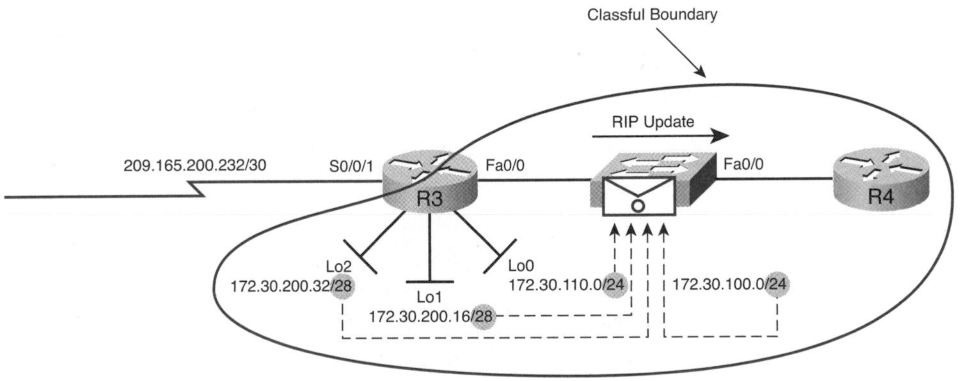

However, with RIPv2, R3 can now include all the 172.30.0.0 subnets in its routing updates to R4, as shown in the **debug** output in Example 7-31. This is because RIPv2 can include the proper subnet mask with the network address in the update.

In the **debug** output shown in Example 7-31, you can see that RIPv2 is including the networks and their subnet masks in its routing updates.

Example 7-31 debug ip rip Output Verifies That Network and Subnet Mask
Information Is Included in Routing Updates

```
R3# debug ip rip

RIP: sending v2 update to 224.0.0.9 via FastEthernet0/0 (172.30.100.1)
RIP: build update entries
        10.1.0.0/16 via 0.0.0.0, metric 2, tag 0
        172.30.1.0/24 via 0.0.0.0, metric 3, tag 0
        172.30.2.0/24 via 0.0.0.0, metric 3, tag 0
        172.30.110.0/24 via 0.0.0.0, metric 1, tag 0
        172.30.200.16/28 via 0.0.0.0, metric 1, tag 0
        172.30.200.32/28 via 0.0.0.0, metric 1, tag 0
        192.168.0.0/16 via 0.0.0.0, metric 2, tag 0
        209.165.200.228/30 via 0.0.0.0, metric 2, tag 0
        209.165.200.232/30 via 0.0.0.0, metric 1, tag 0
```

RIPv2 and CIDR

One of the goals of CIDR as stated by RFC 1519 is "to provide a mechanism for the aggregation of routing information." This goal includes the concept of supernetting. A *supernet* is a block of contiguous classful networks that is addressed as a single network. On R2, we configured a supernet—a static route to a single network that is used to represent multiple networks or subnets.

Supernets have masks that are smaller than the classful mask (/16 here, instead of the classful /24). For the supernet to be included in a routing update, the routing protocol must have the capability of carrying that mask. In other words, it must be a classless routing protocol, like RIPv2.

The static route that was configured on R2 does include a mask that is less than the classful mask:

```
R2(config)# ip route 192.168.0.0 255.255.0.0 Null0
```

In a classful environment, the 192.168.0.0 network address would be associated with the Class C mask /24, or 255.255.255.0. In today's networks, you no longer associate network addresses with classful masks. In this example, the 192.168.0.0 network has a /16, or 255.255.0.0, mask. This route could represent a series of 192.168.0.0/24 networks or any number of different address ranges. The only way this route can be included in a dynamic routing update is with a classless routing protocol that includes the /16 mask.

Using the **debug ip rip** command in Example 7-32, you can see that this CIDR supernet is included in the routing update sent by R2. Automatic summarization does not have to be disabled on RIPv2 or any classless routing protocol for supernets to be included in the updates.

Example 7-32 R2 **debug ip rip** Output Verifies That Supernet Is Sent in Routing
              Update

```
R2# debug ip rip

RIP protocol debugging is on
R2#
RIP: sending v2 update to 224.0.0.9 via Serial0/0/0 (209.165.200.229)
RIP: build update entries
        10.1.0.0/16 via 0.0.0.0, metric 1, tag 0
        172.30.100.0/24 via 0.0.0.0, metric 2, tag 0
        172.30.110.0/24 via 0.0.0.0, metric 2, tag 0
        172.30.200.16/28 via 0.0.0.0, metric 2, tag 0
        172.30.200.32/28 via 0.0.0.0, metric 2, tag 0
        192.168.0.0/16 via 0.0.0.0, metric 1, tag 0
        209.165.200.232/30 via 0.0.0.0, metric 1, tag 0
<output omitted for brevity>
R2#
```

The routing table for R1 in Example 7-33 shows that it has received the supernet route
from R2.

Example 7-33 R1's Routing Table Has a Route to Supernet 192.168.0.0/16

```
R1# show ip route

!Code output omitted

Gateway of last resort is not set

     172.30.0.0/16 is variably subnetted, 6 subnets, 2 masks
R        172.30.200.32/28 [120/2] via 209.165.200.229, 00:00:01, Serial0/0/0
R        172.30.200.16/28 [120/2] via 209.165.200.229, 00:00:01, Serial0/0/0
C        172.30.2.0/24 is directly connected, Loopback0
C        172.30.1.0/24 is directly connected, FastEthernet0/0
R        172.30.100.0/24 [120/2] via 209.165.200.229, 00:00:01, Serial0/0/0
R        172.30.110.0/24 [120/2] via 209.165.200.229, 00:00:01, Serial0/0/0
     209.165.200.0/30 is subnetted, 2 subnets
R        209.165.200.232 [120/1] via 209.165.200.229, 00:00:02, Serial0/0/0
C        209.165.200.228 is directly connected, Serial0/0/0
     10.0.0.0/16 is subnetted, 1 subnets
R        10.1.0.0 [120/1] via 209.165.200.229, 00:00:02, Serial0/0/0
R        192.168.0.0/16 [120/1] via 209.165.200.229, 00:00:02, Serial0/0/0
```

Verifying and Troubleshooting RIPv2

Many times, configuring a routing protocol is fairly straightforward. Understanding the effects and results of these configuration commands can be much more complex. This is why we discuss the protocols in such detail. It is done to help give you the knowledge and tools to verify and troubleshoot these routing protocols.

Verification and Troubleshooting Commands

There are several ways to verify and troubleshoot RIPv2. Many of the same commands used for RIPv2 can be used to verify and troubleshoot other routing protocols.

It is always best to begin with the basics:

- Make sure that all the links (interfaces) are up and operational.

- Check the cabling.

- Make sure that you have the correct IP address and subnet mask on each interface.

- Remove any configuration commands that are no longer necessary or have been replaced by other commands.

show ip route Command

The **show ip route** command is the first command to use to check for network convergence, as demonstrated in Example 7-34. As you examine the routing table, it is important to look for the routes that you expect to be in the routing table as well as for those that should not be in the routing table.

Example 7-34 Verify Convergence with the **show ip route** Command

```
R1# show ip route

!Code output omitted

Gateway of last resort is not set

     172.30.0.0/16 is variably subnetted, 6 subnets, 2 masks
R       172.30.200.32/28 [120/2] via 209.165.200.229, 00:00:01, Serial0/0/0
R       172.30.200.16/28 [120/2] via 209.165.200.229, 00:00:01, Serial0/0/0
C       172.30.2.0/24 is directly connected, Loopback0
C       172.30.1.0/24 is directly connected, FastEthernet0/0
R       172.30.100.0/24 [120/2] via 209.165.200.229, 00:00:01, Serial0/0/0
R       172.30.110.0/24 [120/2] via 209.165.200.229, 00:00:01, Serial0/0/0
```

```
      209.165.200.0/30 is subnetted, 2 subnets
R        209.165.200.232 [120/1] via 209.165.200.229, 00:00:02, Serial0/0/0
C        209.165.200.228 is directly connected, Serial0/0/0
      10.0.0.0/16 is subnetted, 1 subnets
R        10.1.0.0 [120/1] via 209.165.200.229, 00:00:02, Serial0/0/0
R     192.168.0.0/16 [120/1] via 209.165.200.229, 00:00:02, Serial0/0/0
```

show ip interface brief Command

If a network is missing from the routing table, it is often because an interface is down or incorrectly configured. The **show ip interface brief** command quickly verifies the status of all interfaces, as demonstrated in Example 7-35.

Example 7-35 Verify Interface Status with the **show ip interface brief** Command

```
R1# show ip interface brief

Interface          IP-Address      OK? Method Status                Protocol
FastEthernet0/0    172.30.1.1      YES NVRAM  up                    up
FastEthernet0/1    172.30.2.1      YES NVRAM  up                    up
Serial0/0/0        209.165.200.230 YES NVRAM  up                    up
Serial0/0/1        unassigned      YES NVRAM  down                  down
```

show ip protocols Command

The **show ip protocols** command verifies several critical items, including whether RIP is enabled, the version of RIP, the status of automatic summarization, and the networks that were included in the **network** statements, as demonstrated in Example 7-36. The Routing Information Sources listed at the bottom of the output are the RIP neighbors from which this router is currently receiving updates.

Example 7-36 Verify Routing Protocols Configuration with the **show ip protocols** Command

```
R1# show ip protocols

Routing Protocol is "rip"
  Sending updates every 30 seconds, next due in 29 seconds
  Invalid after 180 seconds, hold down 180, flushed after 240
  Outgoing update filter list for all interfaces is not set
```

```
   Incoming update filter list for all interfaces is not set
   Redistributing: rip
   Default version control: send version 2, receive version 2
     Interface              Send  Recv  Triggered RIP  Key-chain
     FastEthernet0/0          2    2
     FastEthernet0/1          2    2
     Serial0/0/0              2    2
   Automatic network summarization is not in effect
   Maximum path: 4
   Routing for Networks:
     172.30.0.0
     209.165.200.0
   Routing Information Sources:
     Gateway          Distance       Last Update
     209.165.200.229     120         00:00:18
   Distance: (default is 120)
```

debug ip rip Command

As demonstrated throughout the chapter and again in Example 7-37, **debug ip rip** is an excellent command to use to examine the contents of the routing updates that are sent and received by a router. There can be times when a route is received by a router but is not added to the routing table. One reason for this could be that a static route is also configured for the same advertised network. By default, a static route has a lower administrative distance than any dynamic routing protocol and will take precedence in being added to the routing table.

Example 7-37 Monitoring RIP Operation with the **debug ip rip** Command

```
R1# debug ip rip

RIP protocol debugging is on
R1#
RIP: sending v2 update to 224.0.0.9 via FastEthernet0/1 (172.30.2.1)
RIP: build update entries
        10.1.0.0/16 via 0.0.0.0, metric 2, tag 0
        172.30.1.0/24 via 0.0.0.0, metric 1, tag 0
        172.30.100.0/24 via 0.0.0.0, metric 3, tag 0
        172.30.110.0/24 via 0.0.0.0, metric 3, tag 0
        172.30.200.16/28 via 0.0.0.0, metric 3, tag 0
        172.30.200.32/28 via 0.0.0.0, metric 3, tag 0
        192.168.0.0/16 via 0.0.0.0, metric 2, tag 0
```

```
            209.165.200.228/30 via 0.0.0.0, metric 1, tag 0
            209.165.200.232/30 via 0.0.0.0, metric 2, tag 0
R1#
RIP: received v2 update from 209.165.200.229 on Serial0/0/0
      10.1.0.0/16 via 0.0.0.0 in 1 hops
      172.30.100.0/24 via 0.0.0.0 in 2 hops
      172.30.110.0/24 via 0.0.0.0 in 2 hops
      172.30.200.16/28 via 0.0.0.0 in 2 hops
      172.30.200.32/28 via 0.0.0.0 in 2 hops
      192.168.0.0/16 via 0.0.0.0 in 1 hops
      209.165.200.232/30 via 0.0.0.0 in 1 hops
R1#
RIP: sending v2 update to 224.0.0.9 via FastEthernet0/0 (172.30.1.1)
RIP: build update entries
          10.1.0.0/16 via 0.0.0.0, metric 2, tag 0
          172.30.2.0/24 via 0.0.0.0, metric 1, tag 0
          172.30.100.0/24 via 0.0.0.0, metric 3, tag 0
          172.30.110.0/24 via 0.0.0.0, metric 3, tag 0
          172.30.200.16/28 via 0.0.0.0, metric 3, tag 0
          172.30.200.32/28 via 0.0.0.0, metric 3, tag 0
          192.168.0.0/16 via 0.0.0.0, metric 2, tag 0
          209.165.200.228/30 via 0.0.0.0, metric 1, tag 0
          209.165.200.232/30 via 0.0.0.0, metric 2, tag 0
R1#
RIP: sending v2 update to 224.0.0.9 via Serial0/0/0 (209.165.200.230)
RIP: build update entries
          172.30.1.0/24 via 0.0.0.0, metric 1, tag 0
          172.30.2.0/24 via 0.0.0.0, metric 1, tag 0
```

ping Command

An easy way to verify round-trip connectivity is with the **ping** command, as shown in
Example 7-38. If end-to-end connectivity is not successful, begin by pinging the local interfaces. If successful, ping the remote router interfaces on the directly connected networks. If
that is also successful, continue pinging interfaces on each successive router. When a ping
is unsuccessful, examine both routers and all the routers in between to determine where and
why the ping is failing.

Example 7-38 Verifying Round-Trip Connectivity with the **ping** Command

```
R2# ping 172.30.2.1

Type escape sequence to abort.
Sending 5, 100-byte ICMP Echos to 172.30.2.1, timeout is 2 seconds:
```

```
!!!!!
Success rate is 100 percent (5/5), round-trip min/avg/max = 28/28/28 ms
R2#ping 172.30.100.1

Type escape sequence to abort.
Sending 5, 100-byte ICMP Echos to 172.30.100.1, timeout is 2 seconds:
!!!!!
Success rate is 100 percent (5/5), round-trip min/avg/max = 28/28/28 ms
R1# ping 172.30.100.1

Type escape sequence to abort.
Sending 5, 100-byte ICMP Echos to 172.30.100.1, timeout is 2 seconds:
!!!!!
Success rate is 100 percent (5/5), round-trip min/avg/max = 56/56/60 ms
R3# ping 172.30.1.1

Type escape sequence to abort.
Sending 5, 100-byte ICMP Echos to 172.30.1.1, timeout is 2 seconds:
!!!!!
Success rate is 100 percent (5/5), round-trip min/avg/max = 56/56/60 ms
```

show running-config Command

The **show running-config** command is the last one you should use to verify and troubleshoot your configuration. Usually, other commands are more efficient and provide more information than a simple listing of the current configuration. However, the **show running-config** command can be used to verify all the commands currently configured, as demonstrated in Example 7-39.

Example 7-39 show running-config Output Helps to Verify All Configuration
                 Components

```
R1# show running-config

Building configuration...
!
hostname R1
!
interface FastEthernet0/0
 ip address 172.30.1.1 255.255.255.0
!
interface FastEthernet0/1
 ip address 172.30.2.1 255.255.255.0
!
```

```
interface Serial0/0/0
 ip address 209.165.200.230 255.255.255.252
 clock rate 64000
!
router rip
 version 2
 network 172.30.0.0
 network 209.165.200.0
 no auto-summary
!
<some output omitted for brevity>
!
end
```

Common RIPv2 Issues

When troubleshooting issues specific to RIPv2, there are several areas to examine:

- **Version:** A good place to begin troubleshooting a network that is running RIP is to verify that the **version 2** command is configured on all routers. Although RIPv1 and RIPv2 can be made compatible with additional commands beyond the scope of this course, RIPv1 does not support discontiguous subnets, VLSM, or CIDR supernet routes. It is always better to use the same routing protocol on all routers unless there is a specific reason not to do so.

- **network statements:** Another source of problems might be incorrectly configured or missing network statements configured with the **network** command. Remember, the **network** command does two things:

  - It enables the routing protocol to send and receive updates on any local interfaces that belong to that network.

  - It includes the configured network in its routing updates to its neighboring routers.

  A missing or incorrect network statement will result in missed routing updates and routing updates not being sent or received on an interface.

- **Automatic summarization:** If there is a need or expectation for sending specific subnets and not just summarized routes, make sure that automatic summarization has been disabled with the **no auto-summary** command.

Authentication

Most routing protocols send their routing updates and other routing information using IP (in IP packets). IS-IS is the notable exception and is discussed in CCNP courses. A security concern of any routing protocol is the possibility of accepting invalid routing updates. The source of these invalid routing updates could be an attacker maliciously attempting to disrupt the network or trying to capture packets by tricking the router into sending its updates to the wrong destination. Another source of invalid updates could be a misconfigured router or even a host computer that is running the routing protocol unbeknownst to its user.

For example, in Figure 7-10, R1 is propagating a default route to all other routers in this routing domain. However, someone has mistakenly added Router R4 to the network, which is also propagating a default route. Some of the routers might forward default traffic to R4 instead of to the real gateway router, R1. These packets could be "black holed" and never seen again.

Figure 7-10   Why Authenticating Routing Information Is Important

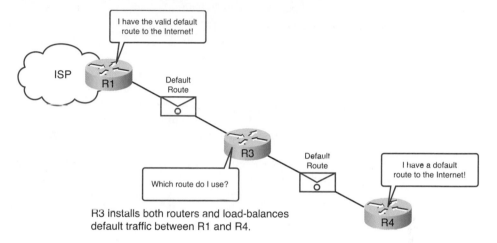

Whatever the reason, it is good practice to authenticate routing information. RIPv2, EIGRP, OSPF, IS-IS, and Border Gateway Protocol (BGP) can be configured to encrypt and authenticate routing information. This practice hides the content of the routing information, and routers will only accept routing information from other routers that have been configured with the same password or authentication information.

Note

The commands to configure authentication for routing protocols are discussed in another course.

Packet Tracer
☐ **Activity**

Routing Table Corruption (7.4.3)

This activity focuses on how Internet service providers use static routes to communicate with their customers, and how customers use the default route to communicate with their service providers. The activity shows how the area border router builds a default route and propagates it to all other routers in the routing domain. After the network has been established a new router R4 is added to the network, but this router has an erroneous default route not pointing to the ISP. You will view the routing table entries to determine the result this has on your network, and examine ping responses. Initially, all interfaces have been configured with correct addressing. RIP will be configured as the routing protocol. Use file e2-743.pka on the CD-ROM that accompanies this book to perform this activity using Packet Tracer.

Summary

Classless IP addressing is implemented with VLSM and CIDR. The subnet mask is no longer assumed by using the value of the first octet of the IP address. Because the subnet mask cannot be automatically determined by a router by looking solely at the network address, classless IP addressing requires that the subnet mask is included in any routing updates. A classless routing protocol includes the subnet mask with the network address in the routing update.

Because the subnet mask is included in the routing update, classless routing protocols like RIPv2, EIGRP, and OSPF can be used to implement discontiguous addressing schemes and VLSM networks. The inclusion of the subnet mask also allows the propagation of CIDR supernets: a summarized route with a mask that is less than the classful mask.

RIPv1 is a classful routing protocol, whereas RIPv2 is a classless routing protocol. Configuring RIPv2 requires adding the **version 2** command. By default, automatic summarization is in effect for RIPv2. The **no auto-summary** command is used to disable the automatic summarization of subnets to their classful network address at boundary routers.

The commands **show ip route**, **show ip protocols**, **show ip interface brief**, **show running-config**, **ping**, and **debug ip rip** can all be used to verify and help troubleshoot RIP.

Chapter 9, "EIGRP," and Chapter 11, "OSPF," will continue the study of the classless routing protocols EIGRP and OSPF, respectively.

Activities and Labs

The activities and labs available in the companion *Routing Protocols and Concepts, CCNA Exploration Labs and Study Guide* (ISBN 1-58713-204-4) provide hands-on practice with the following topics introduced in this chapter.

Lab 7-1: RIPv2 Basic Configuration (7.5.1)

In this lab, you will work with a discontiguous network that is subnetted using VLSM. As you have seen throughout this chapter and Chapter 5, this can be an issue when the routing protocol used does not include enough information to distinguish the individual subnets. To solve this problem, you will configure RIPv2 as the classless routing protocol to provide subnet mask information in the routing updates.

Lab 7-2: RIPv2 Challenge Configuration (7.5.2)

In this lab activity, you are given a network address that must be subnetted using VLSM to complete the addressing of the network. A combination of RIP Version 2 and static routing will be required so that hosts on networks that are not directly connected will be able to communicate with each other and the Internet.

Lab 7-3: RIPv2 Troubleshooting (7.5.3)

In this lab, you begin by loading configuration scripts on each of the routers. These scripts contain errors that will prevent end-to-end communication across the network. After loading the corrupted scripts, troubleshoot each router to determine the configuration errors, and then use the appropriate commands to correct the configurations. When you have corrected all the configuration errors, all the hosts on the network should be able to communicate with each other.

Many of the hands-on labs include Packet Tracer Companion Activities, where you can use Packet Tracer to complete a simulation of the lab. Look for this icon in *Routing Protocols and Concepts, CCNA Exploration Labs and Study Guide* (ISBN 1-58713-204-4) for hands-on labs that have a Packet Tracer Companion.

Check Your Understanding

Complete all the review questions listed here to test your understanding of the topics and concepts in this chapter. Answers are listed in the appendix, "Check Your Understanding and Challenge Questions Answer Key."

1. How do you disable automatic summarization in RIPv2?

   A. Router(config)# **no auto-summary**

   B. Router(config-router)# **no auto-summary**

   C. Router(config-if)# **no auto-summary**

   D. It is not recommended that you disable automatic summarization.

2. Which of the following describes a discontiguous network?

   A. A classful network that has subnets separated by one or more different major networks

   B. A classful network with VLSM

   C. A network subnetted with a mask less than the classful mask

3. When would you disable automatic summarization on RIPv2? (Choose all that apply.)

   A. When you want to minimize the size of the routing tables

   B. When you have discontiguous networks

   C. When you are using VLSM

   D. When there is a need to propagate individual subnets

4. What is the defining characteristic of a classless routing protocol?

   A. The capability of sending a nonsummarized subnet address

   B. The capability of including the subnet mask in the route advertisement

   C. Sending routing updates as link-state advertisements

   D. Using a metric other than hop count

5. What is the default behavior of RIPv2 regarding automatic summarization?

   A. By default, automatic summarization is enabled in RIPv2.

   B. By default, automatic summarization is disabled in RIPv2.

   C. There is no automatic summarization in RIPv2. Summarization can only be done manually.

6. True or False: RIPv2 does not include the subnet mask in the routing update if the network has been summarized.

   A. True

   B. False

Challenge Questions and Activities

These questions require a deeper application of the concepts covered in this chapter and are similar to the style of questions you might see on a CCNA certification exam. You can find the answers to these questions in the appendix, "Answers to Check Your Understanding and Challenge Questions and Activities."

Figure 7-11   Figure Used in Chapter 7 Challenge Questions

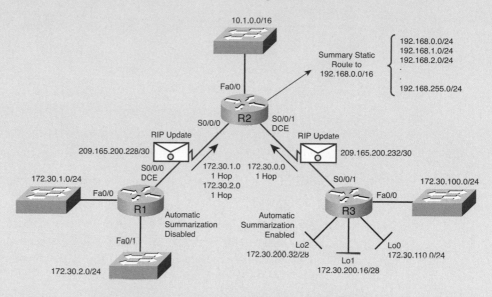

1. In Figure 7-11, all routers are running RIPv2. R1 has automatic summarization disabled, but Router R3 has automatic summary still enabled. What 172.30.0.0 routes do you expect to see in the routing table for R2? (Choose all that apply.)

   A. 172.30.0.0/16

   B. 172.30.1.0/24

   C. 172.30.2.0/24

   D. 172.30.100.0/24

   E. 172.30.110.0/24

   F. 172.30.200.16/28

   G. 172.30.200.32/28

2. Using Figure 7-11, if R2 has a packet destined for 172.30.1.10, will the packet be consistently forwarded to the proper Router R1?

3. RouterX is running the classful routing protocol RIPv1. RouterX has VLSM subnets in its routing table that are all part of the 10.0.0.0/8 network. If RouterX is sending updates out an interface with the address 10.10.10.1/24, which 10.0.0.0 subnets will be sent out that interface?

   A. All 10.0.0.0 subnets but without their subnet masks.

   B. All 10.0.0.0 subnets including their subnet masks.

   C. Only the 10.0.0.0 subnets that have a /24 mask. The subnet mask is not included.

   D. Only the 10.0.0.0 subnets that have a /24 mask. The subnet mask is included.

   E. The summarized network 10.0.0.0. The subnet mask is not included.

4. RouterX is running the classful routing protocol RIPv1. RouterX has VLSM subnets in its routing table that are all part of the 10.0.0.0/8 network. If RouterX is sending updates out an interface with the address 192.168.1.1/24, which 10.0.0.0 subnets will be sent out that interface?

    A. All 10.0.0.0 subnets but without their subnet masks.

    B. All 10.0.0.0 subnets including their subnet masks.

    C. Only the 10.0.0.0 subnets that have a /24 mask. The subnet mask is not included.

    D. Only the 10.0.0.0 subnets that have a /24 mask. The subnet mask is included.

    E. The summarized network 10.0.0.0. The subnet mask is not included.

5. What command is necessary in both versions of RIP to propagate a static default route?

6. Refer to the following output. Packets routed through R2 to hosts on the 172.30.0.0/16 network are not always reaching their destination, with some packets succeeding and others failing. What is the most likely problem? What is the solution if RIPv1 is the routing protocol being used? What is the solution if RIPv2 is the routing protocol being used?

    ```
    R2# show ip route

    !Code output omitted

    Gateway of last resort is not set

    R    172.30.0.0/16 [120/1] via 209.165.200.230, 00:00:09, Serial0/0/0
                        [120/1] via 209.165.200.234, 00:00:11, Serial0/0/1
         209.165.200.0/30 is subnetted, 2 subnets
    C       209.165.200.232 is directly connected, Serial0/0/1
    C       209.165.200.228 is directly connected, Serial0/0/0
         10.0.0.0/16 is subnetted, 1 subnets
    C       10.1.0.0 is directly connected, FastEthernet0/0
    S    192.168.0.0/16 is directly connected, Null0
    ```

To Learn More

Requests For Comments (RFC) are a series of documents submitted to the IETF (Internet Engineering Task Force) to propose an Internet standard or convey new concepts, information, or occasionally even humor. RFC 1723 is the RFC for RIP Version 2.

RFCs can be accessed from several websites, including http://www.ietf.org/rfc/rfc1723.txt. Read all or parts of RFC 1723 to learn more about RIPv2.

Use Packet Tracer to create two discontiguous classful networks. Each discontiguous network should have several routers and subnets, one using VLSM. Between the two groups of discontiguous networks, add another router linking the two discontiguous networks. Be sure to use a different major network between this router and each of the two discontiguous networks.

Use this scenario to examine the issues with RIPv1 and determine how RIPv2 can be used to solve these routing issues.

CHAPTER 8

The Routing Table: A Closer Look

Objectives

Upon completion of this chapter, you should be able to answer the following questions:

- What are the various route types found in the routing table structure?

- What is the route lookup process?

- How would you describe the typical routing behavior in a routed network?

Key Terms

This chapter uses the following key terms. You can find the definitions in the Glossary at the end of the book.

level 1 route   page 342

level 1 parent route   page 344

level 2 route   page 345

level 2 child route   page 346

Previous chapters examined the routing table using the **show ip route** command. You saw how directly connected, static, and dynamic routes are added and deleted from the routing table.

As a network administrator, it is important to know the routing table in depth when troubleshooting network issues. Understanding the structure and lookup process of the routing table will help you diagnose any routing table issue, regardless of your level of familiarity with a particular routing protocol. For example, you might encounter a situation in which the routing table has all of the routes you would expect to see, but packet forwarding is not performing as expected. Knowing how to step through the lookup process of a destination IP address for a packet will enable you to determine whether the packet is being forwarded as expected, if and why the packet is being sent elsewhere, or whether the packet has been discarded.

This chapter takes a closer look at the routing table. The first part of the chapter focuses on the structure of the Cisco IP routing table. You examine the format of the routing table and learn about level 1 and level 2 routes. The second part of the chapter analyzes the lookup process of the routing table. In this chapter, you learn about classful routing behavior and classless routing behavior, which use the **no ip classless** and **ip classless** commands.

Many of the details regarding the structure and lookup process of the Cisco IP routing table have been omitted from this chapter. If you are interested in reading more about this subject and the inner workings of Cisco IOS software, as it pertains to routing, see *Cisco IP Routing*, by Alex Zinin (ISBN 0-201-60473-6).[1]

Note

This book is not a beginner's book on routing protocols—it is a thorough examination of the protocols, processes, and algorithms used by Cisco IOS software.

The Routing Table Structure

The structure or format of the routing table might seem obvious until you take a closer look. Understanding the structure of the routing table will help you verify and troubleshoot routing issues because you will understand the routing table lookup process. You will know exactly what the Cisco IOS software does when it searches for a route.

Lab Topology

For the purpose of understanding the routing table structure and lookup process, refer to the simple three-router network shown in Figure 8-1.

Figure 8-1 Lab Topology

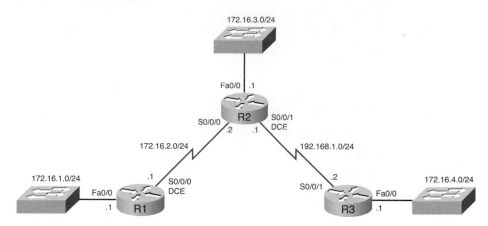

Router R1 and R2 share a common 172.16.0.0/16 network that is divided into /24 subnets. R2 and R3 are connected by the 192.168.1.0/24 network. Notice that R3 also has a 172.16.4.0/24 subnet that is disconnected, or discontiguous, from the 172.16.0.0 network that R1 and R2 share. The effects of this discontiguous subnet are examined later in this chapter when you look at the route lookup process.

The interface configurations for R1 and R3 are also shown in Examples 8-1 and 8-2, respectively. In a later section, you configure the interfaces for R2.

Example 8-1 R1 Configuration

```
R1(config)#interface FastEthernet0/0
R1(config-if)#ip address 172.16.1.1 255.255.255.0
R1(config-if)#no shutdown
R1(config-if)#interface Serial0/0/0
R1(config-if)#ip address 172.16.2.1 255.255.255.0
R1(config-if)#clock rate 64000
R1(config-if)#no shutdown
R1(config-if)#end
R1#copy run start
```

Example 8-2 R3 Configuration

```
R3(config)#interface FastEthernet0/0
R3(config-if)#ip address 172.16.4.1 255.255.255.0
R3(config-if)#no shutdown
R3(config-if)#interface Serial0/0/1
```

```
R3(config-if)#ip address 192.168.1.2 255.255.255.0
R3(config-if)#no shutdown
R3(config-if)#end
R3#copy run start
```

Routing Table Entries

The sample routing table in Example 8-3 consists of route entries from the following sources:

- Directly connected networks

- Static routes

- Dynamic routing protocols

Example 8-3 Sample Routing Table

```
Router#show ip route
Codes: C - connected, S - static, I - IGRP, R - RIP, M - mobile,
<output omitted>

Gateway of last resort is not set

     172.16.0.0/24 is subnetted, 4 subnets
S       172.16.4.0 is directly connected, Serial0/0/1
R       172.16.1.0 [120/1] via 172.16.2.1, 00:00:08, Serial0/0/0
C       172.16.2.0 is directly connected, Serial0/0/0
C       172.16.3.0 is directly connected, FastEthernet0/0
     10.0.0.0/16 is subnetted, 1 subnets
S       10.1.0.0 is directly connected, Serial0/0/1
C     192.168.1.0/24 is directly connected, Serial0/0/1
S     192.168.100.0/24 is directly connected, Serial0/0/1
```

The source of the route—directly connected, static, or dynamic—does not affect the structure of the routing table. The output in Example 8-3 shows a sample routing table with directly connected, static, and dynamic routes. Notice that the 172.16.0.0/24 subnets have a combination of all three types of routing sources.

Note

The routing table hierarchy in Cisco IOS software was originally implemented with the classful routing scheme. Although the routing table incorporates both classful and classless addressing, the overall structure is still built around this classful scheme.

Level 1 Routes

Routers R1 and R3 already have their interfaces configured with the appropriate IP addresses and subnet masks. We will now configure the interfaces for R2 and use **debug ip routing** to view the routing table process that is used to add these entries.

Example 8-4 shows what happens as the Serial 0/0/1 interface for R2 is configured with the 192.168.1.1/24 address.

Example 8-4 Level 1 Route Added to Routing Table

```
R2#debug ip routing
IP routing debugging is on
R2#conf t
R2(config)#interface serial 0/0/1
R2(config-if)#ip address 192.168.1.1 255.255.255.0
R2(config-if)#clock rate 64000
R2(config-if)#no shutdown
R2(config-if)#
00:11:06: %LINK-3-UPDOWN: Interface Serial0/0/1, changed state to up
R2(config-if)#
RT: add 192.168.1.0/24 via 0.0.0.0, connected metric [0/0]
RT: interface Serial0/0/1 added to routing table
R2(config-if)#end
R2#undebug all
All possible debugging has been turned off
```

As soon as **no shutdown** is entered, the output from **debug ip routing** shows that this route has been added to the routing table.

In Example 8-5, **show ip route** displays the directly connected network in the routing table that was just added to R2.

Example 8-5 Verify Route Is in Routing Table

```
R2#show ip route
Codes: C - connected, S - static, I - IGRP, R - RIP, M - mobile, B - BGP
<output omitted>

Gateway of last resort is not set

C    192.168.1.0/24 is directly connected, Serial0/0/1
```

The Cisco IP routing table is not a flat database. The routing table is actually a hierarchical structure that is used to speed up the lookup process when locating routes and forwarding packets. Within this structure, the hierarchy includes several levels. For simplicity, we discuss all routes as one of two levels: level 1 or level 2.

Let's learn about level 1 and level 2 routes by reviewing the following routing table entry in more detail:

```
C     192.168.1.0/24 is directly connected, Serial0/0/1
```

A *level 1 route* is a route with a subnet mask equal to or less than the classful mask of the network address. 192.168.1.0/24 is a level 1 network route because the subnet mask is equal to the network's classful mask. /24 is the classful mask for Class C networks, such as the 192.168.1.0 network.

A level 1 route can function as any of the following:

- **Default route:** A default route is a static route with the address 0.0.0.0/0.

- **Supernet route:** A supernet route is a network address with a mask less than the classful mask.

- **Network route:** A network route is a route that has a subnet mask equal to that of the classful mask. A network route can also be a parent route. Parent routes are discussed in the next section.

The source of the level 1 route can be a directly connected network, a static route, or a dynamic routing protocol.

Figure 8-2 introduces the beginning of a chart that will be used throughout this chapter. At this point, Figure 8-2 is displaying an example of level 1 routes.

The level 1 route 192.168.1.0/24 can be further defined as an ultimate route, as shown in Figure 8-3.

An ultimate route is a route that includes one or both of the following:

- A next-hop IP address (another path)

- An exit interface

The directly connected network 192.168.1.0/24 is a level 1 network route because it has a subnet mask that is the same as its classful mask. This same route is also an ultimate route because it contains the exit interface Serial 0/0/1:

```
C     192.168.1.0/24 is directly connected, Serial0/0/1
```

As shown in the next section, level 2 routes are also ultimate routes.

Figure 8-2   Routing Table: Level 1 Routes

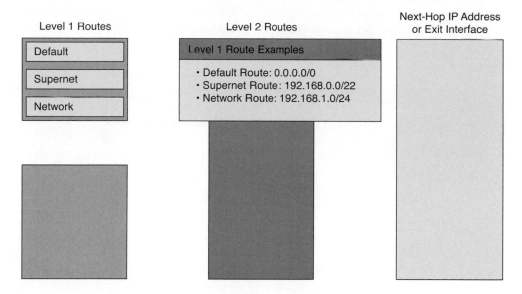

Figure 8-3   Routing Table: Level 1 Routes as Ultimate Routes

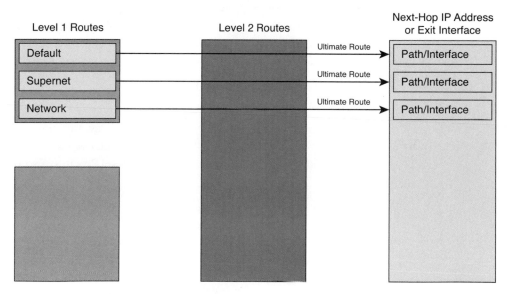

Parent and Child Routes: Classful Networks

In the previous topic, you saw a level 1 network route that was also an ultimate route. Now, take a look at another type of level 1 network route, a parent route. Example 8-6 shows the configuration of the 172.16.3.1/24 interface on R2 and the output from the **show ip route** command.

Example 8-6 Parent and Child Routes

```
R2(config)#interface fastethernet 0/0
R2(config-if)#ip address 172.16.3.1 255.255.255.0
R2(config-if)#no shutdown
R2(config-if)#end
R2#show ip route
Codes: C - connected, S - static, I - IGRP, R - RIP, M - mobile,
<text omitted>


Gateway of last resort is not set


     172.16.0.0/24 is subnetted, 1 subnets
C       172.16.3.0 is directly connected, FastEthernet0/0
C    192.168.1.0/24 is directly connected, Serial0/0/1
```

Notice that there are actually two additional entries in the routing table, as highlighted in the example. When the 172.16.3.0 subnet was added to the routing table, another route, 172.16.0.0, was also added. This first entry does not contain a next-hop IP address or exit interface information. This route is known as a *level 1 parent route*.

Indented under the parent route is the second entry, 172.16.3.0, which is the child route. Why were two entries added rather than one?

Refer to Figure 8-4. There are two entries because a level 1 parent route is a network route that does not contain a next-hop IP address or exit interface for a network. A parent route is actually a heading that indicates the presence of level 2 routes, also known as *child routes*.

A level 1 parent route is automatically created any time a subnet is added to the routing table. In other words, a parent route is created whenever a route with a mask greater than the classful mask is entered into the routing table. The subnet 172.16.3.0 is the level 2 child route of the parent route 172.16.0.0. In this case, the level 1 parent route that was automatically created is as follows:

```
172.16.0.0/24 is subnetted, 1 subnets
```

Figure 8-4   Routing Table: Parent/Child Relationship

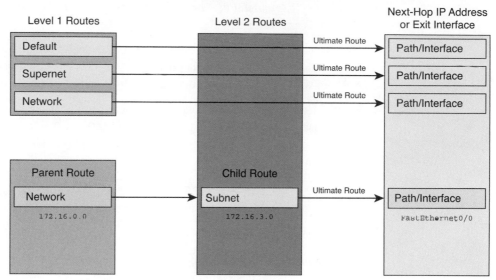

```
        172.16.0.0/24 is subnetted, 1 subnets
C       172.16.3.0 is directly connected, FastEthernet0/0
```

A *level 2 route* is a route that is a subnet of a classful network address. Like a level 1 route, the source of a level 2 route can be a directly connected network, a static route, or a dynamic routing protocol. In this case, the level 2 route is the actual subnet route that was added to the network when we configured the Fast Ethernet 0/0 interface.

Note

Remember that the routing table hierarchy in Cisco IOS software has a classful routing scheme. A level 1 parent route is the classful network address of the subnet route. This is the case even if a classless routing protocol is the source of the subnet route.

Use Figure 8-5 to analyze the routing table entries for both the level 1 parent route and the level 2 child route (subnet) as described in the sections that follow.

Figure 8-5   Parent and Child Route Details

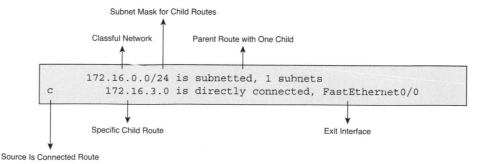

Level 1 Parent Route

The parent route in Figure 8-5 contains the following information:

- **172.16.0.0:** The classful network address for our subnet. Remember, the Cisco IP routing table is structured in a classful manner.

- **/24:** The subnet mask for all the child routes. If the child routes have variable-length subnet masks (VLSM), the subnet mask will be excluded from the parent route and included with the individual child routes. This is shown in a later section.

- **is subnetted, 1 subnets:** This part of the route specifies that this is a parent route and in this case has one child route (that is, one subnet).

Level 2 Child Route

The second entry in Figure 8-5, 172.16.3.0, is the actual route for our directly connected network. This level 2 child route contains the following information:

- **C:** The route code for a directly connected network.

- **172.16.3.0:** The specific route entry.

- **is directly connected:** Along with the route code of C, this specifies that this is a directly connected network with an administrative distance of 0.

- **FastEthernet0/0:** The exit interface for forwarding packets that match this specific route entry.

The level 2 child route is the specific route entry for the 172.16.3.0/24 subnet. Notice that the subnet mask is not included with the subnet, the level 2 child route. The subnet mask for this child route is the /24 mask included in its parent route, 172.16.0.0.

A *level 2 child route* contains the route source and the network address of the route. Level 2 child routes are also considered ultimate routes because they contain the next-hop IP address or exit interface.

Example 8-7 shows the configuration of the Serial 0/0/0 interface on R2.

Example 8-7 Add Another Child Route

```
R2(config)#interface serial 0/0/0
R2(config-if)#ip address 172.16.2.2 255.255.255.0
R2(config-if)#no shutdown
R2(config-if)#end
R2#show ip route
Codes: C - connected, S - static, I - IGRP, R - RIP, M - mobile,
<text omitted>
```

```
Gateway of last result is not set

     172.16.0.0/24 is subnetted, 2 subnets
C       172.16.2.0 is directly connected, Serial0/0/0
C       172.16.3.0 is directly connected, FastEthernet0/0
C     192.168.1.0/24 is directly connected, Serial0/0/1
```

The routing table shows two child routes for the same 172.16.0.0/24 parent route. Both 172.16.2.0 and 172.16.3.0 are members of the same parent route because they are both members of the 172.16.0.0/16 classful network.

Because both child routes have the same subnet mask, the parent route still maintains the /24 mask but now shows two subnets. The role of the parent route is examined when we discuss the route lookup process.

Figure 8-6 shows the relationship between the level 1 parent route and the level 2 child routes using the example from the routing table.

Figure 8-6   Routing Table: Parent/Child Relationship

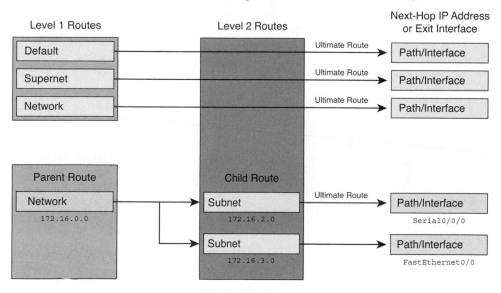

Note

If there is only a single level 2 child route and that route is removed, the level 1 parent route is automatically deleted. A level 1 parent route exists only when there is at least one level 2 child route.

Parent and Child Routes: Classless Networks

For this discussion, we switch briefly to the RouterX topology shown in Figure 8-7.

Figure 8-7   Parent and Child Routes with VLSM

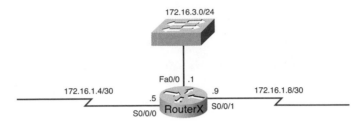

Using RouterX with the VLSM configuration shown, we can examine the effect of VLSM on the routing table. RouterX has three directly connected networks. All three subnets belong to the classful network 172.16.0.0/16 and are therefore level 2 child routes.

In Example 8-8, notice that the child routes do not share the same subnet mask, as was the case in the classful example. In this case, we are implementing a network addressing scheme with VLSM.

Example 8-8 Parent and Child Routes with VLSM

```
RouterX#show ip route
Codes: C - connected, S - static, I - IGRP, R - RIP, M - mobile, B - BGP
<output omitted>


Gateway of last resort is not set


     172.16.0.0/16 is variably subnetted, 3 subnets, 2 masks
C        172.16.1.4/30 is directly connected, Serial0/0/0
C        172.16.1.8/30 is directly connected, Serial0/0/1
C        172.16.3.0/24 is directly connected, FastEthernet0/0
RouterX#
```

Whenever there are two or more child routes with different subnet masks belonging to the same classful network, the routing table presents a slightly different view, which states that this parent network is **variably subnetted**.

Although the parent/child relationship uses a classful structure to display networks and their subnets, this format can be used with both classful and classless addressing. Regardless of the addressing scheme used by the network (classless or classful), the routing table structure uses a classful scheme.

Figure 8-8 shows the details of the parent/child route relationship in a classless environment.

Figure 8-8   Parent and Child Route Details in a Classless Environment

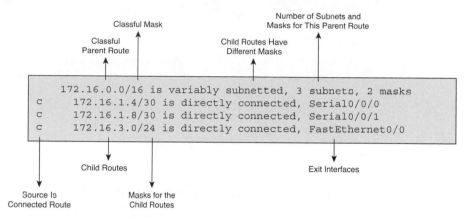

There are several distinct differences with this parent route and its child routes compared to the classful example discussed earlier. First, the parent route of 172.16.0.0 now contains the classful mask /16. In the classful example shown earlier in Figure 8-5, the classful mask was not displayed.

Also notice that the parent route states that the child routes are **variably subnetted**. Like the classful example, the parent route displays the number of subnets (**3 subnets**), but now it also includes the number of different masks of the child routes (**2 masks**).

The final difference between classful and classless networks exists in the child routes. Each child route now contains the subnet mask for that specific route. In the non-VLSM example shown in Figure 8-5, both child routes shared the same subnet mask, and the parent displayed their common subnet mask. With VLSM, the various subnet masks are displayed with the specific child routes.

The parent route in Figure 8-8 contains the following information:

- **172.16.0.0:** The parent route, the classful network address associated with all child routes

- **/16:** The classful subnet mask of the parent route

- **variably subnetted:** States that the child routes are variably subnetted and that there are multiple masks for this classful network

- **3 subnets, 2 masks:** Indicates the number of subnets and the number of different subnet masks for the child routes under this parent route

Using one of the child routes as an example in Figure 8-8, we can see the following information:

- **C:** The route code for a directly connected network

- **172.16.1.4:** The specific route entry

- **/30:** The subnet mask for this specific route

- **is directly connected:** Along with the route code of C, specifies that this is a directly connected network with an administrative distance of 0

- **Serial0/0/0:** The exit interface for forwarding packets that match this specific route entry

So, why does Cisco use the classful routing table format? Let's investigate the routing table lookup process.

Routing Table Lookup Process

Now that you understand the structure of the routing table, the next section will help you understand the routing table lookup process. When a router receives a packet on one of its interfaces, the routing table lookup process compares the destination IP address of the incoming packet with the entries in the routing table. The best match between the packet's destination IP address and the route in the routing table is used to determine to which interface to forward the packet.

Steps in the Route Table Lookup Process

Returning to the topology shown earlier in Figure 8-1, Routing Information Protocol Version 1 (RIPv1), a classful routing protocol, is now configured. We have specifically chosen a classful routing protocol with our discontiguous 172.16.0.0 subnets. The reason for this will become evident in a later section.

Example 8-9 shows the RIP configuration on all three routers. Examples 8-10, 8-11, and 8-12 show the resulting routing tables.

Example 8-9 RIPv1 Configurations

```
R1(config)#router rip
R1(config-router)#network 172.16.0.0
R2(config)#router rip
R2(config-router)#network 172.16.0.0
R2(config-router)#network 192.168.1.0
R3(config)#router rip
R3(config-router)#network 172.16.0.0
R3(config-router)#network 192.168.1.0
```

Example 8-10   R1 Routing Table

```
R1#show ip route
Codes: C - connected, S - static, I - IGRP, R - RIP, M - mobile, B - BGP
        <output omitted>


Gateway of last resort is not set

     172.16.0.0/24 is subnetted, 3 subnets
C        172.16.1.0 is directly connected, FastEthernet0/0
C        172.16.2.0 is directly connected, Serial0/0/0
R        172.16.3.0 [120/1] via 172.16.2.2, 00:00:25, Serial0/0/0
R     192.168.1.0/24 [120/1] via 172.16.2.2, 00:00:25, Serial0/0/0
```

Example 8-11   R2 Routing Table

```
R2#show ip route
Codes: C - connected, S - static, I - IGRP, R - RIP, M - mobile, B - BGP
        <output omitted>


Gateway of last resort is not set

     172.16.0.0/24 is subnetted, 3 subnets
R        172.16.1.0 [120/1] via 172.16.2.1, 00:00:07, Serial0/0/0
C        172.16.2.0 is directly connected, Serial0/0/0
C        172.16.3.0 is directly connected, FastEthernet0/0
C     192.168.1.0/24 is directly connected, Serial0/0/1
```

Example 8-12   R3 Routing Table

```
R3#show ip route
Codes: C - connected, S - static, I - IGRP, R - RIP, M - mobile, B - BGP
        <output omitted>


Gateway of last resort is not set

     172.16.0.0/24 is subnetted, 1 subnets
C        172.16.4.0 is directly connected, FastEthernet0/0
C     192.168.1.0/24 is directly connected, Serial0/0/1
```

As you would expect with this addressing scheme and a classful routing protocol, there are reachability problems. Neither R1 nor R2 has a route to 172.16.4.0. Also, R3 does not have routes to subnets 172.16.1.0/24, 172.16.2.0/24, or 172.16.3.0/24.

R1 and R2 do not include R3's 172.16.4.0 subnet because R3 only sent a summary route of 172.16.0.0 with a metric of one hop. Because R2 already has directly connected interfaces, which are part of this 172.16.0.0 network, it does not add the RIP summary route to its routing table. The same process occurs for R3. R3 only receives a 172.16.0.0 summary route from R2.

Let's examine in more depth how the routers determine the best routes to use when sending packets and why classful routing protocols do not work with discontiguous designs. We will consider the following:

- What happens when a router receives an IP packet, examines the IP destination address, and looks up that address in the routing table?

- How does the router decide which route in the routing table is the best match?

- What effect does the subnet mask have on the routing table lookup process?

- How does the router decide whether to use a supernet or default route if a better match is not found?

Let's begin to answer these questions by examining the steps in the route lookup process.

The Route Lookup Process

Follow the steps in Figure 8-9 through Figure 8-19 to see the route lookup process. Don't worry about fully understanding the steps right now. You will better understand this process when we examine a few examples in the following sections.

Step 1.   The router examines level 1 routes, including network routes and supernet routes, for the best match with the destination address of the IP packet (see Figure 8-9).

Figure 8-9   Routing Table Lookup Process: Step 1

Step 1: Examine level 1 routes for best match with the packet's destination address.

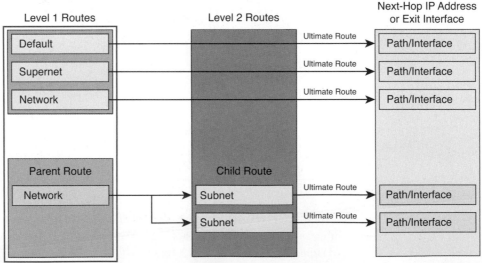

Step 1a. If the best match is a level 1 ultimate route—a classful network, supernet, or default route—this route is used to forward the packet (see Figure 8-10).

Figure 8-10   Routing Table Lookup Process: Step 1a

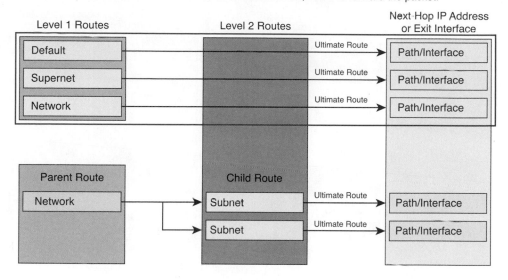

Step 1a: If the best match is a level 1 ultimate route, use it to forward the packet.

Step 1b. If the best match is a level 1 parent route, proceed to Step 2 (see Figure 8-11).

Figure 8-11   Routing Table Lookup Process: Step 1b

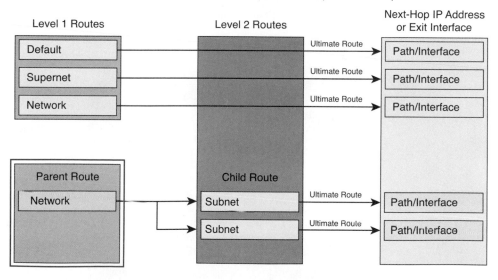

Step 1b: If the best match is a level 1 parent route, proceed to Step 2.

Step 2. The router examines child routes (the subnet routes) of the parent route for a best match (see Figure 8-12).

Figure 8-12 Routing Table Lookup Process: Step 2

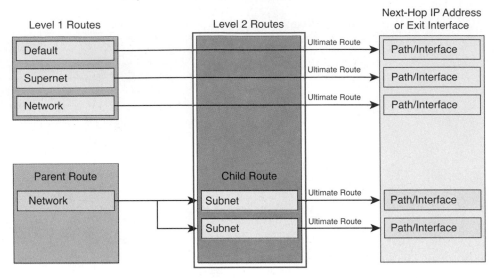

Step 2: Child routes are examined for a best match.

Step 2a. If there is a match with a level 2 child route, that subnet is used to forward the packet (see Figure 8-13).

Figure 8-13 Routing Table Lookup Process: Step 2a

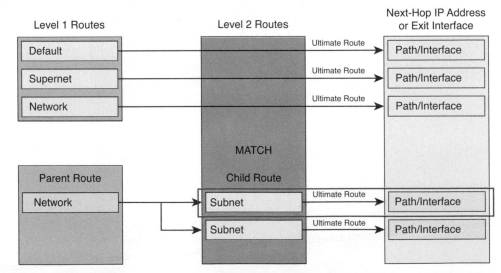

Step 2a: Match! Use this subnet to forward the packet.

Step 2b. If there is not a match with any of the level 2 child routes, proceed to Step 3 (see Figure 8-14).

Figure 8-14   Routing Table Lookup Process: Step 2b

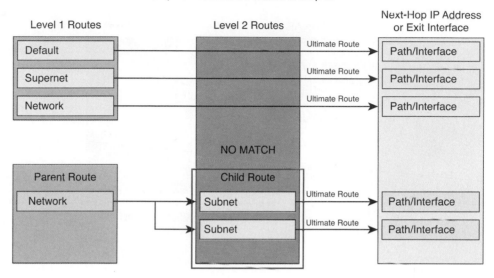

Step 2b: No match. Proceed to Step 3.

Step 3.   Is the router implementing classful or classless routing behavior (see Figure 8-15)?

Figure 8-15   Routing Table Lookup Process: Step 3

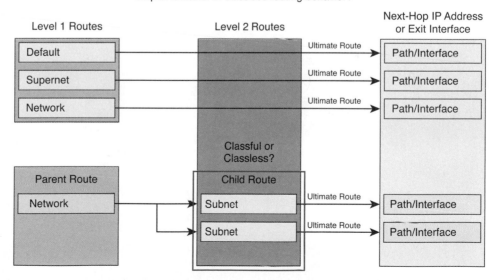

Step 3: Classful or classless routing behavior?

Step 3a. If *classful* routing behavior is in effect, terminate the lookup process and drop the packet (see Figure 8-16).

Figure 8-16   Routing Table Lookup Process: Step 3a

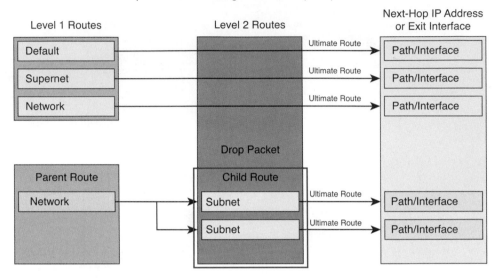

Step 3a: Classful routing behavior: Drop the packet.

Step 3b. If *classless* routing behavior is in effect, continue searching level 1 supernet routes in the routing table for a match, including the default route, if there is one (see Figure 8-17).

Figure 8-17   Routing Table Lookup Process: Step 3b

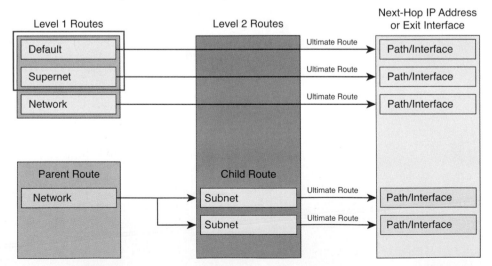

Step 3b: Classless routing behavior: Search level 1 routes.

Step 4.   If there is now a lesser match with a level 1 supernet or default routes, the router uses that route to forward the packet (see Figure 8-18).

Figure 8-18   Routing Table Lookup Process: Step 4

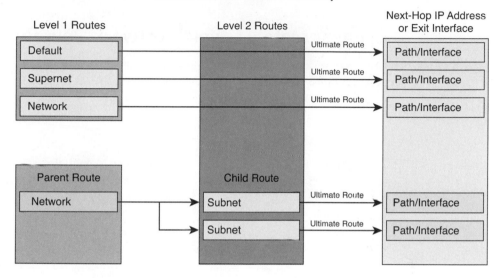

Step 4: Match with supernet or default. Use it to forward packet. Supernets are checked first, then default if necessary.

Step 5.   If there is not a match with any route in the routing table, the router drops the packet (see Figure 8-19).

Figure 8-19   Routing Table Lookup Process: Step 5

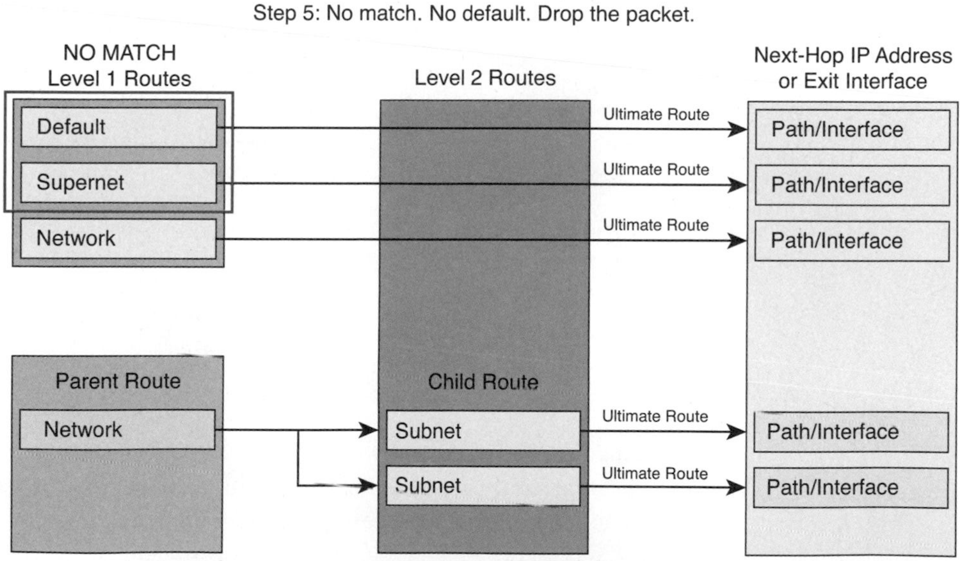

Step 5: No match. No default. Drop the packet.

Classful and classless routing behavior is discussed in more detail in a later section.

Note

A route referencing only a next-hop IP address and not an exit interface must be resolved to a route with an exit interface. A recursive lookup is performed on the next-hop IP address until the route is resolved to an exit interface.

Longest Match: Level 1 Network Routes

Exactly how does the routing table lookup process determine whether the packet's destination IP address matches a route in the routing table? What if there are more than one route entry matches? Let's take a look.

Longest Match

The term *best match* was used in the previous route lookup discussion. Best match is also referred to as longest match. Digressing from the topology for a moment, Figure 8-20 shows that Route 3, 172.16.0.0/26, has the longest match. What is meant by the longest match?

Figure 8-20   Longest Match Is the Preferred Route

IP Packet Destination	172.16.0.10	10101100.00010000.00000000.00001010
Route 1	172.16.0.0/12	10101100.00010000.00000000.00000000
Route 2	172.16.0.0/18	10101100.00010000.00000000.00000000
Route 3	172.16.0.0/26	10101100.00010000.00000000.00000000

Longest Match to IP Packet Destination

First of all, what is a match? For there to be a match between the destination IP address of a packet and a route in the routing table, a minimum number of leftmost bits must match between the IP address of the packet and the route in the routing table. The subnet mask of the route in the routing table is used to determine the minimum number of leftmost bits that must match. (Remember, an IP packet only contains the IP address and not the subnet mask.)

The best match or longest match is the route in the routing table that has the greatest number of leftmost matching bits with the destination IP address of the packet. The route with the greatest number of equivalent leftmost bits, or the longest match, is always the preferred route. The numbers of bits of the subnet mask not only specify the minimum number of leftmost matching bits, but are the only bits considered when looking for a match.

In Figure 8-20, we have a packet destined for 172.16.0.10. Many possible routes could match this packet. Three possible routes are shown that do match this packet: 172.16.0.0/12, 172.16.0.0/18, and 172.16.0.0/26. Of the three routes, 172.16.0.0/26 has the longest match. Remember, for any of these routes to be considered a match, there must be at least the number of matching bits indicated by the subnet mask of the route.

It should be mentioned that Figure 8-20 is an unusual example, used only to illustrate the concept of longest match. In this case, the 172.16.0.0/12 and 172.16.0.0/18 would never be considered because the longest match would always be 172.16.0.0/26. This is because all three routes share the same 32 identical bits. If there are multiple routes with the same network address, but different size subnet masks, the routing table lookup process always uses the route with the larger mask. In this case, the routing table lookup process will always use the 172.16.0.0/26 route.

Example: Level 1 Ultimate Route

The subnet mask that is used to determine the longest match is not always obvious. Let's examine this concept in more detail, using several examples.

In Figure 8-21, PC1 sends a ping to 192.168.1.2, the serial interface on R3.

Figure 8-21   Example: Level 1 Ultimate Route

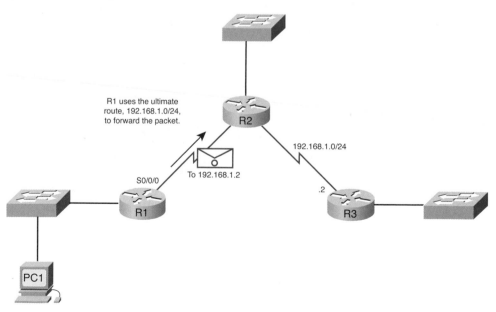

R1 receives the packet. Example 8-13 shows the routing table for R1.

Example 8-13   R1 Routing Table

```
R1#show ip route
Codes: C - connected, S - static, I - IGRP, R - RIP, M - mobile, B - BGP
       <some output omitted>


Gateway of last resort is not set


     172.16.0.0/24 is subnetted, 3 subnets
C       172.16.1.0 is directly connected, FastEthernet0/0
C       172.16.2.0 is directly connected, Serial0/0/0
R       172.16.3.0 [120/1] via 172.16.2.2, 00:00:25, Serial0/0/0
R     192.168.1.0/24 [120/1] via 172.16.2.2, 00:00:25, Serial0/0/0
```

Remember the first part of Step 1 in the route lookup process? Figure 8-22 demonstrates this step to show the routing table lookup process for the 192.168.2.1 packet.

Figure 8-22   Routing Table Lookup Process: Step 1

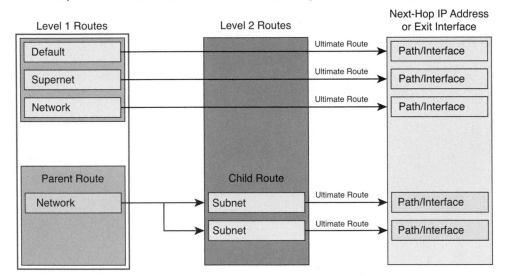

The router first examines level 1 routes for the best match. In our example, there is a match between the destination IP address 192.168.1.2 and the level 1 ultimate route of 192.168.1.0/24:

```
R     192.168.1.0/24 [120/1] via 172.16.2.2, 00:00:25, Serial0/0/0
```

Step 1a in Figure 8-23 shows that R1 uses this route and forwards the packet out interface Serial 0/0/0.

Figure 8-23   Routing Table Lookup Process: Step 1a

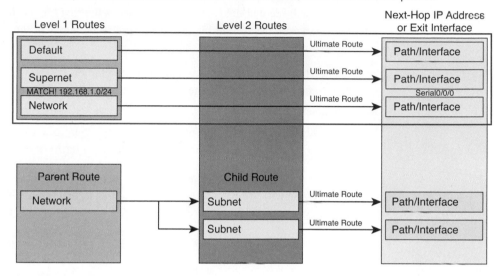

Why is there a match with the 192.168.1.0/24 level 1 route and not with one of the 172.16.0.0 subnets? This might seem obvious. We say, "Of course the router will use 192.168.1.0/24." But, the lookup process is comparing 32-bit addresses to 32-bit route entries, looking for the longest match.

The algorithm used by Cisco IOS software to search the routing table is beyond the scope of this chapter. What is important is to understand why a route entry matches or doesn't match the packet's destination IP address.

Why is there not a match with any of the 172.16.0.0/24 subnets in the routing table? Refer to Figure 8-24.

Figure 8-24   172.16.0.0/16 Level 1 Parent Route

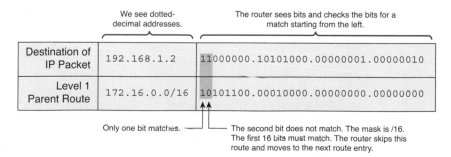

172.16.0.0/24 is a parent route of three subnets or child routes. Before a child route is examined for a match, there must be at least a match between the destination IP address of the packet and the classful address of the parent route, or 172.16.0.0/16.

Do at least 16 of the leftmost bits of the parent route match the first 16 bits of the packet's destination IP address of 192.168.1.2? The answer, no, is obvious to us. In Figure 8-24, however, you will see that the router actually checks the first bit and finds a match. The router then moves to the second bit. Because there is not a match, the lookup process will search other route entries.

Now let's see how the router finds a match between the packet's destination IP address of 192.168.1.2 and the next route in the routing table, 192.168.1.0/24, an ultimate route:

```
R       192.168.1.0/24 [120/1] via 172.16.2.2, 00:00:25, Serial0/0/0
```

The route, 192.168.1.0, is a level 1 ultimate route and, therefore, it also contains the subnet mask, /24. In Figure 8-25, notice that at least the first 24 leftmost bits match.

Figure 8-25   192.168.1.0/24 Level 1 Ultimate Route

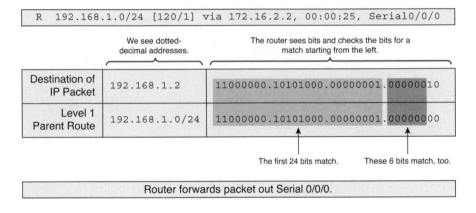

Not only does the minimum of 24 bits match, but a total of 30 bits match, as shown in the figure. Is this important? As shown later, there can be situations in which there are multiple matching routes in the routing table for the same destination IP address. Which one is the preferred route? It is the one with the greatest number of matching bits, the longest match.

In this example, there is a match between the destination IP address 192.168.1.0 and the level 1 ultimate route 192.168.1.0/24. Because there is not a longer, more specific match, the packet is forwarded out the exit interface Serial 0/0/0.

Note

Remember that the route lookup process will need to do a recursive lookup on any route that references only a next-hop IP address and not an exit interface. For a review of recursive lookups, refer to Chapter 2, "Static Routing."

Longest Match: Level 1 Parent and Level 2 Child Routes

Let's examine what happens when there is a match with a level 1 parent route.

First, notice in Example 8-14 that a parent route does not include a next-hop address or an exit interface but is only a "header" for its level 2 child routes, the subnets.

Example 8-14   Level 1 Parent Route and Level 2 Child Routes

```
R1#show ip route
Codes: C - connected, S - static, I - IGRP, R - RIP, M - mobile, B - BGP
         <output omitted>


Gateway of last resort is not set

       172.16.0.0/24 is subnetted, 3 subnets
C        172.16.1.0 is directly connected, FastEthernet0/0
C        172.16.2.0 is directly connected, Serial0/0/0
R        172.16.3.0 [120/1] via 172.16.2.2, 00:00:25, Serial0/0/0
R     192.168.1.0/24 [120/1] via 172.16.2.2, 00:00:25, Serial0/0/0
```

The subnet mask for the child routes, /24 in Example 8-14, is displayed in the parent route, 172.16.0.0, for subnets that use the same subnet mask.

Before any level 2 child routes are examined for a match, there must be a match between the classful address of the level 1 parent route and the destination IP address of the packet.

Example: Level 1 Parent Route and Level 2 Child Routes

In Figure 8-26, PC1 sends a ping to PC2 at 172.16.3.10. R1 receives the packet and forwards it to R2. Let's discuss R1's search of the routing table to find a route.

Step 1b.   (See Figure 8-27.) The first match that occurs is with the level 1 parent route, 172.16.0.0. Remember, with non-VLSM subnets, the classful mask of the parent is not displayed. Before any child routes (subnets) are examined for a match, there must be a match with the classful address of the parent route. In this example, because 172.16.0.0 is a Class B address, 16 leftmost bits must match. (The complete steps in the route lookup process were described earlier in the chapter.)

Figure 8-26   Example: Level 1 Parent Route and Level 2 Child Routes

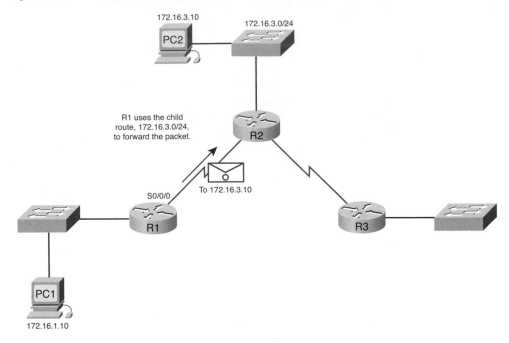

Figure 8-27   Routing Table Lookup Process: Step 1b

Step 1b: If the best match is a level 1 parent route, proceed to Step 2.

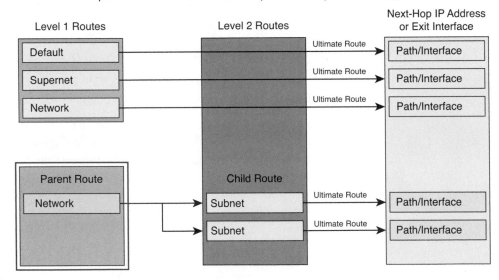

Because the first route entry is a level 1 parent route that matches the destination address (Step 1b of the route lookup process), the route lookup process moves to Step 2.

Step 2.   (See Figure 8-28.) Because there is a match with the parent route, the level 2 child routes will be examined for a match. However, this time the actual subnet mask of /24 is used for the minimum number of leftmost bits that must match.

Figure 8-28   Routing Table Lookup Process: Step 2

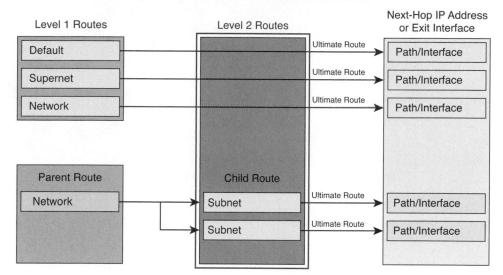

Step 2: Child routes are examined for a best match.

Step 2a.   (See Figure 8-29.) The route lookup process searches the child routes for a match. In this case, there must be a minimum of 24 bits that match.

Using Figure 8-30, let's see how the router finds a match with one of the level 2 child routes.

First, the router examines the parent route for a match. In this example, the first 16 bits of the IP address must match that of the parent route. The leftmost 16 bits must match because that is the classful mask of the parent route, /16.

If there is a match with the parent route, the router checks the 172.16.1.0 route. Child routes are only examined when there is a match with the classful mask of the parent.

Checking the first subnet, 172.16.1.0, the twenty-third bit does not match; therefore, this route is rejected because the first 24 bits do not match.

Figure 8-29   Routing Table Lookup Process: Step 2a

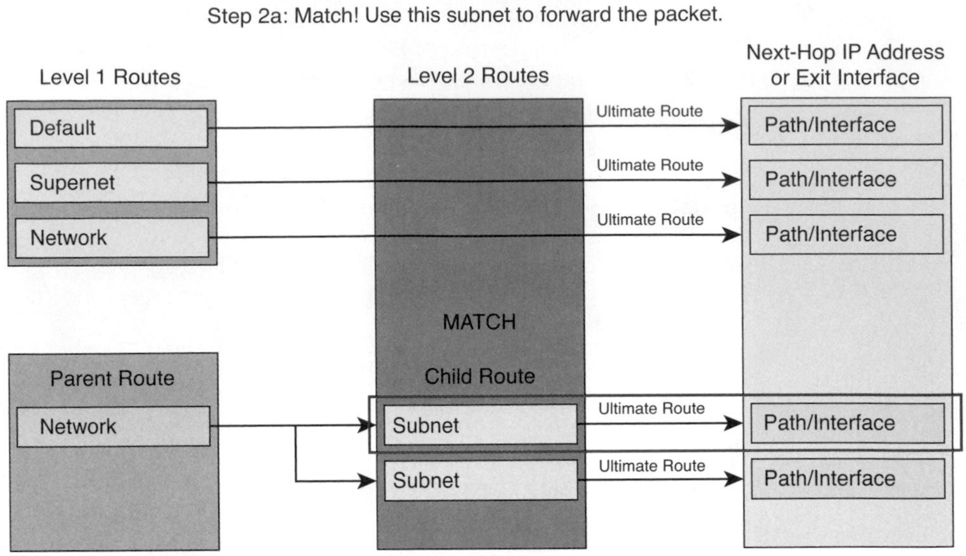

Step 2a: Match! Use this subnet to forward the packet.

Figure 8-30   172.16.3.0/24 Level 2 Child Route

Destination of IP Packet	172.16.3.10	10101100.00010000.00000011.00001010
Level 1 Parent Route	172.16.0.0/16	10101100.00010000.00000000.00000000
Level 2 Child Route	172.16.2.0/24	10101100.00010000.00000010.00000000
Level 2 Child Route	172.16.2.0/24	10101100.00010000.00000010.00000000
Level 2 Child Route	172.16.3.0/24	10101100.00010000.00000011.00000000

172.16.3.0/24 has the longest match.

Next, the router checks the 172.16.2.0/24 route. Because the twenty-fourth bit does not match, this route is also rejected. All 24 bits must match.

The router checks the last child route for 172.16.3.0/24 and finds a match. The first 24 bits do match. The routing table process will use this route, 172.16.3.0/24, to forward the packet with the destination IP address of 172.16.3.10 out the exit interface of Serial 0/0/0:

```
R    172.16.3.0 [120/1] via 172.16.2.2, 00:00:25, Serial0/0/0
```

If this child route did not have an exit interface and only included a next-hop IP address, the next-hop IP address would need to be resolved to an exit interface. The lookup process would need to start from the beginning, this time searching the routing table for the next-hop IP address.

What happens if the router does not have a route? In this scenario, it discards the packet.

Example: Route Lookup Process with VLSM

What about our RouterX topology, repeated here in Figure 8-31, which is using a VLSM addressing scheme? How does this change the lookup process?

Figure 8-31   Route Lookup Process with VLSM

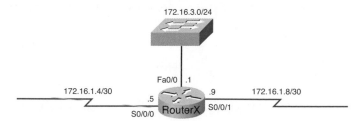

Using Example 8-15, let's see how the router finds a match with one of the level 2 VLSM child routes.

Example 8-15   RouterX Routing Table

```
RouterX#show ip route
Codes: C - connected, S - static, I - IGRP, R - RIP, M - mobile, B - BGP
<output omitted>


Gateway of last resort is not set

     172.16.0.0/16 is variably subnetted, 3 subnets, 2 masks
C       172.16.1.4/30 is directly connected, Serial0/0/0
C       172.16.1.8/30 is directly connected, Serial0/0/1
C       172.16.3.0/24 is directly connected, FastEthernet0/0
RouterX#
```

Using VSLM does not change the lookup process. With VLSM, the /16 classful mask is displayed with the level 1 parent route (172.16.0.0/16 in the example).

As with non-VLSM networks, if there is a match between the packet's destination IP address and the classful mask of the level 1 parent route, the level 2 child routes are searched.

The only difference with VLSM is that child routes display their own specific subnet masks. These subnet masks are used to determine the number of leftmost bits that must match the packet's destination IP address. For example, for there to be a match with the 172.16.1.4 child route, a minimum of 30 leftmost bits must match because the subnet mask is /30.

Routing Behavior

What happens when there is a match between the packet's destination IP address and a level 1 parent route, but there is not a match with any of the level 2 child routes? We might assume the routing table lookup process continues looking for a less-specific match in the routing table. However, you will see that this might or might not be the case depending on the configuration of the router.

Classful and Classless Routing Behavior

The next step in the route lookup process (Step 3) looks at routing behavior. Routing behavior influences the process of searching for the preferred route using the **no ip classless** or **ip classless** commands (see Figure 8-32).

Figure 8-32   Routing Protocols vs. Routing Behaviors

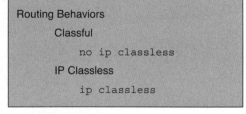

Routing Sources
   Directly Connected Networks
   Static Routes
   Classful Routing Protocols
      RIPv1
      IGRP
   Classless Routing Protocols
      RIPv2
      EIGRP
      OSPF
      IS-IS

• Routing sources (including protocols) are
  used to build the routing table.
• Multiple sources and routing protocols
  can be used.

Routing Behaviors
   Classful
      no ip classless
   IP Classless
      ip classless

• Routing behaviors are used to locate
  information in the routing table.
• Only a single routing behavior can be used.

Classless and classful routing behaviors are not the same as classless and classful routing protocols. Classful and classless routing protocols affect how the routing table is populated. Classful and classless routing behaviors determine how the routing table is searched after it is populated. In Figure 8-32, the routing sources (including classful and classless routing protocols) are the inputs used to populate the routing table. The routing behavior, specified by the **ip classless** or **no ip classless** commands, determines how the route lookup process will proceed at Step 3.

As you can see in Figure 8-32, routing protocols and routing behaviors are completely independent of each other. The routing table could be populated with routes from a classless routing protocol such as RIPv2 yet implement classful routing behavior because the **no ip classless** command is configured.

Topology Changes

Figure 8-33 shows a modified topology using RIPv1 between R1 and R2, and static routes between R2 and R3.

Figure 8-33   Modified Topology

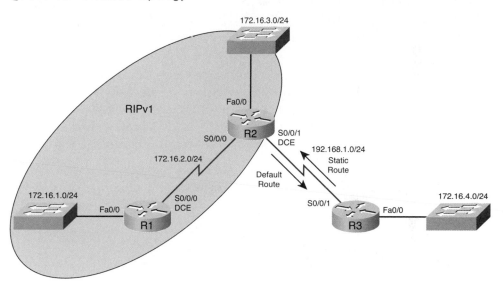

In Chapter 7, "RIPv2," we learned that classful routing protocols such as RIPv1 do not support discontiguous networks. Even though our current topology has discontiguous networks, we can configure static routes to reach those networks.

Example 8-16 shows the configuration changes for R2.

```
Example 8-16    R2 Configuration
R2(config)#ip route 0.0.0.0 0.0.0.0 s0/0/1
R2(config)#router rip
R2(config-router)#default-information originate
R2(config-router)#no network 192.168.1.0
R2(config-router)#end
R2#show ip route
Codes: C - connected, S - static, I - IGRP, R - RIP, M - mobile, B - BGP
<output omitted>
       * - candidate default, U - per-user static route, o - ODR
<output omitted>


Gateway of last resort is 0.0.0.0 to network 0.0.0.0

     172.16.0.0/24 is subnetted, 3 subnets
R        172.16.1.0 [120/1] via 172.16.2.1, 00:00:00, Serial0/0/0
C        172.16.2.0 is directly connected, Serial0/0/0
C        172.16.3.0 is directly connected, FastEthernet0/0
C     192.168.1.0/24 is directly connected, Serial0/0/1
S*    0.0.0.0/0 is directly connected, Serial0/0/1
```

First, we add a static "quad zero" route on R2 for sending default traffic to R3. We then add the **default-information originate** command to the RIP routing process so that R2 will send R1 the default route. This will allow R1 and R2 the capability of reaching all other networks, including 172.16.4.0/24 on R3. Finally, we enter the command **no network 192.168.1.0** because we no longer want to exchange RIP updates with R3.

Example 8-17 shows the configuration changes for R3. We remove RIP routing on R3 and add a static route on R3 for sending traffic for the major network 172.16.0.0/16, which does not have a longer match in the routing table, to R2.

```
Example 8-17    R3 Configuration
R3(config)#ip route 172.16.0.0 255.255.0.0 s0/0/1
R3(config)#no router rip
R3(config-router)#end
R3#show ip route
Codes: C - connected, S - static, I - IGRP, R - RIP, M - mobile, B - BGP
<output omitted>

Gateway of last resort is not set
```

```
        172.16.0.0/16 is variably subnetted, 2 subnets, 2 masks
C          172.16.4.0/24 is directly connected, FastEthernet0/0
S          172.16.0.0/16 is directly connected, Serial0/0/1
C       192.168.1.0/24 is directly connected, Serial0/0/1
```

We are not going to test the connectivity at this time. Connectivity is tested in the following sections.

Classful Routing Behavior: no ip classless

We now focus on Step 3 in the route lookup process: namely, what happens after Step 2b when there is not a match with any of the level 2 child routes of the parent. Later, you will see a specific example.

As you recall from the previous section, in Steps 1 and 2, the router examines level 1 and child routes looking for the best match with the IP packet's destination address. Let's assume there is no match and resume our review of the route lookup process with Step 3.

Steps 3 and 3a in Figures 8-34 and 8-35 shows how classful routing behavior impacts the route lookup process.

Step 3.   (See Figure 8-34.) Is the router implementing classful or classless routing behavior?

Figure 8-34   Routing Table Lookup Process: Step 3

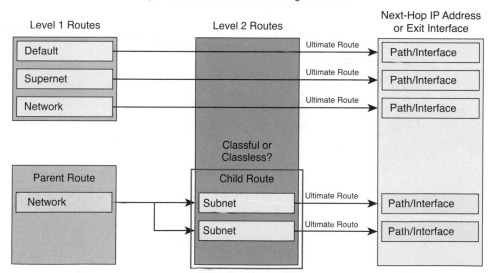

Step 3: Classful or classless routing behavior?

Step 3a.   (See Figure 8-35.) If classful routing behavior is in effect, terminate the lookup process and drop the packet.

Figure 8-35   Routing Table Lookup Process: Step 3a

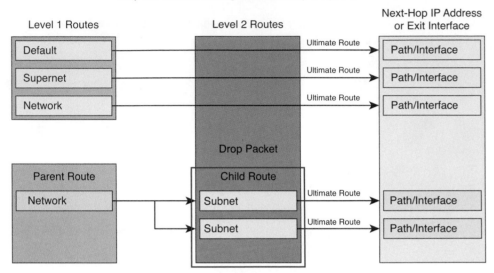

Step 3a: Classful routing behavior: Drop the packet.

> **Note**
>
> Under classful routing behavior, the process never goes to Step 4.

Before Cisco IOS Software Release 11.3, **no ip classless** was the default behavior for Cisco routers. The command **no ip classless** means that the route lookup process uses classful routing table lookups by default. This is explained in the following sections.

The commands **no ip classless** and **ip classless** are global configuration commands and can be viewed by entering **show running-config**. In Cisco IOS Software Release 11.3 and later, the command **ip classless** is the default, implementing a classless route lookup process.

What is the effect of classful routing behavior when all the routers are configured with the **no ip classless** command?

```
R1(config)#no ip classless
R2(config)#no ip classless
R3(config)#no ip classless
```

Let's examine what happens when the router is performing classful routing behavior—that is, when the **no ip classless** command is configured.

Classful Routing Behavior: Search Process

In our routing table lookup process, Step 3a states that when classful routing behavior is in effect (**no ip classless**) the process will not continue searching level 1 routes in the routing table. If a packet doesn't match a child route for the parent network route, the router drops the packet. Let's see an example.

Example: R2 Operating with Classful Routing Behavior

In this example (see Figure 8-36), R2 receives a packet destined for PC3 at 172.16.4.10.

Figure 8-36   R2 Receives Traffic for 172.16.4.10

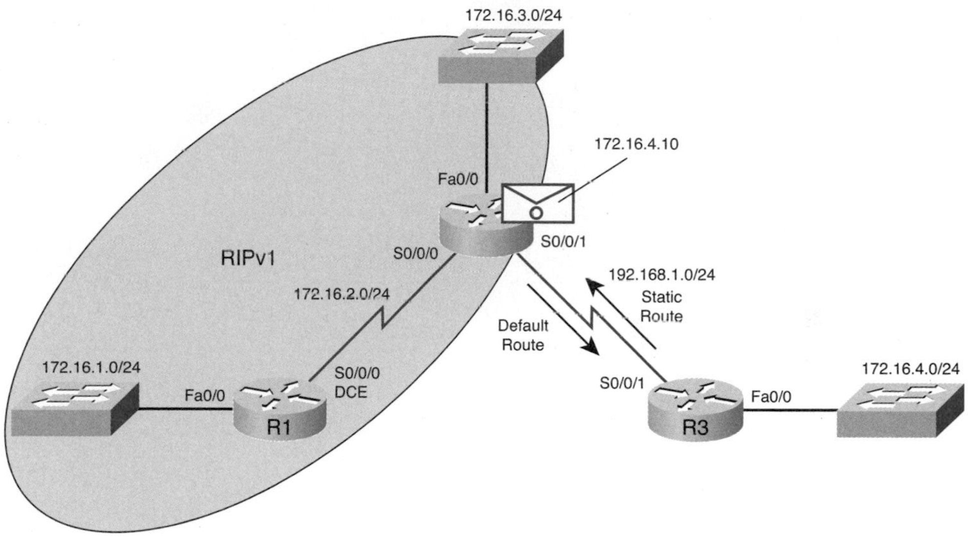

Look at the routing table of R2 in Example 8-18.

Example 8-18   R2 Routing Table

```
R2#show ip route
Codes: C - connected, S - static, I - IGRP, R - RIP, M - mobile, B - BGP
        <output omitted>


Gateway of last resort is 0.0.0.0 to network 0.0.0.0


     172.16.0.0/24 is subnetted, 3 subnets
R       172.16.1.0 [120/1] via 172.16.2.1, 00:00:12, Serial0/0/0
C       172.16.2.0 is directly connected, Serial0/0/0
```

```
C        172.16.3.0 is directly connected, FastEthernet0/0
C     192.168.1.0/24 is directly connected, Serial0/0/1
S*    0.0.0.0/0 is directly connected, Serial0/0/1
```

The routing process searches the routing table in Example 8-18 and finds a 16-bit match with the parent route 172.16.0.0, as shown in Figure 8-37.

Figure 8-37   Example: Level 1 Parent Route and Level 2 Child Routes

Destination matches the parent route. R2 will now check the child routes.		

Destination of IP Packet	172.16.4.10	10101100.00010000.00000100.00001010

Level 1 Parent Route	172.16.0.0/16	10101100.00010000.00000000.00000000
Level 2 Child Route	172.16.1.0/24	10101100.00010000.00000001.00000000
Level 2 Child Route	172.16.2.0/24	10101100.00010000.00000010.00000000
Level 2 Child Route	172.16.3.0/24	10101100.00010000.00000011.00000000

According to Step 1b of the routing process, if a match is made in the parent route, the child routes are checked.

Now let's look at the actual bit-matching process that is taking place as the child routes are checked.

Notice that none of the child routes have 24 leftmost bits that match the 24 leftmost bits of the destination IP address 172.16.4.10. At most, only 21 leftmost bits match. There is no match with the level 2 child routes.

So, what happens next? Router R2 drops the packet.

As shown in Figure 8-38, because Router R2 is using classful routing behavior (**no ip classless**), the router will not search beyond the child routes for a lesser match.

The routing table process will not use the default route, 0.0.0.0/0, or any other route.

A common error is to assume that a default route will always be used if the router does not have a better route. In our example, R2's default route is neither examined nor used, although it is a match. This is often a surprising result when a network administrator does not understand the difference between classful and classless routing behavior.

Figure 8-38   R2 Drops the Packet

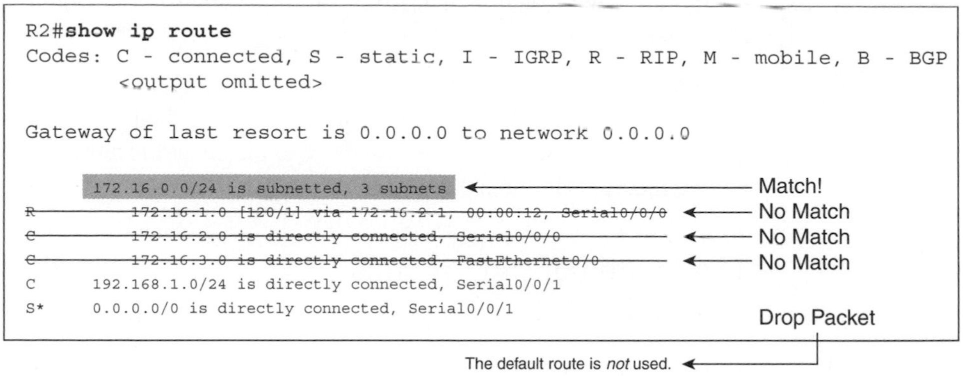

```
R2#show ip route
Codes: C - connected, S - static, I - IGRP, R - RIP, M - mobile, B - BGP
       <output omitted>

Gateway of last resort is 0.0.0.0 to network 0.0.0.0

       172.16.0.0/24 is subnetted, 3 subnets   ◄─────────────── Match!
R         172.16.1.0 [120/1] via 172.16.2.1, 00:00:12, Serial0/0/0   ◄─── No Match
C         172.16.2.0 is directly connected, Serial0/0/0   ◄─── No Match
C         172.16.3.0 is directly connected, FastEthernet0/0   ◄─── No Match
C      192.168.1.0/24 is directly connected, Serial0/0/1
S*     0.0.0.0/0 is directly connected, Serial0/0/1         Drop Packet
```

The default route is *not* used. ◄──────────

Note

You will also see another example in Chapter 9, "EIGRP," where understanding the routing table lookup process will assist you in troubleshooting why a default route does not get used—even with classless routing behavior.

Why does classful routing behavior perform like this? The general idea of classful routing behavior comes from the time when all networks were of a classful nature. At the beginning of the Internet's growth, an organization received a Class A, Class B, or Class C major network address. When an organization had a classful IP major network address, that organization would also administer all the subnets for that classful address. All routers belonging to the organization would know about all the subnets for the major network. If a subnet was not in the routing table, the subnet did not exist. As you learned in Chapter 6, "VLSM and CIDR," IP addresses are no longer allocated based on class.

Classless Routing Behavior: ip classless

Starting with Cisco IOS Software Release 11.3, Cisco changed the default routing behavior from classful to classless. The **ip classless** command is configured by default. The **show running-config** command displays the routing behavior. Classless routing behavior means that the routing process no longer assumes that all subnets for a major classful network can be reached only within the child routes of the parent. Classless routing behavior works well for discontiguous networks and classless interdomain routing (CIDR) supernets.

In this section, we examine the effect of classless routing behavior. All routers are configured with the **ip classless** command:

```
R1(config)#ip classless
```

```
R2(config)#ip classless
```

```
R3(config)#ip classless
```

We will discuss what happens to a packet when there is a match with a level 1 parent route but there is not a match with any of the level 2 child routes or subnets. This takes us to Step 3b, classless routing behavior.

As you recall from the routing table process, in Steps 1 and 2, the routing table process examines level 1 and level 2 child routes looking for the best match with the IP packet's destination address. Let's assume there is no match and resume our review of the route lookup process with Step 3.

The Route Lookup Process

Follow these steps in the figure to see the route lookup process:

Step 3.   (See Figure 8-39.) Is the router implementing classful or classless routing behavior?

Figure 8-39   Routing Table Lookup Process: Step 3

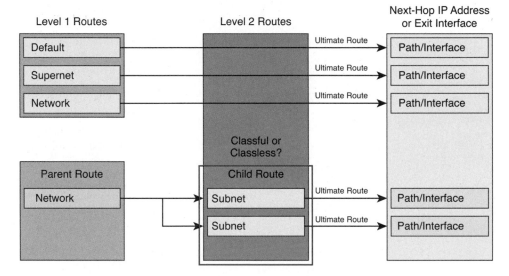

Step 3a.   (See Figure 8-40.) If classful routing behavior is in effect, terminate the lookup process and drop the packet.

Figure 8-40   Routing Table Lookup Process: Step 3a

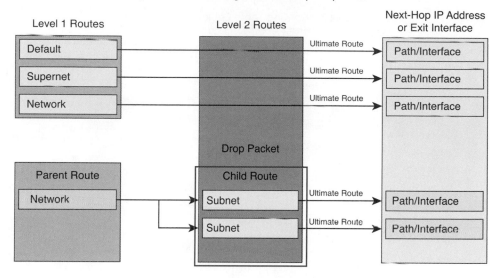

Step 3a: Classful routing behavior: Drop the packet.

Step 3b.   (See Figure 8-41.) If classless routing behavior is in effect, continue searching
level 1 supernet routes in the routing table for a match, including the default
route, if there is one.

Figure 8-41   Routing Table Lookup Process: Step 3b

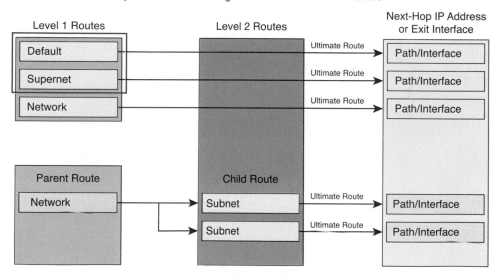

Step 3b: Classless routing behavior: Search level 1 routes.

Step 4.   (See Figure 8-42.) If there is now a lesser match with a level 1 supernet or default routes, the router uses that route to forward the packet.

Figure 8-42   Routing Table Lookup Process: Step 4

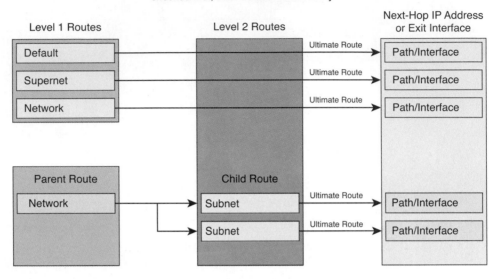

Step 4: Match with supernet or default. Use it to forward packet. Supernets are checked first, then default if necessary.

Step 5.   (See Figure 8-43.) If there is not a match with a route in the routing table, the router drops the packet.

Figure 8-43   Routing Table Lookup Process: Step 5

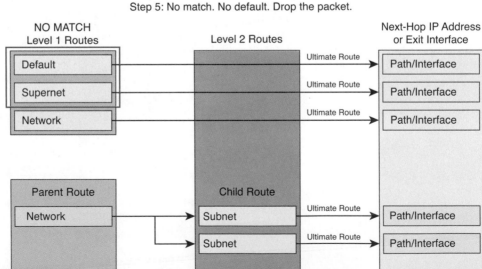

Step 5: No match. No default. Drop the packet.

Classless Routing Behavior: Search Process

Let's revisit our sample topology shown earlier in Figure 8-36 and look at the bit matching that happens when classless routing behavior (**ip classless**) is in effect.

Example: R2 Operating with Classless Routing Behavior

Look at the routing table for R2 in the earlier Example 8-18. Again, R2 receives a packet destined for PC3 at 172.16.4.10. Just as it did with the classful routing behavior, the router searches the routing table and finds a 16-bit match with the parent route 172.16.0.0, as shown earlier in Figure 8-37. According to Step 1b of the routing process, if there is a match with a parent route, the child routes are checked.

As before, no child route has 24 leftmost bits that match the 24 leftmost bits of the destination IP address 172.16.4.10. At most, only the first 21 leftmost bits match. There is no match with the level 2 child routes. With **no ip classless** configured, the R2 dropped the packet.

However, because we now are using classless routing behavior (**ip classless**), the router continues searching the routing table, beyond this parent route and its child routes. The routing process will continue to search the routing table for a route with a subnet mask fewer than the 16 bits of the previous parent route. In other words, the router will now continue to search the other routes in the routing table where there might be fewer bits that match, but still a match.

Again, referring to Example 8-18, the next route in the routing table is 192.168.1.0/24:

```
C    192.168.1.0/24 is directly connected, Serial0/0/1
```

Figure 8-44 shows the 192.168.1.0/24 route does not have 24 leftmost bits that match the destination IP address. Although this might seem obvious, remember that the router will check every network until it finds a match or drops the packet.

Figure 8-44   Classless Routing Behavior: Check the 192.168.1.0/24 Route

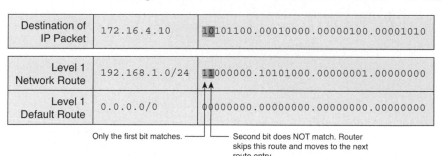

How about the default route? How many bits need to match?

```
S*    0.0.0.0/0 is directly connected, Serial0/0/1
```

In Figure 8-45, you can see that the mask is /0, which means that zero or no bits need to match. A default route will be the lowest-bit match. In classless routing behavior, if no other route matches, the default route will match.

Figure 8-45   Classless Routing Behavior: Default Route Matches

A /0 mask means that no bits have to match to use the default route. R2 uses the default route and forwards the packet.		
Destination of IP Packet	172.16.4.10	10101100.00010000.00000100.00001010
Level 1 Network Route	192.168.1.0/24	11000000.10101000.00000001.00000000
Level 1 Default Route	0.0.0.0/0	00000000.00000000.00000000.00000000

In this case, the router will use the default route because it is the best match (Figure 8-46). The packet will be forwarded out the Serial 0/0/1 interface.

Classful Route on R3

What does R3 do with return traffic back to PC2 at 172.16.2.10? Refer to the routing table for R3 in Figure 8-46.

Figure 8-46   R3 Routing Table Lookup for Return Traffic

```
R3#show ip route
Codes: C - connected, S - static, I - IGRP, R - RIP, M - mobile, B - BGP
       D - EIGRP, EX - EIGRP external, O - OSPF, IA - OSPF inter area
       N1 - OSPF NSSA external type 1, N2 - OSPF NSSA external type 2
       E1 - OSPF external type 1, E2 - OSPF external type 2, E - EGP
       i - IS-IS, L1 - IS-IS level-1, L2 - IS-IS level-2, ia - IS-IS
inter area
       * - candidate default, U - per-user static route, o - ODR
       P - periodic downloaded static route

Gateway of last resort is not set

     172.16.0.0/16 is variably subnetted, 2 subnets, 2 masks       Match!
C       172.16.4.0/24 is directly connected, FastEthernet0/0       No Match
S       172.16.0.0/16 is directly connected, Serial0/0/1           Child Match!
C    192.168.1.0/24 is directly connected, Serial0/0/1
```

R3 uses the 172.16.0.0/16 child route and forwards the packet to R2.

Notice that both the 172.16.4.0/24 subnet route and the 172.16.0.0/16 classful network route are level 2 child routes of the 172.16.0.0/16 parent route. Whenever there are routes for both the subnets of a classful network and a route for the classful network route itself, the classful route is considered a level 2 child route, just like the subnets.

Why are there two 172.16.0.0/16 routes in this routing table? The first 172.16.0.0/16 route is a parent route that was automatically created when the 172.16.4.0/24 child route was added to the routing table.

The 172.16.0.0/16 static route is a little more interesting. If there were no 172.16.0.0/16 parent route (which means no 172.16.4.0/24 child route), this static route would be a level 1 ultimate route. Because there is a 172.16.0.0/16 parent route, this 172.16.0.0/16 static route gets added as a child route within the 172.16.0.0/16 parent route. Remember, the routing table process wants to choose the best route, the one with the longest match. By having the 172.16.0.0/16 static route be a child route with the 172.16.4.0/24 route, it guarantees that the 172.16.4.0/24 child route will be examined for the longer 24 bit match before the 172.16.0.0/16 static route is considered.

In this case, R3 uses the 172.16.0.0/16 child route and forwards the traffic out Serial 0/0/1 back to R2.

Classful vs. Classless Routing Behavior in the Real World

Remember that classful and classless routing behaviors are independent from classful and classless routing protocols. A router could be configured with classful routing behavior (**no ip classless**) and a classless routing protocol, such as RIPv2. A router could also be configured with classless routing behavior (**ip classless**) and a classful routing protocol, such as RIPv1.

In today's networks, it is recommended to use classless routing behavior so that supernet and default routes can be used whenever needed.

Summary

Understanding the structure and lookup process of the routing table can be an important tool in verifying and troubleshooting networks. Knowing which routes should be included and which routes should not be included in the routing table is a critical skill when troubleshooting routing issues.

The Cisco IP routing table is structured in a classful manner, which means that it uses the default, classful addresses, to organize the route entries. The source of a routing entry can be a directly connected network, a static route, or a route learned dynamically from a routing protocol.

In this chapter, you learned that there are level 1 and level 2 routes. A level 1 route can be either an ultimate route or a parent route. A level 1 ultimate route is a route with a subnet mask equal to, or less than, the default classful mask of the network. For example, a route learned through RIP with the network address of 192.168.1.0 and a /24 network mask is a level 1 ultimate route because it includes an exit interface. These routes are displayed in the routing table as a single route entry, as follows:

```
R       192.168.1.0/24 [120/1] via 172.16.2.2, 00:00:25, Serial0/0/0
```

Another type of level 1 route is a parent route. A level 1 parent route is automatically created when a subnet route is added to the routing table. The subnet route is known as a level 2 child route. The parent route is a header for level 2 child routes. Here is an example of a level 1 parent route and a level 2 child route:

```
        172.16.0.0/24 is subnetted, 1 subnets
R          172.16.1.0 [120/1] via 172.16.2.1, 00:00:07, Serial0/0/0
```

The subnet mask of the child routes is displayed in the parent route unless VLSM is used. With VLSM, the parent route displays the default classful mask, and the subnet mask is included with the individual VLSM route entries.

You were also introduced to the routing table lookup process in this chapter. When a packet is received by the router, it looks for the longest match with one of the routes in the routing table. The longest match is the route with the largest number of leftmost bits that match between the destination IP address of the packet and the network address of the route in the routing table. The subnet mask associated with the network address in the routing table defines the minimum number of bits that must match for that route to be a match.

Before examining any level 2 child routes (subnets) for a match, there must be a match with the level 1 parent route. The classful mask of the parent determines how many bits must match the parent route. If there is a match with the parent route, the child routes will be searched for a match.

What happens when there is a match with the parent route but none of the child routes? If the router is using classful routing behavior, no other routes are searched, and the packet is discarded. Classful routing behavior was the default routing behavior on Cisco routers before Cisco IOS Software Release 11.3. Classful routing behavior can be implemented using the **no ip classless** command.

Starting with Cisco IOS Software Release 11.3, classless routing behavior became the default. If there is a match with a parent route but none of the child routes, the routing table process continues to search other routes in the routing table, including a default route and supernet route should one exist. To implement classless routing behavior, use the **ip classless** command.

Routes to networks get added to the routing table from various sources, including directly connected networks, static routes, classful routing protocols, and classless routing protocols. The lookup process, classful or classless routing behavior, is independent of the source of the route. A routing table might have routes learned from a classful routing protocol such as RIPv1 but use classless routing behavior, **no ip classles**s, for the lookup process.

Activities and Labs

The activities and labs available in the companion *Routing Protocols and Concepts, CCNA Exploration Labs and Study Guide* (ISBN 1-58713-204-4) provide hands-on practice with the following topics introduced in this chapter:

Lab 8-1: Investigating the Routing Table Lookup Process (8.4.1)

In this lab, you investigate classless and classful routing behavior.

Lab 8-2: The show ip route Challenge Lab (8.4.2)

In this lab, you determine the topology of a network using the outputs from the **show ip route** command.

Packet Tracer
☐ Companion

Many of the Hands-on Labs include Packet Tracer Companion Activities where you can use Packet Tracer to complete a simulation of the lab. Look for this icon in the *Labs and Study Guide* (ISBN 1-58713-204-4) for Hands-on Labs that have a Packet Tracer Companion.

Check Your Understanding

Complete all the review questions listed here to test your understanding of the topics and concepts in this chapter. Answers are listed in the appendix, "Check Your Understanding and Challenge Questions Answer Key."

1. Refer to the following output. What three types of routes are displayed in this routing table? (Choose three.)

```
<output omitted>
     10.0.0.0/16 is subnetted, 1 subnets
S       10.1.0.0 is directly connected, Serial0/0/1
     172.16.0.0/24 is subnetted, 4 subnets
R       172.16.1.0 [120/1] via 172.16.2.1, 00:00:12, Serial0/0/0
S       172.16.2.0 is directly connected, Serial0/0/0
C       172.16.3.0 is directly connected, FastEthernet0/0
R       172.16.4.0 [120/1] via 172.16.2.1, 00:00:12, Serial0/0/1
C     192.168.1.0/24 is directly connected, Serial0/0/1
<output omitted>
```

A. Networks local to this router

B. The default route for this router

C. Static routes on this router

D. Mobile routes

E. Routes learned from dynamic routing protocols

F. Routes learned from a non-Cisco router

2. Which characteristic can be used to determine whether a route is an ultimate route?

A. The route displays a subnet mask.

B. The route is a parent route.

C. The route was configured by an administrator.

D. The route includes an exit interface.

3. Refer to the following output. Which two routes are considered parent routes? (Choose two.)

```
<output omitted>
      10.0.0.0/16 is subnetted, 1 subnets
S        10.1.0.0 is directly connected, Serial0/0/1
      172.16.0.0/24 is subnetted, 4 subnets
R        172.16.1.0 [120/1] via 172.16.2.1, 00:00:12, Serial0/0/0
S        172.16.2.0 is directly connected, Serial0/0/0
C        172.16.3.0 is directly connected, FastEthernet0/0
R        172.16.4.0 [120/1] via 172.16.2.1, 00:00:12, Serial0/0/1
C     192.168.1.0/24 is directly connected, Serial0/0/1
<output omitted>
```

   A. 172.16.0.0/24

   B. 172.16.4.0

   C. 172.16.1.0

   D. 10.0.0.0/16

   E. 192.168.1.0/24

   F. 192.168.100.0/24

4. Router R1 is configured with **R1(config)#ip classless** and **R1(config)#ip route 0.0.0.0 0.0.0.0 s0/0/0**. What will R1 do with a packet that matches a parent route but does not match any associated child routes?

   A. Forward the packet using the longest parent route match

   B. Forward the packet via the default route

   C. Return the packet with an ICMP "Destination Unreachable" message to the source address

   D. Drop the packet

5. What action will enable classful routing behavior on a router?

   A. Configuring RIPv1 or IGRP

   B. Configuring a link-state routing protocol

   C. Using only classful netmasks on all networks

   D. Issuing the **no ip classless** command

6. In the route lookup process, what constitutes the preferred route?

   A. The ultimate route

   B. The longest match of leftmost bits

   C. The shortest prefix length

   D. The first route that resolves to an exit interface

7. If a packet matches a level 1 parent route in the routing table, what occurs next in the lookup process?

   A. The router drops the packet because level 1 requires an exit interface.

   B. The router looks for the level 2 child route with an exit interface.

   C. The router sends the packet out all interfaces except the one in which it was received.

   D. The router ARPs all connected networks to find the interface with the destination on it.

8. What do the **ip classless** and **no ip classless** commands do?

   A. Determine the address lookup behavior of the routing process

   B. Specify whether the router will accept subnet masks in routing updates

   C. Restrict the use of classful or classless routing protocols

   D. Allow the router to accept or not accept VLSM for interface addresses

9. Router R1 is configured with **R1(config)#no ip classless** and **R1(config)#ip route 0.0.0.0 0.0.0.0 s0/0/0**. What will R1 do with a packet that matches a parent route but does not match any associated child routes?

   A. Forward the packet using the longest parent route match

   B. Forward the packet via the default route

   C. Return the packet with an ICMP "Destination Unreachable" message to the source address

   D. Drop the packet

10. Refer to the following output. RouterC is running Cisco IOS Software Release 12.3. The router receives a packet with a destination of 172.16.1.130. Which route will RouterC use to forward the packet?

```
RouterC#show ip route
<output omitted>

Gateway of last resort is 0.0.0.0 to network 0.0.0.0

     172.16.0.0/13 is subnetted, 1 subnets
S       172.16.0.0 is directly connected, FastEthernet0/0
     172.16.0.0/16 is variably subnetted, 3 subnets, 2 masks
R       172.16.0.0/24 [120/3] via 172.16.1.1, 00:00:12, FastEthernet0/0
C       172.16.1.0/25 is directly connected, FastEthernet0/0
     172.17.0.0/25 is subnetted, 1 subnets
C       172.17.1.0 is directly connected, FastEthernet0/1
S*   0.0.0.0/0 is directly connected, FastEthernet0/0
```

   A. C   172.16.1.0/25 is directly connected, FastEthernet0/0.

   B. 172.16.0.0/16 is variably subnetted, 3 subnets, 2 masks.

   C. R   172.16.0.0/24 [120/3] via 172.16.1.1, 00:00:12, FastEthernet0/0.

   D. 172.16.0.0/13 is subnetted, 1 subnet.

   E. S   172.16.0.0 is directly connected, FastEthernet0/0.

   F. None. It will drop the packet.

11. What makes a level 1 or level 2 route an ultimate route?

12. When is the subnet mask displayed with the child route and not the parent route?

13. Does the network administrator configure the parent route?

14. Can there be a parent route without any child routes?

15. Before any level 2 child routes are examined for a match, what must match?

16. What determines how many bits must match between the destination IP address of a packet and a route in the routing table?

17. What is the current default routing behavior on Cisco routers, and what command can be used to modify this?

Challenge Questions and Activities

These questions require a deeper application of the concepts covered in this chapter and are similar to the style of questions you might see on a CCNA certification exam. You can find the answers to these questions in the appendix, "Answers to Check Your Understanding and Challenge Questions and Activities."

Refer to the following output to answer Questions 1–4:

```
     172.16.0.0/24 is subnetted, 3 subnets
R       172.16.1.0 [120/1] via 172.16.2.1, 00:00:00, Serial0/0/0
C       172.16.2.0 is directly connected, Serial0/0/0
C       172.16.3.0 is directly connected, FastEthernet0/0
     172.30.0.0/16 is variably subnetted, 3 subnets, 2 masks
R       172.30.1.4/30 [120/1] via 172.16.2.1, 00:00:00, Serial0/0/0
R       172.30.1.8/30 [120/1] via 172.16.2.1, 00:00:00, Serial0/0/0
R       172.30.3.0/24 [120/1] via 172.16.2.1, 00:00:00, Serial0/0/0
C    192.168.1.0/24 is directly connected, Serial0/0/1
S*   0.0.0.0/0 is directly connected, Serial0/0/1
```

1. Which of the routes are considered level 2 child routes, and what is their level 1 parent route?

2. Before the 172.16.1.0, 172.16.2.0, and 172.16.3.0 routes can be examined for a match, what route must match? How many bits must match this route before the subnets are examined?

3. If the command **no ip classless** were configured on this router, what would happen to a packet with the destination IP address 172.16.4.5? What route would it use, if any? Would any of the level 1 parent routes have its child routes examined for a match?

4. If the command **ip classless** were configured on this router, what would happen to a packet with the destination IP address 172.16.4.5? What route would it use, if any? Would any of the level 1 parent routes have its child routes examined for a match?

To Learn More

An excellent source on the routing table structure and the lookup process is Alex Zinin's book, *Cisco IP Routing*, which goes into more detail than was discussed in this chapter.[1] In particular, Chapter 4 from that book, "Routing Table Maintenance," covers the following topics:

- Comparison of route sources

- Representation of routing information and interfaces

- Routing table structure

- Route source selection
- Routing table initialization
- Asynchronous table maintenance
- Route resolvability
- Dynamic route processing
- Static route processing
- Manual routing table clearance
- Default route selection

End Notes

[1] Zinin, Alex. *Cisco IP Routing: Packet Forwarding and Intra-domain Routing Protocols*. Addison-Wesley, 2002.

Objectives

Upon completion of this chapter, you should be able to answer the following questions:

- What is the background and history of EIGRP?

- What are the features and operations of EIGRP?

- What commands are used in configuring basic EIGRP, and what are their purposes?

- How is the composite metric calculated for EIGRP?

- What are the concepts and operation of DUAL?

- Which additional commands can be used in the configuration of EIGRP, and what are their uses?

Key Terms

This chapter uses the following key terms. You can find the definitions in the Glossary at the end of the book.

Enhanced Interior Gateway Routing Protocol (EIGRP) is a distance vector, classless routing protocol (see Figure 9-1) that was released in 1992 with Cisco IOS Software Release 9.21. As its name suggests, EIGRP is an enhancement of Cisco Interior Gateway Routing Protocol (IGRP). Both are Cisco proprietary protocols and operate only on Cisco routers.

Figure 9-1   Classification of Routing Protocols

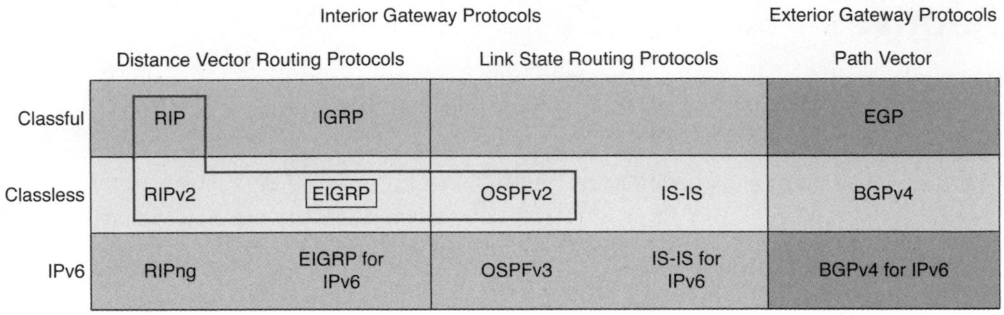

	Interior Gateway Protocols			Exterior Gateway Protocols
	Distance Vector Routing Protocols	Link State Routing Protocols		Path Vector
Classful	RIP IGRP			EGP
Classless	RIPv2 EIGRP	OSPFv2	IS-IS	BGPv4
IPv6	RIPng EIGRP for IPv6	OSPFv3	IS-IS for IPv6	BGPv4 for IPv6

The main purpose in Cisco's development of EIGRP was to create a classless version of IGRP. EIGRP includes several features that are not commonly found in other distance vector routing protocols such as Routing Information Protocol (RIPv1 and RIPv2) and IGRP. These features include the following:

- Reliable Transport Protocol
- Bounded updates
- Diffusing Update Algorithm
- Establishing adjacencies
- Neighbor and topology tables

Although EIGRP might act like a link-state routing protocol, it is still a distance vector routing protocol.

Note

The term *hybrid routing protocol* is sometimes used to define EIGRP. However, this term is misleading because EIGRP is not a hybrid between distance vector and link-state routing protocols—it is solely a distance vector routing protocol. Therefore, Cisco is no longer using this term to refer to EIGRP.

There is another protocol called RTP, Real-time Transport Protocol. This is a different protocol and is used for delivering audio and video over networks.

In this chapter, you learn how to configure EIGRP and verify your EIGRP configuration with new **show** commands. You also learn the formula used by EIGRP to calculate this composite metric.

Unique to EIGRP is its Reliable Transport Protocol (RTP). This Layer 4 protocol can provide either reliable or unreliable delivery of packets, similar to TCP and User Datagram Protocol (UDP). In addition, EIGRP establishes relationships with directly connected routers that are also enabled for EIGRP. Neighbor relationships are used to track the status of these neighbors. RTP and the tracking of neighbor adjacencies set the stage for the EIGRP workhorse, the Diffusing Update Algorithm (DUAL).

As the computational engine that drives EIGRP, DUAL resides at the center of the routing protocol, guaranteeing loop-free paths and backup paths throughout the routing domain. You will learn exactly how DUAL selects a route to install in the routing table and what DUAL does with potential backup routes.

Like RIPv2, EIGRP can operate with classful or classless routing behavior. In this chapter, you learn how to disable automatic summarization, and then how to manually summarize networks to reduce the size of routing tables. Finally, you learn how to use default routing with EIGRP.

Introduction to EIGRP

This section introduces some of the terms and concepts used by EIGRP. Each of these items is discussed in more detail later in the chapter.

EIGRP: An Enhanced Distance Vector Routing Protocol

Although EIGRP is described as an enhanced distance vector routing protocol, it is still a distance vector routing protocol. This can sometimes be a source of confusion. To appreciate enhancements of EIGRP and eliminate confusion, you must first look at its predecessor, IGRP.

Roots of EIGRP: IGRP

Cisco developed the proprietary IGRP in 1985, in response to some of the limitations of RIPv1, including the use of the hop-count metric and the maximum network size of 15 hops.

Instead of hop count, both IGRP and EIGRP use metrics composed of bandwidth, delay, reliability, and load. By default, both routing protocols use only bandwidth and delay. However, because IGRP is a classful routing protocol that uses the Bellman-Ford algorithm and periodic updates, its usefulness is limited in many of today's networks.

Therefore, Cisco enhanced IGRP with a new algorithm, DUAL, and other features. The commands for both IGRP and EIGRP are similar, and in many cases identical. This allows for easy migration from IGRP to EIGRP. Cisco discontinued IGRP starting with Cisco IOS Software Release 12.2(13)T and 12.2(R1s4)S.

Although discussed in more detail throughout this chapter, let us examine some of the differences between a traditional distance vector routing protocol such as RIP and IGRP, and the enhanced distance vector routing protocol, EIGRP.

Table 9-1 summarizes the main differences between a traditional distance vector routing protocol, such as RIP, and the enhanced distance vector routing protocol EIGRP.

Table 9-1   Comparing Traditional Distance Vector and EIGRP

Traditional Distance Vector Routing Protocols	Enhanced Distance Vector Routing Protocol: EIGRP
Uses the Bellman-Ford or Ford-Fulkerson algorithm.	Uses DUAL.
Ages out routing entries and uses periodic updates.	Does not age out routing entries or use periodic updates.
Keeps track of only the best routes; the best path to a destination network.	Maintains a topology table separate from the routing table, which includes the best path and any loop-free backup paths.
When a route becomes unavailable, the router must wait for a new routing update.	When a route becomes unavailable, DUAL uses a backup path if one exists in the topology table.
Slower convergence due to hold-down timers.	Faster convergence because of the absence of hold-down timers and a system of coordinated route calculations.

The Algorithm

Traditional distance vector routing protocols use some variant of the Bellman-Ford or Ford-Fulkerson algorithm. These protocols, such as RIP and IGRP, age out individual routing entries, and therefore need to periodically send routing table updates.

EIGRP uses DUAL. Although still a distance vector routing protocol, EIGRP with DUAL implements features not found in traditional distance vector routing protocols. EIGRP does not send periodic updates, and route entries do not age out. Instead, EIGRP uses a lightweight hello protocol to monitor connection status with its neighbors. Only changes in the routing information, such as a new link or a link becoming unavailable, cause a routing update to occur. EIGRP routing updates are still vectors of distances transmitted to directly connected neighbors.

Path Determination

Traditional distance vector routing protocols such as RIP and IGRP keep track of only the preferred routes, the best path to a destination network. If the route becomes unavailable, the router waits for another routing update with a path to this remote network.

EIGRP's DUAL maintains a topology table separate from the routing table, which includes both the best path to a destination network and any backup paths that DUAL has determined to be loop-free. *Loop-free* means that the neighbor does not have a route to the destination network that passes through this router.

Later in this chapter, you will see that for a route to be a considered as a valid loop-free backup path by DUAL, it must meet a requirement known as the feasibility condition. Any backup path that meets this condition is guaranteed to be loop-free. Because EIGRP is a distance vector routing protocol, it is possible that there might be loop-free backup paths to a destination network that do not meet the feasibility condition. These paths are therefore not included in the topology table as a valid loop-free backup path by DUAL.

If a route becomes unavailable, DUAL searches its topology table for a valid backup path. If one exists, that route is immediately entered into the routing table. If one does not exist, DUAL performs a network discovery process to see whether there happens to be a backup path that did not previously meet the feasibility condition, a condition that checks for the possibility of routing loops. This process is discussed more thoroughly later in this chapter.

Convergence

Traditional distance vector routing protocols such as RIP and IGRP use periodic updates. Because of the unreliable nature of periodic updates, traditional distance vector routing protocols are prone to routing loops and the count-to-infinity problem. RIP and IGRP use several mechanisms to help avoid these problems, including *hold-down timers*, which cause long convergence times.

EIGRP does not use hold-down timers. Instead, loop-free paths are achieved through a system of route calculations (diffusing computations) that are performed in a coordinated fashion among the routers. The detail of how this is done is beyond the scope of this course, but the result is faster convergence than traditional distance vector routing protocols.

EIGRP Message Format

Figure 9-2 shows an example of an encapsulated EIGRP message.

Figure 9-2   Encapsulated EIGRP Message

Data Link Frame Header	IP Packet Header	EIGRP Packet Header	Type/Length/Values Types

Data Link Frame
MAC Source Address = Address of Sending Interface
MAC Destination Address = Multicast: 01-00-5E-00-00-0A

IP Packet
IP Source Address = Address of Sending Interface
IP Destination Address = Multicast: 224.0.0.10
Protocol Field = 88 for EIGRP

EIGRP Packet Header
Opcode for EIGRP Packet Type
AS Number

TLV Types
Some Types Include:

0x0001 EIGRP Parameters
0x0102 IP Internal Routes
0x0103 IP External Routes

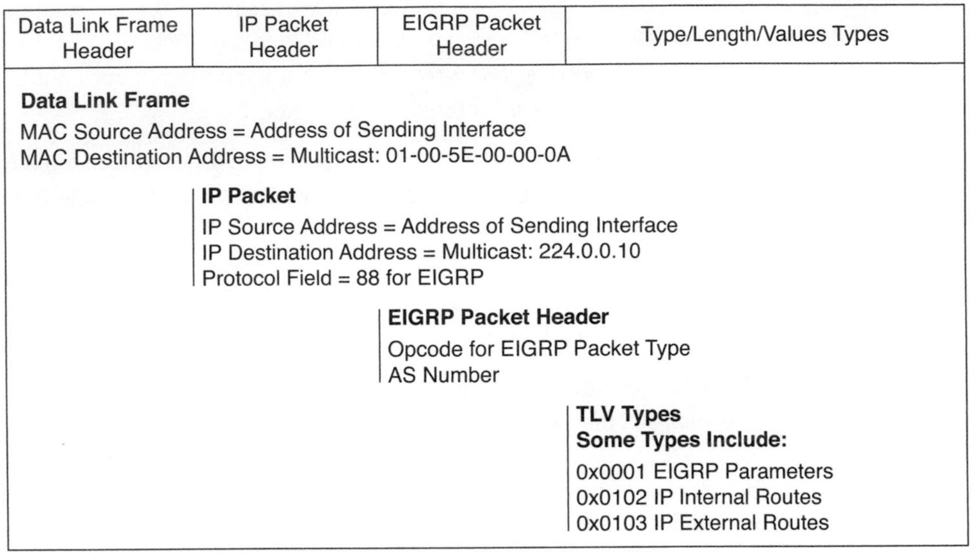

The data portion of an EIGRP message is encapsulated in a packet. This data field is called Type/Length/Value, or *TLV*. As shown in Figure 9-2, the types of TLVs relevant to this course are EIGRP Parameters, IP Internal Routes, and IP External Routes.

The EIGRP packet header is included with every EIGRP packet, regardless of its type. The EIGRP packet header and TLV are then encapsulated in an IP packet. In the IP packet header, the protocol field is set to 88 to indicate EIGRP, and the destination address is set to the multicast 224.0.0.10. If the EIGRP packet is encapsulated in an Ethernet frame, the destination MAC address is also a multicast address: 01-00-5E-00-00-0A.

> **Note**
>
> In the following discussion of EIGRP messages, many fields are beyond the scope of this course. All fields are shown to provide an accurate picture of the EIGRP message format. However, only the fields relevant to the CCNA candidate are discussed.
>
> EIGRP packets can be either multicast or unicast depending on the packet type and the situation. This is beyond the scope of this book and is discussed in CCNP.

Every EIGRP message includes the header, as shown in Figure 9-3.

Figure 9-3   EIGRP Packet Header

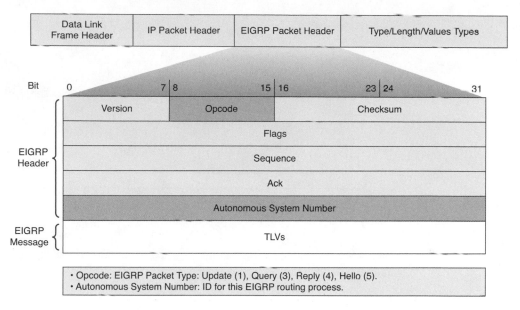

• Opcode: EIGRP Packet Type: Update (1), Query (3), Reply (4), Hello (5).
• Autonomous System Number: ID for this EIGRP routing process.

Important fields for our discussion include the Opcode field and the Autonomous System Number field. Opcode specifies the EIGRP packet type as one of the following:

- Update

- Query

- Reply

- Hello

The autonomous system number specifies the EIGRP routing process. Unlike RIP, Cisco routers can run multiple instances of EIGRP. The autonomous system number is used to track multiple instances of EIGRP.

EIGRP packet types are discussed later in this chapter.

Encapsulated in the EIGRP packet header is the EIGRP TLV, as shown in Figure 9-4.

This EIGRP parameters message includes the weights that EIGRP uses for its composite metric. By default, only bandwidth and delay are weighted. Both are equally weighted; therefore, both the K1 field for bandwidth and the K3 field for delay are set to 1. The other K values are set to 0. Metric calculations are further discussed later in this chapter.

The *hold time* is the amount of time the EIGRP neighbor receiving this message should wait before considering the advertising router to be down. Hold time is discussed in more detail later in this chapter.

Figure 9-4   EIGRP Parameters TLV

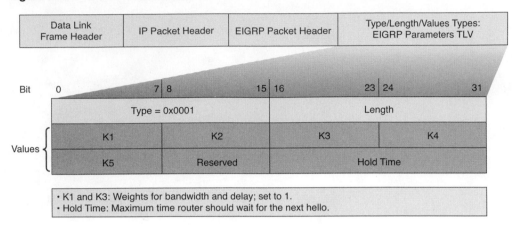

Figure 9-5 shows the IP Internal message that is used to advertise EIGRP routes within an autonomous system.

Figure 9-5   IP Internal Routes TLV

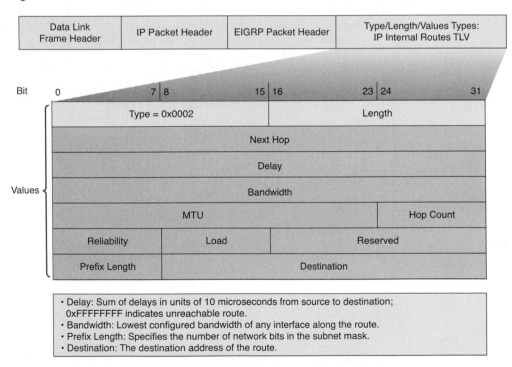

Important fields for our discussion include the following:

- **The metric fields (Delay and Bandwidth):** Delay is calculated as the sum of delays from source to destination in units of 10 microseconds. Bandwidth is the lowest configured bandwidth of any interface along the route.

- **The subnet mask field (Prefix Length):** The subnet mask is specified as the prefix length or the number of network bits in the subnet mask. For example, the prefix length for the subnet mask 255.255.255.0 is 24 because 24 is the number of network bits.

- **The Destination field:** The Destination field stores the address of the destination network. Although only 24 bits are shown in this figure, this field varies based on the value of the network portion of the 32-bit network address. For example, the network portion of 10.1.0.0/16 is 10.1. Therefore, the Destination field stores the first 16 bits. Because the minimum length of this field is 24 bits, the remainder of the field is padded with 0s. If a network address is longer than 24 bits (192.168.1.32/27, for example), the Destination field is extended for another 32 bits (for a total of 56 bits), and the unused bits are padded with 0s.

Figure 9-6 shows the IP External message that is used when external routes are imported into the EIGRP routing process.

Figure 9-6   IP External Routes TLV

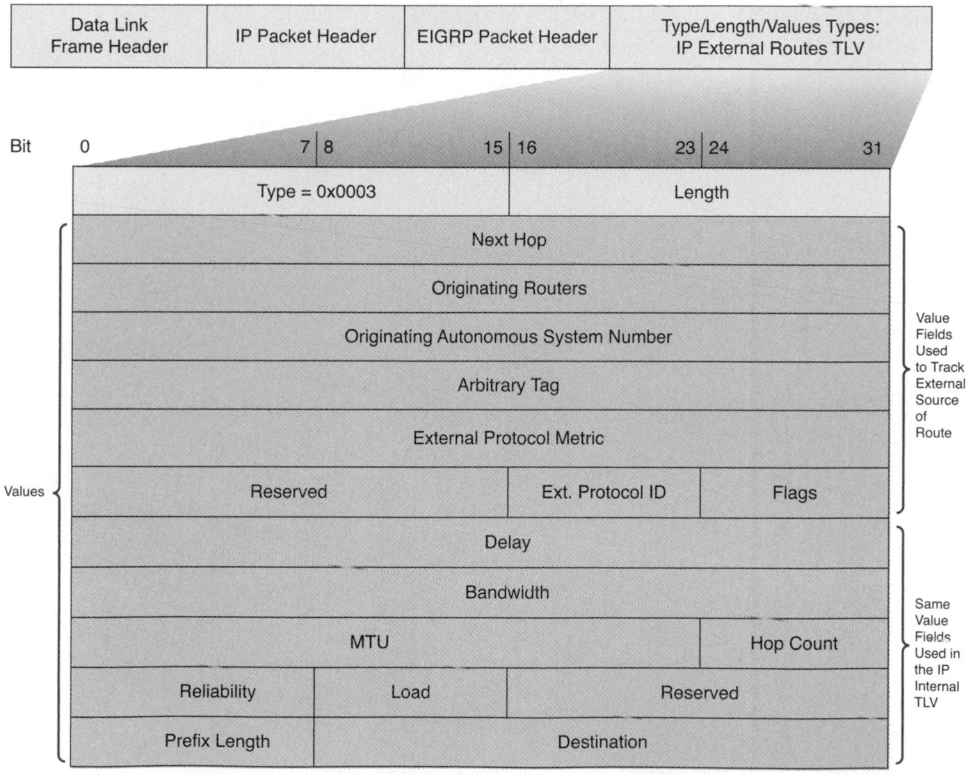

In this chapter, we import or redistribute a default static route into EIGRP. Notice that the bottom half of the IP External TLV includes all the fields used by the IP Internal TLV.

Note

Some EIGRP literature might incorrectly state that the maximum transmission unit (MTU) is one of the metrics used by EIGRP. MTU is not a metric used by EIGRP. The MTU is included in the routing updates, but it is not used to determine the routing metric.

Protocol-Dependent Modules

EIGRP has the capability for routing several different protocols, including IP, Internetwork Packet Exchange (IPX), and AppleTalk, using protocol-dependent modules (PDM), as shown in Figure 9-7.

Figure 9-7   EIGRP Protocol-Dependent Modules

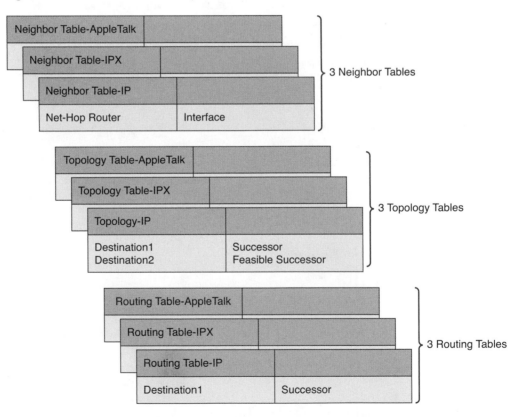

PDMs are responsible for the specific routing tasks for each network layer protocol.

For example:

- The IP-EIGRP module is responsible for sending and receiving EIGRP packets that are encapsulated in IP and for using DUAL to build and maintain the IP routing table. As you can see in Figure 9-7, EIGRP uses different EIGRP packets and maintains separate neighbor, topology, and routing tables for each network layer protocol.

- The IPX EIGRP module is responsible for exchanging routing information about IPX networks with other IPX EIGRP routers. IPX EIGRP and AppleTalk EIGRP are not included in this course.

RTP and EIGRP Packet Types

Reliable Transport Protocol (RTP) is the protocol used by EIGRP for the delivery and reception of EIGRP packets. EIGRP was designed as a network layer -independent routing protocol; therefore, it cannot use the services of UDP or TCP because IPX and AppleTalk do not use protocols from the TCP/IP protocol suite. Figure 9-8 shows conceptually how RTP operates.

Figure 9-8   EIGRP Replaces TCP with RTP

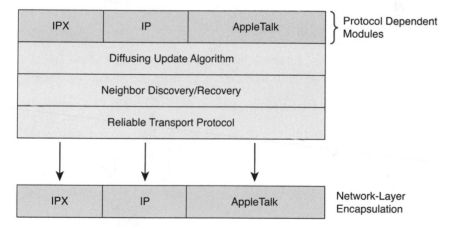

Although *reliable* is part of its name, RTP includes both reliable delivery and unreliable delivery of EIGRP packets, similar to TCP and UDP, respectively. Reliable RTP requires an acknowledgment to be returned by the receiver to the sender. An unreliable RTP packet does not require an acknowledgment.

RTP can send packets either as a unicast or a multicast. Multicast EIGRP packets use the reserved multicast address of 224.0.0.10.

EIGRP Packet Types

EIGRP uses five different packet types, some in pairs.

Figure 9-9 demonstrates an EIGRP hello packet traveling between EIGRP neighbors.

Figure 9-9   EIGRP Hello Packet

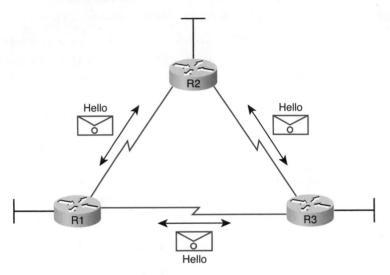

Hello packets are used by EIGRP to discover neighbors and to form adjacencies with those neighbors. EIGRP hello packets are multicasts and use unreliable delivery, so no response is required from the recipient. EIGRP hello packets are discussed in a later section.

In Figure 9-10, update packets are used by EIGRP to propagate routing information.

Figure 9-10   EIGRP Update and Acknowledgment Packets

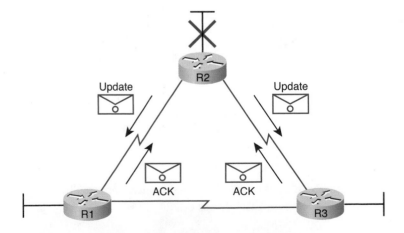

Unlike RIP, EIGRP does not send periodic updates. Update packets are sent only when necessary. EIGRP updates contain only the routing information needed (a change occurs) and are sent only to those routers that require it. EIGRP update packets use reliable delivery. Update packets are sent as a multicast when required by multiple routers, or as a unicast when required by only a single router. In Figure 9-10, because the links are point to point, the updates are sent as unicasts.

Acknowledgment (ACK) packets are sent by EIGRP when reliable delivery is used. RTP uses reliable delivery for EIGRP update, query, and reply packets. EIGRP acknowledgment packets are always sent as an unreliable unicast. EIGRP acknowledgment packets use unreliable delivery.

In Figure 9-10, Router R2 has lost connectivity to the LAN attached to its Fast Ethernet interface. R2 immediately sends a triggered update to R1 and R3 noting the downed route. R1 and R3 respond with an acknowledgment.

Figure 9-11 demonstrates query and reply packets used by DUAL when searching for networks and other tasks.

Figure 9-11   EIGRP Query and Reply Packets

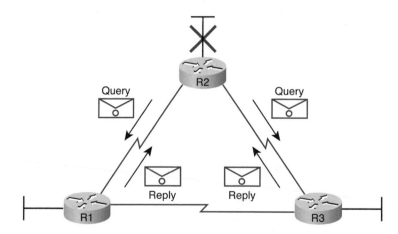

Query Packet

• Used by DUAL when searching for networks or other tasks. Reply packet.
• Automatically sent in response to query packet acknowledgement (ACK) packet.
• Automatically sent back when reliable RTP is used.

Queries and replies use reliable delivery. Queries can use multicast or unicast, whereas replies are always sent as unicast. DUAL is discussed in a later section. Query and reply packets are discussed in more detail in CCNP.

In Figure 9-11, R2 has lost connectivity to the LAN, and it sends out queries to all EIGRP neighbors searching for any possible routes to the LAN. Because queries use reliable delivery, the receiving router must return an EIGRP acknowledgment. (To keep this example simple, acknowledgments were omitted in the graphic.)

All neighbors must send a reply regardless of whether they have a route to the downed network. Because replies also use reliable delivery, routers, such as R2, must send an acknowledgment.

Note

You might be wondering why R2 would send out a query for a network it knows is down. Actually, only the interface attached to the network is down. Another router could be attached to the same LAN. Therefore, R2 queries for such a router before completely removing the network from its database.

Hello Protocol

Before any EIGRP packets can be exchanged between routers, EIGRP must first discover its neighbors. EIGRP neighbors are other routers running EIGRP on shared, directly connected networks.

EIGRP routers discover neighbors and establish adjacencies with neighbor routers using the hello packet. On most networks, EIGRP hello packets are sent every 5 seconds. On multipoint nonbroadcast multiaccess (NBMA) networks such as X.25, Frame Relay, and ATM interfaces with access links of T1 (1.544 Mbps) or slower, hellos are unicast every 60 seconds. An EIGRP router assumes that as long as it is receiving hello packets from a neighbor, the neighbor and its routes remain viable.

Hold time tells the router the maximum time the router should wait to receive the next hello before declaring that neighbor as unreachable. By default, the hold time is 3 times the hello interval, or 15 seconds on most networks and 180 seconds on low-speed NBMA networks. If the hold time expires, EIGRP declares the route as down, and DUAL searches for a new path in the topology table or by sending out queries.

Table 9-2 shows the default hello intervals and hold times for EIGRP.

Table 9-2   Default Hello Intervals and Hold Times for EIGRP

Bandwidth	Example Link	Default Hello Interval	Default Hold Time
1.544 Mbps or slower	Multipoint Frame Relay	60 seconds	180 seconds
Greater than 1.544 Mbps	T1, Ethernet	5 seconds	15 seconds

EIGRP Bounded Updates

EIGRP uses the terms *partial* and *bounded* when referring to its update packets. Unlike RIP, EIGRP does not send periodic updates. Instead, EIGRP sends its updates only when the metric for a route changes.

The term *partial* means that the update only includes information about the route changes. EIGRP sends these incremental updates when the state of a destination changes, instead of sending the entire contents of the routing table.

The term *bounded* refers to the propagation of partial updates sent only to those routers that are affected by the change. The partial update is automatically "bounded" so that only those routers that need the information are updated.

By sending only the routing information that is needed and only to those routers that need it, EIGRP minimizes the bandwidth required to send EIGRP packets.

DUAL: An Introduction

Diffusing Update Algorithm (DUAL) is the convergence algorithm used by EIGRP rather than the Bellman-Ford and Ford Fulkerson algorithms used by other distance vector routing protocols, such as RIP. DUAL is based on research conducted at SRI International, using calculations that were first proposed by E. W. Dijkstra and C. S. Scholten. The most prominent work with DUAL has been done by J. J. Garcia-Luna-Aceves.

Routing loops, even temporary ones, can be extremely detrimental to network performance. Distance vector routing protocols such as RIP prevent routing loops with hold-down timers and split horizon. Although EIGRP uses both of these techniques, it uses them somewhat differently; the primary way that EIGRP prevents routing loops is with the DUAL algorithm.

Figures 9-12 through 9-15 demonstrate the sequence of EIGRP updates, queries, replies, and acknowledgments used by DUAL when there is a change in the topology:

1. A directly connected network on R2 goes down. R2 sends an EIGRP update message to its neighbors indicating the network is down (see Figure 9-12).

2. R1 and R3 return an EIGRP acknowledgment indicating that they have received the update from R2 (see Figure 9-13).

3. R2 does not have an EIGRP backup route known as a feasible successor. (This will be explained later in the chapter.) So, R2 sends an EIGRP query to its neighbors asking them whether they have a route to this downed network.

4. R1 and R3 return an EIGRP acknowledgment indicating that they have received the query from R2 (see Figure 9-14).

Figure 9-12   DUAL Operation: R2 Sends Update

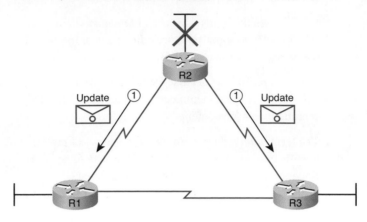

Figure 9-13   DUAL Operation: R1 and R3 Send Replies

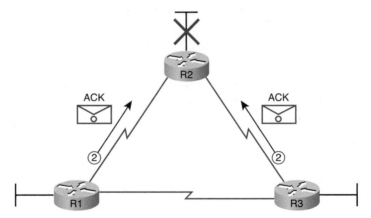

Figure 9-14   DUAL Operation: R2 Sends Queries; R1 and R3 Send Acknowledgments

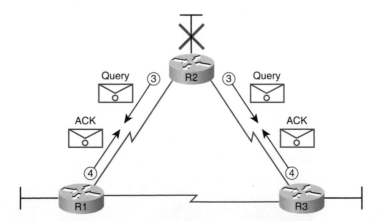

5. R1 and R3 send an EIGRP reply message in response to the query sent by R2. In this case, the query would state that the router does not have a route to this network.

6. R2 returns an acknowledgment indicating that it received the reply (see Figure 9-15).

Figure 9-15   DUAL Operation: R1 and R3 Send Replies; R2 Sends Acknowledgment

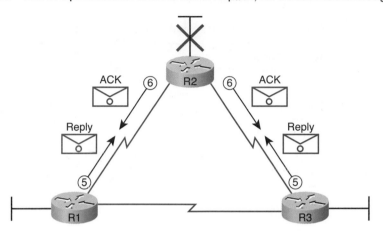

DUAL is used to obtain loop-freedom at every instant throughout a route computation. This allows all routers involved in a topology change to synchronize at the same time. Routers that are not affected by the topology changes are not involved in the recomputation. This method provides EIGRP with faster convergence times than other distance vector routing protocols.

The decision process for all route computations is done by the DUAL Finite State Machine. In general terms, a finite state machine (FSM) is a model of behavior composed of a finite number of states, transitions between those states, and events or actions that create the transitions.

The DUAL FSM tracks all routes, uses its metric to select efficient, loop-free paths, and selects the routes with the least-cost path to insert into the routing table. The DUAL FSM is discussed in more detail later in this chapter.

Because recomputation of DUAL can be processor intensive, it is advantageous to avoid recomputation whenever possible. Therefore, DUAL maintains a list of backup routes it has already determined to be loop-free. If the primary route in the routing table fails, the best backup route is immediately added to the routing table.

Administrative Distance

As you know from Chapter 3, "Introduction to Dynamic Routing Protocols," administrative distance (AD) is the trustworthiness (or preference) of the route source. EIGRP has a default AD of 90 for internal routes and 170 for routes imported from an external source, such as default routes. When compared to other interior gateway protocols (IGP), EIGRP is the most preferred by the Cisco IOS software because it has the lowest AD.

Notice in Table 9-3 that EIGRP has a third AD value, of 5, for summary routes. Later in this chapter, you learn how to configure EIGRP summary routes.

Table 9-3   Default Administrative Distances

Route Source	AD
Connected	0
Static	1
EIGRP summary route	5
External BGP	20
Internal EIGRP	90
IGRP	100
OSPF	110
IS-IS	115
RIP	120
External EIGRP	170
Internal BGP	200

Authentication

Like other routing protocols, EIGRP can be configured for authentication. RIPv2, EIGRP, Open Shortest Path First (OSPF) Protocol, Intermediate System–to–Intermediate System (IS-IS), and Border Gateway Protocol (BGP) can all be configured to encrypt and authenticate their routing information.

It is good practice to authenticate transmitted routing information. This practice ensures that routers will accept routing information only from other routers that have been configured with the same password or authentication information.

Note

When authentication is configured on a router, the router authenticates the source of each routing update packet that it receives. However, authentication does not encrypt the router's routing table.

As stated in previous chapters, configuring routing protocols to use authentication is discussed in a later course.

Basic EIGRP Configuration

This section discusses the basics of EIGRP configuration. There are many similarities with the commands used in configuring other routing protocols such as RIP.

EIGRP Network Topology

Figure 9-16 shows the topology from previous chapters, which now includes the addition of the ISP router. Table 9-4 shows the addressing scheme.

Figure 9-16   EIGRP Topology

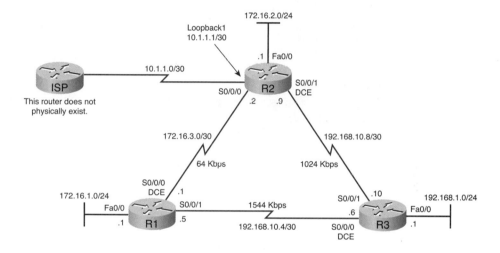

Table 9-4   Addressing Table for EIGRP

Device	Interface	IP Address	Subnet Mask
R1	Fa0/0	172.16.1.1	255.255.255.0
	S0/0/0	172.16.3.1	255.255.255.252
	S0/0/1	192.168.10.5	255.255.255.252
R2	Fa0/0	172.16.2.1	255.255.255.0
	S0/0/0	172.16.3.2	255.255.255.252
	S0/0/1	192.168.10.9	255.255.255.252
	Lo1	10.1.1.1	255.255.255.252
R3	Fa0/0	192.168.1.1	255.255.255.0
	S0/0/0	192.168.10.6	255.255.255.252
	S0/0/1	192.168.10.10	255.255.255.252

Notice that both the R1 and R2 routers have subnets that are part of the 172.16.0.0/16 classful network, a Class B address. The fact that 172.16.0.0 is a Class B address is only relevant because EIGRP automatically summarizes at classful boundaries, similar to RIP.

Examples 9-1, 9-2, and 9-3 show the starting configuration for R1, R2, and R3.

Example 9-1 R1 Starting Configuration

```
R1#show startup-config

<some output omitted>
!
hostname R1
!
interface FastEthernet0/0
 ip address 172.16.1.1 255.255.255.0
!
interface Serial0/0/0
 ip address 172.16.3.1 255.255.255.252
 clock rate 64000
!
interface Serial0/0/1
ip address 192.168.10.5 255.255.255.252
 !
end
```

Example 9-2 R2 Starting Configuration

```
R2#show startup-config

<some output omitted>
!
hostname R2
!
interface Loopback1
 ip address 10.1.1.1 255.255.255.252
 description Simulated ISP
!
interface FastEthernet0/0
 ip address 172.16.2.1 255.255.255.0
!
interface Serial0/0/0
 ip address 172.16.3.2 255.255.255.252
 !
```

```
interface Serial0/0/1
 ip address 192.168.10.9 255.255.255.252
 clockrate 64000
!
end
```

Example 9-3 R3 Starting Configuration

```
R3#show startup-config

<some output omitted>
!
hostname R3
!
interface FastEthernet0/0
 ip address 192.168.1.1 255.255.255.0
!
interface Serial0/0/0
 ip address 192.168.10.6 255.255.255.252
 clockrate 64000
!
interface Serial0/0/1
 ip address 192.168.10.10 255.255.255.252
!
end
```

Notice that the ISP router does not physically exist in our configurations. The connection between R2 and ISP is represented with a loopback interface on Router R2. The use of a loopback interface to represent the connection to ISP allows this scenario to be configured using only three routers. Remember from Chapter 7, "RIPv2," that a loopback interface can be used to represent an interface on a router that does not have an actual connection to a physical link on the network. You can verify a *loopback address* with the **ping** command included in routing updates.

Note

Loopback interfaces also have specific uses with some routing protocols, as you will see in Chapter 11, "OSPF."

Autonomous Systems and Process IDs

This section discusses the difference between an autonomous system and a process ID.

Autonomous System

An *autonomous system* is a collection of networks under the administrative control of a single entity that presents a common routing policy to the Internet. In Figure 9-17, Company A, B, C, and D are all under the administrative control of ISP1. ISP1 "presents a common routing policy" for all of these companies when advertising routes to ISP2.

Figure 9-17   Autonomous Systems

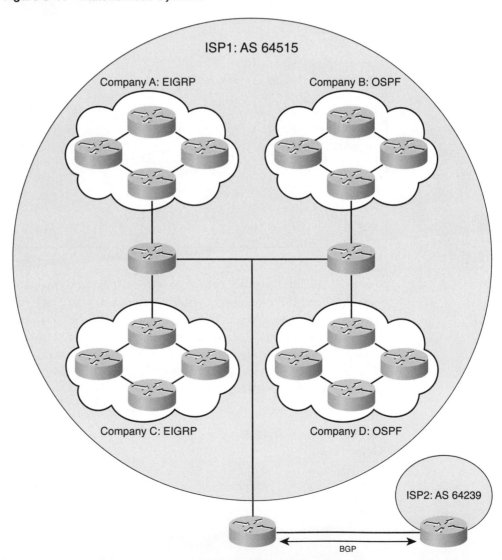

The guidelines for the creation, selection, and registration of an autonomous system are described in RFC 1930. Autonomous system numbers are assigned by the Internet Assigned Numbers Authority (IANA) and its Regional Internet Registries (RIR), the same authority that assigns IP address space. The local RIR is responsible for assigning an autonomous system number to an entity from its block of assigned autonomous system numbers. Before 2007, autonomous system numbers were 16-bit numbers, ranging from 0 to 65,535. Now 32-bit autonomous system numbers are assigned, increasing the number of available autonomous system numbers to more than 4 billion.

Who needs an autonomous system number? Usually, it is Internet service providers (ISPs), Internet backbone providers, and large institutions connecting to other entities that also have an autonomous system number. These ISPs and large institutions use the exterior gateway routing protocol BGP to propagate routing information. BGP is the only routing protocol that uses an actual autonomous system number in its configuration.

The vast majority of companies and institutions with IP networks do not need an autonomous system number because they come under the control of a larger entity such as an ISP. These companies use interior gateway protocols such as RIP, EIGRP, OSPF, and IS-IS to route packets within their own networks. They are one of many independent and separate networks within the autonomous system of the ISP. The ISP is responsible for the routing of packets within its autonomous system and between two other autonomous systems.

Process ID

Both EIGRP and OSPF use a process ID to represent an instance of their respective routing protocol running on the router:

```
Router(config)#router eigrp autonomous-system
```

Although EIGRP refers to the parameter as an "autonomous-system" number, it actually functions as a process ID. This number is not associated with an autonomous system number discussed previously and can be assigned any 16-bit value as demonstrated here:

```
Router(config)#router eigrp 1
```

The number 1 identifies the particular EIGRP process running on this router.

To establish neighbor adjacencies, EIGRP requires all routers in the same routing domain to be configured with the same process ID, as Figure 9-18 illustrates. Typically, only a single process ID of any routing protocol would be configured on a router.

> **Note**
>
> RIP does not use process IDs; therefore, it can support only a single instance of RIP. Both EIGRP and OSPF can support multiple instances of each routing protocol, although this type of multiple routing protocol implementation is not usually needed or recommended.

Figure 9-18   Single Process IDs

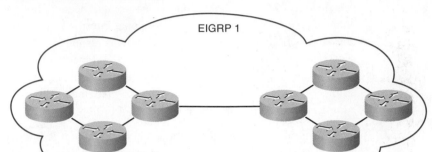

The router eigrp Command

The **router eigrp** *autonomous-system* global configuration command enables EIGRP. The autonomous system parameter is a number chosen by the network administrator between 1 and 65,535. The number chosen is the process ID number and is important because all routers in this EIGRP routing domain must use the same process ID number (autonomous system number).

As you can see from the router output in Example 9-4, EIGRP is enabled on all three routers using the process ID of 1.

Example 9-4   Enabling EIGRP Routing

```
R1(config)#router eigrp 1
R1(config-router)#
R2(config)#router eigrp 1
R2(config-router)#
R3(config)#router eigrp 1
R3(config-router)#
```

The network Command

The **network** command in EIGRP has the same function as in other IGP routing protocols:

- Any interface on this router that matches the network address in the **network** command will be enabled to send and receive EIGRP updates.

- This network (or subnet) will be included in EIGRP routing updates.

The **network** command is used in router configuration mode:

```
Router(config-router)#network network-address
```

The *network-address* is the classful network address for this interface. A single classful network statement is used on R1 to include both 172.16.1.0/24 and 172.16.3.0/30 subnets:

```
R1(config-router)#network 172.16.0.0
```

When EIGRP is configured on R2, DUAL sends a notification message to the console stating that a neighbor relationship with another EIGRP router has been established:

```
R2(config-router)#network 172.16.0.0
%DUAL-5-NBRCHANGE: IP-EIGRP 1: Neighbor 172.16.3.1 (Serial0/0) is up: new adjacency
```

This new *adjacency* happens automatically because both R1 and R2 are using the same EIGRP 1 routing process and both routers are now sending updates on the 172.16.0.0 network.

The network Command with a Wildcard Mask

By default, when the **network** command and a classful network address such as 172.16.0.0 are used, all interfaces on the router that belong to that classful network address will be enabled for EIGRP. However, there may be times when the network administrator does not want to include all interfaces within a network when enabling EIGRP. To configure EIGRP to advertise specific subnets only, use the *wildcard-mask* option with the network command:

```
Router(config-router)#network network-address [wildcard-mask]
```

Think of a *wildcard mask* as the inverse of a subnet mask. The inverse of subnet mask 255.255.255.252 is 0.0.0.3. To calculate the inverse of the subnet mask, subtract the subnet mask from 255.255.255.255:

```
   255.255.255.255
-  255.255.255.252  Subtract the subnet mask
   ——————-·
     0.  0.  0.  3  Wildcard mask
```

R2 is configured with the subnet 192.168.10.8 and the wildcard mask 0.0.0.3:

```
R2(config-router)#network 192.168.10.8 0.0.0.3
```

Some Cisco IOS software versions also let you just enter the subnet mask. For example, you might enter the following:

```
R2(config-router)#network 192.168.10.8 255.255.255.252
```

However, Cisco IOS software then converts the command to the wildcard mask format, as can be verified with the **show running-config** command shown in Example 9-5.

Example 9-5 Verifying EIGRP Configuration with **show run**

```
R2#show running-config
<some output omitted>
!
router eigrp 1
 network 172.16.0.0
 network 192.168.10.8 0.0.0.3
 auto-summary
!
```

Note

The **passive-interface** command should not be used with EIGRP. When the **passive-interface** command is configured, EIGRP stops sending hello packets on that interface. When this happens, the router is not able to form EIGRP neighbor adjacencies on that interface, and therefore is unable to send or receive routing updates.

Example 9-6 shows the configuration for R3. As soon as the classful network 192.168.10.0 is configured, R3 establishes adjacencies with both R1 and R2.

Example 9-6 EIGRP Configuration for R3

```
R3(config)#router eigrp 1
R3(config-router)#network 192.168.10.0
%DUAL-5-NBRCHANGE: IP-EIGRP 1: Neighbor 192.168.10.5 (Serial0/0/0) is up: new
  adjacency
R3(config-router)#
%DUAL-5-NBRCHANGE: IP-EIGRP 1: Neighbor 192.168.10.9 (Serial0/0/1) is up: new
  adjacency
R3(config-router)#network 192.168.1.0
```

Verifying EIGRP

Before any updates can be sent or received by EIGRP, routers must establish adjacencies with their neighbors. EIGRP routers establish adjacencies with neighbor routers by exchanging EIGRP hello packets.

Use the **show ip eigrp neighbors** command to view the neighbor table and verify that EIGRP has established an adjacency with its neighbors. For each router, you should be able to see the IP address of the adjacent router and the interface that this router uses to reach that EIGRP neighbor. Figure 9-19 shows how to use the **show ip eigrp neighbors** command to verify that R2 has established the necessary adjacencies with R1 and R3. If you were to enter the same command on R1 and R3, you would see that each router has two neighbors listed in the neighbor table.

Figure 9-19   Neighbor Table

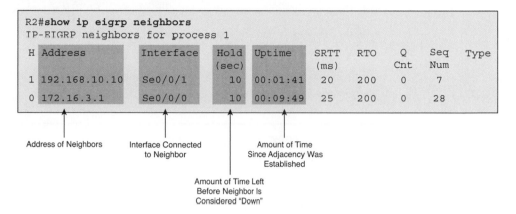

The output from the **show ip eigrp neighbors** command includes the following:

- **H column:** Lists the neighbors in the order they were learned.

- **Address:** The IP address of the neighbor.

- **Interface:** The local interface on which this hello packet was received.

- **Hold:** The current hold time. Whenever a hello packet is received, this value is reset to the maximum hold time for that interface and then counts down to zero. If zero is reached, the neighbor is considered "down."

- **Uptime:** Amount of time since this neighbor was added to the neighbor table.

- **SRTT (Smooth Round Trip Timer) and RTO (Retransmit Interval):** Used by RTP to manage reliable EIGRP packets. SRTT and RTO are discussed further in CCNP courses.

- **Queue Count:** Should always be zero. If more than zero, EIGRP packets are waiting to be sent. Queue count is discussed further in CCNP courses.

- **Sequence Number:** Used to track updates, queries, and reply packets. Sequence numbers are discussed further in CCNP courses.

The **show ip eigrp neighbors** command is very useful for verifying and troubleshooting EIGRP. If a neighbor is not listed after adjacencies have been established with a router's neighbors, check the local interface to make sure it is activated with the **show ip interface brief** command. If the interface is active, try pinging the IP address of the neighbor. If the ping fails, it means that the neighbor interface is down and needs to be activated. If the ping is successful and EIGRP still does not see the router as a neighbor, examine the following configurations:

- Are both routers configured with the same EIGRP process ID?

- Is the directly connected network included in the EIGRP **network** statements?

- Is the **passive-interface** command inappropriately configured, thus preventing EIGRP hello packets on the interface?

As with RIP, you can use the **show ip protocols** command to verify that EIGRP is enabled, as demonstrated in Example 9-7.

Example 9-7 show ip protocols Command

```
R1#show ip protocols
Routing Protocol is "eigrp 1"
  Outgoing update filter list for all interfaces is not set
  Incoming update filter list for all interfaces is not set
  Default networks flagged in outgoing updates
  Default networks accepted from incoming updates
  EIGRP metric weight K1=1, K2=0, K3=1, K4=0, K5=0
  EIGRP maximum hopcount 100
  EIGRP maximum metric variance 1
  Redistributing: eigrp 1
  Automatic network summarization is in effect
  Automatic address summarization:
    192.168.10.0/24 for FastEthernet0/0, Serial0/0/0
      Summarizing with metric 2169856
    172.16.0.0/16 for Serial0/0/1
      Summarizing with metric 28160
  Maximum path: 4
  Routing for Networks:
    172.16.0.0
    192.168.10.0
  Routing Information Sources:
    Gateway         Distance      Last Update
    (this router)         90      00:03:29
    192.168.10.6          90      00:02:09
    Gateway         Distance      Last Update
    172.16.3.2            90      00:02:12
  Distance: internal 90 external 170
```

The **show ip protocols** command displays different types of output specific to each routing protocol.

Notice that the output specifies the process ID used by EIGRP:

```
Routing Protocol is "eigrp 1"
```

Remember, the process ID must be the same on all routers for EIGRP to establish neighbor adjacencies and share routing information.

EIGRP's internal and external ADs are also displayed:

```
Distance: internal 90 external 170
```

Examining the Routing Table

Another way to verify that EIGRP and other functions of the router are configured properly is to examine the routing tables with the **show ip route** command.

Examples 9-8, 9-9, and 9-10 show the routing tables for R1, R2, and R3.

Example 9-8 R1 Routing Table

```
R1#show ip route
Codes: C - connected, S - static, I - IGRP, R - RIP, M - mobile, B - BGP
       D - EIGRP, EX - EIGRP external, O - OSPF, IA - OSPF inter area
       N1 - OSPF NSSA external type 1, N2 - OSPF NSSA external type 2
<Output omitted>

Gateway of last resort is not set

     192.168.10.0/24 is variably subnetted, 3 subnets, 2 masks
D       192.168.10.0/24 is a summary, 00:03:50, Null0
C       192.168.10.4/30 is directly connected, Serial0/0/1
D       192.168.10.8/30 [90/2681856] via 192.168.10.6, 00:02:43, Serial0/0/1
     172.16.0.0/16 is variably subnetted, 4 subnets, 3 masks
D       172.16.0.0/16 is a summary, 00:10:52, Null0
C       172.16.1.0/24 is directly connected, FastEthernet0/0
D       172.16.2.0/24 [90/2172416] via 172.16.3.2, 00:10:47, Serial0/0/0
C       172.16.3.0/30 is directly connected, Serial0/0/0
D    192.168.1.0/24 [90/2172416] via 192.168.10.6, 00:02:31, Serial0/0/1
```

Example 9-9 R2 Routing Table

```
R2#show ip route
<Output omitted>

Gateway of last resort is not set

     192.168.10.0/24 is variably subnetted, 3 subnets, 2 masks
D       192.168.10.0/24 is a summary, 00:04:13, Null0
D       192.168.10.4/30 [90/2681856] via 192.168.10.10, 00:03:05, Serial0/0/1
C       192.168.10.8/30 is directly connected, Serial0/0/1
     172.16.0.0/16 is variably subnetted, 4 subnets, 3 masks
D       172.16.0.0/16 is a summary, 00:04:07, Null0
D       172.16.1.0/24 [90/2172416] via 172.16.3.1, 00:11:11, Serial0/0/0
C       172.16.2.0/24 is directly connected, FastEthernet0/0
C       172.16.3.0/30 is directly connected, Serial0/0/0
     10.0.0.0/30 is subnetted, 1 subnets
C       10.1.1.0 is directly connected, Loopback1
D    192.168.1.0/24 [90/2172416] via 192.168.10.10, 00:02:54, Serial0/0/1
```

Example 9-10   R3 Routing Table

```
R3#show ip route
<Output omitted>

Gateway of last resort is not set

     192.168.10.0/24 is variably subnetted, 3 subnets, 2 masks
D       192.168.10.0/24 is a summary, 00:03:11, Null0
C       192.168.10.4/30 is directly connected, Serial0/0/0
C       192.168.10.8/30 is directly connected, Serial0/0/1
D    172.16.0.0/16 [90/2172416] via 192.168.10.5, 00:03:23, Serial0/0/0
                    [90/2172416] via 192.168.10.9, 00:03:23, Serial0/0/1
C    192.168.1.0/24 is directly connected, FastEthernet0/0
```

By default, EIGRP automatically summarizes routes at the major network boundary. You can disable the automatic summarization with the **no auto-summary** command, just as you can for RIPv2.

Notice that EIGRP routes are denoted in the routing table with a D, which stands for DUAL.

Remember, because EIGRP is a classless routing protocol (includes the subnet mask in the routing update), it supports variable-length subnet masks (VLSM) and classless interdomain routing (CIDR). You can see in the routing table for R1 that the 172.16.0.0/16 parent network is variably subnetted with three child routes using either a /24 or /30 mask.

Introducing the Null0 Summary Route

Example 9-11 shows the routing table for R2 with two entries highlighted. Notice that EIGRP has automatically included a summary route to Null0 for the classful networks 192.168.10.0/24 and 172.16.0.0/16.

Example 9-11   R2 Routing Table with Null0 Summary Routes

```
R2#show ip route
<Output omitted>

Gateway of last resort is not set

     192.168.10.0/24 is variably subnetted, 3 subnets, 2 masks
D       192.168.10.0/24 is a summary, 00:04:13, Null0
D       192.168.10.4/30 [90/2681856] via 192.168.10.10, 00:03:05, Serial0/0/1
C       192.168.10.8/30 is directly connected, Serial0/0/1
     172.16.0.0/16 is variably subnetted, 4 subnets, 3 masks
D       172.16.0.0/16 is a summary, 00:04:07, Null0
D       172.16.1.0/24 [90/2172416] via 172.16.3.1, 00:11:11, Serial0/0/0
C       172.16.2.0/24 is directly connected, FastEthernet0/0
C       172.16.3.0/30 is directly connected, Serial0/0/0
     10.0.0.0/30 is subnetted, 1 subnets
C       10.1.1.0 is directly connected, Loopback1
D    192.168.1.0/24 [90/2172416] via 192.168.10.10, 00:02:54, Serial0/0/1
```

Remember from Chapter 7 that Null0 is not an actual interface. Notice that the summary routes are sourced from Null0; this is because these routes are used for advertisement purposes. The 192.168.10.0/24 and 172.16.0.0/16 routes do not actually represent a path to reach the parent networks. If a packet does not match one of the level 2 child routes, it is sent to the Null0 interface. In other words, if the packet matches the level 1 parent (the classful network address), but none of the subnets, the packet is discarded.

Note

EIGRP automatically includes a Null0 summary route as a child route whenever both of the following conditions exist:

- There is at least one subnet that was learned via EIGRP.
- Automatic summarization is enabled.

You will see that the Null0 summary route is removed when automatic summary is disabled.

R3 Routing Table

The routing table for R3 in Example 9-12 shows that both R1 and R2 are automatically summarizing the 172.16.0.0/16 network and sending it as a single routing update. R1 and R2 are not propagating the individual subnets because of automatic summarization. We will turn off automatic summarization later. Because R3 is getting two equal-cost routes for 172.16.0.0/16 from both R1 and R2, both routes are included in the routing table.

Example 9-12   R3 Routing Table with Summarized 172.16.0.0/16

```
R3#show ip route
<Output omitted>

Gateway of last resort is not set

     192.168.10.0/24 is variably subnetted, 3 subnets, 2 masks
D       192.168.10.0/24 is a summary, 00:03:11, Null0
C       192.168.10.4/30 is directly connected, Serial0/0/0
C       192.168.10.8/30 is directly connected, Serial0/0/1
D    172.16.0.0/16 [90/2172416] via 192.168.10.5, 00:03:23, Serial0/0/0
                    [90/2172416] via 192.168.10.9, 00:03:23, Serial0/0/1
C    192.168.1.0/24 is directly connected, FastEthernet0/0
```

Configure and Verify EIGRP Routing (9.2.6)

Use the Packet Tracer Activity to configure and verify basic EIGRP routing. Detailed instructions are provided within the activity. Use file e2-926.pka on the CD-ROM that accompanies this book to perform this activity using Packet Tracer.

EIGRP Metric Calculation

Remember from Chapter 5, "RIP Version 1" that RIP uses hop count as its metric. Although EIGRP includes hop count in its routing updates, hop count is not used as part of the EIGRP composite metric. This section examines the values used in the EIGRP metric and how EIGRP performs the calculation to arrive at the metric displayed in the routing table.

EIGRP Composite Metric and the K Values

EIGRP uses the following values in its composite metric to calculate the preferred path to a network:

- Bandwidth

- Delay

- Reliability

- Load

Note

As mentioned earlier in this chapter, although MTU is included in the routing table updates, it is not a routing metric used by EIGRP or IGRP. By default, only bandwidth and delay are used to calculate the metric. Cisco recommends that reliability and load are not used unless the administrator has an explicit need to do so.

The Composite Metric

Figure 9-20 shows the composite metric formula used by EIGRP. The formula consists of values K1 through K5, known as *EIGRP metric weights*. By default, K1 and K3 are set to 1, and K2, K4, and K5 are set to 0. The result is that only the bandwidth and delay values are used in the computation of the default composite metric.

Figure 9-20   EIGRP Composite Metric

Default Composite Formula:
metric = [K1*bandwidth + K3*delay]

Complete Composite Formula:
metric = [K1*bandwidth + (K2*bandwidth)/(256 – load) + K3*delay] * [K5/(reliability + K4)]
(Not used if "K" values are 0)

Default Values:
K1 (bandwidth) = 1
K2 (load) = 0
K3 (delay) = 1
K4 (reliability) = 0
K5 (reliability) = 0

"K" values can be changed with the **metric weights** command.

```
Router(config-router)#metric weights tos k1 k2 k3 k4 k5
```

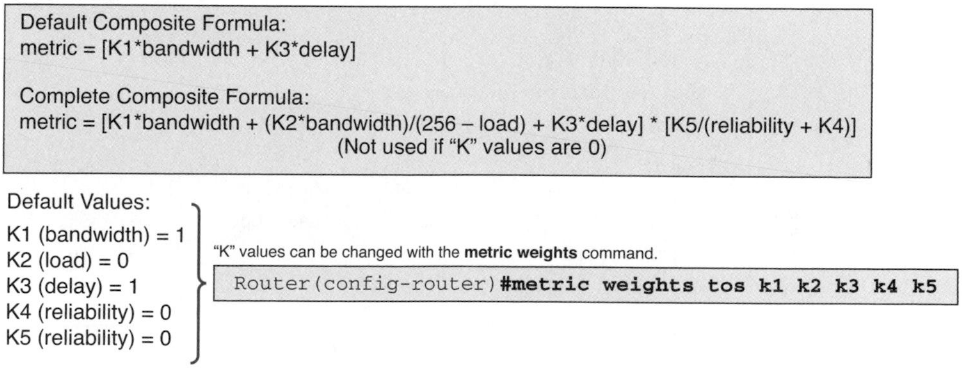

The default K values can be changed with the following EIGRP router command:

```
Router(config-router)#metric weights tos k1 k2 k3 k4 k5
```

Note

Modifying the metric weights is beyond the scope of this course, but their relevance is important in establishing neighbors and is discussed in a later section. The **tos** (type of service) value is left over from IGRP and was never implemented. The **tos** value is always set to 0.

Verifying the K Values

The **show ip protocols** command is used to verify the K values, as demonstrated in Example 9-13 for Router R1. Notice that the K values on R1 are set to the default. Again, changing these values to other than the default is not recommended unless the network administrator has a very good reason to do so.

Example 9-13   Verifying K Values with the **show ip protocols** Command

```
R1#show ip protocols
Routing Protocol is "eigrp 1"
  Outgoing update filter list for all interfaces is not set
  Incoming update filter list for all interfaces is not set
  Default networks flagged in outgoing updates
  Default networks accepted from incoming updates
  EIGRP metric weight K1=1, K2=0, K3=1, K4=0, K5=0
  EIGRP maximum hopcount 100
  EIGRP maximum metric variance 1
  Redistributing: eigrp 1
  Automatic network summarization is in effect
  Automatic address summarization:
    192.168.10.0/24 for FastEthernet0/0, Serial0/0/0
      Summarizing with metric 2169856
    172.16.0.0/16 for Serial0/0/1
      Summarizing with metric 28160
  Maximum path: 4
  Routing for Networks:
    172.16.0.0
    192.168.10.0
  Routing Information Sources:
    Gateway         Distance      Last Update
    (this router)         90      00:03:29
    192.168.10.6          90      00:02:09
    Gateway         Distance      Last Update
    172.16.3.2            90      00:02:12
  Distance: internal 90 external 170
```

EIGRP Metrics

The EIGRP composite metric consists of bandwidth, delay, reliability, and load. This section discusses how to display and interpret these interface values.

Examining the Metric Values

You now know the defaults for the K values. By using the **show interface** command, you can examine the actual values used for bandwidth, delay, reliability, and load in the computation of the routing metric.

The output in Example 9-14 highlights the values used in the composite metric for the serial 0/0/0 interface on R1.

Example 9-14   Verifying Metric Values with the **show interface** Command

```
R1#show interface serial 0/0/0
Serial0/0/0 is up, line protocol is up
  Hardware is GT96K Serial
  Description: Link to R2
  Internet address is 172.16.3.1/30
  MTU 1500 bytes, BW 1544 Kbit, DLY 20000 usec,
     reliability 255/255, txload 1/255, rxload 1/255
  Encapsulation HDLC, loopback not set
  Keepalive set (10 sec)
  Last input 00:00:00, output 00:00:01, output hang never
  Last clearing of "show interface" counters 3d22h
  Input queue: 0/75/0/0 (size/max/drops/flushes); Total output drops: 0
  Queueing strategy: fifo
  Output queue: 0/40 (size/max)
  5 minute input rate 0 bits/sec, 0 packets/sec
  5 minute output rate 0 bits/sec, 0 packets/sec
     112522 packets input, 7303722 bytes, 0 no buffer
     Received 40016 broadcasts, 0 runts, 0 giants, 0 throttles
     0 input errors, 0 CRC, 0 frame, 0 overrun, 0 ignored, 0 abort
     112601 packets output, 7280131 bytes, 0 underruns
     0 output errors, 0 collisions, 2 interface resets
     0 output buffer failures, 0 output buffers swapped out
     12 carrier transitions
     DCD=up  DSR=up  DTR=up  RTS=up  CTS=up
```

Bandwidth

The bandwidth metric (1544 Kbps) is a static value used by some routing protocols such as EIGRP and OSPF to calculate their routing metric. The bandwidth is displayed in kilobits per second (Kbps):

```
MTU 1500 bytes, BW 1544 Kbit, DLY 20000 usec,
   reliability 255/255, txload 1/255, rxload 1/255
```

Most serial interfaces use the default bandwidth value of 1544 Kbps or 1,544,000 bps (1.544 Mbps). This is the bandwidth of a T1 connection. However, some serial interfaces use a different default bandwidth value. Always verify bandwidth with the **show interface** command.

The value of the bandwidth might or might not reflect the actual physical bandwidth of the interface. Modifying the bandwidth value does not change the actual bandwidth of the link. If actual bandwidth of the link differs from the default bandwidth value, you should modify the bandwidth value, as you will see in a later section.

Delay

Delay is a measure of the time it takes for a packet to traverse a route. The delay (DLY) metric is a static value based on the type of link to which the interface is connected and is expressed in microseconds:

```
MTU 1500 bytes, BW 1544 Kbit, DLY 20000 usec,
    reliability 255/255, txload 1/255, rxload 1/255
```

Delay is not measured dynamically. In other words, the router does not actually track how long packets are taking to reach the destination. The delay value, much like the bandwidth value, is a default value that can be changed by the network administrator.

Table 9-5 shows the default delay values for various interfaces. Notice that the default value is 20,000 microseconds for serial interfaces and 100 microseconds for Fast Ethernet interfaces.

Table 9-5   Default Values in Microseconds

Media	Delay (in μs)
100M ATM	100
Fast Ethernet	100
FDDI	100
HSSI	20,000
16M *Token Ring*	630
Ethernet	1,000
T1 (Serial Default)	20,000
512K	20,000
DS0	20,000
56K	20,000

Reliability

Reliability is a measure of the probability that the link will fail or how often the link has experienced errors. Unlike delay, reliability is measured dynamically with a value between 0 and 255, with 1 being a minimally reliable link and 255 being 100 percent reliable. Reliability is calculated on a 5-minute weighted average to avoid the sudden impact of high (or low) error rates:

```
MTU 1500 bytes, BW 1544 Kbit, DLY 20000 usec,
    reliability 255/255, txload 1/255, rxload 1/255
```

Reliability is expressed as a fraction of 255; the higher the value, the more reliable the link. So, 255/255 would be 100 percent reliable, whereas a link of 234/255 would be 91.8 percent reliable.

Remember that by default EIGRP does not use reliability in its metric calculation.

Load

Load reflects the amount of traffic using the link. Like reliability, load is measured dynamically with a value between 0 and 255:

```
MTU 1500 bytes, BW 1544 Kbit, DLY 20000 usec,
    reliability 255/255, txload 1/255, rxload 1/255
```

Similar to reliability, load is expressed as a fraction of 255. However, in this case, a lower load value is more desirable because it indicates less load on the link. So, 1/255 would be a minimally loaded link. 40/255 is a link at 16 percent capacity, and 255/255 is a link that is 100 percent saturated.

Load is displayed as both an outbound, or transmit, load value (txload) and an inbound, or receive, load value (rxload). This value is calculated on a 5-minute weighted average to avoid the sudden impact of high (or low) channel usage.

Remember that by default EIGRP does not use load in its metric calculation.

Using the bandwidth Command

On most serial links, the bandwidth metric defaults to 1544 Kbps. Because both EIGRP and OSPF use bandwidth in default metric calculations, a correct value for bandwidth is very important to the accuracy of routing information. But, what do you do if the actual bandwidth of the link does not match the default bandwidth of the interface?

Use the interface command **bandwidth** to modify the bandwidth metric:

```
Router(config-if)#bandwidth kilobits
```

Use the interface command **no bandwidth** to restore the default value.

In the chapter topology shown earlier in Figure 9-16, the link between R1 and R2 has a bandwidth of 64 Kbps, and the link between R2 and R3 has a bandwidth of 1024 Kbps. Example 9-15 shows the configurations used on all three routers to modify the bandwidth on the appropriate serial interfaces.

Example 9-15   bandwidth Command

```
R1(config)#inter s 0/0/0
R1(config-if)#bandwidth 64
R2(config)#inter s 0/0/0
R2(config-if)#bandwidth 64
R2(config)#inter s 0/0/1
R2(config-if)#bandwidth 1024
R3(config)#inter s 0/0/1
R3(config-if)#bandwidth 1024
```

You can verify the change using the **show interface** command, as demonstrated in Example 9-16. It is important to modify the bandwidth metric on both sides of the link to ensure proper routing in both directions.

Example 9-16   Verifying the Bandwidth Value

```
R2#show interface serial 0/0/0
Serial0/0/0 is up, line protocol is up
  Hardware is PowerQUICC Serial
  Internet address is 172.16.3.2/30
  MTU 1500 bytes, BW 64 Kbit, DLY 20000 usec,
     reliability 255/255, txload 1/255, rxload 1/255
  Encapsulation HDLC, loopback not set
<some output omitted>
R2#show interface serial 0/0/1
Serial0/0/1 is up, line protocol is up
  Hardware is PowerQUICC Serial
  Internet address is 192.168.10.9/30
  MTU 1500 bytes, BW 1024 Kbit, DLY 20000 usec,
     reliability 255/255, txload 1/255, rxload 1/255
  Encapsulation HDLC, loopback not set
```

Calculating the EIGRP Metric

Figure 9-21 shows the composite metric used by EIGRP. Using the default values for K1 and K3, you can simplify this calculation to the slowest bandwidth (or minimum bandwidth) plus the cumulative sum of all the delays.

Figure 9-21   Calculating the EIGRP Default Metric

```
Default metric = [K1*bandwidth + K3*delay] * 256

Because both K1 and K3 equal 1, the formula simplifies to: bandwidth + delay

bandwidth = speed of slowest link in route to the destination
      delay = sum of delays of each link in route to the destination
```

```
Slowest bandwidth:               (10,000,000/bandwidth kbps) * 256
Plus the sum of the delays: + (sum of delay/10) * 256
                            = EIGRP metric
```

```
R2#show ip route
<output omitted>

D   192.168.1.0/24 [90/3014400] via 192.168.10.10, 00:02:14, Serial0/0/1
```

In other words, by examining the bandwidth and delay values for all the outgoing interfaces of the route, you can determine the EIGRP metric:

How To

Step 1.   Determine the link with the slowest bandwidth. That bandwidth is used for the (10,000,000/bandwidth) * 256 portion of the formula.

Step 2.   Determine the delay value for each outgoing interface on the way to the destination.

Step 3.   Sum the delay values and divide by 10 (sum of delay/10), and then multiply by 256 (* 256).

Step 4.   Add the bandwidth and sum of delay values to obtain the EIGRP metric.

The routing table output for R2 shows that the route to 192.168.1.0/24 has an EIGRP metric of 3,014,400. Let's see exactly how EIGRP calculated this value.

Bandwidth

Example 9-17 displays partial output from the **show interface** commands for R1 and R3.

Example 9-17   Finding the Slowest Bandwidth and Summing the Delays

```
R2#show inter ser 0/0/1
Serial0/0/1 is up, line protocol is up
  Hardware is PowerQUICC Serial
  Internet address is 192.168.10.9/30
  MTU 1500 bytes, BW 1024 Kbit, DLY 20000 usec,
     reliability 255/255, txload 1/255, rxload 1/255
  Encapsulation HDLC, loopback not set
<remaining output omitted>
```
```
R3#show inter fa 0/0
FastEthernet0/0 is up, line protocol is up
  Hardware is AmdFE, address is 0002.b9ee.5ee0 (bia 0002.b9ee.5ee0)
  Internet address is 192.168.1.1/24
  MTU 1500 bytes, BW 100000 Kbit, DLY 100 usec,
     reliability 255/255, txload 1/255, rxload 1/255
  Encapsulation ARPA, loopback not set
<remaining output omitted>
```

Because EIGRP uses the slowest bandwidth in its metric calculation, you can find the slowest bandwidth by examining each interface between R2 and the destination network 192.168.1.0. The serial 0/0/1 interface on R2 has a bandwidth of 1024 Kbps, or 1,024,000 bps. The Fast Ethernet 0/0 interface on R3 has a bandwidth of 100,000 Kbps, or 100 Mbps. Therefore, the slowest bandwidth is 1024 Kbps and is used in the calculation of the metric.

EIGRP takes the *reference bandwidth* value of 10,000,000 and divides it by the bandwidth value in kilobits per second. This will result in higher bandwidth values receiving a lower metric and lower bandwidth values receiving a higher metric.

The value of 10,000,000 is divided by 1024. If the result is not a whole number, the value is rounded down. In this case, 10,000,000 divided by 1024 equals 9765.625. The .625 is dropped before multiplying by 256. The bandwidth portion of the composite metric is 2,499,840.

Delay

Using the same outgoing interfaces and the output shown in Example 9-17, you can also determine the delay value.

EIGRP uses the cumulative sum of delay metrics of all the outgoing interfaces. The serial 0/0/1 interface on R2 has a delay of 20,000 microseconds. The Fast Ethernet 0/0 interface on R3 has a delay of 100 microseconds.

Each delay value is divided by 10 and then summed: 20,000/10 + 100/10 results in a value of 2010. This result is then multiplied by 256. The delay portion of the composite metric is 514,560.

Adding Bandwidth and Delay

Simply add the two values together, 2,499,840 + 514,560, to obtain the EIGRP metric of 3,014,400. This value matches the value shown in the routing table for R2. This is a result of the slowest bandwidth and the sum of the delays

Example 9-18 shows the route entry for 192.168.1.0/24 and its EIGRP metric of 3,014,400.

```
Example 9-18    Adding Bandwidth and Delay
R2#show ip route
<code output omitted>


Gateway of last resort is not set


     192.168.10.0/24 is variably subnetted, 3 subnets, 2 masks
D        192.168.10.0/24 is a summary, 00:00:15, Null0
D        192.168.10.4/30 [90/21024000] via 192.168.10.10, 00:00:15, Serial0/0/1
C        192.168.10.8/30 is directly connected, Serial0/0/1
     172.16.0.0/16 is variably subnetted, 4 subnets, 3 masks
D        172.16.0.0/16 is a summary, 00:00:15, Null0
D        172.16.1.0/24 [90/40514560] via 172.16.3.1, 00:00:15, Serial0/0/0
C        172.16.2.0/24 is directly connected, FastEthernet0/0
C        172.16.3.0/30 is directly connected, Serial0/0/0
     10.0.0.0/30 is subnetted, 1 subnets
C        10.1.1.0 is directly connected, Loopback1
D    192.168.1.0/24 [90/3014400] via 192.168.10.10, 00:00:15, Serial0/0/1
```

Packet Tracer
☐ Activity

Calculating the EIGRP Metric (9.3.4)

The purpose of this lab is to modify the EIGRP metric formula. The EIGRP metric formula consists of values K1 through K5, known as EIGRP metric weights. By default, K1 and K3 are set to 1 and K2, K4, and K5 are set to 0. The result is that only the bandwidth and delay are used to compute the default composite metric. Detailed instructions are provided within the activity. Use file e2-934.pka on the CD-ROM that accompanies this book to perform this activity using Packet Tracer.

DUAL

As stated in a previous section, the Diffusing Update Algorithm is the algorithm used by EIGRP. This section discusses how DUAL determines the best loop-free path and loop-free backup paths.

DUAL Concepts

DUAL provides the following:

- Loop-free paths
- Loop-free backup paths, which can be used immediately
- Fast convergence
- Minimum bandwidth usage with bounded updates

DUAL uses several terms that are discussed in more detail throughout this section:

- Successor
- Feasible distance
- Feasible successor
- Reported distance or advertised distance
- Feasible condition or feasibility condition

These terms and concepts are at the center of DUAL's loop-avoidance mechanism. The sections that follow examine them in more depth.

Successor and Feasible Distance

A *successor* is a neighboring router that is used for packet forwarding and is the least-cost route to the destination network. The IP address of a successor is shown in a routing table entry right after the word *via*.

Feasible distance (FD) is the lowest calculated metric to reach the destination network. FD is the metric listed in the routing table entry as the second number inside the brackets. As with other routing protocols, this is also known as the metric for the route.

Examining the routing table for R2 in Example 9-19, you can see that EIGRP's best path for the 192.168.1.0/24 network is through router R3, the successor for the route. The FD is 3014400—the same metric calculated in the previous topic.

Example 9-19   Feasible Distance and Successor

```
R2#show ip route
<code output omitted>

Gateway of last resort is not set

     192.168.10.0/24 is variably subnetted, 3 subnets, 2 masks
D       192.168.10.0/24 is a summary, 00:00:15, Null0
D       192.168.10.4/30 [90/21024000] via 192.168.10.10, 00:00:15, Serial0/0/1
C       192.168.10.8/30 is directly connected, Serial0/0/1
     172.16.0.0/16 is variably subnetted, 4 subnets, 3 masks
D       172.16.0.0/16 is a summary, 00:00:15, Null0
D       172.16.1.0/24 [90/40514560] via 172.16.3.1, 00:00:15, Serial0/0/0
C       172.16.2.0/24 is directly connected, FastEthernet0/0
C       172.16.3.0/30 is directly connected, Serial0/0/0
     10.0.0.0/30 is subnetted, 1 subnets
C       10.1.1.0 is directly connected, Loopback1
D    192.168.1.0/24 [90/3014400] via 192.168.10.10, 00:00:15, Serial0/0/1
```

Other successors and FDs are also shown in the routing table. Can you answer the following questions?

What is the IP address of the successor for network 172.16.1.0/24?

Answer: 172.16.3.1, which is R1

What is the feasible distance to 172.16.1.0/24?

Answer: 40514560.

Feasible Successors, Feasibility Condition, and Reported Distance

One of the reasons DUAL can converge quickly after a change in the topology is because it can use backup paths to other routers known as feasible successors without having to recompute DUAL.

Examine the feasible successor in Figure 9-22.

Figure 9-22 Finding the Feasible Successor

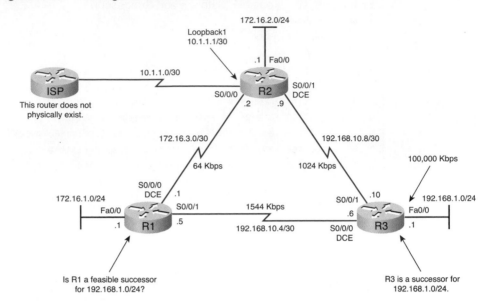

A *feasible successor (FS)* is a neighbor who has a loop-free backup path to the same network as the successor by satisfying the feasibility condition. In the topology, would R2 consider R1 to be a feasible successor to network 192.168.1.0/24? To be a feasible successor, R1 must satisfy the *feasibility condition (FC)*.

The FC is met when a neighbor's *reported distance (RD)* to a network is less than the local router's FD to the same destination network. The reported distance or advertised distance is simply an EIGRP neighbor's FD to the same destination network. The RD is the metric that a router reports to a neighbor about its own cost to that network.

If R3 is the successor, can the neighbor R1 be an FC to this same 192.161.0/24 network? In other words, if the link between R2 and R3 fails, can R1 immediately be used as a backup path without a recomputation of DUAL? R1 can only be an FS if it meets the FC (see Figure 9-23).

Example 9-20 shows R1's routing table entry for network 192.168.1.0. R1 is reporting to R2 that its FD to 192.168.1.0/24 is 2172416. From R2's perspective, 2172416 is R1's RD. From R1's perspective, 2172416 is its FD.

Figure 9-23   Determining the Feasible Successor

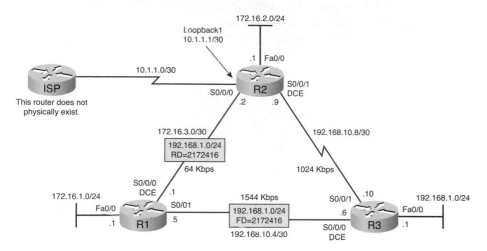

Example 9-20   R1's Feasible Distance Is the Reported Distance to R2

```
R1#show ip route
<output omitted>


D     192.168.1.0/24 [90/2172416] via 192.168.10.6, 01:12:26, Serial0/0/1
```

R2 examines the RD of 2172416 from R1. Because the RD of R1 is less than R2's own FD of 3014400, R1 meets the feasibility condition. R1 is now an FS for R2 to the 192.168.1.0/24 network.

Why isn't R1 the successor if its RD is less than R2's FD to 192.168.1.0/24? Because of the total cost for R2, its FD to reach 192.168.1.0/24 is greater through R1 than it is through R3. In other words, the total cost for R2 to reach the 192.168.1.0/24 network is a better, smaller metric through R3 than it is through R1.

Topology Table: Successor and Feasible Successor

The successor, FD, and any FSs with their RDs are kept by a router in its EIGRP topology table or *topology database*. As shown in the Example 9-21, you can display the topology table by using the **show ip eigrp topology** command.

Example 9-21   show ip eigrp topology Command

```
R2#show ip eigrp topology
IP-EIGRP Topology Table for AS(1)/ID(10.1.1.1)


Codes: P - Passive, A - Active, U - Update, Q - Query, R - Reply,
       r - reply Status, s - sia Status


<output omitted>
P 192.168.1.0/24, 1 successors, FD is 3014400
          via 192.168.10.10 (3014400/28160), Serial0/0/1
          via 172.16.3.1 (41026560/2172416), Serial0/0/0
P 192.168.10.8/30, 1 successors, FD is 3011840
          via Connected, Serial0/1
<output omitted>
```

The topology table lists all successors and FSs that DUAL has calculated to destination networks. Figure 9-24 labels each part of the **show ip eigrp topology** command output for the 192.168.1.0/24 network.

Figure 9-24   Table Entry for 192.168.1.0/24

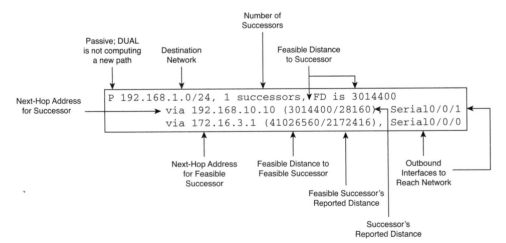

A detailed description of each part of the topology table entry shown in Figure 9-24 is as follows:

The first line displays the following:

- **P:** This route is in the passive state. When DUAL is not performing its diffusing computations to determine a path for a network, the route is in a stable mode, known as the *passive state*. If DUAL is recalculating or searching for a new path, the route is in an *active state*. All routes in the topology table should be in the passive state for a stable routing domain. DUAL displays an *A* if the route is "Stuck in Active," which is a CCNP level troubleshooting issue.

- **192.168.1.0/24:** This is the destination network that is also found in the routing table.

- **1 successors:** This shows the number of successors for this network. If there are multiple equal-cost paths to this network, there will be multiple successors.

- **FD is 3014400:** This is the FD, the EIGRP metric to reach the destination network.

The first entry shows the successor:

- **via 192.168.10.10:** This is the next-hop address of the successor, R3. This address is shown in the routing table.

- **3014400:** This is the FD to 192.168.1.0/24. It is the metric shown in the routing table.

- **28160:** This is the RD of the successor and is R3's cost to reach this network.

- **Serial0/0/1:** This is the outbound interface used to reach this network, also shown in the routing table.

The second entry shows the feasible successor, R1. (If there is not a second entry, there are no FSs.)

- **via 172.16.3.1:** This is the next-hop address of the FS, R1.

- **41026560:** This would be R2's new FD to 192.168.1.0/24 if R1 became the new successor.

- **2172416:** This is the RD of the FS or R1's metric to reach this network. This value, RD, must be less than the current FD of 3014400 to meet the FC.

- **Serial0/0/0:** This is the outbound interface used to reach the FC, if this router becomes the successor.

To view detailed information about the metrics of a specific entry in the topology table, add the optional parameter [*network*] to the **show ip eigrp topology** command, as shown in Example 9-22.

Example 9-22   *network* Option for the **show ip eigrp topology** Command

```
R2#show ip eigrp topology 192.168.1.0
IP-EIGRP topology entry for 192.168.1.0/24
  State is Passive, Query origin flag is 1, 1 Successor(s), FD is 3014400
  Routing Descriptor Blocks:
```

```
192.168.10.10 (Serial0/0/1), from 192.168.10.10, Send flag is 0x0
    Composite metric is (3014400/28160), Route is Internal
    Vector metric:
        Minimum bandwidth is 1024 Kbit
        Total delay is 20100 microseconds
        Reliability is 255/255
        Load is 1/255
        Minimum MTU is 1500
        Hop count is 1
172.16.3.1 (Serial0/0/0), from 172.16.3.1, Send flag is 0x0
    Composite metric is (41026560/2172416), Route is Internal
    Vector metric:
        Minimum bandwidth is 64 Kbit
        Total delay is 40100 microseconds
        Reliability is 255/255
        Load is 1/255
        Minimum MTU is 1500
        Hop count is 2
```

Remember that EIGRP is a distance vector routing protocol. This command lists the full list of distance vector metrics available to EIGRP even though, by default, EIGRP uses only bandwidth and delay, which are highlighted in Example 9-22. It also displays other information included in the routing update but not included in the composite metric: minimum MTU and hop count.

Topology Table: No Feasible Successor

To continue your understanding of DUAL and its use of successors and feasible successors, look at the routing table for R1 shown in Example 9-23.

Example 9-23   R1 Routing Table

```
R1#show ip route
Codes: C - connected, S - static, R - RIP, M - mobile, B - BGP
       <output omitted>


Gateway of last resort is not set

     192.168.10.0/24 is variably subnetted, 3 subnets, 2 masks
D       192.168.10.0/24 is a summary, 00:45:09, Null0
C       192.168.10.4/30 is directly connected, Serial0/0/1
D       192.168.10.8/30 [90/3523840] via 192.168.10.6, 00:44:56, Serial0/0/1
```

```
       172.16.0.0/16 is variably subnetted, 4 subnets, 3 masks
D        172.16.0.0/16 is a summary, 00:46:10, Null0
C        172.16.1.0/24 is directly connected, FastFthernet0/0
D        172.16.2.0/24 [90/40514560] via 172.16.3.2, 00:45:09, Serial0/0/0
C        172.16.3.0/30 is directly connected, Serial0/0/0
D      192.168.1.0/24 [90/2172416] via 192.168.10.6, 00:44:55, Serial0/0/1
```

The highlighted route to 192.168.1.0/24 shows that the successor is R3 via 192.168.10.6 with an FD of 2172416.

Now examine the topology table shown in Example 9-24 to see whether there are any FSs for this route.

Example 9-24   R1 Topology Table

```
R1#show ip eigrp topology
IP-EIGRP Topology Table for AS(1)/ID(192.168.10.5)

Codes: P - Passive, A - Active, U - Update, Q - Query, R - Reply,
       r - reply Status, s - sia Status

P 192.168.10.0/24, 1 successors, FD is 2169856
        via Summary (2169856/0), Null0
P 192.168.10.4/30, 1 successors, FD is 2169856
        via Connected, Serial0/0/1
P 192.168.1.0/24, 1 successors, FD is 2172416
        via 192.168.10.6 (2172416/28160), Serial0/0/1
P 192.168.10.8/30, 1 successors, FD is 3523840
        via 192.168.10.6 (3523840/3011840), Serial0/0/1
<output omitted>
```

The topology table only shows the successor 192.168.10.6. There are no FSs. By looking at the actual physical topology or network diagram, it is obvious that there is a backup route to 192.168.1.0/24 through R2. Why isn't R2 listed as an FS? R2 is not an FS because it does not meet the FC.

Although looking at the topology it is obvious that R2 is a backup route, EIGRP does not have a map of the network topology. EIGRP is a distance vector routing protocol and only knows about remote network information through its neighbors.

Therefore, DUAL does not store the route through R2 in the topology table. However, you can view all possible links whether they satisfy the feasible condition or not by adding the [**all-links**] option to the **show ip eigrp topology** command, as shown in Example 9-25.

Example 9-25 R1 Topology Table with All Possible Links Shown

```
R1#show ip eigrp topology all-links
IP-EIGRP Topology Table for AS(1)/ID(192.168.10.5)

Codes: P - Passive, A - Active, U - Update, Q - Query, R - Reply,
       r - reply Status, s - sia Status

P 192.168.10.0/24, 1 successors, FD is 2169856, serno 3
        via Summary (2169856/0), Null0
        via 172.16.3.2 (41024000/3011840), Serial0/0/0
P 192.168.10.4/30, 1 successors, FD is 2169856, serno 1
        via Connected, Serial0/0/1
P 192.168.1.0/24, 1 successors, FD is 2172416, serno 5
        via 192.168.10.6 (2172416/28160), Serial0/0/1
        via 172.16.3.2 (41026560/3014400), Serial0/0/0
P 192.168.10.8/30, 1 successors, FD is 3523840, serno 11
        via 192.168.10.6 (3523840/3011840), Serial0/0/1
<output omitted>
```

The **show ip eigrp topology all-links** command shows all possible paths to a network, including successors, FSs, and even those routes that are not FSs. R1's FD to 192.168.1.0/24 is 2172416 via the successor R3. For R2 to be considered an FS, it must meet the FC. R2's FD to reach 192.168.1.0/24 must be less than R1's current FD. As you can see in Example 9-25, R2's FD is 3014400, which is higher than R1's FD of 2172416.

Even though R2 looks like a viable backup path to 192.168.1.0/24, R1 has no idea that its path is not a potential loop back through itself. EIGRP is a distance vector routing protocol, without the ability to see a complete, loop-free topological map of the network. DUAL's method of guaranteeing that a neighbor has a loop-free path is that the neighbor's metric must satisfy the feasibility condition. By ensuring that the RD of the neighbor is less than its own FD, the router can assume that this neighboring router is not part of its own advertised route, thus always avoiding the potential for a loop.

Does this mean R2 cannot be used if the successor fails? No, R3 can be used, but there will be a longer delay before adding it to the routing table. Before this can happen, DUAL will need to do some further processing, which is explained in the next topic.

Finite State Machine

The centerpiece of EIGRP is DUAL and its EIGRP route-calculation engine. The actual name of this technology is DUAL Finite State Machine (FSM). This FSM contains all the logic used to calculate and compare routes in an EIGRP network. Figure 9-25 shows a simplified version of the DUAL FSM.

Figure 9-25   DUAL Finite State Machine

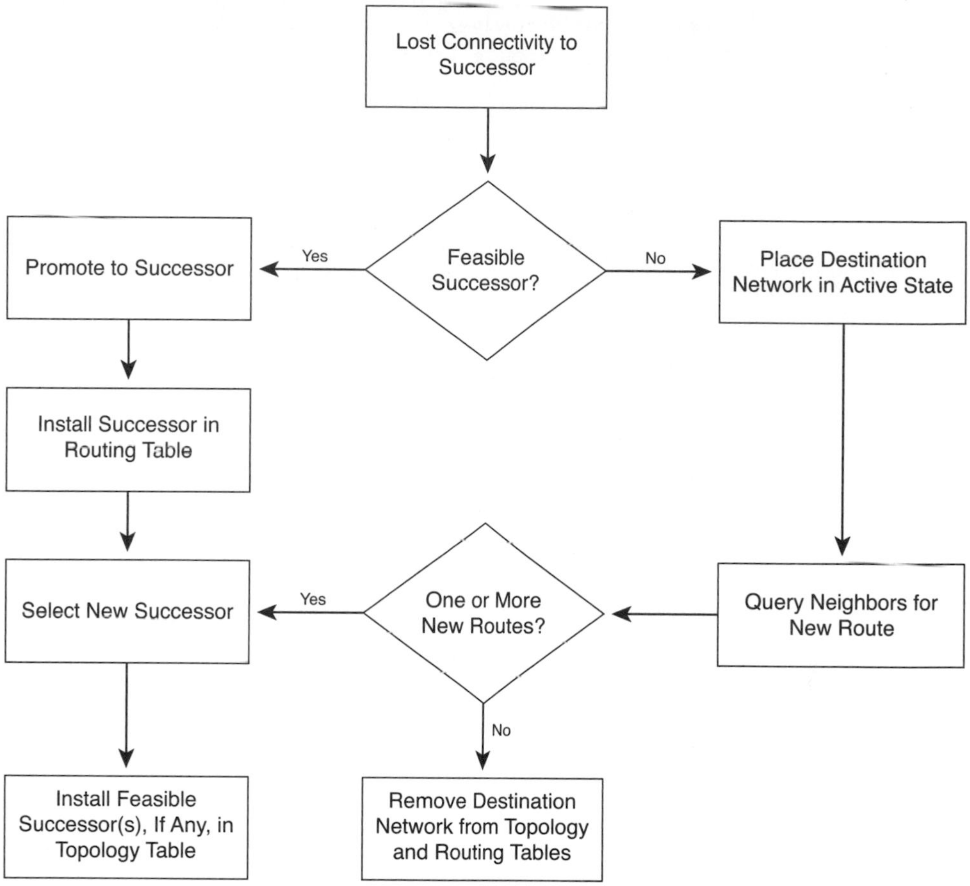

DUAL FSM

An FSM is an abstract machine, not a mechanical device with moving parts. FSMs define a set of possible states that something can go through, what events cause those states, and what events result from those states. Designers use FSMs to describe how a device, computer program, or routing algorithm will react to a set of input events. FSMs are beyond the scope of this course; however, we introduce the concept to examine some of the output from EIGRP's FSM using **debug eigrp fsm**. Let's use the command to watch what DUAL does when a route is removed from the routing table.

Example 9-26 shows the EIGRP topology table for R2.

Example 9-26 R2 Topology Table with R3 as Successor to 192.168.1.0

```
R2#show ip eigrp topology
IP-EIGRP Topology Table for AS(1)/ID(10.1.1.1)


Codes: P - Passive, A - Active, U - Update, Q - Query, R - Reply,
       r - reply Status, s - sia Status


P 192.168.10.0/24, 1 successors, FD is 3011840
        via Summary (3011840/0), Null0
        via 172.16.3.1 (41024000/2169856), Serial0/0/0
P 192.168.10.4/30, 1 successors, FD is 3523840
        via 192.168.10.10 (3523840/2169856), Serial0/0/1
P 192.168.1.0/24, 1 successors, FD is 3014400
        via 192.168.10.10 (3014400/28160), Serial0/0/1
        via 172.16.3.1 (41026560/2172416), Serial0/0/0
P 192.168.10.8/30, 1 successors, FD is 3011840
        via Connected, Serial0/1
P 172.16.0.0/16, 1 successors, FD is 28160
        via Summary (28160/0), Null0
P 172.16.1.0/24, 1 successors, FD is 40514560
        via 172.16.3.1 (40514560/28160), Serial0/0/0
P 172.16.2.0/24, 1 successors, FD is 28160
        via Connected, FastEthernet0/0
P 172.16.3.0/30, 1 successors, FD is 40512000
        via Connected, Serial0/0
```

Remember from previous discussions that R2 is currently using R3 as the successor to 192.168.1.0/24. In addition, R2 currently lists R1 as an FS. Watch what happens when you simulate a failure of the link between R2 and R3, as shown in Example 9-27.

Example 9-27 R2 DUAL FSM in Action: Promoting R2 as Successor

```
R2#debug eigrp fsm
EIGRP FSM Events/Actions debugging is on
R2#conf t
Enter configuration commands, one per line.  End with CNTL/Z.
R2(config)#int s0/0/1
R2(config-if)#shutdown
<some debug output omitted>

DUAL: Find FS for dest 192.168.1.0/24. FD is 3014400, RD is 3014400
DUAL:    192.168.10.10 metric 4294967295/4294967295
DUAL:    172.16.3.1 metric 41026560/2172416 found Dmin is 41026560
```

```
DUAL: Removing dest 192.168.1.0/24, nexthop 192.168.10.10
DUAL: RT installed 192.168.1.0/24 via 172.16.3.1

R2(config-if)#end
R2#undebug all
All possible debugging has been turned off

R2#show ip route
<some output omitted>

D    192.168.1.0/24 [90/41026560] via 172.16.3.1, 00:08:58, Serial0/0
```

First, you turn on DUAL debugging with the **debug eigrp fsm** command. Then, you simulate a link failure using the **shutdown** command on the Serial 0/0/1 interface on R2.

When you do this on a real router or Packet Tracer, you will see all the activity generated by DUAL when a link goes down. R2 must inform all EIGRP neighbors of the lost link and must take care of updating its own routing and topology tables. The **debug** output in Example 9-27 only shows selected **debug** output. In particular, notice that the DUAL FSM searches for and finds an FS for the route in the EIGRP topology table. The FS, R1, now becomes the successor and is installed in the routing table as the new best path to 192.168.1.0/24.

In Example 9-28, the topology table for R2 now shows R1 as the successor and shows that there are no new feasible successors.

Example 9-28   R2 Topology Table with R1 as the New Successor to 192.168.1.0

```
R2#show ip eigrp topology
IP-EIGRP Topology Table for AS(1)/ID(10.1.1.1)

Codes: P - Passive, A - Active, U - Update, Q - Query, R - Reply,
       r - reply Status, s - sia Status

P 192.168.10.0/24, 1 successors, FD is 41024000
         via 172.16.3.1 (41024000/2169856), Serial0/0
P 192.168.1.0/24, 1 successors, FD is 3014400
         via 172.16.3.1 (41026560/2172416), Serial0/0
P 172.16.1.0/24, 1 successors, FD is 40514560
         via 172.16.3.1 (40514560/28160), Serial0/0
P 172.16.2.0/24, 1 successors, FD is 28160
         via Connected, FastEthernet0/0
P 172.16.3.0/30, 1 successors, FD is 40512000
         via Connected, Serial0/0
```

If you are following along on routers or Packet Tracer, be sure to restore the original topology by reactivating the Serial 0/0/1 interface on R2 with the **no shutdown** command.

No Feasible Successor

What if the path to the successor fails and there are no FSs? Remember, just because DUAL does not have an FS does not mean that there is not another path to the network. It just means that DUAL does not have a guaranteed loop-free backup path to the network, so it wasn't added to the topology table as an FS. If there are no FSs in the topology table, DUAL puts the network into the active state. DUAL will actively query its neighbors for a new successor.

Example 9-29 shows the EIGRP topology table for R1.

Example 9-29   R1 Topology Table with R3 as Successor to 192.168.1.0

```
R1#show ip eigrp topology
IP-EIGRP Topology Table for AS(1)/ID(192.168.10.5)

Codes: P - Passive, A - Active, U - Update, Q - Query, R - Reply,
       r - reply Status, s - sia Status

P 192.168.10.0/24, 1 successors, FD is 2169856
        via Summary (2169856/0), Null0
P 192.168.10.4/30, 1 successors, FD is 2169856
        via Connected, Serial0/0/1
P 192.168.1.0/24, 1 successors, FD is 2172416
        via 192.168.10.6 (2172416/28160), Serial0/0/1
P 192.168.10.8/30, 1 successors, FD is 3523840
        via 192.168.10.6 (3523840/3011840), Serial0/0/1
P 172.16.0.0/16, 1 successors, FD is 28160
        via Summary (28160/0), Null0
P 172.16.1.0/24, 1 successors, FD is 28160
        via Connected, FastEthernet0/0
P 172.16.2.0/24, 1 successors, FD is 40514560
        via 172.16.3.2 (40514560/28160), Serial0/0/0
P 172.16.3.0/30, 1 successors, FD is 40512000
        via Connected, Serial0/0/0
```

R1 is currently using R3 as the successor to 192.168.1.0/24. However, R1 does not have R2 listed as an FS because R2 does not satisfy the FC. Watch what happens when you simulate a failure of the link between R1 and R3, as shown in Example 9-30.

Example 9-30 R1 DUAL FSM in Action: Querying Neighbors to Find New Successor

```
R1#debug eigrp fsm
EIGRP FSM Events/Actions debugging is on
R1#conf t
Enter configuration commands, one per line.  End with CNTL/Z.
R1(config)#int s0/0/1
R1(config-if)#shutdown
<some debug output omitted>


DUAL: Find FS for dest 192.168.1.0/24. FD is 2172416, RD is 2172416
DUAL:    192.168.10.6 metric 4294967295/4294967295
DUAL:    172.16.3.2 metric 41026560/3014400 not found Dmin is 41026560
DUAL: Dest 192.168.1.0/24 entering active state.
DUAL: rcvreply: 192.168.1.0/24 via 172.16.3.2 metric 41026560/3014400
DUAL: Find FS for dest 192.168.1.0/24. FD is 4294967295, RD is 4294967295 found
DUAL: Removing dest 192.168.1.0/24, nexthop 192.168.10.6
DUAL: RT installed 192.168.1.0/24 via 172.16.3.2


R1(config-if)#end
%SYS-5-CONFIG_I: Configured from console by console
R1#undebug all
All possible debugging has been turned off

R1#show ip route
<some output omitted>


D    192.168.1.0/24 [90/41026560] via 172.16.3.2, 00:00:17, Serial0/0/0
```

First, you turn on DUAL debugging with the **debug eigrp fsm** command. Then, you simulate a link failure using the **shutdown** command on the Serial 0/0/1 interface on R1.

The selected **debug** output shows the 192.168.1.0/24 network put into the active state and shows that EIGRP queries are sent to other neighbors. R2 replies with a path to this network, which becomes the new successor and is installed into the routing table.

When the successor is no longer available and there is no FS, DUAL puts the route into active state. DUAL will send EIGRP queries asking other routers for a path to this network. Other routers return EIGRP replies, letting the sender of the EIGRP query know whether they have a path to the requested network. If none of the EIGRP replies have a path to this network, the sender of the query will not have a route to this network.

If the sender of the EIGRP queries receives EIGRP replies that include a path to the requested network, the preferred path is added as the new successor and added to the routing table. This process takes longer than if DUAL had an FS in its topology table and was able to quickly add the new route to the routing table.

Note

DUAL FSM and the process of queries and replies is beyond the scope of this course.

In Example 9-31, the topology table for R1 now shows R2 as the successor and shows that there are no new feasible successors.

Example 9-31   R1 Topology Table with R2 as the New Successor to 192.168.1.0

```
R1#show ip eigrp topology
IP-EIGRP Topology Table for AS(1)/ID(192.168.10.5)


Codes: P - Passive, A - Active, U - Update, Q - Query, R - Reply,
       r - reply Status, s - sia Status


P 192.168.10.0/24, 1 successors, FD is 41024000
        via 172.16.3.2 (41024000/3011840), Serial0/0/0
P 192.168.1.0/24, 1 successors, FD is 41026560
        via 172.16.3.2 (41026560/3014400), Serial0/0/0
P 172.16.1.0/24, 1 successors, FD is 28160
        via Connected, FastEthernet0/0
P 172.16.2.0/24, 1 successors, FD is 40514560
        via 172.16.3.2 (40514560/28160), Serial0/0/0
P 172.16.3.0/30, 1 successors, FD is 40512000
        via Connected, Serial0/0/0
```

If you are following along on routers or Packet Tracer, be sure to restore the original topology by reactivating the Serial 0/0/1 interface on R1 with the **no shutdown** command.

Packet Tracer
☐ Activity

Investigating Successors and Feasible Successors (9.4.6)

The purpose of this activity is to modify the EIGRP metric formula to cause a change in the topology. Debug outputs will be used to see how EIGRP reacts when a neighbor goes down due to unforeseen circumstances. You will use the **debug** command to view topology changes and how the DUAL Finite Machine determines successor and feasible successor paths. Detailed instructions are provided within the activity. Use file e2-946.pka on the CD-ROM that accompanies this book to perform this activity using Packet Tracer.

More EIGRP Configurations

This section discusses the commands used for EIGRP route summarization, propagating a default route, and EIGRP fine-tuning.

The Null0 Summary Route

Analyzing a routing table containing EIGRP routes can be confusing because of EIGRP's automatic inclusion of Null0 summary routes. In Example 9-32, you have already learned that R1's routing table contains two routes that have an exit interface of Null0.

Example 9-32   R1 Routing Table

```
R1#show ip route
Codes: C - connected, S - static, R - RIP, M - mobile, B - BGP
       D - EIGRP, EX - EIGRP external, O - OSPF, IA - OSPF inter area
       N1 - OSPF NSSA external type 1, N2 - OSPF NSSA external type 2
       E1 - OSPF external type 1, E2 - OSPF external type 2
       i - IS-IS, su - IS-IS summary, L1 - IS-IS level-1, L2 - IS-IS level-2
       ia - IS-IS inter area, * - candidate default, U - per-user static route
       o - ODR, P - periodic downloaded static route

Gateway of last resort is not set

     192.168.10.0/24 is variably subnetted, 3 subnets, 2 masks
D        192.168.10.0/24 is a summary, 00:45:09, Null0
C        192.168.10.4/30 is directly connected, Serial0/0/1
D        192.168.10.8/30 [90/3523840] via 192.168.10.6, 00:44:56, Serial0/0/1
     172.16.0.0/16 is variably subnetted, 4 subnets, 3 masks
D        172.16.0.0/16 is a summary, 00:46:10, Null0
C        172.16.1.0/24 is directly connected, FastEthernet0/0
D        172.16.2.0/24 [90/40514560] via 172.16.3.2, 00:45:09, Serial0/0/0
C        172.16.3.0/30 is directly connected, Serial0/0/0
D     192.168.1.0/24 [90/2172416] via 192.168.10.6, 00:44:55, Serial0/0/1
```

Remember from Chapter 7 that the Null0 interface is simply a route to nowhere, commonly known as "the bit bucket." So by default, EIGRP uses the Null0 interface to discard any packets that match the parent route but do not match any of the child routes.

You might think that if you configure classless routing behavior with the **ip classless** command, EIGRP would not discard that packet but would continue looking for a default or supernet route. However, notice that the EIGRP *Null0 summary route* is a child route indented under the parent route. This Null0 summary route is a child route that will match any possible packets of the parent route that do not match another child route. Even with classless routing behavior (**ip classless**), where you would expect the route lookup process to check for supernets and default routes, EIGRP will use the Null0 summary route and discard the packet because this route will match any packets of the parent that do not have a child route.

Regardless of whether classful or classless routing behavior is being used, the Null0 summary will be used and therefore denying the use of any supernet or default route.

Looking at the routing table in Example 9-32, R1 will discard any packets that match the parent 172.16.0.0/16 classful network but do not match one of the child routes 172.16.1.0/24, 172.16.2.0/24, or 172.16.3.0/24. For example, a packet to 172.16.4.10 would be discarded. Even if a default route were configured, R1 would still discard the packet because it matches the Null0 summary route to 172.16.0.0/16:

```
D       172.16.0.0/16 is a summary, 00:46:10, Null0
```

> **Note**
>
> EIGRP automatically includes a Null0 summary route as a child route whenever both of the following conditions exist:
>
> - There is at least one subnet that was learned via EIGRP.
> - Automatic summarization is enabled.

Like RIP, EIGRP automatically summarizes at major network boundaries. You might have already noticed in the **show run** output that EIGRP, by default, uses the **auto-summary** command. In the next topic, you will see that disabling automatic summarization will remove the Null0 summary route and allow EIGRP to look for a supernet or default route when an EIGRP child route does not match a destination packet.

Disabling Automatic Summarization

Like RIP, EIGRP automatically summarizes at major network boundaries using the default **auto-summary** command. You can see the result of this by looking at the routing table for R3 in Example 9-33.

```
Example 9-33    R3 Routing Table
R3#show ip route

     192.168.10.0/24 is variably subnetted, 3 subnets, 2 masks
D       192.168.10.0/24 is a summary, 01:08:35, Null0
C       192.168.10.4/30 is directly connected, Serial0/0/0
C       192.168.10.8/30 is directly connected, Serial0/0/1
D    172.16.0.0/16 [90/2172416] via 192.168.10.5, 01:08:30, Serial0/0/0
C       192.168.1.0/24 is directly connected, FastEthernet0/0
```

Notice that R3 is not receiving individual routes for the 172.16.1.0/24, 172.16.2.0/24, and 172.16.3.0/24 subnets. Both R1 and R2 automatically summarized those subnets to the 172.16.0.0/16 classful boundary when sending EIGRP update packets to R3. The result is that R3 has one route to 172.16.0.0/16 through R1. R1 is the successor because of the difference in bandwidth.

You can quickly see that this route is not optimal. R3 will route all packets destined for 172.16.2.0 through R1. R3 does not know that R1 will then have to route these packets across a very slow link to R2. The only way R3 can learn about this slow bandwidth is if R1 and R2 send individual routes for each of the 172.16.0.0/16 subnets. In other words, R1 and R2 must stop automatically summarizing 172.16.0.0/16.

As in RIPv2, automatic summarization can be disabled with the **no auto-summary** command, as shown in Example 9-34. The router configuration command **eigrp log-neighbor-changes** is on by default on some IOS implementations. If on, you will see output similar to that shown for R1.

Example 9-34   Disabling Automatic Summarization

```
R1#conf t
R1(config)#router eigrp 1
R1(config-router)#no auto-summary
%DUAL-5-NBRCHANGE: IP-EIGRP(0) 1: Neighbor 172.16.3.2 (Serial0/0/0) is resync:
  summary configured
%DUAL-5-NBRCHANGE: IP-EIGRP(0) 1: Neighbor 192.168.10.6 (Serial0/0/1) is resync:
  summary configured
%DUAL-5-NBRCHANGE: IP-EIGRP(0) 1: Neighbor 172.16.3.2 (Serial0/0/0) is down: peer
  restarted
%DUAL-5-NBRCHANGE: IP-EIGRP(0) 1: Neighbor 172.16.3.2 (Serial0/0/0) is up: new
  adjacency
%DUAL-5-NBRCHANGE: IP-EIGRP(0) 1: Neighbor 192.168.10.6 (Serial0/0/1) is down:
  peer restarted
%DUAL-5-NBRCHANGE: IP-EIGRP(0) 1: Neighbor 192.168.10.6 (Serial0/0/1) is up: new
  adjacency
R2#conf t
R2(config)#router eigrp 1
R2(config-router)#no auto-summary
R3#conf t
R3(config)#router eigrp 1
R3(config-router)#no auto-summary
```

DUAL takes down all neighbor adjacencies and then reestablishes them so that the effect of the **no auto-summary** command can be fully realized. All EIGRP neighbors will immediately send out a new round of updates that will not be automatically summarized.

Examples 9-35, 9-36, and 9-37 show the routing tables for all three routers.

Example 9-35   R1 Routing Table with Automatic Summarization Disabled

```
R1#show ip route
Codes: C - connected, S - static, R - RIP, M - mobile, B - BGP
       <output omitted>


Gateway of last resort is not set

     192.168.10.0/30 is subnetted, 2 subnets
C       192.168.10.4 is directly connected, Serial0/0/1
D       192.168.10.8 [90/3523840] via 192.168.10.6, 00:16:55, Serial0/0/1
     172.16.0.0/16 is variably subnetted, 3 subnets, 2 masks
C       172.16.1.0/24 is directly connected, FastEthernet0/0
D       172.16.2.0/24 [90/3526400] via 192.168.10.6, 00:16:53, Serial0/0/1
C       172.16.3.0/30 is directly connected, Serial0/0/0
D    192.168.1.0/24 [90/2172416] via 192.168.10.6, 00:16:52, Serial0/0/1
```

Example 9-36   R2 Routing Table with Automatic Summarization Disabled

```
R2#show ip route
Codes: C - connected, S - static, I - IGRP, R - RIP, M - mobile, B - BGP
       <output omitted>


Gateway of last resort is not set

     192.168.10.0/30 is subnetted, 2 subnets
D       192.168.10.4 [90/3523840] via 192.168.10.10, 00:15:44, Serial0/0/1
C       192.168.10.8 is directly connected, Serial0/0/1
     172.16.0.0/16 is variably subnetted, 3 subnets, 2 masks
D       172.16.1.0/24 [90/3526400] via 192.168.10.10, 00:15:44, Serial0/0/1
C       172.16.2.0/24 is directly connected, FastEthernet0/0
C       172.16.3.0/30 is directly connected, Serial0/0/0
     10.0.0.0/30 is subnetted, 1 subnets
C       10.1.1.0 is directly connected, Loopback1
D    192.168.1.0/24 [90/3014400] via 192.168.10.10, 00:15:44, Serial0/0/1
```

Example 9-37   R3 Routing Table with Automatic Summarization Disabled

```
R3#show ip route
Codes: C - connected, S - static, I - IGRP, R - RIP, M - mobile, B - BGP
       <output omitted>


Gateway of last resort is not set


     192.168.10.0/30 is subnetted, 2 subnets
C       192.168.10.4 is directly connected, Serial0/0/0
C       192.168.10.8 is directly connected, Serial0/0/1
     172.16.0.0/16 is variably subnetted, 3 subnets, 2 masks
D       172.16.1.0/24 [90/2172416] via 192.168.10.5, 00:00:11, Serial0/0/0
D       172.16.2.0/24 [90/3014400] via 192.168.10.9, 00:00:12, Serial0/0/1
D       172.16.3.0/30 [90/41024000] via 192.168.10.5, 00:00:12, Serial0/0/0
                      [90/41024000] via 192.168.10.9, 00:00:12, Serial0/0/1
C    192.168.1.0/24 is directly connected, FastEthernet0/0
```

You can see in these routing tables that EIGRP is now propagating individual subnets. Notice that EIGRP no longer includes the Null0 summary route, because automatic summarization has been disabled with **no auto-summary**. As long as the default classless routing behavior (**ip classless**) is in effect, supernet and default routes are used when there is not a match with a subnet route.

Because routes are no longer automatically summarized at major network boundaries, the EIGRP routing and topology tables also change.

Examples 9-38, 9-39, and 9-40 show the EIGRP topology tables for all three routers.

Example 9-38   R1 Topology Table with Automatic Summarization Disabled

```
R1#show ip eigrp topology
IP-EIGRP Topology Table for AS(1)/ID(192.168.10.5)


Codes: P - Passive, A - Active, U - Update, Q - Query, R - Reply,
       r - reply Status, s - sia Status


P 192.168.10.4/30, 1 successors, FD is 2169856
        via Connected, Serial0/0/1
P 192.168.1.0/24, 1 successors, FD is 2172416
        via 192.168.10.6 (2172416/28160), Serial0/0/1
P 192.168.10.8/30, 1 successors, FD is 3523840
        via 192.168.10.6 (3523840/3011840), Serial0/0/1
        via 172.16.3.2 (41024000/3011840), Serial0/0/0
```

```
P 172.16.1.0/24, 1 successors, FD is 28160
        via Connected, FastEthernet0/0
P 172.16.2.0/24, 1 successors, FD is 3526400
        via 192.168.10.6 (3526400/3014400), Serial0/0/1
        via 172.16.3.2 (40514560/28160), Serial0/0/0
P 172.16.3.0/30, 1 successors, FD is 40512000
        via Connected, Serial0/0/0
```

Example 9-39   R2 Topology Table with Automatic Summarization Disabled

```
R2#show ip eigrp topology
IP-EIGRP Topology Table for AS(1)/ID(10.1.1.1)

Codes: P - Passive, A - Active, U - Update, Q - Query, R - Reply,
       r - reply Status, s - sia Status

P 192.168.10.4/30, 1 successors, FD is 3523840
        via 192.168.10.10 (3523840/2169856), Serial0/0/1
        via 172.16.3.1 (41024000/2169856), Serial0/0/0
P 192.168.1.0/24, 1 successors, FD is 3014400
        via 192.168.10.10 (3014400/28160), Serial0/0/1
        via 172.16.3.1 (41026560/2172416), Serial0/0/0
P 192.168.10.8/30, 1 successors, FD is 3011840
        via Connected, Serial0/0/1
P 172.16.1.0/24, 1 successors, FD is 3526400
        via 192.168.10.10 (3526400/2172416), Serial0/0/1
        via 172.16.3.1 (40514560/28160), Serial0/0/0
P 172.16.2.0/24, 1 successors, FD is 28160
        via Connected, FastEthernet0/0
P 172.16.3.0/30, 1 successors, FD is 40512000
        via Connected, Serial0/0/0
```

Example 9-40   R3 Topology Table with Automatic Summarization Disabled

```
R3#show ip eigrp topology
IP-EIGRP Topology Table for AS(1)/ID(192.168.10.10)

Codes: P - Passive, A - Active, U - Update, Q - Query, R - Reply,
       r - reply Status, s - sia Status
```

```
P 192 168.10.4/30, 1 successors, FD is 2169856
        via Connected, Serial0/0/0
P 192.168.1.0/24, 1 successors, FD is 28160
        via Connected, FastEthernet0/0
P 192.168.10.8/30, 1 successors, FD is 3011840
        via Connected, Serial0/0/1
P 172.16.1.0/24, 1 successors, FD is 2172416
        via 192.168.10.5 (2172416/28160), Serial0/0/0
P 172.16.2.0/24, 1 successors, FD is 3014400
        via 192.168.10.9 (3014400/28160), Serial0/0/1
P 172.16.3.0/30, 2 successors, FD is 41024000
        via 192.168.10.9 (41024000/40512000), Serial0/0/1
        via 192.168.10.5 (41024000/40512000), Serial0/0/0
```

Without automatic summarization, R3's routing table now includes the three subnets: 172.16.1.0/24, 172.16.2.0/24, and 172.16.3.0/24. Why does R3's routing table now have two equal-cost paths to 172.16.3.0/24? Shouldn't the best path only be through R1 with the 1544-Mbps link?

Remember that EIGRP only uses the link with the slowest bandwidth when calculating the composite metric. The slowest link is the 64-Kbps link that contains the 172.16.3.0/30 network. In this example, the 1544-Mbps link and the 1024-Kbps link are irrelevant in the calculation as far as the bandwidth metric is concerned. Because both paths have the same number and types of outgoing interfaces, the delay values end up being the same. As a result, the EIGRP metric for both paths is the same, even though the path through R1 would actually be the "faster" path.

Manual Summarization

EIGRP can be configured to summarize routes, whether or not automatic summarization (**auto-summary**) is enabled. Because EIGRP is a classless routing protocol and includes the subnet mask in the routing updates, manual summarization can include supernet routes. Remember, a supernet is an aggregation of multiple major classful network addresses.

Figure 9-26 shows the modified topology.

Suppose you were to add two more networks, as shown in Example 9-41, to router R3 using loopback interfaces: 192.168.2.0/24 and 192.168.3.0/24. You also configure networks in R3's EIGRP routing process with network commands so that R3 will propagate these networks to other routers.

Figure 9-26   Modified Network Topology for Manual Summarization

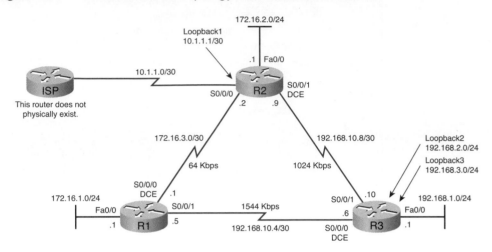

Example 9-41   Adding Loopbacks to R3

```
R3(config)#interface loopback 2
R3(config-if)#ip address 192.168.2.1 255.255.255.0
R3(config-if)#interface loopback 3
R3(config-if)#ip address 192.168.3.1 255.255.255.0
R3(config-if)#router eigrp 1
R3(config-router)#network 192.168.2.0
R3(config-router)#network 192.168.3.0
```

To verify that R3 sent EIGRP update packets to R1 and R2, you check the routing tables. In Example 9-42, only the pertinent routes are shown.

Example 9-42   R1 and R2 Routes for 192.168

```
R1#show ip route
<output limited to 192.168 routes>


Gateway of last resort is not set


D     192.168.1.0/24 [90/2172416] via 192.168.10.6, 02:07:38, Serial0/0/1
D     192.168.2.0/24 [90/2297856] via 192.168.10.6, 00:00:34, Serial0/0/1
D     192.168.3.0/24 [90/2297856] via 192.168.10.6, 00:00:18, Serial0/0/1
R2#show ip route
<output limited to 192.168 routes>
```

```
Gateway of last resort is not set

D    192.168.1.0/24 [90/3014400] via 192.168.10.10, 02:08:50, Serial0/0/1
D    192.168.2.0/24 [90/3130840] via 192.168.10.10, 00:01:46, Serial0/0/1
D    192.168.3.0/24 [90/3139840] via 192.168.10.10, 00:01:30, Serial0/0/1
```

R1 and R2 routing tables show these additional networks in their routing tables: 192.168.2.0/24 and 192.168.3.0/24. Instead of sending three separate networks, R3 can summarize the 192.168.1.0/24, 192.168.2.0/24, and 192.168.3.0/24 networks as a single route.

Determining the Summary EIGRP Route

First, determine what the summary of these three networks would be using the same method used to determine summary static routes in Chapter 2, "Static Routing":

Step 1. Write out the networks that you want to summarize in binary.

Step 2. To find the subnet mask for summarization, start with the leftmost bit.

Step 3. Work your way to the right, finding all the bits that match consecutively.

Step 4. When you find a column of bits that do not match, stop. You are at the summary boundary.

Step 5. Now, count the number of leftmost matching bits, which in this example is 22. This number becomes your subnet mask for the summarized route: /22 or 255.255.252.0.

Step 6. To find the network address for summarization, copy the matching 22 bits and add all 0 bits to the end to make 32 bits.

The result is the summary network address and mask for 192.168.0.0/22, as shown in Figure 9-27.

Figure 9-27 Calculating the Summary Route

```
192.168.1.0:  11000000 . 10101000 . 00000001 . 00000000
192.168.2.0:  11000000 . 10101000 . 00000010 . 00000000
192.168.3.0:  11000000 . 10101000 . 00000011 . 00000000
              ◄──────── 22 Matching Bits ──────►
```

22 Matching Bits = a /22 Subnet Mask or 255.255.252.0

Configure EIGRP Manual Summarization

To establish EIGRP manual summarization on all interfaces that send EIGRP packets, use the following interface command:

```
Router(config-if)#ip summary-address eigrp as-number network-address subnet-mask
```

Because R3 has two EIGRP neighbors, the EIGRP manual summarization in configured on both Serial 0/0/0 and Serial 0/0/1, as shown in Example 9-43.

Example 9-43   Configuring Summary Routes for EIGRP Propagation

```
R3(config)#interface serial 0/0/0
R3(config-if)#ip summary-address eigrp 1 192.168.0.0 255.255.252.0
R3(config-if)#interface serial 0/0/1
R3(config-if)#ip summary-address eigrp 1 192.168.0.0 255.255.252.0
```

Examples 9-44 and 9-45 show that the routing tables of R1 and R2 now no longer include the individual 192.168.1.0/24, 192.168.2.0/24, and 192.168.3.0/24 networks. Instead, they show a single summary route of 192.168.0.0/22.

Example 9-44   R1 Routing Table with Summary Route Installed

```
R1#show ip route
<output omitted>

Gateway of last resort is not set

 192.168.10.0/30 is subnetted, 2 subnets
C       192.168.10.4 is directly connected, Serial0/0/1
D       192.168.10.8 [90/3523840] via 192.168.10.6, 00:01:34, Serial0/0/1
     172.16.0.0/16 is variably subnetted, 3 subnets, 2 masks
C       172.16.1.0/24 is directly connected, FastEthernet0/0
D       172.16.2.0/24 [90/3526400] via 192.168.10.6, 00:01:12, Serial0/0/1
C       172.16.3.0/30 is directly connected, Serial0/0/0
D    192.168.0.0/22 [90/2172416] via 192.168.10.6, 00:01:11, Serial0/0/1
```

Example 9-45   R2 Routing Table with Summary Route Installed

```
R2#show ip route
<output omitted>

Gateway of last resort is not set
```

```
      192.168.10.0/30 is subnetted, 2 subnets
D        192.168.10.4 [90/3523840] via 192.168.10.10, 00:00:23, Serial0/0/1
C        192.168.10.8 is directly connected, Serial0/0/1
      172.16.0.0/16 is variably subnetted, 3 subnets, 2 masks
D        172.16.1.0/24 [90/3526400] via 192.168.10.10, 00:00:23, Serial0/0/1
C        172.16.2.0/24 is directly connected, FastEthernet0/0
C        172.16.3.0/30 is directly connected, Serial0/0/0
      10.0.0.0/30 is subnetted, 1 subnets
C        10.1.1.0 is directly connected, Loopback1
D     192.168.0.0/22 [90/3014400] via 192.168.10.10, 00:00:23, Serial0/0/1
```

As you learned in Chapter 2, summary routes lessen the number of total routes in routing tables, which makes the routing table lookup process more efficient. Summary routes also require less bandwidth utilization for the routing updates because a single route can be sent rather than multiple individual routes.

EIGRP Default Route

Using a static route to 0.0.0.0/0 as a default route is not routing protocol dependent. The "quad zero" static default route can be used with any currently supported routing protocols. The static default route is usually configured on the router that has a connection to a network outside the EIGRP routing domain, for example, to an ISP. Example 9-46 shows the default static route configuration on R2.

Example 9-46   Configuring and Redistributing a Default Route in EIGRP

```
R2(config)#ip route 0.0.0.0 0.0.0.0 loopback 1
R2(config)#router eigrp 1
R2(config-router)#redistribute static
```

EIGRP requires the use of the **redistribute static** command to include this static default route with its EIGRP routing updates. The **redistribute static** command tells EIGRP to include this static route in its EIGRP updates to other routers. The example shows the configuration of the static default route and the **redistribute static** command on Router R2.

Note

The static default route is using the exit interface of Loopback1. This is because the ISP router in our topology does not physically exist. By using a loopback interface, you can simulate a connection to another router.

Examples 9-47, 9-48, and 9-49 show the routing tables for R1, R2, and R3. The routing tables now show a static default route, and a gateway of last resort is now set.

Example 9-47   R1 Routing Table with Default Route Installed

```
R1#show ip route
Codes: C - connected, S - static, R - RIP, M - mobile, B - BGP
       D - EIGRP, EX - EIGRP external, O - OSPF, IA - OSPF inter area
       N1 - OSPF NSSA external type 1, N2 - OSPF NSSA external type 2
       E1 - OSPF external type 1, E2 - OSPF external type 2, E - EGP
       i - IS-IS, L1 - IS-IS level-1, L2 - IS-IS level-2, ia - IS-IS inter area
       * - candidate default, U - per-user static route, o - ODR
       P - periodic downloaded static route

Gateway of last resort is 192.168.10.6 to network 0.0.0.0

     192.168.10.0/30 is subnetted, 2 subnets
C       192.168.10.4 is directly connected, Serial0/0/1
D       192.168.10.8 [90/3523840] via 192.168.10.6, 01:06:01, Serial0/0/1
     172.16.0.0/16 is variably subnetted, 3 subnets, 2 masks
C       172.16.1.0/24 is directly connected, FastEthernet0/0
D       172.16.2.0/24 [90/3526400] via 192.168.10.6, 01:05:39, Serial0/0/1
C       172.16.3.0/30 is directly connected, Serial0/0/0
D*EX 0.0.0.0/0 [170/3651840] via 192.168.10.6, 00:02:14, Serial0/0/1
D       192.168.0.0/22 [90/2172416] via 192.168.10.6, 01:05:38, Serial0/0/1
```

Example 9-48   R2 Routing Table with Default Route Installed

```
R2#show ip route
Codes: C - connected, S - static, I - IGRP, R - RIP, M - mobile, B - BGP
       D - EIGRP, EX - EIGRP external, O - OSPF, IA - OSPF inter area
       N1 - OSPF NSSA external type 1, N2 - OSPF NSSA external type 2
       E1 - OSPF external type 1, E2 - OSPF external type 2, E - EGP
       i - IS-IS, L1 - IS-IS level-1, L2 - IS-IS level-2, ia - IS-IS inter area
       * - candidate default, U - per-user static route, o - ODR
       P - periodic downloaded static route

Gateway of last resort is 0.0.0.0 to network 0.0.0.0

     192.168.10.0/30 is subnetted, 2 subnets
D       192.168.10.4 [90/3523840] via 192.168.10.10, 01:03:26, Serial0/0/1
C       192.168.10.8 is directly connected, Serial0/0/1
     172.16.0.0/16 is variably subnetted, 3 subnets, 2 masks
```

```
D        172.16.1.0/24 [90/3526400] via 192.168.10.10, 01:03:26, Serial0/0/1
C        172.16.2.0/24 is directly connected, FastEthernet0/0
C        172.16.3.0/30 is directly connected, Serial0/0/0
     10.0.0.0/30 is subnetted, 1 subnets
C        10.1.1.0 is directly connected, Loopback1
S*    0.0.0.0/0 is directly connected, Loopback1
D     192.168.0.0/22 [90/3014400] via 192.168.10.10, 01:03:26, Serial0/0/1
```

Example 9-49   R3 Routing Table with Default Route Installed

```
R3#show ip route
Codes: C - connected, S - static, I - IGRP, R - RIP, M - mobile, B - BGP
       D - EIGRP, EX - EIGRP external, O - OSPF, IA - OSPF inter area
       N1 - OSPF NSSA external type 1, N2 - OSPF NSSA external type 2
       E1 - OSPF external type 1, E2 - OSPF external type 2, E - EGP
       i - IS-IS, L1 - IS-IS level-1, L2 - IS-IS level-2, ia - IS-IS inter area
       * - candidate default, U - per-user static route, o - ODR
       P - periodic downloaded static route

Gateway of last resort is 192.168.10.9 to network 0.0.0.0

     192.168.10.0/30 is subnetted, 2 subnets
C        192.168.10.4 is directly connected, Serial0/0/0
C        192.168.10.8 is directly connected, Serial0/0/1
     172.16.0.0/16 is variably subnetted, 3 subnets, 2 masks
D        172.16.1.0/24 [90/2172416] via 192.168.10.5, 01:04:48, Serial0/0/0
D        172.16.2.0/24 [90/3014400] via 192.168.10.9, 01:04:50, Serial0/0/1
D        172.16.3.0/30 [90/41024000] via 192.168.10.5, 01:04:50, Serial0/0/0
                       [90/41024000] via 192.168.10.9, 01:04:50, Serial0/0/1
C     192.168.1.0/24 is directly connected, FastEthernet0/0
C     192.168.2.0/24 is directly connected, Loopback2
C     192.168.3.0/24 is directly connected, Loopback3
D*EX 0.0.0.0/0 [170/3139840] via 192.168.10.9, 00:01:25, Serial0/0/1
D     192.168.0.0/22 is a summary, 01:04:48, Null0
```

In the routing tables for R1 and R3, notice the routing source and AD for the new static default route. The entry for the static default route on R1 is the following:

```
D*EX 0.0.0.0/0 [170/3651840] via 192.168.10.6, 00:01:08, Serial0/1
```

- **D:** This static route was learned from an EIGRP routing update.

- ***:** The route is a candidate for a default route.

- **EX:** The route is an external EIGRP route, in this case a static route outside of the EIGRP routing domain.

- **170:** This is the AD of an external EIGRP route.

Default routes provide a default path to outside the routing domain and, like summary routes, minimize the number of entries in the routing table.

Note

There is another method to propagate a default route in EIGRP, using the **ip default-network** command. More information on this command can be found at this site:

http://www.cisco.com/en/US/tech/tk365/technologies_tech_note09186a0080094374.shtml

---

Fine-Tuning EIGRP

The last two topics of this chapter discuss two fundamental ways to fine-tune EIGRP operations. First, you learn EIGRP bandwidth utilization. Next, you learn how to change the default hello and holdtime values.

EIGRP Bandwidth Utilization

By default, EIGRP uses only up to 50 percent of the bandwidth of an interface for EIGRP information. This prevents the EIGRP process from overutilizing a link and not allowing enough bandwidth for the routing of normal traffic. The **ip bandwidth-percent eigrp** command can be used to configure the percentage of bandwidth that may be used by EIGRP on an interface.

```
Router(config-if)#ip bandwidth-percent eigrp as-number percent
```

R1 and R2 share a very slow 64-Kbps link. The configuration to limit how much bandwidth EIGRP uses is shown in Example 9-50, along with the **bandwidth** command.

Example 9-50   EIGRP Bandwidth Utilization

```
R1(config)#interface serial 0/0/0
R1(config-if)#bandwidth 64
R1(config-if)#ip bandwidth-percent eigrp 1 50
R2(config)#interface serial 0/0/0
R2(config-if)#bandwidth 64
R2(config-if)#ip bandwidth-percent eigrp 1 50
```

The **ip bandwidth-percent eigrp** command uses the amount of configured bandwidth (or the default bandwidth) when calculating the percent that EIGRP can use. In the example, you are limiting EIGRP to no more than 50 percent of the link's bandwidth. Therefore, EIGRP will never use more the 32 Kbps of the link's bandwidth for EIGRP packet traffic.

Configuring Hello Intervals and Hold Times

Hello intervals and hold times are configurable on a per-interface basis and do not have to match with other EIGRP routers to establish adjacencies. The command to configure a different hello interval is this:

```
Router(config-if)#ip hello-interval eigrp as-number seconds
```

If you change the hello interval, make sure that you also change the hold time to a value equal to or greater than the hello interval. Otherwise, neighbor adjacency will go down after the hold time expires and before the next hello interval. The command to configure a different hold time is as follows:

```
Router(config-if)#ip hold-time eigrp as-number seconds
```

The *seconds* value for both hello and holdtime intervals can range from 1 to 65,535. This range means that you can set the hello interval to a value of just over 18 hours, which might be appropriate for an expensive dialup link. However, in Example 9-51, you configure both R1 and R2 to use a 60-second hello interval and 180-second hold time.

Example 9-51   Changing the Hello Intervals and Hold Time

```
R1(config)#int s0/0/0
R1(config-if)#ip hello-interval eigrp 1 60
R1(config-if)#ip hold-time eigrp 1 180
R1(config-if)#end
R2(config)#int s0/0/0
R2(config-if)#ip hello-interval eigrp 1 60
R2(config-if)#ip hold-time eigrp 1 180
R2(config-if)#end
```

The **no** form can be used on both of these commands to restore the default values.

Summary

EIGRP is a classless, distance vector routing protocol released in 1992 by Cisco Systems. EIGRP is a Cisco proprietary routing protocol and an enhancement of another Cisco propriety protocol, IGRP. IGRP is a classful, distance vector routing protocol that is no longer supported by Cisco. EIGRP uses the source code of *D* for DUAL in the routing table. EIGRP has a default AD of 90 for internal routes and 170 for routes imported from an external source, such as default routes.

EIGRP used PDMs, giving it the capability to support different Layer 3 protocols, including IP, IPX, and AppleTalk. EIGRP uses RTP as the transport layer protocol for the delivery of EIGRP packets. EIGRP uses reliable delivery for EIGRP updates, queries, and replies, and it uses unreliable delivery for EIGRP hellos and acknowledgments. Reliable RTP means an EIGRP acknowledgment must be returned.

Before any EIGRP updates are sent, a router must discover its neighbors. This is done with EIGRP hello packets. On most networks, EIGRP sends hello packets every 5 seconds. On NBMA networks such as X.25, Frame Relay, and ATM interface with access links of T1 (1.544 Mbps) or slower, hellos are sent every 60 seconds. The hold time is 3 times the hello, or 15 seconds on most networks and 180 seconds on low-speed NBMA networks.

The hello and hold-down values do not need to match for two routers to become neighbors. The **show ip eigrp neighbors** command is used to view the neighbor table and verify that EIGRP has established an adjacency with its neighbors.

EIGRP does not send periodic updates like RIP. EIGRP sends partial and bounded updates. *Partial* means the update includes only the route changes. *Bounded* means the update is only sent to those routers that are affected by the change. The EIGRP composite metric uses bandwidth, delay, reliability, and load to determine best path. By default, only bandwidth and delay are used. The default calculation is the slowest bandwidth plus the sum of the delays of the outgoing interfaces from the router to the destination network.

At the center of EIGRP is DUAL. The DUAL FSM is used to determine the best path and potential backup paths to every destination network. The successor is a neighboring router that is used to forward the packet using the least-cost route to the destination network. FD is the lowest calculated metric to reach the destination network through the successor. An FS is a neighbor who has a loop-free backup path to the same network as the successor and also meets the FC. The FC is met when a neighbor's RD to a network is less than the local router's FD to the same destination network. The RD is simply an EIGRP neighbor's FD to the destination network.

EIGRP is configured with the **router eigrp autonomous-system** command. The *autonomous-system* value is actually a process ID and must be the same on all routers in the EIGRP routing domain. The **network** command is similar to that used with RIP. The network is the classful network address of the directly connected interfaces on the router. A wildcard mask is an optional parameter that can be used to include only specific interfaces.

There are several ways to propagate a static default route with EIGRP. The **redistribute static** command in EIGRP router mode is a common method.

Activities and Labs

The activities and labs available in the companion *Routing Protocols and Concepts, CCNA Exploration Labs and Study Guide* (ISBN 1-58713-204-4) provide hands-on practice with the following topics introduced in this chapter:

Lab 9-1: Basic EIGRP Configuration (9.6.1)

In this lab, you learn how to configure the routing protocol EIGRP. A loopback address is used on the R2 router to simulate a connection to an ISP, where all traffic that is not destined for the local network will be sent. Some segments of the network have been subnetted using VLSM. EIGRP is a classless routing protocol that can be used to provide subnet mask information in the routing updates. This will allow VLSM subnet information to be propagated throughout the network.

Lab 9-2: Challenge EIGRP Configuration (9.6.2)

In this lab activity, you are given a network address that must be subnetted using VLSM to complete the addressing of the network. A combination of EIGRP routing and static routing is required so that hosts on networks that are not directly connected will be able to communicate with each other. EIGRP must be configured so that all IP traffic takes the shortest path to the destination address.

Lab 9-3: Troubleshooting EIGRP Configuration (9.6.3)

In this lab, you begin by loading corrupted configuration scripts on each of the routers. These scripts contain errors that will prevent end-to-end communication across the network. You need to troubleshoot each router to determine the configuration errors and then use the appropriate commands to correct the configurations. When you have corrected all the configuration errors, all the hosts on the network should be able to communicate with each other.

Many of the Hands-on Labs include Packet Tracer Companion Activities where you can use Packet Tracer to complete a simulation of the lab. Look for this icon in the *Labs and Study Guide* (ISBN 1-58713-204-4) for Hands-on Labs that have a Packet Tracer Companion.

Check Your Understanding

Complete all the review questions listed here to test your understanding of the topics and concepts in this chapter. Answers are listed in the appendix, "Check Your Understanding and Challenge Questions Answer Key."

1. What is the purpose of the EIGRP PDM?

    A. PDM is the Layer 4 protocol EIGRP uses to share routing information.

    B. PDM is the mechanism that EIGRP uses to ensure the availability of neighboring routers.

    C. PDM is the algorithm engine used by EIGRP to create routing tables.

    D. PDM provides modular support for Layer 3 protocols.

    E. PDM is the distance to a destination as reported by a neighboring router.

2. Match the EIGRP terms and concepts with their correct descriptions.

    Terms and concepts:

    Neighbor table

    Topology table

    Routing table

    Successor

    Feasible successor router

    Descriptions:

    A. Contains the EIGRP routes to be used for packet forwarding

    B. The primary route to be used; selected by DUAL

    C. Important EIGRP data source; lists adjacent routers

    D. Backup path to a destination network

    E. Contains all learned routes to all destination networks

3. What type of EIGRP packet is used to discover, verify, and rediscover neighboring routers?

    A. Acknowledgment

    B. Hello

    C. Query

    D. Reply

4. If an EIGRP route goes down and a feasible successor is not found in the topology table, how does DUAL flag the route that has failed?

A. Recomputed

B. Passive

C. Active

D. Down

E. Unreachable

F. Successor

5. Which of the following tables does a router running EIGRP maintain? (Choose three.)

A. DUAL table

B. Feasible distance table

C. Neighbor table

D. OSPF table

E. Routing table

F. Topology table

6. What is the purpose of the EIGRP neighbor and topology tables?

A. The neighbor and topology tables are used by DUAL to build the routing table.

B. The neighbor table is sent to all neighboring routers, which use it to build topology tables.

C. The topology table is sent to all routers listed in the neighbor table.

D. The neighbor table is used by DUAL to create the topology table.

E. The neighbor table is broadcast to neighbor routers, and the topology table is broadcast to all other routers.

7. Refer to Example 9-52. What does the 255/255 value in the output represent?

Example 9-52   Check Your Understanding, Question 7

```
R1#show interface serial 0/0/0
Serial0/0/0 is up, line protocol is up
  Hardware is GT96K Serial
  Description: Link to R2
  Internet address is 172.16.3.1/30
  MTU 1500 bytes, BW 1544 Kbit, DLY 20000 usec,
     reliability 255/255, txload 1/255, rxload 1/255
  Encapsulation HDLC, loopback not set
```

    A. The number of times that the link was operational during 255 polls

    B. The link failure rate over 255 seconds

    C. The probability that the link will continue to be operational

    D. A static value representing the normal reliability of an interface type

8. Match the EIGRP term with its correct description.

    Terms:

    Feasible successor

    Successor

    Feasible distance

    Routing table

    Topology table

    Definitions:

    A. A viable backup path to a network

    B. A route that is used for packet forwarding and is the least-cost route

    C. The lowest calculated metric to reach destination network

    D. A table that contains successors and feasible successors

    E. A table that contains only successors

9. A network administrator is troubleshooting an EIGRP routing issue. What command will show the administrator all possible paths to a destination?

   A. **show ip route**

   B. **show ip eigrp topology active**

   C. **show ip eigrp neighbors detail**

   D. **show ip eigrp topology all-links**

   E. **show ip eigrp topology summary**

10. Refer to Example 9-53. What reported distance is the feasible successor to network 192.168.1.0 advertising?

Example 9-53   Check Your Understanding, Question 10

```
R1#show ip eigrp topology

<output omitted>

P 192.168.10.0/24, 1 successors, FD is 3011840
        via Summary (3011840/0), Null0
        via 172.16.3.1 (41024000/2169856), Serial0/0/0
P 192.168.10.4/30, 1 successors, FD is 3523840
        via 192.168.10.10 (3523840/2169856), Serial0/0/1
P 192.168.1.0/24, 1 successors, FD is 3014400
        via 192.168.10.10 (3014400/28160), Serial0/0/1
        via 172.16.31 (41026560/2172416), Serial0/0/0
<output omitted>
```

   A. 28160

   B. 3014400

   C. 2172416

   D. 41026560

11. What routing algorithm does EIGRP use?

12. Does EIGRP send periodic updates?

13. What command enables you to verify that EIGRP has established relationships with its directly connected neighbors?

14. What metrics does the EIGRP composite metric use? Which ones are used by default?

15. What is the feasibility condition?

16. Does EIGRP use automatic summarization similar to RIP? If so, how can it be disabled?

Challenge Questions and Activities

These questions require a deeper application of the concepts covered in this chapter and are similar to the style of questions you might see on a CCNA certification exam. You can find the answers to these questions in the appendix, "Answers to Check Your Understanding and Challenge Questions and Activities."

1. When enabling EIGRP with the router mode command **router eigrp** *autonomous-system*, what are the requirements regarding the *autonomous-system* parameter?

2. The following is output from the **show ip eigrp topology** command. Does this output show a feasible successor? How can you tell?

```
P 192.168.10.4/30, 1 successors, FD is 3523840
          via 192.168.10.10 (3523840/2169856), Serial0/1
          via 172.16.3.1 (41024000/2169856), Serial0/0
```

3. Under what conditions is a Null0 summary route sometimes automatically included by EIGRP?

To Learn More

Routing TCP/IP, Volume I

There are several good sources to learn more about DUAL. *Routing TCP/IP, Volume I*, Second Edition, by Jeff Doyle and Jennifer Carroll, includes an excellent section on the Diffusing Update Algorithm, including two diffusing computation examples.

J.J. Garcia-Luna-Aceves

DUAL was first proposed by E. W. Dijkstra and C. S. Scholten, with the most prominent work done by J. J. Garcia-Luna-Aceves. J. J. Garcia-Luna-Aceves is the Jack Baskin Chair of Computer Engineering at the University of California, Santa Cruz (UCSC) and is a Principal Scientist at the Palo Alto Research Center (PARC). Several of J. J. Garcia-Luna-Aceves's published articles, including his work done on DUAL, "Loop-Free Routing Using Diffusing Computations," IEEE/ACM Transactions on Networking, Vol. 1, No. 1, February 1993, can be found at http://www.soe.ucsc.edu/research/ccrg/publications.html.

CHAPTER 10

Link-State Routing Protocols

Objectives

Upon completion of this chapter, you should be able to answer the following questions:

- What are the basic features and concepts of link-state routing protocols?

- What are the benefits and requirements of link-state routing protocols?

Key Terms

This chapter uses the following key terms. You can find the definitions in the Glossary at the end of the book.

link-state routing protocol   *page 470*

shortest path first (SPF) algorithm   *page 470*

link-state packet (LSP)   *page 474*

link-state database   *page 480*

In Chapter 3, "Introduction to Dynamic Routing Protocols," you learned the difference between link-state and distance vector routing with an analogy. The analogy stated that distance vector routing protocols are like using road signs to guide you on your way to a destination, only giving you information about distance and direction. However, link-state routing protocols are like using a map. With a map, you can see all the potential routes and determine your own preferred path.

Distance vector routing protocols are like road signs because routers must make preferred path decisions based on a distance or metric to a network. Just as travelers trust a road sign to accurately state the distance to the next town, a distance vector router trusts that another router is advertising the true distance to the destination network.

Link-state routing protocols take a different approach. Link-state routing protocols are more like a road map because they create a topological map of the network and each router uses this map to determine the shortest path to each network. Just as you refer to a map to find the route to another town, link-state routers use a map to determine the preferred path to reach another destination.

Routers running a *link-state routing protocol* send information about the state of their links to other routers in the routing domain. The state of those links refers to its directly connected networks and includes information about the type of network and any neighboring routers on those networks—hence the name link-state routing protocol.

The ultimate objective is that every router receives all the link-state information about all other routers in the routing area. With this link-state information, each router can create its own topological map of the network and independently calculate the shortest path to every network.

This chapter introduces the concepts of link-state routing protocols. In Chapter 11, "OSPF," we will apply these concepts to Open Shortest Path First (OSPF).

Link-State Routing

Distance vector routing protocols are thought to be simple to understand, whereas link-state routing protocols have the reputation of being very complex, even intimidating. However, link-state routing protocols and concepts are not difficult to understand. In many ways, the link-state process is simpler to understand than distance vector concepts.

Link-State Routing Protocols

Link-state routing protocols are also known as shortest path first protocols and are built around Edsger Dijkstra's *shortest path first (SPF) algorithm*. The SPF algorithm will be discussed in more detail in a later section.

Figure 10-1 illustrates the IP link-state routing protocols:

- Open Shortest Path First (OSPF)

- Intermediate System–to–Intermediate System (IS-IS)

Figure 10-1 Classification of Routing Protocols

| | Interior Gateway Protocols | | | | Exterior Gateway Protocols |
	Distance Vector Routing Protocols		Link-State Routing Protocols		Path Vector
Classful	RIP	IGRP			EGP
Classless	RIPv2	EIGRP	OSPFv2	IS-IS	BGPv4
IPv6	RIPng	EIGRP for IPv6	OSPFv3	IS-IS for IPv6	BGPv4 for IPv6

Link-state routing protocols have the reputation of being much more complex than their distance vector counterparts. However, the basic functionality and configuration of link-state routing protocols are not complex. Even the algorithm itself can be easily understood, as you will see in the next topic. Basic OSPF operations can be configured with a **router ospf process-id** command and a network statement, similar to other routing protocols such as Routing Information Protocol (RIP) and Enhanced Interior Gateway Routing Protocol (EIGRP).

Note

OSPF is discussed in Chapter 11, and IS-IS is discussed in the CCNP curricula. There are also link-state routing protocols for non-IP networks. These include DEC's DNA Phase V and Novell's NetWare Link Services Protocol (NLSP), which are not part of the CCNA or CCNP curriculum.

Introduction to the SPF Algorithm

Dijkstra's algorithm is commonly referred to as the shortest path first (SPF) algorithm. This algorithm accumulates costs along each path, from source to destination. Although Dijkstra's algorithm is known as the shortest path first algorithm, this is in fact the purpose of every routing algorithm.

In Figure 10-2, each path is labeled with an arbitrary value for cost. The cost of the shortest path for R2 to send packets to the LAN attached to R3 is 27 (20 + 5 + 2 = 27). Notice that this cost is not 27 for all routers to reach the LAN attached to R3. Each router determines its own cost to each destination in the topology. In other words, each router calculates the SPF algorithm and determines the cost from its own perspective. This will become more evident later in this chapter.

Figure 10-2   Dijkstra's Shortest Path First Algorithm

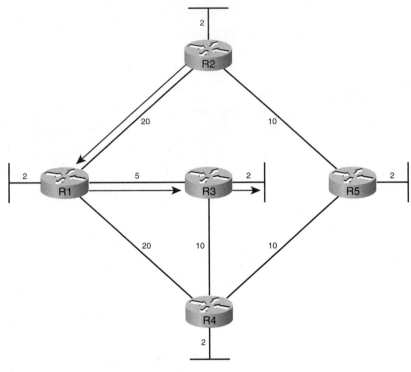

Shortest Path for Host on R2 LAN to Reach Host on R3 LAN:
R2 to R1 (20) + R1 to R3 (5) + R3 to LAN (2) = 27

Table 10-1 lists, for R1, the shortest path to each LAN, along with the cost.

Table 10-1   SPF Tree for R1

Destination	Shortest Path	Cost
R2 LAN	R1 to R2	22
R3 LAN	R1 to R3	7
R4 LAN	R1 to R3 to R4	17
R5 LAN	R1 to R3 to R4 to R5	27

The shortest path is not necessarily the path with the least number of hops. For example, look at the path to the R5 LAN. You might think that R1 would send directly to R4 instead of to R3. However, the cost to reach R4 directly (22) is higher than the cost to reach R4 through R3 (17).

Observe the shortest path for each router to reach each of the LANs, as shown in Tables 10-2 through 10-5.

Table 10-2 SPF Tree for R2

Destination	Shortest Path	Cost
R1 LAN	R2 to R1	22
R3 LAN	R2 to R1 to R3	27
R4 LAN	R2 to R5 to R4	22
R5 LAN	R2 to R5	12

Table 10-3 SPF Tree for R3

Destination	Shortest Path	Cost
R1 LAN	R3 to R1	7
R2 LAN	R3 to R1 to R2	27
R4 LAN	R3 to R4	12
R5 LAN	R3 to R4 to R5	22

Table 10-4 SPF Tree for R4

Destination	Shortest Path	Cost
R1 LAN	R4 to R3 to R1	17
R2 LAN	R4 to R5 to R2	22
R3 LAN	R4 to R3	12
R5 LAN	R4 to R5	12

Table 10-5 SPF Tree for R5

Destination	Shortest Path	Cost
R1 LAN	R5 to R4 to R3 to R1	27
R2 LAN	R5 to R2	12
R3 LAN	R5 to R4 to R3	22
R4 LAN	R5 to R4	12

Link-State Routing Process

So exactly how does a link-state routing protocol work? The following list summarizes the link-state routing process. All routers in the topology will complete the following generic link-state routing process to reach a state of convergence:

1. Each router learns about its own links, its own directly connected networks. This is done by detecting that an interface is in the up state, including a Layer 3 address.

2. Each router is responsible for meeting its neighbors on directly connected networks. Similar to EIGRP, link-state routers do this by exchanging Hello packets with other link-state routers on directly connected networks.

3. Each router builds a *link-state packet (LSP)* containing the state of each directly connected link. This is done by recording all the pertinent information about each neighbor, including neighbor ID, link type, and bandwidth.

4. Each router floods the LSP to all neighbors, who then store all LSPs received in a database. Neighbors then flood the LSPs to their neighbors until all routers in the area have received the LSPs. Each router stores a copy of each LSP received from its neighbors in a local database.

5. Each router uses the database to construct a complete map of the topology and computes the best path to each destination network. Like having a road map, the router now has a complete map of all destinations in the topology and the routes to reach them. The SPF algorithm is used to construct the map of the topology and to determine the best path to each network. All routers will have a common map or tree of the topology, but each router will independently determine the best path to each network within that topology.

The sections that follow discuss the different steps of the process in more detail.

Step 1: Learning About Directly Connected Networks

The topology now shows the network addresses for each link. Referring to Step 1 in the list summarizing the link-state routing process, *each router learns about its own links, its own directly connected networks.* This is done in the same way as was discussed in Chapter 1, "Introduction to Routing and Packet Forwarding." When a router interface is configured with an IP address and subnet mask, the interface becomes part of that network.

When you correctly configure and activate the interfaces, the router learns about its own directly connected networks, as shown in Figure 10-3.

Regardless of the routing protocols used, these directly connected networks are now part of the routing table. For the purposes of our discussion, we will focus on the link-state routing process from the perspective of R1.

Figure 10-3   R1 Learns About Directly Connected Networks

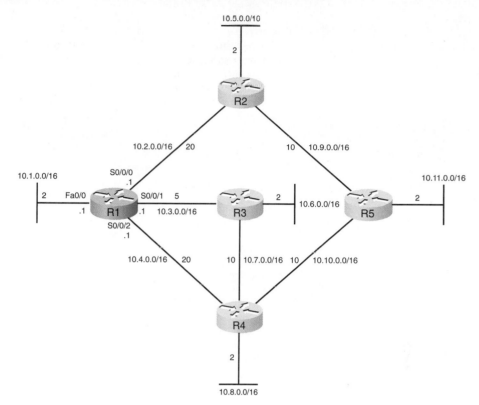

Links

With link-state routing protocols, a link is an interface on a router. As with distance vector protocols and static routes, the interface must be properly configured with an IP address and subnet mask, and the link must be in the up state before the link-state routing protocol can learn about a link. Also, like distance vector protocols, the interface must be included in one of the network statements before it can participate in the link-state routing process.

Figure 10-4 shows R1 linked to four directly connected networks:

- FastEthernet 0/0 interface on the 10.1.0.0/16 network

- Serial 0/0/0 network on the 10.2.0.0/16 network

- Serial 0/0/1 network on the 10.3.0.0/16 network

- Serial 0/0/2 network on the 10.4.0.0/16 network

Figure 10-4   Link-State Information for R1

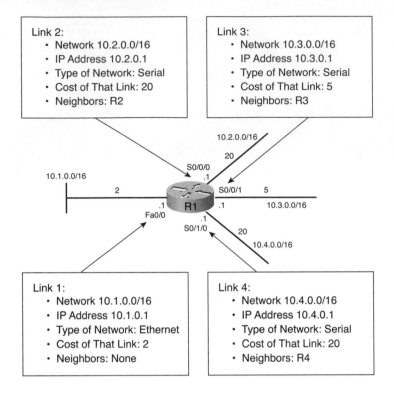

Link 2:
- Network 10.2.0.0/16
- IP Address 10.2.0.1
- Type of Network: Serial
- Cost of That Link: 20
- Neighbors: R2

Link 3:
- Network 10.3.0.0/16
- IP Address 10.3.0.1
- Type of Network: Serial
- Cost of That Link: 5
- Neighbors: R3

Link 1:
- Network 10.1.0.0/16
- IP Address 10.1.0.1
- Type of Network: Ethernet
- Cost of That Link: 2
- Neighbors: None

Link 4:
- Network 10.4.0.0/16
- IP Address 10.4.0.1
- Type of Network: Serial
- Cost of That Link: 20
- Neighbors: R4

Link States

Information about the state of a router's links is known as *link states*. As you can see from Figure 10-4, this information includes

- The interface's IP address and subnet mask

- The type of network, such as Ethernet (broadcast) or serial point-to-point link

- The cost of that link

- Any neighbor routers on that link

Note

Initially, the router will not be aware of any neighbor routers on the link. Not until the router receives a Hello packet from the adjacent neighbor does it learn about that neighbor. Hello packets are discussed in the following section.

You will see that the Cisco implementation of OSPF specifies the cost of the link, the OSPF routing metric, as the bandwidth of the outgoing interface. But for the purposes of this chapter, we are using arbitrary cost values to simplify our demonstration.

Step 2: Sending Hello Packets to Neighbors

The second step in the link-state routing process is as follows:

Each router is responsible for meeting its neighbors on directly connected networks.

Routers with link-state routing protocols use a Hello protocol to discover any neighbors on their links. A neighbor is any other router that is enabled with the same link-state routing protocol.

Figure 10-5 shows R1 sending Hello packets out its links (interfaces) to discover whether there are any neighbors. R2, R3, and R4 reply to the Hello packet with their own Hello packets because these routers are configured with the same link-state routing protocol. There are no neighbors out the FastEthernet 0/0 interface. Because R1 does not receive a Hello on this interface, it will not continue with the link-state routing process steps for the FastEthernet 0/0 link.

Figure 10-5   R1 Discovers Neighbors on Directly Connected Networks

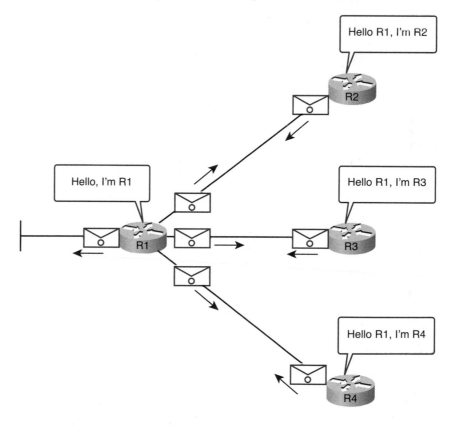

Similar to EIGRP's Hello packets, when two link-state routers learn that they are neighbors, they form an adjacency. These small Hello packets continue to be exchanged between two adjacent neighbors, which serve as a "keepalive" function to monitor the state of the neighbor. If a router stops receiving Hello packets from a neighbor, that neighbor is considered unreachable and the adjacency is broken. In this example, R1 forms an adjacency with all three routers.

Step 3: Building the Link-State Packet

We are now at the third step in the link-state routing process:

> Each router builds a link-state packet (LSP) containing the state of each directly connected link.

After a router has established its adjacencies, it can build its LSPs, which contain the link-state information about its links. The router only sends LSPs out interfaces where it has established adjacencies with other routers. Notice that R1 does not send LSPs out its Ethernet interface. Figure 10-6 shows a simplified version of the LSPs from R1 as

1. R1; Ethernet network 10.1.0.0/16; Cost 2

2. R1 -> R2; Serial point-to-point network; 10.2.0.0/16; Cost 20

3. R1 -> R3; Serial point-to-point network; 10.3.0.0/16; Cost 5

4. R1 -> R4; Serial point-to-point network; 10.4.0.0/16; Cost 20

Figure 10-6   R1 Builds a Link-State Packet

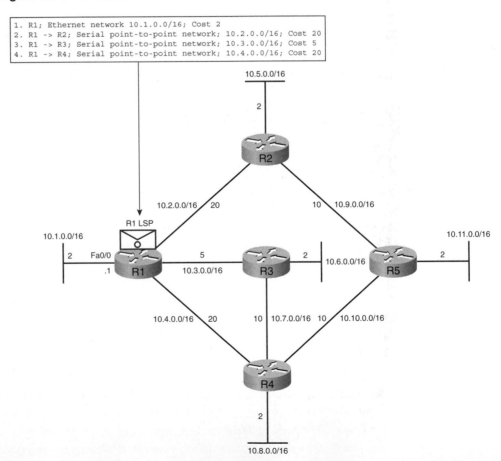

Step 4: Flooding Link-State Packets to Neighbors

The fourth step in the link-state routing process is as follows:

> Each router floods the LSP to all neighbors, who then store all LSPs received in a database.

Each router floods its link-state information to all other link-state routers in the routing area. Whenever a router receives an LSP from a neighboring router, it immediately sends that LSP out all other interfaces, except the interface that received the LSP. This process creates a flooding effect of LSPs from all routers throughout the routing area.

As you can see in Figure 10-7, the LSPs from R1 are flooded throughout the network. When a router receives an LSP, it forwards it almost immediately without intermediate calculations. The LSP is therefore quickly dispersed through the entire network.

Figure 10-7   LSP from R1 Is Flooded to All Neighbors

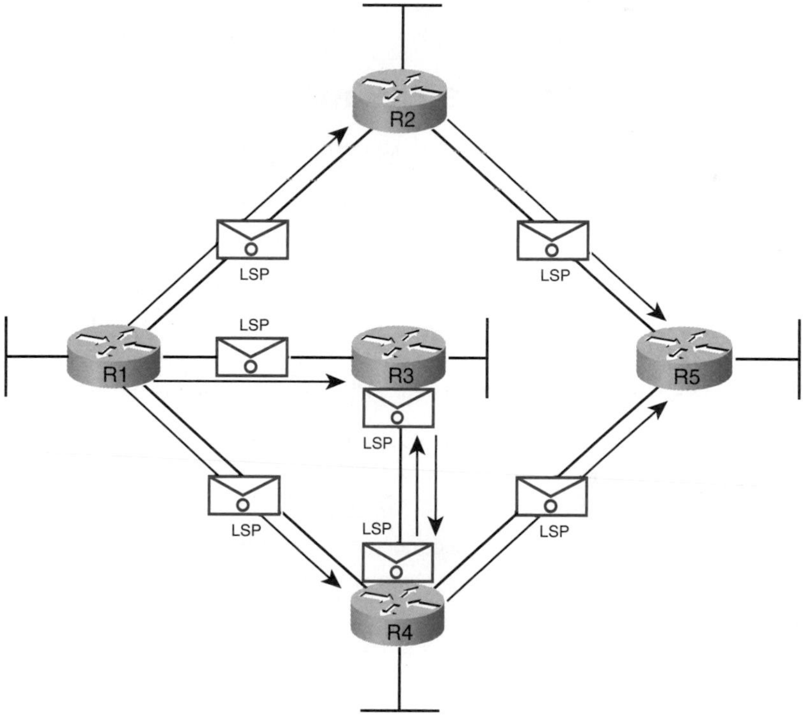

Unlike distance vector routing protocols that must first run the Bellman-Ford algorithm to process routing updates before sending them to other routers, link-state routing protocols calculate the SPF algorithm after the flooding is complete. As a result, link-state routing protocols reach convergence much faster than distance vector routing protocols.

Remember that LSPs do not need to be sent periodically, unlike Hello packets. An LSP needs to be sent only

- During initial startup of the router or of the routing protocol process on that router

- Whenever there is a change in the topology, including a link going down or coming up, or a neighbor adjacency being established or broken

In addition to the link-state information, other information is included in the LSP—such as sequence numbers and aging information—to help manage the flooding process. This information is used by each router to determine whether it has already received the LSP from another router or whether the LSP has newer information than what is already contained in the *link-state database*. This process allows a router to keep only the most current information in its link-state database.

> **Note**
>
> How these sequence numbers and aging information are used is beyond the scope of this curriculum. Additional information can be found in *Routing TCP/IP*, by Jeff Doyle.

Step 5: Constructing a Link-State Database

The final step in the link-state routing process is as follows:

> Each router uses the database to construct a complete map of the topology and computes the best path to each destination network.

After each router has propagated its own LSPs using the link-state flooding process, each router will then have an LSP from every link-state router in the routing area. These LSPs are stored in the link-state database. Each router in the routing area can now use the SPF algorithm to construct the SPF trees that you saw earlier.

Table 10-6 lists all the links that R1 now has in its link-state database.

Table 10-6   Link-State Database for R1

LSPs from R2	Connected to neighbor R1 on network 10.2.0.0/16, cost of 20
	Connected to neighbor R5 on network 10.9.0.0/16, cost of 10
	Has a network 10.5.0.0/16, cost of 2
LSPs from R3	Connected to neighbor R1 on network 10.3.0.0/16, cost of 5
	Connected to neighbor R4 on network 10.7.0.0/16, cost of 10
	Has a network 10.6.0.0/16, cost of 2

LSPs from R4	Connected to neighbor R1 on network 10.4.0.0/16, cost of 20
	Connected to neighbor R3 on network 10.7.0.0/16, cost of 10
	Connected to neighbor R5 on network 10.10.0.0/16, cost of 10
	Has a network 10.8.0.0/16, cost of 2
LSPs from R5	Connected to neighbor R2 on network 10.9.0.0/16, cost of 10
	Connected to neighbor R4 on network 10.10.0.0/16, cost of 10
	Has a network 10.11.0.0/16, cost of 2
R1 link states	Connected to neighbor R2 on network 10.2.0.0/16, cost of 20
	Connected to neighbor R3 on network 10.3.0.0/16, cost of 5
	Connected to neighbor R4 on network 10.4.0.0/16, cost of 20
	Has a network 10.1.0.0/16, cost of 2

Table 10-7 shows the SPF tree that results from the calculation of the SPF algorithm. This is the same table you saw earlier in Table 10-1.

Table 10-7   SPF Tree for R1

Destination	Shortest Path	Cost
R2 LAN	R1 to R2	22
R3 LAN	R1 to R3	7
R4 LAN	R1 to R3 to R4	17
R5 LAN	R1 to R3 to R4 to R5	27

As a result of the flooding process, Router R1 has learned the link-state information for each router in its routing area. The figure shows the link-state information that R1 has received and stored in its link-state database. Notice that R1 also includes its own link-state information in the link-state database.

With a complete link-state database, R1 can now use the database and the shortest path first (SPF) algorithm to calculate the preferred path or shortest path to each network. Notice that R1 does not use the path between itself and R4 to reach any LAN in the topology, including the LAN attached to R4. The path through R3 has a lower cost. Also, R1 does not use the path between R2 and R5 to reach R5. The path through R3 has a lower cost. Each router in the topology determines the shortest path from its own perspective.

> **Note**
>
> The link-state database and the SPF tree would still include those directly connected networks, those links that have been shaded in Table 10-6.

Shortest Path First (SPF) Tree

Remember from the introduction that Dijkstra's algorithm is commonly referred to as the shortest path first (SPF) algorithm. This algorithm accumulates costs along each path, from source to destination.

Building the SPF Tree

Figure 10-8 shows R1's current topology at the beginning of the tree-construction process. Notice that the tree (topology) only includes its directly connected neighbors.

Figure 10-8   R1 Links Only

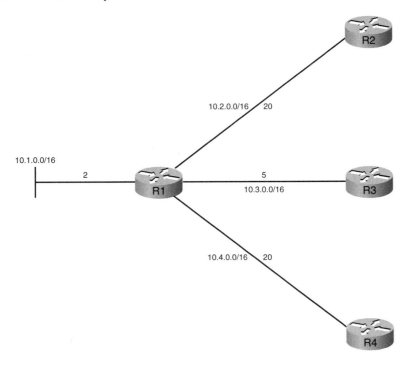

However, using the link-state information from all other routers, R1 can now begin to construct an SPF tree of the network with itself at the root of the tree.

Note

The process described in this section is only a conceptual form of the SPF algorithm and SPF tree to help make them more understandable.

The SPF algorithm begins by processing the following LSP information from R2:

- Connected to neighbor R1 on network 10.2.0.0/16, cost of 20

- Connected to neighbor R5 on network 10.9.0.0/16, cost of 10

- Has a network 10.5.0.0/16, cost of 2

Figure 10-9 shows the new links R1 learned from R2.

Figure 10-9   R1 Processes the LSPs from R2

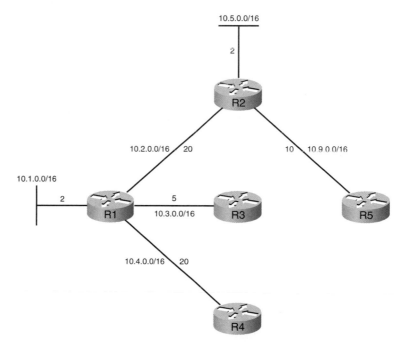

R1 can ignore the first LSP, because R1 already knows that it is connected to R2 on network 10.2.0.0/16 with a cost of 20. R1 can use the second LSP and create a link from R2 to another router, R5, with the network 10.9.0.0/16 and a cost of 10. This information is added to the SPF tree. Using the third LSP, R1 has learned that R2 has a network 10.5.0.0/16 with a cost of 2 and with no neighbors. This link is added to R1's SPF tree.

The SPF algorithm now processes the LSPs from R3 as follows:

- Connected to neighbor R1 on network 10.3.0.0/16, cost of 5

- Connected to neighbor R4 on network 10.7.0.0/16, cost of 10

- Has a network 10.6.0.0/16, cost of 2

Figure 10-10 shows the new links R1 learned from R3.

Figure 10-10 R1 Processes the LSPs from R3

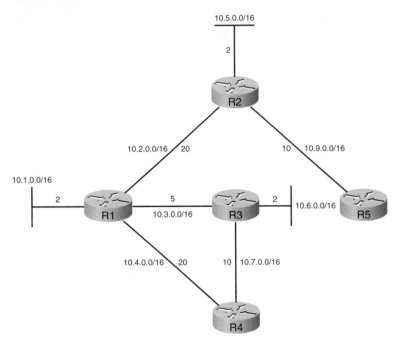

R1 can ignore the first LSP, because R1 already knows that it is connected to R3 on network 10.3.0.0/16 with a cost of 5. R1 can use the second LSP and create a link from R3 to Router R4, with the network 10.7.0.0/16 and a cost of 10. This information is added to the SPF tree. Using the third LSP, R1 has learned that R3 has a network 10.6.0.0/16 with a cost of 2 and with no neighbors. This link is added to R1's SPF tree.

The SPF algorithm now processes the LSPs from R4 as follows:

- Connected to neighbor R1 on network 10.4.0.0/16, cost of 20

- Connected to neighbor R3 on network 10.7.0.0/16, cost of 10

- Connected to neighbor R5 on network 10.10.0.0/16, cost of 10

- Has a network 10.8.0.0/16, cost of 2

Figure 10-11 shows the new links R1 learned from R4.

Figure 10-11 R1 Processes the LSPs from R4

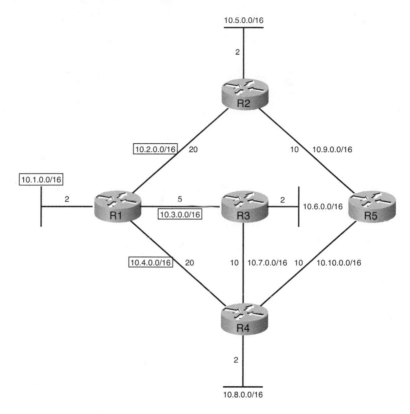

R1 can ignore the first LSP because R1 already knows that it is connected to R4 on network 10.4.0.0/16 with a cost of 20. R1 can also ignore the second LSP because SPF has already learned about the network 10.6.0.0/16 with a cost of 10 from R3.

However, R1 can use the third LSP to create a link from R4 to Router R5, with the network 10.10.0.0/16 and a cost of 10. This information is added to the SPF tree. Using the fourth LSP, R1 learns that R4 has a network 10.8.0.0/16 with a cost of 2 and with no neighbors. This link is added to R1's SPF tree.

The SPF algorithm now processes the final LSPs from R5 as follows:

- Connected to neighbor R2 on network 10.9.0.0/16, cost of 10

- Connected to neighbor R4 on network 10.10.0.0/16, cost of 10

- Has a network 10.11.0.0/16, cost of 2

Figure 10-12 shows the new links R1 learned from R5.

Figure 10-12 R1 Processes the LSPs from R5

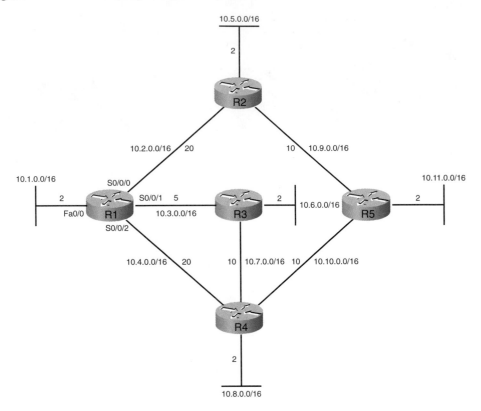

R1 can ignore the first two LSPs (for the networks 10.9.0.0/16 and 10.10.0.0/16), because SPF has already learned about these links and added them to the SPF tree. R1 can process the third LSP, learning that R5 has a network 10.11.0.0/16 with a cost of 2 and with no neighbors. This link is added to the SPF tree for R1.

Determining the Shortest Path

Because all LSPs have been processed using the SPF algorithm, R1 has now constructed the complete SPF tree. The 10.4.0.0/16 and 10.9.0.0/16 links are not used to reach other networks, because lower-cost or shorter paths exist. However, these networks still exist as part of the SPF tree and are used to reach devices on those networks.

Note

The actual SPF algorithm determines the shortest path as it is building the SPF tree. We have done it in two steps to simplify the understanding of the algorithm.

Table 10-8 repeats the SPF tree for R1 that you have already seen.

Table 10-8   SPF Tree for R1

Destination	Shortest Path	Cost
R2 LAN	R1 to R2	22
R3 LAN	R1 to R3	7
R4 LAN	R1 to R3 to R4	17
R5 LAN	R1 to R3 to R4 to R5	27

Using this tree, the SPF algorithm results indicate the shortest path to each network. Only the LANs are shown in the table, but SPF can also be used to determine the shortest path to each WAN link network in Figure 10-12, shown earlier. In this case, R1 determines that the shortest path for each network is as follows:

- Network 10.5.0.0/16 via R2 Serial 0/0/0 at a cost of 22
- Network 10.6.0.0/16 via R3 Serial 0/0/1 at a cost of 7
- Network 10.7.0.0/16 via R3 Serial 0/0/1 at a cost of 15
- Network 10.8.0.0/16 via R3 Serial 0/0/1 at a cost of 17
- Network 10.9.0.0/16 via R2 Serial 0/0/0 at a cost of 30
- Network 10.10.0.0/16 via R3 Serial 0/0/1 at a cost of 25
- Network 10.11.0.0/16 via R3 Serial 0/0/1 at a cost of 27

Each router constructs its own SPF tree independently from all other routers. To ensure proper routing, the link-state databases used to construct those trees must be identical on all routers. In Chapter 11, we will examine this in more detail.

Generating a Routing Table from the SPF Tree

Using the shortest path information determined by the SPF algorithm, these paths listed previously can now be added to the routing table.

The routing table will also include all directly connected networks and routes from any other sources, such as static routes. Packets will now be forwarded according to these entries in the routing table.

Implementing Link-State Routing Protocols

Chapter 11 discusses the implementation and configuration of a link-state routing protocol, OSPF. The following sections discuss the advantages, requirements, and comparisons of link-state routing protocols.

Advantages of a Link-State Routing Protocol

There are several advantages of link-state routing protocols compared to distance vector routing protocols.

Builds a Topological Map

Link-state routing protocols create a topological map, or SPF tree, of the network topology. Distance vector routing protocols do not have a topological map of the network. Routers implementing a distance vector routing protocol only have a list of networks, which includes the cost (distance) and next-hop routers (direction) to those networks. Because link-state routing protocols exchange link states, the SPF algorithm can build an SPF tree of the network. Using the SPF tree, each router can independently determine the shortest path to every network.

Fast Convergence

There are several reasons why a link-state routing protocol converges faster than a distance vector routing protocol. When receiving a link-state packet (LSP), link-state routing protocols immediately flood the LSP out all interfaces except for the interface from which the LSP was received. A router using a distance vector routing protocol needs to process each routing update and update its routing table before flooding them out other interfaces, even with triggered updates. Faster convergence is achieved with link-state routing protocols. A notable exception is EIGRP.

Another reason that a link-state protocol converges faster is the lack of a hold-down timer, which is a distance vector routing protocol feature designed to give the network time to converge. Link-state routing protocols do not use a hold-down timer because any changes in the topology are flooded immediately with the entire routing domain using LSPs.

Event-Driven Updates

After the initial flooding of LSPs, link-state routing protocols only send out an LSP when there is a change in the topology. The LSP contains only the information regarding the affected link. Unlike some distance vector routing protocols, link-state routing protocols do not send periodic updates.

Note

OSPF routers do flood their own link states every 30 minutes. This is known as a *paranoid update* and is discussed in the following chapter. Also, not all distance vector routing protocols send periodic updates. RIP and IGRP send periodic updates; however, EIGRP does not.

Hierarchical Design

Link-state routing protocols such as OSPF and IS-IS use the concept of areas. Multiple areas create a hierarchical design to networks, allowing better route aggregation (summarization) and the isolation of routing issues within an area. Multi-area OSPF and IS-IS are discussed further in CCNP.

The advantages of link-state routing protocols are summarized in the following list:

- Each router builds its own topological map of the network to determine the shortest path.

- Immediate flooding of LSPs achieves faster convergence.

- LSPs are sent only when there is a change in the topology and contain only the information regarding that change.

- Hierarchical design is used when implementing multiple areas.

Requirements of a Link-State Routing Protocol

Modern link-state routing protocols are designed to minimize the effects on memory, CPU, and bandwidth usage. The use and configuration of multiple areas can reduce the size of the link-state databases. Multiple areas can also limit the amount of link-state information flooding in a routing domain and send LSPs only to those routers that need them.

For example, when there is a change in the topology, only those routers in the affected area receive the LSP and run the SPF algorithm. This can help isolate an unstable link to a specific area in the routing domain. In Figure 10-13, there are three separate routing domains: Area 1, Area 0, and Area 51.

If a network in Area 51 goes down, the LSP with the information about this downed link is only flooded to other routers in that area. Only routers in Area 51 will need to update their link-state databases, rerun the SPF algorithm, create a new SPF tree, and update their routing tables. Routers in other areas will learn that this route is down, but this will be done with a type of link-state packet that is essentially a distance vector technique and that does not cause them to rerun their SPF algorithm. Routers in other areas can update their routing tables directly and do not need the processing resources required to rerun the SPF algorithm.

Figure 10-13 Multiple Areas and the SPF Algorithm

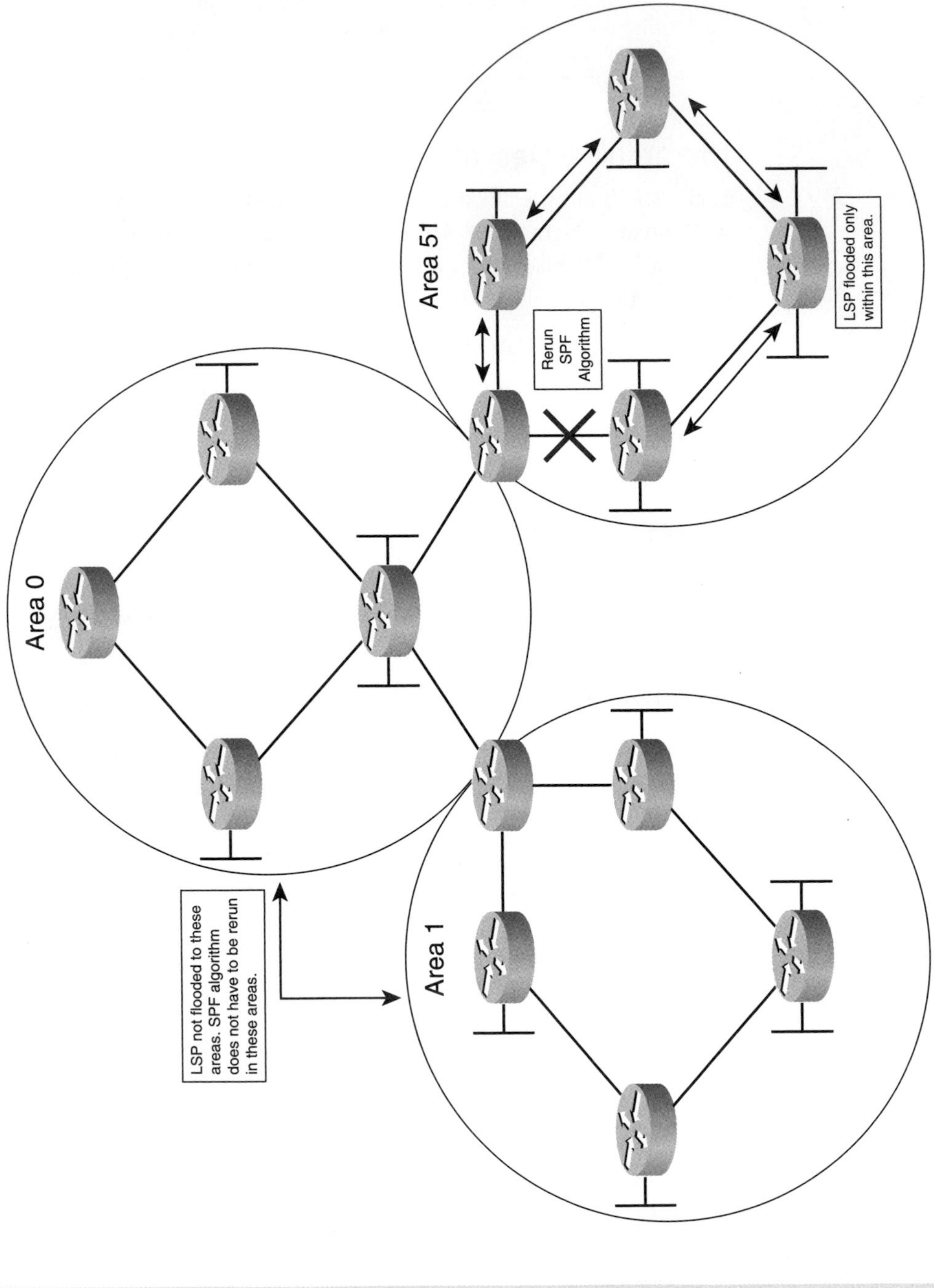

Note

Multiple areas with OSPF and IS-IS are discussed in CCNP-level routing protocol books.

Memory Requirements

Link-state routing protocols typically require more memory, more CPU processing, and at times, more bandwidth than distance vector routing protocols. The memory requirements are because of the use of link-state databases and the creation of the SPF tree.

Processing Requirements

Link-state protocols can also require more CPU processing than distance vector routing protocols. The SPF algorithm requires more CPU time than distance vector algorithms such as Bellman-Ford because link-state protocols build a complete map of the topology.

Bandwidth Requirements

The flooding of link-state packets can adversely affect the available bandwidth on a network. This should only occur during initial startup of routers, but it can also be an issue on unstable networks.

Comparison of Link-State Routing Protocols

There are two link-state routing protocols used for routing IP today:

- **Open Shortest Path First (OSPF):** OSPF was designed by the IETF (Internet Engineering Task Force) OSPF Working Group, which still exists today. The development of OSPF began in 1987, and there are two current versions in use:

  - **OSPFv2:** OSPF for IPv4 networks (RFC 1247 and RFC 2328)

  - **OSPFv3:** OSPF for IPv6 networks (RFC 2740)

  Most of the work on OSPF was done by John Moy, author of most of the RFCs regarding OSPF. His book, *OSPF, Anatomy of an Internet Routing Protocol*, provides interesting insight into the development of OSPF.

- **Intermediate System–to–Intermediate System (IS-IS):** IS-IS was designed by the ISO (International Organization for Standardization) and is described in ISO 10589. The first incarnation of this routing protocol was developed at DEC (Digital Equipment Corporation) and is known as DECnet Phase V. Radia Perlman was the chief designer of the IS-IS routing protocol.

  IS-IS was originally designed for the OSI protocol suite and not the TCP/IP protocol suite. Later, Integrated IS-IS, or Dual IS-IS, included support for IP networks. Although IS-IS has been known as the routing protocol used mainly by ISPs and carriers, more enterprise networks are beginning to use IS-IS.

OSPF and IS-IS have many similarities and also have many differences. Many pro-OSPF and pro-IS-IS factions discuss and debate the advantages of one routing protocol over the other. Both routing protocols provide the necessary routing functionality. You can learn more about IS-IS and OSPF in CCNP and begin to make your own determination about whether one protocol is more advantageous than the other.

Note

OSPF is discussed in the following chapter. Multiple Area OSPF and OSPFv3 are discussed in CCNP-level routing protocol books.

Summary

Link-state routing protocols are also known as shortest path first protocols and are built around Edsger Dijkstra's shortest path first (SPF) algorithm. There are two link-state routing protocols for IP: OSPF (Open Shortest Path First) and IS-IS (Intermediate System–to–Intermediate System).

The link-state process can be summarized as follows:

1. Each router learns about its own directly connected networks.

2. Each router is responsible for "saying hello" to its neighbors on directly connected networks.

3. Each router builds a link-state packet (LSP) containing the state of each directly connected link.

4. Each router floods the LSP to all neighbors, who then store all LSPs received in a database.

5. Each router uses the database to construct a complete map of the topology and computes the best path to each destination network. The best path can then be added to the routing table. This depends on whether this is the only source of the route. If this is not the only source, the source with the lowest administrative distance will have its route added to the routing table.

A link is an interface on the router. A link state is the information about that interface, including its IP address and subnet mask, the type of network, the cost associated with the link, and any neighbor routers on that link.

Each router determines its own link states and floods the information to all other routers in the area. As a result, each router builds a link-state database (LSDB) containing the link-state information from all other routers. Each router will have identical LSDBs. Using the information in the LSDB, each router will run the SPF algorithm. The SPF algorithm will create an SPF tree, with the router at the root of the tree. As each link is connected to other links, the SPF tree is created. After the SPF tree is completed, the router can determine on its own the best path to each network in the tree. This best-path information is then stored in the router's routing table.

Link-state routing protocols build a local topology map of the network that allows each router to determine the best path to a given network. A new LSP is sent only when there is a change in the topology. When a link is added, removed, or modified, the router will flood the new LSP to all other routers within the same area. When a router receives the new LSP, it will update its LSDB, rerun the SPF algorithm, create a new SPF tree, and update its routing table.

Link-state routing protocols tend to have a faster convergence time than distance vector routing protocols. A notable exception is EIGRP. However, link-state routing protocols do require more memory and processing requirements. This is usually not an issue with today's newer routers.

In the next and final chapter of this course, you will learn about the link-state routing protocol OSPF.

Activities and Labs

The activities and labs available in the companion *Routing Protocols and Concepts, CCNA Exploration Labs and Study Guide* (ISBN 1-58713-204-4) provide hands-on practice. There are no hands-on labs or activities related to this chapter's topics; however, you will find coverage of the hands-on labs or activities associated with the other chapters, where applicable.

Check Your Understanding

Complete all the review questions listed here to test your understanding of the topics and concepts in this chapter. The answers are listed in the appendix, "Check Your Understanding and Challenge Questions Answer Key."

1. Which routing protocol is considered a link-state protocol?

    A. RIPv1

    B. RIPv2

    C. EIGRP

    D. IS-IS

    E. BGP

2. Which of the following mechanisms are used by link-state routing protocols to build and maintain routing tables? (Choose three.)

   A. Service network advertisements

   B. Hello packets

   C. Link-state packets

   D. Routing table broadcasts

   E. Shortest path first algorithm

   F. Spanning Tree Protocol

3. For each attribute, determine whether it is associated with a distance vector routing protocol or link-state routing protocol.

   Hardware intensive:

   Uses Bellman-Ford algorithm:

   Fast convergence:

   Uses timed updates:

   Builds complete topology:

   Referred to at times as "routing by rumor":

   Uses Dijkstra's algorithm:

4. What is one advantage of link-state protocols over most distance vector protocols?

   A. Ability to route IPX

   B. Continual route checking with periodic updates

   C. Faster convergence

   D. Lower hardware requirements

5. Why do link-state protocols converge faster than most distance vector protocols?

   A. Distance vector protocols compute their routing tables before sending routing updates; link-state protocols do not.

   B. Link-state protocols have lower computing requirements than distance vector protocols.

   C. Link-state protocols send updates out more often than distance vector protocols.

   D. Distance vector protocols receive more packets per update than link-state protocols.

6. Refer to Figure 10-14. If all routers are using a link-state routing protocol, which routers does Router A send Hello packets to?

Figure 10-14 Check Your Understanding, Question #6

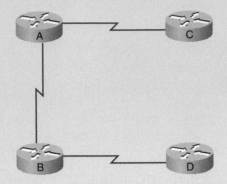

A. B, C

B. B, C, D

C. Only the DR

D. Only the BR and BDR

7. What information is contained in LSPs sent by link-state routers to their neighbors?

A. A copy of the routing table

B. A copy of the topology database

C. The state of directly connected links

D. The most current version of the SPF tree

8. What is one disadvantage of link-state protocols over distance vector protocols?

A. Slow convergence

B. Flat network topology

C. Periodic updates

D. Higher processing requirements

9. After two OSPF routers have exchanged Hello packets and formed an adjacency, what is the next thing to occur?

A. They will take turns broadcasting their entire routing table to each other.

B. They will start sending link-state packets to each other.

C. They negotiate to determine which will be the root router of the OSPF domain.

D. They will adjust their Hello timers so that they don't collide with each other.

10. How does a router learn about a directly connected network?

    A. When the administrator configures a static route

    B. When the administrator configures a dynamic routing protocol

    C. When the administrator assigns an IP address and subnet mask to the interface

    D. When a broadcast address is discovered on a specific interface

11. Why is a distance vector routing protocol like a road sign?

12. Why is a link-state routing protocol like a road map?

13. What algorithm do link-state routing protocols use?

14. In link-state routing terminology, what is a link?

15. In link-state routing terminology, what is a link state?

16. In link-state routing terminology, what is a neighbor, and how are neighbors discovered?

17. What does the link-state flooding process do? What is the end result of this process?

18. Where are LSPs stored, and how are they used?

Challenge Questions and Activities

These questions require a deeper application of the concepts covered in this chapter and are similar to the style of questions you might see on a CCNA certification exam. You can find the answers to these questions in the appendix, "Answers to Check Your Understanding and Challenge Questions and Activities."

1. Do link-state routing protocols send out periodic updates?

2. What are the advantages of a link-state routing protocol compared to a distance vector protocol?

3. What are the requirements of using a link-state routing protocol? What can help minimize these requirements?

4. What are two common link-state routing protocols used today for routing IP?

To Learn More

Suggested Books

Understanding the SPF algorithm is not difficult. There are several good books and online resources that explain Dijkstra's algorithm and describe how it is used in networking. There are several websites devoted to explaining how these algorithms work. Seek out some of the resources, and familiarize yourself with how this algorithm works.

Here are some suggested resources:

- *Interconnections, Bridges, Routers, Switches, and Internetworking Protocols*, by Radia Perlman
- *Cisco IP Routing*, by Alex Zinin
- *Routing the Internet*, by Christian Huitema

Classroom Analogy

An exercise to help you understand the SPF algorithm can be done with a classroom of students and a set of index cards. Each student gets a set of four index cards. On the first index card, the student will write down her name along with the name of the student sitting to her left. If no student is there, she should write the word *none*. On the next card, the student will do the same thing but for the student on her right. The next two cards are for the students sitting in front and sitting in back. These index cards are representative of link-state information.

For example, Teri has a set of four cards with the following information:

- Teri —-> Jen
- Teri —-> Pat
- Teri —-> Rick
- Teri —-> Allan

After all the students in the classroom have filled out the index cards, the instructor collects the index cards. This is similar to the link-state flooding process. The stack of index cards is similar to the link-state database. In a network, all routers would have this identical link-state database.

The instructor takes each card and lists the name and the neighbor student on the board, with a line between them. After all the index cards are transcribed to the board, the result will be a map of the students in the classroom. To make it easier, the instructor should map the names similarly to how students are sitting in the classroom, for example, Jen is sitting to the left of Teri. This is similar to the SPF tree that a link-state routing protocol creates.

Using this topology map on the board, the instructor can see all the paths to the various students in the class.

OSPF

Objectives

Upon completion of this chapter, you should be able to answer the following questions:

- What is the history and background of OSPF?

- What are the basic features of OSPF?

- Can you describe, modify, and calculate the metric used by OSPF?

- What is the Designated Router and Backup Designate Backup Router process in multiaccess networks?

- How is the **default-information originate** command configured in OSPF to propagate a default route?

Key Terms

This chapter uses the following key terms. You can find the definitions in the Glossary at the end of the book.

The Open Shortest Path First Protocol (OSPF) is a link-state routing protocol that was developed as a replacement for the distance vector routing protocol Routing Information Protocol (RIP) (see Figure 11-1).

Figure 11-1   Classification of Routing Protocols

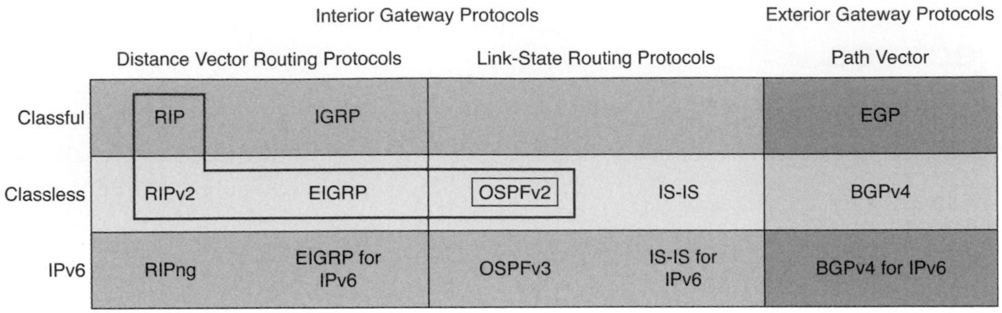

	Interior Gateway Protocols				Exterior Gateway Protocols
	Distance Vector Routing Protocols		Link-State Routing Protocols		Path Vector
Classful	RIP	IGRP			EGP
Classless	RIPv2	EIGRP	OSPFv2	IS-IS	BGPv4
IPv6	RIPng	EIGRP for IPv6	OSPFv3	IS-IS for IPv6	BGPv4 for IPv6

RIP was an acceptable routing protocol in the early days of networking and the Internet, but its reliance on hop count as the only measure for choosing the best route quickly became unacceptable in larger networks that needed a more robust routing solution. OSPF is a classless routing protocol that uses the concept of areas for scalability. RFC 2328 defines the OSPF metric as an arbitrary value called cost. Cisco IOS software uses bandwidth to calculate the OSPF cost metric.

OSPF's major advantages over RIP are its fast convergence and its scalability to much larger network implementations. In this final chapter of the Routing Protocols and Concepts course, you will learn basic, single-area OSPF implementations and configurations. More complex OSPF configurations and concepts are reserved for CCNP-level courses.

Introduction to OSPF

This section introduces some of the concepts and protocols that are used in this chapter. Some of these, such as the Hello protocol, are discussed in more detail later in the chapter. All of these topics are examined in much more detail in CCNP.

Background of OSPF

The initial development of OSPF began in 1987 by the Internet Engineering Task Force (IETF) OSPF Working Group. At that time, the Internet was largely an academic and research network funded by the U.S. government.

In 1989, the specification for OSPFv1 was published in RFC 1131. There were two implementations written: one to run on routers, and the other to run on UNIX workstations. The latter implementation later became a widespread UNIX process known as GATED. OSPFv1 was an experimental routing protocol that was never deployed.

In 1991, OSPFv2 was introduced in RFC 1247 by John Moy. OSPFv2 offered significant technical improvements over OSPFv1. At the same time, the International Organization for Standardization (ISO) was working on a link-state routing protocol of its own, Intermediate System–to–Intermediate System (IS-IS). IETF chose OSPF as its recommended IGP (interior gateway protocol).

In 1998, the OSPFv2 specification was updated in RFC 2328 and is the current RFC for OSPF. RFC 2328, *OSPF Version 2*, is on the IETF website at http://www.ietf.org/rfc/rfc2328.

Note

In 1999, OSPFv3 for IPv6 was published in RFC 2740. RFC 2740 was written by John Moy, Rob Coltun, and Dennis Ferguson. OSPFv3 is discussed in CCNP.

OSPF Message Encapsulation

The data portion of an OSPF message is encapsulated in a packet. This data field can include one of five OSPF packet types. Each packet type is briefly discussed in the next topic.

Figure 11-2 shows an encapsulated OSPF message in an Ethernet frame.

Figure 11-2   Encapsulated OSPF Message

Data Link Frame Header	IP Packet Header	OSPF Packet Header	OSPF Packet Type-Specific Data

Data Link Frame (Ethernet Fields Shown Here)
MAC Source Address = Address of Sending Interface
MAC Destination Address = Multicast: 01-00-5E-00-00-05 or 01-00-5E-00-00-06

IP Packet
IP Source Address = Address of Sending Interface
IP Destination Address = Multicast: 224.0.0.5 or 224.0.0.6
Protocol Field = 89 for OSPF

OSPF Packet Header
Type Code for OSPF Packet Type
Router ID and Area ID

OSPF Packet Types
0x01 Hello
0x02 Database Description
0x03 Link State Request
0x04 Link State Update
0x05 Link State Acknowledgment

The OSPF packet header is included with every OSPF packet, regardless of its type. The OSPF packet header and packet type-specific data are then encapsulated in an IP packet. In the IP packet header, the protocol field is set to 89 to indicate OSPF, and the destination address is typically set to one of two multicast addresses: 224.0.0.5 or 224.0.0.6. If the OSPF packet is encapsulated in an Ethernet frame, the destination MAC address is also a multicast address: 01-00-5E-00-00-05 or 01-00-5E-00-00-06.

OSPF Packet Types

In the preceding chapter, you learned about link-state packets (LSP). The following list describes the five different types of OSPF LSPs. This is only an overview of these packet types. Some of these packet types are discussed later in this chapter, and all of them are discussed in much more detail in CCNP. Each packet serves a specific purpose in the OSPF routing process:

- **Hello:** Hello packets are used to establish and maintain adjacency with other OSPF routers. The Hello protocol is discussed in detail in the next topic.

- **DBD:** The *database description (DBD)* packet contains an abbreviated list of the sending router's link-state database and is used by receiving routers to check against the local link-state database.

- **LSR:** Receiving routers can then request more information about any entry in the DBD by sending a *link-state request (LSR)*.

- **LSU:** *Link-state update (LSU)* packets are used to reply to LSRs and to announce new information. LSUs contain seven different types of *link-state advertisements (LSA)*. LSUs and LSAs are briefly discussed in a later topic.

- **LSAck:** When an LSU is received, the router sends a *link-state acknowledgment (LSAck)* to confirm receipt of the LSU.

Hello Protocol

Figure 11-3 shows the OSPF packet header and Hello packet. The highlighted fields are discussed in more detail later in the chapter. For now, let's focus on the uses of the Hello packet.

OSPF packet Type 1 is the OSPF Hello packet. Hello packets are used to do the following:

- Discover OSPF neighbors and establish neighbor adjacencies

- Advertise parameters on which two routers must agree to become neighbors

- Elect the Designated Router and Backup Designated Router on *multiaccess networks* such as Ethernet and Frame Relay

Figure 11-3   OSPF Packet Header and Hello Packet

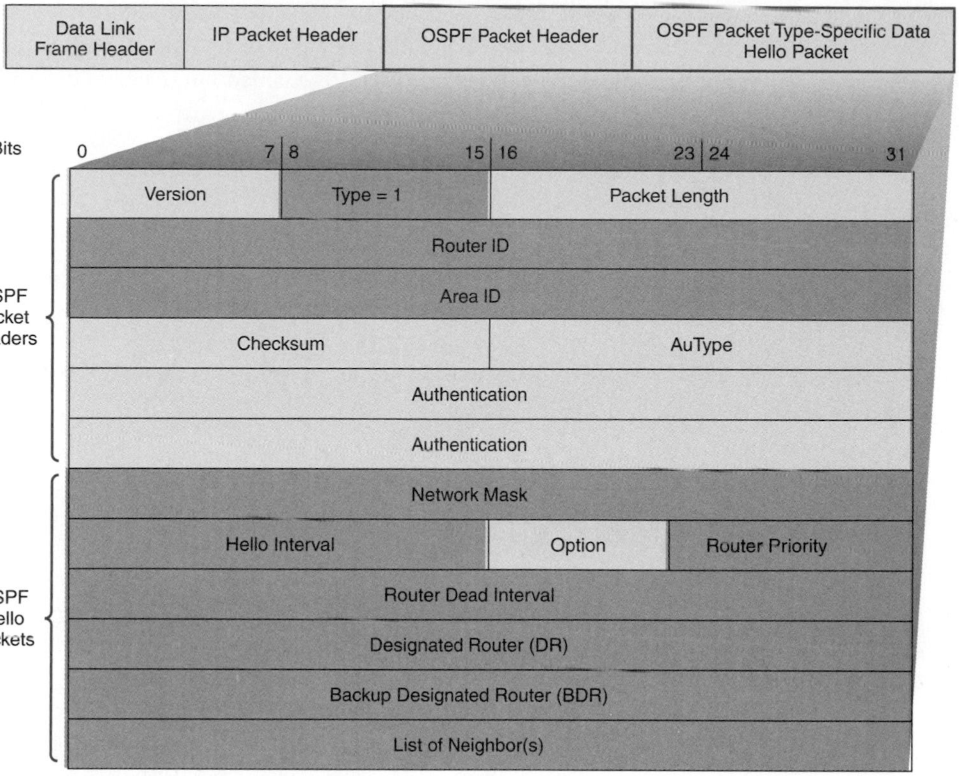

Important fields shown in the figure include the following:

- **Type:** OSPF packet type: Hello (Type 1), DBD (Type 2), LS Request (Type 3), LS Update (Type 4), LS ACK (Type 5)

- **Router ID:** ID of the originating router

- **Area ID:** Area from which the packet originated

- **Network Mask:** Subnet mask associated with the sending interface

- **Hello Interval:** Number of seconds between the sending router's Hellos

- **Router Priority:** Used in DR/BDR election (discussed later)

- **Designated Router (DR):** Router ID of the DR, if any

- **Backup Designated Router (BDR):** Router ID of the BDR, if any

- **List of Neighbors:** Lists the OSPF Router ID of the neighboring router(s)

Neighbor Establishment

Before an OSPF router can flood its link states to other routers, it must determine whether there are any other OSPF neighbors on any of its links. In Figure 11-4, the OSPF routers are sending Hello packets on all OSPF-enabled interfaces to determine whether there are any neighbors on those links.

Figure 11-4   Hello Protocol

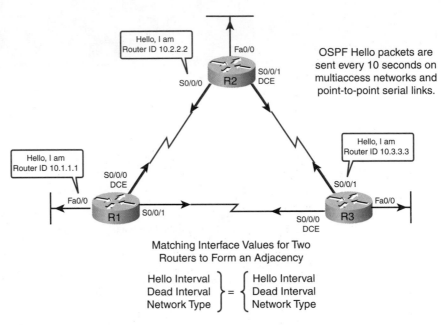

The information in the OSPF Hello includes the OSPF router ID of the router sending the Hello packet. (Router ID is discussed later in this chapter.) Receiving an OSPF Hello packet on an interface confirms for a router that there is another OSPF router on this link. OSPF then establishes adjacency with the neighbor. Although the routers are not considered fully adjacent, at this point each router is aware of the other OSPF router on the link. For example, in the figure, R1 will establish adjacencies with R2 and R3.

Full adjacency happens after both routers have exchanged any necessary LSUs and have identical link-state databases. This process is discussed further in CCNP.

OSPF Hello and Dead Intervals

Before two routers can form an OSPF neighbor adjacency, they must agree on three values: Hello interval, Dead interval, and network type. The OSPF Hello interval indicates how often an OSPF router transmits its Hello packets. By default, OSPF Hello packets are sent every 10 seconds on multiaccess and point-to-point segments and every 30 seconds on *non-broadcast multiaccess (NBMA)* segments (Frame Relay, X.25, ATM).

In most cases, OSPF Hello packets are sent as multicast to an address reserved for *ALLSPFRouters* at 224.0.0.5. The source router can save CPU processing time and network bandwidth by transmitting one packet to all destinations instead of one packet to each destination. The receiving devices save CPU processing time by ignoring packets that are not addressed to them. Because multicast realizes both CPU and bandwidth savings throughout, it is the preferred choice in broadcast networks such as Ethernet. For example, using a multicast address allows a device to ignore the packet if its interface is not enabled to accept OSPF packets. This saves CPU processing time on non-OSPF devices.

The *Dead interval* is the period, expressed in seconds, that the router will wait to receive a Hello packet before declaring the neighbor "down." Cisco uses a default of four times the Hello interval. For multiaccess and point-to-point segments, this period is 40 seconds. For NBMA networks, the Dead interval is 120 seconds.

If the Dead interval expires before the routers receive a Hello packet, OSPF removes that neighbor from its link-state database. The router floods the link-state information about the "down" neighbor out all OSPF-enabled interfaces.

Network types are discussed later in the chapter.

Note

Also, before two routers can establish an OSPF adjacency, both the interfaces on the two routers must be part of the same network, including having the same subnet mask.

Electing a DR and BDR

To reduce the amount of OSPF traffic on multiaccess networks, OSPF elects a *Designated Router (DR)* and *Backup Designated Router (BDR)*. The DR is responsible for updating all other OSPF routers (called *DROther*s) when a change occurs in the multiaccess network. The BDR monitors the DR and takes over as DR if the current DR fails.

In Figure 11-4, R1, R2, and R3 are connected through point-to-point links. Therefore, no DR/BDR election occurs. The DR/BDR election and processes is discussed in a later topic, and the topology will be changed to a multiaccess network.

Note

The Hello packet is discussed in more detail in CCNP, along with the other types of OSPF packets.

OSPF LSUs

Link-state updates (LSU) are the packets used for OSPF routing updates. An LSU packet can contain 11 different types of LSAs, as shown in Figure 11-5.

Figure 11-5   LSUs Contain LSAs

Type	Packet Name	Description
1	Hello	Discovers neighbors and builds adjacencies between them.
2	DBD	Checks for database synchronization between routers.
3	LSR	Requests specific link-state records from router to router.
4	LSU	Sends specifically requested link-state records.
5	LSAck	Acknowledges the other packet types.

The acronyms LSA and LSU are often used interchangeably.

An LSU contains one or more LSAs.

LSAs contain route information for destination networks.

LSA specifics are discussed in CCNP.

LSA Type	Description
1	Router LSAs
2	Network LSAs
3 or 4	Summary LSAs
5	Autonomous System External LSAs
6	Multicast OSPF LSAs
7	Defined for Not-So-Stubby Areas
8	External Attributes LSA for Border Gateway Protocol (BGP)
9, 10, 11	Opaque LSAs

The difference between the terms *link-state update* and *link-state advertisement* can sometimes be confusing. At times, these terms are used interchangeably. An LSU contains one or more LSAs, and either term can be used to refer to link-state information propagated by OSPF routers.

Note

The different types of LSAs are discussed in CCNP.

OSPF Algorithm

Figure 11-6 shows an overview of the OSPF process of gathering link-state information to populating the routing table, which was discussed in Chapter 10, "Link-State Routing Protocols."

Each OSPF router maintains a link-state database containing the LSAs received from all other routers. When a router has received all the LSAs and built its local link-state database, OSPF uses Dijkstra's shortest path first (SPF) algorithm to create an SPF trec. The SPF tree is then used to populate the IP routing table with the best paths to each network.

Figure 11-6   OSPF Uses Dijkstra's Shortest Path First Algorithm

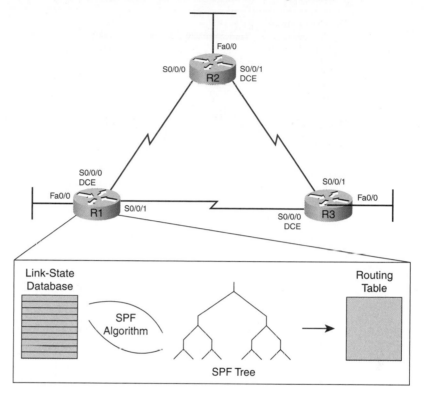

Administrative Distance

As you know from Chapter 3, "Introduction to Dynamic Routing Protocols," administrative distance (AD) is the trustworthiness (or preference) of the route source. OSPF has a default AD of 110. As you can see in Table 11-1, when compared to other IGPs, OSPF is preferred over IS-IS and RIP.

Table 11-1   Default Administrative Distances

Route Source	AD
Connected	0
Static	1
EIGRP summary route	5
External BGP	20

continues

Table 11-1   Default Administrative Distances   *continued*

Route Source	AD
Internal EIGRP	90
IGRP	100
OSPF	110
IS-IS	115
RIP	120
External EIGRP	170
Internal BGP	200

Authentication

As stated in previous chapters, configuring routing protocols to use authentication is discussed in a later course. Like other routing protocols, OSPF can be configured for authentication.

It is good practice to authenticate transmitted routing information. RIPv2, EIGRP, OSPF, IS-IS, and BGP can all be configured to encrypt and authenticate their routing information. This practice ensures that routers will only accept routing information from other routers that have been configured with the same password or authentication information.

Note

Authentication does not encrypt the router's routing table.

Basic OSPF Configuration

This section discusses the commands used for basic OSPF configuration. As you will see, the commands used are not much different from the commands you have already used in other routing protocols. Later in this chapter, you learn more about the OSPF metric calculation and other OSPF processes that are critical for understanding, implementing, and troubleshooting OSPF.

Lab Topology

Figure 11-7 shows the topology for this chapter. Notice that the addressing scheme is discontiguous. OSPF is a classless routing protocol. Therefore, we will configure the mask as part of our OSPF configuration. As you know, doing this overcomes the problem with discontiguous addressing. Also, notice in this topology that there are three serial links of various bandwidths and that each router has multiple paths to each remote network.

Table 11-2 shows the addressing scheme used in the topology. Examples 11-1, 11-2, and 11-3 show the starting configurations for Routers R1, R2, and R3, respectively.

Figure 11-7 OSPF Topology

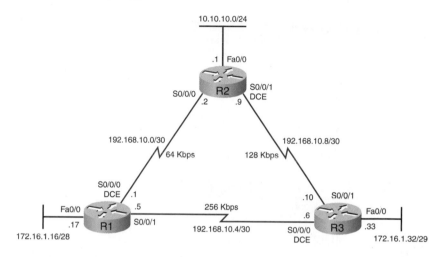

Table 11-2 Addressing Table for OSPF

Device	Interface	IP Address	Subnet Mask
R1	Fa0/0	172.16.1.17	255.255.255.240
	S0/0/0	192.168.10.1	255.255.255.252
	S0/0/1	192.168.10.5	255.255.255.252
R2	Fa0/0	10.10.10.1	255.255.255.0
	S0/0/0	192.168.10.2	255.255.255.252
	S0/0/1	192.168.10.9	255.255.255.252
R3	Fa0/0	172.16.1.33	255.255.255.248
	S0/0/0	192.168.10.6	255.255.255.252
	S0/0/1	192.168.10.10	255.255.255.252

Example 11-1   R1 Starting Configuration

```
R1#show startup-config

Current configuration : 1344 bytes
!
<some output omitted>
!
hostname R1
!
!
!
interface FastEthernet0/0
 description R1 LAN
 ip address 172.16.1.17 255.255.255.240
!
interface Serial0/0/0
 description Link to R2
 ip address 192.168.10.1 255.255.255.252
 clock rate 64000
!
interface Serial0/0/1
 description Link to R3
 ip address 192.168.10.5 255.255.255.252
!
end
```

Example 11-2   R2 Starting Configuration

```
R2#show startup-config

Current configuration : 1343 bytes
!
<some output omitted>
!
hostname R2
!
!
!
interface FastEthernet0/0
 description R2 LAN
 ip address 10.10.10.1 255.255.255.0
!
interface Serial0/0/0
```

```
 description Link to R1
 ip address 192.168.10.2 255.255.255.252
!
interface Serial0/0/1
 description Link to R3
 ip address 192.168.10.9 255.255.255.252
 clock rate 64000
!
end
```

Example 11-3   R3 Starting Configuration

```
R3#show startup-config

Current configuration : 1342 bytes
!
<some output omitted>
!
hostname R3
!
interface FastEthernet0/0
 description R3 LAN
 ip address 172.16.1.33 255.255.255.248
!
interface Serial0/0/0
 description Link to R1
 ip address 192.168.10.6 255.255.255.252
 clockrate 64000
!
interface Serial0/0/1
 description Link to R2
 ip address 192.168.10.10 255.255.255.252
!
end
```

The **clock rate** command in these configurations is used only to provide a signal for the serial link. This is for lab purposes only and is not necessarily representative of the actual bandwidth of the link.

The current configurations do not include the **interface bandwidth** command. This means that the bandwidth value on the serial interfaces is set to the default value of 1544 Kbps.

The router ospf Command

OSPF is enabled with the **router ospf** *process-id* global configuration command:

```
R1(config)#router ospf 1
R1(config-router)#
```

The *process-id* is a number between 1 and 65,535 and is chosen by the network administrator. The process ID is locally significant, which means that it does not have to match other OSPF routers to establish adjacencies with those neighbors. This differs from EIGRP. The EIGRP process ID or autonomous system number does need to match for two EIGRP neighbors to become adjacent.

In our topology, we will enable OSPF on all three routers using the same process ID of 1. We are using the same process ID simply for consistency.

The network Command

The **network** command used with OSPF has the same function as when used with other IGP routing protocols:

- Any interfaces on a router that match the network address in the **network** command will be enabled to send and receive OSPF packets.

- This network (or subnet) will be included in OSPF routing updates.

The **network** command is used in router configuration mode:

```
Router(config-router)#network network-address wildcard-mask area area-id
```

The OSPF **network** command uses a combination of *network-address* and *wildcard-mask* similar to that which can be used by EIGRP. Unlike EIGRP, however, OSPF requires the wildcard mask. The network address, along with the wildcard mask, is used to specify the interface or range of interfaces that will be enabled for OSPF using this **network** command.

As with EIGRP, the wildcard mask can be configured as the inverse of a subnet mask. For example, R1's FastEthernet 0/0 interface is on the 172.16.1.16/28 network. The subnet mask for this interface is /28 or 255.255.255.240. The inverse of the subnet mask results in the wildcard mask:

```
  255.255.255.255
- 255.255.255.240   Subtract the subnet mask
  --------------
    0.  0.  0. 15   Wildcard mask
```

Note

Like EIGRP, some Cisco IOS software versions allow you to simply enter the subnet mask instead of the wildcard mask. The Cisco IOS software then converts the subnet mask to the wildcard mask format.

The **area** *area-id* refers to the *OSPF area*. An OSPF area is a group of routers that share link-state information. All OSPF routers in the same area must have the same link-state information in their link-state databases. This is accomplished by routers flooding their individual link states to all other routers in the area. In this chapter, we configure all the OSPF routers within a single area. This is known as *single-area OSPF*.

An OSPF network can also be configured as multiple areas. There are several advantages to configuring large OSPF networks as multiple areas, including smaller link-state databases and the ability to isolate unstable network problems within an area. Multi-area OSPF is covered in CCNP.

When all the routers are within the same OSPF area, the **network** commands must be configured with the same area ID on all routers. Although any area ID can be used, it is good practice to use an area ID of 0 with single-area OSPF. This convention makes it easier if the network is later configured as multiple OSPF areas where area 0 becomes the backbone area.

Example 11-4 shows the **network** commands for all three routers, enabling OSPF on all interfaces. At this point, all routers should be able to ping all networks.

Example 11-4   Configuring OSPF Networks

```
R1(config)#router ospf 1
R1(config-router)#network 172.16.1.16 0.0.0.15 area 0
R1(config-router)#network 192.168.10.0 0.0.0.3 area 0
R1(config-router)#network 192.168.10.4 0.0.0.3 area 0
R2(config)#router ospf 1
R2(config-router)#network 10.10.10.0 0.0.0.255 area 0
R2(config-router)#network 192.168.10.0 0.0.0.3 area 0
R2(config-router)#network 192.168.10.8 0.0.0.3 area 0
R3(config)#router ospf 1
R3(config-router)#network 172.16.1.32 0.0.0.7 area 0
R3(config-router)#network 192.168.10.4 0.0.0.3 area 0
R3(config-router)#network 192.168.10.8 0.0.0.3 area 0
```

OSPF Router ID

The OSPF router ID plays an important role in OSPF. This section discusses the determination and configuration of the router ID. Later in this chapter, you will see how the router ID is used in the DR and BDR process.

Determining the Router ID

The OSPF router ID is used to uniquely identify each router in the OSPF routing domain. A router ID is simply an IP address. Cisco routers derive the router ID based on three criteria and with the following precedence:

1. Use the IP address configured with the OSPF **router-id** command.

2. If the router ID is not configured, the router chooses the highest IP address of any of its loopback interfaces.

3. If no loopback interfaces are configured, the router chooses the highest active IP address of any of its physical interfaces.

Highest Active IP Address

If an OSPF router is not configured with an OSPF **router-id** command and there are no loopback interfaces configured, the OSPF router ID will be the highest active IP address on any of its interfaces. The interface does not need to be enabled for OSPF, meaning that it does not need to be included in one of the OSPF **network** commands. However, the interface must be active; that is, it must be in the up state.

Using the criteria for determining the router ID, can you determine the router IDs for R1, R2, and R3 using the topology in Figure 11-7 and IP addresses in Table 11-2?

Verifying the Router ID

Because we have not configured router IDs or loopback interfaces on our three routers, the router ID for each router is determined by the third criterion in the preceding list: the highest active IP address on any of the router's physical interfaces. As shown in the figure, the router ID for each router is as follows:

- **R1:** 192.168.10.5, which is higher than either 172.16.1.17 or 192.168.10.1

- **R2:** 192.168.10.9, which is higher than either 10.10.10.1 or 192.168.10.2

- **R3:** 192.168.10.10, which is higher than either 172.16.1.33 or 192.168.10.6

One command you can use to verify the current router ID is **show ip protocols**. Some Cisco IOS software versions do not display the router ID, as shown in Example 11-5. In those cases, use the **show ip ospf** or **show ip ospf interface** commands to verify the router ID.

Example 11-5   Verifying the Router ID with **show ip protocols**

```
R1#show ip protocols
Routing Protocol is "ospf 1"
  Outgoing update filter list for all interfaces is not set
  Incoming update filter list for all interfaces is not set
```

```
    Router ID 192.100.10.5
    Number of areas in this router is 1. 1 normal 0 stub 0 nssa
<output omitted>
```
```
R2#show ip protocols
Routing Protocol is "ospf 1"
  Outgoing update filter list for all interfaces is not set
  Incoming update filter list for all interfaces is not set
    Router ID 192.168.10.9
    Number of areas in this router is 1. 1 normal 0 stub 0 nssa
<output omitted>
```
```
R3#show ip protocols
Routing Protocol is "ospf 1"
  Outgoing update filter list for all interfaces is not set
  Incoming update filter list for all interfaces is not set
    Router ID 192.168.10.10
    Number of areas in this router is 1. 1 normal 0 stub 0 nssa
<output omitted>
```

Loopback Address

If the OSPF **router-id** command is not used and loopback interfaces are configured, OSPF chooses the highest IP address of any of its loopback interfaces. A loopback address is a virtual interface and is automatically in the up state when configured. You already know the commands to configure a loopback interface:

```
Router(config)#interface loopback number
Router(config-if)#ip address ip-address subnet-mask
```

All three routers have been configured with loopback addresses to represent the OSPF router IDs. Figure 11-8 shows the loopbacks added to the topology, and Example 11-6 shows the loopback interface configuration on all three routers.

Example 11-6   Loopback Configurations

```
R1(config)#interface loopback 0
R1(config-if)#ip address 10.1.1.1 255.255.255.255
```
```
R2(config)#interface loopback 0
R2(config-if)#ip address 10.2.2.2 255.255.255.255
```
```
R3(config)#interface loopback 0
R3(config-if)#ip address 10.3.3.3 255.255.255.255
```

Figure 11-8   Topology with Loopback Interfaces

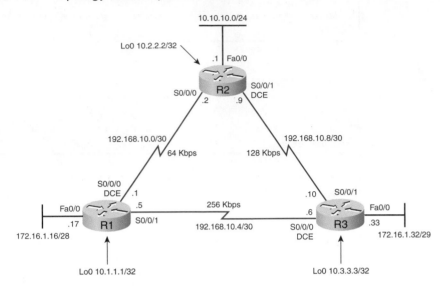

The advantage of using a loopback interface is that, unlike physical interfaces, it cannot fail. There are no actual cables or adjacent devices on which the loopback interface depends for being in the up state. Therefore, using a loopback address for the router ID provides stability to the OSPF process. Because the OSPF **router-id** command, which is discussed next, is a fairly recent addition to Cisco IOS software, it is more common to find loopback addresses used for configuring OSPF router IDs.

OSPF **router-id** Command

The OSPF **router-id** command was introduced in Cisco IOS Software Release 12.0(T) and takes precedence over loopback and physical interface IP addresses for determining the router ID. The command syntax is as follows:

```
Router(config)#router ospf process-id
Router(config-router)#router-id ip-address
```

Modifying the Router ID

The router ID is selected when OSPF is configured with its first OSPF **network** command. If the OSPF **router-id** command or the loopback address is configured after the OSPF **network** command, the router ID is derived from the interface with the highest active IP address.

The router ID can be modified with the IP address from a subsequent OSPF **router-id** command by reloading the router or by using the following command:

```
Router#clear ip ospf process
```

Note

Modifying a router ID with a new loopback or physical interface IP address may require reloading the router.

Duplicate Router IDs

When two routers have the same router ID in an OSPF domain, routing might not function properly. If the router ID is the same on two neighboring routers, the neighbor establishment might not occur. When duplicate OSPF router IDs occur, Cisco IOS software displays a message similar to this:

```
%OSPF-4-DUP_RTRID1: Detected router with duplicate router ID
```

To correct this problem, configure all routers so that they have unique OSPF router IDs.

Because some Cisco IOS versions do not support the **router-id** command, we will use the loopback address method for assigning router IDs. An IP address from a loopback interface will usually only replace a current OSPF router ID by reloading the router. In Example 11-7, the routers have been reloaded, and the **show ip protocols** command is used to verify that each router is now using the loopback address for the router ID.

Example 11-7   Verifying the New Router IDs with **show ip protocols**

```
R1#show ip protocols
Routing Protocol is "ospf 1"
  Outgoing update filter list for all interfaces is not set
  Incoming update filter list for all interfaces is not set
  Router ID 10.1.1.1
  Number of areas in this router is 1. 1 normal 0 stub 0 nssa
<output omitted>
R2#show ip protocols
Routing Protocol is "ospf 1"
  Outgoing update filter list for all interfaces is not set
  Incoming update filter list for all interfaces is not set
  Router ID 10.2.2.2
  Number of areas in this router is 1. 1 normal 0 stub 0 nssa
<output omitted>
R3#show ip protocols
Routing Protocol is "ospf 1"
  Outgoing update filter list for all interfaces is not set
  Incoming update filter list for all interfaces is not set
  Router ID 10.3.3.3
  Number of areas in this router is 1. 1 normal 0 stub 0 nssa
<output omitted>
```

Verifying OSPF

The **show ip ospf neighbor** command shown in Example 11-8 enables you to verify and troubleshoot OSPF neighbor relationships.

Example 11-8   Verifying Neighbor Adjacency with the **show ip ospf neighbor** Command

```
R1#show ip ospf neighbor

Neighbor ID     Pri   State          Dead Time   Address         Interface
10.3.3.3          1   FULL/   -      00:00:30    192.168.10.6    Serial0/0/1
10.2.2.2          1   FULL/   -      00:00:33    192.168.10.2    Serial0/0/0
R2#show ip ospf neighbor

Neighbor ID     Pri   State          Dead Time   Address         Interface
10.3.3.3          1   FULL/   -      00:00:36    192.168.10.10   Serial0/0/1
10.1.1.1          1   FULL/   -      00:00:37    192.168.10.1    Serial0/0/0
R3#show ip ospf neighbor

Neighbor ID     Pri   State          Dead Time   Address         Interface
10.2.2.2          1   FULL/   -      00:00:34    192.168.10.9    Serial0/0/1
10.1.1.1          1   FULL/   -      00:00:38    192.168.10.5    Serial0/0/0
```

For each neighbor, this command displays the following output:

- **Neighbor ID:** The router ID of the neighboring router.

- **Pri:** The OSPF priority of the interface. This is discussed in a later section.

- **State:** The OSPF state of the interface. FULL state means that the router's interface is fully adjacent with its neighbor and they have identical OSPF link-state databases. OSPF states are discussed in CCNP.

- **Dead Time:** The amount of time remaining that the router will wait to receive an OSPF Hello packet from the neighbor before declaring the neighbor down. This value is reset when the interface receives a Hello packet.

- **Address:** The IP address of the neighbor's interface to which this router is directly connected.

- **Interface:** The interface on which this router has formed adjacency with the neighbor.

When troubleshooting OSPF networks, you can use the **show ip ospf neighbor** command to verify that the router has formed an adjacency with its neighboring routers. If the router ID of the neighboring router is not displayed, or if it does not show as a state of FULL, the two routers have not formed an OSPF adjacency. If two routers do not establish adjacency, link-state information will not be exchanged. Incomplete link-state databases can cause inaccurate SPF trees and routing tables. Routes to destination networks might not exist or might not be the optimum path.

> **Note**
>
> On multiaccess networks such as Ethernet, two routers that are adjacent may have their states displayed as 2WAY. This is discussed in a later section.

Two routers may not form an OSPF adjacency if any one of the following conditions is present:

- The subnet masks do not match, causing the routers to be on separate networks.

- OSPF Hello or Dead timers do not match.

- OSPF network types do not match.

- There is a missing or incorrect OSPF **network** command.

Other powerful OSPF troubleshooting commands include the following:

```
show ip protocols
show ip ospf
show ip ospf interface
```

As shown in Example 11-9 for R1, the **show ip protocols** command is a quick way to verify vital OSPF configuration information, including the OSPF process ID, the router ID, networks the router is advertising, the neighbors the router is receiving updates from, and the default AD, which is 110 for OSPF.

Example 11-9   show ip protocols Command

```
R1#show ip protocols
Routing Protocol is "ospf 1"
  Outgoing update filter list for all interfaces is not set
  Incoming update filter list for all interfaces is not set
  Router ID 10.1.1.1
  Number of areas in this router is 1. 1 normal 0 stub 0 nssa
  Maximum path: 4
  Routing for Networks:
    172.16.1.16 0.0.0.15 area 0
    192.168.10.0 0.0.0.3 area 0
    192.168.10.4 0.0.0.3 area 0
  Reference bandwidth unit is 100 mbps
  Routing Information Sources:
    Gateway         Distance      Last Update
    10.2.2.2             110      11:29:29
    10.3.3.3             110      11:29:29
  Distance: (default is 110)
```

The **show ip ospf** command shown in Example 11-10 for R1 can also be used to examine the OSPF process ID and router ID. In addition, this command displays the OSPF area information and the last time the SPF algorithm was calculated.

```
Example 11-10   show ip ospf Command
R1#show ip ospf
 <some output omitted>
 Routing Process "ospf 1" with ID 10.1.1.1
 Start time: 00:00:19.540, Time elapsed: 11:31:15.776
 Supports only single TOS(TOS0) routes
 Supports opaque LSA
 Supports Link-local Signaling (LLS)
 Supports area transit capability
 Router is not originating router-LSAs with maximum metric
 Initial SPF schedule delay 5000 msecs
 Minimum hold time between two consecutive SPFs 10000 msecs
 Maximum wait time between two consecutive SPFs 10000 msecs
 Incremental-SPF disabled
 Minimum LSA interval 5 secs
 Minimum LSA arrival 1000 msecs
 Area BACKBONE(0)
        Number of interfaces in this area is 3
        Area has no authentication
        SPF algorithm last executed 11:30:31.628 ago
        SPF algorithm executed 5 times
        Area ranges are
        <output omitted>
```

As you can see from the sample output, OSPF is a very stable routing protocol. The only OSPF-related event that R1 has participated in during the past 11.5 hours is to send small Hello packets to its neighbors.

Note

Additional information displayed by the **show ip ospf** command is discussed in CCNP courses.

The command output includes important SPF algorithm information, which includes the SPF schedule delay:

```
Initial SPF schedule delay 5000 msecs
Minimum hold time between two consecutive SPFs 10000 msecs
Maximum wait time between two consecutive SPFs 10000 msecs
```

Any time a router receives new information about the topology (addition, deletion, or modification of a link), the router must rerun the SPF algorithm, create a new SPF tree, and update the routing table. The SPF algorithm is CPU intensive, and the time it takes for calculation depends on the size of the area. The size of an area is measured by the number of routers and the size of the link-state database.

A network that cycles between an up state and a down state is referred to as a *flapping link*. A flapping link can cause OSPF routers in an area to constantly recalculate the SPF algorithm, preventing proper convergence. To minimize this problem, the router waits 5 seconds (5000 ms) after receiving an LSU before running the SPF algorithm. This is known as the *SPF schedule delay*. To prevent a router from constantly running the SPF algorithm, there is an additional hold time of 10 seconds (10,000 ms). The router waits 10 seconds after running the SPF algorithm before rerunning the algorithm.

The quickest way to verify Hello and Dead intervals is to use the **show ip ospf interface** command. As shown in Example 11-11 for R1, adding the interface name and number to the command displays output for a specific interface.

```
Example 11-11  show ip ospf interface Command
R1#show ip ospf interface serial 0/0/0
Serial0/0/0 is up, line protocol is up
  Internet Address 192.168.10.1/30, Area 0
  Process ID 1, Router ID 10.1.1.1, Network Type POINT_TO_POINT, Cost: 64
  Transmit Delay is 1 sec, State POINT_TO_POINT,
  Timer intervals configured, Hello 10, Dead 40, Wait 40, Retransmit 5
    oob-resync timeout 40
    Hello due in 00:00:07
  Supports Link-local Signaling (LLS)
  Index 2/2, flood queue length 0
  Next 0x0(0)/0x0(0)
  Last flood scan length is 1, maximum is 1
  Last flood scan time is 0 msec, maximum is 4 msec
  Neighbor Count is 1, Adjacent neighbor count is 1
    Adjacent with neighbor 10.2.2.2
  Suppress hello for 0 neighbor(s)
```

These intervals are included in the OSPF Hello packets sent between neighbors. OSPF may have different Hello and Dead intervals on various interfaces, but for OSPF routers to become neighbors, their OSPF Hello and Dead intervals must be identical. Refer to the highlighted portion of the command output in Example 11-11. R1 is using a Hello interval of 10 and a Dead interval of 40 on the Serial 0/0/0 interface. R2 must also use the same intervals on its Serial 0/0/0 interface; otherwise, the two routers will not form an adjacency.

Examining the Routing Table

As you know, the quickest way to verify OSPF convergence is to look at the routing table for each router in the topology.

Examples 11-12, 11-13, and 11-14 show the routing tables for R1, R2, and R3, respectively.

Example 11-12 R1 Routing Table

```
R1#show ip route
Codes: <some code output omitted>
        D - EIGRP, EX - EIGRP external, O - OSPF, IA - OSPF inter area

Gateway of last resort is not set

     192.168.10.0/30 is subnetted, 3 subnets
C        192.168.10.0 is directly connected, Serial0/0/0
C        192.168.10.4 is directly connected, Serial0/0/1
O        192.168.10.8 [110/128] via 192.168.10.2, 14:27:57, Serial0/0/0
     172.16.0.0/16 is variably subnetted, 2 subnets, 2 masks
O        172.16.1.32/29 [110/65] via 192.168.10.6, 14:27:57, Serial0/0/1
C        172.16.1.16/28 is directly connected, FastEthernet0/0
     10.0.0.0/8 is variably subnetted, 2 subnets, 2 masks
O        10.10.10.0/24 [110/65] via 192.168.10.2, 14:27:57, Serial0/0/0
C        10.1.1.1/32 is directly connected, Loopback0
```

Example 11-13 R2 Routing Table

```
R2#show ip route
Codes: <some code output omitted>
        D - EIGRP, EX - EIGRP external, O - OSPF, IA - OSPF inter area

Gateway of last resort is not set

     192.168.10.0/30 is subnetted, 3 subnets
C        192.168.10.0 is directly connected, Serial0/0/0
O        192.168.10.4 [110/128] via 192.168.10.1, 14:31:18, Serial0/0/0
C        192.168.10.8 is directly connected, Serial0/0/1
     172.16.0.0/16 is variably subnetted, 2 subnets, 2 masks
O        172.16.1.32/29 [110/65] via 192.168.10.10, 14:31:18, Serial0/0/1
O        172.16.1.16/28 [110/65] via 192.168.10.1, 14:31:18, Serial0/0/0
     10.0.0.0/8 is variably subnetted, 2 subnets, 2 masks
C        10.2.2.2/32 is directly connected, Loopback0
C        10.10.10.0/24 is directly connected, FastEthernet0/0
```

Example 11-14 R3 Routing Table

```
R3#show ip route
Codes: <some code output omitted>
         D - EIGRP, EX - EIGRP external, O - OSPF, IA - OSPF inter area

Gateway of last resort is not set

     192.168.10.0/30 is subnetted, 3 subnets
O       192.168.10.0 [110/845] via 192.168.10.9, 14:31:52, Serial0/0/1
                        [110/845] via 192.168.10.5, 14:31:52, Serial0/0/0
C       192.168.10.4 is directly connected, Serial0/0
C       192.168.10.8 is directly connected, Serial0/1
     172.16.0.0/16 is variably subnetted, 2 subnets, 2 masks
C       172.16.1.32/29 is directly connected, FastEthernet0/0
O       172.16.1.16/28 [110/782] via 192.168.10.5, 14:31:52, Serial0/0/0
     10.0.0.0/8 is variably subnetted, 2 subnets, 2 masks
C       10.3.3.3/32 is directly connected, Loopback0
O       10.10.10.0/24 [110/782] via 192.168.10.9, 14:31:52, Serial0/0/1
```

You can use the **show ip route** command to verify that OSPF is sending and receiving routes via OSPF. The letter *O* at the beginning of each route indicates that the route source is OSPF. The routing table and OSPF will be examined more closely in the following section. However, you should immediately notice two distinct differences in the OSPF routing table compared to routing tables you have seen in previous chapters. First, notice that each router has four directly connected networks because the loopback interface counts as the fourth network. These loopback interfaces are not advertised in OSPF. Therefore, each router lists seven known networks. Second, unlike RIPv2 and EIGRP, OSPF does not automatically summarize at major network boundaries. OSPF is inherently classless.

Configure and Verify OSPF Routing (11.2.6)

Use the Packet Tracer Activity to configure and verify basic OSPF routing. Detailed instructions are provided within the activity. Use file e2-1126.pka on the CD-ROM that accompanies this book to perform this activity using Packet Tracer.

The OSPF Metric

The OSPF metric is called cost. The following passage is from RFC 2328:

> A cost is associated with the output side of each router interface. This cost is configurable by the system administrator. The lower the cost, the more likely the interface is to be used to forward data traffic.

Notice that RFC 2328 does not specify which values should be used to determine the cost.

OSPF Metric

Cisco IOS software uses the cumulative bandwidths of the outgoing interfaces from the router to the destination network as the cost value. At each router, the cost for an interface is calculated using the following formula:

```
Cisco IOS Cost for OSPF = 10⁸/bandwidth in bps
```

In this calculation, the value 10^8 is known as the *reference bandwidth*. Dividing 10^8 by the interface bandwidth is done so that interfaces with the higher bandwidth values will have a lower calculated cost. Remember, in routing metrics, the lowest-cost route is the preferred route. (For example, with RIP, 3 hops is better than 10 hops.) Table 11-3 shows the default OSPF costs for several types of interfaces.

Table 11-3   Cisco IOS OSPF Cost Values

Interface Type	10^8/bps = Cost
Fast Ethernet and faster	10^8/100,000,000 bps = 1
Ethernet	10^8/10,000,000 bps = 10
E1	10^8/2,048,000 bps = 48
T1	10^8/1,544,000 bps = 64
128 Kbps	10^8/128,000 bps = 781
64 Kbps	10^8/64,000 bps = 1562
56 Kbps	10^8/56,000 bps = 1785

Reference Bandwidth

The reference bandwidth defaults to 10^8, which is 100,000,000 bps or 100 Mbps. This results in interfaces with a bandwidth of 100 Mbps and higher having the same OSPF cost of 1. The reference bandwidth can be modified to accommodate networks with links faster than 100,000,000 bps (100 Mbps) using the OSPF command **auto-cost reference-bandwidth**. When this command is necessary, it is recommended that it is used on all routers so the OSPF routing metric remains consistent.

OSPF Accumulates Cost

The cost of an OSPF route is the accumulated value from one router to the destination network. For example, the following output is from R1's routing table in Example 11-12, which shows a cost of 65 to reach the 10.10.10.0/24 network on R2:

```
O        10.10.10.0/24 [110/65] via 192.168.10.2, 14:27:57, Serial0/0/0
```

Figure 11-9 shows the cost values of each link between R1 and network 10.10.10.0/24.

Figure 11-9   OSPF Accumulates Cost

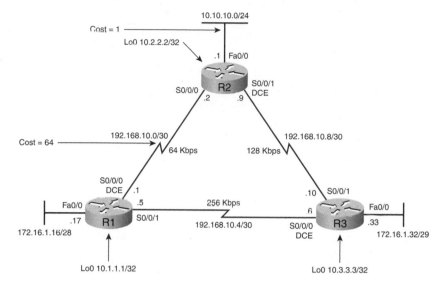

Because 10.10.10.0/24 is attached to a Fast Ethernet interface, R2 assigns the value 1 as the cost for 10.10.10.0/24. R1 then adds the additional cost value of 64 to send data across the default T1 link between R1 and R2. The "Cost = 64" in Figure 11-9 refers to the default cost of the serial interface, $10^8/1{,}544{,}000$ bps = 64, and not to the actual 64-Kbps "speed" of the link.

Default Bandwidth on Serial Interfaces

You might recall from Chapter 9, "EIGRP," that you can use the **show interface** command to view the bandwidth value used for an interface. On Cisco routers, the bandwidth value on many serial interfaces defaults to T1 (1.544 Mbps). However, some serial interfaces may default to 128 Kbps. Therefore, never assume that OSPF is using any particular bandwidth value. Always check the default value with the **show interface** command.

Remember, this bandwidth value does not actually affect the speed of the link; it is used by some routing protocols to compute the routing metric. Most likely, on serial interfaces the actual speed of the link is different from the default bandwidth. It is important that the bandwidth value reflect the actual speed of the link so that the routing table has accurate best path information. For example, you might only be paying for a fractional T1 connection from your service provider, one-fourth of a full T1 connection (384 Kbps). However, for routing protocol purposes, Cisco IOS software assumes a T1 bandwidth value even though the interface is actually only sending and receiving one-fourth of a full T1 connection (384 Kbps).

Example 11-15 shows the output for the serial 0/0/0 interface on R1. In the previous figure, Figure 11-9, notice that all the serial links have actual bandwidths that are possibly different from the default.

Example 11-15 Differences Between Default and Actual Bandwidth

```
R1#show interface serial 0/0/0
Serial0/0/0 is up, line protocol is up
  Hardware is GT96K Serial
  Description: Link to R2
  Internet address is 192.168.10.1/30
  MTU 1500 bytes, BW 1544 Kbit, DLY 20000 usec,
      reliability 255/255, txload 1/255, rxload 1/255
  Encapsulation HDLC, loopback not set
  <output omitted>
```

Notice that the default bandwidth value in the command output for R1 is 1544 Kbps. However, the actual bandwidth of this link, as labeled in Figure 11-9, is 64 Kbps. This means that the router has routing information that does not accurately reflect the network topology.

Example 11-16 displays partial output of the routing table for R1.

Example 11-16 Inaccuracies in the Routing Table for R1

```
R1#show ip route
Codes: <some code output omitted>
        D - EIGRP, EX - EIGRP external, O - OSPF, IA - OSPF inter area


<route ouput omitted>


O       192.168.10.8 [110/128] via 192.168.10.6, 14:27:57, Serial0/0/1
                     [110/128] via 192.168.10.2, 14:27:57, Serial0/0/0
```

R1 believes that both of its serial interfaces are connected to T1 links, although one of the links is a 64 Kbps link and the other one is a 256 Kbps link. This results in R1's routing table having two equal-cost paths to the 192.168.8.0/30 network, when Serial 0/0/1 is actually the better path.

The calculated OSPF cost of an interface can be verified with the **show ip ospf interface** command, as shown in the partial output in Example 11-17.

Example 11-17   Verifying Calculated Cost with the **show ip ospf interface**
                    Command

```
R1#show ip ospf interface serial 0/0/0
Serial0/0/0 is up, line protocol is up
  Internet Address 192.160.10.1/30, Area 0
  Process ID 1, Router ID 10.1.1.1, Network Type POINT_TO_POINT, Cost: 64
  <output omitted>
```

With this command, we can verify that R1 is indeed assigning a cost of 64 to the Serial
0/0/0 interface. Although you might think that this is the correct cost because this interface
is attached to a 64-Kbps link, remember that cost is derived from the cost formula. The cost
of a 64-Kbps link is 1562 (100,000,000/64,000). The value of 64 displayed corresponds to
the cost of a T1 link. In the next topic, you learn how to modify the cost of all the links in
the topology.

Modifying the Cost of the Link

When the serial interface is not actually operating at the default T1 speed, the interface
requires manual modification. Both sides of the link should be configured to have the same
value. Both the **bandwidth interface** command and the **ip ospf cost interface** command
achieve this purpose: an accurate value for use by OSPF in determining the best route.

The **bandwidth** Command

The **bandwidth** command is used to modify the bandwidth value used by the Cisco IOS
software in calculating the OSPF cost metric. The interface command syntax is the same
syntax that you learned in Chapter 9:

```
Router(config-if)#bandwidth bandwidth-kbps
```

Example 11-18 shows the **bandwidth** commands used to modify the costs of all the serial
interfaces in the topology. For R1, the **show ip ospf interface** command shows that the
cost of the Serial 0/0/0 link is now 1562, the result of the Cisco OSPF cost calculation
10^8/64,000 bps.

Example 11-18 bandwidth Command

```
R1(config)#inter serial 0/0/0
R1(config-if)#bandwidth 64
R1(config-if)#inter serial 0/0/1
R1(config-if)#bandwidth 256
```

```
R1(config-if)#end
R1#show ip ospf interface serial 0/0/0
Serial0/0 is up, line protocol is up
  Internet Address 192.168.10.1/30, Area 0
  Process ID 1, Router ID 10.1.1.1, Network Type POINT_TO_POINT, Cost: 1562
  Transmit Delay is 1 sec, State POINT_TO_POINT,
  <output omitted>
R2(config)#inter serial 0/0/0
R2(config-if)#bandwidth 64
R2(config-if)#inter serial 0/0/1
R2(config-if)#bandwidth 128
R3(config)#inter serial 0/0/0
R3(config-if)#bandwidth 256
R3(config-if)#inter serial 0/0/1
R3(config-if)#bandwidth 128
```

The **ip ospf cost** Command

An alternative method to using the **bandwidth** command is to use the **ip ospf cost** command, which allows you to directly specify the cost of an interface. For example, on R1, we could configure Serial 0/0/0 with the following command:

```
R1(config)#interface serial 0/0/0
R1(config-if)#ip ospf cost 1562
```

Obviously, this would not change the output of the **show ip ospf interface** command, which still shows the cost as 1562, as shown in Example 11-19. This is the same cost calculated by Cisco IOS software when we configured the bandwidth as 64.

Example 11-19 ip ospf cost Command

```
R1(config)#inter serial 0/0/0
R1(config-if)#ip ospf cost 1562
R1(config-if)#end
R1#show ip ospf interface serial 0/0/0
Serial0/0 is up, line protocol is up
  Internet Address 192.168.10.1/30, Area 0
  Process ID 1, Router ID 10.1.1.1, Network Type POINT_TO_POINT, Cost: 1562
  Transmit Delay is 1 sec, State POINT_TO_POINT,
  <output omitted>
```

The **bandwidth** Command vs. the **ip ospf cost** Command

The **ip ospf cost** command is useful in multivendor environments where non-Cisco routers use a metric other than bandwidth to calculate the OSPF costs. The main difference between the two commands is that the **bandwidth** command uses the result of the cost calculation to determine the cost of the link. The **ip ospf cost** command bypasses this calculation by directly setting the cost of the link to a specific value.

Table 11-4 shows the two alternatives that can be used in modifying the costs of the serial links in the topology. The right side shows the **ip ospf cost** command equivalents of the **bandwidth** commands on the left.

Table 11-4   Equivalent **bandwidth** and **ip ospf cost** Commands

bandwidth Commands	ip ospf cost Commands
Router R1	**Router R1**
R1(config)#**interface serial 0/0/0**	= R1(config)#**interface serial 0/0/0**
R1(config-if)#**bandwidth 64**	R1(config-if)#**ip ospf cost 1562**
R1(config)#**interface serial 0/0/1**	= R1(config)#**interface serial 0/0/1**
R1(config-if)#**bandwidth 256**	R1(config-if)#**ip ospf cost 390**
Router R2	**Router R2**
R2(config)#**interface serial 0/0/0**	= R2(config)#**interface serial 0/0/0**
R2(config-if)#**bandwidth 64**	R2(config-if)#**ip ospf cost 1562**
R2(config)#**interface serial 0/0/1**	= R2(config)#**interface serial 0/0/1**
R2(config-if)#**bandwidth 128**	R2(config-if)#**ip ospf cost 781**
Router R3	**Router R3**
R3(config)#**interface serial 0/0/0**	= R3(config)#**interface serial 0/0/0**
R3(config-if)#**bandwidth 256**	R3(config-if)#**ip ospf cost 390**
R3(config)#**interface serial 0/0/1**	= R3(config)#**interface serial 0/0/0**
R3(config-if)#**bandwidth 128**	R3(config-if)#**ip ospf cost 781**

Modifying the Cost of the Link (11.3.2)

Use the Packet Tracer Activity to modify the cost values for OSPF. Detailed instructions are provided within the activity. Use file e2-1132.pka on the CD-ROM that accompanies this book to perform this activity using Packet Tracer.

OSPF and Multiaccess Networks

A *multiaccess network* is a network with more than two devices on the same shared media. Examples of multiaccess networks include Ethernet, Token Ring, and Frame Relay. Token Ring is LAN technology that is for the most part obsolete. Frame Relay is a WAN technology that is discussed in a later CCNA course.

Challenges in Multiaccess Networks

In the top portion of Figure 11-10, the Ethernet LAN attached to R1 is extended to show possible devices that might be attached to the 172.16.1.16/28 network.

Figure 11-10 Multiaccess vs. Point-to-Point Networks

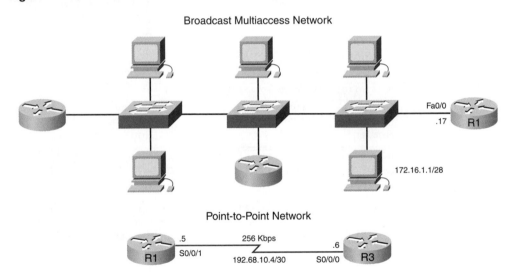

Ethernet LANs are an example of a broadcast multiaccess network. They are broadcast networks because a single device is capable of sending a single frame that has all devices on the network as its destination. They are multiaccess networks because there may be numerous hosts, printers, routers, and other devices that are members of the same network.

In contrast, on a point-to-point network, there are only two devices on the network, one at each end. The WAN link between R1 and R3 is an example of a point-to-point link. The bottom portion of Figure 11-10 shows the point-to-point link between R1 and R3.

OSPF defines five network types:

- Point to point

- Broadcast multiaccess

- Nonbroadcast multiaccess

- Point to multipoint

- Virtual links

NBMA and point-to-multipoint networks include Frame Relay, ATM, and X.25 networks. NBMA networks are discussed in another CCNA course. Point-to-multipoint networks are discussed in CCNP. Virtual links are a special type of link that can be used in multiarea OSPF. OSPF virtual links are discussed in CCNP.

Figure 11-11 shows that the topology uses both point-to-point and broadcast networks.

Figure 11-11 OSPF Network Types Used in the Topology

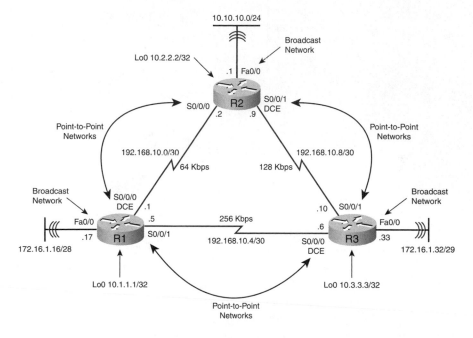

Multiaccess networks can create two challenges for OSPF regarding the flooding of LSAs:

- Creation of multiple adjacencies, one adjacency for every pair of routers

- Extensive flooding of LSAs

Multiple Adjacencies

The creation of an adjacency between every pair of routers in a network would create an unnecessary number of adjacencies. This would lead to an excessive number of LSAs passing between routers on the same network.

To understand the problem with multiple adjacencies, we need to study a formula. For any number of routers (designated as *n*) on a multiaccess network, there will be $n(n-1)/2$ adjacencies. Figure 11-12 shows a simple topology of five routers, all of which are attached to the same multiaccess Ethernet network.

Figure 11-12 Five-Router Multiaccess Network

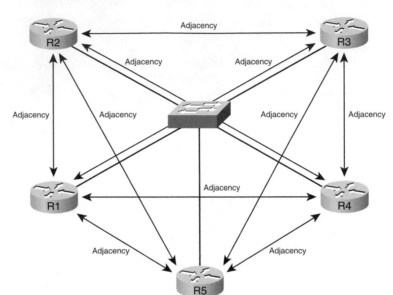

Without some type of mechanism to reduce the number of adjacencies, collectively these routers would form 10 adjacencies: $5(5-1)/2 = 10$. This might not seem like much, but as routers are added to the network, the number of adjacencies increases dramatically. Although the 5 routers in Figure 11-36 will only need 10 adjacencies, you can see that 10 routers would require 45 adjacencies. Twenty routers would require 190 adjacencies! Table 11-5 shows how the number of adjacencies would grow exponentially.

Table 11-5 Number of Adjacencies Grows Exponentially as Routers Are Added

Routers	Adjacencies
n	$n(n-1)/2$
5	10
10	45
20	190
100	4950

Flooding of LSAs

Remember from Chapter 10, "Link-State Routing Protocols," that link-state routers flood their link-state packets when OSPF is initialized or when there is a change in the topology.

In a multiaccess network, this flooding can become excessive. In Figure 11-13, R2 sends out an LSA that is then flooded by the switch in Figure 11-14.

Figure 11-13 R2 Sends Out an LSA

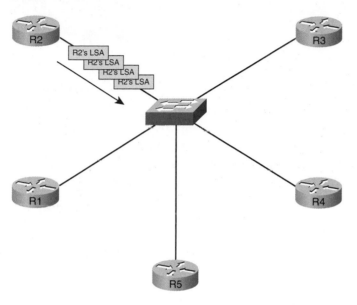

Figure 11-14 The Switch Floods the LSA Out All Ports

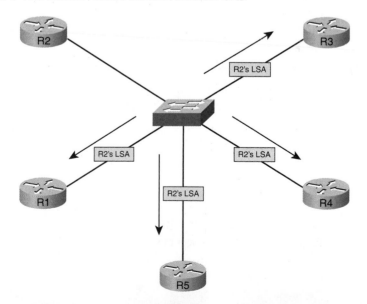

This event triggers every other router to also send out an LSA, as shown in Figure 11-15.

Figure 11-15 R1, R3, R4, and R5 Send Out LSAs

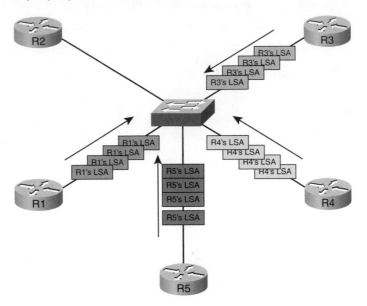

Not shown in the figures are the required acknowledgments sent for every LSA received. If every router in a multiaccess network had to flood and acknowledge all received LSAs to all other routers on that same multiaccess network, the network would become overburdened with LSAs and might cause other network traffic to be delayed or lost.

To illustrate this point, imagine that you are in a room with a large number of people. What if everyone had to introduce himself or herself individually to everyone else? Not only would each person have to tell everyone his or her name, but whenever one person learned another person's name, that person would then have to tell everyone else in the room, one person at a time. As you can see, this process would be a burden for everyone in the room!

Solution: Designated Router

The solution to managing the number of adjacencies and the flooding of LSAs on a multiaccess network is the Designated Router (DR). Continuing our previous example, this solution is analogous to electing someone in the room to go around and learn everyone's names and then announce these names to everyone in the room at once.

On multiaccess networks, OSPF elects a DR to be the collection and distribution point for LSAs sent and received. A Backup Designated Router (BDR) is also elected in case the DR fails. All other routers become DROthers. (This indicates a router that is neither the DR nor the BDR.)

Figures 11-16 and 11-17 show the role of the DR and BDR. Routers on a multiaccess network elect a DR and BDR.

Figure 11-16 R1 Sends LSAs Only to DR and BDR

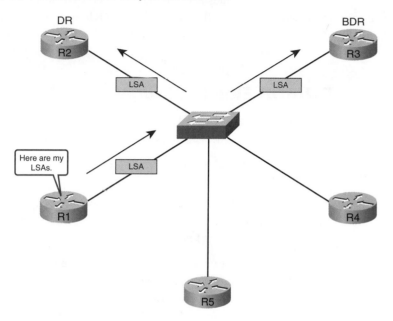

Figure 11-17 DR Sends Out Any LSAs to All Other Routers

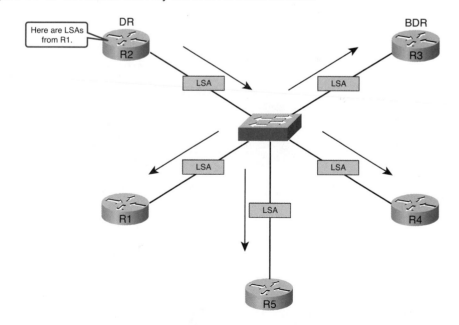

DROthers only form full adjacencies with the DR and BDR in the network. This means that instead of flooding LSAs to all routers in the network, DROthers only send their LSAs to the DR and BDR using the multicast address 224.0.0.6 (ALLDRouters, all DR routers). In Figure 11-16, R1 sends LSAs to the DR. The BDR listens, too. In Figure 11-17, the DR is responsible for forwarding the LSAs from R1 to all other routers. The DR uses the multicast address 224.0.0.5 (AllSPFRouters, all OSPF routers). The result is that there is only one router doing all the flooding of all LSAs in the multiaccess network.

DR/BDR Election Process

How does a router become the DR or BDR? The following section describes this process and how specific routers can be configured to be the DR or BDR.

Topology Change

DR/BDR elections do not occur in point-to-point networks. Therefore, in our standard three-router topology, R1, R2, and R3 do not need to elect a DR and BDR because the links between these routers are not multiaccess networks.

For the rest of the discussion on DR and BDR, we use the multiaccess topology shown in Figure 11-18. The names of the routers are different, solely to emphasize that this topology is not the same three-router topology we have been using up to this point. We return to our chapter topology, Figure 11-7, after the discussion of the DR/BDR election process.

Figure 11-18 Multiaccess Three-Router Topology

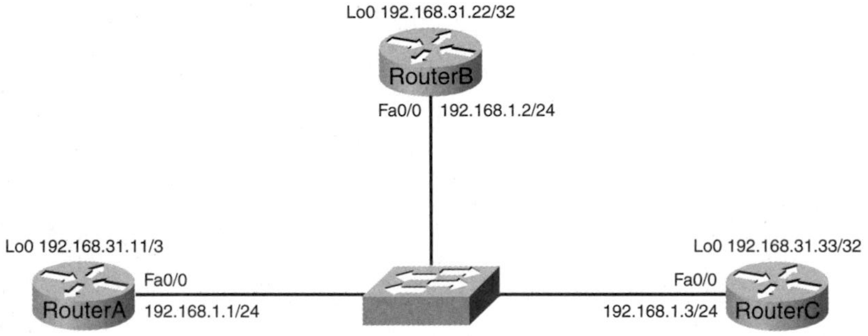

In this new topology, we have three routers sharing a common Ethernet multiaccess network, 192.168.1.0/24. Each router is configured with an IP address on the Fast Ethernet interface and a loopback address for the router ID.

DR/BDR Election

How do the DR and BDR get elected? The following criteria are applied:

1. DR: Router with the highest OSPF interface priority.
2. BDR: Router with the second highest OSPF interface priority.
3. If OSPF interface priorities are equal, the highest router ID is used to break the tie.

In this example, the default OSPF interface priority is 1. As a result, based on the selection criteria listed above, the OSPF router ID is used to elect the DR and BDR. As you can see in Figure 11-19, RouterC becomes the DR and RouterB, with the second highest router ID, becomes the BDR. Because RouterA is not elected as either the DR or BDR, it becomes the DROther.

Figure 11-19 DR/BDR Election

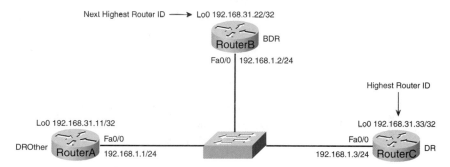

DROthers only form *full* adjacencies with the DR and BDR but will still form a neighbor adjacency with any DROthers that join the network. This means that all DROther routers in the multiaccess network still receive Hello packets from all other DROther routers. In this way, they are aware of all routers in the network. When two DROther routers form a neighbor adjacency, the neighbor state is displayed as 2WAY. The different neighbor states are discussed in CCNP.

The **show ip ospf neighbor** command output in Example 11-20 displays the neighbor adjacency of each router on the multiaccess network.

Example 11-20 Verifying DR and BDR with the **show ip ospf neighbor** Command

```
RouterA#show ip ospf neighbor

Neighbor ID     Pri   State      Dead Time   Address       Interface
192.168.31.33    1    FULL/DR    00:00:39    192.168.1.3   FastEthernet0/0
192.168.31.22    1    FULL/BDR   00:00:36    192.168.1.2   FastEthernet0/0
RouterB#show ip ospf neighbor
```

```
Neighbor ID        Pri    State          Dead Time    Address        Interface
192.168.31.33       1     FULL/DR        00:00:34     192.168.1.3    FastEthernet0/0
192.168.31.11       1     FULL/DROTHER   00:00:38     192.168.1.1    FastEthernet0/0
RouterC#show ip ospf neighbor


Neighbor ID        Pri    State          Dead Time    Address        Interface
192.168.31.22       1     FULL/BDR       00:00:35     192.168.1.2    FastEthernet0
192.168.31.11       1     FULL/DROTHER   00:00:32     192.168.1.1    FastEthernet0
```

Notice for RouterA that it shows that the DR is RouterC with the router ID of 192.168.31.33 and that the BDR is RouterB with the router ID of 192.168.31.22. Also, notice that the priority for all routers is the default 1.

Because RouterA shows both its neighbors as the DR and BDR, RouterA is a DROther. This can be verified using the **show ip ospf interface fastethernet 0/0** command on RouterA, as shown in Example 11-21. This command shows the DR, BDR, or DROTHER state of this router, along with the router ID of the DR and BDR on this multiaccess network.

Example 11-21 Verifying Router States with the **show ospf interface** Command

```
RouterA#show ip ospf interface fastethernet 0/0
FastEthernet0/0 is up, line protocol is up
  Internet Address 192.168.1.1/24, Area 0
  Process ID 1, Router ID 192.168.31.11, Network Type BROADCAST, Cost: 1
  Transmit Delay is 1 sec, State DROTHER, Priority 1
  Designated Router (ID) 192.168.31.33, Interface address 192.168.1.3
  Backup Designated router (ID) 192.168.31.22, Interface address 192.168.1.2
  Timer intervals configured, Hello 10, Dead 40, Wait 40, Retransmit 5
    oob-resync timeout 40
    Hello due in 00:00:06
  Supports Link-local Signaling (LLS)
  Index 1/1, flood queue length 0
  Next 0x0(0)/0x0(0)
  Last flood scan length is 0, maximum is 1
  Last flood scan time is 0 msec, maximum is 0 msec
  Neighbor Count is 2, Adjacent neighbor count is 2
    Adjacent with neighbor 192.168.31.22  (Backup Designated Router)
    Adjacent with neighbor 192.168.31.33  (Designated Router)
  Suppress hello for 0 neighbor(s)
```

Timing of DR/BDR Election

The DR and BDR election process takes place as soon as the first router with an OSPF-enabled interface is active on the multiaccess network. This can happen when the routers are powered on or when the OSPF **network** command for that interface is configured. The election process only takes a few seconds. If not all the routers on the multiaccess network have finished booting, it is possible that a router with a lower router ID will become the DR. This could be a lower-end router that took less time to boot, which might not be the best router to handle the functions of the DR.

When the DR is elected, it remains the DR until one of the following conditions occurs:

- The DR fails.

- The OSPF process on the DR fails.

- The multiaccess interface on the DR fails.

In the following figures, an *X* indicates one or more of these failures.

Figure 11-19 shows the topology with the current DR and BDR.

If the DR fails, the BDR assumes the role of DR, and an election is held to choose a new BDR. In Figure 11-20, RouterC fails and the former BDR, RouterB, becomes DR. The only other router available to be BDR is RouterA.

Figure 11-20 The Current DR, RouterC, Fails

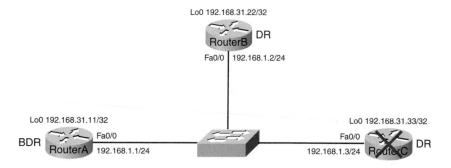

In Figure 11-21, RouterD joins the network. If a new router enters the network after the DR and BDR have been elected, it will not become the DR or the BDR even if it has a higher OSPF interface priority or router ID than the current DR or BDR. The new router can be elected the BDR if the current DR or BDR fails. If the current DR fails, the BDR will become the DR, and the new router can be elected the new BDR.

After the new router becomes the BDR, if the DR fails, the new router will become the DR.

Figure 11-21 RouterD Joins the Network

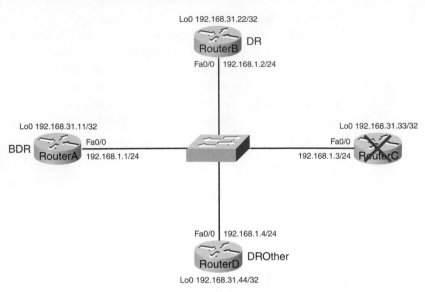

Even though its router ID, 192.168.31.44, is higher than the current DR and BDR routers, RouterD assumes the role of a DROther.

A previous DR does not regain DR status if it returns to the network. In Figure 11-22, RouterC has finished a reboot and becomes a DROther even though its router ID, 192.168.31.33, is higher than the current DR and BDR.

Figure 11-22 Previous DR Does Not Resume DR State

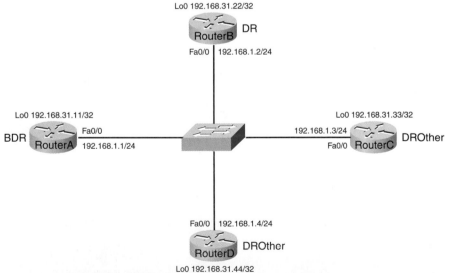

If the BDR fails, an election is held among the DROthers to see which router will be the new BDR. In Figure 11-23, the BDR router fails. An election is held between RouterC and RouterD. RouterD wins the election with the higher router ID.

Figure 11-23 BDR Elections Are Held When Current BDR Fails

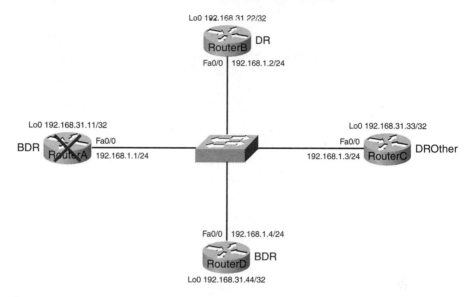

In Figure 11-24, RouterB fails. Because RouterD is the current BDR, it is promoted to DR. RouterC becomes the BDR.

Figure 11-24 Both DR and BDR Fail

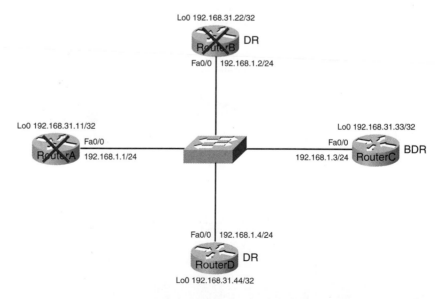

So, how do you make sure that the routers you want to be DR and BDR win the election? Without further configurations, the solution is to do either of the following:

- Boot up the DR first, followed by the BDR, and then boot all other routers.

- Shut down the interface on all routers, followed by a **no shutdown** on the DR, then the BDR, and then all other routers.

However, as you might have already guessed, we can change the OSPF interface priority to better control our DR/BDR elections.

OSPF Interface Priority

Because the DR becomes the focal point for the collection and distribution of LSAs, it is important for this router to have sufficient CPU and memory capacity to handle the responsibility. Instead of relying on the router ID to decide which routers are elected the DR and BDR, it is better to control the election of these routers with the **ip ospf priority** interface command.

```
Router(config-if)#ip ospf priority {0 - 255}
```

In our previous discussion, the OSPF priority was equal. This is because the priority value defaults to 1 for all router interfaces. Therefore, the router ID determined the DR and BDR. If you change the default value from 1 to a higher value, however, the router with the highest priority becomes the DR, and the router with the next highest priority becomes the BDR. A value of 0 makes the router ineligible to become a DR or BDR.

Because priorities are an interface-specific value, they provide better control of the OSPF multiaccess networks. They also allow a router to be the DR in one network and a DROther in another.

To simplify our discussion, we removed RouterD from the topology, as shown in Figure 11-25.

Figure 11-25 Multiaccess Topology

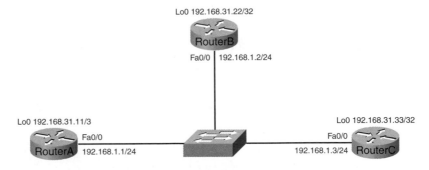

The OSPF interface priority can be viewed using the **show ip ospf interface** command. In Example 11-22, we can verify that the priority on RouterA is at the default value of 1.

Example 11-22 Verifying Priority with the **show ip ospf interface** Command

```
RouterA#show ip ospf interface fastethernet 0/0
FastEthernet0/0 is up, line protocol is up
  Internet Address 192.168.1.1/24, Area 0
  Process ID 1, Router ID 192.168.31.11, Network Type BROADCAST, Cost: 1
  Transmit Delay is 1 sec, State DROTHER, Priority 1
  Designated Router (ID) 192.168.31.33, Interface address 192.168.1.3
  Backup Designated router (ID) 192.168.31.22, Interface address 192.168.1.2
  Timer intervals configured, Hello 10, Dead 40, Wait 40, Retransmit 5
    oob-resync timeout 40
    Hello due in 00:00:06
  Supports Link-local Signaling (LLS)
  Index 1/1, flood queue length 0
  Next 0x0(0)/0x0(0)
  Last flood scan length is 0, maximum is 1
  Last flood scan time is 0 msec, maximum is 0 msec
  Neighbor Count is 2, Adjacent neighbor count is 2
    Adjacent with neighbor 192.168.31.22  (Backup Designated Router)
    Adjacent with neighbor 192.168.31.33  (Designated Router)
  Suppress hello for 0 neighbor(s)
```

Example 11-23 shows the OSPF interface priorities of RouterA and RouterB modified so that RouterA with the highest priority becomes the DR and Router B becomes the BDR. The OSPF interface priority of RouterC remains at the default value of 1.

Example 11-23 Modifying the OSPF Interface Priority

```
RouterA(config)#interface fastethernet 0/0
RouterA(config-if)#ip ospf priority 200
RouterB(config)#interface fastethernet 0/0
RouterB(config-if)#ip ospf priority 100
```

Example 11-24 shows how to force the election process. After doing a **shutdown** and a **no shutdown** on the Fast Ethernet 0/0 interfaces of all three routers, we see the result of the change of OSPF interface priorities.

Example 11-24 Forcing a DR/BDR Election

```
RouterA(config)#interface fastethernet 0/0
RouterA(config-if)#shutdown
RouterA(config-if)#no shutdown
RouterA(config-if)#end
RouterA#show ip ospf neighbor

Neighbor ID     Pri  State        Dead Time   Address      Interface
192.168.31.22   100  FULL/BDR     00:00:30    192.168.1.2  FastEthernet0/0
192.168.31.33     1  FULL/DROTHER 00:00:30    192.168.1.3  FastEthernet0/0
RouterB(config)#interface fastethernet 0/0
RouterB(config-if)#shutdown
RouterB(config-if)#no shutdown
RouterB(config-if)#end
RouterB#show ip ospf neighbor

Neighbor ID     Pri  State        Dead Time   Address      Interface
192.168.31.11   200  FULL/DR      00:00:37    192.168.1.1  FastEthernet0/0
192.168.31.33     1  FULL/DROTHER 00:00:38    192.168.1.3  FastEthernet0/0
RouterC(config)#interface fastethernet 0/0
RouterC(config-if)#shutdown
RouterC(config-if)#no shutdown
RouterC(config-if)#end
RouterC#show ip ospf neighbor

Neighbor ID     Pri  State        Dead Time   Address      Interface
192.168.31.22   100  FULL/BDR     00:00:32    192.168.1.2  FastEthernet0/0
192.168.31.11   200  FULL/DR      00:00:31    192.168.1.1  FastEthernet0/0
```

The **show ip ospf neighbor** command on RouterC now shows that RouterA (Router ID 192.168.31.11) is the DR with the highest OSPF interface priority of 200 and that Router B (Router ID 192.168.31.22) is still the BDR with the next highest OSPF interface priority of 100. Notice from RouterA's output of **show ip ospf neighbor** that it does not show a DR, because RouterA is the actual DR on this network.

Configuring the OSPF interface priority does not resolve the issue of the first router booting possibly becoming the DR.

Determining the DR and BDR (11.4.3)

When you first open the file in Packet Tracer, you might notice that the link lights for the switch are amber. All routers are attached to the switch in the middle. These link lights will stay amber for 50 seconds while the switch makes sure that one of the routers is not another switch. You will learn more about this loop avoidance technique in another course. For now, just know that it will take a few minutes for OSPF to converge. In this activity, you will examine current DR and BDR roles, watch the roles change, and then force new roles by changing priority. Detailed instructions are provided within the activity. Use file e2-1143.pka on the CD-ROM that accompanies this book to perform this activity using Packet Tracer.

More OSPF Configuration

The previous section discussed basic OSPF configuration. The following section discusses other OSPF configuration commands, including redistributing a default route, modifying the reference bandwidth, and modifying timers.

Redistributing an OSPF Default Route

As with other routing protocols, OSPF has the ability to propagate a default route.

Topology

Using Figure 11-26, let's return to the earlier topology, which now includes a new link to ISP.

Figure 11-26 Topology with ISP Connection

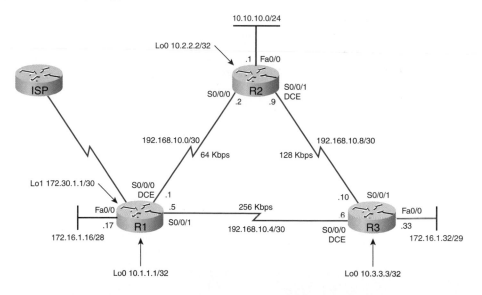

As with RIP and EIGRP, the router connected to the Internet is used to propagate a default route to other routers in the OSPF routing domain. This router is sometimes called the edge, entrance, or gateway router. However, in OSPF terminology, the router located between an OSPF routing domain and a non-OSPF network is called the *Autonomous System Boundary Router (ASBR)*. In this topology, the Loopback1 (Lo1) represents a link to a non-OSPF network. We will not configure the 172.30.1.1/30 network as part of the OSPF routing process.

Example 11-25 shows the ASBR (R1) configured with the Loopback1 IP address and static default route forwarding traffic toward the ISP router.

Example 11-25 ASBR Static Default Route Configuration

```
R1(config)#interface loopback 1
R1(config-if)#ip add 172.30.1.1 255.255.255.252
R1(config-if)#exit
R1(config)#ip route 0.0.0.0 0.0.0.0 loopback 1
R1(config)#router ospf 1
R1(config-router)#default-information originate
```

Note

The static default route is using the loopback as an exit interface because the ISP router in this topology does not physically exist. By using a loopback interface, we can simulate the connection to another router.

Like RIP, OSPF requires the use of the **default-information originate** command to advertise the 0.0.0.0/0 static default route to the other routers in the area. If the **default-information originat**e command is not used, the default "quad zero" route will not be propagated to other routers in the OSPF area.

Examples 11-26, 11-27, and 11-28 show the routing tables for R1, R2, and R3. All three routers now have a "gateway of last resort" set in the routing table.

Example 11-26 R1 Routing Table with Default Route

```
R1#show ip route
Codes: <some code output omitted>
        D - EIGRP, EX - EIGRP external, O - OSPF, IA - OSPF inter area
        E1 - OSPF external type 1, E2 - OSPF external type 2

Gateway of last resort is 0.0.0.0 to network 0.0.0.0

     192.168.10.0/30 is subnetted, 3 subnets
C        192.168.10.0 is directly connected, Serial0/0/0
C        192.168.10.4 is directly connected, Serial0/0/1
O        192.168.10.8 [110/1171] via 192.168.10.6, 00:00:58, Serial0/0/1
     172.16.0.0/16 is variably subnetted, 2 subnets, 2 masks
```

```
O          172.16.1.32/29 [110/391] via 192.168.10.6, 00:00:58, Serial0/0/1
C          172.16.1.16/28 is directly conncoted, FastEthernet0/0
      172.30.0.0/30 is subnetted, 1 subnets
C          172.30.1.0 is directly connected, Loopback1
      10.0.0.0/8 is variably subnetted, 2 subnets, 2 masks
O          10.10.10.0/24 [110/1172] via 192.168.10.6, 00:00:58, Serial0/0/1
C          10.1.1.1/32 is directly connected, Loopback0
S*    0.0.0.0/0 is directly connected, Loopback1
```

Example 11-27 R2 Routing Table with Default Route

```
R2#show ip route
Codes: <some code output omitted>
        D - EIGRP, EX - EIGRP external, O - OSPF, IA - OSPF inter area
        E1 - OSPF external type 1, E2 - OSPF external type 2

Gateway of last resort is 192.168.10.10 to network 0.0.0.0

      192.168.10.0/30 is subnetted, 3 subnets
C         192.168.10.0 is directly connected, Serial0/0/0
O         192.168.10.4 [110/1171] via 192.168.10.10, 00:00:25, Serial0/0/1
C         192.168.10.8 is directly connected, Serial0/0/1
      172.16.0.0/16 is variably subnetted, 2 subnets, 2 masks
O         172.16.1.32/29 [110/782] via 192.168.10.10, 00:00:25, Serial0/0/1
O         172.16.1.16/28 [110/1172] via 192.168.10.10, 00:00:25, Serial0/0/1
      10.0.0.0/8 is variably subnetted, 2 subnets, 2 masks
C         10.2.2.2/32 is directly connected, Loopback0
C         10.10.10.0/24 is directly connected, FastEthernet0/0
O*E2 0.0.0.0/0 [110/1] via 192.168.10.10, 00:00:13, Serial0/0/1
```

Example 11-28 R3 Routing Table with Default Route

```
R3#show ip route
Codes: <some code output omitted>
        D - EIGRP, EX - EIGRP external, O - OSPF, IA - OSPF inter area
        E1 - OSPF external type 1, E2 - OSPF external type 2

Gateway of last resort is 192.168.10.5 to network 0.0.0.0

      192.168.10.0/30 is subnetted, 3 subnets
O         192.168.10.0 [110/1952] via 192.168.10.5, 00:00:38, Serial0/0/0
C         192.168.10.4 is directly connected, Serial0/0/0
C         192.168.10.8 is directly connected, Serial0/0/1
```

```
        172.16.0.0/16 is variably subnetted, 2 subnets, 2 masks
C          172.16.1.32/29 is directly connected, FastEthernet0/0
O          172.16.1.16/28 [110/391] via 192.168.10.5, 00:00:38, Serial0/0/0
        10.0.0.0/8 is variably subnetted, 2 subnets, 2 masks
C          10.3.3.3/32 is directly connected, Loopback0
O          10.10.10.0/24 [110/782] via 192.168.10.9, 00:00:38, Serial0/0/1
O*E2 0.0.0.0/0 [110/1] via 192.168.10.5, 00:00:27, Serial0/0/0
```

Notice the default route in R2 and R3 with the routing source OSPF, but with the additional code, **E2**. For R2, the route is as follows:

```
O*E2 0.0.0.0/0 [110/1] via 192.168.10.10, 00:05:34, Serial0/0/1
```

E2 denotes that this route is an OSPF External Type 2 route.

OSPF external routes fall in one of two categories: External Type 1 (E1) or External Type 2 (E2). The difference between the two is in the way the OSPF cost of the route is calculated at each router. OSPF accumulates cost for an E1 route as the route is being propagated throughout the OSPF area. This process is identical to cost calculations for normal OSPF internal routes. However, the cost of an E2 route is always the external cost, irrespective of the interior cost to reach that route. In this topology, because the default route has an external cost of 1 on the R1 router, R2 and R3 also show a cost of 1 for the default E2 route. E2 routes at a cost of 1 are the default OSPF configuration. Changing these defaults, and more external route information, is discussed in CCNP.

Fine-Tuning OSPF

The next section discusses modifying the reference bandwidth and the timers. Whenever modifying defaults, be sure to understand the consequences and to add these commands to the appropriate routers.

Reference Bandwidth

As you remember, Cisco OSPF cost uses accumulated bandwidth. The cost value of each interface is calculated using 100,000,000/bandwidth; 100,000,000 or 10^8 is known as the reference bandwidth.

Therefore, 100,000,000 is the default bandwidth referenced when the actual bandwidth is converted into a cost metric. As you know from previous studies, we now have link speeds that are much faster than Fast Ethernet speeds, including Gigabit Ethernet and 10GigE. Using a reference bandwidth of 100,000,000 results in interfaces with bandwidth values of 100 Mbps and higher having the same OSPF cost of 1.

To obtain more accurate cost calculations, it might be necessary to adjust the reference bandwidth value. The reference bandwidth can be modified to accommodate these faster links by using the OSPF command **auto-cost reference-bandwidth**:

```
R1(config-router)#auto-cost reference-bandwidth ?
1-4294967 The reference bandwidth in terms of Mbits per second.
```

When this command is necessary, use it on all routers so that the OSPF routing metric remains consistent.

Notice that the value is expressed in megabits per second. Therefore, the default value is equivalent to 100. To increase it to 10GigE (10 Gbps Ethernet) speeds, you need to change the reference bandwidth to 10000:

```
R1(config-router)#auto-cost reference-bandwidth 10000
```

Again, make sure you configure this command on all routers in the OSPF routing domain. Cisco IOS Software might also remind you, as shown in Example 11-29.

Example 11-29 Configuring the Reference Bandwidth

```
R1(config-if)#router ospf 1
R1(config-router)#auto-cost reference-bandwidth ?
  <1-4294967>  The reference bandwidth in terms of Mbits per second

R1(config-router)#auto-cost reference-bandwidth  10000
% OSPF: Reference bandwidth is changed.
        Please ensure reference bandwidth is consistent across all routers.
R2(config-if)#router ospf 1
R2(config-router)#auto-cost reference-bandwidth  10000
% OSPF: Reference bandwidth is changed.
        Please ensure reference bandwidth is consistent across all routers.
R3(config-if)#router ospf 1
R3(config-router)#auto-cost reference-bandwidth  10000
% OSPF: Reference bandwidth is changed.
        Please ensure reference bandwidth is consistent across all routers.
```

The routing table for R1 in Example 11-30 shows the change in the OSPF cost metric.

Example 11-30 R1 Routing Table with Cost Metrics Adjusted to New Reference Bandwidth

```
R1#show ip route
Codes: <some code output omitted>
        D - EIGRP, EX - EIGRP external, O - OSPF, IA - OSPF inter area
        E1 - OSPF external type 1, E2 - OSPF external type 2
```

```
Gateway of last resort is 0.0.0.0 to network 0.0.0.0

     192.168.10.0/30 is subnetted, 3 subnets
C        192.168.10.0 is directly connected, Serial0/0/0
C        192.168.10.4 is directly connected, Serial0/0/1
O        192.168.10.8 [110/104597] via 192.168.10.6, 00:01:33, Serial0/0/1
     172.16.0.0/16 is variably subnetted, 2 subnets, 2 masks
O        172.16.1.32/29 [110/39162] via 192.168.10.6, 00:01:33, Serial0/0/1
C        172.16.1.16/28 is directly connected, FastEthernet0/0
     172.30.0.0/30 is subnetted, 1 subnets
C        172.30.1.0 is directly connected, Loopback1
     10.0.0.0/8 is variably subnetted, 2 subnets, 2 masks
O        10.10.10.0/24 [110/65635] via 192.168.10.2, 00:01:33, Serial0/0/0
C        10.1.1.1/32 is directly connected, Loopback0
S*   0.0.0.0/0 is directly connected, Loopback1
```

Notice that the values are much larger cost values for OSPF routes than are shown in
Example 11-26. For example, before modifying the reference bandwidth in Example 11-29,
the cost to 10.10.10.0/24 is 1172. After configuring a new reference bandwidth, the cost for
the same route is now 65635, as shown in Example 11-30.

Modifying OSPF Intervals

In Example 11-31, the **show ip ospf neighbor** command on R1 verifies that R1 is adjacent
to R2 and R3. Notice in the output that the Dead time is counting down from 40 seconds.
By default, this value is refreshed every 10 seconds when R1 receives a Hello from the
neighbor.

Example 11-31 Verifying Dead Time with the **show ip ospf neighbor** Command

```
R1#show ip ospf neighbor

Neighbor ID     Pri   State          Dead Time   Address         Interface
10.3.3.3          0   FULL/  -       00:00:35    192.168.10.6    Serial0/0/1
10.2.2.2          0   FULL/  -       00:00:36    192.168.10.2    Serial0/0/0
```

It might be desirable to change the OSPF timers so that routers will detect network failures
in less time. Doing this will increase traffic, but sometimes there is a need for quick convergence that outweighs the extra traffic. Before changing any timer default values, be sure to
give it careful consideration and understand the effects of making those changes.

OSPF Hello and Dead intervals can be modified manually using the following interface commands:

```
Router(config-if)#ip ospf hello-interval seconds
Router(config-if)#ip ospf dead-interval seconds
```

Example 11-32 shows the Hello and Dead intervals modified to 5 seconds and 20 seconds, respectively, on the Serial 0/0/0 interface for R1.

Example 11-32 Modifying Hello and Dead Intervals on R1

```
R1(config)#interface serial 0/0/0
R1(config-if)#ip ospf hello-interval 5
R1(config-if)#ip ospf dead-interval 20
R1(config-if)#end

<Wait 20 seconds for IOS message>

%OSPF-5-ADJCHG: Process 1, Nbr 10.2.2.2 on Serial0/0/0 from FULL to DOWN, Neighbor
  Down:

Dead timer expired
```

Immediately after changing the Hello interval, Cisco IOS Software automatically modifies the Dead interval to four times the Hello interval. However, it is always good practice to explicitly modify the timer instead of relying on an automatic Cisco IOS feature so that modifications are documented in the configuration.

After 20 seconds, the Dead timer on R1 expires. R1 and R2 lose adjacency. We only modified the values on one side of the serial link between R1 and R2:

```
%OSPF-5-ADJCHG: Process 1, Nbr 10.2.2.2 on Serial0/0/0 from FULL to DOWN, Neighbor
  Down: Dead timer expired
```

Remember, OSPF Hello and Dead intervals must be equivalent between neighbors. You can verify the loss of adjacency with the **show ip ospf neighbor** command on R1, as shown in Example 11-33.

Example 11-33 R1 Loses Adjacency with R2

```
R1#show ip ospf neighbor

Neighbor ID     Pri   State           Dead Time   Address         Interface
10.3.3.3          0   FULL/   -       00:00:35    192.168.10.6    Serial0/0/1
```

Notice that the 10.2.2.2 neighbor is no longer present. However, 10.3.3.3 or R3 is still a neighbor. The timers set on Serial 0/0/0 do not affect the neighbor adjacency with R3.

Example 11-34 shows that the mismatching Hello and Dead intervals can be verified on R2 using the **show ip ospf interface serial 0/0/0** command.

Example 11-34 Verifying Hello and Dead Intervals with the **show ip ospf interface** Command

```
R2#show ip ospf interface serial 0/0/0
Serial0/0/0 is up, line protocol is up
  Internet Address 192.168.10.2/30, Area 0
  Process ID 1, Router ID 10.2.2.2, Network Type POINT_TO_POINT, Cost: 65535
  Transmit Delay is 1 sec, State POINT_TO_POINT,
  Timer intervals configured, Hello 10, Dead 40, Wait 40, Retransmit 5
    oob-resync timeout 40
    Hello due in 00:00:09
  Supports Link-local Signaling (LLS)
  Index 2/2, flood queue length 0
  Next 0x0(0)/0x0(0)
  Last flood scan length is 1, maximum is 1
  Last flood scan time is 0 msec, maximum is 0 msec
  Neighbor Count is 0, Adjacent neighbor count is 0
  Suppress hello for 0 neighbor(s)
```

The interval values on R2, Router ID 10.2.2.2, are still set with a Hello interval of 10 seconds and a Dead interval of 40 seconds.

To restore adjacency between R1 and R2, modify the Hello and Dead intervals on the Serial 0/0/0 interface on R2 to match the intervals on the Serial 0/0/0 interface on R1, as shown in Example 11-35.

Example 11-35 Restore Adjacency by Configuring Matching Hello and Dead Intervals on R2

```
R2(config)#interface serial 0/0/0
R2(config-if)#ip ospf hello-interval 5
R2(config-if)#ip ospf dead-interval 20
R2(config-if)#end
%OSPF-5-ADJCHG: Process 1, Nbr 10.1.1.1 on Serial0/0/0 from LOADING to FULL,
  Loading Done
```

Cisco IOS software displays a message that adjacency has been established with a state of
FULL.

Verify that neighbor adjacency is restored with the **show ip ospf neighbor** command on
R1, as demonstrated in Example 11-36.

Example 11-36 Verifying Adjacency Is Restored with the **show ip ospf neighbor**
Command

```
R1#show ip ospf neighbor

Neighbor ID     Pri   State        Dead Time   Address         Interface
10.3.3.3          0   FULL/  -     00:00:36    192.168.10.6    Serial0/0/1
10.2.2.2          0   FULL/  -     00:00:17    192.168.10.2    Serial0/0/0
```

Notice that the Dead time for Serial 0/0/0 is now much lower because it is counting down
from 20 seconds rather than the default 40 seconds. Serial 0/0/1 is still operating with
default timers.

Note

OSPF requires that the Hello and Dead intervals match between two routers for them to become
adjacent. This differs from EIGRP, where the hello and hold-down timers do not need to match for
two routers to form an EIGRP adjacency.

Default Routing and Fine-Tuning OSPF (11.5.2)

Use the Packet Tracer Activity to configure a default route and propagate it within the
OSPF routing process. Also, practice changing the reference bandwidth and the Hello and
Dead intervals. Detailed instructions are provided within the activity. Use file e2-1152.pka
on the CD-ROM that accompanies this book to perform this activity using Packet Tracer.

Summary

OSPF is a classless, link-state routing protocol. The current version of OSPF for IPv4 is OSPFv2, introduced in RFC 1247 and updated in RFC 2328 by John Moy. In 1999, OSPFv3 for IPv6 was published in RFC 2740.

OSPF has a default AD of 110 and is denoted in the routing table with a route source code of *O*. OSPF is enabled with the **router ospf** *process-id* global configuration command. The process ID is locally significant, which means that it does not have to match other OSPF routers to establish adjacencies with those neighbors.

The **network** command used with OSPF has the same function as when used with other IGP routing protocols, but with slightly different syntax:

```
Router(config-router)#network network-address wildcard-mask area area-id
```

The *wildcard-mask* is the inverse of the subnet mask, and the *area-id* should be configured to match the routers in the area. Although any area ID can be used, it is good practice to use an area ID of 0 with single-area OSPF.

OSPF does not use a transport layer protocol because OSPF packets are sent directly over IP. The OSPF Hello packet is used by OSPF to establish neighbor adjacencies. By default, OSPF Hello packets are sent every 10 seconds on multiaccess (Ethernet) and point-to-point segments, and every 30 seconds on NBMA segments (Frame Relay, X.25, ATM). The Dead interval is the period of time an OSPF router will wait before terminating adjacency with a neighbor. The Dead interval is four times the Hello interval, by default. For multiaccess and point-to-point segments, this period is 40 seconds. For NBMA networks, the Dead interval is 120 seconds.

For routers to become adjacent, their Hello interval, Dead interval, network types, and subnet masks must match. The **show ip ospf neighbors** command can be used to verify OSPF adjacencies.

The OSPF router ID is used to uniquely identify each router in the OSPF routing domain. Cisco routers derive the router ID based on three criteria, and with the following precedence:

1. Use the IP address configured with the OSPF **router-id** command.

2. If the router ID is not configured, the router chooses the highest IP address of any of its loopback interfaces.

3. If no loopback interfaces are configured, the router chooses the highest active IP address of any of its physical interfaces.

RFC 2328 does not specify which values should be used to determine the cost. Cisco IOS software uses the cumulative bandwidths of the outgoing interfaces from the router to the destination network to calculate the cost value.

Multiaccess networks can create two challenges for OSPF regarding the flooding of LSAs: the creation of multiple adjacencies, one adjacency for every pair of routers; and extensive flooding of LSAs. OSPF elects a DR to act as collection and distribution point for LSAs sent and received in the multiaccess network. A BDR is elected to take over the role of the DR should the DR fail. All other routers are known as DROthers. All routers send their LSAs to the DR, which then floods the LSA to all other routers in the multiaccess network.

The router with the highest router ID is the DR, and the router with the second highest router ID is the BDR. This can be superseded by the **ip ospf priority** command on that interface. By default, the **ip ospf priority** is 1 on all multiaccess interfaces. If a router is configured with a new priority value, the router with the highest priority value is the DR, and the next highest is the BDR. A priority value of 0 means the router is ineligible to become the DR or BDR.

A default route is propagated in OSPF similar to that of RIP. The OSPF router mode command **default-information originate** is used to propagate a static default route.

The **show ip protocols** command is used to verify important OSPF configuration information, including the OSPF process ID, the router ID, and the networks the router is advertising.

Activities and Labs

The activities and labs available in the companion *Routing Protocols and Concepts, CCNA Exploration Labs and Study Guide* (ISBN 1-58713-204-4) provide hands-on practice with the following topics introduced in this chapter:

Lab 11-1: Basic OSPF Configuration (11.6.1)

In this lab activity, there are two separate scenarios. In the first scenario, you learn how to configure the routing protocol OSPF using the network shown in the Topology Diagram in Scenario A. The segments of the network have been subnetted using VLSM. OSPF is a classless routing protocol that can be used to provide subnet mask information in the routing updates. This will allow VLSM subnet information to be propagated throughout the network.

In the second scenario, you learn to configure OSPF on a multiaccess network. You also learn to use the OSPF election process to determine the DR, BDR, and DROther states.

Lab 11-2: Challenge OSPF Configuration (11.6.2)

In this lab activity, you are given a network address that must be subnetted using VLSM to complete the addressing of the network shown in the Topology Diagram. A combination OSPF routing and static routing is required so that hosts on networks that are not directly connected will be able to communicate with each other. An OSPF area ID of 0 and a process ID of 1 will be used in all OSPF configurations.

Lab 11-3: OSPF Troubleshooting (11.6.3)

In this lab, you begin by loading configuration scripts on each of the routers. These scripts contain errors that will prevent end-to-end communication across the network.

You need to troubleshoot each router to determine the configuration errors, and then use the appropriate commands to correct the configurations.

When you have corrected all the configuration errors, all the hosts on the network should be able to communicate with each other.

Many of the Hands-on Labs include Packet Tracer Companion Activities where you can use Packet Tracer to complete a simulation of the lab. Look for this icon in the *Labs and Study Guide* (ISBN 1-58713-204-4) for Hands-on Labs that have a Packet Tracer Companion.

Check Your Understanding

Complete all the review questions listed here to test your understanding of the topics and concepts in this chapter. Answers are listed in the appendix, "Check Your Understanding and Challenge Questions Answer Key."

1. Which of the following statements are true regarding routing protocols that use the link-state routing algorithm? (Choose three.)

    A. They are known collectively as link-state routing protocols.

    B. They learn routes and send them to directly connected neighbors.

    C. They maintain a database of the network topology.

    D. They are based on the Dijkstra algorithm.

    E. They are considered a good choice for small networks with low-end routers.

2. Match the OSPF description with the proper term.

    OSPF descriptions:

    Creates and maintains neighbor adjacencies

    Triggered when a topology change has occurred

    Description of an interface and its relationship to other routers

    Calculates the best path to each destination network

    OSPF terms:

    A. LSA

    B. State of the link

    C. SPF algorithm

    D. Hello packet

3. What reasons would a network administrator have for using loopback interfaces when configuring OSPF? (Choose two.)

   A. Loopbacks are logical interfaces and do not go down.

   B. Only loopback addresses can be used for an OSPF router ID.

   C. Loopback interfaces are used to set the OSPF metric.

   D. The loopback address will be used as the router ID, overriding the physical IP address values.

   E. OSPF error checking is enabled by loopback addresses.

   F. The loopback address will override the configured router priority value.

4. In which of the following types of networks will OSPF designated routers not be elected? (Choose two.)

   A. Point to point

   B. Point to multipoint

   C. Broadcast multiaccess

   D. Nonbroadcast multiaccess

5. A network administrator enters the **router ospf 100** command. What is the function of the number **100** in this command?

   A. Autonomous system number

   B. Metric

   C. Process ID

   D. Administrative distance

6. On a router running OSPF, what is the purpose of entering the **bandwidth 56** command on a serial interface?

   A. Changes the cost value

   B. Functions only as a description

   C. Changes the throughput of the interface to 56 Kbps

   D. Is necessary for the DUAL algorithm

7. What factor does the Cisco implementation of OSPF use to pick the best route?

   A. Uptime

   B. Reliability

   C. Bandwidth

   D. Load

   E. Shortest number of hops

8. Which command allows a router to advertise default static routes via OSPF?

   A. **redistribute static**

   B. **network 0.0.0.0 0.0.0.0 area 0**

   C. **default-information originate**

   D. Default routes are local only and cannot be advertised using OSPF.

9. During an OSPF DR/BDR election, what is used to determine the DR or BDR when participating OSPF routers have identical interface priorities?

   A. The highest OSPF process ID

   B. The lowest interface IP address

   C. The lowest interface cost

   D. The router ID

10. Which packet type is invalid for OSPF?

    A. Hello

    B. LRU

    C. LSR

    D. LSAck

    E. DBD

11. In the **router ospf** command, does the process ID need to match on all routers?

12. Given the following configuration, what is the OSPF router ID of RouterA?

```
RouterA(config)#interface serial 0/0/0
RouterA(config-if)#ip add 192.168.2.1 255.255.255.252
RouterA(config)#interface loopback 0
RouterA(config-if)#ip add 10.1.1.1 255.255.255.255
RouterA(config)#router ospf 1
RouterA(config-if)#network 192.168.2.0 0.0.0.3 area 0
```

13. What command enables you to verify or determine the bandwidth value of an interface used by the OSPF metric?

14. What command enables you to modify the OSPF cost of an interface without modifying the bandwidth value of that interface?

15. What is the default Hello interval on Ethernet networks and serial point-to-point networks? What is the default Hello interval on NBMA networks?

16. What values must match before two routers will form an OSPF adjacency?

17. What problems does electing a DR and BDR solve?

18. How are the DR and BDR elected?

Challenge Questions and Activities

These questions require a deeper application of the concepts covered in this chapter and are similar to the style of questions you might see on a CCNA certification exam. You can find the answers to these questions in the appendix, "Answers to Check Your Understanding and Challenge Questions and Activities."

1. When the DR fails, how is the new DR determined?

2. What happens when a router with a higher OSPF interface priority is added to a network that already has a DR and BDR?

3. What significance does an OSPF interface priority of 0 have?

4. What command must be used to propagate a default route using OSPF?

To Learn More

RFC 2328 OSPF Version 2

RFCs are a series of documents submitted to the IETF (Internet Engineering Task Force) to propose an Internet standard or convey new concepts, information, or occasionally even humor. RFC 2328 is the current RFC for OSPFv2.

RFCs can be accessed from several websites, including http://www.ietf.org. Read all or parts of RFC OSPF to learn more about this classless, link-state routing protocol.

Multiarea OSPF

Some of the real advantages of OSPF, especially in large networks, can be seen with multiarea OSPF. Multiarea OSPF is discussed in CCNP, but you might be interested in looking at some of these new concepts now.

Suggested Resources

- *Routing TCP/IP, Volume I,* by Jeff Doyle and Jennifer Carroll

- *OSPF, Anatomy of an Internet Routing Protocol,* by John Moy

Check Your Understanding and Challenge Questions Answer Key

Chapter 1

Check Your Understanding

1. D. Both the routing table and ARP cache are stored in RAM. These tables are not saved after the router is powered off. The bootstrap program is stored in ROM, the startup configuration file is stored in NVRAM, and the operating system image is stored in flash. These files are permanently stored in these locations after the router is powered off.

2. A, E. The **show interfaces** and **show ip interface brief** commands include the interfaces and their IP addresses in the output. The other choices are not valid commands.

3. A. The correct command to configure a privileged mode password is **enable secret** *password*.

4. C. The three routing table principles, as described by Alex Zinin in his book *Cisco IP Routing*, are as follows:

   - Every router makes its decision alone, based on the information it has in its own routing table.

   - The fact that one router has certain information in its routing table does not mean that other routers have the same information.

   - Routing information about a path from one network to another does not provide routing information about the reverse, or return, path.

5. B, D. One task that routing protocols are responsible for is discovering networks and adding those networks to the routing table. After those routes are added to the routing table, the routing protocol is responsible for updating and maintaining the routes in the routing table. Routing protocols are not responsible for discovering hosts, propagating a default gateway for hosts, or assigning IP addresses.

6. C. At this point, only the router's directly connected networks are in the routing table. Remote networks can only be added by configuring static routes or by using a dynamic routing protocol.

7. B, D. All packets that are forwarded by the router must be resolved to an exit interface in the routing table. If a route only has a next-hop IP address, that next-hop address must eventually be resolved to another route in the routing table that does include an exit interface, such as a directly connected network.

8. A. A metric is used by routing protocols as a quantitative value used to measure the distance to a remote network.

9. B. S* 0.0.0.0/0 is directly connected, Serial0/0/0

10. Router hardware components are described as follows:

- Central processing unit (CPU): Executes operating system instructions, such as system initialization, routing functions, and network interface control.

- Random-access memory (RAM): Stores the routing table and other data structures that the router needs when forwarding packets.

- Read-only memory (ROM): Holds basic diagnostic software used when the router is powered on.

- Nonvolatile RAM (NVRAM): Stores the startup configuration, including IP addresses, routing protocol, and other related information. NVRAM is a portion of the boot ROM chip.

- Flash memory: Stores the operating system (Cisco IOS) and other files.

- LAN interfaces, such as Ethernet and Fast Ethernet interfaces.

- WAN interfaces, such as serial, ISDN, and Frame Relay interfaces.

11. Test router hardware:

1. Perform POST.
2. Execute bootstrap loader.

Locate and load the Cisco IOS Software:

3. Locate the IOS.
4. Load the IOS.

Locate and load the startup configuration file or enter setup mode:

5. Locate the configuration file.
6. Execute the configuration file.
7. Enter setup mode.

12. A router adds the following features:

- Determines the best path to send packets

- Forwards packets toward their destination

13. The steps to apply a basic configuration are as follows:

1. Name the router.
2. Set passwords.
3. Configure interfaces.
4. Configure a banner.
5. Save changes on a router.
6. Verify basic configuration and router operations.

14. A routing table provides the router with the necessary information to carry out its primary function: forwarding packets toward the destination network.

15. A router learns about networks in the following ways:

   ■ Connected routes

   ■ Static routes

   ■ Dynamic routes

16. The most relevant fields are as follows:

   ■ Version: Version of IP currently used (IPv4)

   ■ Time to Live (TTL): Number of routers a packet can traverse before being dropped

   ■ Source IP address: 32-bit source IP address

   ■ Destination IP address: 32-bit destination IP address

17. The source encapsulates data in a packet with source and destination IP addresses. It then encapsulates the packet into a frame with source and destination MAC addresses and sends the frame out as bits on the wire. The frame is received by the source's gateway—a router—and is decapsulated. If the destination MAC address is the router, the router will search the routing table for an outgoing interface to the destination, encapsulate the packet in the appropriate frame format for the outgoing interface with new source and destination Layer 2 addresses, and forward the frame out the interface. This process is repeated at each router along the path until the packet reaches the destination. From source to destination, the Layer 2 addresses change at each hop. However, the Layer 3 source and destination IP addresses do not change.

Challenge Questions and Activities

1. Your answer should revolve around the understanding that a router is a single-purpose device and a computer is a multipurpose device. The router's main purpose is to forward packets across different Layer 3 networks. A typical PC will most likely have several purposes, including word processing, gaming, and Internet access.

2. Answers will vary. Currently, CLI is the preferred configuration method on Cisco routers, and for many operations, it is the only method. Some of the more complex security operations can be configured on some Cisco routers using the Cisco Security Device Manager (SDM). SDM is a web-based device-management tool for Cisco routers that can improve the productivity of network managers, simplify router deployments, and help troubleshoot complex network and VPN (Virtual Private Network) connectivity issues. For the foreseeable future, it will be important for a network administer to be comfortable with using the Cisco CLI.

3. Answers will vary. Your description should include a step-by-step process. To see pseudocode for current routing algorithms, search the web for Bellman-Ford and Dijkstra algorithms.

4. A hierarchical structure is common to all Layer 3 addressing protocols. Each one identifies a network portion and a host portion. How each does this is different. For example, Novell's Internet Packet Exchange uses an 80-bit address. The first 32 bits are designated network bits and are determined by the administrator. The remaining 48 bits are the same as the MAC address of the host.

Chapter 2

Check Your Understanding

1. A, D. The **ip route 10.0.0.0 255.0.0.0 172.16.40.2** command is used by Router A to reach Router B's remote network. The **ip route 192.168.1.0 255.255.255.0 172.16.40.1** command is used by Router B to reach Router A's remote network. Both commands used the IP address of the next-hop router.

2. C. All routes in the routing table must be resolved to an exit interface in the routing table. If a route only has a next-hop IP address, that next-hop address must eventually be resolved to another route in the routing table that does include an exit interface, such as a directly connected network. Some static routes, such as those with Ethernet exit interfaces, can include both an exit interface and a next-hop IP address.

3. C. The 10.0.0.0/8 route is a static route. The way to remove a static route is to use the static route command prefaced with the **no** option.

4. A. This output was displayed using the **traceroute** command. The numbers in the column on the left indicate a router in the path.

5. D. R1(config)# **ip route 0.0.0.0 0.0.0.0 2.1.1.2** is the correct command because it is configured from global configuration mode, uses the network/mask of 0.0.0.0 0.0.0.0, and uses 2.1.1.2 as the correct next-hop IP address.

6. A, D, E. Configuring a static route does not ensure that the path is always available. If the exit interface or next-hop IP address is in the up state, the static route will be included in the routing table, regardless of whether the destination network is available. Dynamic routing protocols are typically a better option when there are multiple routes to the same destination network. The routing protocol will be able to automatically determine the best path.

7. A. The **show cdp neighbors** command displays the port type and platform of neighboring Cisco routers. It will not necessarily show non-Cisco devices.

8. D. This is a DTE end of a smart serial cable. It is a DTE end because the connector is male.

9. D. Directly connected networks will only be added to the routing table when the interface and line protocol are up, which can be displayed using the **show interface** command. For the interface and line protocol to be up, the interface must be configured with an IP address and subnet mask.

10. Enter global configuration mode: D

    Enter interface configuration mode: A

    Configure an IP address: B

    Activate the interface: G

11. **show ip route**: A

    show ip interface brief: D

    show interfaces: B

    show controllers: F

    debug ip routing: C

    show cdp neighbors: E

12. Straight-through cables are used to connect PCs and routers to hubs and switches. Crossover cables are used to connect PCs to routers, hubs to switches, routers to routers, and switches to switches.

13. **show interfaces**, **show ip interface brief**, **show running-config**

14. In a production environment, serial interfaces are attached to service provider equipment. Normally, the service provider sets the clocking speed. In a lab environment, routers are directly connected through the serial interface. Therefore, one of the routers must provide the clocking speed.

15. CDP, or Cisco Discovery Protocol, is a proprietary protocol for gathering information about directly connected Cisco devices. For example, both a Cisco router and a Cisco switch send CDP advertisements by default over the data link layer of the shared link that is active. The information revealed in CDP advertisements (including IP addresses, device platform, and IOS versions) presents a security risk. CDP can be disabled on an interface-by-interface basis or disabled globally.

16.

```
Router(config)# ip route network-address subnet-mask {ip-address ¦ exit-interface}
```

17. A recursive route lookup is another search of the routing table to find an exit interface for an outbound packet. A recursive route lookup occurs when the initial route lookup resolves to an IP address for the next hop. Because IOS needs an exit interface, it must look up the exit interface for the next-hop IP address.

18. A static route cannot just be changed. The original route must also be removed from the configuration. Otherwise, both the original route and the new route will be stored in the configuration.

19. Summary and default routes decrease the size of the routing tables. If a router has a large collection of static routes pointing out the same interface, sometimes these routes can be summarized into one routing table entry. Without default routing, every router would need a route to every location in the network.

20. ping, **traceroute**, **show ip route**, **show ip interface brief**, **show cdp neighbors**

Challenge Questions and Activities

1. In older computers, only a crossover cable would work between two computers. However, many manufacturers (Dell, for example) are designing the on-board NIC to autodetect what type of device is on the other end of the connection and then internally switch the transmit and receive pins, if necessary. For example, connecting two newer Dell computers directly will work with a straight-through cable. One of the computers switches the 1 and 3 pins to be the receive pair, which creates the same connection as a crossover cable.

2. R2 and R3 are sharing the same IP address on the 192.168.1.0/24 network. When R1 pings R3 at 192.168.1.1, R2 replies, not R3. To see this, the network administrator would have to traceroute to 192.168.1.1. When R3 pings R1, the ping is sourced from the Serial 0/0/1 interface with an IP address 192.168.1.1 as the source address. R1 receives the ping request and replies. However, R2 accepts the ping reply sent to 192.168.1.1 as belonging to R2. Therefore, the ping reply is not routed to R2. To fix the problem, configure R2 with a different IP address from the 192.168.1.0/24 network. (192.168.1.2 is used in the chapter example.)

3. **Figure A-1**   Topology for Challenge Question #3

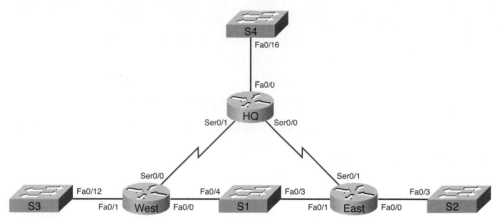

4. Branch1, Branch2, and Branch3 all have the same default static route:

   ```
   ip route 0.0.0.0 0.0.0.0 s0/0/0
   ```

   RegionA has the following static route configuration:

   ```
   ip route 0.0.0.0 0.0.0.0 serial 0/0/3
   ip route 172.16.0.0 255.254.0.0 serial0/0/0
   ip route 172.18.0.0 255.254.0.0 serial0/0/1
   ip route 172.24.0.0 255.248.0.0 serial0/0/2
   ```

   HQ has the following static route configuration:

   ```
   ip route 0.0.0.0 0.0.0.0 serial 0/0/1
   ip route 172.16.0.0 255.240.0.0 serial0/0/0
   ```

   ISP has the following static route configuration:

   ```
   ip route 172.16.0.0 255.240.0.0 serial0/0/0
   ```

Chapter 3

Check Your Understanding

1. B, D. Static routes are considered more secure because they are not propagated between routers and therefore are not susceptible to snooping or malicious attacks. Dynamic routes can be secured using authentication. Static routes require no computing overhead because they are not propagated between routers. Note: There is some computing overhead with static routes, but it is minimal.

2. Answers:

   A. Path vector exterior routing protocol: BGP

   B. Cisco advanced interior routing protocol: EIGRP

   C. Link-state interior routing protocol: OSPF

   D. Distance vector interior routing protocol: RIP

   E. Cisco distance vector interior routing protocol: IGRP

3. B. Convergence is the time required by routers to have complete and accurate information about the network.

4. A, C. Hop count is used by RIP. Bandwidth is used by IGRP, EIGRP, and OSPF. The other choices are not valid routing protocol metrics.

5. A. Given these choices, EIGRP internal routes are the most trustworthy, with the lowest administrative distance of 90. IS-IS has an administrative distance of 115, OSPF has an administrative distance of 110, and RIP, which includes both version 1 and 2, has an administrative distance of 120.

6. C. By default, Cisco routers can load-balance up to four equal-cost paths. The maximum number of equal-cost paths depends on the routing protocol and IOS version.

7. B. The **show ip route** command displays route entry information, including the administrative distance. The administrative distance is the first number in brackets, followed by the metric. For example, [120/2] shows an administrative distance of 120 (RIP) and a metric of 2 (hop count).

8. D. A directly connected network will appear in the routing table when it is addressed and operational at Layer 3—in other words, when it has been configured with an IP address and subnet mask, and the interface and line protocol are both in the up state.

9. A. Whenever any routing protocol has multiple paths to the same network, it will choose the path with the lowest metric. This is the route that is added to the routing table.

10. Answers:

    A. eBGP: 20

    B. EIGRP (Internal): 90

    C. EIGRP (External): 170

    D. IS-IS: 115

    E. OSPF: 110

    F. RIP: 120

11. Answers:

    A. Does not support discontiguous networks: classful routing protocol

    B. EIGRP, OSPF, and BGP: classless routing protocol

    C. Sends subnet mask in its routing updates: classless routing protocol

    D. Supports discontiguous networks: classless routing protocol

    E. RIP version 1 and IGRP: classful routing protocol

    F. Does not send subnet mask in its routing updates: classful routing protocol

12. Static routing is more secure, uses less router computational power, and is easier to understand. It is more secure because routers do not advertise routing information to other routers. It uses less router resources than dynamic routing, which requires the implementation of algorithms and the processing of update packets. It is often easier to understand than some of the more complex routing protocols.

13. Dynamic routing protocols can be classified as either interior or exterior, distance vector or link-state, classful or classless, and by speed of convergence.

14. Hop count, bandwidth, delay, and cost.

15. Administrative distance is a measure of the trustworthiness of a route source. It is used when a router has learned routes to the same destination from two different route sources. It is important because not all route sources are equal. For example, you certainly would not want a router sending traffic to another router if the destination is a directly connected network! Administrative distance ensures that this does not happen because directly connected routes are trusted over all other route sources.

Challenge Questions and Activities

1. Every router that forwards user traffic to the Internet will have at least one static route. That static route would be a default route. Every household that has a router to connect to the Internet uses a static default route to send all traffic to the ISP.

2. Hop count can use the better path if the path chosen by a bandwidth metric is saturated with traffic.

Chapter 4

Check Your Understanding

1. A, C, D, F. Because of slow convergence, distance vector routing protocols do not scale well. RIPv2 does multicast its updates; however, RIPv1 uses broadcasts in its updates.

2. B, C, D. Most distance vector routing protocols will send a triggered update when they sense a change in the topology, such as a new link becoming active. When a triggered update is received by a router, it will immediately forward that update to other routers. Some distance vector routing protocols, such as RIP and IGRP, send periodic updates. An update timer is used to determine the interval of these routing updates. A hold-down timer expiring will not cause new updates to be sent. The hold-down timer is used to determine how long to keep a route in the hold-down state.

3. D, F. EIGRP does not send periodic updates. EIGRP updates are only sent when there is a topology change and is only sent to those routers that need the updated information.

4. B. Cisco IOS uses the random variable RIP-JITTER, which varies the 30-second update interval from 25 to 30 seconds.

5. A, C. RIP uses several timers, including the invalid, flush, route update, and hold-down timers.

6. C. Distance vector routing protocols have the reputation of being easier to configure. Although this is true, link-state routing protocols are only slightly more difficult to configure. The ease of implementation should not usually be the basis for deciding which routing protocol to use.

7. C. Instead of propagating potentially incorrect information, the hold-down timer will cause the route to be marked as unreachable for a period of time, giving the network time to converge.

8. A. Using the split horizon rule, R4 will not send R5 an update regarding the 10.0.0.0 network because R4 received that update from R5.

9. B. Route poisoning is used to mark a route as unreachable. RIP marks a route as unreachable by advertising a metric of "infinity," or 16.

10. C. The value of the TTL (Time to Live) is set by the source. As each router receives the packet, the TTL is decreased by 1. If the TTL reaches 0, the router drops that packet.

11. Answer:

Split horizon: A

Route poisoning: B

Hold-down timers: D

Triggered updates: C

Challenge Questions and Activities

1. RIP and IGRP are distance vector routing protocols characterized by periodic updates that are broadcast to directly connected neighbors. The entire routing table is sent in the update.

2. Convergence occurs when all routers in the network have consistent and correct information about how to reach destination networks. A network is not completely operable until it has converged; therefore, routing protocols require short convergence times.

3. Answer:

   Update timer: (30 seconds) Used to time when to send the next update

   Invalid timer: (180 seconds) Counts how long it has been since the last update for a route

   Hold-down timer: (180 seconds) The amount of time an unreachable route is in hold-down

   Flush timer: (240 seconds) Time until a route is removed from the routing table

4. Answer:

   Defining maximum metric to prevent count to infinity

   Hold-down timers

   Split horizon

   Route poisoning or poison reverse

   Triggered updates

Chapter 5

Check Your Understanding

1. B. The **debug ip rip** command displays RIP updates sent and received by the router's interfaces. This can be a useful command to verify whether the router is sending or receiving RIP updates.

2. B. The **passive-interface** command prevents RIP updates from being sent out an interface. However, this command does not prevent RIP updates from being received on that interface.

3. B. A boundary router has interfaces on more than one major classful network. For example, a router with the Serial 0/0/0 interface on the 172.16.1.0/24 network and the Serial 0/0/1 interface on the 172.30.1.0/24 network would be considered a boundary

router. The 172.16.1.0/24 network is part of the 172.16.0.0/16 major classful network, whereas 172.30.1.0/24 is part of the 172.30.0.0/16 major network. Both are Class B networks but are different major networks.

4. D. The **default-information originate** command will propagate a candidate default route, a default static route, to other routers through RIP.

5. D. The candidate default route is configured using a default static route.

6. C. The 10.16.1.0/27 network and the 10.16.1.64/27 network are both 10.0.0.0 Class A networks separated by other major classful networks, such as 192.16.9.0/30 and 192.168.10.4/30.

7. C. If the route belongs to the same major classful network as the interface, RIPv1 will use the subnet mask of the interface. If the route belongs to a different major classful network than the interface address, RIPv1 will use the default classful mask of the route.

8. E. The route source of this route entry is RIP, and the administrative distance of RIP is 120. The second value in the bracket, 1, is the metric.

9. D. The **network** command is used to enable RIP on any interfaces that belong to that network address and to include those interface addresses in the RIP updates.

10. **debug ip rip**: C

    show ip protocols: D

    show running-config: A

    show ip route: E

    show interfaces: B

11. Explanation:

    - RIP is a distance vector routing protocol.
    - RIP uses hop count as its only metric for path selection.
    - Advertised routes with hop counts greater than 15 are unreachable.
    - Update messages are broadcast every 30 seconds.

12. Explanation:

```
BR1(config)# router rip
BR1(config-router)# network 192.168.0.0
BR1(config-router)# network 192.168.1.0
```

13. Explanation:

   - **show ip route**

   - **show ip protocols**

   - **debug ip rip**

14. The **passive-interface** command is used to stop RIP updates from being sent out an interface where RIP updates are not needed. For example, a LAN interface would only need to send out RIP updates if there is another RIP-enabled device on the LAN.

    ```
    BR1(config-router)# passive-interface fa 0/0
    ```

15. ISP routers have routes to all other destinations on the Internet. Because the ISP is the default router for all traffic for which you do not have routes, the best solution is to configure a default route pointing to the ISP. The alternative is to exchange routing updates, have your routers build huge routing tables, and end up sending externally bound traffic to the ISP anyway.

Challenge Questions and Activities

1. Explanation:

   ```
   HQ(config)# router rip
   HQ(config-router)# network 192.168.0.0
   HQ(config-router)# default-information originate
   HQ(config-router)# exit
   HQ(config)# ip route 0.0.0.0 0.0.0.0 s0/0/0
   ```

2. The LAN for R3 is not being advertised in RIP updates. Because this LAN is also missing from the routing table for BR3, the interface is not active. Activating the interface would be the first step to solving the convergence problem. As long as BR3 is configured to advertise 192.168.3.0 in RIP updates, convergence should be achieved.

   ```
   R3(config)# interface fa0/0
   R3(config-if)# ip address 192.168.3.65 255.255.255.192
   R3(config-if)# no shutdown
   ```

   If necessary, add 192.168.3.0 to the RIP process.

   ```
   R3(config)# router rip
   R3(config-router)# network 192.168.3.0
   ```

3. Explanation:

   ```
   ISP(config)# ip route 192.168.0.0 255.255.252.0 s0/0/0
   ```

Chapter 6

Check Your Understanding

1. Answer:

   RIPv1: non-VLSM

   EIGRP: VLSM

   IGRP: non-VLSM

   IS-IS: VLSM

   OSPF: VLSM

   RIPv2: VLSM

   Classful routing protocols such as RIPv1 and IGRP do not support VLSM. Classless routing protocols such as RIPv2, EIGRP, OSPF, and IS-IS do support VLSM. To support VLSM, a routing protocol must include the subnet mask in the routing update. Therefore, only classless routing protocols support VLSM.

2. Combining several IP network addresses in one IP address: route summarization

   Ability to specify a different subnet mask for the same network number and different subnets: VLSM

   Used in supernetting: route summarization

   Conserves address space: VLSM

   Used to reduce the number of entries in a routing table: route summarization

3. A, C. Variable-length subnetting allowed networks to be subnetted with various numbers of hosts, therefore making better use of network address space. Private addressing with Network Address Translation/Port Address Translation (NAT/PAT) allowed networks to have a larger number of hosts than the public network address they were allocated.

4. A, C, D. 255.255.255.252 is equivalent to /30, 255.255.255.240 is equivalent to /28, and 255.255.255.192 is equivalent to /26.

5. A. A Class A network has a default subnet mask of 255.0.0.0. The first octet represents the network portion of the address and the last three octets represent the host portion.

6. 172.16.64.0/18: E

    172.16.16.64/30: A

    172.16.128.0/19: D

    172.16.18.0/24: C

    172.16.5.128/26: B

    By examining each of the subnet masks, you can determine how many bits are available for the hosts. For example, a /30 subnet mask has 30 bits for the network address, leaving 2 bits for the hosts. Two bits gives a total of four hosts, but the first host address is used for the subnet or network address and the last host address is used for the broadcast address, leaving you with two usable hosts.

7. C. If you write out all the addresses in binary, you will notice that the first 21 bits match, or a /21 subnet mask. Copy the matching bits and add all 0s to the end, and this will give you the summary address of 192.168.0.0.

8. E. IPv4 uses 32-bit addresses (four octets of 8 bits each).

9. 191.254.45.0: Class B

    123.90.78.45: Class A

    128.44.0.23: Class B

    129.68.11.45: Class B

    126.0.0.0: Class A

    125.33.23.56: Class A

    Class A addresses range from 0.0.0.0 to 127.255.255.255. Class B addresses range from 128.0.0.0 to 191.255.255.255.

10. A. CIDR allows route aggregation or route summarization. The 172.16.0.0/16, 172.17.0.0/16, and 172.18.0.0/16 networks can be summarized to 172.16.0.0/14. The /14 is a mask that is less than the classful mask, so this would be considered a supernet.

11. A classless routing protocol includes the subnet mask in the routing update.

12. Classless routing protocols allow the use of VLSM and CIDR within the routing domain.

13. If the network address in the routing update is on the same major classful network as the receiving interface, the classful routing protocol will use the same mask as the interface; otherwise, it will use the default classful mask.

14. The Internet routers' routing tables were experiencing very fast growth. There needed to be a way to summarize the routes in the routing table.

Because classful addressing only provided /8, /16, or 24 masks, the IPv4 address space was becoming depleted.

15. VLSM

Challenge Questions and Activities

1. 172.16.10.0/24 could be subnetted using the /26 subnet mask.

<-Network-> | <-Host->

172.16.10. 0 0|0 0 0 0 0

172.16.10. 0 1|0 0 0 0 0

172.16.10. 1 0|0 0 0 0 0

172.16.10. 1 1|0 0 0 0 0

This would give four subnets with the maximum number of hosts. You cannot do three subnets; the next lower number of subnets would be two.

2. 172.16.10.0/28

172.16.10.208/28

172.16.10.224/28

3. Supernetting refers to the ability to summarize networks less than the classful default mask. Classless routing protocols are able to propagate a supernet route because they include the subnet mask with the summarized network address.

4. 192.168.64.0/18

Chapter 7

Check Your Understanding

1. B. The **no auto-summary** command is used to disable automatic summarization and is executed at the router mode prompt. To reenable automatic summarization, use the **auto-summary** command, also at the router mode prompt.

2. A. A discontiguous network is a classful network address that has subnets separated by at least one other major network address. This causes the subnets of the classful network to be separated.

3. B, D. Automatic summarization should be disabled when there are discontiguous networks; otherwise, routers will receive the same summary route from both boundary routers. Automatic summarization should also be disabled when there is a need to propagate the individual subnets instead of the classful network address.

4. B. A classless routing protocol includes the subnet mask in its routing updates. RIPv2, EIGRP, OSPF, IS-IS, and BGP are all classless routing protocols.

5. A. By default, automatic summarization is enabled with RIPv2. The behavior can be disabled with the **no auto-summary** command.

6. B. This is false. RIPv2, as with all classless routing protocols, includes the subnet mask in the routing update, whether or not the route has been summarized. When automatic summarization is enabled with RIPv2, the routing update will include both the classful network address and the default classful mask.

Challenge Questions and Activities

1. A, B, C. R2's routing table:

    172.30.0.0/16 is variably subnetted, 3 subnets, 2 masks

    R   172.30.0.0/16 [120/1] via 209.165.200.234, 00:00:18, Serial0/1

    R   172.30.2.0/24 [120/1] via 209.165.200.230, 00:00:09, Serial0/0

    R   172.30.1.0/24 [120/1] via 209.165.200.230, 00:00:09, Serial0/0

    The 172.30.1.0/24 and 172.30.2.0/24 networks are sent nonsummarized from R1. Because these are routes of the 172.30.0.0/16 network, a 172.16.0.0/16 parent route is also created. This is the first route shown in our routing table. R3 sends a summary route of 172.16.0.0/16. This route is included with the two subnetted routes, 172.16.1.0/24 and 172.16.2.0/24. (The routing table is discussed in more detail in Chapter 8.)

2. Yes. When R2 receives both routing updates, it will include both the summary router 172.16.0.0/16, forwarding packets to R3, and the specific subnets 172.30.1.0/24 and 172.30.2.0/24, forwarding those packets to R1. The routing table process will always choose the more specific route over the less specific, summary route.

3. C. RIPv1 is a classful routing protocol and does not support VLSM. Because the subnet mask is not included in the routing update, RouterX will only send 10.0.0.0 subnets with a /24 mask out an interface with a /24 mask. This is because the receiving router can only apply its own /24 interface mask to these updates.

4. E. The interface with the address 192.168.1.1/24 belongs to the 192.168.1.0/24 major classful network. Because the 10.0.0.0/8 network is a different major classful network from this interface, RouterX will send the summary network address of 10.0.0.0. RIPv1 is a classful routing protocol and does not include the subnet mask. The receiving router will apply the classful /8 mask to this update.

5. Both RIPv1 and RIPv2 require the default **information-originate** command in router configuration mode.

6. The problem is most likely a discontiguous network, with some subnets through Serial 0/0/0 and some subnets through Serial 0/0/1. If RIPv1 is the current routing protocol, the adjacent routers need to be configured for RIPv2 with automatic summarization disabled. If RIPv2 is the current routing protocol, the adjacent routers need to be configured with automatic summarization disabled.

Chapter 8

Check Your Understanding

1. A, C, E. Using the codes for the route source, C are directly connected networks, S are static routes, and R are RIP routes, a dynamic routing protocol.

2. D. Ultimate routes are routes that include a next-hop IP address or an exit interface. Parent routes cannot be ultimate routes because they do not include either of these.

3. A, D. Parent routes do not have a next-hop IP address or an exit interface. Parent routes contain at least one level 2 child route.

4. B. The **ip classless** command signifies that classless routing behavior is being used. With classless routing behavior, if there is not a match with a child route, the routing table process will continue searching other level 1 routes for a lesser match. This includes the default route.

5. D. The **no ip classless** command enables classful routing behavior. The **ip classless** command enables classless routing behavior.

6. B. The best match or longest match is the route that has the most leftmost bits that match the destination IP address of the packet.

7. B. If there is a match with a level 1 parent route, the routing table process then searches the level 2 child routes.

8. A. These commands determine whether the routing table lookup process uses classful routing behavior (**no ip classless**) or classless routing behavior (**ip classless**).

9. D. The **no ip classless** command signifies that classful routing behavior is being used. With classful routing behavior, if there is not a match with a child route, the routing table process does not continue searching other level 1 routes for a lesser match. If there is not a match with any of the level 2 child routes, the packet is dropped.

10. E. The first route that matches is the parent route 172.16.0.0/13 because 16 bits match the 172.16.1.130 destination IP address. The child static route 172.16.0.0 matches because 13 bits match the destination IP address. This is the route used to forward the packet. Although there is a match with the parent route of 172.16.0.0/16, there is not a match with either of the child routes. The 172.16.0.0/24 route does not match the required 24 bits, and the 172.16.1.0/25 does not match the required 25 bits.

11. When the route also contains a next-hop IP address or an exit interface.

12. When using VLSM, a subnet mask displayed with the child route and not the parent route.

13. No, it is created when the subnet (level 2 child) route is added to the routing table.

14. No. Parent routes do not contain a next-hop address or an exit interface. This information is contained in the child routes.

15. There must be a match with the level 1 parent route.

16. The subnet mask for that entry in the routing table determines how many bits must match between the destination IP address of a packet and a route in the routing table.

17. The default routing behavior is classless. The **no ip classless** command can be used to modify the routing behavior.

Challenge Questions and Activities

1. Answer:

Parent: 172.16.0.0/24 is subnetted, 3 subnets

Child: R 172.16.1.0 [120/1] via 172.16.2.1, 00:00:00, Serial0/0/0

Child: C 172.16.2.0 is directly connected, Serial0/0/0

Child: C 172.16.3.0 is directly connected, FastEthernet0/0

Parent: 172.30.0.0/16 is variably subnetted, 3 subnets, 2 masks

Child: R 172.30.1.4/30 [120/1] via 172.16.2.1, 00:00:00, Serial0/0/0

Child: R 172.30.1.8/30 [120/1] via 172.16.2.1, 00:00:00, Serial0/0/0

Child: R 172.30.3.0/24 [120/1] via 172.16.2.1, 00:00:00, Serial0/0/0

2. There must first be a match with the 172.16.0.0 parent route, and 16 bits must match the parent route; /16 is the classful mask of the parent.

3. The packet would be dropped. The packet would match the level 1 parent 172.16.0.0 but not match any of the child routes. Because of classful routing behavior, the routing table lookup process would not continue searching supernet and default routes.

4. The packet would be forwarded using the default route. The packet would match the level 1 parent 172.16.0.0 but not match any of the child routes. Because of classless routing behavior, the routing table lookup process would continue to search supernet and default routes.

Chapter 9

Check Your Understanding

1. D. PDM, or protocol dependent modules, gives EIGRP the capability to support different Layer 3 protocols such as IPv4, IPX, and AppleTalk.

2. Answer:

   Neighbor table: C

   Topology table: E

   Routing table: A

   Successor: B

   Feasible successor router: D

3. B. EIGRP uses hello packets to discover neighbors and to form adjacencies with those neighbors. EIGRP hello packets are multicasts and use unreliable delivery. An EIGRP router assumes that as long as it is receiving hello packets from a neighbor, the neighbor and its routes remain viable.

4. C. When a route has failed and there is not a feasible successor in the topology table, DUAL puts the route into active state as it queries its neighbors looking for a new successor.

5. C, E, F. Besides the IP routing table, EIGRP maintains a separate neighbor table and topology table.

6. A. Before any EIGRP exchanges routing updates with other routers, it must first discover its neighbors. These neighbors are added to the neighbor table. EIGRP also maintains a topology table with the successors and feasible successors. Only the successors are entered into the routing table.

7. C. The value of 255/255 represents a link that is 100 percent reliable. Reliability is a measurement of the probability that the link will fail or how often the link has experienced errors.

8. Feasible successor: A

   Successor: B

   Feasible distance: C

   Routing table: E

   Topology table: D

9. D. The command **show ip eigrp topology all-links** will show successors, feasible successors, and next-hop routers that need not meet the feasibility condition.

10. C. The feasible successor is the second entry, via 172.16.3.1 because its feasible distance is higher than the via 192.168.10.10 entry. The first value 41026560 would be the feasible distance to 192.168.1.0/24 should Router1 use this path as the successor. The second value 2172416 is the reported distance. The reported distance or advertised distance is simply an EIGRP neighbor's feasible distance to the same destination network. The reported distance is the metric that a router reports to a neighbor about its own cost to that network.

11. DUAL (Diffusing Update Algorithm)

12. No, EIGRP sends nonperiodic bounded updates, only the routing information that is needed and only to those routers that need it. *Nonperiodic* means that the updates are not sent at regular intervals, and are only sent when there is a metric change.

13. **show ip eigrp neighbors**

14. Bandwidth, delay, reliability, and load. Only bandwidth and delay are used by default.

15. When the neighbor's reported distance (RD) to a network is less that this router's feasible distance (FD) to the same destination network.

16. Yes. Automatic summarization can be disabled using the **no auto-summary** command.

Challenge Questions and Activities

1. The autonomous system needs to be the same on all routers in the EIGRP routing domain. The autonomous system number does not need to be an actual autonomous system number.

2. Yes, 172.16.3.1 is a feasible successor. This is because the RD of 2169856 is less than the successor 192.168.10.10 FD of 3523840.

3. A Null0 summary route is automatically added to the routing table by EIGRP when there is at least one child route with a routing source of EIGRP and the default **auto-summary** command is used.

Chapter 10

Check Your Understanding

1. D. Both IS-IS and OSPF are link-state routing protocols. RIPv1, RIPv2, IGRP, and EIGRP are distance vector routing protocols. BGP is a path vector routing protocol.

2. B, C, E. Link-state routing protocols use Hello packets to discover neighbors and form adjacencies, link-state packets propagate link-state information, and the shortest path first algorithm determines the best path to remote networks.

3. Hardware intensive: Link-state

   Uses Bellman-Ford algorithm: Distance vector

   Fast convergence: Link-state

   Uses timed updates: Distance vector

   Builds complete topology: Link-state

   Referred to at times as "routing by rumor": Distance vector

   Uses Dijkstra's algorithm: Link-state

4. C. Link-state routing protocols typically converge faster than distance vector routing protocols for several reasons, including the fact that link-state routing protocols immediately flood the LSP out all interfaces except for the interface from which the LSP was received.

5. A. One of the reasons why link-state routing protocols converge faster is that distance vector routing protocols compute the routing table first and then send out their routing updates. Link-state routing protocols forward link-state packets (LSP) immediately out all interfaces, except the incoming interface, immediately upon receiving that LSP.

6. A. Router A will send Hello packets out all directly connected networks, which in this example means that both Router B and Router C will receive those updates.

7. C. LSPs contain the state of the directly connected links or network. This can include the interface's IP address and mask, the type of link such as Ethernet, the cost of the link, and any neighboring routers on that link.

8. D. The SPF algorithm requires higher processing requirements than the Bellman-Ford algorithm used by distance vector routing protocols.

9. B. After OSPF routers form an adjacency, the routers will start exchanging LSPs to begin building their link-state databases. In actuality, there are several other steps that OSPF routers can perform before exchanging LSPs, which is beyond the scope of this curriculum and is discussed in CCNP.

10. C. A router learns about its directly connected network when the interface has an IP address and subnet mask and becomes active.

11. Routers that use distance vector routing protocols only have information regarding distance (metric) of the network and which next-hop router (vector) to forward those packets to. These routers do not see the network beyond their directly connected neighbors.

12. Routers using link-state routing protocols exchange link-state information. This allows the SPF algorithm to build an SPF tree or a topological map of the network. These routers can see the network beyond their directly connected neighbors.

13. Link-state routing protocols use the shortest path first (SPF) algorithm, which was developed by E.W. Dijkstra. This algorithm is also known as Dijkstra's algorithm.

14. A link is an interface on a router.

15. A link state is the information regarding that link. This can include the router's IP address, the type of network, the cost of the link, and whether any neighboring routers are on that link.

16. A neighbor is a router that shares a link, a directly connected network, with another router. Routers discover their neighbors by using the Hello packets of a specific routing protocol.

17. Whenever a router receives an LSP from another neighbor, it immediately sends this LSP out all interfaces except for the interface from which it was received. The result is that all routers in the routing area will receive this LSP.

18. Routers store LSPs in link-state databases, also known as topological databases. The SPF algorithm is run using these LSPs to create the SPF tree and determine the shortest path to each network.

Challenge Questions and Activities

1. No, link-state routing protocols do not send out typical periodic updates like RIP and IGRP do. OSPF routers do send out their own LSPs every 30 minutes; however, this is used differently from a periodic update. Paranoid updates are discussed in the chapter on OSPF. Remember, not all distance vector routing protocols send out periodic updates either. EIGRP does not send out periodic updates.

2. Explanation:

   - Use of a topological map, SPF tree of the network.

   - Faster convergence.

   - No periodic updates, unlike some distance vector routing protocols.

   - Specific LSPs are flooded only when there is a change in the topology.

3. The requirements are as follows:

   - More memory for link-state databases

   - More CPU processing for the SPF algorithm

   - More bandwidth for flooding of LSPs

   Multiple areas can be used to minimize these requirements.

4. Explanation:

   - Open Shortest Path First (OSPF)

   - Intermediate System–to–Intermediate System (IS-IS)

Chapter 11

Check Your Understanding

1. A, C, D. Link-state routing protocols use a link-state routing algorithm, as compared to distance vector routing protocols, which use some form of the Bellman-Ford algorithm. Link-state routing protocols base their algorithm on Dijkstra's algorithm. This algorithm uses a database of link-state information to determine the shortest path to each network.

2. Creates and maintains neighbor adjacencies: D

   Triggered when a topology change has occurred: A

   Description of an interface and its relationship to other routers: B

   Calculates the best path to each destination network: C

3. A, D. Loopback addresses are commonly used to configure the router ID in OSPF. One of their main benefits is that these interfaces cannot go down, which creates a stable and predictable OSPF router ID.

4. A, B. The DR and BDR are only elected on multiaccess networks such as Ethernet.

5. C. The number 100 represents the OSPF process ID. This value has local significance only and does not need to match the process ID on other routers in the OSPF routing domain.

6. A. The **bandwidth** command is used to modify the value of the interface used in determining the OSPF routing metric. It does not have an effect on the actual speed of the link. The bandwidth value should reflect the actual speed of the link; otherwise, the routing tables might not reflect the best paths to networks.

7. C. The RFC for OSPF states cost of an interface for the routing metric. However, the RFC does not specify how to determine that cost. Cisco IOS software uses the cumulative bandwidths of the outgoing interfaces from the router to the destination network to calculate the cost value.

8. C. Similar to RIP, OSPF uses the **default-information originate** command to propagate a default route within the OSPF routing domain.

9. D. If OSPF interface priorities are equal, which they are by default with a value of 1, the router with the highest router ID becomes the DR, and the router with the second highest router ID becomes the BDR.

10. B. Hello, LSR (link-state request), LSAck (LSA acknowledgment), and DBD (database description) are all valid OSPF packets. LRU is not a valid OSPF packet, but LSU (link-state update) would be.

11. No, unlike EIGRP, the OSPF is locally significant and does not need to match other OSPF routers.

12. The OSPF router ID is 10.1.1.1, the highest loopback address in the absence of the OSPF **router-id** command.

13. **show interface**

14. The **ip ospf cost** interface command.

15. By default, OSPF Hello packets are sent every 10 seconds on multiaccess and point-to-point segments and every 30 seconds on NBMA segments (Frame Relay, X.25, ATM).

16. Hello interval

    Dead interval

    Network type

    Subnet masks

17. Creation of multiple adjacencies, one adjacency for every pair of routers. Extensive flooding of LSAs (link state advertisements).

18. DR is the router with the highest OSPF interface priority, and the BDR has the second highest OSPF interface priority. If the OSPF interface priorities are equal, the highest router ID is used to break the tie.

Challenge Questions and Activities

1. The BDR becomes the new DR, and an election takes place for a new BDR.

2. Nothing. The DR and BDR only lose their role if the router or the multiaccess interface fails.

3. This router's interface is ineligible to become a DR or BDR.

4. The OSPF command **default-information originate**

Glossary of Key Terms

This glossary defines many of the terms and abbreviations related to networking. It includes all the key terms used throughout the book. As with any growing technical field, some terms evolve and take on several meanings. Where necessary, multiple definitions and abbreviation expansions are presented.

A

active state   A state in which there is no feasible successor in the topology table and the local router goes into active state and queries its neighbors for routing information.

adjacency   A relationship formed between selected neighboring routers and end nodes for the purpose of exchanging routing information. Adjacency is based on the use of a common media segment.

administrative distance   Rating of the trustworthiness of a routing information source. Administrative distance (AD) is often expressed as a numerical value between 0 and 255. The higher the value, the lower the trustworthiness rating. If a router has multiple routing protocols in its routing table, it will select the route with the lowest administrative distance.

algorithm   Well-defined rule or process for arriving at a solution to a problem. In networking, algorithms are commonly used to determine the best route for traffic from a particular source to a particular destination.

ALLSPFRouters   A multicast group used in the OSPF routing protocol. The ALLSPFRouters address is 224.0.0.5.

ARP   Address Resolution Protocol. Internet protocol used to map an IP address to a MAC address. Defined in RFC 826.

asymmetric routing   When a path from network 1 to network 2 is different from the path from network 2 to network 1.

Asynchronous Transfer Mode (ATM)   The international standard for cell relay in which multiple service types (such as voice, video, or data) are conveyed in fixed-length (53-byte) cells. Fixed-length cells allow cell processing to occur in hardware, thereby reducing transit delays. ATM is designed to take advantage of high-speed transmission media, such as E3, SONET, and T3.

automatic summarization   Consolidation of networks and advertised in classful network advertisements. In RIP, this causes a single summary route to be advertised to other routers.

autonomous system (AS)   A collection of networks under a common administration sharing a common routing strategy. Autonomous systems are subdivided by areas. An autonomous system must be assigned a unique 16-bit number by the IANA.

Autonomous System Boundary Router (ASBR) The OSPF router located between an OSPF autonomous system network and a non-OSPF network. ASBRs run both OSPF and another routing protocol, such as RIP. ASBRs must reside in a non-stub OSPF area.

B

backup designated router (BDR)   A router that becomes the designated router if the current designated router fails. The BDR is the OSPF router with the second-highest priority at the time of the last DR election.

Bellman-Ford (Algorithm)   Class of routing algorithms that iterate on the number of hops in a route to find a shortest-path spanning tree. Distance vector routing algorithms call for each router to send its entire routing table in each update, but only to its neighbors. Distance vector routing algorithms can be prone to routing loops but are computationally simpler than link-state routing algorithms.

best path   The fastest path to a certain destination. The fastest path is based on the routing protocol's metric.

BGP   Border Gateway Protocol. Interdomain routing protocol that replaces EGP. BGP exchanges reachability information with other BGP systems. It is defined by RFC 1163.

boundary router   A router that sits on the edge of two discontiguous classful networks. A boundary router can also be known as a router that sits on the edge of two different networks that have different routing protocols. Sometimes the term *boundary router* is loosely used when discussing OSPF and Autonomous System Boundary Routers.

bounded updates   Updates that are bounded to those very routers that need the updated information instead of sending updates to all routers.

C

cable   Transmission medium of copper wire or optical fiber wrapped in a protective cover.

CIDR   Classless interdomain routing. Technique supported by BGP4 and based on route aggregation. CIDR allows routers to group routes to reduce the quantity of routing information carried by the core routers. With CIDR, several IP networks appear to networks outside the group as a single, larger entity. With CIDR, IP addresses and their subnet masks are written as four octets, separated by periods, followed by a forward slash and a two-digit number that represents the subnet mask.

Cisco Discovery Protocol (CDP)   A Cisco-proprietary protocol that defines a set of messages that Cisco devices send. The messages include a basic statement about the device sending the message, such as the device's name, OS level, type of device, and other configuration information. Cisco devices on neighboring data links receive these multicast CDP messages and learn about the neighboring devices.

classful IP addressing   In the early days of IPv4, IP addresses were divided into five classes, namely, Class A, Class B, Class C, Class D, and Class E.

classful routing protocols   Routing protocols that use classful IP addressing. They do not use subnet mask information in their routing operation. They automatically assume classful masks.

classless routing protocols   Routing protocols that include the subnet mask in their routing operation.

clocking   The configuration of a clock rate on the DCE interface of a serial connection.

clocking signal   A signal used to coordinate the transmission on two or more circuits.

console port DTE port through which commands are entered into a host.

contiguous Consistent or adjacent. In terms of contiguous networks, the word *contiguous* means network blocks that are hierarchical in nature.

converged The past tense of converge. When all intermediate devices have the same consistent network topology in their routing tables, they have converged.

convergence Speed and ability of a group of internetworking devices running a specific routing protocol to agree on the topology of an internetwork after a change in that topology.

cost An arbitrary value, typically based on hop count, media bandwidth, or other measures, that is assigned by a network administrator and used to compare various paths through an internetwork environment. Routing protocols use cost values to calculate the most favorable path to a particular destination: the lower the cost, the better the path.

count to infinity Problem that can occur in routing algorithms that are slow to converge, in which routers continuously increment the hop count to particular networks. Typically, some arbitrary hop-count limit is imposed to prevent this problem.

D

data link Layer 2 of the OSI reference model. Provides reliable transit of data across a physical link. The data link layer is concerned with physical addressing, network topology, line discipline, error notification, ordered delivery of frames, and flow control. The IEEE divided this layer into two sublayers: the MAC sublayer and the LLC sublayer.

Sometimes simply called the link layer. Roughly corresponds to the data link control layer of the SNA model.

database description (DBD) A packet used in OSPF that contains link-state advertisement (LSA) headers only and describes the contents of the entire link-state database. Routers exchange DBDs during the exchange phase of adjacency creation.

datagram Logical grouping of information sent as a network layer unit over a transmission medium without prior establishment of a virtual circuit. IP datagrams are the primary information units in the Internet. The terms *cell*, *frame*, *message*, *packet*, and *segment* are also used to describe logical information groupings at various layers of the OSI reference model and in various technology circles.

debug To locate and analyze possible problems in certain processes. For instance, when using the **debug** command on a router, it provides output that shows the certain process for the debug parameter that is input. This allows you to analyze and find possible reasons for a problem that you are trying to diagnose.

designated router (DR) OSPF router that generates LSAs for a multiaccess network and has other special responsibilities in running OSPF. Each multiaccess OSPF network that has at least two attached routers has a designated router that is elected by the OSPF Hello protocol. The designated router enables a reduction in the number of adjacencies required on a multiaccess network, which in turn reduces the amount of routing protocol traffic and the size of the topological database.

Diffusing Update Algorithm (DUAL)
Convergence algorithm used in Enhanced IGRP that provides loop-free operation at every instant throughout a route computation. Allows routers involved in a topology change to synchronize at the same time, while not involving routers that are unaffected by the change.

discontiguous   Components that are fragmented. For example, a discontiguous network is composed of a major network that separates another major network.

discontiguous address assignment   A fragmented network assignment that does not follow a consistent pattern.

discontiguous network   Fragmented network addressing. Networks that do not have a hierarchical scheme.

distance vector   *See* Bellman-Ford (Algorithm).

DROthers   Routers that are not a DR or BDR. They are the other routers in the OSPF network.

DSL   Digital subscriber line. Network technology that delivers high bandwidth over conventional copper wiring at limited distances. There are four types of DSL: ADSL, HDSL, SDSL, and VDSL. All are provisioned through modem pairs, with one modem located at a central office and the other at the customer site. Because most DSL technologies do not use the whole bandwidth of the twisted pair, there is room remaining for a voice channel.

dynamic routing protocols   Routing that adjusts automatically to network topology or traffic changes. Also called *adaptive routing*.

E

EIGRP   Enhanced Interior Gateway Routing Protocol. Advanced version of IGRP developed by Cisco. Provides superior convergence properties and operating efficiency, and combines the advantages of link-state protocols with those of distance vector protocols.

equal-cost load balancing   When a router utilizes multiple paths with the same administrative distance and cost to a destination.

equal-cost metric   A metric that has the same value on multiple paths to the same destination. When multiple paths have equal-cost metrics, a router can execute equal-cost load balancing among those paths.

Ethernet   Baseband LAN specification invented by Xerox Corporation and developed jointly by Xerox, Intel, and Digital Equipment Corporation. Ethernet networks use CSMA/CD and run over a variety of cable types at 10 Mbps. Ethernet is similar to the IEEE 802.3 series of standards.

exterior gateway protocols (EGP)   Routing protocols used to route between autonomous systems. The current exterior routing protocol of the Internet is BGP.

F–G

FDDI   Fiber Distributed Data Interface. LAN standard, defined by ANSI X3T9.5, specifying a 100-Mbps token-passing network using fiber-optic cable, with transmission distances of up to 2 km. FDDI uses dual-ring architecture to provide redundancy.

feasibility condition (FC)   If the receiving router has a feasible distance to a particular network and it receives an update from a neighbor with a lower advertised distance (reported distance) to that network, there is a feasibility condition. Used in EIGRP routing.

feasible distance (FD)   The metric of a network advertised by the connected neighbor plus the cost of reaching that neighbor. The path with the lowest metric is added to the routing table and is called FD or feasible distance. Used in EIGRP routing.

feasible successor (FS)   A next-hop router that leads to a certain destination network. The feasible successor can be thought of as a backup next hop if the primary next hop (successor) goes down. Used in EIGRP routing.

flapping link   Routing problem where an advertised route between two nodes alternates (flaps) back and forth between two paths because of a network problem that causes intermittent interface failures.

flash   A variation of electrically erasable programmable read-only memory, which is nonerasable. Flash memory is erasable and writable. In the context of this course, flash is the storage card where the router stores the IOS image.

Frame Relay   A packet-switched data link layer protocol that handles multiple virtual circuits used between connected devices. Frame Relay is more efficient than X.25, the protocol for which it generally is considered a replacement.

gateway   A device on a network that serves as an access point to other networks. A default gateway is used by a host when an IP packet's destination address belongs to someplace outside the local subnet. A router is a good example of a default gateway.

H

high-order bit   The bit of a binary number that carries the most weight, the one written farthest to the left. High-order bits are the 1s in the network mask.

hold time   The maximum time a router waits to receive the next Hello packet or routing update. When the hold-time counter expires, that route will become unreachable.

hold-down timers   Timers that a route is placed in so that routers neither advertise the route nor accept advertisements about the route for a specific length of time (the hold-down period). Holddown is used to flush bad information about a route from all routers in the network. A route typically is placed in holddown when a link in that route fails.

host   Computer system on a network. Similar to node, except that host usually implies a computer system, whereas node generally applies to any networked system, including access servers and routers.

hub-and-spoke   A WAN topology in which various branch offices are connected through a centralized hub or headquarters.

I

ICMP   Internet Control Message Protocol. Network layer Internet protocol that reports errors and provides other information relevant to IP packet processing. Documented in RFC 792.

IGRP   Interior Gateway Routing Protocol. IGP developed by Cisco to address the issues associated with routing in large, heterogeneous networks.

interior gateway protocol (IGP)   Internet protocol used to exchange routing information within an autonomous system. Examples of common Internet IGPs include IGRP, OSPF, and RIP.

Internet service provider (ISP)   A company that provides access to the Internet to individuals or companies.

IP   Network layer protocol in the TCP/IP stack offering a connectionless internetwork service. IP provides features for addressing, type-of-service specification, fragmentation and reassembly, and security. Defined in RFC 791.

IPv6   A network layer protocol for packet-switched internetworks. This is the successor of IPv4 for general use on the Internet.

IPX   Internetwork Packet Exchange. NetWare network layer (Layer 3) protocol used for transferring data from servers to workstations. IPX is similar to IP and XNS.

ISDN   Integrated Services Digital Network. Communication protocol offered by telephone companies that permits telephone networks to carry data, voice, and other source traffic.

IS-IS   The Intermediate System–to–Intermediate System (IS-IS) Protocol is based on a routing method known as DECnet Phase V routing, in which routers known as intermediate systems exchange data about routing using a single metric to determine the network topology. IS-IS was developed by the International Organization for Standardization (ISO) as part of its Open Systems Interconnection (OSI) model.

L

LAN   High-speed, low-error data network covering a relatively small geographic area (up to a few thousand meters). LANs connect workstations, peripherals, terminals, and other devices in a single building or other geographically limited area. LAN standards specify cabling and signaling at the physical and data link layers of the OSI model.

LED   Light emitting diode. Semiconductor device that emits light produced by converting electrical energy.

level 1 parent route   A first-level route in the routing table that has subnets "catalogued" under it. A first-level parent route does not contain a next-hop IP address or exit interface information, but serves as a type of header information for the child routes.

level 1 route   A route with a subnet mask equal to or less than the classful mask of the network address.

level 2 child route   The subnets that belong to the parent route.

level 2 route   A subnet is the level 2 route of the parent route.

link state   Refers to the status of a link, including the interface IP address/subnet mask, type of network, cost of the link, and any neighbor routers on that link.

link-state acknowledgment (LSAck)   Acknowledges receipt of LSA (link-state advertisement) packets. Link-state acknowledgment packets are Type 5 OSPF packets.

link-state advertisement (LSA)   Broadcast packet used by link-state protocols that contains information about neighbors and path costs. LSAs are used by the receiving routers to maintain their routing tables.

link-state database A table used in OSPF that is a representation of the topology of the autonomous system. It is the method by which routers "see" the state of the links in the autonomous system.

link-state packet (LSP) *See* link-state advertisement.

link-state request (LSR) Link-state request packets are Type 3 OSPF packets. The link-state request packet is used to request the pieces of the neighbor's database that are more up to date.

link-state router A router that uses a link-state routing protocol.

link-state routing protocol A routing protocol in which routers exchange information with one another about the reachability of other networks and the cost or metric to reach the other networks. Link-state routers use Dijkstra's algorithm to calculate shortest paths to a destination, and normally update other routers with whom they are connected only when their own routing tables change.

link-state update (LSU) Link-state update packets are Type 4 OSPF packets. A link-state update packet carries a collection of link-state advertisements one hop farther from its origin.

load balancing In routing, the capability of a router to distribute traffic over all its network ports that are the same distance from the destination address. Good load-balancing algorithms use both line speed and reliability information. Load balancing increases the use of network segments, thus increasing effective network bandwidth.

longest match A route in the routing table that has a closer match of leftmost bits with the destination IP address in the IP packet.

loop-free Free of loops.

loopback address 127.0.0.1 is an IP address available on all devices to test whether the NIC on that device is functioning. If you send a packet to 127.0.0.1, it "loops back" on itself, thereby sending the data to the NIC on that device. If you get a positive response to a **ping 127.0.0.1** command, you know that your NIC is up and running.

loopback interface A virtual interface used for management purposes. Unlike a proper loopback interface, this loopback device is not used to talk with itself.

M

MAC address Standardized data link layer address that is required for every port or device that connects to a LAN. Other devices in the network use these addresses to locate specific ports in the network and to create and update routing tables and data structures. MAC addresses are 6 bytes long and are controlled by the IEEE.

media In the context of this course, media (the plural form of medium) are various physical environments through which transmission signals pass. Common network media include twisted-pair, coaxial, and fiber-optic cable, and the atmosphere (through which microwave, laser, and infrared transmission occurs). Sometimes called *physical media*.

metric Method by which a routing algorithm determines that one route is better than another. This information is stored in routing tables. Metrics include bandwidth, communication cost, delay, hop count, load, MTU, path cost, and reliability.

multiaccess network Network that allows multiple devices to connect and communicate simultaneously.

N

NAT   Network Address Translation. Mechanism for reducing the need for globally unique IP addresses. NAT allows an organization with addresses that are not globally unique to connect to the Internet by translating those addresses into globally routable address space.

neighbor   In OSPF, two routers that have interfaces to a common network. On multiaccess networks, neighbors are discovered dynamically by the OSPF Hello protocol.

network prefix   Number of bits that defines the subnet mask. For example, the subnet mask 255.255.0.0 is a /16 prefix.

next hop   The next point of routing. When routers are not directly connected to the destination network, they will have a neighboring router that provides the next step in routing the data to its destination.

NIC   Network interface card. Computer hardware that is designed to allow computers to communicate over a computer network.

nonbroadcast multiaccess (NBMA) network   Term describing a multiaccess network that either does not support broadcasting (such as X.25) or in which broadcasting is not feasible (for example, an SMDS broadcast group or an extended Ethernet that is too large).

null interface   Provides an alternative method of filtering traffic. You can avoid the overhead involved with using access lists by directing undesired network traffic to the null interface. This interface is always up and can never forward or receive traffic. Think of it as a black hole.

null0 summary routes   Another mechanism to prevent routing loops. EIGRP always creates a route to the Null0 interface when it summarizes a group of routes. This is because whenever a routing protocol summarizes, the router might receive traffic for any IP address within that summary. Because not all IP addresses are always in use, there is a risk of looping packets in case default routes are used on the router that receives the traffic for the summary route.

NVRAM   Nonvolatile random-access memory. Random-access memory that retains its contents when the power is shut off.

O

operating system   Software that performs basic tasks such as controlling and allocating memory, prioritizing system requests, controlling input and output devices, facilitating networking, and managing file systems.

OSPF   Open Shortest Path First. Link-state, hierarchical IGP routing algorithm proposed as a successor to RIP in the Internet community. OSPF features include least-cost routing, multipath routing, and load balancing. OSPF was derived from an early version of the IS-IS Protocol.

OSPF area   A logical set of network segments (CLNS-, DECnet-, or OSPF-based) and their attached devices. Areas are usually connected to other areas through routers, making up a single autonomous system.

P

packet   Logical grouping of information that includes a header containing control information and (usually) user data. Packets most often are used to refer to network layer units of data. The terms *datagram*, *frame*, *message*, and *segment* are also used to describe logical information groupings at various layers of the OSI reference model and in various technology circles.

passive state   A state when the router has identified the successor(s) for a certain destination and it becomes stable. A term used in conjunction with EIGRP.

path vector protocol   A routing protocol that marks and shows the path that update information takes as it diffuses through the network. BGP is a user of this kind of protocol because it verifies what autonomous systems the update has passed through to verify loops.

Point-to-Point Protocol (PPP)   Successor to SLIP that provides router-to-router and host-to-network connections over synchronous and asynchronous circuits. Whereas SLIP was designed to work with IP, PPP was designed to work with several network layer protocols, such as IP, IPX, and ARA. PPP also has built-in security mechanisms, such as CHAP and PAP. PPP relies on two protocols: LCP and NCP.

poison reverse   A variation of the split horizon technique that specifies that all routes should be included in an update out a particular interface, but that the metric should be set to infinity for those routes acquired over that interface.

power-on self test (POST)   Set of hardware diagnostics that runs on a hardware device when that device is powered up.

prefix aggegation   Also known as *network summarization*. Multiple IP addresses and IP prefixes can be summarized into a single IP prefix and be announced to other routers as only the resulting less-specific prefix (aggregated prefix) instead of the more specific IP addresses and prefixes that it covers. For example, the 172.16.1.0/24, 172.16.2.0/24, and 172.16.3.0/24 networks can all be summarized as a single 172.16.0.0/22 network.

private address   An address that is used for internal networks. This address follows RFC 1918 addressing. Not routable on the Internet.

privileged EXEC mode   The administration mode for the router or switch. This mode allows you to view router settings that are considered only accessible to the administrator. This mode also allows you to enter global configuration mode. To enter privileged EXEC mode, you must use the **enable** command.

protocol-dependent module   A component that depends on a certain routed protocol. For example, protocol-dependent modules in EIGRP allow it to work with various routed protocols. PDMs allow EIGRP to keep a topology table for each routed protocol such as IP, IPX RIP, AppleTalk Routing Table Maintenance Protocol (RTMP), and IGRP.

Q–R

quad-zero route   Default route, 0.0.0.0, representing either the network address or the subnet mask.

quality of service (QoS)   Measure of performance for a transmission system that reflects its transmission quality and service availability.

RAM   Volatile memory that can be read and written to by a microprocessor.

recursive route lookup   A route lookup that occurs to resolve the next-hop IP address of a previous route.

redistribution   Allowing routing information discovered through one routing protocol to be distributed in the update messages of another routing protocol. Sometimes called *route redistribution*.

reference bandwidth   The bandwidth referenced by the SPF algorithm when calculating the shortest path. In OSPF, the reference bandwidth is 10^8 divided by the actual interface bandwidth.

reported distance (RD)   The total metric along a path to a destination network as advertised by an upstream neighbor in EIGRP.

RIP   Routing Information Protocol. IGP supplied with UNIX BSD systems. The most common IGP in the Internet. RIP uses hop count as a routing metric.

ROM   Nonvolatile memory that can be read, but not written to, by the microprocessor.

route poisoning   Routing updates that explicitly indicate that a network or subnet is unreachable, rather than implying that a network is unreachable by not including it in updates. Poison reverse updates are sent to defeat large routing loops. The Cisco IGRP implementation uses poison reverse updates.

route summarization   Consolidation of advertised addresses in OSPF and IS-IS. In OSPF, this causes a single summary route to be advertised to other areas by an area border router.

router   Network layer device that uses one or more metrics to determine the optimal path along which network traffic should be forwarded. Routers forward packets from one network to another based on network layer information. Occasionally called a *gateway* (although this definition of gateway is becoming increasingly outdated).

routing domain   *See* autonomous system.

routing table   A table stored in the memory of a router or some other internetworking device that keeps track of routes to particular network destinations. A router uses this list of networks to determine where to send data.

S

scale   To alter to a certain size according to need. For example, a routing protocol is scalable when the router's routing table grows according to the addition of new networks.

serial   Method of data transmission in which the bits of data characters are transmitted sequentially over a single channel.

setup mode   When a Cisco router boots up and does not find a configuration file in NVRAM, it enters setup mode. Setup mode is a dialogue of questions that the administrator must answer to set up a basic router configuration.

shortest path first (SPF) algorithm   Routing algorithm that iterates on the length of path to determine a shortest-path spanning tree. Commonly used in link-state routing algorithms. Sometimes called *Dijkstra's algorithm*.

Smart Serial   Cisco smart serial interfaces have 26-pin connectors and can automatically detect RS-232, RS-449, RS-530, X.21, or V.35 connectors.

SPF schedule delay   After executing the **show ip ospf** command, you will see the parameter "SPF schedule delay *X* secs." (*X* indicates the number of seconds.) This is the delay time of SPF calculations.

split horizon   Routing technique in which information about routes is prevented from exiting the router interface through which that information was received. Split horizon updates are useful in preventing routing loops.

static routing   Routing that depends on manually entered routes in the routing table.

stub network   A network that only has a single exit point to the Internet or other networks.

stub router   A router that is connected to only one other router.

successor   The path to a destination. The successor is chosen using DUAL from all the known paths or feasible successors to the end destination. Used in EIGRP.

summary route   A summary route is the result of route summarization. Route summarization reduces the number of routes that a router must maintain. It is a method of representing a series of network addresses as a single summary address. A summary route would be a single route representing multiple, more specific routes. For example, the networks 172.16.1.0/24, 172.16.2.0/24, and 172.16.3.0/24 can be summarized into a single 172.16.0.0/22 network. The 172.16.0.0/22 network can then be advertised as a single summary route for all three networks.

supernet   Aggregation of IP network addresses advertised as a single classless network address. For example, given four Class C IP networks—192.0.8.0, 192.0.9.0, 192.0.10.0, and 192.0.11.0—each having the intrinsic network mask of 255.255.255.0, one can advertise the address 192.0.8.0 with a subnet mask of 255.255.252.0.

supernetting   Combining several IP network addresses into one IP address. Supernetting reduces the number of entries in a routing table and is done in CIDR addressing as well as in internal networks.

T

Telnet   Standard terminal emulation protocol in the TCP/IP protocol stack. Telnet is used for remote terminal connection, enabling users to log in to remote systems and use resources as if they were connected to a local system. Telnet is defined in RFC 854.

TLV   Type/Length/Value. The data portion of the EIGRP packet. All TLVs begin with a 16-bit Type field and a 16-bit Length field. Different TLV values exist according to the routed protocol. There is, however, a general TLV that describes generic EIGRP parameters such as Sequence (used by Cisco Reliable Multicast) and EIGRP software version.

Token Ring   Token-passing LAN developed and supported by IBM. Token Ring runs at 4 or 16 Mbps over a ring topology. Similar to IEEE 802.5.

topology database   Also known as the topology table, the topology database holds the information about the successor, feasible distance, and any feasible successors with their reported distances. Used in EIGRP routing.

topology table   *See* topology database.

triggered update   A routing update that is triggered by an event in the network.

TTL   Time to Live. Field in an IP header that indicates how long a packet is considered valid.

U

ultimate route   Also known as a *level 1 route*, an ultimate route is a route in the routing table that includes a next-hop address and an outgoing interface.

unequal-cost load balancing   Load balancing that uses multiple paths to the same destination that have different costs or metrics. EIGRP uses unequal-cost load balancing with the **variance** command.

unified communications   A communications system for voice, video, and data. The system integrates wired, wireless, and mobile devices to create a secure solution for enterprise networks.

V

vector   A quantity characterized by a magnitude (for example, hops in a path) and a direction.

VLSM   Variable-length subnet mask(ing). Capability to specify a different subnet mask for the same network number on different subnets. VLSM can help optimize available address space.

W

WAN   Data communications network that serves users across a broad geographic area and often uses transmission devices provided by common carriers. Frame Relay, SMDS, and X.25 are examples of WANs.

wildcard mask   A 32-bit quantity used in conjunction with an IP address to determine which bits in an IP address should be ignored when comparing that address with another IP address. A wildcard mask is specified when setting up access lists.

X–Z

XNS   Xerox Network Systems. A protocol stack developed by Xerox that contains network protocols that closely resemble IP and TCP. XNS was one of the first protocol stacks used in the first local-area network implementations.

Index